Organizational
Behavior

St. Clair Press Titles
In Management and Organizations

Organizational Behavior

Stephen J. Carroll
University of Maryland

Henry L. Tosi
Michigan State University

St. Clair Press
4 East Huron Street
Chicago, Illinois 60611

The material on management by objectives (MBO) throughout this book is drawn
extensively from the authors' book *Management by Objectives: Applications and
Research* (Macmillan, 1973), and "Setting Goals in Management by Objectives,"
with John Rizzo, in *California Management Review* (Sept., 1970).

Library of Congress Catalog Card Number 76-29491
ISBN 0-914292-08-0

St. Clair Press
4 East Huron Street
Chicago, Illinois 60611

To
Edna W. Freeman,
Nellie Mondlak,
and
Frank Mondlak

Contents

Preface

This book is about the human problems of management. It focuses on people and organizations, and the many ways these interact to result in varying levels of organizational effectiveness—which is usually judged in terms of profits, efficiency, benefits produced, and the like. This book is a prescriptive book; that is, we write about what we think is the best way to manage different kinds of people in different types of organizations.

Figure 1 shows the basic plan of this book. After an introduction (Part 1) which examines the historical development of management thinking and different research approaches to studying organizational behavior, Part II of the text (chaps. 3, 4, 5) analyzes individuals and groups. The basic thesis of Part II is that, because of different early life experiences—and different basic personalities—individuals come to organizations with different values, attitudes, and objectives. The organizations they come into also differ. These organization differences, and some of their causes, are analyzed in detail in Part III (chaps. 6 and 7), which posits four basic organization types.

In Part IV (chaps. 8, 9, 10, 11, and 12) we turn our analysis to what managers do—the processes of leadership, communication, acquiring and maintaining human resources, developing organizational control systems, and securing cooperation of organization members. But for managers to operate effectively, these processes must be varied by them according to the type of organization. Thus in chapters 13, 14, and 15 (Part V) we suggest strategies for using these processes in the basic organization types: hierarchical, dynamic, and two mixed-form. Finally, in chapters 16, 17, and 18, we deal with organizational change.

We have tried to draw together the essential ideas about managing human behavior within organizations and weave them into "managerial process contingency theory," in order to make sense for the manager, the person who must ultimately function face to face with a subordinate, a superior, or customers, and still get things done—and get them done effectively. That is why this book takes a prescriptive point of view. We did not want to write a social psychology text for managers. Our starting point was the question, "What do managers need to know from the behavioral sciences to make their work easier?" To the best of our ability and knowledge, we have tried to answer this question.

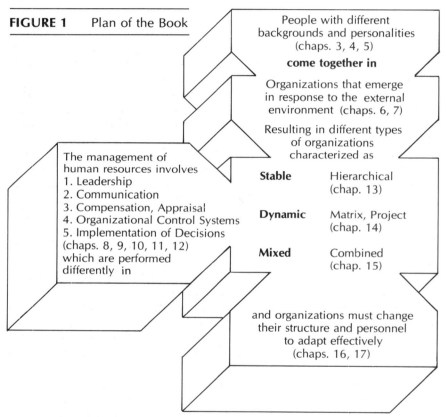

FIGURE 1   Plan of the Book

People with different backgrounds and personalities (chaps. 3, 4, 5)

come together in

Organizations that emerge in response to the external environment (chaps. 6, 7)

Resulting in different types of organizations characterized as

Stable	Hierarchical (chap. 13)	
Dynamic	Matrix, Project (chap. 14)	
Mixed	Combined (chap. 15)	

The management of human resources involves
1. Leadership
2. Communication
3. Compensation, Appraisal
4. Organizational Control Systems
5. Implementation of Decisions
(chaps. 8, 9, 10, 11, 12) which are performed differently in

and organizations must change their structure and personnel to adapt effectively (chaps. 16, 17)

This book, then, is our point of view, our theory of management and organizational behavior. In it we attempt to show how the various topics that fall within any broad, general concept of organizational behavior relate to each other in an integrated framework. The particular conceptual model underlying this book is Henry Tosi's, but each of us regards the other not simply as co-author, but as a collaborator without equal. We include some chapters from our earlier book, *Man-*

agement: *Contingencies, Structure, and Process*, but this book is directed at different course requirements and disciplinary interests than *Management*. This book was written because of numerous suggestions made to the authors that its point of view would be of value to teachers of organizational behavior.

Finally, a word about the question of the social responsibility of managers: We believe managers should be socially responsible. For that matter, we believe *everyone* should be, and we hope that this belief informs every relevant area discussed in this text. We also believe that of course the managerial role can be performed as adequately by females as by males. But in this book we have generally used the convention of the masculine pronoun because we know of no English-language singular that includes both sexes. We have, however, occasionally used female examples for various occupations to underscore our view that good management is nondiscriminatory.

We wish to express our deep gratitude to our publisher, Robert G. St. Clair, and to our editor, Curt Johnson, for their contributions to this book. Authors could not ask for more competent and helpful individuals than these.

It remains to make the conventional but necessary disclaimer that we take responsibility for all errors of logic, omission, or commission.

Stephen J. Carroll
Henry L. Tosi

Part I
Introduction

The premise of this book is that to manage effectively, different approaches are needed in different organizations because the character of work to be done and people are different. Such an approach is called the "management process contingency approach" (Tosi and Carroll, 1976). In chapter 1, we show how the different approaches (or schools of thought) have fed this contingency stream of thinking. In chapter 2, an overview of research and theory is presented to acquaint the reader with the way concepts are developed and tested in the field of organizational behavior.

Chapter 1
Organizational Behavior: Background

It is people—men and women—who make the world work. It is people trying to influence other people—and succeeding or failing—which brings about harmony and peace or disruption and conflict. As much as (maybe more than) anything else, effective management requires the understanding of people. It also requires the understanding of organizations, for managers work, usually, in organizations, and that fact limits their freedom of action.

In this book we will study organizations and describe ways that the human factor can be managed to increase organizational effectiveness. We will give the manager a set of concepts—a toolbag—which can be used to manage better (that is, to achieve improved outcomes). This is, we think, a testable question, boiling down to the issue of whether one approach, say *Method A*, is better than another, say *Method B*, to achieve desired results. We will try to avoid as much as possible specifying what organizations should seek to achieve, what desired results *should be*, for these are value judgments, questions of preference, and there is no way to resolve differences in value judgments save through social processes ranging from taking votes to waging war. In the final analysis it is the culture—the society—that makes the judgment of desirability of ends either individual or organizational, but in an organizational context the two must coincide. And achieving that coincidence is what this book is about.

Behavior in Organizations: Organizational Psychology

This book is concerned with human action (behavior) in organizations. An organization is a group of people who interact to achieve some purpose. The interaction is patterned (somewhat predictable, that is) and occurs over a period of time long enough for an observer to discern the patterns. To understand behavior in organizations, we must examine characteristics of individuals (behavior, attitudes, perceptions, motivation) separately and in groups. But we must also pay attention to the context within which behavior occurs, the organizational setting. Finally we suggest ways for a manager to improve performance (results).

Consideration of the human factors and their relationship to organizational effectiveness, forms the general content of this book. This book's ideas are drawn primarily from industrial psychology and industrial sociology. The psychologists contribute concepts for understanding individuals, while sociologists have added substantively to understanding the workings of organized systems. These perspectives converge with others which have been more sharply directed at managing. Some of the main themes which led to the present state of knowledge about behavior in organizations come from other diverse starting points. These starting points, called "schools of management thought," are scientific management, administrative theory, management science, the behavioral school, and the contingency approach.

In this book we integrate ideas from two of these schools—the contingency and the behavioral. The behavioral school focuses on individuals and groups, with particular emphases on motivation, leadership, attitudes, and the like. Basic theoretical ideas and managerial applications of these concepts are discussed, but the particular application of a concept—say that of leadership—depends on several factors, and we deal with this "contingency" aspect in our discussions. The "best" style of leadership, for instance, depends—and the contingency approach seeks to define upon what it depends. But while we use notions from the contingency school to develop the context within which organizational behavior occurs, all of the different schools of thought provide ideas that reinforce the discussion.

Some Antecedents of Modern Management Thinking

Since man first grouped together, he has tried to organize his own activities and those of others so that they are more efficient. Hoagland (1964), for example, shows how a famous study by Frederick Taylor (who is called the "father of scientific management," because his writings at the turn of the century were seminal to the contemporary study of management problems) can be traced back at least to the Renaissance. One of Taylor's most famous studies centered on the task of "shoveling." Concerned with increasing the productivity of common laborers, Taylor conducted research to determine the most efficient way to perform this task. Hoagland, through historical documents, traces the genesis of this study back to Taylor's teachers in the mid-19th century and farther back to work on the same problem by many others, including Leonardo da Vinci. In this chapter, we present some of the more important historical antecedents of modern management and organizational theory.

In the ancient world, management techniques were used to achieve religious, military, and political goals. (Much of this discussion follows George [1972].) It was in such organizations that management thinking originated, and writing on the art of management, as well as the development of various managerial tools and procedures, was about and for such organizations. There were few, if any, economic organizations of the kind we know today.

Complex economic organizations first began to develop during the Middle Ages. Organizations quite modern in character originated in Italy during this period, and became especially advanced in Venice by the 15th century. Many merchants of Venice formed partnerships, joint ventures, and trading companies. There were some obvious advantages to this form of economic ownership. Since much business was in sea trade, losses were often very substantial when ships were lost. Financing a particular expedition by several families, rather than by only one, reduced the risks involved in such an undertaking. The profits were also reduced by spreading the risk, of course, but joint financing made possible far more extensive undertakings than would otherwise have been the case.

The Industrial Revolution

The Industrial Revolution came to different parts of the world at different times. In the late 1700s, it may be said to have begun in England with the invention of the steam engine. This provided a simple, flexible means of converting natural materials such as coal into energy to drive belts, turn wheels, and provide other forms of mechanical motion. Since the steam engine provided such energy anywhere, factories of considerable size could be located in many different places. About the same time came new methods of smelting iron, which also facilitated industrial growth.

But harnessing power with a steam engine was only part of the impetus to economic growth during the Industrial Revolution. About the same time that Watt invented the steam engine, another important event took place that shaped men's thinking about how economic affairs should be arranged. Adam Smith, an economic philosopher published *The Wealth of Nations*.

This book, along with other ideas about industrial freedom and liberty that were gaining acceptance at this time, spurred a change in thinking that was to have a profound impact on the economic sectors of society. Prior to the late 1700s, it was generally held that economic decisions should be made by the state. Resource allocations were decided by a small cadre of men around the king, or simply by the king himself. Smith believed that these decisions were better made by individuals acting in their own self-interest. Under these conditions, he asserted, the common good would be enhanced. This concept forms the basic assumptions underlying classic economic theory of markets, especially the competitive model.

The concept is based on the conviction that men and institutions must be free to compete, because competition is in accord with natural law. Men, institutions, and ideas, through competition, prove their fitness for survival. Free competition and free markets lead to the maximum benefit for mankind. The self-interests of various segments of the economy striving to maximize their own well-being will lead to a self-regulation of the economic system. There is no need for political interference. The economy will be guided by the "invisible hand," not the heavy hand of the sovereign. As Smith put it:

> Every individual endeavors to employ his capital so that its produce may be of greatest value. He generally neither intends to promote the public interest, nor knows how much he is promoting it. He intends only his own security, only his own gain. And he is in this led by an *invisible hand* to promote an end which was no part of his intention. By pursuing his own interest he frequently promotes that of society more effectively than when he really intends to promote it.

Smith also convincingly argued that the wealth of a nation did not rest in the quantities of gold it held. The idea that it did had led to wars and explorations in which the primary purpose was to increase a nation's storehouse of gold. Smith showed how the wealth of a nation could be advanced by increasing the productivity of the capital and productive components of society.

The new economic philosophy, coupled with advancing technology, shifted the wealth in the society. A new class emerged in England and in the other countries where similar developments took place. The new class came into conflict (still not fully resolved) with the old, landed class for political and economic supremacy. The new industrialists had a different set of ideas about "right," "wrong," and "importance" than did the old, landed class. The new class emphasized individual initiative and individual responsibility. The old, landed class felt more responsibility for their workers than did the new class. The newer class had a much stronger work orientation than did the landed class, and it did not emphasize intellectual, cultural, and recreational pursuits to the same degree as the landed gentry.

The Growth of Industry in the United States

Before the American Revolution there was little industry in the Colonies, largely because of the sparse population, the lack of capital, and restrictive legislation from England which hindered manufacturing. The Revolution gave some impetus to industry, however, and manufacturing grew slowly until the 1820s, when a number of inventions and technical advances stimulated its growth. In the first half of the 19th century, most U.S. factories were small, and corporate ownership was not nearly as popular as individual or partnership forms. Labor was scarce. In fact, about half of all factory workers were children. In the 1840s and 1850s the construction of new roads, railroads, and canals stimulated industrial growth. About the same time, increased immigration furnished the large labor force necessary for work in factories, railroads, and coal mines.

The Civil War increased the rate of U.S. industrial growth even further, especially in steel, textiles, leather, meat packing, and prepared foods. The railroads opened the West, stimulating demand for many products manufactured in the East, and inventions and other innovative developments also fostered increased industrialization.

As in England, the spirit of laissez-faire capitalism characterized U.S. economic life. The owners of large firms became known as "robber barons" and were accused of having little concern for anything except wealth and power. A flaw was becoming apparent in the theory of competition. Adam Smith's argument had been that if individuals were left alone to compete freely, the general well-being would be served, but this conclusion was based on the assumption that there would be a *large* number of buyers *and* a *large* number of sellers. As huge fortunes were accumulated in the United States, many smaller sellers were consolidated into fewer larger ones, and the *monopoly*—a case in which a single firm has almost complete control of the quality and price of its goods and services—emerged. When goods or services such as oil, steel, and rail transportation are vital to the society, those who control them have enormous power, and can misuse it. In time, U.S. monopolies were accused of practices harmful to society: fixing prices, rather than having them result from competitive market forces, and forcing raw material producers to accept the monopolist's price, since there were few other customers.

The Sherman Anti-Trust Act was passed in 1890 as a response to these practices. It prohibited monopoly or tendency toward monopoly. While it is considered by many to be the beginning of a too extensive government regulation of business, the Sherman Act was designed to produce the same result as laissez-faire capitalism—increased social benefits, since the economy, unregulated, was not working as intended in theory. In any event, the Sherman Act significantly affected what an industrialist could do. With its enactment there was no longer unbridled freedom to act only in the best interests of a given firm. There were now some things that a businessman couldn't do, and these constraints made it more difficult to maximize profit. For instance, the Act made it illegal to form a trust to raise prices arbitrarily. As a result, owners had to begin to focus more sharply on managing the resources of the business.

Just as U.S. industry grew after the Civil War, so did the unrest of U.S. labor. By the mid-1870s, workers were beginning to react against extremely difficult and often unreasonable working conditions. Because of increased immigration after the war, there was a vast labor supply available to industry. Because workers had both better working conditions in the United States than they had in Europe, and the promise and hope of further improvement, they tended to be somewhat more tolerant of difficult working conditions. But by the 1880s, poor working conditions, low wages, and an almost total lack of job security were stimulating intensive union activity, especially in the coal-mining industry. Unions were not widely successful in obtaining contracts, but they were instrumental in bringing about legislation covering working conditions. Like the Sherman Act, these laws were a constraint on the decisions that a businessman could make. Industry was powerful, but abrasive; growing, but inefficient. It drew recklessly on the vast human and physical resources available to it.

It was in this societal and economic milieu of a growing economy, increased regulation, and advancing unionism that the scientific management movement began.

Contemporary Management Movements

The times were ripe, then, for the emergence of people such as Frederick W. Taylor and his colleagues in scientific management. Around 1900 managers began to experiment with ways to use raw materials, men, and equipment more efficiently. When their experiments met with success, their ideas were sought out by others who had similar problems. Since that time, numerous practitioners and theorists have contributed to the present state of the modern art and practice of management. They came from diverse backgrounds, ranging from engineering to journalism, and in a short history it is impossible to give all of them the kind of treatment they deserve. As George (1968) has noted, to "write a history of management is to write a history of man." In this section, we want to point out the *major* approaches and *some* of the important contributors to each.

FIGURE 1.1 Sources of Modern Management Ideas

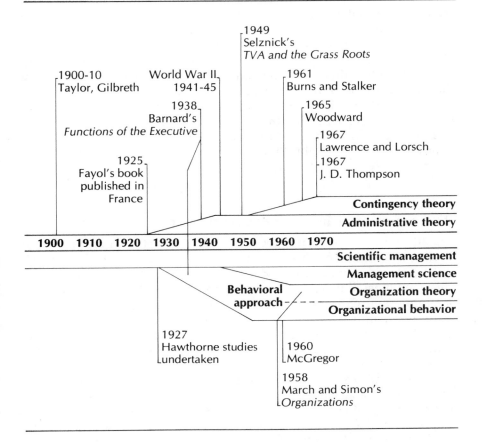

There are five major schools of thought about management: (1) scientific management, (2) administrative theory, (3) management science, (4) the behavioral approach, and (5) the contingency approach. We discuss some of the major ideas of and contributions to each school of thought in this section. Figure 1.1 depicts the development of management thinking since 1900. The primary thrust comes from the *scientific management* movement and the work of Taylor.

The year 1925, with the publication of Henri Fayol's *General and Industrial Management* in France, marked the beginning of the *administrative theory* era. The behavioral approach to management (also called the "human relations" approach) is generally acknowledged to have begun around 1927, with the advent of the Hawthorne studies, while World War II saw the birth of operations research or *management science*. Interdisciplinary teams were brought together to solve major war problems. Psychologists, economists, but especially engineers and mathematicians, contributed to this line of thinking.

The *contingency approach* can be traced back to at least 1949 and Selznick's study, *TVA and the Grass Roots*. Later studies and theory development in this area provided a basis for potential integration of the varied strains of thought from the other approaches.

The major ideas from the five different points of view are discussed here. The reader will note the divergencies. By the mid-1960s, there was a great deal of confusion in management thinking because of the many schools of thought. Perhaps we are closer today to achieving a degree of integration of them.

The Scientific Management Approach

Scientific management was focused on the lowest level of the organization, the worker and his boss. The basic question to which most scientific management research was addressed was: "How can the job be designed most efficiently?" Taylor, who was born to a well-to-do Philadelphia family, but who was unable to complete college because of poor eyesight, was the best known of these researchers. He took a job in industry as an apprentice at the Midvale Steel Company in 1878, and quickly rose through the ranks to become chief engineer in 1884, at the age of 28.

Based on his experiences and studies, Taylor developed many ideas to increase management efficiency, and became widely sought as a consultant to other firms. His ideas, when applied, met with considerable success. He presented papers reporting his results to professional engineering societies and later in several books (Taylor, 1947).

Henry L. Gantt was a colleague of Taylor's and worked with him on several consulting projects. Frank and Lillian Gilbreth were also leaders in the scientific management movement. Together the Gilbreths worked to develop scientific approaches to measuring work and designing efficient work practices. Scientific management is a collection of ideas on management by these, and other writers.

Some of the more important ideas of scientific management are these:

1. *Current management practice was inefficient.* Taylor argued that the economic success of a firm was not indicative of its efficiency. A firm could be successful, even though inefficient, if it had a patent, a location advantage, or if its competitors were equally inefficient. Gantt felt that the abundance of natural resources in the nation, rather than the quality of its management, accounted for its high standard of living.

2. *Management must adopt the scientific method in industry.* A tenet of Taylor and his colleagues was the use of "scientific method." The scientific method involves solving problems by research, rather than relying on experience or intuition. It requires evaluation of alternatives by making systematic and objective comparisons among them to see which is best. One example was Taylor's famous metal-cutting experiments, which started in 1880 and lasted 26 years. The purpose was to find the optimum method for cutting metal through the use of science rather than to continue to rely upon experience, as in the past.

3. *Specialization should be practiced.* Taylor and his colleagues believed that each individual in an organization should be a specialist. This would insure that a person knew his job well and would make it easier to train and select employees. Taylor believed in specialization for management as well. For example, he advocated the use of "functional foremanship," where each employee would be supervised by several different foremen, each with distinct responsibilities. One foreman would be in charge of machine speeds, another of discipline, another of planning, and so on.

4. *Planning and scheduling were essential.* In scientific management, there was a very strong emphasis on planning. It was considered to be the essence of management. Everything was to be done according to a plan. Yearly plans were to be broken down into monthly, weekly, and daily plans. Plans for a whole organization were to be broken down into plans for smaller units, and even further to individuals.

Planning techniques were devised. Gantt devised the "Gantt Chart," which not only helped a manager to make optimum use of his resources by carefully scheduling jobs among available equipment, but helped to ascertain at a glance whether certain jobs were behind schedule or not.

Planning and scheduling meant obtaining materials at the right time, right place, and in the right condition for efficient use. Frank Gilbreth especially was concerned with this problem. He invented the movable scaffold so that the bricks could be delivered at the most efficient height for a bricklayer. Gilbreth even had the bricks placed on the scaffold with the good side of the brick facing upward so that the bricklayer could place it without first inspecting it. This increased speed without sacrificing quality.

5. *Proper selection should be done.* It was important that the right man was selected for each job. Taylor believed there were first-class men, second-class men, and so on, depending upon their qualifications for a task. Just as a draft horse and a race horse were fitted for particular types of work, in Taylor's view, so were people best fitted for some jobs but unsuited for others. Taylor advised the use of tests to identify whether or not a person had the critical attributes for a particular job. For example, he devised a test for measuring the perceptual speed and reaction time of quality inspectors.

6. *The standard method should be found.* Scientific management emphasized finding through research the best way to perform a given task. Those assigned to that task would then be required to carry it out in the prescribed manner. This standard method was to be used until a better one was developed. To improve methods, workers were studied by observers, or by motion pictures, making it possible to analyze a task in slow motion. A work method was carefully studied to see if certain motions could be combined, shifted to another part of the body, or eliminated, or if the work place could be redesigned for greater efficiency.

7. *Standard times for each task should be established.* Taylor believed a primary barrier to greater efficiency was management's lack of knowledge about what constituted a fair performance level for an employee. Believing that the output of most workers was below their capability, he did not think that historical productivity records used by management could be accurate indicators of how long it should take to complete a task.

8. *Wage incentives should be utilized.* A basic premise of most scientific management pioneers was that a man should be paid on the basis of what he does, rather than the amount of time he puts into the job. Many wage incentive plans were devised and implemented. These incentive wage plans generally paid workers a bonus if they reached or surpassed the standard time established by time-study procedures.

Results under Scientific Management. The application of these scientific management action principles resulted in significant productivity increases. In his most famous case, Taylor significantly improved productivity of the loading of pig iron bars into railroad cars. In the well-known shoveling experiment, Taylor found, through experimentation, that the optimum size shovel for handling material carried about 21 pounds of material, and was able to increase productivity from 16 to 59 tons of material shoveled per day, while the number of shovelers needed per day was decreased from 500 to 140.

The Gilbreths, in a number of applications of their work redesign methods, also demonstrated spectacular increases in productivity. Frank Gilbreth was able to increase the average productivity of bricklayers from 120 to 350 bricks per hour. This was accomplished in part by decreasing the number of motions used in bricklaying from 18 to 5. While in London at a Japanese-British exposition, Gilbreth observed a worker in an exhibition booth who was acknowledged to be extremely productive at attaching labels on boxes. She worked at the rate of 24 boxes in 40 seconds. Gilbreth suggested some changes in her methods, and in her first attempt with the new method she disposed of 24 boxes in 26 seconds. In her second attempt, the time was reduced to 20 seconds.

Such results were typical when scientific management was applied, and they led to a strong advocacy of scientific management methods. The analysis and redesign of work was widely applied in industry. As Daniel Bell (1975) says of this movement:

> ... The prophet of modern work was Frederick W. Taylor, and the stop watch was his rod. If any social upheaval can ever be attributed to one man, the logic of efficiency as a mode of life is due to Taylor. With "scientific management," as formulated by Taylor in 1893, we pass far beyond the old, rough computations of the division of labor and more into the division of time itself. ...

> There is no little irony in the fact that one of Taylor's chief admirers was Lenin. In a notable speech in June 1919, Lenin urged "the study and teaching of the Taylor system and its systematic trial and adaptation." The logic of efficiency knows no social boundaries.

Administrative Theory

By the late 1920s, a group of managers had begun to write about the job of the administrator. They began to analyze the basic task of management. They were also concerned with the development of princi-

ples of management—guides for designing and managing an organization. Most of these writers worked independently of the others but
nevertheless came to similar conclusions about management. Two of
the more promininent earlier contributors were Henri Fayol (1949)
and Chester Barnard (1938; 1947).

ITEM 1.1   Henri Fayol

A Business Scientist

From his practical experience Fayol
developed a framework for a unifying
doctrine of administration that might
hold good wherever the art of government had to be exercised. He originated
the symbol of formal organization, the
organization chart, which, with his organization manual of job descriptions,
remains the chief instrument of business
management. He produced ideas on
human relationships. . . . Not least, he
was a firm advocate of the view that
management can and should be taught.
This was a revolutionary idea when he
first propounded it in 1908.

Fayol's first paper on management
theory was read to the *Congrès des
Mines et de la Métallurgie* in 1900. He
followed this with his "Discourse on the
General Principles of Administration" at
the Jubilee Congress of the *Société de
l'Industrie Minérale* in 1908, a paper
which appeared in the third number of
the *Bulletin de la Société de l'Industrie
Minérale* for 1916 and was published as
a book by Dunod of Paris. This was
translated into English by Conbrough in
1929, and again by Constance Storrs in
1949. It is the latter translation which is
in widespread use under the title *General and Industrial Management,* and by
which Fayol is primarily known to the
British and American reader.

Fayol was born in 1841 of the French
petite bourgeoisie. . . .

His working life fell into four periods.
For twelve years from 1860 he was a
junior executive interesting himself in
the problems of mining engineering,
especially fire hazards. Promoted to
Manager of a group of pits in 1872, he
became concerned chiefly with the factors determining the economic life of the
pits in his charge. This not only stimulated him to write a geological monograph but aroused his interest in thinking
and planning ahead. In 1888 he was
appointed Managing Director of the
combine, taking over when the undertaking was on the verge of bankruptcy.
He closed uneconomic metallurgical
works, replaced exhausted mines with
rich acquisitions and expanded the
whole organization. When he retired in
1918 the financial position of the combine was impregnable. It had made a
contribution of the greatest value to the
allied cause in the First World War, and
it had an administrative, technical and
scientific staff famous throughout France.

In his retirement Fayol devoted his
time to the popularization of his own
views on management and to the development of theoretical studies. He immediately founded the Centre for Administrative Studies, which had a profound
influence on business, the Army, and the
Navy in France, and attempted to persuade the French government to pay attention to principles of administration.
By invitation of the Under-Secretary of
State for Posts and Telegraphs he under-
took an investigation of this department.
At the time of his death in 1925 he was

engaged in investigating the organization of the French tobacco industry. . . .

Fayol's Contribution. Henri Fayol was an able man whose talents had a fertile field for development in the social and economic environment of France between 1860 and 1925. His abilities placed him in the *élite* comprised of those who had attended the *grandes écoles,* the most senior administrators in business, government, the armed forces and in other fields. At the time he commenced his business career the French economy had "taken off" and was passing through [a] period of rapid growth [in which] there was a sense in which French business needed a theory of management, as did American business in a similar stage of development. Fayol's work in France, a country with a long tradition of administration, was complementary to that of Taylor in the U.S.A., a nation which revered the principle of "coming up the hard way". That Taylor worked primarily on the operative level, from the bottom of the hierarchy upwards, while Fayol concentrated on the senior manager and worked downwards, was not merely a reflection of their different careers; it was also a reflection of the political and social history of the two nations.

Fayol's views on management theory contain some weaknesses of analysis and assessment. His principles, elements and duties overlap; he confused structure and process; and there is a vagueness and superficiality about some of his terms and definitions. He hinted at, but did not elaborate, the limitations of his view that management can and should be taught. Senior managers and administrators he imagined as an intellectual élite, a view which could not be supported universally although true of his own circle and still largely obtaining in France today. He placed a higher value on management theory than it could be expected to support, in 1924 addressing a conference on the importance of administrative doctrine as a contribution to peace.

Nevertheless Fayol's contribution to management theory is unique and valuable. He was a generation ahead of his time in proclaiming its significance and he propounded many views which have been attributed to others who followed. While acclaimed for originating the organization chart, the job specification and the concept of management education and training, he has been underestimated. His views on human relationships at work anticipated many of the basic findings of industrial psychology. His idea of flexible planning at all levels lies behind the development of the *Commissariat du Plan* which has played such a significant part in the recent expansion of the French economy.

Although it is clear that he was exceptionally gifted, Fayol maintained that his phenomenal business success was due primarily not to his personal qualities but to the application of simple principles which could be taught and learned. These constituted his theory of management. It exercised, and continues to exercise, a profound influence on efforts to clarify thinking on organization, and is one of the foundations of organization theory. His emphasis on unremitting effort has the flavor of Samuel Smiles of latter nineteenth century Britain, but it is probable that his biological model could only have been produced by a Frenchman. . . .—Norman H. Cuthbert

Scientific Business, February 1964

Copyright © 1964 by MCB Journals.

Henri Fayol. Fayol (see item 1.1) distinguished management activities from technical activities, pointing out that managerial activities increased in importance and technical activities decreased in importance as we move from the lowest to the highest level of an organization. He felt that management could, and should, be taught at all educational levels. Only the lack of a management theory, which he would help create, prevented this from occurring.

Fayol proposed 14 principles of management. He stressed the importance of specialization of labor to make the best use of human resources, although he warned that this could be carried too far. Fayol also proposed that responsibility must increase as authority increases, discipline or obedience is essential in any prosperous enterprise, and that organizational members should receive orders from only one superior. He stressed the importance of determining the proper organization level at which managerial decisions are made.

Fayol was concerned about the use of human resources as well. Equality of treatment was to him very important. To facilitate motivation, the wage payment system, he believed, must fit the type of job and situation and supervisors must encourage initiative among their subordinates.

Chester Barnard. Barnard (1938), another important management theorist, perceived the organization differently than Fayol, who stressed designing an organization in a rational and systematic way and then fitting individuals to it. Barnard paid more attention to human factors. He saw organizations evolving out of the attempt to reconcile organizational needs with individual needs.

Organizations, to Barnard, are systems of cooperative effort and coordinated activities. They are formed, or develop, to overcome the inherent limitations of an individual's capacity; that is, when the task to be done requires more than one person, organized effort is necessary.

Like Fayol, Barnard was aware of the formal, designated structure of organization—but he recognized that what really occurred in the context of any organization was different from the charts, job specifications, and procedures specified by management. He made it clear in his analysis that there were informal organizations that existed side by side with the formal. These resulted from different human needs that could not be dealt with by the formal system.

Barnard, in his exposition of this concept, provided groundwork for later analysis which examined the interrelationship of individuals and groups with organizations. Much of what transpires at work can be accounted for by the formal organization. Much, however, can only be understood if the psychological and sociological aspects of organizational life are more fully considered.

He also examined the structure of organization in terms of decision making. Top-level management set objectives. The next management level established plans to achieve them. Then the next lower level developed more detailed plans, until the operating level was reached.

Barnard, like Fayol, also described what executives must do to manage an organization efficiently. The executive functions, according to Barnard, are:

1. *Maintaining organization communication.* This involves integrating managers and their jobs in the system. Competent managers, compatible to the needs of the organization, should be able to communicate effectively to achieve organization purpose.

2. *Securing the essential services of individuals.* Managers are responsible for recruiting, or inducing individuals to join an organization, as well as seeing to it that they produce once they join.

3. *Formulating purpose and objectives.* Managers are responsible for stating, in operational terms, the goals of the organization, then breaking them down into subgoals to be assigned to lower-level units.

The Administrative Point of View.   Some of the major ideas that flow from the administrative approach to management are the treatment of authority, management functions, principles of management, organization structure, and emphasis on objectives.

In the administrative approach, *authority* and *responsibility* are seen as rights and obligations of employees and managers. Authority is the right of a manager to decide about resource allocation. Responsibility is the obligation to perform according to job requirements. Authority and responsibility are associated with a position and should be co-equal; that is, a person should not be responsible for those things about which he has no authority. Line authority flows down, according to the administrative school, from the top of the hierarchy to the lowest managerial level.

An *emphasis on objectives* is required to develop a rational relationship among activities. When goals are clearly defined and stated, other resources can be arranged in such a way as to maximize the possibility of attainment. Managers, the administrative theorists believed, would be able to select the best alternative from those available only when goals are known.

One of the more important contributions of the administrative school to management theory is *organization structure*, or guidance on how to design an organization. Many principles of management deal with this problem. Davis (1951), for example, states the principle of *functional homogeneity*. "Duties should be grouped in a manner which will provide the greatest functional similarity." Such grouping would result in lower costs and better performance. Relationships *between* activities, he said, should be governed by the principle of *complementary functions:* "The functions involved in the completion of a project, and their performance factors, must be related in a manner that will facilitate the cumulation of results into the effective, economical accomplishment of the final objectives." Davis then goes on to detail the things that make functions complementary. This design aspect of administrative theory gives a great deal of help in defining an organization system.

Principles of management were both a strength and a weakness of the administrative approach. Principles were seen by the administrative school as guides to action for managers. Drawn from real-world experiences, they were meant to facilitate high performance. The message from the administrative school was "Follow the principles, and success will very likely come."

Yet many critics, such as March and Simon (1958), attacked these principles because they were based on observation, not research, and they were "proverbs." But many of the principles have extremely sound bases. For instance the *unity of command* principle states that a person should receive orders from only one superior. This "proverb," based on the experience of the administrative theorists, has a more glamorous conceptual formulation by the social scientist; he calls it avoiding *role conflict.* Role conflict occurs when a person receives inconsistent demands from two or more others so that complying with one of the demands precludes compliance with another. Research has shown the negative effects on individuals of high role conflict (Rizzo et al.; Tosi, 1970).

Management functions are those activities which all executives perform in whole or part. The administrative theorists did the most extensive early analysis of what these functions are. Managerial functions are planning, organizing, and controlling. *Planning* is the determining, in advance of activity execution, what factors are required to achieve goals. The planning function includes defining the objective and determining what resources are necessary. *Organizing* is the function of acquiring and assembling resources in proper relationship to each other to achieve objectives. *Controlling* is insuring that activities, when carried out, conform to plans, to achieve objectives.

The administrative theory school, then, stresses a rational approach to management: If we define our objective, then it is possible to organize resources to achieve it. This is what scientific management was concerned with, also.

The Management Science Movement

Management science, or operations research, grew out of World War II research on the application of quantitative methods to military and logistical decision problems. Some of the earliest projects were to increase bombing accuracy, to develop search methods for submarines, to minimize ship loss due to submarine attacks, and to improve methods for loading and unloading ships. This approach to problem solving is interdisciplinary. Problems are attacked by teams, and team members come from a wide variety of fields, though for the most part they are engineers, mathematicians, statisticians, economists, and psychologists.

Miller and Starr (1964) consider operations research to be applied decision theory. It uses "any scientific, mathematical, or logical means to attempt to cope with problems that confront the executive when he tries to achieve a thoroughgoing rationality in dealing with his decision problems." But, how does this differ from some of the other points of view of the scientific management and administrative theory schools? Miller and Starr offer this way of distinguishing operations research approaches from these others:

> Management science differs from Taylor's scientific management in many ways. It is not concerned primarily with production tasks and the efficiency of men and machines. Rather, the efficiency is a secondary achievement which should follow adequate planning. In other words, poor decisions can be implemented in an efficient way.

Thus, the operations research movement tries to marry the concern of the scientific management school with production and efficiency, with the planning approach and the emphasis on objectives of the administrative theory school. This is attempted, however, with an eye toward integrating several fields of knowledge and using systematic analytical techniques, especially quantitative methods, to deal with problems facing managers and organizations. Management scientists use models (representations of real life) with computers to make the necessary and often quite complex mathematical computations to optimize the attainment of a given set of objectives. Today, basic techniques such as linear programming, game theory, queuing theory, and statistical decision theory are being applied to many business problems.

However, management science does not eliminate from consideration the effects of behavioral problems. Miller and Starr note that "management science is essentially quantitative; however, the important problems that cannot be quantified are handled qualitatively. Whether quantitative or qualitative methods are applied, operations research is used to produce rational decisions and logical plans of action."

The Behavioral Approach

The scientific management movement analyzed the activities of workers; the administrative management writers focused on the activities of managers. The behavioral approach to management sought to understand how human psychological processes—such as motivation and attitude—interact with what one does—activities—to affect performance.

The behavioral approach is probably more fragmented than either the scientific management or administrative management approaches. Behavioralists come from many different social science disciplines (political science, sociology, psychology, and anthropology), and while there are varying emphases among them, they can be generally grouped into three categories: (1) the human relations perspective, based on the Hawthorne studies, (2) the industrial psychology perspective, which focused on the optimal fit between a person and the job, and (3) organizational theory, which tends to consider the organization—its structure and functioning—as the focal point.

The Human Relations Perspective.   In the early years of the scientific management movement, behavioral scientists were deeply involved. Their concern was with problems such as worker fatigue, boredom, and job design. Quite a different perspective emerged after the Hawthorne experiment at Western Electric in the late 1920s, which gave rise to the "human relations" approach (Roethlisberger and Dickson, 1939).

The Hawthorne experiment was carried out in the Hawthorne plant of Western Electric, an AT&T subsidiary in Cicero, Illinois. The Hawthorne studies (started in 1927) were prompted by an experiment which was carried out by the company's engineers between 1924 and 1927. The engineers, in the best tradition of scientific management, were seeking the answers to industrial questions through research. They studied two groups to determine the effects of different levels of illumination on worker performance. In one group the level of illumination was changed, while in the other it was not. They found that when illumination was increased, the level of performance increased.

But productivity also increased when the level of illumination decreased, even down to the level of moonlight. Moreover, productivity
also increased in the control group. These results seemed contrary to
reason, and so the engineers examined other factors which might have
affected the results. The workers in the experiment were the center of
attention. They appeared to react as they thought they should react.

The researchers concluded that the way people were treated made
an important difference in performance. Obviously, the subjects were
responding not to the level of light, but to the experiment itself and to
their involvement in it. They were responding in a way that they
thought the experimenters wanted and because they were the center
of attention. Since that time, this effect in research has been known as
the "Hawthorne Effect."

The Hawthorne studies which followed the experiment were conducted by a team of researchers headed by Elton Mayo and F. J. Roethlisberger, from Harvard. The results of these studies are summarized
here.

1. *The First Relay Assembly Group.* The first study investigated the
effects on worker output of variations in the physical conditions of
work, such as rest pauses, hours of work, temperature, and humidity.
The study group consisted of six experienced female operators who
assembled telephone relays. When each relay was assembled it was
dropped down a chute, at which time a mechanism punched a hole in
a piece of moving tape. Productivity could be accurately measured by
counting the number of holes in the tape and, since it moved at a constant speed, one could later determine productivity levels for any particular time period.

Over a two-year period, many changes were made in the working
conditions, especially with respect to rest pauses. Two five-minute,
then two ten-minute, then six five-minute rest pauses were tried. Food
was served with the rest pauses. The work day and the work week
were shortened, first by one-half hour a day, then by one hour, then to
a five-day instead of a six-day week. Each change in the physical
working conditions was made separately and lasted several weeks.

In addition to these changes, the task was simplified somewhat.
Workers in the room were put on an incentive wage plan which en-
abled them to earn more money if the performance level of the group
increased. The approach to supervision in the room was different than
in the previous work location. In the relay assembly room, much more
attention, interest, and consideration was shown to the workers than
on their previous jobs.

In addition, records were kept on temperature, humidity, hours of sleep, food eaten and so on. The data amassed in this study was extensive and detailed.

Over the two-year period, productivity *generally* went up steadily, no matter what changes in working conditions were made. At the end of the study the investigators formulated five hypotheses to account for the increased production: (1) improved methods of work, (2) reduction in fatigue with changes in rest pauses and shorter hours, (3) reduction in monotony due to rest pauses and hour changes, (4) effect of a wage incentive plan, and (5) effect of the new method of supervision. The first three hypotheses were rejected by the investigators, leaving wage incentives and the method of supervision to be tested in further studies.

2. *The Second Relay Assembly Group.* To test the effects of wage incentives, a group of workers was selected who remained in the regular work department, but were taken off the regular wage plan and put on a group incentive plan. Productivity increased in the study group by 13 percent, as did their earnings. But the study was terminated after nine weeks because of the resentment of other workers in the department. The investigators concluded, perhaps unwisely, that group rivalry was the cause of the increased production rather than the incentive wage plan.

3. *The Mica-splitting Test Room.* To examine the effects of different supervision, another group of workers already on piecework was studied. The change in supervision seemed, at first, to make a difference in performance. But with worsening of economic conditions accompanying the Depression, productivity declined and remained stable for a long period of time.

4. *The Interviewing Program.* The investigators had rejected all their hypotheses about a single cause of the increased productivity. They decided that employee behavior was the result of a reaction to a complex social system made up of several interdependent elements. An interviewing program was initiated in 1928 which lasted several years, and which involved more than 21,000 interviews with workers to try to understand some of these complex interrelationships. In this study, several conclusions were reached:

a) Morale is improved when individuals have a chance to air their grievances.
b) Complaints are not objective statements of fact.
c) Workers are influenced in their job demands by experiences outside the work situation.
d) Worker satisfaction is influenced by how the employee views his social status relative to others.

5. *The Bank Wiring Observation Room.* In this study, 14 male workers were formed into a work group and closely observed for 7 months. The researchers, in observing the group, saw the emergence of a social system when these workers were placed together. The social system influenced worker behavior considerably. This study will be described in detail in chapter 4 because it highlights concepts useful to understanding how and why groups affect the behavior of individuals.

The Hawthorne studies seemed to point up the importance of leadership practices and work-group pressures on employee satisfaction and performance. They downgraded the importance of economic incentives in worker motivation. They also stressed the importance of examining the effect of any one factor, such as pay, in terms of a whole social system, pointing out that employees react to a whole complex of forces together, rather than to one factor alone.

While the Hawthorne studies represent the main point of departure for the behavioral approach, both the research methods and the conclusions have been questioned (Carey, 1967; Sykes, 1965; Kerr, 1953; Bendix and Fisher, 1949). For instance, it is said that the research had a management bias, striving to increase productivity without regard to the welfare of workers. Criticism has also been leveled at the research method; for example, that samples were too small, the questions vague. Others criticize the fact that the results were misinterpreted. For example, in the second relay assembly study, production increased with incentives, yet the researchers concluded that group rivalry was the cause. Some questioned the conclusion that management and workers have similar rather than contradictory objectives. Regardless of the merit of the criticisms, the research had a significant impact on thinking about management problems. It provided the impetus for critics of the scientific management movement to argue that any effort to develop a science of management without taking the human factor into account would be fruitless.

Industrial Psychology. At about the same time that the scientific management movement began to gain impetus (around 1900), industrial psychology began its growth. The driving initial force in this discipline was Hugo Munsterberg. According to Miner (1969), Munsterberg's work, before World War I was in a "direct line with the development of personnel management." Munsterberg's work was directed at finding the most effective and productive relationship between human and physical resources. Daniel Wren (1972), an historian of management thought claims that

Munsterberg's *Psychology and Industrial Efficiency* was directly related to Taylor's proposals and contained three broad parts: (1) "The best possible man," (2) "The best possible work," and (3) "The best possible effect" .... Munsterberg outlined definite proposals for the use of tests in worker selection, for the application of research on learning in training industrial personnel, and for the study of psychological techniques which increased worker's motives and reduced fatigue ... Munsterberg illustrated his proposals with his own evidence gathered from the study of trolley motormen, telephone operators, and ships' officers.

Taylor and others ... had envisioned contributions from psychologists for research in the human factor. Munsterberg fitted into this scheme and the ethic of scientific management was readily apparent in (1) the focus on the individual, (2) the emphasis on efficiency and (3) the social benefits to be derived from the application of the scientific method.

An early success for this relatively infant field was the selection and placement of personnel for the U.S. Army in World War I. Faced with the problem of drafting, inducting, and placing millions of men, the army sought the assistance of the American Psychological Association. A group of psychologists under the leadership of Walter Dill Scott responded (Ling, 1965). To cope with the selection problem, the Army Alpha Test was developed. It was an intelligence test which could be administered to a large number of people at one time and it proved "extremely valuable in placing draftees and is estimated to have saved ... many millions of dollars" (Miner, 1969). A companion test, the Army Beta, was constructed to evaluate the intelligence of those who did not have reading and writing skills to take the Alpha. Miner (1969) believes that these tests led to a judgment that though illiteracy was widespread, individuals were bright enough that they would respond to training, which was subsequently developed by the military. These training programs formed the basis for much industrial training to follow.

The second contribution of industrial psychology to World War I was the development of personnel classification and assessment procedures. This development was spearheaded by Walter Dill Scott. Scott worked on methods for evaluation of officers for both promotion and assignment. (For his work he was awarded the Distinguished Service Medal.)

After World War I, much of what had been learned and applied to the military was directed toward the private sector. For the most part, industrial psychologists were concerned with selection and placement problems. Companies became increasingly concerned with personnel management problems. Sweeping changes in labor legislation in the 1930s increased management's concern with cost reduction through both industrial engineering and industrial psychology.

World War II had another sharp impact on the development of industrial psychology. The same selection and placement problems of World War I existed, but by now psychology had developed refined techniques to improve these processes. For instance, screening instruments were developed which were used to predict the probability of success at completing different types of military training.

Because of the large-scale production effort to produce defense materials during World War II, under conditions where workers had been lost to the armed services, new techniques for training employees had to be developed. Women were used extensively in heavy manufacturing jobs which were earlier the province of men alone. One of the more important results of World War II for psychology was the growth of interest in leadership. The military and industry recognized the importance of leadership. If more could be understood about it, perhaps leadership training and selection could be improved. Major research projects were undertaken at The Ohio State University and the University of Michigan in the late 1940s which have set the tone of research and theory to this date. The training and experience that industrial psychologists received, however, were still fundamentally in the vein of Munsterberg.

Organizational Theory. The administrative theorists were concerned with describing primarily what managers do and proposing "rules" or principles of organization, such as the principle of unity of command. They were concerned with the question of how an organization could be designed to operate more effectively to achieve objectives in a "rational" way. They looked at organization problems rather than at human problems. This broad view could also be found in the behavioral schools, largely based on the work of Max Weber. This German sociologist, whose emphasis was on bureaucracy, was an important influence on writing and theory about the study of organization.

Max Weber's analysis considered organizations as part of broader society (Handers and Parsons, 1947). He described the characteristics of the bureaucracy, which he viewed as the most efficient form for large complex organizations such as business, government, and the military. The bureaucratic form of organization, as described by Weber, uses extensive formal rules and procedures to govern the job be-

havior of organizational members. Organizational positions are ar-
rayed in a hierarchy, each with a particular established amount of
authority and responsibility. Promotion to higher positions is based
on technical competence, objectively judged. Weber felt that this type
of organization emphasized predictability of behavior and results and
showed great stability over time. He suggested that organizations naturally evolved toward this rational form.

Chester Barnard, as we mentioned earlier, was identified with the
administrative theory school. However, much of his work had a significant effect on the behavioral approach, especially in the area of organization theory. He added much to the thinking about organization
with such concepts as "the linking pin," "the zone of indifference,"
and "the acceptance theory of authority."

The "linking pin" concept was a way of considering organizational
relationships between superiors and subordinates in organizations.

> The executives of several unit organizations, as a group, usually
> with at least one other person as a superior, form an executive or-
> ganization. Accordingly, persons specializing in executive functions
> ... are "members of" or contributors to, two units of organization in
> one complex organization—first, the so-called "working" unit and
> second, the executive unit (Barnard, 1938).

The "zone of indifference" and the "acceptance theory of authority"
contributed substantially to the view of how compliance was obtained. In the administrative school's view, authority was seen as the
right of a superior. Barnard maintained that authority works when it is
accepted, and that it is accepted often because a communication from
a superior falls within the recipient's "zone of indifference," which
means substantially that the person is willing to comply.

Using concepts from Barnard, March and Simon surveyed a wide
range of empirical work in psychology and sociology, as well as economic theory to write the book, *Organizations* (1958). This book was
stimulated by feelings that the existing research and theory about organization and management were inadequate.

The classical principles of management as formulated by Fayol and
others were attacked, as we noted earlier; March and Simon contended that such principles were not only logically inconsistent, but
oversimplified. They extended the Barnard view of the organization as
a social system. Following Barnard, they presented a more elaborate
motivational theory for organizational members than the classical
writers. They emphasized individual decision making as a basis for

understanding behavior in organizations. One of the salient points they developed was that of "bounded rationality." To make the optimal decisions suggested by the administrative theorists, they said, the manager would have to select the best of *all* possible alternatives. But the executive, as an "administrative man," is limited by his own perceptions. He has limited knowledge in making organizational decisions and cannot, therefore, make optimal decisions.

ITEM 1.2   Sibyl of a Modern Science

Mary Parker Follett was a pioneer. It was her work that spanned the gap between scientific management, as advocated by Frederick W. Taylor and his brother engineers, and the new social psychology of the 1920s, which made better human relations in industry a first concern of modern management.

Miss Follett's success as an organization expert, as a counselor to top executives here and abroad, and as an advocate of professionalized management, reached a peak more than 40 years ago. Her papers on management and organization, collected by Henry C. Metcalf and Lyndall Urwick under the title *Dynamic Administration,* are conceded to be classics.

Credit lines. The footnotes to Follett that still sprinkle the pages of management research papers have long ceased to tell more than the lady's sex—and often enough Metcalf and Urwick run off with the citations. The casual reader might be even more confused to know that Mary Follett was neither a psychologist nor an engineer and that she never met a payroll in her life. What's more, management didn't discover her until she was in her mid-50s, at the peak of her fame as a political philosopher and social critic.

No one ever spent a longer life backing into management. Few ever offered a better example of the fortunate timing of chance. But then, no one before her had had the chance to offer

management a package of pure logic and idealism, and win praise for being so realistic and understanding.

Proper background. No one in Quincy, Mass., could have guessed in the years following the Civil War that Mary Follett would someday become one of the management movement's foremost philosophers. Miss Follett had a proper background, the advantages of schooling at Thayer Academy in nearby Braintree, the privilege of entering in 1888 "The Annexe" (to Harvard University) which later became Radcliffe College.

Scientific management had not yet been invented, and Mary Parker Follett couldn't have cared less. She was studying economics and government and looking forward to her junior year abroad. At Newnham College, Cambridge, in 1891 she read a paper before the Historical Society on The Speaker of the House of Representatives. The paper was published and she had become a recognized scholar.

Natural sequence. Graduation from Radcliffe in 1898, summa cum laude, followed naturally, as did postgraduate work in France. And in Boston at the turn of the century it was no surprise to see a highly educated young gentlewoman undertake a life of private culture and public service. It was this passion for good works that, 20 years later, would lead to fame as management's favorite friend and philosopher.

In 1900, Mary Follett was a novice social worker, busy organizing a debating club in the Roxbury Neighborhood House. By 1933, she was addressing the new Dept. of Business Administration at the London School of Economics as one of the world's leading authorities on the theory of organization. Oxford had already heard her more than once.

Back in 1909, she may have thought she had achieved success in becoming chairman of the school-house subcommittee of the Women's Municipal League of Boston—her first recognition as a leader.

Revolutionist. It wasn't until 1920 that her scholarship and her concern for social reform finally found expression in a book, *The New State*. This suddenly made her a woman to reckon with, one who knew she had the answer to the stupidities of waste and war.

With unquestionable humanitarianism, irreproachable erudition, and the courage to criticize every sacred cow supporting organized society, she called for a revolutionary new principle of association "because we have not yet learned to live together."

Miss Follett, the settlement house worker, found it in the group principle: "Group organization is to be the new method in politics, the basis for our future industrial system, the foundation of international order." Her searching examination of human relations was, perhaps, the first to promote "togetherness" and "group thinking"—using precisely those terms.

She castigated "ballot-box democracy," advocated the approach of scientific management to government, criticized men who, like C. H. Harriman, told his board of directors: "Gentlemen, we must have cooperation," only later to admit honestly that what he meant by cooperation was: "Do as I say and do it damned quick."

Business testing ground. From then on, Miss Follett looked at business sometimes to illustrate error but more often for evidence that her utopia of individual satisfaction through group organization could be achieved. She was overjoyed to discover that "cutthroat competition is beginning to go out of fashion." She was pleased with the arrangement effected between "most of our large printers in Boston not to outbid one another."

"People are beginning to see that industrial organization must be based on the community idea," she wrote. So she criticized collective bargaining just because it remained bargaining and rested on concession and compromise. Real harmony between capital and labor must depend upon an integration of motives and interests that will make them into one group.

New principles. Businessmen were not put off by Miss Follett's collectivism or her mysticism. Nor did they criticize her for planning a world entirely made up of superior people like herself—sincere, unselfish, and trusting. Indeed, they were intrigued all the more, four years later, when she turned herself into a one-woman interdisciplinary task force representing all the social sciences and single-handedly sought to solve the whole problem of human relations—especially in industry.

Creative Experience argued that through conference and cooperation people could evoke each other's latent ideas and become united in pursuit of their goals. The principle again was that of psychical interpenetration—the confronting and integrating of desires as a continuous and reciprocal process—with a resulting growth in creativity and the development of new powers. This was the doctrine of circular or spiral behavior, and Miss Follett never let go of her theory.

Mutual admiration. It was this theory that swung Mary Follett into the mainstream of progressive management thinking, for businessmen were already looking beyond scientific management for help with their problems of administration. How could they better achieve coordination and control? How should they motivate and organize? How might they exercise authority?

They scrambled to take her to lunch and tell her their troubles. They listened to her quotations from Fichte and Freud and her other mentors in philosophy and psychology. And they came away with ideas that worked, despite their novelty. As for Mary Follett, she confessed: "I never had such interesting meals."

It was the beginning of a mutual admiration society that at once taught the lady philosopher the facts of business life and offered executives an objective appraisal of themselves and their problems that emphasized the values of professionalism, participation, creativity, humanitarianism, and scientific management—all of them reciprocally related and circularly integrated.

Ahead of her time. In the last nine years of her life—years largely spent in England—she published more than 20 papers on business organization and management. She anticipated much that even now is considered new departures in management: the need to depersonalize authority in recognition of "the law of the situation," the significance of management training and development, the application of behavioral science to problems of organization, the constructive uses of conflict, the psychology of power, the nature of horizontal communication and of multiple management and, above all, the social responsibilities of management.

Miss Follett liked businessmen as much as they liked her. "It is among businessmen, not all, but a few," she said, "that I find the greatest vitality of thinking today, and I like to do my thinking where it is the most alive." And she added: "Moreover, I find the thinking of businessmen today in line with the deepest and best thinking we have ever had."

So Mary Parker Follett could be optimistic and confident when she reminded executives that "there is no one else in the world but yourselves to create the science, the art, the profession of business management." And for this they must prepare themselves "seriously."

But would it be worth the effort? Miss Follett was sure of it: "No occupation can make a more worthy appeal to the imagination either from the point of view of the service it can perform, or from the tremendous interest in the job itself, than business management."

Business Week, Nov. 21, 1964

Organizational Behavior—The Emergence. March and Simon were not the only ones who felt that the principles of management and organization defined by the scientific and administrative schools were limited. There was developing a feeling that the bureaucratic structure was a limited form of organization that would work under some, but not all circumstances. In fact, critics of this persuasion argued that rigid job specifications, rules, and policies stifled the creativity, growth, development, and general effectiveness of the human side of the organization.

Of course such restrictions on human activity *were* unproductive. More important, some felt that the scientific and administrative theory perspective never really dealt with ways to integrate the interests of workers with those of management; that in fact scientific management approaches fostered divisiveness between management and workers.

In the early 1930s Mary Parker Follett was proposing ways to bring diverse interests together (see item 1.2). She had a significant impact on management thinking, especially in terms of viewing the nature of the authority relationship. Authority, she stated, should be founded not in position but in knowledge and information. If this could be achieved, then there would be a high level of integration of the interests of all parties involved in the work organization.

Douglas McGregor, in *The Human Side of Enterprise* (1960) said that most managers made a set of incorrect assumptions about those who worked for them. He called these assumptions, collectively, Theory X. Theory X assumed that man was lazy, personal goals ran counter to the organization's, and that, because of this, man had to be controlled externally. In a work context, this meant close supervision and guidance so that management would insure high performance. Theory Y assumptions, on the other hand, were based on greater trust in others. Man was more mature, self-motivated, and self-controlled than Theory X gave him credit for. McGregor suggested that there was little need for either rigid organization or interpersonal controls.

Chris Argyris (1957, 1965) also made a strong case for reducing the amount of organizational control. He believed that many constraints placed by organization structure on human beings were self-defeating to organizational goals of effectiveness and efficiency. The basic thrust of this argument, along with McGregor's, is that the bureaucratic form of organization is incongruent with the basic needs of the healthy individual. Argyris maintains that the bureaucratic form of organization treats lower organizational members like children. This fosters dependence and leads to the frustration of the higher-order human needs. This frustration expresses itself in lack of work involvement and antiorganizational activities such as sabotage.

In 1961 Rensis Likert, a psychologist, published *New Patterns of Management,* a book which was to have a powerful impact on thinking about human problems of management. Likert was the Director of the Institute for Social Research (ISR) at the University of Michigan, which was heavily involved in leadership research after World War II. Likert believed that "managers with the best record of performance in American business and government are in the process of pointing the way to an appreciably more effective system of man-

agement than now exists" (Likert, 1961). Relying on much of the research conducted at ISR, he proposed an approach which was based
on the premise that leaders (or managers) will be most effective using
a "supportive approach." This means that they must create a work
environment in which the individual sees his "experiences (in terms
of his values, goals, expectations and aspirations) as contributing to
and maintaining his sense of personal worth and importance" (Likert,
1961). Likert went on to detail the characteristics of managers and
organizations that would be "supportive" to individuals and, hence,
effective organizationally.

Another leadership researcher and psychologist, Ralph Stogdill,
drew on the work at Ohio State to formulate a broad-ranging theory of
individual behavior and group achievement (Stogdill, 1959). Stogdill
was one of the first to blend skillfully the results of social science research with some of the theories of administrative and scientific management.

The important aspect of the work of McGregor, Likert, Argyris, and
Stogdill is that it (and other work like it) broadened the scope of traditional industrial psychology from selection and placement to issues
such as organization structure and design. This work strongly affected
the field of organizational behavior (or organizational psychology) as
we know it today.

Contingency Theories of Management

At the point we have now reached in our short history, the field of
management was in a state of turmoil and confusion. Advocates of
one point of view criticized, often mistakenly, other approaches. The
administrative theorists argued that the behavioral approach propo-
nents did not understand the realities of the world of business and
administration. Critics of "principles" said principles were limited
because there were many ways to organize and be successful. Every
approach and everyone involved with them were wrong; psychologists were too narrow, sociologists too broad, principles inapplicable,
and management science approaches capable of dealing only with
trivial problems.

There was also a profound change in the approach to teaching management in university schools of business administration. In 1959 the
Carnegie Report and the Gordon and Howell Report (both on the education of businessmen) provided pressures for increased training and
emphasis on fundamental areas of quantitative analysis, organization
theory, managment principles, and human relations (Wren, 1972).

These reports had the effect of reducing the emphasis that business schools had placed on functional areas such as marketing, finance, and accounting—though these functional and skill areas are, of course, still extremely important—and shifting the focus toward the underlying disciplines of mathematics and psychology. This shift brought psychologists, especially industrial psychologists, into the business schools.

All the critics of views that differed from their own were right, of course, and all were wrong. The major problem was that critics tended to disparage other contributions without really understanding them. No one took the time to develop an integrated approach to fit together the pieces of the puzzle in a systematic way.

This sorting, sifting, and reformulation of ideas, bringing threads from all the contributing areas and weaving them into a more general approach is what contingency theories of management seek to do. Critics of the administrative and scientific management theorists were correct. There *is* no one best way to manage. But the critics never really told anyone how to proceed to develop a proper managerial strategy. It *did* all depend—but on what?

Some of the answers began to emerge, though in a very basic way, from a study of the Tennessee Valley Authority by Selznick, *TVA and the Grass Roots* (1949). He showed how various other organizations and interest groups in the outside environment of the TVA affected managerial decisions. The structure of any organization is subjected to many such outside restraints, he claimed, so the organization develops both formal and informal systems which help it to adapt to the outside environment, and thus to survive. Selznick made it clear on what the formal structure depended. Not only that, but he described how and through what kind of strategy the adjustment took place. James D. Thompson (1967), an important organization scholar in this tradition, suggests that the basic task of an administrator is the co-alignment of environmental factors with the internal technology, organizational structure, and human resources.

In 1961, Burns and Stalker published a study of British industry. They found differences in the structures of the firms they studied, and traced these differences to the nature of the technology used and the markets served. When the technological and market environments were uncertain, a loose organization was found. When the environment was more predictable, a more traditional bureaucracy seemed to be most effective. Burns and Stalker not only saw the environment effect as important, but specified more precisely than had been done before what the internal structure should look like, given a certain kind of environment.

Another English study reported by Woodward (1965), following the Burns and Stalker model, showed that the type of organizational structure used was related to a firm's economic performance when type of technology was taken into account.

Lawrence and Lorsch (1967) studied a highly effective and a less effective organization in three different industries: plastics, food, and container. These industries were chosen because they operated in environments which differed with respect to rate of technological change for the products they produced and the production methods used. The industries also differed with respect to the type of competitive situation they were in. These factors led to differences in the amount of environmental uncertainty. Lawrence and Lorsch found that in the plastics and food industry, companies were faced with much change and uncertainty, while the container industry was much more stable and predictable. They concluded that the closer the organizational structure matched the requirements imposed on it by the environment, the more successful was the firm. The effective organization had, for example, a high degree of coordinated effort when the environment required it. And a high degree of task specialization was present in high-performance firms when the environment demanded this. In general, they concluded that organizations in a stable environment are more effective if they have more detailed procedures and more centralization of the decision-making process, while organizations in an unstable environment have decentralization, participation, and less emphasis on rules and standard procedures.

The work of Selznick, Burns and Stalker, Lawrence and Lorsch, and Woodward primarily dealt with organization structure or design. The concern was with organizational theory in the tradition of Weber and Barnard—a view that tends to have a sociological perspective. A similar contingency perspective was beginning to be taken by the psychologists. In 1961 Vroom reported research which showed that there was not a simple relationship between job performance and the individual's degree of participation in determining job requirements. He found that the personality of the individual made a difference in how participation and job performance were related. Thus, the way one managed a subordinate should depend on the characteristics of the subordinate.

But an even stronger impact was made by Fred Fiedler. He had for a number of years been involved, as Stogdill and Likert were, in the study of leadership. In 1967 his *Theory of Leadership Effectiveness* presented a contingency view of leadership. Fiedler amassed some evidence to show how the impact of a manager's behavioral style was affected by the degree of routineness of subordinates' work, how much formal authority the manager had, and how well he got along with the group members. In 1974, Tosi and Hamner published an integration of these two perspectives; that is, the broad organization view with the topics that had been typically the concern of organizational psychologists: groups, motivation, attitudes, perception, and organization change.

Plan of This Book

The insights of the contingency view have had a marked impact on the writing of this book. We believe that the studies by Selznick, Burns and Stalker, Woodward, and Lawrence and Lorsch, along with the work of James Thompson, enable the manager to see fairly clearly how the environment affects the structure of an organization. These concepts are discussed in chapters 6 and 7. At the same time, the manager must be aware that ideas from the administrative school can be put to good use in management structure and strategy. In chapters 8, 9, 10, 11, and 12 we show various ways that managers can deal with others to influence them to implement decisions and how managers can develop systems for managing human resources. Concepts that consider individual and group processes are examined in chapters 3, 4, and 5. Attitudes, values, group characteristics, and motivation theories developed by the behavioral approach describe what kind of internal psychological factors seem related to high performance in different types of organizations, and this information, too, can be of great value to the manager. These concepts are all brought into our analysis and in chapters 13, 14, and 15 we show how they can be related to each other to understand how to manage different levels of people in different organizations. This approach is one aspect of a broader theory of management described by Tosi and Carroll (1975) as the "managerial process contingency approach."

Finally, the book examines organization change. The manner in which the internal structure of an organization may change to adapt more effectively to its external environment is considered in chapter 16, along with problems associated with growth, organizational strategy, and organizational design. In chapter 17, the focus is on techniques and methods of changing the human factors in an organization.

Chapter 18 provides a brief discussion of the characteristics of the effective organization and some of the environmental issues and problems which effective organizations must relate to in the near future.

All of the studies reviewed in this book reveal facets of the problem of managing people. We have tried to synthesize the constructs, ideas, and principles that seem to emerge as most effective from these studies—that is, from what is known about organizations, individuals, and managing—and show how this synthesis can be effectively applied in the various circumstances in which organizations and individuals find themselves. To conclude our short history, then, the purpose of this book is to specify, as well as can be done at this stage of the art, how a manager can more effectively manage those who work in organizations.

Discussion Questions

1. If so much thought was given to management problems before the 20th century, what made the Frederick Taylor era the starting point of scientific management?

2. Think about the points of view of the administrative theorists and the scientific management writers. How are they similar? Different?

3. How do you feel about the basic prescriptions of scientific management outlined in this chapter? Do they make sense to you as a manager? As an employee?

4. What is your opinion of the importance of the behavioral approach? How can an understanding of human behavior facilitate the manager's job?

5. Some have said that managers are concerned with manipulation of people. What schools of thought would contribute the knowledge one needs to "manipulate" others?

Chapter 2
Theory and Research in Organizational Behavior

Common to all the schools of management thought is their stress on the need for the use of the scientific method in the study of management problems. While there may be disagreement on the important variables or main thrust of the research (e.g., an emphasis on technological vs. human variables, or a psychological vs. an administrative approach), advocates of all approaches argue vigorously for systematic observation of organizational and individual activities. Obviously there is some disagreement over the nature of this systematic observation.

In this chapter, we describe the way that knowledge in the field of organization behavior is developed and organized. It is developed through science, created in research, and organized into theories.

The Scientific Method

The scientific method is a way of going about solving problems—of acquiring knowledge. It is a way of *thinking,* not necessarily the use of specific tools or techniques such as laboratories, statistics, or research designs. It is not even related to the ability to measure precisely a factor we wish to study. Techniques are used to implement a scientific approach, but techniques alone don't make science.

More than anything, the scientific method is a perspective—a way of looking at problems and their answers as tentative. Current knowledge is seen as being in a state of transition, always open to change.

With a scientific perspective, one is concerned with *what is,* rather than with *what should be.* The emphasis is on what is occurring, not on trying to judge whether the occurrence is good or bad, since evaluative judgments reflect personal values and tend to hinder scientific inquiry.

The position we take in this book about the scientific method was well summarized by Kerlinger (1967):

First there is doubt, a barrier, an indeterminate situation crying out, so to speak, to be made determinate. The scientist experiences vague doubts, emotional disturbance, inchoate ideas. He struggles to formulate the problems, even if inadequately. He studies the literature, scans his own experience and the experience of others. Often he simply has to wait for an inventive leap of the mind. Maybe it will occur; maybe not. With the problem formulated, with the basic question or questions properly asked, the rest is much easier. Then the hypothesis is constructed, after its implications are deduced, mainly along experimental lines. In this process the original problem, and of course the original hypothesis, may be changed. It may be broadened or narrowed. It may even be abandoned. Lastly, but not finally, the relation expressed by the hypothesis is tested by observation and experimentation. On the basis of the research evidence, the hypothesis is accepted or rejected. This information is then fed back to the original problem and it is kept or altered as dictated by the evidence.... What is important is the overall fundamental idea of scientific research as a controlled rational process of reflective inquiry, the interdependent nature of the parts of the process, and the paramount importance of the problem and its statement.

Theory and Organizational Behavior

Theory is important to the scientific method. Formulating a theory is a way of organizing knowledge about something. A theory is an abstraction of real life, a way of defining a system into variables and their relationships. A theory is a set of interrelated concepts, definitions, and propositions about relationships between the concepts. In organizational behavior, theories present a systematic view of individuals, groups, and subgroups and how they interact in some relatively patterned behavior sequence to achieve a goal.

The purpose of theory is to explain, predict, and guide research. Theory can have prescriptive or descriptive utility. Some theoretical approaches to organizational behavior present normative prescriptions about what conditions and relationships should exist in organizations. For example, how should work be organized? How should authority and responsibility be assigned? What are the "principles" that should be complied with? Normative (or prescriptive) theory has value in determining and prescribing organizational conditions in order to avoid certain problems or to obtain certain outcomes. It can throw up a "red flag," suggesting that when prescriptions are violated, problems *may* develop. Prescriptive theory, then, has a predictive aspect to it. For instance, the "traditional" concept of unity of command leads to a general prediction of role conflict (inconsistent demands on a person from different sources) if violated.

Some theories are descriptive; that is, they are directed to the *explanation* of behavior in organizations, treating, for instance, individual reactions to different degrees of behavioral prescription or organizational considerations. Such theories focus on human variables affected by structural considerations. Both descriptive and prescriptive approaches have the fundamental goal of understanding why specific things occur as they do in organizations. Theory enables us to organize concepts, to have a systematic body of knowledge.

Theory should also serve as the basis for research. The explicit and implicit propositions and hypotheses in theory provide direction for empirical efforts toward verification or rejection of the theory itself, or its important hypothetical substructures.

Development of Theory

Science rests on theory, a proposed explanation of something. A theory defines variables (or concepts) and the relationships among them. It describes a "suggested" way that something operates. It is like a picture or diagram. For example, if one did not know how the insides of a clock worked, but could only see the hands moving around a face at a certain rate, he might develop a theory (or picture) of the underlying components and their relationship to each other. This theory would help him understand. A theory is a way to capture the real world, to identify what is related to what, and how.

Everyone has personal theories for guidance in daily actions. Whenever a person makes assumptions about how a chain of events will occur to produce a certain effect, that person is using a theory. Managers have always used theories to manage, whether they were aware of it or not. In establishing a price, a manager assumes this will trigger a set of reactions resulting in a particular response from customers, or perhaps competitors. When a company establishes an employee profit-sharing plan, it often does so because it believes this will result in increased employee morale and/or more productive effort.

Formal theory is more widely used in science and research than personal theories. Formal theory may be *deductive* or *inductive*. A deductive theory is one which starts with a set of postulates or axioms; that is, it starts with assumptions taken without proof and which are considered to be self-evident. From these *postulates* or *ax-*

ioms, a set of conclusions are derived (or deduced) about the nature of reality, and how things relate to each other. Theories in organizational behavior, however, tend to be inductive. Inductive theories are built from observation and research. Both deductive and inductive thought processes are typically involved in the development of theory, as will be seen in the discussion below of the typical steps in the development of theory in the field of organizational behavior.

Observation—The Development of Concepts. A theory begins by observing some phenomena. These observations may be quite imprecise, only the casual observations of an interested individual. From these observations, concepts or constructs may emerge. A concept (construct) is a mental image. It is formed after a set of observations has been made. It is a definition providing a label for and a meaning to the reality observed. It is developed after careful study of some phenomena. In the physical sciences "atom," "molecule," and "gravity" are examples of such concepts. In the behavioral sciences, "achievement needs" "self-esteem," "intelligence," and "status" are examples. Concepts help individuals to perceive and classify the world around them. Given the tremendous amount of information brought to the brain by the senses, it is impossible to make sense of the world without using concepts.

An example of two important concepts in organizational behavior is "consideration" and "initiating structure" in leadership research. For many years, individuals speculated on the characteristics of "effective" or "ineffective" leaders. Early lists of effective leadership behaviors were very long (Stogdill, 1974), probably because those observing particular leaders saw that they exhibited a very wide variety of different and specific behaviors. Gradually, however, many leader behaviors were classified into two categories. One category was related to the task or work activities. The other was related to the morale or satisfaction of followers or subordinates. Such concepts as "task-centered" and "employee-centered" leadership behavior came to be studied more closely. From some of these studies, the concept "leader initiating structure" was developed to describe task-oriented activities such as scheduling work, assigning tasks, specifying procedures, and communicating performance-level expectations. Another concept, leader "consideration," included people-oriented behaviors such as being friendly and approachable, looking out for the personal welfare of the group, and giving advance notice of change.

Development and Testing of Hypotheses. In a theory, concepts are related to other concepts. These relationships are tentative. They are

Hypotheses vs. Propositions

hypotheses. Hypotheses are conditional predictions about the relationship between two concepts or variables. They state how the concepts in a theory go together, and they form the basis for research efforts to test and refine the theory. Over the years in leadership research, "consideration" and "initiating structure" were correlated with many different types of attitudes, behaviors, and performances. This research resulted in a further clarification, elaboration, and development of "initiating structure" and "consideration."

In research, hypotheses are formed, the concepts are assessed, and then they are examined. The results are used to accept or refute the hypotheses. To identify the nature of the relationship between two or more concepts, they must be put into operational terms and measured. This is difficult, because many concepts are quite difficult to measure. Love, for example. How is it to be measured? Number of kisses and/or number of affectionate glances per unit of time might be two ways of operationalizing this concept. How about intelligence? Performance on several problems with different levels of difficulty might be one way. The concept of status might be measured by obtaining rankings of groups by members of other groups, or by observing communication patterns, or by noting who influences whom.

Often research is unsuccessful; it fails to find a predicted relationship between concepts because the operationalization of those concepts is inadequate or insufficient. The concept, as conceived, may be broader, richer, and more complex than the measuring devices used in an attempt to convert it into operational terms.

Development of Propositions.   After several studies have been completed to test various hypotheses about the relationship of one concept to another, a proposition may be formulated. A *proposition* describes the relationships among a group of concepts or variables. A proposition is a formal statement about the state of reality. It might be considered a statement about the truth of the matter as a particular individual sees it. Sometimes propositions are called *truth statements.* They may also be seen as *if-then* statements, since they are often in the form of: *If* certain conditions are present, *then* particular results will occur. Of course a proposition is only an individual's belief about how things in reality are related to each other. The proposition may not be necessarily true. Propositions are developed to be tested to determine their validity. Often the propositions go far *beyond* the previous research on which they are based. They may be much more general and abstract than a particular hypothesis. When a number of propositions *that are not inconsistent with each other* are put together, a theory exists.

An example of the use of propositions can be seen in House's (1971) "path-goal theory of leader effectiveness." House attempted to reconcile contradictory findings in previous leadership research. In this previous research, for example, it was sometimes found that leader "initiating structure" was related to higher subordinate satisfaction. But sometimes leader "initiating structure" was related to lower subordinate satisfaction. House believed that the effect of "initiating structure" on subordinate satisfaction and motivation was significantly influenced by the nature of the subordinate's task. He reasoned that if the task was ambiguous and uncertain, subordinates would appreciate the leader's efforts to clarify it and to tell them what to do and how to do it. On the other hand, if the task was simple, routine, and well understood by the subordinates, then the leader's efforts to clarify it (initiating structure) would be viewed as unnecessary—and perhaps insulting—by the subordinates, and their satisfaction would be low. One of his propositions states:

> Where leader attempts to clarify path-goal relationships are redundant with existing conditions, that is, where path-goal relationships are apparent because of the routine of the tasks or objective system-fixed controls, attempts by the leader to clarify path-goal relationships will result in increased externally imposed control and will be seen by subordinates as redundant. Although such control may increase performance, it will also result in decreased satisfaction. (House, 1971).

This proposition states that if a supervisor tries to clarify the task (high initiating structure leader behavior) where the task is already highly structured, those who work for him will view his behavior as unnecessary. Their satisfaction will decrease. This proposition is a general statement about the relationship among variables (leader behavior, satisfaction, and task characteristics). It is of the "if-then" variety. It states that *if* something increases (initiating structure) in a certain environment, *then* something else (satisfaction) will decrease. The proposition also explains why it happens.

Testing Propositions. If the proposition is correct, then the researcher would expect to find a certain relationship between concepts or variables. The researcher states—in the form of an hypothesis—what the proposition leads him to expect. The researcher then designs a study and research instruments, collects and analyzes his data, and comes to certain conclusions about the validity of the hypothesis. The results confirm or disconfirm the proposition. For example, Schuler (1973) tested the proposition of House that when the way to do a job was already clear, because the job was highly routine, leader behavior which was directive (i.e., tried to clarify the path/goal relationship) would likely result in high performance but low satisfaction. Schuler found, for instance, that high performance in repetitive jobs was associated with high leader guidance (contrary to the House proposition) for workers who were high in motivation, and proposed a reformulation of the House (1971) proposition:

> Highly motivated subordinates working for leaders who are highly initiating on (highly repetitive tasks) have higher levels of performance than highly motivated subordinates working for leaders who are less initiating . . . (Schuler, 1973).

Theory Revision. If the proposition in a theory is disconfirmed, this does not mean the underlying theory, of which the proposition is a part, is disconfirmed, since the validity of a theory may rest on several propositions. Also, the proposition may be only partially disconfirmed and may be reformulated. Then the reformulated proposition can be tested again.

Thus the theory, due to testing of its original propositions and reformulation of them, is under continual revision. If, however, sufficient disconfirmation occurs, then validity of the theory is cast in serious doubt and, in general, it will not be used.

What Is a "Good" Theory?

There are often several alternative theories which treat a particular phenomena. This is particularly true in organizational behavior. There are several leadership theories (House, 1971; Fiedler, 1965), for example. And there are competing theories, such as expectancy theories, need theories, and reinforcement theories, to explain motivation. One way to judge the merits of competing theories is to consider each's capacity to predict, the ease of testing their hypotheses, their consistency with other theories, and their parsimony.

Predictability. How well a theory explains is not as important as how well it predicts. Prediction is much more difficult than explanation. For any phenomena that one sees, there may be many different explanations, all of which may seem equally plausible. Human knowledge advances when a wide range of different explanations become narrowed or reduced. Scientific research generally aims to eliminate alternative explanations for phenomena.

By sharpening the predictive capacity of a theory (one of the aims of science), prediction and control of an uncertain environment is facilitated. When outcomes can be predicted more accurately, the accomplishment of more specific goals is eased.

Testability. Theories which can be tested are more valuable than those which cannot be. Unless the concepts in a theory can be measured, the theory cannot be revised or discarded if found wanting. Many behavioral theories of the past are difficult to test. In Freudian theory, for example, it is assumed that certain behaviors are the result of basic drives (libido) in the individual, that they are stored in the id, and that they are blocked or modified by societal or parental restrictions. This and other Freudian concepts are quite difficult, if not impossible, to operationalize or measure. Such theories, however, even though difficult to operationalize and test, may last a long time, especially when they are valuable to many, say psychotherapists, for their explanatory power.

Consistency with Other Theories. Any proposed theory gains in acceptability if it is congruent with other theories which themselves have been partially validated. Theories which seem to contradict knowledge already accumulated are not as likely to find acceptance among scientists as are theories which are in congruence with theories partially supported by research evidence. Also, theories which are congruent with other theories can perhaps be combined with them to create an even better theory in the sense of increased predictive power.

Parsimony. The criterion of parsimony is useful in comparing alternative theories which attempt to explain or predict the same type of behavior. In general, scientists feel that if one theory uses fewer concepts or propositions than another but *predicts* as well, then it is the superior theory. Some feel the emphasis should be on prediction, however, rather than on parsimony and explanation, because many brief theories explain something that has already happened but are not useful in predicting the future since the terms they use are very general or abstract and cover many more specific behaviors. A very early theory of human behavior, derived from Greek philosophy (from Epicurus and Aristippus), was that man is motivated to achieve pleasure and to avoid pain—hedonism. Centuries later, Adam Smith

(1759) and Jeremy Bentham (1789) made hedonism the basis for their economic theories. Thorndike's (1911) Law of Effect was also derived from hedonistic notions. It states that a new behavior is learned if it enables the organism to achieve pleasure or to avoid pain. As Thorndike put it: "Pleasure stamps in; pain stamps out." Hedonism is a very parsimonious explanation for past behavior, but it is not particularly useful for predicting future behavior unless we know in advance what particular behaviors will give a specific individual pleasure or pain.

The Research Process

If developing theory is forming the question, then research is systematically seeking the answers. Some research questions may be quite parochical, of interest only to a few people in a particular organization. Other research questions are broader and their answers may greatly advance the welfare of mankind. The basic steps in the research process are essentially the same, however, whether simple or complex questions are involved.

Identify General Research Objective. A study may be initiated to obtain an answer to a specific organizational question—for example, to identify the job satisfactions and dissatisfactions of employees in particular organizational units. Or some organizations may wish more information on current industry practices—for example, wage levels and wage techniques used by other organizations similar to their own.

A theory describes the assumed relationship between things that exist in reality. A simple theory might describe the relationship between two factors, while a more complex theory might describe the relationship between a number of factors that vary. Some theories may be quite personal, such as those we hold as individuals, while others are more widely held. Some theories have a good deal of evidence in their favor, while others do not.

In organizational behavior, most research is aimed at the development of better theory. Studies are undertaken to improve the formulation of concepts and to test propositions and generally increase a theory's predictive capacity.

Establish Specific Research Questions and Hypotheses. Before seeking an answer through research, one should know precisely what the question is. The nature of the question guides the investigation. An individual must be aware of what he wants to know so he can know how and where to look.

An hypothesis is a conditional prediction about the relationship between two or more things. An hypothesis states the expected relationship between the presumed causal factor (the independent variable) and the presumed effect (the dependent variable). For instance, an investigator may hypothesize that increasing the level of performance standards will result in better performance. The level of performance standard would be the independent variable; the level of performance, the dependent variable.

Develop Research Design. A research design is the plan which will be used to obtain the answers to the questions or to test the hypotheses. Each research design is unique, to some degree, to the problem being studied. In the research design, independent variables are manipulated, or related to variations in dependent variables. In a typical research design, the subjects, or individuals, to be studied are put in one of two groups—an experimental group of a control group. Individuals in both groups are measured or given one or more pretests on the dependent variable or variables of interest to the researcher—at time one (T_1). Next, the experimental group—but not the control group—is given some type of treatment. Then the individuals in the two groups are measured or given a post-test on the variable of interest at time two (T_2). This research design uses the *experimental* approach. The experimental approach involves an attempt to hold constant all possible causal variables except the one the investigator wishes to manipulate (the treatment) in order to determine clearly if variations on the factor have an effect on the dependent variable.

Develop Research Instruments. Measurement is usually necessary to carry out research. For anything to have meaning to human minds, it must be compared or related to something else. Research questions, or hypotheses, are usually stated in terms of how differences in the magnitude of some variable (such as age or intelligence) is related to variation in the magnitude of some other variable (such as satisfaction or performance).

Research instruments measure the variables studied. These research instruments may be psychological tests to measure such things as intelligence or aggressiveness. They may be questions formed to obtain information on personal characteristics or attitudes. They may be electronic devices to measure such factors as skin temperature or eye movements.

Any measurement should have *reliability* and *validity*, two fundamental prerequisites for measures of anything. Reliability refers to consistency in measurement. One type of reliability, test–retest, is the consistency or stability of a measurement over time. So long as what is being measured does not change in magnitude over time, repeated measurements should produce the same score. If this is so, then one can have faith in a measure taken at one point.

Alternate-form reliability is another way to assess consistency. Reliability is sometimes measured by giving two equivalent forms of the measure to the same group of individuals. If the measure is reliably measuring some characteristic, for example, a particular individual should get about the same relative score on both measures.

Validity refers to accuracy in measurement. Does the measure actually measure the factor being studied? A measure can be reliable but have low validity when it consistently yields the same, but inaccurate, score for an individual. There are many ways to determine validity. A test for finger dexterity may be validated by giving it to a group of watch makers and a group of foundry workers. If the watchmakers score higher on this measure, this would be congruent with what you would expect when measuring finger dexterity.

Choose a Sample. The researcher will generally be unable to study *all* the phenomena of the world in which he is interested. He therefore must study a sample, or smaller group, in order to generate conclusions to apply to a larger population. It is of course necessary that the smaller group be as representative as possible of the larger population. The more representative the sample, the more likely it is that conclusions about the population are justified. This representativeness is most likely to be achieved when the sample is drawn by random means from the population. If a sample is drawn by random means, then each and every member of the population has an equal probability of being drawn.

Any sample from a given population will not be exactly representative of the whole population, and therefore any measurements taken of that sample are not likely to be exactly the same as those taken of the population as a whole. The measurements taken in a sample will deviate from those taken in the population because of sampling error. The larger the sample taken and the more random the sampling process, the less the sampling error.

Choose Method for Analyzing Data. Hypotheses are accepted if statistical facts support them. A statistic is a value calculated from a sample. Statistical analysis is often necessary to make inferences or conclusions from a sample about a larger group or population. If the magnitude of the results, or the statistical facts, are such that they are too large to be accounted for by sampling error alone, we say that they are "statistically significant." Thus if a researcher obtains differences in the average productivity of two groups of workers, say those raised in rural areas and those raised in an urban area, and these differences are sufficiently large so that it is unlikely that they can be attributed to sampling error alone, a statistically significant result is obtained. This means that the differences are real. But it is possible that even though the differences are real, they are not sufficiently large to be of practical importance.

Conduct a Pilot Study and Make Changes as Necessary. After the research design has been developed and the measuring instruments and methods of analysis have been determined, a pilot study is often conducted to test the research approach. In the pilot study a very small group is measured and the results analyzed to test the feasibility of the study as planned. At this point it may be found that the subjects being studied do not understand the questions asked of them. Or it may be found that they do not vary on the concepts studied. Perhaps the planned statistical analysis is inappropriate for this type of study. In a pilot study the researcher seeks to test the research strategy to see if changes in the research plan are necessary.

Collect and Analyze Data. The next step is to collect and analyze the data. This step may involve very little of the total amount of time of a research project, but it is of critical importance. In collecting the data, a researcher could bias the results by letting the subjects know, for example, what he wishes to find. The subjects might then try to answer the research instruments as they think the researcher wants them to, and this will bias the measurement. And in analyzing the data it is easy to make many classification and computational errors so that the results are incorrect. While data analysis is often a very routine phase of the research process, it is an extremely critical one, and great care must be taken with it to prevent a simple error, such as a computational mistake, which would lead to incorrect conclusions.

Draw Conclusions. The researcher can now arrive at conclusions about his questions or hypotheses (and on the basis of his conclusions, revise his previous beliefs or opinions). Of course in drawing conclusions many factors must be considered. The methodology employed in the study and various possible sources of error, such as low reliability or a contamination in the study itself, could affect the results. There are also many problems which emerge in carrying out a study which were not anticipated when it was planned. Measurements may be in error because of faulty equipment or because the subjects did not understand the questions asked of them. Perhaps the subjects lied to the investigators or misled them in some way. Perhaps satisfactory responses were received from only a small proportion of the sample studied, making it very difficult to generalize from the sample to the population. Sometimes after a study has been completed, a reassessment of the whole research process will lead to a conclusion that the instruments measured something other than what the researchers intended. When conditions such as this exist, the conclusions should be drawn to reflect the differences in concepts.

Finally, a research report is prepared. Such a report should describe the research questions, or hypotheses, and why they were chosen. The research procedures used for data analysis should be explained. The results are then presented and explained, and finally the conclusions of the investigator are set forth.

The description of the study should be complete so that the reader can evaluate the validity of the methodology employed and the conclusions of the investigators. It is quite possible that the reader of a research report may arrive at conclusions quite different from those of the original investigators. Another reason for the precise description of the research methodology is so that the study can be repeated (replicated) by others. Replication is an important check in science. It is one reason why the scientific perspective or approach has resulted in a great advancement of knowledge. Finally, the researcher must subject his work to scrutiny and criticism from his fellow professionals, making him careful and cautious in his work.

Research Methods in Organizational Behavior

As we have said, research is nothing more than a way to view experiences in a systematic, logical, and controlled fashion in order to increase the likelihood that the conclusion drawn about a relationship between factors is correct. Research which flows from theory is based on the scientific method, the logic applied to the study of a problem. Scientific techniques are the tools used to implement the scientific method. Statistical methods and research designs are techniques, and how they are used often differs between various disciplines, especially between the social sciences and the natural sciences. The important difference in technique between the natural and social sciences is in measurement of the concepts. In the natural sciences there is more precision in measurement than in the social sciences, but the essense of science remains method, not technique. In this section we examine several techniques for studying organizational behavior to show that a particular problem can be studied many different ways.

Consistent research findings from several different techniques provide a basis for strong corroboration of a theory. To illustrate this, we will briefly describe several different kinds of studies on management by objectives (MBO). MBO is an approach to managing in which a superior and subordinate develop a clear understanding of the subordinate's goals, and these goals are used for evaluation of the subordinate's performance. The basic activities in MBO are setting specific goals, getting agreement on them between a superior and subordinate, and using them to provide performance feedback to the subordinate.

Many of these MBO activities, such as goal setting, have been studied in different ways, often in some other context than MBO. Some have been studied in laboratory research and others have been examined in field research. The basic distinction between laboratory research and field research is that in field research the investigator goes into the "real" world where events are going on and attempts to determine, through different observational strategies, how factors are related. In laboratory research, on the other hand, the factors are studied under controlled conditions so that the researcher can draw conclusions that are free from the effects of contaminating factors that might be present in field research.

Laboratory Research

In laboratory studies, the researcher attempts to minimize the effects of extraneous, and perhaps influential, factors irrelevant to the problem by isolating the research setting from the ordinary situation in which it occurs. Then the variables with which the researcher is concerned are carefully manipulated under controlled conditions to determine their effect.

For instance, suppose you are concerned with studying how difficult task (work) goals affect job performance. One way to do this would be to ask a group of workers how difficult their work goals are and then relate their answers to how well they do their job. (This is a *field study*). But there are a number of reasons which might cause a worker to respond to your question ("How difficult are your work goals?") in different ways. For example, does the person understand what you mean by "difficult" or "work goals"? You might mean "Did your boss require you to produce 20 percent above standard for this week?" Perhaps the worker you spoke with thought you were asking,

"In general, how hard is your job?" To eliminate problems of this type, it may be desirable to perform this research in a laboratory.

This is exactly what E. A. Locke did. Locke (1968) reports several experiments in which he studied the effects of goal difficulty on performance. He secured the cooperation of college students as subjects. In each study, the students were broken down into three groups. One group was assigned "hard" goals, another "medium," and the third "easy" goals. The experimental task to perform was to list words describable by adjectives such as "heavy," or thinking of several different uses for common objects. Locke concluded from his studies using college students as laboratory experiment subjects that the harder the assigned goal, the higher the level of performance. The procedure used in a similar laboratory study is described in item 2.1.

ITEM 2.1   A Laboratory Study

Procedure

Subject Pool. The original S pool consisted of 10 male and 10 female paid college student volunteers from the University of Maryland.

Task and Rating Scales. The task was simple addition, each problem consisting of three two-digit numbers. Each S was presented with a booklet containing a separate sheet(s) of addition problems for each trial. The number of problems per page varied according to trial length and to the arrangement of the problems on the page. The arrangement was such as to prevent Ss from keeping track of their scores.

Separating each trial sheet was a page consisting of four attitude rating scales. The Interest-Boredom scale was a bipolar, vertical, graphic scale anchored at various points by statements ranging from "it was extremely boring" to "it was fascinating." There were two Task Focus scales, one asking for the *percentage of time S* felt he was focused on the task and the other asking how *intensely S* felt he was focusing. The Effort scale asked S to indicate the percentage of his maximum possible effort exerted during the trial. The S was told to rate the experience of effort and not to make an induction from performance.

There were 12 trials of steadily increasing length. Trials 1-4 lasted 15 sec., Trials 5-6 were 30 sec. long, followed by Trials 7-12 which were, respectively, 1, 2, 4, 8, 16, and 32 min. in length. The Ss had 30 sec. between trials to fill out the four rating scales. The purpose of the differing trial lengths was to allow the selection of Ss who were similar in performance rate on the shorter trials ("maximal ability") but different on the longer trials, a drop on the latter being taken as indicative of lowered motivation to perform.

Method. *Test I.* The experiment was introduced as a study of attitudes as a function of trial length. All Ss were instructed to "do their best." It was added that they should try to work at a steady pace, exerting the same amount of effort per time unit on every trial.

Test II. Two to three wk. after taking Test I, the Goal and Do-Best Ss returned for Test II, which was identical to Test I. The instructions for the Do-Best group were the same as those given to all Ss before Test I, though it was suggested that they might find the going a little faster this time since they had worked these same problems previously. The Goal Ss were told that on Test I they had slowed down in performance during the longer trials as compared to the Do-Best

Of the original 20 Ss taking Test I, 12 were selected for Tests II and III. The six Ss having the uniformly lowest performance slopes and lowest scores on the attitude scales were placed in the *Goal* condition for the next two tests. The six Ss having the uniformly highest scores on these measures were placed in the *Do-Best* condition for Tests II and III. The differences between the two groups on total scores on the rating scales on Test I were all significant at the .05 level or better (t's = 2.49, 3.15, 3.63, and 4.20 for the boredom-interest, percent focus, intensity of focus, and effort measures, respectively). The difference between the groups in total performance on Test I was not significant (t = 1.34), but generally the performance rate (in terms of mean problems correct per minute) of the low-motivation Ss decreased more than did the performance of the high-motivation Ss (the two groups had identical performance means on the four 15-sec. trials). Thus the two groups were of the same "maximal ability" as indicated by their performance on the shortest trials, but the one group dropped off more on the longer trials and showed less interest in and focus on the task on Test I, as a whole, than did the other. Ss and to try and improve their perfor-

mance on Test II by trying to reach the specific goals which had been set for them on each trial. They were told that the goals on the short (15-sec.) trials were set at about the same place that they had reached on Test I, but that the goals for the longer trials were set above what they had done previously, since their performance had been poorer on these trials.

The goals for the Goal group were marked by a red circle placed around the problem the S was to try to reach by the end of the trial. These goals were determined by taking the mean number done correctly by S on the four 15-sec. trials on Test I as the base rate and making each subsequent goal an appropriate multiple of this so that S would have to maintain his initial rate to reach each subsequent goal.

Test III. Two to five wk. (M = 2.5) after Test II, the Goal and Do-Best Ss returned to take the identical test again. The instructions for the Do-Best group were the same as those used in Tests I and II. The Goal Ss were told that they had raised their performance on Test II but to try to further improve their performance on Test III by trying for new goals. These new goals were set 10% above their own best previous performance (on Test I or II) on each trial. (The goals were again marked by red circles on the worksheets.) This new method of setting goals was used here, because it was found that the method used for Test II yielded goals that were too hard on the longer trials.— Judith F. Bryan and Edwin A. Locke

Journal of Applied Psychology, 1967, vol. 51, no. 3

Advantages and Disadvantages.

The most obvious criticism of laboratory research is that (1) it is an artificially contrived setting, (2) it generally uses subjects who are not representative of the group to whom we would wish to apply the results, and (3) the tasks are contrived, routine, simple, and meaningless. Do college undergraduates in psychology react to goal difficulty in the same way as workers in the real world? Probably not. And when Locke sets "difficult" goals (which means a longer list of items for subjects under the "high goal" treatment), is that the same as raising a worker's piece quota 20 percent, or a salesman's sales quota 15 percent? Does it have the same effect?

But there are some important advantages to work done in the laboratory. Situations can be isolated, and variables can be manipulated and controlled more easily than out of the lab. In other words, the researcher can come much closer to controlling conditions in such a way as to eliminate the impact of extraneous factors—that is, factors other than the independent variables being manipulated.

Field Research

One characteristic of laboratory research is that it allows the conditions to be controlled closely. Another is that it allows the manipulation of a variable under study (as, for example, Locke was able to manipulate "goal difficulty"). This permits the researcher to draw conclusions about the effects of the factor (goal difficulty). But often this same kind of manipulation is possible outside the laboratory. When this condition exists, the research is called a field experiment (as opposed to the field study, in which there is no attempt made to control any variables; in a field study, the variables are observed to determine how they are related to each other).

Field Experiments.   In the field experiment, the investigator attempts to systematically observe the effects of one variable (e.g., participation in goal setting) on another (e.gm, performance). But this is done by seeking to control the conditions under which the experiment occurs. One such study, on an aspect of MBO (participation), is reported by French, Kay, and Meyer (1965). Some managers were assigned goals by their superiors. Other managers participated with their superiors in setting goals. The superior was instructed on how to set goals (either directive or participative). French, Kay, and Meyer found little difference in performance between the two groups of managers as a result of the way their goals were set, but when there were specific goals, higher performance was reported. Another field study on management by objectives was carried out by Muczyk (1973), who divided all the branches of a large bank in the suburbs of Washington D.C. into control and experimental groups. He then obtained measures of the branch's performance. Next he persuaded the branch managers in the "experimental" branches to use the MBO approach for one year. He then compared the performance of the branches using a management by objectives approach with those which did not. He found that performance improvement in the experimental branches was not large enough to be statistically significant. Further investigation by Muczyk suggested that perhaps the reason for this was that most of the goals set in the experimental branches were not difficult. This field experiment is described in item 2.2. In addition to clarifying the nature of a field experiment, item 2.2 also demonstrates that sometimes research efforts do not yield the kind of findings which are of interest to the researcher.

ITEM 2.2 A Field Experiment

Management by objectives (MBO) is a subject about which a great deal has been written in textbooks and in journals spanning the entire gamut from the most mundane trade journals to esoteric academic ones. The popularity of MBO is not restricted to the United States alone. It appears to be accepted even more in England.

Regrettably, most of the conclusions drawn with regard to the efficacy of MBO are a product of either opinion or research of a low level of rigor (e.g., case studies and personal testimony.) The few better studies neglect "hard" measures of economic performance. What is needed at the present time is a well controlled field experiment—that is, a study in an actual firm conducted by the exacting rules of experimental design.

Three such studies were conducted— one in a 41-branch bank and two in a railroad company. The control and experimental groups in the bank were constituted through matching branches on economic variables. The branch was selected as the economic unit to be studied since ample economic performance measures existed for each branch. Two facets of the operations of the railroad company were examined with a control and experimental group in

each. Two identical car repair shops constituted one study, while two similar automated track maintenance gangs comprised the second experimental situation. Objective measures of productivity existed in both operations.

In the bank study, the criterion variables were: number of checking accounts, number of savings accounts, number of other time deposits, number of installment loans, dollar value of checking accounts, dollar value of savings accounts, dollar value of other time deposits, dollar value of installment loans, interest on commercial loans, and dollar value of the tellers' adjustment accounts. The experimental treatment group and the control group were compared on the ten criterion variables at the six-month level and at the end of the study (12 mos.). Change scores were used to control for any initial differences. No significant differences were found between the experimental and the control groups on both occasions.

In the two railroad studies, objective measures existed as well. Although the management by objectives groups had higher performance, the differences were insufficiently large to be significant at the .05 level of confidence.

In addition to testing MBO's impact

on "hard" measures of performance, the researcher tested its effect in the bank study on the following psychological variables: role conflict, role ambiguity, job involvement, perceived importance of skills and contributions in determining pay, job satisfaction, self-actualization needs, autonomy needs, esteem needs, social needs, and security needs. Change scores were used to control for any initial differences between the two groups. Though the mean change scores were in favor of the MBO group, the differences did not reach significance at the .05 level of confidence.

The smallness of the samples in all three studies militated against statistical significance.—Jan P. Muczyk **Dissertation abstract, Univ. of Maryland**

A variant, and quite a neat one, of field experiments is the "natural" field experiment. In this type of study, the researcher must be lucky enough to find a situation which lends itself to experimental research. One such study is reported by Ivancevich (1970) studying the implementation of MBO in two production units of plants which had different degrees of support for MBO. In one, managers received much encouragement from higher levels to use MBO. In the second, there was no encouragement. A third plant in which there was no formal MBO at all, was used as a control, a base line against which to compare the other two. Ivancevich found that performance was highest for that plant in which there was a great deal of encouragement to use MBO.

Field Studies. Perhaps field studies are the most common types of studies reported in the organizational behavior research literature. They are "ex post facto scientific inquiries aimed at discovering the relations and interactions among sociological [and] psychological . . . variables in real social structures" (Kerlinger, 1967). The researcher looks at sets of variables and how they are related to each other, generally at one particular ioint in time. For instance, in one very extensive study of MBO, Carroll and Tosi (1973) examined how goal characteristics, superior-subordinate relationships, and feedback were related to reported managerial changes in attitudes and performance. They studied managers in the Black and Decker Manufacturing Company. The managers completed a questionnaire with scales measuring these variables. One study reported from this research is described in item 2.3.

Advantages and Disadvantages of Field Research. The major problem with field research is the possible contamination by other factors of the variables under study. Even in a field experiment there are many possible factors beyond the control and the awareness of the researcher which may systematically bias the results. The real world setting, however, gives field research a credibility for applications to

ITEM 2.3   A Field Study

The objective of the study was to identify the characteristics of the superior and his situation that were related to the manner in which he established goals and reviewed the performance of his subordinates. Such a study has implications for management effectiveness, since previous research by the authors has indicated that the manner of carrying out the Management by Objectives (MBO) process is related to results obtained with this approach.

METHOD

Sample. The sample, containing 112 managers, was analyzed to identify superior/subordinate pairs for which research data were available. Seventy-seven such pairs were identified. The rest of the managers in the sample did not have a superior or a subordinate among the managerial respondents.

Data Collection. For each manager in the superior/subordinate pairs, there was available a 50-item questionnaire. The items in this questionnaire were used to construct scales measuring various aspects of the goal-setting process and various aspects of the performance review process. Also, the questionnaire was used to develop scales measuring reactions to the MBO program, attitudes toward the superior and the organization, and results obtained by the subordinate under the MBO program. In addition to the questionnaire, the Ghiselli Self-Description Inventory, a forced-choice type of personality inventory, was completed by all managerial respondents. Eight personality scales of the Ghiselli were used in the analysis. Ratings on performance and promotability were also available for about 40 managers in the total sample. The data available for each superior and his subordinate were punched on the same card.

Hypotheses. A number of general hypotheses were developed to provide guides for the selection of variables to be analyzed. These hypotheses were derived from results of previous research studies and on an a priori basis.

Analysis of the Data. A number of different types of analyses were made depending on the specific hypothesis in question. Typically, correlation analysis was used, but chi square and the t test were also employed. The sample size also varied from one analysis to another since in some cases data were available for only a certain number of managers and because in the total sample some superiors had more than one subordinate and it was considered desirable to handle "unique" superior/subordinate pairs only in some of the analyses.

RESULTS

Hypothesis 1. This general hypothesis stated that a subordinate's manner of carrying out the MBO process is related to the way his superior carries out the MBO process with him. It was tested by correlating how the MBO process was carried out for the superiors to how the MBO process was carried out for their subordinates. The analysis generally supported the hypothesis. For example, goal clarity for the superior correlated .30 to goal clarity for the subordinate. Subordinate participation in the establishing of goals for the superior correlated .28 with subordinate participation in the establishing of goals for managers reporting to these superiors. The frequency of performance review for the superior correlated .38 with the frequency of performance review for the subordinates. The establishment of priorities for goals for the superior correlated .27 with the establishment of priorities for goals for the subordinate. All of these correlations are significant at the .01 level. Difficulty of goals and number of goals for the superior were not significantly related to difficulty and number of goals for the subordinate, as might be expected.

Hypothesis 2. The second hypothesis was that superiors are more effective in carrying out the MBO process if they feel the organization supports the MBO program. It was tested by correlating the superior's perceptions of organizational support for the MBO program to his subordinate's reports on goal clarity, goal difficulty, and frequency of performance review. Higher amounts of these factors have been found to be related to more effectiveness in an MBO program in previous research conducted by the authors. In this analysis, organizational support for the MBO program as perceived by the superior correlated .16 for goal clarity, .17 for goal difficulty, and .27 for frequency of review for the subordinates of this superior. Only the latter correlation for frequency of review is statistically significant, although the first two correlations only barely miss significance at the .05 level. Thus, there does appear to be some limited support for this hypothesis.

Hypothesis 3. The third hypothesis stated that superiors with higher job satisfaction are more effective in carrying out the MBO program. This was tested by correlating satisfaction of the superior with his boss and situation (job and pay) to the clarity and difficulty of assigned goals and to the frequency of performance review as reported by the subordinate. The superior's satisfaction with his superior correlated .24 with goal clarity, .28 with goal difficulty, and .14 with frequency of performance review for the subordinate. Only the latter correlation is not statistically significant. Satisfaction with the situation for the superior was not significantly related to goal clarity, goal difficulty, or frequency of performance review for the subordi-

nate. Thus, satisfaction with the boss but not satisfaction with the situation did seem to have a limited relationship to more superior effectiveness in carrying out the MBO process.

Hypothesis 4. This hypothesis stated that managers carry out the MBO process more effectively with their subordinates if they feel their bosses would be concerned if they failed to achieve their goals. Here the superior's perception of the degree of concern that the superior's boss would feel if the superior did not meet his goals was correlated to goal clarity, goal difficulty, and frequency of performance review for the subordinate. In this analysis, the perceived degree of concern of the superior's boss for the superior's goal failure correlated .16 with goal clarity, .22 with goal difficulty, and .24 with frequency of performance review for the superior's subordinates. Only the first of these correlations is not statistically significant at the .05 level, but does approach statistical significance. There is, then, limited support for this hypothesis.

Hypothesis 5. The fifth hypothesis was that the competence of the subordinate is related to how his superior carries out the MBO process. In testing this hypothesis, the promotability and performance ratings given to subordinates were correlated to how goals were established and how frequently performance was reviewed. Promotability and performance ratings were in the form of four category scales and were available for 40 managers only. Promotability ratings correlated .31 with subordinate influence in establishing goals. This is statistically significant at the .05 level. The relationship between current performance ratings and subordinate influence in setting goals was .22, which only approaches significance at the .05 level with a sample of 40 members. These competence ratings were not significantly related to any other MBO process variables. Thus, the quality of the subordinate was somewhat related to how much participation his superior allows him in the establishment of goals for his position.

Hypothesis 6. This is a very general hypothesis that states that the personality of the superior is related to how he carries out the MBO process with his subordinates. It was felt that the personality traits generally associated with greater managerial effectiveness would especially be related to how the MBO process was carried out. This hypothesis was tested by correlating the scores on different scales on the Ghiselli Self-Description Inventory for the superior to the manner in which he established goals and reviewed performance as reported by his subordinates.

This analysis indicated the superior's personality trait that was most consistently related to how the MBO process was carried out was "decision-making approach," which measures degrees of decisiveness vs. cautiousness in decision making. Higher decisiveness and less cautiousness for superiors correlated positively to goal clarity ($r = .19$), goal difficulty ($r = .24$), subordinate participation in establishing goals ($r = .37$), and number of goals ($r = .26$). All these correlations are statistically significant at the .05 level.

In addition, self-assurance, which is a measure of confidence in one's ability to solve problems that confront one, correlated .24 with goal clarity, .31 with goal difficulty, .27 with number of goals, and .25 with frequency of feedback. All of these correlations are significant at the .05 level of significance. The other personality characteristics measured were not related to more than one or two of the MBO process scales. Both decisiveness and self-assurance have been found to be predictive of general managerial effectiveness in previous research.— Stephen J. Carroll, Dennis Cintron, and Henry L. Tosi
Proceedings, 79th Annual Convention, APA, 1971

---

real world problems far beyond that of research done in laboratory settings. This is especially true, we think, for research in organizational behavior that must ultimately be translated to some real world application if it is to be useful. We reiterate here a point made earlier: Only when findings have been reproduced in many research settings can they have high credibility. Many of the topics which we discuss in subsequent chapters of this book have been studied in a number of ways.

Application of Organizational Behavior Research

Does the tine and effort spent developing theory and conducting research have a payoff for the world in which managers operate? Some of it does, and a high payoff at that. For instance, from the MBO research reported by Carroll and Tosi (1973), a number of changes in MBO were suggested for the firm where the research was conducted. From the research, a "diagnostic change program" was implemented, with the goal of increasing acceptance of MBO and stimulating greater involvement in it. This change effort consisted of (1) feedback of research results to managers, (2) changing the MBO reporting system, and (3) a more systematic approach to setting goals. As a result of this change effort, managers were more participative in goal setting, they saw goals more clearly, and they sensed a greater level of top management support for MBO (Tosi and Carroll, 1973).

Another area of widespread use of research results is in training and development. For instance, Norman Maier has conducted numerous studies on the effect of group participation in problem solving. (These results form much of our discussion of implementation of decisions, chap. 12). Maier found the kind of problems that are most effectively worked on in groups. For example, better decisions are made when the group is facing a problem which personally affects them. In fact, Maier found that when decisions about these problems are made unilaterally, they are less well received than when the same decision is reached by a group. Using his research results, Maier has developed "role playing" as a form of managerial training. From extensive research he has constructed carefully contrived role-playing exercises which focus on many different problems that managers face.

This book's conclusions and suggestions are based upon the application of research and theory to organization problems. Throughout, we draw heavily from any research or theory which we believe helps suggest a more effective way to manage.

Discussion Questions

1. Some have criticized the scientific approach for being restrictive of thinking and idea development. Why would such a criticism be possibly true? What is your assessment?

2. When you read later sections of this book, you may have this reaction: "It's too theoretical." What does that mean? Of what use is theory? Can theory be of benefit to the practicing manager? How?

3. We stated that the essence of the scientific method is logic, not technique. Does this mean that technique is unimportant? What do you think we mean by technique anyway?

4. Laboratory studies are contrived situations and many of those studied in these situations are not managers. What utility do such studies have beyond providing the researcher with a "publication"?

5. Can you define a situation in which you were involved which would have made a "natural field experiment"? What would you have studied? How would you have designed your study?

Part II
Individuals

Perhaps the most difficult part of any manager's job is dealing with people. Unlike machines, there is a great deal of variability in human beings. Part II explores this issue of how people become different and why they react to situations differently.

In chapter 3, we examine different individual orientations to organizations and how they develop. Since people work together in groups, the impact of groups on individuals is considered in chapter 4. Chapter 5 brings together individual and group concepts and examines the problems of what factors—technical and human—affect individual performance in organizations.

Chapter 3
Development of Work Motives, Values, and Attitudes

Human beings are involved with their work in different ways. They have different values, outlooks, and attitudes, and these cause different individuals to react in different ways to identical situations. Why is it that when a supervisor gives the same order to two subordinates, one will comply and the other will look for ways to avoid the work? The answer is that they are different people—meaning they have brought different characteristics to the job. This chapter discusses the different kinds of human characteristics which have a significant impact, when brought to the job, on the effectiveness of managerial practices. The manager must understand something about these different characteristics in order to manage well.

First, we will focus on how individuals develop certain attitudes and values. This process is more easily understood if we know some of the fundamental ideas behind learning theory and perception. We will also discuss what some of the individual characteristics are and how they emerge, and we will show how these individual characteristics affect a person's affiliation with work organizations, and how the organization affects different kinds of individuals.

Behavioral Model of Human Beings

Thought of in a behavioral sense, an individual has at least the following: (1) skills, ability, and knowledge, (2) self-concept, (3) attitudes, (4) values, and (5) needs or motives. These are shaped over a person's lifetime, and their content and strength determine not only what a person feels (emotions), but also what he is (behavior), and what he may be (potential). These elements differ between individuals. The differences constitute the uniqueness of each human being.

Figure 3.1 represents our general behavioral model, considering the human as being made up of, at least, the elements mentioned above. The model is similar to one proposed by March and Simon (1958), and it operates in this way: The individual perceives a *stimulus*, or

cue, in the environment. The cue triggers a certain set of values, attitudes, and behavior (the *evoked set*). When a person acts, his action is
the *response*. If the response is *reinforced* positively, then the likelihood of that cue triggering a similar response in the future is increased.

FIGURE 3.1   A General Model of an Individual

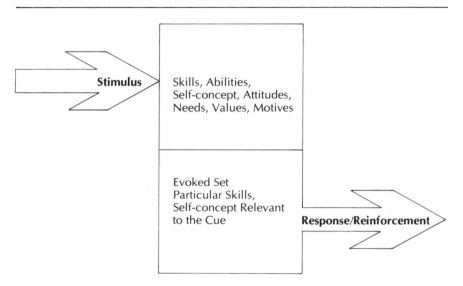

Stimuli.   A stimulus is a factor or a condition that triggers behavior.
It precedes behavior. Stimuli, or cues, are those "aspects of the environment that have a significant impact on behavior in the next time
interval" (March and Simon, 1958). A stimulus is perceived by an
individual and he reacts to it. The stimulus can be fairly simple—say
a whistle that signals a lunch break in a factory. Or it may be complex
—a disciplinary interview in which a superior provides information
in the form of verbal criticism (what he says), as well as information
by how he says it (e.g., with a frown and harsh tone of voice).

Evoked Set.   Stimuli act on the individual, but not on all his values,
attitudes, and behavioral alternatives. A cue evokes only the particular set of these elements that the individual associates with the cue.
The set it acts upon is called the "evoked set," the set that contains
the response of the person to the cue. For example, when the lunch

whistle blows, it triggers a whole group of attitudes and behaviors—workers pick up their lunch buckets, head for the eating area, and so on.

Response. Part of the evoked set contains the response of the individual. The response may be behavior or it may be an emotional reaction. It can be relatively simple (such as going to eat when the lunch whistle blows), or complex (such as changing the way an individual does a job after a disciplinary interview).

Reinforcement. A stimulus induces tension to act—the individual feels the need to do something or say something. (If an inducement of tension does not occur, it is not proper to conceive of the event as a stimulus.) When we respond to a cue with a behavior (verbal or physical) or the expression of an attitude, and the tension is reduced, and we associate this reduction of tension with the cue, positive reinforcement has occurred. (In some instances, however, negative reinforcement may take place. We will discuss the differences between these two types of reinforcement in the next section.)

Over time, as a person experiences reinforcements, patterns or regularities of behavior begin to emerge. A certain behavioral response (behavior or emotion) becomes regularly associated with a cue.

Behavior patterns are learned. An understanding of learning theory, will show us how.

Learning Theory

Learning theory is a set of concepts which deals with how individuals respond to cues in their environment. It provides an explanation of how behavioral patterns develop, and this explanation is helpful in many ways. First, we can use it to understand how skills, values, and attitudes are acquired. Second, it is essential to an understanding of why individuals in a work situation behave as they do. Finally, from it, we can gain insights into how to change the environment (cues) or the reinforcements in order to bring about behavior change to improve organization performance.

Positive and Negative Reinforcement

An individual may associate either positive feelings or negative feelings with a particular behavior. Both associations are reinforcements. A response is *positively* reinforced when the probability of its future occurrence with the same cue present is increased. That is, behavior is likely to be repeated in the future if it is associated with a positive result—a reward. A positive reinforcement may be a smile, or a pay increase, or it may be the termination of an unpleasant stimulus (such as the departure from the room of another person who has been berating you). A response is *negatively reinforced* when the probability of its future occurrence is decreased. When a response is sanctioned, or punished (as perceived by the individual) he will try to figure out other ways of responding. A third possibility is *nonreinforcement.* This occurs when neither reward nor punishment follows an individual's behavioral response. Here, as with negative reinforcement, the probability of the response occurring in the future is decreased.

For something to act as a reinforcer, it must be linked to a specific behavior. This means t at the individual must perceive the link between the reinforcement and the response. An employee, for instance, may engage in a variety of behaviors which are then followed either by praise or by censure from a superior. Often the employee does not know for sure which of several behaviors resulted in the superior's approval or disapproval. Unfortunately, individuals often believe it was one kind of behavior that solicited approval when actually it was quite another. Therefore individuals often act in ways they believe pleasing to others, when actually those ways are not pleasing.

Reinforcement Schedules

The frequency and rate at which various reinforcements (rewards or punishments) are associated with particular responses is called the *reinforcement schedule.* This schedule affects the speed with which responses are learned, or behavior changes. Rewarding every correct response is 100 percent reinforcement. With 100 percent reinforcement, new behavior is learned very quickly. However, if individuals become used to being rewarded every time they make a certain type of response, they stop behaving that way very quickly if the reinforcement stops. The nonreinforcement is very obvious to the individual.

On the other hand, if the responses of the individual are reinforced or rewarded only intermittently, it takes longer for new behavior to develop, but stopping the reinforcement will not stop the behavior immediately. The individual will continue to anticipate the reward, even though it is not forthcoming, since the nonreinforcement is not obvious. Research has shown that an intermittent and variable reinforcement schedule is slow to bring about new behaviors, but very effective for maintaining a particular type of behavioral response once it is learned (Nord, 1969).

Behavioral Change

An individual may learn to respond in a particular way in one situation, and then find himself in another, similar situation in which the old response is not positively reinforced, or perhaps is negatively reinforced. If now a new behavior, or even the opposite behavior, is positively reinforced, the individual will behave differently. This is, by definition, behavior change. For example, let us say that a student grows up in a household where to the stimulus (or cue) "labor union," the response of expressing negative attitudes toward unions is rewarded with signs of approval. At college, however, when he expresses negative attitudes toward labor unions his position is met with disapproval from his fellow students or from his professors. Since he may wish to elicit approval (rewards) instead of disapproval (punishments), he may begin to express positive attitudes toward labor unions—and at college he may be positively rewarded. Ultimately, in order to justify the contradictory attitudes he expresses in two situations—home and college—he may take a middle position, saying that labor unions have both good and bad features. His behavior in what he *says* about unions has changed.

Reinforcement in Everyday Life

Obviously we are all subjected to reinforcements all the time. Whenever we say something and another person important to us shows approval or disapproval, our behavior is influenced. Whenever we show signs of approval or disapproval of what others say or do, we are reinforcing a particular action of theirs. Of course, what constitutes positive and negative reinforcement lies in the mind of the person reinforcing or being reinforced. A compliment from a hated supervisor may be negatively rather than positively reinforcing. By the same token, an expression of disapproval from a disliked professor may be positively reinforcing to the student, especially when the negative response meets with the approval of other students, with whom he identifies. Since we are often unaware of the perspectives of others, we are often unable to determine when a reaction to a particular behavioral response reinforces it positively or negatively.

Clearly, the concept of reinforcement can provide a manager with a useful motivational tool. These ideas will be discussed in further detail in chapter 5, "Motivation and Performance," and in later chapters on the management of different types of organizations.

Perception

Perception is the way we assimilate and organize the information that surrounds us in the environment. To respond to a stimulus, it must be observed in the world around us. Individuals *perceive* cues. They also perceive reinforcements to a particular response. And, as mentioned, often a reinforcement is perceived to be associated with a different behavior than a manager might intend.

Individuals notice only certain aspects of their environments. Each person's perception of the same situation may be different because of this selective perception. Each of several individuals in a group, or organization, will have a somewhat different perception of the group, or organization, than others. It is, of course, not possible for a person to perceive and evaluate all of the information available from the environment at any one point in time, so he must be selective. This being so, what are some of the factors which influence this selectivity?

Stimulus Factors

Reinforcement has its effect when an event is associated with a behavior. This association of reward or sanction with the behavior is a function of perception. What is it about a cue that is likely to cause it to be seen as a cue? Newcomb and his colleagues (1965) suggest that the characteristics of cues which are related to perception are (1) primacy (2) vividness, and (3) frequency. (The following discussion is based on concepts developed extensively in Newcombe et al., 1965.)

The relative timing by which information about a particular set of circumstances is received is called primacy. Information received early is more likely to have an effect than that received later. First impressions, for example, are likely to be long-lasting and difficult to change. For example, the first time a manager meets someone applying for a job in his department, he forms an impression about the applicant that may affect his judgment about the other person for a long time.

Vividness has to do with the degree to which an event is markedly different from what the individual believes it should be. Circumstances that are unusual, extreme, or that deviate from this notion of "should be" trigger a response. Vividness is not necessarily a function of the magnitude of difference alone, however. It is also related to the extent to which the individual can sense deviations, however small. For instance, an experienced manager might sense that a problem exists, while a less experienced manager in the same situation might believe that everything is as it should be.

Frequency of cues also affects perception. If an event occurs a number of times, especially in some regular fashion, an individual is more likely to be aware of it as something to which he should respond than if it happens less frequently.

Personal Factors

Since perception is defined as an individual, personal process, it follows that individuals perceive or see things differently. Some of the individual factors that affect perception are listed by Newcomb and his colleagues (1965) as follows; (1) the temporary psychological state of an individual, (2) well-established attitudes, (3) the relationship of cues to other specific factors, and (4) the personality characteristics of the individual.

Temporary psychological state refers to the emotional, mental and/or psychological condition of a person at a particular point in time. Human beings are not always hungry, but when they are, food stimuli are more likely to be perceived than other stimuli. If a person is angry, and as a result feels tense and anxious, he may impute meanings to behavior of others that are not intended. A manager, for example, may find that one of his most effective subordinates has failed to follow through on a project, a failure that is not consistent with the subordinate's past behavior. The subordinate, however, may have a major personal problem at home—say a divorce—which is altering his work behavior. The interests and needs of a person influence what he notices in his outside environment. If he is insecure, he may look for information about where he stands with his superior. If he is dissatisfied with his pay, he may try to discover what others are receiving in salary. Sometimes this process is called "selective sensitivity," since the individual is sensitive only to certain aspects of his environment (Costello and Zalkind, 1963).

The well-established attitudes of a person are important because they serve as a frame of reference from which information inputs are organized and interpreted. Individuals with favorable attitudes toward their work and their company will be alert to cues to improve performance. Those with negative attitudes may not sense work-oriented cues, or even if they do, may react in a way different than that intended by the cue-sender.

The relationship of cues to other specific factors, or how an individual perceives data to be organized for him, is important because cues occur in a context, and the individual creates this context. For instance, the behavior of a person who displays gentleness and quietness may be associated by an observer with the general belief—the sterotype—that such traits are those of a weak person. This context will affect the manner in which the cue is interpreted and, consequently, the response of the other person.

The personality of an individual is also important. The personality of an individual refers to their uniqueness; it is often defined in such terms as aggressive, shy, loud, dependent, and so forth. Individuals with dogmatic and structured personalities will usually classify information into categories, rather than trying to see it as it is—as a less-structured personality might. Structured personalities will tend to resist information that would cause them to change previous perceptions. Or, to take another example, individuals with little self-confidence may be unwilling to accept negative information about themselves from the outside world, and therefore they will selectively distort incoming information so that it conforms to a favorable self-image.

The Socialization Process—
Personality Development

Socialization is the process by which a culture, or society, or other institution conditions the behavior of individuals. It can be understood in terms of learning theory and perception. Certain responses (behavior or feelings) become associated with particular situations (cues). When the learner perceives a cue, his response occurs. Over time, these responses become regularly associated with the cue by the person. The unique set of values, attitudes, and behaviors of individuals in their adult lives begin their formation in early experiences. From the time a person is born until his death, he is subjected to the pressure of group norms and values, cues, and reinforcements that over a period of time develop and shape his behavior and attitudes. He develops certain modes of adapting to situations he encounters. This *pattern of adaptation* is called "personality." In general, personality is considered to be the unique pattern of psychological and behavioral characteristics of a single individual. The characteristics, as we stated earlier, are: (1) skills, ability, and knowledge, (2) self-concept, (3) attitudes, (4) values, and (5) needs or motives.

Most of those who have studied personality believe that once it is formed, it is resistant to change. They have emphasized the importance of childhood experiences in personality formation; that is, individual psychological and behavioral patterns that persist in the adult reflect the experiences he had as a child. The adult learned then—or did not learn—how to solve some basic problems. There are those who believe personality is set by six years of age. Erik Erikson (1959),

---

FIGURE 3.2 Erickson's Stages of Personality Development

Approximate Chronological Phase	Specific Problem	Resolution
Infancy	Trust vs. mistrust	From and through his parents. the child hopefully concludes that the world is not a hostile or random place, and some people can be trusted.
Young childhood	Autonomy vs. shame Initiative vs. guilt	Again from and through parents. (mainly in the conflict over toilet training and freedom to explore his house), the child should learn that he is an autonomous person who can and should exercise his independence without guilt.
Childhood and adolescence	Industry vs. inferiority	Success in exercising initiative tends to reinforce itself; the young person should become energetic and confident in seeking productive activity and challenge.
Adolescence	Identity vs. confusion	From examples of his elders and personal exploration, the young person should come to know who he is and what he can do.
Young adulthood	Intimacy vs. isolation	Clarity about self should facilitate the ability of the person to enter into close relationships with others.
Adulthood and middle age	Generativity vs. stagnation	With success and maturity, the individual faces the problem of maintaining effort and interest.
Old age	Ego integrity vs. despair	With declining physical and mental states, the individual struggles to maintain a sense of self-worth and optimism.

Reprinted from "Identity and the Life Cycle" by Erik H. Erikson. From *Psychological Issues*, vol. 1, no. 1. By permission of W. W. Norton & Company, Inc. Copyright © 1959 by International Universities Press, Inc.

the psychiatrist, points out that the orderly development of a healthy personality requires the successive resolution of certain conflicts at each stage of personality development. His life stages and their particular problems are shown in figure 3.2.

Certain aspects of the personality take on special importance in the world of work. For example, people differ in their reaction to authority. This is so because of differences in their early conditioning. And reaction to authority plays a significant role in organization performance. All organizations have authority systems, and authority issues pervade their day-to-day functioning. Reactions to authority learned by a child in coping with demands of parents, teachers, and other authority figures determine, to a great degree, responses as a superior or subordinate later in life.

Early Socialization Experiences

An infant has very simple needs: to be fed and protected. When he is hungry, he cries. Hearing the cry, the parents feed the child. Feeding reduces the tension (reinforcement). The infant learns that crying behavior will result in satisfaction of the hunger need. While a child is being fed, other events also take place. One of these, for instance, may be a display of affection. The infant will in time begin to associate affection with feeding, and, secondarily, with crying. He is getting affection at the same time his hunger need is being satisfied. When he was hungry, he cried. This led to his hunger need being satisfied. But when he cried, he also got affection. Eventually, he generalizes this reinforcement so that affection itself can reduce his anxiety or tension. (affection is reinforcing now, in addition to feeding). So the child learns to cry to get affection. He also learns other ways to get the same reinforcement. He begins to seek the affection of his parents in order to reduce anxiety.

From this relatively simple sequence, a whole range of potential responses may develop. For instance, the child may learn that to get the affection, he may have to resort to what would generally be regarded as "bad" behavior. The child cries. He may become aggressive, but ultimately he obtains some kind of response from his parents, and this may be what he is seeking.

Parents are "authority figures." Authority figures have power. They can give rewards or withhold them. They can administer punishment or refrain from its use. Parents as authority figures can provide a wide range of need gratification to a child by virtue of the way in which they allocate the rewards and sanctions at their disposal.

In his very early years, the child begins to learn how to respond to authority and authority figures. As he grows, he continues to learn how to adapt to and cope with the world. The responses to authority figures learned at home become further developed and reinforced later in churches, schools, and other organizations, such as the Boy Scouts or Girl Scouts.

These early experiences and what is learned from them carry on into later life. A child who has learned that he can obtain affection from his parents by compliance is very likely to do what he is told by teachers in school. If he follows their directions, he will win recognition. He will try to please his teachers. Doing this will result in positive reinforcement, probably praise. This increases the likelihood he will do as he is told later. As he continues to comply with teachers, he continues to be rewarded. A cycle develops. Children who are "good" students are rewarded and reinforced—and they become "better" students. Teachers look for "good student" behaviors to reward. Often they ignore the "bad" behavior of good students. They may selectively perceive only "good student" cues.

There is a reverse side to this coin, and it is the one in which a child is unable to get attention by compliance. Suppose a young girl has a smaller sister. When she is told to be "good," she does so—but sees her parents spending time with her smaller sister, even so. The older child's reinforcement for being good is perceived as having her mom and dad ignore her—no affection. In time she learns that to get reinforcement (attention), it is better not to be "good." She learns that she must compete for her parents' time, and that this can be done most effectively by being a problem, by adopting an alternate mode of behavior from that of complying. She becomes aggressive, a problem child.

When the child goes to school, she carries this pattern of behavior to the classroom. The teacher expects a certain behavior, and this child acts in the opposite way. There may be negative reinforcement of this behavior from the teacher, but the child's fellow students may positively reinforce her. Thus, when the teacher publicly calls attention to her behavior this may, in a sense, be the very recognition she is seeking before her fellow students. This double reinforcement increases the likelihood that her "undesirable" behavior will continue. In time, teachers come to expect her to be "bad," and they will look for that particular behavior and reinforce it accordingly. So will her peers.

Thus, from early life, people develop individual ways of coping with and adjusting to the world around themselves—and to authority figures. As we have said, these patterns of accommodation have special importance in the world of work.

The Unique Individual—The Results of Socialization

The general pattern of individual reaction and response in coping with the world is a manifestation of an individual's personality. We judge another's personality by what we see him do and hear him say. As we have more and more experiences with people, we learn that most of them have patterns to their responses. A person may be energetic, shy, confident, dominant, friendly, truculent, independent, and so on. If a person consistently strikes out at others when confronted with a problem, he is characterized as an "aggressive personality." If he consistently feels that he is the object of intended harm, he may be regarded as "paranoid."

Skills, Ability, and Knowledge

Some people have high levels of competence in certain areas, say mathematics, while others have great difficulty understanding the subject. Others have the ability to perform physical activities well, while others don't. Some people have extremely high finger dexterity, others fumble putting on gloves. Human beings differ widely in the knowledge, abilities, and aptitudes they bring to a job. Knowledge is an acquaintance with facts or principles. Ability is the capacity to do something. Aptitude is the *potential* to develop future skills or knowledge.

Managers (and others as well, of course) often underestimate the magnitude of individual differences. Even within a group of ostensibly similar people there may be wide differences among individuals on some characteristics. In a group of highly trained scientists, for example, there can be substantial differences in the degree *and* the type of knowledge. The widest differences, however, are typically found in lower occupational groups, since in higher-level occupations, minimal ability standards may be a requirement for admittance.

Some aptitudes and skills are inherited. (A person's finger dexterity, for example, cannot be changed significantly by special training.) And while there is a great deal of controversy about the relative effects of heredity and environment on intelligence, it is clear that certain levels of intelligence make it easier to acquire certain levels of specialized knowledge. Thus, intelligence tests are often good predictors of who can successfully complete a particular course of instruction.

Individual differences in tested abilities can be overemphasized on the job, however. Quite often a difference in aptitudes, skills, or knowledge in one area has no effect on performance because that area is not relevant to the task. Differences in intelligence, say, in applicants may not be relevant on a job which requires only finger dexterity. Also, the differences may not be extensive enough to matter. A person with an IQ of 140 may perform a job no better than one with a score of 130.

Research shows that the typical individual varies, within himself, from one aptitude to another (Tyler, 1958). Thus, one person may be very high on finger dexterity, medium on color discrimination, and low on intelligence. What is important to management is that characteristics relevant to a job be determined and that they be measured specifically and accurately.

Self-concept

A person's self-concept is the way a person perceives and evaluates himself. Individuals bring a self-concept with them to the job which can have an effect on how they perform. Some see themselves as competent and are willing to undertake tasks which have an element of uncertainty in them. Others see themselves as leaders and attempt to dominate interpersonal relationships. Others may not evaluate their abilities very highly. They may be afraid to assume certain responsibilities. These self-perceptions are, of course, formed over a person's lifetime, largely on the basis of how others react to him. The individual obtains feedback from others about his impact on them and this information is used to find out about himself. Also, at work, some people assume a self-concept which is congruent with their stereotype of an occupation, such as "research scientist," say. Such a person may feel a responsibility to behave as he believes a research scientist should in a particular set of circumstances.

Attitudes

An attitude refers to an individual's feelings and beliefs about other persons, objects, events, and activities. Attitudes are learned, or develop, over time. These feelings and beliefs about persons, objects, events, and activities can be positive or negative and are the *affective component* of an attitude. The affective component is the emotion generated by the object or event. It means simply that we feel some preference—like or dislike toward an object. This affective component develops because we associate, or "perceive," positively, or negatively, the reinforcing circumstances of the object.

What we see and evaluate is the *cognitive component* of the attitude. It is what we believe to be true or not true about the object. So if we find that a certain behavior is positively reinforced, not only is it likely that we will respond similarly to a similar cue, but we will also develop stronger feelings toward the object and the circumstances. We develop a positive, or favorable attitude toward the situation when there is positive reinforcement, or tension reduction.

Attitudes are learned in a variety of ways. In the many groups to which an individual belongs, certain expressed attitudes are continually reinforced positively or negatively. In a work group, for example, an employee's peers will show approval and disapproval after the expression of attitudes about management, unions, work procedures, performance standards, and other matters. Since most of us seek social acceptance, it is not surprising that the group has an influence over attitudes. The expression of attitudes was, of course, also reinforced in our homes as children, as well as in our present neighborhood and home situation. Certain attitudes develop out of personal experiences with an event in question. If some object, for instance, has contributed to a person's failure, it is likely that he will have negative attitudes toward that object.

Most managers believe that attitudes have a significant influence on work behavior. They believe that the way an individual behaves toward an object or event is substantially affected by that person's attitudes. Attitudes are thus considered to have an *action* component. The way a person feels about something—and what he believes about it—determines how he will behave toward it. It is assumed that attitudes precede behavior, and indeed some research has shown that the changing of attitudes toward a person can change behavior toward the same person (Zimbardo and Ebbeson, 1970). On the other hand, some students of the subject do not believe that attitudes cause behavior, although it must be recognized that attitudes are difficult to measure accurately and that therefore the validity of this belief is open to question.

Research has also shown that a change in behavior can lead to a change in attitude. For example, in one study a group of workers' attitudes were measured. Later, some of these workers became foremen. They then were acting as managers, not as workers, and when their attitudes were resurveyed they were found to have changed to be more like those of management. Other workers in the study became union officials. Their attitudes became different from that of the workers, more like those of union officials (Lieberman, 1956). Thus, when an individual behaves in a particular way, his attitudes change so that they are consistent with what he does. For example, if an employee finds himself alongside a member of a group toward which he has a negative attitude, but treats the other in a way consistent with a favorable feeling about the person as a person, he is more likely than not to develop favorable attitudes toward the entire group. This is because individuals attempt to maintain some consistency between their behavior and their attitudes (Festinger, 1957). In general, a person must be able to justify his behavior with an appropriate attitude, and that behavior influences the attitude—which in turn influences future behavior. There is, then, a reciprocal relationship between attitudes and behavior.

Human beings have many attitudes toward different things. We have attitudes toward work, politics, education, sex, leisure, and so on. These different attitudes tend to be consistent with each other as well as with behavior. This consistency helps us make sense of the world and to behave consistently. The attitude system is therefore one guide to reality.

Attitudes are important factors in a person's identification with a particular group. Holding attitudes in common with others contributes to a strong sense of unity with them. Because attitudes perform so many valuable functions for us, it is hardly surprising that we strongly resist attempts to change them.

Values

Values are more deeply ingrained and more general than attitudes (which are aimed at quite specific individuals or objects). Values are what an individual considers good or bad, important or unimportant. They serve as a means or a standard for evaluating objects and events and therefore they help a person to deal with his environment. They are especially useful in comparing alternatives, since the alternatives can be scaled against values.

Many values come from an individual's background—for example, his religious and ethical upbringing. Some come from the culture itself. For example, in the United States a high value is placed on competition, while in Japan, the opposite is true (Whitehill and Takezawa, 1968). Values also reflect the individual's psychological needs and are part of the action component of such needs.

Needs or Motives

Most people who study human behavior believe that a large part of it is goal-directed, that we behave as we do to satisfy some individual human need. Just what is meant by a "need"? Needs, or motives, refer to goal states that an individual strives to achieve. A need exists when an individual determines that his present state of being is not what he desires it to be. When the difference between what is and what is desired is great enough, the person acts to reduce the disparity. This is goal-directed behavior.

There are many ways to conceive of human needs. Some attempts to categorize them describe very specific needs (such as the need for water), while others are more general (relatedness or existence needs). A popular and widely accepted approach to the human need structure is that of Maslow (1943), who describes five categories of needs (see fig. 3.3).

FIGURE 3.3 Maslow's Need Hierarchy

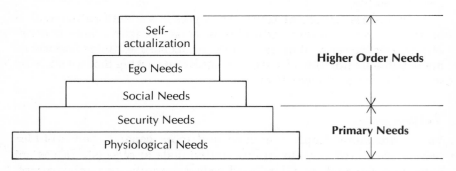

1. *Physiological Needs.* Physiological needs refer to the basic requirements for survival. Man must have food in order to live. He must find some shelter to protect him from the elements. His physical wellbeing must be provided for before anything else can assume importance.

2. *Security Needs.* Once a person has food and found shelter, he can worry whether or not he will have them in the future. He desires protection against loss of shelter, food, and other basic requirements for survival. The security needs also involve the desire to live in a stable and predictable environment. It may involve a preference for order and for structure.

3. *Social Needs.* The need to interact with others and have some social acceptance and approval is generally shared by most people. For some, this need may be satisfied by joining groups. Others may find sufficient affection from their family members or other individuals, without joining groups.

4. *Ego Needs.* The ego needs have to do with the human desire to be respected by others, the need for a positive self-image. Individuals strive to increase their status in the eyes of others, to attain prestige or a certain reputation or a high ranking in a group. Self-confidence is increased when the self-esteem needs are satisfied. The thwarting of these needs produces feelings of inferiority or weakness.

5. *Self-actualization.* Maslow describes the need for self-actualization as the individual's desire to do what he is fitted for. Individuals want to achieve their potential. This is called the "highest-order need."

A distinction is often made between *primary* and *higher-order needs.* Primary needs usually refer to physiological and security needs. Primary needs are satisfied in fairly standardized ways among people, especially people from the same culture. They are easiest to satisfy in a reasonably active economy, so long as adequate income is provided. That is, an individual with income can obtain the kind of food and shelter that he chooses, within wage limitations, and security needs may be partially satisfied through union contracts or work agreements, as well as social programs such as unemployment compensation and welfare benefits. Letting an employee know what is expected of him also helps satisfy primary needs.

The higher-order needs are more psychological in nature. Different people want different things, and this is precisely the reason why the need hierarchy is difficult to translate into a motivational strategy for the manager. There is no way that managerial strategy or policy can be tailored to meet the very nature of higher-order needs, which include social, ego, and self-actualization needs.

From figure 3.3 it can be seen that an individual's needs form a hierarchy, or ladder. Maslow claims that the higher-level needs are not considered important by an individual until the lower-lever needs are at least partially satisfied. In other words, an individual will not be concerned with social needs if he does not have adequate food or shelter, or if security needs have not been met. Maslow also feels that a person is not motivated by a need that is satisfied. Once a need is satisfied, the person is concerned with the next level of the hierarchy. A person seeks to move up the hierarchy of needs, always striving to satisfy the deficiency at the next highest level. Maslow hypothesized that unsatisfied needs dominate the individual's thoughts and are reflected in what the person is concerned about. (Most attempts to measure needs try to gather information about an individual's thoughts and perceptions.)

A reformulation of the Maslow hierarchy has been proposed by

Alderfer (1972). Alderfer collapses the Maslow need structure of five into three: (1) existence needs, (2) relatedness needs, and (3) growth needs. *Existence needs* encompass Maslow's physiological needs and some aspects of the security needs; *relatedness needs* include the desire for social acceptance and status in a group; and *growth needs* focus on self-esteem and self-actualization.

From research on how the satisfaction of a need influences its importance and the importance of other needs, it appears that as the need becomes satisfied, it becomes less important, with the exception of the self-actualization needs (Alderfer, 1972). As Maslow predicted, the self-actualization needs do seem to become *more* important as they are partially satisfied.

Finally, research tends to substantiate that if lower-level needs are highly deficient, there is diminished concern for the higher-order needs. The individual is preoccupied with his lower-level need problems (Lawler and Suttle, 1972). This has been shown to be true for individuals who are known to be very hungry, for example, or who have found their jobs threatened, as when a firm faces bankruptcy. Thus, extreme fear or anxiety about lower-level needs precludes thoughts and concerns about higher-order ones. Alderfer's research shows that the relatedness needs may be especially critical for satisfaction of other needs (Alderfer, 1972). If they are not satisfied, the individual may become concerned almost entirely with lower-level needs. If the relatedness needs are satisfied, however, the person becomes primarily involved with the higher-level needs.

An individual's need structure is determined by his socialization, or early learning experiences, and thus there are many differences among individuals with respect to the needs that are important to them. More important, there are many ways in which a particular kind of need may be satisfied. For instance, one person's ego needs may be satisfied by being recognized as the best worker in a department. Another may find this need satisfied by others' recognition of his dress style—being acknowledged as the sharpest dresser in his group.

The specific manner in which an individual satisfies a particular need is learned by reinforcement experiences early in life. We learn through experience that some situations are more desirable (rewarding) than others, and we seek these out. Other situations are ones we seek to avoid. It may be particularly comfortable, for instance, to interact with others of a certain ethnic or religious background, and very uncomfortable to interact with those from other backgrounds.

There is some evidence of differences in needs among occupational groups. Rank-and-file workers generally consider the lower-level needs to be more important in work situations than do managers (Porter, Lawler and Hackman, 1975). Managers, especially those at the highest echelons, consider the higher-level needs more important than the lower-level needs. All this may mean, however, is that lower-level workers may be stating that they are not concerned with higher-level needs as a type of defense behavior, since they have little opportunity to satisfy these higher needs at work. Workers from urban backgrounds seem to be more concerned with satisfying lower-level needs than do workers from rural backgrounds (Locke, 1975). What this means remains open to interpretation, also.

Frustration and the Inability to Satisfy Needs

Behavior is goal-directed. In general, human beings seek to minimize tension by escaping punishment or by obtaining rewards. As we progress from primary to higher-order needs, the particular situations that can positively reinforce, say, ego needs, are different for various people. For example, one person may have his ego needs satisfied when he is promoted, or given a salary increase. The promotion or raise will increase the probability that he will engage more frequently in the behaviors he believes were responsible for obtaining the rewards, and he will do this in the context of the organization where he received the reward. Another person, however, may try to satisfy ego needs away from work by seeking election to an office in the community. If the second person's major orientation is toward, say, a seat on the library board, then a promotion at work will probably not have the same reinforcing strength within the organizational context as it did for the first person.

Perhaps a woman finds that no matter what she does her superior refuses to treat her in a way consistent with her self-concept. She may see herself as a highly effective manager, but she believes her superior treats her as a "simpering female." What happens, then, when tension cannot be reduced or perhaps even avoided? Or, to put it another way, what will a person do when she finds that a particular behavior does not result in need satisfaction? Suppose that the woman wants a promotion very badly but doesn't get it. If she believes her work deserves and has earned recognition, she may continue her past behavior pattern, hoping to be promoted sometime in the future. If she fails to get the next available promotion, however, she will feel *frustration*. Frustration arises from goal blockage when a person is trying to obtain a personal goal, or satisfy an important need but is prevented from obtaining the goal or satisfying the need by some force beyond her control.

The level of frustration may vary with a number of situational factors. One of these is the expectation of failure. The more an individual expects goal blockage to occur, the less frustration he experiences. Whether or not the individual has alternative goals, or means of achieving them, also influences the level of frustration. In addition, frustration is higher the closer the person is to goal attainment when the blockage occurs, when he has had several recent past frustrations, and when the goals he is seeking are important to him (Costello and Zalkind, 1963). Finally, frustration is higher when the blockage appears to be arbitrary, rather than justified.

Reactions to Frustration

The frustrated individual may react in a number of different ways. He may, of course, alter his behavior patterns in such a way that he can achieve the satisfaction of needs. The manager who desires promotion may find that he was passed over because he did not have certain background qualifications, say competence in accounting and financial management. So he goes to school or transfers to another job where he can acquire this competence. This is constructive behavior. However, frustration may produce some undesirable effects, such as aggression, psychological withdrawal, defensive behavior, and alienation.

Aggression is behavior directed at others with the intent of injuring them. Aggression can take many forms. One is *direct aggression*. For example, a foreman takes a worker off a job he is trying to finish, assigning him to another task. The worker goes back to his original job. After a while the foreman takes him off the job again and assigns him another task. The worker once more returns to his original job, and once again the foreman takes him off it. The worker's response is to solve his problem in a new and more direct way; he flattens the foreman. Direct aggressive tendencies are not always so extreme, of course. They may be verbal, as for instance, gossip about another, spreading malicious stories, or calling another person names. Aggression can also be directed at the organization, and a significant proportion of labor management disputes have their roots in job frustration. Sabotage, stealing, wildcat strikes, slowdowns, sitdowns, and militancy and economic strikes may be the result of worker frustration, and are ways of striking back.

Displaced aggression occurs when the source of the frustration cannot be attacked directly, and aggression is then directed toward an innocent third party. At home, an executive frustrated at work may yell at his wife and children. Conversely, frustrations at home can result in aggression displaced against innocent individuals at work.

A reaction to frustration in which a person simply gives up and does not try anymore is *psychological withdrawal*. The level and frequency of frustration may be so high that the individual says, "What's the use?" He comes to work late, he stands around doing as little as possible, he leaves work early. Others may believe that this worker is uninterested, that he does not like his job.

Perhaps such reactions occur because he is frustrated in his job. He may have wanted to be promoted, and felt that he deserved such recognition, but the rewards were never received. This reaction is seen particularly with underprivileged workers—the subjects often of discriminatory promotion practices. Several studies suggest that psychological withdrawal may set in when an initial high level of motivation is followed by a long series of frustrations (Liebow, 1967).

Sometimes an individual copes with his unsatisfied needs by *defensive behavior*. Such behavior has the function of distorting reality so that self-esteem or esteem in the eyes of others is maintained. It is a result of frustration, especially when failure occurs. Since failure often challenges one's positive self-concept, some method of coping with it must be found. This coping mechanism may take any form— finding excuses for failure in the action of others, forgetting mistakes, or blaming others for failure.

The Development of Orientations Toward Work

As we have said, values, attitudes, needs, abilities differ among individuals. Each of us expects something different from work. Nash and Carroll (1975) in reviewing several research studies conclude that lower occupational groups place a higher value on security and money than do higher occupational groups. It must be kept in mind, of course, that there are many differences in work values within any occupational group.

What an individual values in work reflects his psychological needs. For example, employees with higher needs for security place a higher value on having clear work assignments (Carroll and Tosi, 1973). There is also evidence that among managers there is more concern for security in the early years on the job, when the manager is unsure of organizational expectations and perhaps of his own abilities. (Hall and Nougaim, 1968). Security needs for such individuals then decrease as they grow older, but for rank-and-file workers, concern for security increases with age.

Work values differ from culture to culture as well. For example, need for esteem is more important to Italian managers than to U.S. managers, while concern for security is much higher among managers in underdeveloped countries than those in the United States (Haire, Ghiselli, and Porter, 1966). Some research shows much more respect for authority among Japanese workers than among U.S. workers (Whitehall and Takezawa, 1968).

Work values are also a result of what actually happens to a person on the job. If for example, we have worked hard on a task for little money, then we will perhaps convince ourselves that the task has much more intrinsic satisfaction built into it than it actually has (Zimbardo, 1969). Finally, individuals who have been very successful on a job often come to place a high value on performance itself (Hall and Nougaim, 1968).

Family Characteristics and Work Values

Family background is associated with later work values. The socioeconomic level of the family, for example, is a consistent predictor of such values. In one study, for instance, being a member of a close family, having many close friends, being subjected to parental discipline, and having social activities such as dating and taking part in community projects were all related to placing a high value on job security, a desire for good working conditions, and a desire for having good relations with fellow workers (Paine et al., 1967). A stress on independence and cultural activities in the home, however, was related to more concern with status, responsibility and independence on the job. According to Witkin et al. (1962), individuals raised in a home environment in which independence, achievement, and self-control were emphasized tend to be more active and have a task orientation as an adult. On the other hand they found that individuals raised where family ties are emphasized tend to be passive and socially dependent, and to place a higher value on social acceptance.

Occupational Choice and Work Values

The occupation we choose is also affected by our early socialization experiences. Although there are many chance factors which affect one's career choice, it has been shown that the father's occupation is related to a person's occupation. The sons of individuals in higher-level occupations, for example, tend to end up in higher-level occupations themselves. The offspring of those in lower-level occupations tend to take jobs similar to those of their parents. This tendency, of course, is to some extent determined by the educational opportunities available, which is most often dependent on the income of the family.

Which jobs are the high-status jobs? Professional (scientist, engineer, lawyer, physician) and managerial (bank manager, production manager, etc.) jobs are consistently ranked at the top of the status hierarchy by the general population (Inkeles and Ross, 1956).

Individual factors, however, do play a role in occupational choice, especially in choosing from among occupations with similar educational and experience requirements. One study of those entering the field of management showed that managerial success (given a high level of initial ability) was determined by the capacity to understand one's work environment and demands, competence in handling a wide variety of tasks, willingness to take risks, and ability to learn about oneself and then adapt to change as needed (Dill, Hilton, and Reitman, 1962). Ginzberg (1951) feels that individuals attempt to find occupations consistent with their values, which make use of their abilities, and are in line with their interests. On the other hand, he feels that an occupation ordinarily does not fulfill all of these requirements, so that an individual must compromise among them to some degree. He sees occupational choice process taking place over a long period of time.

Super (1957) also believes that occupational choice is a result of a long developmental process, during which the individual is learning about himself and developing a self-concept. A person in his earlier years (before 25) is attempting to find out what kind of human being he is and where his strengths and weaknesses are, and he utilizes feedback from others in doing this. His self-concept then becomes an important determinant of his occupational choice. An individual's attempts to establish his identity, however, may continue past the time he makes his occupational choice, especially if he is in certain occupations where the demands appear to require contradictory behaviors, such as pharmacists (businessman or professional dispensator of pharmaceuticals?), military chaplains (army officer or man of religion?), insurance salesman (businessman or financial counselor?).

Chance or luck, as well as parental pressures and individual characteristics also play a role in occupational choice. Chance seems especially important in choosing jobs among the lower occupational levels (Myers and Schultz, 1951). Parental pressures are especially important for individuals who have low self-esteem, or a low self-image (Korman, 1966). Previous investments in certain types of socialization education are also important factors in occupational choice.

Occupational Socialization

For individuals who choose occupations for which specialized training is required, educational experiences may be viewed as a form of socialization for the occupation. For some, occupational specialization begins in professional school, where the would-be professional is first exposed to the perspectives, values, and ways of thinking characteristic to the chosen field. A professional set of beliefs is acquired by participation in informal student groups, from taking courses, and through interaction with teachers. These beliefs are internalized; that is, they become part of the needs, attitudes, values, and self-concept of the individual. The person acts as a "professional" without thinking about it. Reinforcements from teachers are especially influential in shaping the new professional, since in many professions, the professor has much to do with the placement of students. The process of developing a professional self-image is a slow one, however, and the student probably does not begin to think of himself as a professional until he is treated as one by those who already have achieved that recognition.

Socialization and Organizational Involvement

So, what we are is what we have been. Parents, school, college, friends all shape our personality. We expect certain things from life and we react according to whether or not we get them. Where we work, and what we work at is a major part of life. How we react to work and the work organization is reflective of our personality.

It is possible to categorize various orientations that people have toward organizations and work that are derived from t eir experiences. Some people are highly committed to the organization, others seem to have little or no interest in their work or the organization. Still others seem to be extremely interested in what they do but have little commitment to the organization in which they work. Presthus (1965) categorizes these different orientations as *upward mobile, indifferent,* and *ambivalent.* We have changed the labels in the discussion that follows, making them more directly refer to individual organization orientations. These categories are a sort of organizational personality stereotype, suffering the limitations of any classification scheme or stereotyping. But they are useful in our later analysis, since these different personality types appear in different proportions in different types of organizations. We expect to find more professionals in some organizations. In others, we expect to find more organizationally-oriented types.

The Organizationalist

Large and small companies, universities, and government agencies all have highly loyal members who function very well within the system. A person highly committed to the place where he works is called an "organizationalist." He does well in the unit in which he works, seeking organizational rewards and advancement and identifying with the system. His self-concept is inextricably tied to the organization. The organizationalist has high morale and job satisfaction. He is likely to have an extremely low tolerance for uncertainty and ambiguity. He wants to know what his job is, for what he is responsible, and to whom he is accountable. The organizationalist is very concerned with the effectiveness and efficiency of the organization. Organizational success is important to him because it is reflective of his own success. He is highly committed to the organization's goals. Identifying with a superior, he finds it easy to rationalize organizational pressures for conformity and performance, since he is seeking promotion and other rewards from the system. Status in the organization is very important to him. His life values may be defined, or reflected by, the level he has achieved in the organization. Because this is so important to him, he probably experiences a great deal of status anxiety, or fears that his position in the organization is threatened in reality or potentially. The organizationalist avoids controversy. He is a stickler for maintaining himself within the "channels" of the system, not readily going outside them to handle problems.

The Socialization of the Organizationalist.   How does the organizationalist get to be what he is? The organizationalist develops an early respect for authority figures. His early experiences lead him to recognize the importance of authority, realizing that authority figures have power to dispense rewards and/or sanctions. Presthus (1965) has suggested that the organizationalist comes from a family in which rewards and sanctions are applied primarily by the father.

Externally-oriented Persons

Some people seem to work just for the pay they receive. They find their jobs acceptable but not a critical part of their lives. They perform well but are not highly committed to the organization. They, in effect, act right but feel wrong. They may be managers, lower-level employees, or highly-trained professionals. For some reason or other they do not actively seek the rewards of the organization or strive for higher position. They accept what they have. Given a choice, they would rather be doing other things. They seek satisfaction of higher-order psychological needs outside the organization by doing things that are not related to where they work or what their work is. This is in marked contrast to the organizationalist, who seeks need satisfaction from his connection with the firm. The externally-oriented person generally prefers to withdraw from work. He may be alienated by the tedium of the work itself. He does not get extensively involved with the work organization, and participates in it only minimally beyond work requirements. There are other, more important things in life than the job and the company. Rather then emphasizing the puritan ethic values of work, as does the organizationalist, the externalist seems more concerned with leisure.

He rejects the status and prestige associated with the job. He separates work from what he regards as the more meaningful aspects of life. He is essentially adapting to his work environment by withdrawing from it as much as possible, seeking his psychological satisfaction from neither the work itself nor the organization.

The Socialization of the Externally-oriented. Presthus (1965) suggests that the externally-oriented person generally comes from the lower middle class. With a limited education, he is restricted in his opportunities for advancement in an organization. If he is in the lower levels of the organization, he is highly likely to stay there.

We must not assume, however, that only lower-level personnel are externalists. Many managers function in this same way. For example, early in a manager's career he may be extremely committed to the organization. He may seek its rewards and want to advance. However, in middle age and in later career life he may find that he has been passed over several times for promotion. Often a person finds that someone else gets the job that he expected to get. When this happens, the person finds other places for positive reinforcement. Thus, it is possible that with their promotion practices organizations may turn managers from highly-committed organizationalists to externally-oriented types. Certainly we would expect to find fewer externalists at higher levels, but it is not uncommon to find them in the higher-management ranks.

Often a person, whether a manager, a specialist, or an operative worker turns the substance of his life to other things. Employees who were once fiercely loyal to the point of following orders without question may change. One such apparent shift in orientation seems to be exemplified in the career of John DeLorean, an ex-employee of General Motors. DeLorean's experiences are described in item 3.1.

ITEM 3.1   Not All Top Managers Are Organizationalists

Reflections on the Abbreviated Career of John DeLorean, a Nonconforming Executive, at General Motors

Three years ago John Zachary DeLorean, then general manager of General Motors' Chevrolet division, ordered members of his research staff to find him the world's best-handling passenger car. They came back with two Mercedes, and DeLorean ordered his engineers to duplicate their suspension and steering characteristics for the 1973 model of Chevrolet's medium-priced specialty car, the Monte Carlo. When the body of the Monte Carlo was restyled, DeLorean carefully avoided all frills, keeping it distinctively sleek and alive. This year the Monte Carlo is being acclaimed as one of the best-looking, easiest-to-handle cars Detroit has ever produced.

But last spring, while thousands of impatient customers were signing their names on waiting lists for the Monte Carlo, DeLorean was walking out of General Motors. At forty-eight, he resigned from a job that paid more than $550,000 in salary and bonuses, ending a career that had seemed to point him toward the presidency of the world's largest and most powerful manufacturing corporation. Instead, he plans to become a Cadillac dealer somewhere.

There is no question that DeLorean's departure was a significant loss to the corporation. Semon E. (Bunkie) Knudsen, who served both G.M. and Ford in high capacities and is now chairman of White Motor Corp., considers him one of the smartest automobile engineers he knows. And Richard C. Gerstenberg, G.M.'s current chairman and chief executive, pays him this tribute: "He was highly regarded by his colleagues and by his dealers. He was good in marketing, too. That's surprising, because he was an engineer, and you don't always find the two going together."

• • • •

In view of his achievements and seemingly brilliant future, DeLorean's departure was not only a surprise, but a mystery.

• • • •

His own stated reason is that he was sick of life at G.M. "The automobile industry has lost its masculinity," he says. "Management's not the same type as when I came here."

The substance of his complaint seems to be that encroaching government regulation has taken the fun out of the business, reducing it to the status of a utility, and that G.M.'s sheer size has led to mind-dulling bureaucratization, which left no room for an individualist like John DeLorean.

• • • •

Lanky, six-feet-four, with friendly blue eyes and a rich, commanding voice, DeLorean practiced the art of nonconformity at G.M. with an intemperance that was downright exuberant. Now that he is out, his daily uniform around Bloomfield Hills, Michigan, is an open-necked sports shirt, faded blue denims, and a well-worn pair of black loafers.

• • • •

He travels in a glittering world of sports stars and movie makers—a group that is decidedly *not* General Motors. Although one divorce is now considered permissible at the company, DeLorean has been married three times, on the last two occasions to actress-models who were in their early twenties.

"A square fellow when I hired him."
The child of parents who separated,

DeLorean spent half his boyhood in Los Angeles, his mother's home, and half in Detroit, where his father was a set-up man in a Ford foundry. A gangly youth, he doesn't remember winning any school-yard fights, but in other ways he soon developed an intense, almost uncontrollable drive to attain perfection. Something of a loner, he stuck to activities in which he excelled, giving up saxophone and clarinet lessions because he realized he would never be a great musician.

After getting an engineering degree at the Lawrence Institute of Technology in 1948, DeLorean went to work for Chrysler. It was an era when automobiles were seen as a glamorous product; schoolboys vied to win the Fisher Body Craftsman Guild design contest, and aspired as much to be president of G.M. as to be President of the U.S. DeLorean saw the business as an important calling, a way to give Americans mobility, and he still retains that view to some degree.

• • • •

By 1952 he had grown restless at Chrysler. "It was too big for me to be noticed," he says, and he switched to Packard.

Four years later, when he was head of research and development, Bunkie Knudsen, then general manager of G.M.'s Pontiac division, offered him a similar post with Pontiac. "He was a pretty square fellow when I hired him," says Knudsen. By then married to a secretary from northern Michigan, DeLorean wore his hair short, and his suits came off the rack.

In 1961, DeLorean became chief engineer, and four years later, at forty, the youngest general manager in Pontiac's history. He was also named a vice president of the corporation.

Building on the momentum Knudsen had created, DeLorean led the division to its most successful year. A rock-music enthusiast, he developed a feeling for what young people wanted. "Automobiles are a fashion thing, like clothing," he says. "And the people who set fashions are really the young people, people up to thirty-five." He crafted his idea of what the young wanted into two fast specialty cars, the Firebird and the Grand Prix.

• • • •

Pontiac became known as just about the best-engineered car in the business. DeLorean tightened the pressure on the dealers, and sales leaped from 688,000 in 1964 to 877,000 in 1968, a record that still stands. The Firebird and the Grand Prix accounted for half the increase.

After a triumph of this magnitude, one might think DeLorean would have been immeasurably happy. But he had begun to have misgivings. Back around 1960, Knudsen had taken him to a Pontiac dealers' conference at the El Dorado Country Club in Palm Springs. The late Harlow Curtice, G.M.'s retired president and chief executive, was vacationing nearby and DeLorean met him at the festivities. A powerful executive, Curtice had run the company almost as a monarchy, and he had done so with spectacular success. "I looked at this guy almost as a god," DeLorean recalls.

Talking with the club's golf pro the next day, DeLorean mentioned Curtice. "That's the loneliest human being who ever lived," said the pro. "He comes into my golf shop for a couple of hours every day and talks to me and my assistant about the automobile business. We don't know anything about the automobile business, but we listen to him. He just seems to want to talk so badly."

DeLorean was shaken. Recounting the episode recently, he said, "You realized he never had been regarded as a human being, but only for his job." Like many other G.M. executives, Curtice had devoted all his hours to The Corporation; his friendships were corporate, even his interests and knowledge were pretty much limited to the affairs of General Motors. Now that G.M. was in the hands of others, Curtice's world had rolled away without him. "What is life all about?" DeLorean asked himself. "You work forty years, and what have you got?"

As DeLorean climbed at General Motors and his annual income broke through the quarter-million mark, he gradually shed any attributes Bunkie Knudsen might have considered square. He was beginning to wear turtleneck sweaters and wide lapels, and he grew his hair long.

• • • •

As his own life changed, DeLorean began questioning what he calls the cloistered life at G.M.'s upper levels. As he saw it, the senior officers spent most of their days confined to meetings on the fourteenth floor of the corporation's headquarters in Detroit. Most executives worked ten-hour days, leaving for home around 7:00 p.m., lugging bulging briefcases. On Saturdays many reappeared in the office, this time in shirtsleeves, to put in a few more hours.

Most G.M. executives lived in Bloomfield Hills or neighboring Birmingham, where they socialized together. When they weren't playing golf with suppliers or dealers, they frequently formed foursomes with one another at the Bloomfield Hills Country Club, because few made close friendships outside General Motors. While debate was allowed within the company, it was never to be aired in public, and since G.M. dominated the field, this meant there was little open self-criticism in the industry. Dinner conversations with G.M. executives, DeLorean felt, tended to concentrate on narrow interests—automobiles or finance or engineering—and to exclude such subjects as films or music.

DeLorean wondered if the kinds of friendships that developed around G.M. were really meaningful. In 1968, when Bunkie Knudsen left to become president of Ford, Knudsen became a nonperson at G.M.—despite the fact that his father had been a president of the company and Bunkie himself had built some lifelong associations there. DeLorean made a point of continuing his friendship with the Knudsens, and spent a lot of his time outside the G.M. community with people whose style of life blended with his own.

• • • •

On January 25, 1969, a Saturday, DeLorean was summoned from the twelfth hole of Palm Springs' Thunderbird Country Club by an urgent call from Roger Kyes, then vice president for the car-and-truck group and DeLorean's boss. Kyes told him to catch the first plane back to Detroit and meet him at President Edward N. Cole's house in Bloomfield Hills at eight o'clock the next morning. There Cole told DeLorean he wanted him to become general manager of Chevrolet.

Chevrolet was in trouble. As one G.M. executive describes it, using a metaphor that DeLorean himself is supposed to have coined, "You were looking at the Penn Central of the automobile industry." Chevy's profits were falling, hundreds of dealers were losing money, and the division's market share was shrinking, from 26 percent in 1965 to 22 percent in 1968. Yet Ford was retaining most of its share, even under the battering of imports. As one Chevy dealer says in retrospect: "G.M. got so conservative and so conscious of the corporate image that Ford was beating them with new products people wanted."

Communications among some of the division's major departments were erratic, primarily because each lived in a state of secluded autonomy. The marketing department had launched an ad campaign for the four-cylinder Nova with little warning to the manufacturing department, which had no chance to plan and had to go on overtime to meet the demand the ads generated. The division had twenty-five computers, and they had not been coordinated into an efficient system. When a new car was designed, its specifications had to be taken from the engineering department's computer and reprogrammed into the manufacturing department's computer. Things broke down altogether when the 1969 models were introduced; the computers failed to invoice hundreds of new cars.

All in all, DeLorean faced a staggering assignment: he was being asked to turn around what amounted to the world's fifth-biggest industrial company. By FORTUNE's estimate, the annual sales of Chevrolet total some $10 billion, about the same as the sales of General Electric.

The tyranny of the perfectionist
DeLorean visited plants and talked to supervisors and workers as he searched for the trouble spots. He met with the dealers, whose low morale had been driven even lower when the division's sales manager told *Automotive News*, the industry's trade paper, that part of Chevy's problem was too many fat-cat dealers.

• • • •

DeLorean fashioned his staff into a dedicated team. He would sit in his office, his feet on the desk, while questioning each new visitor incisively and answering an incessant barrage of telephone calls. He grasped one complex issue after another, as if he were performing a cerebral juggling act. "He wasn't hanging over anybody's shoulder to keep an eye on them," says Gerstenberg. He didn't have to, for he cultivated his people, delegating authority and persuading them that his demands were really their own ideas. But he would brutally tyrannize anyone who didn't measure up to his standards.

• • • •

The division's slide stopped, and its market share leveled off at about 22 percent. Chevy's profits continued to decline during 1969 and 1970, the latter

year because of the long United Auto Workers strike. But they turned up in 1971 and have been growing ever since. Dealers' profits before taxes have doubled since 1969 to more than $400 million in 1972.

• • • •

While absorbed in trying to bring Chevrolet under control, DeLorean was beginning to have problems at home. He was on the road much of the time and worked long hours when he was back in Detroit.

• • • •

To be sure, DeLorean earned more in a year than many people do in their lifetimes. But he was discovering that neither the money nor the position could guarantee happiness. Some dealers he knew, including one of his three brothers, were making as much as he and giving a lot less of themselves to the job. "I make $600,000 a year," he once told a Chevrolet dealer in Illinois. "But I can't play golf next Thursday and you can."

Toward the end of 1970, DeLorean heard that a franchise for a new Cadillac dealership might soon become available in California.

• • • •

DeLorean was promoted to corporate vice president for the car-and-truck group, which accounts for about a quarter of G.M.'s operations. He moved onto the fourteenth floor, where he worked with other senior officials, attending meetings of the many committees that made the decisions at the top. Such a post might be viewed as the place where G.M. puts the final trim on its future presidents. But the change was too much for DeLorean.

• • • •

He found that a group executive, who oversees the division managers, is cut off from sources of information. The committee system so annoyed him that, if a particular meeting seemed to him unimportant, he deliberately stayed away, to the irritation of his superiors.

"You were getting all your input from lower-level specialists," he says. "They provided information in such a way that they would get the answer they wanted. I know, I used to be down below and do it. The feeling I started to get, being suddenly put on the fourteenth floor, was that now I was being presented with information that had limited alternatives. This is totally inconsistent with any thoughtful and creative originality. You never could reflect on and modify a proposal. You couldn't be a planner. You were too harassed and oppressed by committee meetings and paperwork—you just had tons of it. You were cut off from the outside world. You saw only the men on the fourteenth floor. The corporate hierarchy was just reacting to the demands of the organization and responding to some degree to the government and the public. It was like standing in the boiler room and tending a machine and you were just watching it instead of running it."

As high up in the corporation as he was, DeLorean continued to have trouble getting his views across. About three months after his arrival on the fourteenth floor, he proposed that General Motors save what he claimed would amount to $1 billion annually by making a number of changes.

• • • •

But DeLorean's seniors decided that his proposals would not save any money. . . .

"A guy who is giving his life's blood" Perhaps the most controversial issue DeLorean got embroiled in was what position G.M. should take on federal emission standards, and whether it should request a year's extension of the 1975 deadline set by Congress.

• • • •

According to sources within the company, what bothered DeLorean was that General Motors . . . was arguing for the year's delay because it did not know for sure that [its] converters would meet the standards completely. DeLorean contended that instead of asking for the delay, the company should take a more positive and realistic stand and announce that it was willing to *try* to meet the existing standards—even if it could not guarantee 100 percent success—by equipping the 1975 cars with the new converters. Because he was getting nowhere with a lot of his arguments, he became dejected: "When this happens to a guy who recognizes what ought to be done, and who is giving his life's blood and can't get it done, then hell, he ought to go on and do something else."

The longer he inhabited the fourteenth floor, the more DeLorean realized that the rewards he had believed would lie at the top, the immense power and sense of fulfillment, simply were not there. Suppose he did one day become president, what would it mean? Cole was a man who knew the product and its market, yet as president, Cole often seemed to be powerless. Cole had also urged that G.M. be more aggressive in small cars, but lost. DeLorean finally concluded that what he regarded as Cole's predicament would be his own.

In March he told Murphy he wanted a Cadillac franchise that was opening in Florida. Murphy, Gerstenberg, and others tried to dissuade him, but this time they did not push very hard. "After awhile you begin to wonder whether you're wasting his time and ours," says Gerstenberg.—Rush Loving, Jr.

Fortune, Sept. 1973

We must be careful, however, not to jump to the conclusion that the externalist is a less effective employee than an organizationalist. The externalist orientation is a state of mind. It may be only indirectly related to competence or quality of performance. The externalist may not care as much about the organization as the highly committed person, but, if he has high skill levels, he may be able to perform extremely well. Ability, as well as state of mind, is an important component in determining level of performance.

The Professional

Not all those who look outward from an organization are alienated from their work. Professionals have external orientations but are still preoccupied with their jobs or, more specifically, their careers. While the organizationalist has his self-concept linked to *where* he works, the professional has his tied to *what* he does. The professional has probably been heavily exposed to occupational socialization. In many cases the occupational socialization experiences condition him to believe that he must perform his work extremely well. However, in an organization, there must be compromises with the needs of the system. When the professional is subjected to managerial pressure to conform to organization demands that are inconsistent with his professional values, the professionally-oriented person may believe that such directives are not rational. For instance, a researcher working for a pharmaceutical firm may believe that a particular drug needs more extensive testing before it is released in the market. But there are economic considerations in the decision which must be made. The decision to release a drug might be made by a manager who is less technically qualified than the researcher, and the professional may then believe that a bad decision has been made.

Professionals are likely to be particularly disturbed when they believe they are in a situation where they are unable to most effectively utilize all their skills. In such a situation, the professional feels underutilized. Most importantly, his self-esteem may be threatened because he does not have the opportunity to do the things which he has been trained to do best.

Often professionals refuse to play the organizational status game, looking outward to other professional colleagues for approval. The professional would rather not be in the organization. He would rather be operating independently. Yet an organization is necessary to him, since it is imperative that he have a place to work, a base of operations and an economic base for his work. The professor who does not purport to have a high degree of loyalty to his university must still be in some university to do what he wants to do. Otherwise he cannot teach, do research, or engage in those other scholarly activities which the profession requires. The professional must adapt in some way to these supportive needs, and often these accommodation patterns are highly conflictive.

The Socialization of the Professional. Presthus (1965) states that the professionally-oriented person comes from the middle class and has become successful through higher level of education, or by his own efforts to increase his skill. He is likely to have a strong "ideological" orientation and to be extremely concerned that he does well in his chosen field. Success for the professional is usually defined in terms of personal achievement. More than likely it is measured by recognition from external colleagues, rather than by the rewards received internally in the organization. Organizational rewards are not valueless however, since they do represent a way that the professional may estimate the importance of his professional contribution relative to others in the system. His specialty may be extremely fulfilling for him if he is able to operate in an organization where, due to the importance of his professional skills, he is accorded higher status and pay than those in other work groups.

Organization Socialization—The Psychological Contract

To a large degree, the character of a person is fairly well s aped by the time he begins his work life. Early socialization experiences have caused the person to develop some ideas about how he should interact with an organizational system. His early socialization experiences are the basis for his values, expectations, and beliefs about what he should do at work. By the same token, there are expectations by the members of the organization about what employees should do. The *psychological contract* refers to the mutual expectation between an organization and its members about what is expected of each (Schein, 1970). An industrial organization and its employees, whether managers, specialists, or operative workers, have expectations about how much work is to be performed for the pay received. Students and professors have a set of expectations about what is appropriate performance for the other in a course when a grade is to be given. These expectations, however, are not limited to compensation only. They may focus on demands such as loyalty to the firm or the special rights of long-term workers.

Norms are ideas about what kind of behavior patterns and values are acceptable in a group or organization. They are expressed in terms of acceptable performances expected of others. Naturally, there are many norms that apply in any organization. For instance, there are accepted ways of dealing with a superior. In some organizations, certain kinds of dress patterns are appropriate, while others are frowned upon. Dark suits and subdued shirts and ties may be "right." Flowery shirts, open at the neck, and sandals may be "wrong." Some norms are more important than others. Schein (1970) calls the most important norms—those which must be accepted by organizational members—*pivotal* norms. The *peripheral* norms are less important. They may be desired in a member but it is not essential that the person accept them. Schein says there are three models of individual adjustment to an organization: *active rebellion*, when both pivotal and peripheral norms are rejected; *conformity*, when both are accepted; and *creative individualism*, when the pivotal norms are accepted and the peripheral ones rejected. It is more possible for an organization to grow and change itself in a productive way in the creative individualism mode than if the first two adjustment modes prevail.

Schein (1970) points out that the psychological contract between an organization and an individual is informally negotiated over time—at least partly—through the *organization socialization process*. New members learn performance expectations of their superiors, as well as the organizationally-preferred values and ways of doing things. This occurs in a variety of ways, as in the case of early socialization experiences of life. The teaching may be direct, as when a new employee is told about performance standards and rules, or it may be learned through "behavioral modeling," in which the employee imitates others in the organization. Most behaviors, however, are probably learned through reinforcement. Of course, the consequences of certain responses may be mixed—approval for some, disapproval for others— but the individual's future behavior is going to be influenced importantly by reinforcements from his dominant reference group. A new production employee, for example, may be far more concerned with approval from his fellow workers than from his foreman. A student's fraternity brothers or sorority sisters are likely to have more influence on the development of his or her values than will the college dean.

The new organizational member, then, comes to the job with a set of work expectations. He expects certain things about his working conditions, the mode of supervision, type of work assignments, and organization expectations of him. As the individual is socialized to organizational life, he may learn that there is a divergence between what he expected and what the organization expects. In one study of college graduates hired by one of the large automotive companies, typical graduates found most of the job characteristics were worse than expected (Dunnette, Arvey, and Banas, 1973). In this study, it was also found that there was a wider divergence between what the graduate expected and what was present in the job situation for those who terminated as compared to those who stayed. Thus, more often than not, the typical new organizational member has a set of expectations about his job which are somewhat unrealistic in terms of the organization's expectations. A period of adjustment and change takes place, and gradually the organization's expectations become better known to the individual, and management becomes more aware of the individual's expectations. Thus, the stereotyped idea of an individual being simply a pawn molded by an organization is not an appropriate way to view reality. It is certainly true that individuals are shaped by their organizational environments. However, organizations must, of necessity, adapt to the needs and values of various individuals or their very existence is threatened. Unless an organization can continue to secure the services of new members, it will atrophy and die.

When a person changes organizations, he must be "resocialized." Schein (1968) has followed business school graduates through various stages of their careers. He has found, as expected, that the values learned by students in the university setting change once they take jobs elsewhere. When they are in school, the values of the students reflect those of their professors. After a time in an organization, the students' values become significantly less like those of faculty members and more like those of top management personnel in the organizations where they work.

This chapter has discussed how individuals develop attitudes, values, and needs in their early experiences that are important in their affiliations with work organizations later. Three organizational orientations that result from socialization experiences were defined, and we have also discussed briefly the effect of organizational influences on individuals. Later in this book we will suggest how different organizations may, among their personnel, find different compositions of these individual personality patterns. In later chapters, also, many of the concepts sketched in this chapter will be reintroduced and expanded.

In the next chapter, we move to another problem—interaction in groups. Maslow's need hierarchy places social needs in an important position; therefore, group processes must play an important role in individual behavior in an organization and must be understood so that the managerial process can be effectively carried out.

Discussion Questions

1. Can you recall, from your own experience, a situation when you misinterpreted a cue, or stimulus, from another person? Did it get you in trouble? How?

2. Have you ever given someone a compliment (a positive reinforcement) and had that person react differently than you had anticipated?

3. Look around you right now. Select a part of your environment that you weren't aware of when you started reading. Why didn't you see it?

4. Close your eyes and listen to the sounds around you. What is happening? Is anything going on that shouldn't be? Pick up the differences by listening.

5. Parents, teachers, scoutmasters are authority figures. Do you react to your boss at work in the same way you reacted to them?

6. Was there ever an instance in your school days when the teacher disciplined you yet you were a hero to your friends? How did you feel? Would you do again the thing that got you into the predicament?

7. Consider Maslow's "ego" needs. How can yours best be satisfied? How about those of your best friend? Your mother? Father? Boss? Husband? Wife? Other friends?

8. In this chapter, we describe three stereotyped ways of reacting to organizations. Think of two people who fit in each category. Think of an *executive* that you know who would fit in each category. Think of a *professor* for each. Can you think of an "operative employee" or worker for each?

9. What is your reaction to John DeLorean? Did he make a good decision? How would you characterize it? Would you do what he did? What makes you the same? Different?

Chapter 4
Group Behavior

The formal structure of an organization is nothing more than the creation and specification of groups, along with the description of how they should relate to each other, and thus groups of all kinds and sizes abound in work organizations. Departments, committees, integrated task teams and the like are all formally designated groups. Within these units, members may go on to act in ways not specified in their job descriptions. No job description, for example, defines the individuals with whom an employee has lunch or travels to and from work. Yet from these activities may develop lasting relationships which can affect job performance.

Many problems in organizations can only be understood when the group is the unit of reference. Conflict between labor and management, for example, or between production and sales units, or between line and staff may be considered as special cases of group conflict. For these reasons it is important for managers to know something about group characteristics, phenomena, and processes.

All groups start from a collection of individuals assembled for some purpose. The purpose may be to accomplish together some common personal objective of the individuals or to accomplish some temporary or more enduring objective of the organization or of a manager with authority over the individuals that make up the group. For example, a group of workers or managers may voluntarily get together to form a car pool or to discuss possible approaches for obtaining a change in a disliked organizational policy. Or a department head may form a committee of six subordinates to produce a set of recommendations for reducing customer complaints. Or a collection of general lathe operators may be put together in a particular section of a new plant to perform various assigned tasks. These permanent or temporary collections of individuals then develop norms, values, roles, a status hierarchy, and other group characteristics. Then, depending on the degree of attraction the members develop for the group, and the group's success in achieving its objectives and the objectives of its members, the group becomes more or less cohesive over time.

Groups—Primary and Secondary

A group may be defined as a collection of individuals who regularly interact with each other, who are psychologically aware of each other, and who perceive themselves to be a group. There are two kinds of groups: primary and secondary.

Primary Groups

When people interact together on a face-to-face basis and where the relationships between members are personal, the group is called "primary." Primary groups have no formal written rules and procedures. Family and friendship groups are examples of primary groups.

In the work setting, primary groups are usually made up of individuals who feel they have something in common. Perhaps they all come from the same part of town. Primary groups at work might be based on similar racial or ethnic backgrounds. Or the cribbage players, bowlers, or classical music fans may spend time together at work, forming a primary group. Among managerial groups, in some organizations, primary groups may be based on the "old school tie," that is, a common educational and class background.

Secondary Groups

Secondary groups are usually larger and more impersonal than primary groups. They are governed by formal rules, procedures, and policies. The work organization is a secondary group, as are professional associations and unions. Most secondary work groups are fairly stable over time (departments, for example). Others are temporary (committees, for example).

Departments or Permanent Functional Assignments

The formal work assignment of an individual is likely to be related to the manner in which he perceives problems and his perception of his unit's status. For example, Browne and Goliembiewski (1974) found that members of staff or support units saw their "organizational unit as unimportant, impotent, as having an inward orientation. . . ." Operating unit personnel, however, saw their units as "important, powerful, having an outward orientation." Dearborn and Simon (1958) found that executives from different functional areas such as production, marketing, and accounting defined problems in terms of activities and goals of their work assignments.

These studies point up the fact that the nature of the work group, together with the job requirements, can have significant effects on the attitudes and perceptions of individuals. In addition, individuals operating in groups are often strongly influenced by group norms. This is true whether or not the group forms itself or is an organizationally-defined unit.

Committees

Committees are common to all organizations. They are contrived groups, meet only periodically, and are established for a variety of purposes. Committees may investigate problems and report the results of their investigation. They may be used to obtain new ideas: to make decisions; or be created to coordinate the activities of various groups in the organization. A committee is usually a temporary work assignment. Its members meet together to discuss the issues before it.

The effectiveness of a committee in reaching its objectives depends upon a number of factors. For instance, both the structure and composition of the committee and the process of communication and deliberation are important. For greatest effectiveness, committees should not be so large as to preclude involvement of all members; should contain individuals with the necessary authority to implement decisions that are reached by the group; should be motivated to achieve the group task; and should not be made up of members with personal characteristics (such as quite unequal statuses) which might hinder full participation of all members.

Required and Emergent Behavior in Groups

Organizational units such as departments and committees are established on the basis of task requirements, or the job to be done. They are set up as a result of a rational decision-making process or they may in part simply evolve as a response to some organization need. Required behavior refers to that which is established for, and expected of, the members. It is an organizational requirement. Emergent behavior is that behavior which actually occurs in the group. It is a result, not only of job requirements, but of a wide range of individual and group characteristics which we will discuss later in this chapter.

As Homans (1951) points out, emergent behavior is likely to be different from, and more complex than, required behavior, because required behavior only considers the needs of the organization, not the needs of individuals and of the group itself. On the other hand, emergent behavior—the behavior you actually see in a group—is the result of an accommodation between organizational demands and the interests of group members.

Most emergent behavior is probably functional for the group. It helps the group to cope with the stresses arising from the nature of the work and the interaction between individuals in the group. For instance, where workers have a monotonous job, the monotony may lead the workers to trade jobs, gamble, or engage in horseplay and other social activities—all diversions which enable them as a group to cope with the demands placee upon them by boring and repetitive work.

Some emergent behavior of course may be highly undesirable from the organizational point of view. Restriction of production, for example, is organizationally undesirable, but it may also be a way by which workers adjust to managerial pressures which conflict with individual or group needs, a way to avoid threatening comparisons between group members, for instance. Or, since the restriction of production is a group activity, it may provide the excuse for social interaction which gives the group a sense of purpose and a reason for existence. Production may also obviously be restricted in order to protect the jobs and income of group members.

The Effects of Groups at Work—Two Studies

The importance of groups in the work setting is highlighted in the two studies that we discuss here. The first, the Bank Wiring Observation Room study, is part of the Hawthorne studies. It shows how required and emergent behavior exist in the work place. The second, a study of coal-mining methods in England, illustrates how re-forming groups (or departments) can have positive effects on productivity.

The Bank Wiring Observation Room. As part of the Hawthorne studies, the researchers wanted to examine a stable and experienced group of workers which had control over its own output and where it was easy to measure individual output quite precisely (Roethlisberger and Dixon, 1939). The men chosen—nine wiremen, three soldermen, and two inspectors—attached wires to banks of terminals used as parts of switches for central office telephone equipment. To perform this job, each wireman first attached wire by hand to terminals on a plastic bank which was stabilized in a holder. Next, a solderman soldered the wire in place. Then the inspector, using an electrical test set, tested the work.

Before the study began, output records from the department from which the men were chosen were obtained for 18 weeks. In addition, all 32 workers in the department from which the men were chosen were interviewed prior to the study period. During these interviews, the men expressed their attitudes toward their jobs, supervisors, and working conditions. The 14 men chosen were told by their foreman that they were to be studied and were asked to cooperate. The experimental subjects were then introduced to the man who would observe them in the observation room. They were assured that no information obtained by the observer would be used to their disadvantage. All but one of the men studied were between 20 and 26 years of age, and only one had any college education.

The Bank Wiring Observation Room was separated from the main department by high partitions. In it, in addition to the 14 subjects, there was the observer and, for a good part of the time, a trucker who brought in materials and removed completed work, and a group chief, the lowest grade of supervisor. As in the main department, the wiremen who wired "connectors" were placed in the front of the room and the wiremen who wired "selectors" were placed in the back of the room.

Group piecework was the system of wage payment for the department. Each piece of equipment completed by the department as a whole was credited to the department as a fixed sum. Each worker was paid an hourly rate of pay, depending upon his efficiency rating, plus a bonus.

Observation of the group at work showed that the actual behavior of the workers was different from, and more elaborate than, the work behavior described in the official descriptions of the jobs. For example, the men helped each other when someone fell behind in his work, though not all workers were helped and not all workers helped. In addition, the wiremen and the soldermen traded jobs (with the offer to trade being made by the wiremen).

The men also formed *two* friendship cliques within the Bank Wiring Observation Room. Each clique participated in their own games and other social activities. In addition to conversations, there was kidding and horseplay within the groups. The men gambled in a number of different ways. They organized pools and together would choose and place bets on horse races. They also matched coins, shot craps, and played cards. The men bought candy together and shared it, and they ate lunch with each other.

The researchers soon realized that the men in the Bank Wiring Observation Room, as a group, were controlling the rate of production.

They had a definite idea of what constituted "too much" and "too little" work. At times, slower workers were bawled out for not working fast enough.

In addition to setting production norms, the group felt that no worker should "squeal" to higher management about another group member and no group member should attempt to put himself in a superior position in relation to the other workers in the room. One of the inspectors, the oldest man in the room and the only worker with some college education, was teased by the men. They adjusted his test set so that it did not work and reported to their supervisor that he delayed them. He retaliated by reporting the men to a higher level, an act that created so much hostility toward him that he had to be transferred out of the room.

The Bank Wiring Observation Room study ended in May, 1932, after 6½ months. During this time, the researchers observed that the men had created an informal social organization which developed an unwritten but understood set of rules governing the behavior of the men in the group and specifying the nature of the relationships among them. The Bank Wiring Observation Room group illustrates many important characteristics of all groups, characteristics which will be discussed later in this chapter.

Integrated Task Teams. Naturally efforts have been made to more carefully construct work groups and assign work to them to improve performance as well as the satisfaction of members. One such effort is the "integrated task team." It is based on several assumptions (Rice, 1953). The first is that a work group should have just the right number of workers to complete the task efficiently, but be small enough to enable individual members to identify with the group's output, thus allowing them to experience a sense of task completion, of accomplishment, of success, and of satisfaction. To accomplish this means that the tasks assigned to a group must be extensive enough for the group members collectively to feel they have accomplished something worth-while, such as producing an identifiable result.

The second assumption is that work groups will be more cohesive and stable if they can identify with a territory or area different from that occupied by any other workers. This could be accomplished through the use of walls, partitions, special marking on the floor or on the equipment, or by some other means.

The third assumption is that cohesiveness, stability, and satisfaction will be higher in groups with satisfactory interpersonal relationships, with control over their own day-to-day work and organization, and with a fairly narrow range of skill levels and pay differentials within the group.

An investigation was made in the British coal mining industry of the consequences of assigning work to integrated task teams instead of on an individual basis (Trist and Banforth, 1951). Prior to World War I, mining companies in Great Britain obtained coal with the use of small work teams—often consisting of three persons—which worked on a contract basis. Paid according to how much coal they brought to the surface, the teams were very cohesive. This system was replaced by the longwall system under which coal was obtained through specialization. Under the longwall method, each miner was a specialist and each shift did specialized tasks.

In the conventional longwall method, the first shift in each new location bores holes in which to place explosives in the coal face, undercuts the coal face so the coal will drop when the explosives are set off, and takes down the conveyer equipment at the previous location. The second shift reassembles the conveyer at the new location, makes passageways, and props the roof. The third shift takes out the coal and brings it to the surface.

TABLE 4.1

	Conventional Longwall (specialization)	Composite Longwall (integrated task team)
Percentage of time spent reworking tasks done poorly by other shifts	25	5
Absence rate percentage	20	8.2
Productivity as percentage of ideal productivity (perfect efficiency in getting out all coal)	78	95

Source: E. L. Trist and K. Banforth, "Some Social and Psychological Consequences of the Long Wall Method of Coal Getting, *Human Relations* 4 (1951).

In one mine a new system was developed and used which has been called the "composite longwall system." In this system, miners with various job specialties are placed in teams which have the skills to perform all of the necessary tasks in mining the coal. Each team works in the mine as a shift and does whatever tasks are necessary to carry forward the work done by the previous shift. This means that one shift does not have to complete certain tasks before the work of the next shift can commence. In addition, each work team is given autonomy and the right to control its own activities. Each team was also put on a group incentive plan in which all members of the team shared. Table 4.1 presents a comparison of some results achieved under the two systems. Clearly the quality and quantity of work improved significantly and the absence rate decreased when the group was re-formed to use the integrated task team approach.

Some Properties of Groups

Groups, like individuals, can be characterized or described along certain dimensions which are characteristics of the group, not of any single member, characteristics such as group *values, norms, roles,* and *cohesiveness.*

Group Values

Individuals bring values and attitudes to a group and also learn them from the group itself. A group's values refer to what is important or unimportant to, or what is good or bad for, most members of the group. Activities of other groups, the organization, and of its own members are evaluated against the value structure of the group. Some groups place a high value on education, for example, some on money, others on experience. Others place a high value on the establishment of strong personal friendships.

Norms

Group norms refer to the unwritten set of behavioral expectations— what members "ought to do." Norms are rules and standards that govern the conduct of group members. Norms will obviously be congruent with the values of the group, and are a means of social control, a means of evaluating the behavior of others. Norms tell an individual what to do and what not to do.

Learning of Norms. Norms are learned in a variety of ways. They may be learned by simple observation of other group members, by being directly taught, or by conditioning, (as discussed in chap. 3). Conditioning occurs as a result of reinforcement from other group members. When, for instance, a new member works at too fast a pace the first day on the job, he may be subjected to derogatory comments such as "Look at old speed king there," "Look who's trying to make us look bad," "Look who's trying to impress the foreman," "Look at who's trying to make us lose our jobs," and so on. A little of this goes a long way in obtaining compliance with group norms.

Norms of a group are enforced, then, by sanctioning violators. Sanctions may range from communications of disapproval, such as those cited above, to social ostracism, threats, and actual physical attacks, pranks, and the direct sabotage of another's equipment, raw materials, or finished goods. For example, in a steel mill a work team found that the previous shift filled the furnace with grit each morning until they reduced their level of production to the norm of the other furnace teams. A worker in a sweater factory found that other workers cut his yarn and damaged his machine when he worked at a pace which they considered too fast.

Factors Affecting the Level of Compliance. There are usually varying degrees of compliance to group norms. Some individual members are quite conformist, while others are not. A number of personal characteristics seem to be related to susceptibility to group influence. One such personal characteristic is the degree of identification with the group. Some individuals identify strongly with a group, while others do not. A higher level of education, or being of higher social class than most other workers may generate negative identification with the group. In the Bank Wiring Observation Room study, the individual who violated the group norms had a higher level of education and was older than the other group members. Also, most organizational members are the members of several groups. If the norms and values of the other groups conflict with those of organizational groups, a problem is created. This problem often becomes a matter of which group the organizational member primarily identifies with. The group with which an individual identifies most strongly is a primary reference group—the one to which he looks for guidance in his behavior and attitudes. Some research has indicated that the professionals in an organization, such as scientists, engineers, and economists, are more likely to identify with an outside group than are managers. If they identify strongly with their professional colleagues outside the firm, they may, of course, be less loyal to the firm than are managers.

Conforming behavior has also been found to be associated with certain personality characteristics. Individuals with low levels of self-confidence, with high levels of insecurity, or with a fear of being different are likely to be more responsive to group influence than their opposites.

One's position in the group also influences norm conformity. The lower a person's status in the group, the less the other group members expect of him. In general, individuals in high-status positions are expected to be models of conformity to group norms.

The level of norm compliance also depends on factors peculiar to the group itself. All norms are not of equal importance to the group, and all deviations from norms are not equally visible to other group members.

Role and Position

Norms define the kind of behavior another person *should* exhibit. The behavior sequences of an individual's interaction with others is called a "role." ("Role prescription" is another way to define norm.) In a group, formal or nonformal, an individual may interact with several others. For instance, at work a manager may interact with subordinates, fellow managers, and his secretary. The manager's relationship with his subordinates is one role. His relationship with fellow managers is another role. Each of these different role partners have expectations (or norms) about how the manager should act.

All of an individual's group roles, as a cluster, define that individual's *position*. The position, a cluster of related roles performed by an individual in a group, locates him in relation to others "with respect to the job to be done, and the giving and taking of orders" (Katz and Kahn, 1964).

Since different individuals may occupy the same position at different points in time, it is expected that there would be some differences in role behavior between individuals in the same position, but also much similarity. Role behavior would depend upon the role incumbent's own personal characteristics and his perceptions of what others expect in the behavior of a person in his position, as well as the demands of others. Behavior of different individuals in the same position would be similar in many ways because of the expectations of others, and would be different in many ways because of differences in abilities and personality. In the Bank Wiring Observation Room, there were two inspectors, and they perceived their roles quite differently, one ingratiating himself with the group and not carrying out his officially assigned duties; the other acting quite officiously and informing on the men.

An individual may have many roles simultaneously, but in any particular instant of time only one role may be activated. Which one it is depends upon which group an individual is acting with at the time and with which individuals he is interacting.

The roles that an individual may have vary from one group to another and from one group member to another. At times an individual is the superior and at times he is a subordinate. At times he is expected to provide information and at times to receive information. At times he must make a decision and at times he must carry out another person's decision. And at other times, of course, he may be a parent, a Little League umpire, or the secretary of the local bridge club.

The *role set* consists of all those other individuals in the group with which a person has contact and who have expectations about his behavior. He himself is included in his role set. Of course, there may be misunderstanding by a group member of what behavior is expected of him by others in his role set. His role perceptions may differ from what is sent or communicated by members of his role set. Or the group member may understand clearly what the expectations of members of his role set are, but he cannot comply for a number of reasons. One reason may be role conflict. For example, a foreman's subordinates may expect him to ease up on them after an especially difficult day, while his superiors may expect him to increase pressure on his men to get out a particular order.

Status

Role relationships are defined in terms of interaction between incumbents of positions. Roles may also be different in terms of *status* within the group. Status refers to the hierarchical ranking of roles in a group so that some roles may be said to be "higher" than or "superior" to others. Newcomb and his colleagues (1965) note that such distinctions may be functions of "skill, wealth, power, popularity."

Individuals in roles may have high or low status because they belong to particular professions (such as the medical), have a particular formal position (say as the vice-president), have a particularly important skill for the group (say as a computer programmer), or have achieved recognition in another area (such as a professional ballplayer). Having high status gives one a set of rights and obligations. For example, individuals in a high-status position have the right to make suggestions to individuals occupying lower positions. At the same time they may have an obligation to provide certain types of advice and help incumbents of lower-status position. In the Bank Wiring Observation Room, the higher-status wiremen always initiated the request to change jobs with the lower-status soldermen. For a solderman to initiate such a request would be considered inappropriate behavior for a person in the low-status position.

Group Cohesiveness

Both primary and secondary groups differ in their solidarity or cohesiveness. *Cohesiveness* is the ability of the group to maintain itself, or continue to exist, when it is subjected to pressures and stress (Stogdill, 1959). Some groups are closely knit, while others are much less so. A number of factors have been found to be associated with group cohesiveness. Size is an obvious factor; other factors being equal, smaller groups are generally more cohesive than larger. Interaction opportunities contribute to cohesiveness. In many organizations, it may be quite difficult for members to talk to each other or be in close contact. Noise, physical separation by machinery, and other factors may limit interaction.

Cohesiveness generally increases as a group experiences success in its collective activities. Repeated failure often creates internal dissension and bickering within a group, but if a group is successful in meeting its objectives, pride in being a member may increase, and members may increase their commitment to the group. External attacks and pressure may also greatly increase group cohesiveness. To meet a common threat, the members will pull together.

Personal characteristics of members may also influence group cohesiveness. Individuals with similar backgrounds are likely to have common values and are therefore less likely to disagree. A common background may contribute to patterns of similar interests, making communication easier. Similar backgrounds may make individuals more comfortable in one another's presence.

Status factors are also important. If one believes his professional, ethnic, or racial group is superior to those of others, he may not want to associate with those believed to be of lower status. Also, persons may not want to associate with others whose status is ambiguous, because the uncertainty makes them uncomfortable. *Status congruence* means the degree to which the factors associated with group status line up with respect to each other for a particular individual. (Zaleznik et al., 1958). A person has high status congruence if his personal characteristics are consistent in placing him at a high-, a middle-, or at a low-status position in the status hierarchy. Low-status congruence means there are inconsistencies with respect to such factors. The important factor is consistency. For example, assuming that a particular group values individuals with high levels of education, who are older, experienced, can tell funny jokes and have a native American background, a young immigrant with little education or experience, who is not funny, would still have high-status congruence because he is consistently low in all his status factors. On the other hand, another person, well-educated, funny, but young with only a moderate amount of experience would have low-status congruence. It is likely that the first young person would be accepted by the group. Members would find it easy to interact with him because his status position in the group is clear, and one's expected behavior toward him is also unambiguous. The other young person might find only limited acceptance, however, because his status position in the group is unclear and there is uncertainty about how others should behave toward him. The uncertainty is likely to lead to avoidance, since uncertainty contributes to interpersonal anxiety and most individuals attempt to avoid anxiety-producing relationships.

Some Effects of Membership in Groups

Membership in groups has an impact, both positive and negative, on the attitudes and behaviors of members. Groups can be highly satisfying, providing sources of social support, while at the same time be the source of problems for an individual.

Individual Support. An individual becomes a group member to gain the advantages of such membership. The advantages may be many. In the previous chapter we discussed basic human needs. Some of these needs are satisfied in the group. For example, the group provides opportunities for social interaction, which in itself may be satisfying. The individual may find others who care about him and his problems. The group also provides help and assistance to its members. Through the group, the new employee may find out which rules have to be followed and which do not. He is told how to get on the best side of his superior. He gets advice and help with his work.

The group also protects the individual. In unity there is strength. A group can often stand up to a foreman, or to organization pressures, when an individual cannot. The opportunities to exercise leadership and other skills may also exist in a group. A group may be a means of achieving a high individual status, if the group is highly regarded by others. Individuals may grow and develop in groups, and group members may learn from each other.

Secondary groups, as well as primary, are of value to the individual. Obviously, membership in some secondary groups is the means by which one makes a living. Secondary groups may authenticate one's professionalism, and also—along with primary groups—may provide many off-the-job satisfactions.

Effects on Performance and Attitudes. Group members are influenced in their performance by what they perceive others expect and want of them. A cohesive group may perform at a consistently high level as well as at a low level. Seashore (1957) found in a study of 228 groups in a machinery company that attitude toward management was an important determinant of whether performance norms for a group were at a high or low level. It is not known, however, whether the effect of *most* groups is negative or positive with respect to performance level.

Job Satisfaction. The evidence seems clear that workers who are accepted members of industrial work groups have higher job satisfaction (Vroom, 1964; Helmreich, Bakeman, and Schenwitz, 1973). Several studies have shown that as opportunities to interact with other workers are diminished, job satisfaction goes down (Jasinsi, 1956).

Turnover-absenteeism. There is a demonstrably constant and close relationship between satisfaction and turnover and absenteeism. As job satisfaction decreases, absenteeism and turnover increase (Vroom, 1964). Therefore, it is not surprising that a number of studies show that workers who are accepted group members or who have an opportunity for conversation and interaction with other workers have lower absenteeism and turnover rates than those who do not (Porter and Steers, 1973).

Helping Behavior. Helping others seems to be a fairly universal activity in groups. This phenomenon is found in all groups—family groups, college fraternities, military units, industrial work groups, primitive tribes, and so on. Such helping behavior may be of considerable value in improving production. For example, where the work is interdependent, better coordination and team effort can help the job. On the other hand, of course, it is also possible that members may help each other sabotage work.

Tension and Anxiety. Seashore (1954), in his study of 228 industrial work groups in a machinery company, found there was less anxiety among workers in the highly cohesive groups. There is other evidence also that individuals associate being with other people with a reduction in tension and anxiety (Schacter, 1964). Thus, positive mental health benefits may result from the individual employee's acceptance in his work group.

Individual Growth and Development. There is increasing concern today with providing opportunities for personal growth and development in work and social situations. But while individuals may become more competent as a result of group membership, such membership may prove a barrier to self-development efforts. Zaleznik, Christensen, and Roethlisberger (1958) made an intensive study of 50 workers in a manufacturing plant and found that there was a certain amount of suppression of the individual by the group. In some groups, individual members were not allowed to learn new modes of behavior or to adopt new ideas and perspectives.

There is a cost to conformity, and some part of it is a loss of individual freedom in growth and development. The Volvo plant in Sweden, for example, has used a form of job enrichment (see chap. 5) to change its assembly procedures. Rather than a typical assembly line, as found in U.S. auto manufacturing, teams of three of four Volvo workers decide among themselves who will work on the various parts of the engine. A group of visiting U.S. auto assemblers worked in the plant. Some liked the quite different atmosphere, but some felt that "working with a team . . . required accommodating to the habits of others; they preferred to be responsible to themselves."

Problems of Groups

In groups, individuals, as we have noted, do not always find the going easy. Groups can impose many pressures and sanctions on individual members, and thus contribute to individual stress. Also, groups can be a cause of many problems in organizations because they are in conflict with each other. In this section, we will examine two sets of problems. One set deals with stresses on the individual—those of role conflict and role ambiguity. The second set deals with intergroup problems.

Role Conflict and Ambiguity

Katz and Kahn (1964) have treated the problem of role conflict and ambiguity extensively. These stresses to which an individual is exposed in groups, whether a work group or formal departmental assignment, can affect the way group members perform and feel.

Role conflict occurs when a person is subjected to inconsistent demands with respect to his behavior. *Intersender role conflict* occurs when the inconsistent demands come from different individuals in the role set. The salesman, for instance, is under pressure from his superior to get the highest possible price, while the customer presses for a low price. *Intrasender role conflict* occurs when the inconsistent demands come from the same source, as when a manager expects a subordinate to complete a project which requires more personnel to do it, but at the same time refuses to assign added staff to the subordinate's unit. *Interrole conflict* develops when a person outside the role set imposes demands which cause problems within it. The family of a manager may expect the manager to spend time with them, rather than at the office, thus inducing role conflict. *Person-role conflict* occurs when the demands in the role are inconsistent with the individual's own value system. This problem could occur, for example, in cases where a work assignment calls for a legal but perhaps unethical activity which the person feels is wrong.

Role conflicts exist in all organizations, and people learn to adapt to some moderate levels. Organization structures which define jobs and accountability are efforts to minimize this condition.

The condition in which individuals may not be clear as to what the role requirements are—that is, they may not know precisely what to do—is called *role ambiguity*. Two types of role ambiguity may exist. Ambiguity with regard to what behavior, or task, is expected is called *task ambiguity*. Or a person may be unclear about what others think of him. This may be related to how his supervisor rates him, or what his status in a group is. This type of role ambiguity is sometimes called *social-emotional ambiguity*.

Sources of Role Conflict and Ambiguity.   Role problems may occur for a number of reasons. Perhaps an individual is a new group member. It will take him some time to "learn the ropes." Or role relationships may be unclear due to rapidly changing membership in a group. In formal organization structures, we would expect higher levels of role ambiguity when there is rapid growth or change. Role conflict may be high, for example, when the organization structure must be constantly changed to accommodate developing markets or changing technology.

In subsequent chapters we will be more specific about the particular types of role conflict and ambiguity in different kinds of organizations, along with their effects.

Intergroup Conflict

An organization is made up of many different groups. Some of these groups have work which is relatively independent of other groups, while others may be interdependent due to the nature of their work. When the work of different groups is interdependent, the relationships between or among the groups is of critical importance organiza-

tionally. Such relationships may be characterized as being cooperative, helpful, synergistic, or uncooperative, antagonistic, mutually
destructive, and so on.

This does not mean that intergroup cooperation is good and intergroup conflict is bad for an organization. Some conflict is productive
if it results in two conflicting objectives being satisfied. For example,
there may be substantial disagreement in an organization between the
engineering group and the sales group as to whether a product should
be designed with an emphasis on quality or on price. Both quality and
price must be considered and the disagreement between the two
groups may insure that both factors are considered in the design and
production of the product.

On the other hand, two groups may cooperate to the detriment of
the organization by jointly opposing needed changes. Or two groups
may place such a high value on avoiding disagreement that problems
that should be surfaced and discussed are not.

Some Determinants of Group Conflict. A number of different factors
can contribute to intergroup hostility, leading to unproductive results
such as confrontation, maneuvering and marshaling strength to overcome the other.

1. *Competition over Resources.* Groups will find it easier to function and group goals will be easier to achieve when resources, money,
people, or physical assets are plentiful. When a number of groups are
dependent upon a single or otherwise limited resource base, however,
there is likely to be a great deal of competition for resources. This
gives rise to hostility and conflict. In addition, groups will want representation in decision making about resource allocation to insure that
they are equitably treated.

2. *Status Differences and Work Flow.* Group conflict can develop
because of the work-flow sequence in an organization. If work relationships are such that individuals from a low-status group appear to
be telling individuals in a high-status organizational group what to do,
considerable resistance may develop. The higher-status group may
attempt to show its independence and power by doing the opposite of
what is requested, by anger, by ridiculing members of the lower-status
group, or by avoiding contact with representatives of the lower-status
group. If a waitress gives a cook an order from a customer, he may
swear at her just to let her know who is boss. When draftsmen give
suggestions to engineers, when technicians criticize the work of production experts, or when students criticize faculty members, there
may be negative, hostile feelings generated in the higher-status group

member because of what appears to be inappropriate behavior on the part of the lower-status group.

3. *Conflicting Objectives.* Different groups often have different objectives. These may be contradictory, leading to considerable disagreement between two groups which must coordinate their efforts. For example, a production group responsible for minimizing production costs may disagree with a sales group trying to maximize sales revenue by processing customer orders at a faster but more costly rate. Disagreement is especially likely when the two different groups are rewarded or punished for meeting or not meeting their assigned objectives. Such conflict is inevitable because an organization pursues many objectives simultaneously and many of these objectives are contradictory.

Different executives may not agree on the relative importance of different company objectives. Some may stress short-run objectives of the organization, while others may be more concerned with long-run objectives. Such differences in objectives are related to differences in group memberships in the organization, as we have noted earlier. These, in turn, are related to differences in the problems facing different groups and differences in their values.

4. *Different Perceptions.* Even though different groups may interact regularly, members of one group may perceive things differently than members of another. One frequent source of disagreement is the tendency of any group to value its own ideas, proposals, and creations more highly than those of other groups. Each of two groups making a proposal tends to overvalue its own work and to undervalue the work of the other group.

Perceptual differences arise from the tendency of an individual to evaluate things in terms of his own experiences. Since organizational members have had different experiences, training, and education, they tend to perceive problems and their causes differently (Simon and Dearborn, 1958). This is especially likely to occur when the problems or possible causes of a problem are ambiguous.

5. *Ambiguous Authority and Work Assignments.* Many tasks require the work of two or more groups. In such cases it may be difficult to pinpoint responsibility or to correctly allocate credit or blame for good or bad performance. For this reason, members of some groups may not wish to undertake joint assignments. A group may attempt to get another to assume responsibility for the unpleasant, difficult, or unfairly rewarded tasks, while it tries to gain control over the more pleasant, easy, or fairly rewarded tasks. Actions such as these lead to conflict between groups.

6. *Reciprocity.* Gouldner (1960) has noted the importance of reci-

procity in and between groups. Group members feel that they should receive a just return for their services. If the relations between groups are such that one group seems to be always doing something for another group without receiving benefits in return, this gives rise to a feeling of being exploited and the first group will be motivated to terminate the relationship.

Relationships Between Competing Groups. Some research in both organizational and nonorganizational settings shows that competition among groups affects what happens *within* groups and between them (Schein, 1970).

What happens *within* each competing group? Each group becomes more closely knit and elicits greater loyalty from its members. Members close ranks and bury some of their internal differences. The group climate changes from informal, casual, and playful to work- and task-oriented, and concern for members' psychological needs declines, while concern for task accomplishment increases. Leadership patterns tend to change from democratic toward autocratic and the group becomes more willing to tolerate this. Each group becomes more highly structured and organized. More loyalty and conformity are demanded from members in order to be able to present a solid front.

What happens *between* the competing groups? Each group begins to see the other groups as the enemy, rather than merely as a neutral object. The group begins to experience distortions of perception—it tends to perceive only the best parts of itself, denying its weaknesses, and tends to perceive only the worst parts of the other group, denying its strengths. Each group is likely to develop a negative stereotype of the other ("They don't play fair like we do"). Hostility toward the other group increases, while interaction and communication with the other group decreases, making it easier to maintain negative stereotypes and more difficult to correct perceptual distortions. If the groups are forced into interaction—for example, if they are forced to listen to representatives plead their own and the others' cause in reference to some task—each group is likely to listen more closely to their own representative than the representative of the other group, and to find fault with the latter's presentation. In other words, group members tend to hear only that which supports their own position and stereotype. As mentioned earlier, the group that wins in the competitive situation is likely to become more cohesive. The losing group tends toward internal dissension and finding fault with certain of its members.

These concepts about groups and group problems are underlying explanations for many coordinating problems which managers must face. (In chap. 15, for example, we discuss how a manager can approach the job of bringing together, for the purpose of achieving organizational goals, groups with very divergent points of view.) To be an effective manager, it is essential not only to understand a great deal about the nature of individuals, but also a great deal about the nature of groups.

Discussion Questions

1. Are the experiences described in the Bank Wiring Observation Room Study similar to or different from those you have encountered in work groups? Other groups?

2. Think about your experience in observing an ethnic group from a distance. Were the characteristics which you associate with individuals from that ethnic background prominent to you? Did you have positive or negative feelings about the group? Think of how they felt, good or bad, while they were together. When you meet individually with your close friends from that same ethnic background, are they like the "group" you observed?

3. What do your answers to the questions in no. 2 above tell you about
   a) group norms and values?
   b) group pressures?
   c) differences in behavior when alone or in a group?

4. Have you ever experienced *role conflict*? How did you resolve it? Have you ever experienced a role conflict situation in which resolution to the satisfaction of all involved was impossible? How did you decide with whom you would comply?

Chapter 5
Motivation
and Performance

Now that we have considered the questions of how individuals get to be what they are—and how they are—and how groups work together (or don't), we can more closely address the practical consequences of some of these ideas.

Ask a manager what his most common problem is, and he will probably respond, "People. How to get those who work for me to carry out their tasks satisfactorily—how to 'motivate' them to perform well." The ability to motivate subordinates is generally considered an essential management skill. Perhaps not surprisingly, those in top management positions in most organizations tend to feel that *people* seldom perform up to their capacity, the implication being that either people are not working well, or that they are not being managed effectively by lower-level executives. For example, two top managers said this about their work groups:

"I'll tell you my honest opinion. About 5 percent of the people work, 10 percent of the people think they work, and the other 85 percent would rather die than work!"

"There are lots of workers in this plant, hundreds of them, who don't have the capacity to do things other than what they're doing. And they're lazy! They might be able to develop some capacities, although I think there are a lot of them who couldn't even if they wanted to. But *they don't even have the desire*" (Argyris, 1953).

Motivation, then, is a prime concern of today's managers. Managers at all levels believe that if they can only "motivate" their subordinates, those subordinates *will* perform to capacity, and life for everyone will be simpler and better.

This concern with motivation is due, in large part, to the fact that measureable differences in performance between companies, government agencies, departments, and other types of organizational units are more often than not attributed to human factors. If, for example, you were to enter an automobile plant in which all signs and symbols designating the company had been removed, you probably could not differentiate it from the plant of any other auto company. The assembly line at a Chevrolet plant looks very much like that at a Ford plant. Therefore, given this similarity between hardware and technology, it is easy to attribute differences in productivity and performance between a Ford plant and a Chevy plant to human factors—a problem of differences which can be solved, it is commonly thought, by proper motivation of the workers.

Motivation is also a concern in our contemporary culture because of our historic stress on the "work ethic"—the belief that to work is good and that everyone should *want* to work. The socialization experiences of large segments of our society have led them to believe that they should be involved and committed to their work. (This causes some psychological problems for people when they are out of work. At the 1975 convention of the American Psychological Association, for example, Dr. Hannah Levin reported that after interviewing 45 unemployed men and their wives and children in Brooklyn and Staten Island, her finding was that many unemployed look upon themselves as "nonpersons." She said that "lack of work, especially for a male, puts him in a psychological no-man's land. He doesn't feel legitimate anymore, nor adult," and that 90 percent of the 45 unemployed she interviewed felt responsible for their predicament. "'I should have gone to college,' said one. 'Maybe I lacked initiative,' said another. 'I didn't try hard enough,' said a third." This is the work ethic functioning when there is no work.)

Many managers subscribe to the work ethic, and it upsets them to discover that many who work for them do not—may, in fact, be alienated from their work. The most common tactic used (or tried) to counter this alienation is "motivation," because it is widely believed, especially among those who subscribe to the work ethic, that if one is committed to and generally satisfied with his work, he will perform better. If he *thinks* well of his job, he will *do* well at it. This is one concept of motivation frequently held by managers who wish to "motivate" their subordinates. The question is, is it a sound concept?

An oft-cited story whose moral is intended to stress the importance of work involvement has three stonemasons of the Middle Ages working on a cathedral. An onlooker approaches the three and asks the nearest, "What are you doing?"

"I am earning a living," is the reply.

The observer turns to the second and asks the same question.

"I am practicing my craft."

The observer turns to the third mason and again asks the same question.

The third stonemason's reply is: "I am building a cathedral."

The *intended* moral of this anecdote is that the third stonemason has been doing the best job because his work is the most meaningful to him—he is "motivated." It is our guess, however, that if we could find that cathedral, and the three locations where the stonemasons were working, there would be no differences between quality of any of the stone placement. If the anecdote's moral were true, buildings all around us would have bricks falling out of them where the least motivated brick layers toiled. When motivation is defined this way (as job involvement, job satisfaction, or work commitment) it may—or may not—be related to performance. The attitude of an individual worker toward his job, how he thinks about it, may be substantially less important in determining how well or poorly he performs than are a good many other factors.

Motivation—Two Definitions

Perhaps some of the difficulties of understanding the relationship of motivation to work occur because there are several ways this term is used and, often, there is confusion. One way to define motivation is as a *management activity*, or something that a manager does to induce others to act in a way to produce the results required organizationally. In this context we might say, "The teacher tries to motivate the student," or "The role of a manager is to motivate the worker." We use the term in this way when, later in this chapter, we describe several managerial motivation strategies.

We also use it another way. Motivation can also be defined as an internal mental state of an individual which causes him to behave. This is a *psychological* definition of motivation, some facets of which were examined in chapters 3 and 4. Some of these facets will be expanded upon later in this chapter in our discussion of different theories of motivation.

Job Satisfaction, Motivation, and Performance

Job satisfaction may well be the most studied human factor in organizations, with much of the work resulting from the interest generated by the Hawthorne studies and the point of view known as "human relations." The logic underlying the human relations point of view was the assumption that if a worker is committed to his job, he will be more productive. Such a commitment is likely to be made because of, and reflected by, the level of job satisfaction. By increasing job satisfaction, goes the assumption, we will improve performance.

But why *should* satisfaction cause a worker to perform at a higher level? A worker may be perfectly happy in his job while at the same time be wholly uninterested in exerting much effort at it. Or a worker may perform at a very high level even though dissatisfied, because he fears losing his job. Or he may perform well because he believes it is his duty as a responsible person to do the best he can. (Professionals, especially, often feel this way.) He also may work hard because he needs the money to pay his bills.

That satisfaction causes high performance is an intriguing assumption and would be very useful if it were consistent with reality. Victor Vroom (1964) has examined 20 studies in which various measures of job satisfaction (or employee attitudes toward work) were correlated with different measures of performance. He found that the average correlation in these studies between satisfaction and performance was very low, leading him to conclude that:

> There is no simple relationship between job satisfaction and job performance. . . . We do not know yet the conditions which affect the magnitude and direction of relationships between satisfaction and performance.
>
> . . . The absence of a marked or consistent correlation between job satisfaction and performance casts some doubt on the generality or intensity of either effects of satisfaction on performance or performance on satisfaction. It also suggests that the conditions which determine a person's level of job satisfaction and his level of job performance are not identical.

Thus, it would seem, as we have stated, that improving job satisfaction may not in itself necessarily improve job performance. On the other hand, there is some evidence that higher job satisfaction may *follow* better job performance (Greene, 1973). This is likely to happen when the higher performance is followed by receiving rewards important to the employee, such as a promotion when a job is done well by the organizationalist type of employee. In chapter 3 we discussed learning theory and stated that for a reward to be positively reinforcing it must be *associated* with the event by the individual. Thus, the externally-oriented employee who performs well and is promoted may not be as satisfied as the organizationalist, because, as we said, his values lie outside the organization.

At the same time, research has shown a definite and consistent relationship between job satisfaction and the turnover and absenteeism rate among workers (Vroom, 1964). Absenteeism and turnover can both, of course, affect both costs and productivity. If a worker is absent from his job, for example, others may have difficulty performing their jobs because of that absence. If a worker quits, his equipment and machinery stand idle until he is replaced (perhaps by a less experienced worker).

High turnover and absenteeism can be very expensive. Consider, for example, a plant employing 1,000 workers at an average wage (salary and fringe benefits) of $15,000 per employee. If the absentee rate is 5 percent, this means that the plant must hire 50 additional employees at a cost of $750,000 to offset the absenteeism. Conversely, cutting absenteeism by one-fifth (20 percent) would result in a savings of $150,000 a year.

Jeswald (1974) describes some of the costs incurred by organizations due to turnover. Fringe benefits, severance pay, overtime costs, under-utilization of facilities, administrative expenses, training cost, and productivity losses are substantial. Nash and Carroll (1975) estimate that a rank-and-file employee who quits can cost a company at least $3,000. The costs are significantly greater for managers and professional employees. If 10 percent of a rank-and-file work force of 1,000 workers quits each year, then turnover costs will amount to at least $300,000.

So, while it is very difficult to associate job satisfaction with productivity levels, if we accept the idea that it is related to absenteeism and turnover, then it is clear that some substantial costs may be reduced if satisfaction can be increased. We can see that because of high cost associated with job dissatisfaction, leading as it does to turnover and absenteeism, it is necessary to try to determine what factors may increase job satisfaction.

Factors Affecting Job Satisfaction

A person's satisfaction with a job is determined by the difference between the characteristics of the job, what he wants from it, and what he feels he should receive from it.

What an employee wants is determined by his values, and is related to his economic and psychological needs. What he feels he should receive is determined by a personal sense of equity—by his perceptions of what other individuals are receiving for what they do compared to what he believes he does. Thus, if an employee finds out that another worker is earning more than he is, but is not exerting more effort, putting in more hours, or does not have more seniority or education, then he will feel a sense of inequity or injustice and will be dissatisfied. On the other hand, an employee may be satisfied with his pay even if he finds out that other workers doing work similar to his are getting more pay than he is, *if* he perceives that they work harder than he does or have more seniority, education, or ability.

It is also true that in certain circumstances, pay satisfaction or dissatisfaction is not highly related to *overall* job satisfaction. If a worker places relatively little value on pay, as compared to the value he places on other job factors, pay dissatisfaction may not significantly reduce his total job satisfaction. And even when workers on similar jobs receive exactly the same benefits, we would still expect differences in job satisfaction among them because they will have different job values. As mentioned in previous chapters, some individuals place a high value on pay, while others place a lower value on it. Some employees place a high value on using their abilities; some do not. A variety of job satisfaction and dissatisfaction factors, then, and their relationship to one another, must be weighed and reckoned with when devising motivational programs.

All this is to say that if the manager expects to increase satisfaction, *he must work on those factors which make a difference to employees.* In one organization which was experiencing high dissatisfaction, the management believed a "communications" gap existed. They began bombarding the employees with "newsletters" and other informational devices. The general dissatisfaction remained. A more objective assessment by an outside consultant found that the problem came, not from lack of information, but from several policies the workers thought unfair. One cause of discontent was the "parking policy." Certain parking places were *always* restricted, even after working hours. Some employees who worked a later shift thought this unfair, especially since the spaces were generally unused after 5:00 o'clock. A reconsideration of the policy led to a change, removing a cause of dissatisfaction.

Herzberg's Two-factor Theory

Herzberg (1959) argues that satisfaction and dissatisfaction may not be opposites, that the provision of certain job benefits may only serve to minimize dissatisfaction and will not increase satisfaction. For example, making satisfactory parking available to workers may not cause them to be unusually happy, but the lack of satisfactory parking *will*

create dissatisfactions. Herzberg maintains that providing fringe benefits, nice offices, and good vacation plans serves primarily to minimize dissatisfaction and to keep people in the organization; it does
not lead to more work or better performance.

According to Herzberg, job characteristics can be classified as either
"Satisfiers" or "Dissatisfiers," depending on whether they affect satisfaction or dissatisfaction. Dissatisfiers, also called "hygiene" factors,
create dissatisfaction. Some of these hygiene factors are:

1. Technical supervision
2. Interpersonal relationships with peers
3. Salary
4. Working conditions
5. Status
6. Company policy
7. Job security
8. Interpersonal relations with the superior

According to Herzberg, the absence of a certain job factor in this
category—such as good relations with peers—creates dissatisfaction;
but if there are good peer relations, that does not generate satisfaction.

Satisfiers are also called "motivators," because they are related to
high satisfaction and willingness to work harder. These job factors
may induce more effort, but if they are absent, will not produce dissatisfaction in most people. The following characteristics of the work
situation are "motivational" in nature.

1. Responsibility
2. Achievement
3. Advancement
4. The work itself
5. Recognition
6. The possibility of growth

If, then, a person is in a challenging job, he is likely to be satisfied
and motivated to perform better. The lack of challenging work does
not cause dissatisfaction, but merely the absence of satisfaction.

The attractiveness of such an approach for a manager is obvious. It
is very helpful in deciding what to do. For instance, if a high level of
worker dissatisfaction is seen as the major problem, then it is clear
that attention must be given to the hygiene factors. But the manager
knows that this will not be enough to improve performance. To do
this the manager must work on the motivators, and this means
changing the character of the work to make it more challenging and

intrinsically rewarding.

While there is research to support some of Herzberg's claims, most does not, at least not completely. Those studies that do not support Herzberg's theory show that certain job characteristics can produce either satisfaction or dissatisfaction, depending upon their presence or absence, though some factors are more likely to influence dissatisfaction than satisfaction, and vice versa. Table 5.1 summarizes the results of several studies carried out by Locke who used Herzberg's research technique which asks employees to think of days when they felt unusually good or unusually bad about their job. As table 5.1 shows, being given an interesting task activity is associated with satisfaction, as one would suspect. Being assigned an unpleasant task is related to dissatisfaction. Similarly, successfully completing an assignment is related to happy feelings, and failing to complete a task successfully is associated with unhappy feelings. Locke's research (1975; 1976), and that of others, indicates that for most employees, the task is mentioned more often as a source of unusually high or low levels of satisfaction than are other job factors, even pay. This is probably because on most jobs pay does not vary as much as does the nature of the task. Most employees receive a pay increase at regular intervals of time, annually, let us say, and the amount of the increase is anticipated in advance.

TABLE 5.1   Frequency of Motivator and Hygiene Events as Satisfiers and Dissatisfiers for Five Samples

Event Category	Frequency as: Satisfier	Dissatisfier
1. Task Activity	40	39
2. Amount of Work	9	27
3. Smoothness of Work	11	32
4. Achievement/Failure	114	64
5. Promotion	20	13
6. Responsibility	33	8
7. Recognition	81	93
8. Money	35	20
9. Interpersonal Relations	17	40
10. Working Conditions	7	26
All Motivators (1-7)	308	276
All Hygienes (8-10)	59	86

Source: Compiled from E. A. Locke's "Satisfiers and Dissatisfiers Among White-Collar and Blue-Collar Employees," *Journal of Applied Psychology*, 58 (1973):67–76 (copyright 1973 by the American Psychological Association; reprinted by permission) and E. A. Locke and J. Schneider's "A Critique of Herzberg's Incident Classification System and a Suggested Revision," *Organizational Behavior and Human Performance*, 6 (1971):441–57.

The employee's answer when he is asked to think of a time when he felt unusually good or unusually bad about his job is influenced by the employee's memory, what has actually occurred, and his tendency toward selective perception. This leads, using such a research method, to attributing successful events to himself and unsuccessful events to others.

In general, the research suggests that the following job factors are associated with "good" days:

1. Being given an interesting work assignment.
2. A feeling of achievement from success in doing a task well.
3. Recognition from others for good work.
4. An advancement, an unexpected salary increase, or an increase in responsibility.

In general, then, something that the person *himself* can take credit for produces reported satisfaction.

The following tend to be associated with "bad" days:

1. Being assigned unpleasant work.
2. Inability to complete an assignment successfully.
3. Criticism from employer or associates.
4. Failure to receive rewards that are expected.
5. Unfair treatment, unfair distribution of work, etc.

In general, then, bad days are blamed on others.

In reviewing these finding, Locke concluded that a person wants the following from his job:

1. Challenging work he can cope with successfully.
2. Just rewards for performance which are in line with his aspirations.
3. An understanding of what is expected by others.
4. Appreciation and acceptance by supervisor and co-workers.
5. Working facilities and resources which facilitate task performance.

Locke's study shows that the factors listed by Herzberg as satisfiers and dissatisfiers are not as clear-cut and obvious as they may seem on the surface. For example, a person wants "challenging work he can cope with successfully." Self-confidence, as well as skill, will be a determinant here. For instance, one person may find it challenging to repair an automobile engine. The highly-skilled mechanic who views an engine as a problem to be solved will be motivated to work on it. That same engine, broken down, would be avoided by a person who has no knowledge of internal combustion engines, for he knows that if he works on it, the problem will probably become worse.

Motivation and Performance—A Complex Relationship

Pragmatically, the manager must get results from other people. He must structure the work situation, with a mix of people and equipment, to yield some outcome—a product or service—to be used by others. This can happen only when someone works, either physically or mentally.

These results are what we mean when we use the term *performance*. Performance is the result of the application of effort, mental or physical. It is usually evaluated against some standard which may reflect earlier achievement by others, the person himself, or a standard developed from a time study. Performance levels may be stated in terms of quantity or quality, and may reflect some subjective judgment by a manager. A particular level of performance may be considered "high" for one person, but the same level may be only "satisfactory," or perhaps "unsatisfactory," for another. Finally, although performance is the result of effort, it is not correct to think that the level of performance can be raised by more effort. Sometimes a student, for example, receives an A in a course with little work and a D in another in spite of more work on the latter. The level of performance, relative to some standard, is called "productivity."

As mentioned, when the performance of an organization or a subunit is at a lower level than desired, the blame is usually placed on the people who work in it. The manager will want to get "better people," "more motivated personnel." Before a manager concerns himself with "motivation" however, he should attempt to determine what other factors cause poor performance.

If it is truly due to lack of motivation, he should of course, attempt to induce his subordinates to exert more effort, but other factors—such as an individual's ability, the amount of help received from the supervisor, and technological considerations—also affect performance and should be considered when evaluating it. The way we view motivation and performance in this book is shown in figure 5.1. Basically, results at work (performance) are dependent upon the characteristics of the *people* (IA) and the nature of the *technology* required to produce (IB). These are the raw materials with which a manager must work. The manager may do a number of different things in trying to achieve the most effective blending of people and equipment. These are *managerial motivation strategies* (II). What the manager does affects the individual's beliefs about what the work will yield, both for the organization and for himself. These beliefs are called *expectancies* (III) and, according to some research, they seem to be related to levels of performance (Lawler and Suttle, 1973).

FIGURE 5.1 A Motivational Model of Performance

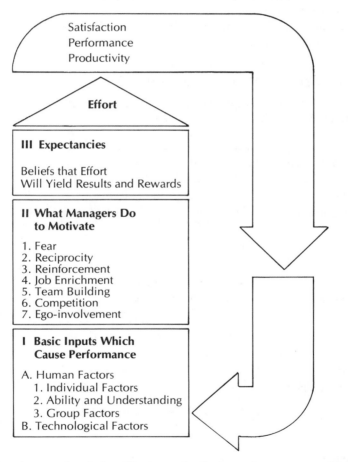

Finally, the result of the effort put forth is *performance*, which has no less than two aspects. The first is *productivity*. Productivity simply means how the results obtained from this effort compares to some standard. Productivity is a measure of the efficiency of resource utilization. Performance also has a *satisfaction* dimension. When we accomplish any task, we have some feelings about it. If we like what we do or how we did it, we feel good. If we expect to be rewarded somehow with pay or recognition, we feel good. If we get these pay-offs, we are *reinforced* and that has an effect on whether or not we will want to put forth the same effort later.

The rest of this chapter discusses the basic components of this motivation-performance model. First, however we must discuss in more detail what we mean by performance and how it ties in with the other factors. Then we consider the inputs (I), managerial strategies (II) and expectancy theory (III).

Performance—A Multidimensional View

What do we mean when we say someone is a good performer? A weak performer? A "star"? Think about *any* person's job. There are many

FIGURE 5.2 A Hypothetical Production Foreman's Job

1. Preparing Work Schedules	Ability: Know Skills of Workers Expectancy: That a Good Schedule Will Result Expectancy: That This Is Important to Superior Superior's Behavior: Very Little Interference
2. Ordering Raw Materials	Ability: Technical Knowledge of Product Specifications Expectancy: This Activity is Critical to Cost Reduction Superior's Behavior: Constant Monitoring of Reports of Raw Materials' Cost
3. Dealing with Subordinates	Ability: Human Skill at Interaction Expectancy: Harmony in Workplace Will Result in Productivity Superior's Behavior: Stresses Need for Better Human Relations
4. Running Departmental Meetings	Ability: Skill in Defining Problems, Handling Participation Expectancy: That Solutions Will Emerge from Meetings Superior's Behavior: Frequently Attends Meetings to Show Belief in their Importance

parts to it. A quarterback of a football team must be able to pass, understand defenses, and run. A professor teaches and carries out research. The manager of an auditing unit must deal with his staff, run meetings, and understand the financial structure of the organization.

The point is that *several* components exist on most jobs. When we speak of performance, we must understand this, because a person may be highly competent in one dimension, not so in another. He may be more motivated (interested) in one than another. A quarterback may be most interested in throwing passes, either because this is the activity in which he is most skilled—or the one that gets the most attention. And there is another point. A superior may view some facets of performance as more important than others. Superiors may focus on, and reinforce, only one aspect of a job. For example, a production foreman's job is complex (see fig. 5.2). Suppose we conceptualize it as being composed of the following activities:

1. Preparing work schedules
2. Ordering raw materials
3. Dealing with subordinates
4. Running departmental meetings

It is possible that top management, being concerned with cost reduction, emphasizes raw materials' costs. Consequently, they create an incentive system which rewards cost reduction. This may cause the foreman to emphasize this aspect of his job, perhaps to the neglect of the other aspects.

From figure 5.2 we can also see that different abilities are required for each of the job components, and these may have a different technological/human mix (as we discussed earlier). For example, running departmental meetings will require more human skills than ordering raw materials. However, ordering raw materials may require the use of computers and the ability to understand materials flow. There are clearly different skills required for the two job components, but the same person is expected to have them.

Similarly, the foreman will have different expectancies about each component of his job. He may feel that if he increases his effort at work scheduling, he will get a smoother flow of work. And if he does, then he may receive a pay increase, which he values. The foreman may thus spend more time on this activity than on the others. He may not have the same feelings about the other task components. He may have low expectations of the payoffs for ordering raw materials. He may know that this area is of great importance to top management, but he may have little control over the activity if he must clear his requests with, say, a purchasing department. The manager of this foreman must, therefore, not look at "performance" in a global sense, but in a specific way, trying to understand the strengths and weaknesses of the individual for each task component. This may mean, for instance, providing help and coaching if the foreman is weak in the use of the computer. At the same time, if he can run meetings well, the foreman may need no help in this area.

Basic Input Factors

For figure 5.1, we show the basic inputs which yield results as *human* and *technological* factors. In chapters 3 and 4, we dealt extensively with factors that affect human inputs. We will be more detailed about technological factors in chapters 6 and 7. Here, however, we can present enough material to indicate how these human and technological factors affect motivation and performance.

Human Factor Inputs

Human factors that affect performance are individual skill and ability, values, attitudes, and the effect of work groups.

Needs and Values. Individual needs, attitudes, and values interact with other factors in the workplace to condition the results. First, they affect the reaction to the strategies used by managers to motivate workers. In addition, work experiences contribute in many ways to the satisfaction of individual needs, often providing an opportunity to fulfill unsatisfied needs. (See the discussion of Maslow's hierarchy of needs in chap. 3). The level of personal satisfaction also follows the attainment of a particular performance level. For example, doing well in a job may make an employee feel more secure, while performing below a certain level may be associated with a fear of job loss or negative reaction from the supervisor.

The relationship of individual needs to job characteristics has been shown in two studies. In one study of 200 employees of a telephone company, it was found that more complex jobs were associated with higher motivation, satisfaction, and quality of performance for those employees who were concerned with higher-order needs (Hackman and Lawler, 1971). In another study (Carroll, 1974) it was found that dental assistants with high accomplishment needs had low job involvement in a clinic where the jobs were well-structured and simple, but high job involvement in a clinic where many of the jobs were expanded to make the tasks more varied and complex. In the more structured unit, those who were primarily concerned with security needs were more involved with their work than were the dental assistants who were primarily concerned with achievement needs.

Achievement needs are of particular importance in managerial effectiveness in increasing performance. McClelland (1965) has demonstrated the relationship of high achievement needs to entrepreneurial behavior. He has extensively studied this particular individual characteristic. Research shows it to be an important factor in organizational effectiveness (Wild and Kempner, 1973).

Individuals high in achievement needs derive a deep feeling of satisfaction from competing against some standard of excellence (McClelland et al., 1953). They seek success for the sense of accomplishment that it gives them and they may perform at high levels even in the absence of material rewards for achievement. The standard of excellence to be obtained may involve an attempt to do better than others, or it may be simply an attempt to improve on earlier performance.

The need for achievement is an internal drive state of the individual —the extent to which he believes success is important and he values it. The level of the individual's need for achievement is related to early socialization experiences (Heckhausen, 1967). One's early success experiences, in frequency and in terms of where they were experienced, determine the level of need achievement. All individuals have some level of achievement need, but this level varies from individual to individual. It may also be directed toward different sources of need satisfaction. For instance, the "organizationalist" may find his achievement needs satisfied by becoming successful within the firm, while the "professional" may seek recognition and achievement within a group of colleagues who are also specialists, as he is. The "externalist" may find his achievement needs satisfied in social organizations outside the work setting.

Some persons have a need to avoid failure, rather than a need for achievement (Atkinson, 1957). Rather than obtaining need satisfaction by seeking to be successful in situations, they do so by attempting to avoid circumstances in which they might fail. Failure avoidance rather than achievement is their main driving motive. These individuals, setting performance goals for themselves, tend to set them at either such a low level that they cannot fail, or at such an impossibly high level that no one expects them to achieve them.

Individuals oriented toward achievement value success and want to do well in competitive situations. They want to win, and they usually exhibit a great deal of drive, initiative, and aggressiveness in their

work. They find a situation in which they cannot be successful dis-
comforting. If placed in such a situation, they will either be frustrated,
or will leave. By the same token, those high in need to avoid failure
will try to stay away from challenging and difficult assignments.
Thus, for the manager there should always be careful consideration of
matching the characteristics of a particular situation with the needs of
the individual. This is not always possible, nor is it easy. The conflicting demands between organizational requirements and the needs
of people may not be highly congruent.

Group Factors. As discussed in chapter 4, groups often develop
production norms—that is, what members consider appropriate performance levels—and they take actions to insure that members conform to these norms. In addition, groups can affect perceptions and
attitudes as well as behavior. Individuals, however, differ in their susceptibility to group pressures. Research indicates that compliance is
greatest when a group's member's previous values and attitudes are
congruent with the compliance attempt and when the individual
places a high value on group acceptance (Helmreich, Bakeman, and
Scherwitz, 1973). The individual then internalizes the group norm,
and it governs his behavior.

Ability and Understanding. A person must have the ability to perform and must understand when those abilities are to be used. Ability
is the capacity to carry out a set of interrelated behavioral, or mental,
sequences to produce a result. One has the ability to play the piano
when he can read music, understand chord structures, and has the
manual dexterity to finger the keyboard appropriately. One has the
ability to operate a computer when he is capable of preparing data,
programming it, and processing it. Ability levels differ among and
within individuals. It is important to be aware of this individual difference, since most jobs have several different characteristics which
require different abilities. For example, the production foreman's job
(fig. 5.2) included the scheduling of work, ordering raw materials,
dealing with subordinates (handling grievances, supervising his
crew), and running departmental meetings. Each of these separate activities requires different skills, and a person may be high in some and
low in others. There may also be a wide range of performance among
individuals who perform similar jobs. Some personnel managers are
better than others. Some carpenters are more skillful than others.
Some musicians perform better than others. Like needs, individual
differences in ability must be taken into account when a manager

makes a job assignment.

Understanding what to do, when something must be done, is also important. The organizational member must know what he is supposed to do, when and how he is supposed to do it, and also must know how well he is doing. The problem of misunderstanding what is to be done is highlighted by some research which indicates that a good deal of disagreement exists between superiors and subordinates with respect to performance expectations (Maier et al., 1961). Many subordinates do not seem to know what their superiors expect of them, and this misunderstanding itself can contribute to poor performance. A number of studies have indicated that when individuals are given specific performance goals rather than being given the more generalized goal of "do your best," performance significantly increases (Locke, 1975). Certainly part of this performance increase is due to the fact that the individual's efforts and energies are directed in specific directions rather than being diffused wastefully over a number of activities. Some of the performance increase can also be attributed to the individual's knowing specifically what will constitute good performance.

One way to increase understanding about work requirements is by providing a person with feedback about previous results. Feedback is necessary since it is sometimes difficult for an organizational member to determine how well he is doing or has done without being told by a superior. Studies have indicated that providing feedback on progress toward goals can improve performance (Carroll and Tosi, 1973; Ronan, Latham, and Kinne, 1973). One reason why feedback helps is because the performance of individuals is selectively perceived by themselves. Individuals tend to rate their own performance higher than do their supervisors. They often tend to assume their performance is adequate when it is not. In addition, if they are having difficulties, they tend to attribute them to outside forces rather than to themselves (Locke, 1975), and thus they are not inclined to take actions themselves to correct such difficulties. In general, then, management can improve performance by taking actions to communicate performance expectations clearly and then by providing appropriate feedback on such performance.

Technological Inputs

The term "technological factors" refers to the tools, machines, facilities, and equipment a person uses in performing a task. Cooks use pots, stoves, and recipes to produce a meal. Auto workers "use" a

complex assembly line with highly interdependent activities to manufacture a car. An artist uses, perhaps, a drawing board, paint, and a
brush. Obviously the technological structure varies tremendously
from one organization to another—as, say, between a steel mill and an
advertising agency—as well as within organizations—as, say, where
one group of employees must use giant computers and another group
simply pencils and paper.

The Dynamics of Technological and Human Inputs.   The manager
must determine which of the two factors—human or technological—
are most important in affecting the level of performance, because efforts to improve performance must be focused correctly.

In some tasks, the individual skill component is the most important
factor. In others, technology may be the most important factor. Consider, for example, the design engineer. His performance is not likely
to be a function of the kind of equipment he has, but rather it will
depend on his personal skill. Giving him better equipment is likely to
have only a marginal effect on his performance.

Contrast this with the assembly-line worker. Perhaps only limited
skills are required in his job. One advantage of an assembly-line technology is that high levels of training and skill are not required. The
most effective method of improving performance here would be to
make substantial improvements in the manner in which the technology is used. Investment in new machines and equipment may be
most appropriate under these sorts of technological constraints.

The manager must analyze the work situation of his subordinates
along these lines. To expect performance to increase simply because
we obtain competent people may result in disappointment when technology is the controlling variable.

Motivation—The Managerial Function

Virtually all writers on management stress that motivation is a function of management, that it is something a manager must do to get
things done through people. This view is appropriate so long as we
remember that managerial motivation strategies are manipulative in
nature. This means simply that a manager is trying to get someone to
do what he, the manager, wants them to do. These manipulative, or
motivational strategies, in and of themselves, cannot be regarded as
either good or bad. Goodness or badness depends upon whether or not
an individual, so motivated by another, is ultimately placed in a position he might not have chosen freely, or is injured. To be "motivated"

by an attractive woman to ask her to dinner may be fully consistent with the desires of a man. To be "motivated" by a superior to do something illegal is entirely another matter. Both the woman and the superior may use similar manipulative strategies. It is the outcome which is the cause of concern.

When a manager attempts to motivate others, he is trying to act primarily on the human input factor within the technological constraints of the situation. Essentially he attempts to increase the individual's drive to perform better. A number of different motivational strategies have been used by managers. Each has its advantages and disadvantages, and each varies in effectiveness from one situation to another. Some of the strategies have been evaluated by Carroll (1973), who surveyed a number of different supervisory groups to assess which of these strategies they believed to be most useful in their work. The ratings given to some of these motivational strategies by several groups are shown in table 5.2.

Fear or Threat. With the fear strategy, an individual is threatened with undesirable consequences unless he complies. "If you're late for work, you will be given a three-day layoff," or "You will be fired if you are insubordinate." The threat may be, then, something very specific, such as the loss of one's job, or it may be unspecified, as when an organizational member complies simply to avoid displeasing a higher level of authority. This approach seems to be fairly widely used, perhaps because it is easy. One study showed that this approach is effective in motivating organizational members to perform at a high level if they have limited alternative employment opportunities (Goode and Fowler, 1949). The approach is not perceived to be effective by supervisors, however, in the typical situations they encounter, as table 5.2 shows.

The use of threats, or fear, is limited. First, it only works in the short run. In the long run, most individuals can find alternative employment opportunities where there is less reliance upon fear as a managerial strategy. Second, it creates anxiety, which may disrupt rather than facilitate performance. (A number of studies indicate that performance is lower under conditions of high anxiety; see Vroom, 1964). Also, threats directed at some employees may increase anxiety in others. Third, to work, the threats must have credibility. This is difficult to achieve where employees are protected by a strong union, by tenure rights, or by other safeguards. In addition, threats induce hostile feelings toward the supervisors who make them, feelings which may be manifested in aggressive acts against either the supervisor or

TABLE 5.2 Supervisory Ratings of Alternative Managerial Strategies

Motivational Approaches	Not Effective	Somewhat Effective	Effective	Very Effective
1. Fear (threat of sanctions)	Police			
	Factory			
	Government			
	Engineering			
	Bank			
2. Reciprocity (exchange favors for performance)	Police			
	Factory			
	Government			
	Engineering			
	Bank			
3. Reinforcement (make performance path to personal goals)	Police			
	Factory			
	Government			
	Engineering			
	Bank			
4. Job Enrichment (motivation through work itself)	Police			
	Factory			
	Government			
	Engineering			
	Bank			
5. Team Building (build team spirit)	Police			
	Factory			
	Government			
	Engineering			
	Bank			
6. Competition (compete for rewards)	Police			
	Factory			
	Government			
	Engineering			
	Bank			
7. Ego-involvement (tie in performance with self-concept)	Police			
	Factory			
	Government			
	Engineering			
	Bank			

Police N=39, Factory N=19, Government N=19, Engineering N=39, Bank N=51 the organization.

Another problem with the fear strategy is that it creates a punitive climate in which individuals are afraid of being different from or of offending others. This diminishes creativity and can lead to intellectual stagnation.

Reciprocity. The expression "If you scratch my back, I'll scratch yours," describes reciprocity. The "norm of reciprocity" states that what one is given, he will repay in approximate equivalence (Gouldner, 1960). Individuals who receive benefits from others feel guilty if they have a chance to reciprocate and do not do so. In fact, they feel a sense of relief at repaying an obligation when they can.

Using reciprocity, a supervisor may attempt to trade certain things of value to subordinates in exchange for satisfactory levels of performance. The commodities traded may include special privileges, special concern for the individual, and the acceptance of rule violations, in addition to more obvious favors.

Reciprocity is widely used and generally seen as effective (see table 5.2). To some degree, the popularity of this approach can be accounted for by its ease of use. But it presents problems. First, there can be disagreement about the value of the things exchanged. For example, a group of workers may feel their supervisor is asking them to do a "big" favor for him when he has done only "little" favors for them. Second, certain favors may become so common that the recipients no longer consider them to be favors. For example, in a case, say, where employees can leave early when their work is done, they may begin to plan on it and not see early departure as a "favor" anymore. The workers may become extremely upset when the supervisor attempts to withhold the favor. Finally, there may be resentment created when a recipient of a favor does not have the ability to repay—a person may feel he is getting more and more committed to do something special for his boss.

The psychological contract, discussed in an earlier chapter, includes the concept of reciprocity. The employee agrees informally to meet some of the organization's performance expectations in return for the benefits the organization provides him. But, as they do with the individual supervisor, organizational members often disagree with the organization as to the value of the benefits exchanged between them.

Reinforcement. With this strategy, the manager attempts to reward workers who perform well, and either not reward or impose sanctions on workers who perform poorly. Behaviors followed by desired rewards are repeated, while behaviors followed by nonreward are extinguished, or not repeated, as noted in chapter 3. Thus, if an individual sees a clear relationship between good work and the attainment of a desired reward, he has a tendency to perform at a high level.

A number of studies have found that people perform at a higher level when they perceive a relationship between high performance and the obtaining of desired rewards, such as pay increases and promotions (Lawler and Suttle, 1973). Experimental studies conducted in the laboratory situation, in the military, in educational organizations, and in industrial organizations demonstrate that using money, tokens, signs of social approval, or surrogate rewards can increase the frequency with which certain desired behaviors occur (Krasner, 1971). Nash and Carroll (1975), after reviewing studies on the effectiveness of incentive wage plans in industry, conclude that, on the average, there is an increase in production when workers are paid by the piece rather than on the basis of the amount of time they work. Item 5.1 describes some recent attempts by industrial firms to tie executive performance to pay incentives. It is, as noted, no easy task, but it has a great deal of appeal.

ITEM 5.1   Incentive Plans

Payoff in "Performance" Bonuses

The Age-old Executive Bonus has a New Look Meeting in the richly appointed Empire Room of New York's Waldorf Astoria Hotel last month, the stockholders of Manufacturers Hanover Corp., holding company for the nation's fifth-largest bank, quickly dispatched their business. Cheered by Chairman Gabriel Hauge's announcement that the corporation had just completed its best quarter in history, they responded by electing management's slate of directors, ratifying its selection of auditors and voting down two proposals from individual shareholders.

Then the company's owners did something more important for the future: They approved a spanking-new bonus plan that will for the first time relate the compensation of its top executives both to corporate performance and to their own performance on the job.

On the face of it, performance-based bonuses would hardly seem worth mentioning in the esoteric world of executive compensation. Nevertheless, they are the hottest thing around right now—not only for banks, which have traditionally lagged behind in awarding incentive extras, but for many industrial companies as well. Just within the past year, performance bonus plans have been installed or improved at such major companies as IBM, Exxon, Bendix, LTV, Gulf & Western, McGraw-Edison, Kennecott Copper, U.S. Steel and Lone Star Industries. "This," declares partner Donald Simpson of Philadelphia consulting firm

Hay Associates, ''is the year for incentive plans based on performance.''

Theoretically, of course, bonuses have always been related to performance. In practice, however, most companies have used them as little more than a way of dividing up the pie at the end of a good year. Soon taken for granted by everybody, they have largely lost all value as an incentive. ''A lot of companies,'' says partner Jack Salwen of consulting firm Rothschild & Salwen, ''got into the bad habit of paying a man a bonus just for showing up in the morning. That, after all, is what you give him a salary for.''

Amid today's pressures, however, all that is changing. In a time of mounting cost-consciousness, top management is eager to get the greatest possible impact from every compensation dollar. Moreover, with the competition for top-notch executives more avid than ever, it is equally eager to attract and retain the best man. For both reasons, companies are now trying to make bonuses more meaningful by using them more selectively than in the past. ''Many companies,'' observes Frederick Teague, compensation specialist for Booz, Allen, Hamilton & Co., ''have decided to make no special effort from now on to retain the executive whose performance is merely average. Instead, they intend to single out for monetary rewards the few who really make the mare go.''

As a result, this season one proxy statement after another is setting forth a new performance-oriented bonus plan for share-holder approval. But that is only part of the story. For one of the quiet attractions of a bonus plan from management's viewpoint is that unlike an option plan, for example, it need not be voted on by the stockholders. The company may choose to submit it to them to get their moral support, but in most cases the step is strictly optional. Consequently, as Donald Simpson puts it, ''The plans you see in this year's proxy

statements are only the tip of the iceberg.''

Bonuses, of course, can be based on either long-term or short-term performance. A company might want to motivate some executives to optimize each year's results, while giving the top people longer-range incentives to make sure that the company does not sacrifice its long-run interests for the sake of one spectacular year. Most of the new bonus plans, though, are being formulated for the short-term, paying off in cash on the barrelhead soon after the end of the year. ''A lot of boards,'' explains President Robert Sibson of consulting firm Sibson & Co., ''have become disenchanted in recent years with long-term incentives because so many things can go wrong along the way.''

Strengthening the push for performance bonus plans right now is the winding down of federal controls on compensation. No one knows for sure whether anything will be left of the Administration's wage and price program after May 1. But clearly the impetus at both ends of Pennsylvania Avenue is to free companies from the rigid controls of the past three years. The recent emphatic vote for decontrol by two committees of Congress suggests that the Cost of Living Council may be totally dismantled. In any case, particularly eager to make up for lost time are the companies that got caught with their plans down when controls were slammed on. ''Ordinarily,'' notes one compensation man, ''a company should change its incentive plan every three years or so—not only because tax laws and accounting rules change, but because as people get used to any plan, it no longer motivates. So a lot of companies will be playing catch up.''

• • • •

Reaching Down While financial-oriented companies are eager newcomers to the bonus lists, manufacturing corporations have of course been at the game for some years. But now there is a new flurry of activity as managements try to make their bonus plans more performance-oriented.

Some companies that have long paid bonuses at the corporate level, like those in the oil, steel and food industries, are now seeking to devise comparable cash incentives for executives who head their best-performing divisions. Others are trying to fine-tune their compensation programs so that they can reward deserving individuals at any level in the corporate hierarchy. As Richard Jamison, compensation director of General Mills, notes: "There is hardly a compensation man today who is not aware of the need to develop rewards more closely related to individual performance."

Among the companies that now reach down two or three echelons to reward a man for a job well done are McGraw-Edison, Colt Industries, J. C. Penney, Bendix, Owens-Illinois, Indian Head, Lone Star Industries, G. D. Searle, du Pont and Thiokol Chemical. Others are clearly moving in that direction. IBM, long a believer in the value of incentives, last year introduced a new plan of this sort. "The corporation," the proxy statement explained, "has decided that the measure of an executive's performance should be more closely related to that part of the corporation's activities for which he is directly responsible." About sixty executives will be eligible for such awards.

Beyond that, the company plans to grant "special supplemental awards to a limited number of executives for extraordinary achievement." Last year was a good one—financially, at least—for the computer giant. And both Chairman Frank T. Cary and Senior Vice President Gilbert E. Jones were awarded bonuses larger than their six-figure salaries.

One unsung company that has been using incentive compensation most effectively at the divisional level is Scovill Manufacturing Co. The Waterbury, Connecticut-based brass manufacturer has had such a plan in use, in one form or another, for about ten years. Scovill has set up its incentives in such a way that the chairman, the president and the other top corporate officers cannot get a bonus equal to more than 25% of their salary, no matter how prosperous a year the company reports. Division managers, in contrast, can earn bonuses of as much as 50% of salary if their divisions top specific goals in pretax profits.

An "Exacting Discipline" As companies generally become more sophisticated about their incentive plans, they are giving increased attention to the process of goal-setting that lies at the heart of it all. For any plan is only as realistic as its goals. Too high, they become a constant discouragement; too low, they simply fail to motivate. "Goal setting is becoming a very exacting discipline," says Robert Sibson. "Goals have to be set shrewdly, be widely known and result in payoff for performance—or else you wind up with a simple profit-sharing scheme, which isn't a motivator at all."

• • • •

The happy thing about the true performance bonus is that it marries so well the interests of the recipient and of the shareholders. For if the bonus plan is skilfully designed, no executive will get any extra pay unless the shareholders, too, have a much better-than-average year. And if the company rings up a truly superlative year, the stockholders should hardly begrudge a bonus—even one in six figures—to the executive chiefly responsible. The man who performs has a right to the payoff.—John C. Perham

Dun's Review, May 1975

In general, managers view the reinforcement approach as effective (see table 5.2), but it too has its problems. First, it is only effective if the rewards used are those desired by the organizational members. Pay increases, promotions, social status symbols (such as office rugs), all may be regarded as different kinds of rewards, but there are substantial individual differences in preferences for payoffs. Some people prefer pay increases. Others seek promotion. Still others may desire new rugs on their office floors. Some may regard compensatory time off as a reward. Individual differences in preferences for rewards make it very difficult for a manager to effectively utilize organizational factors as incentives. The value a person places on different incentives is internal.

Second, linking rewards with performance is especially difficult. This is most likely to be the case for those whose jobs are extremely interdependent. How do you determine the contribution of one worker on an assembly line to the final product? How do you assess the contribution of one research scientist in a team working on environmental pollution controls? It is also extremely difficult to measure individual performance for staff personnel, higher-level managers and many professionals, since there are problems with quantifying results and isolating outcomes that can be associated with an individual.

Most pay systems in organizations violate the principles derived from the theory and research on reinforcement. In the typical organization, pay increases are given at predictable times, without much differentiation between good and bad performers. The research on reinforcement shows that awarding increases at unpredictable times is more effective than giving them at predictable intervals (Nord, 1969). Organizations which reward performers relatively equally, without regard to their performance, are in effect reinforcing the poor performers to maintain their present levels of performance while discouraging the better performers. When a group of employees receives an across-the-board pay increase of, say, 10 percent, the poorer employees are treated in the same way as the good ones.

Job Enrichment. With job enrichment, emphasis is placed on motivating the worker through the task, or job itself. The assumption is that if the work is challenging, then no outside motivational efforts are necessary. This is especially true where the work is routine and/or broken down into such small components that the person cannot see how his work is related to that of others, or to the end product. Job enrichment involves assigning work to individuals in such a way that they have the opportunity to complete an identifiable task from beginning to end. They are then held responsible for successful completion of the task. Basically, the motivational effect of job enrichment flows from the opportunity for personal achievement, challenge, and recognition.

The experiment in job enrichment underway at the Saab-Volvo automobile manufacturers in Sweden (see item 5.2) illustrates rather nicely how job enrichment works. Rather than the monotonous production system which characterizes auto manufacturing in the U.S., at Saab-Volvo they use a team-assembly concept in which workers rotate the tasks required for building an auto. Basically, the entire group is responsible for assembling the entire auto.

Such an approach is being widely experimented with in industry. Companies which have undertaken job enrichment programs are AT&T and Texas Instruments, among others. But these programs have not always met with success (Miner and Dachler, 1973). Research to date suggests that these efforts may improve morale and the quality of work more than the quantity (Miner, 1973).

Job enrichment is generally seen as effective by managers, but is not without its problems, some of which were noted in chapter 4. When workers are given a more complex job, they realistically expect commensurate increases in compensation; otherwise they feel inequitably treated, and some work—such as large-scale assembly operations— may not lend itself to job enrichment.

ITEM 5.2   Job Enrichment

Volvo's Valhalla

To Henry Ford, patron saint of mass production, the new Volvo plant in Kalmar, Sweden, would seem curious indeed. It looks more like a giant repair shop than an auto factory. The working space is airy, uncluttered by stacks of spare parts. The plant is so quiet that workers can chat in normal tones, or hum along with the pop tunes playing on their cassette tape recorders. Troubleshooters on lightweight bicycles ensure a steady flow of spare parts. Sunlight plays against brightcolored walls through huge picture windows looking out on the landscape. But the most puzzling question in Ford's mind would be: What happened to the assembly line?

Busy Interest.   The answer is that it has been changed beyond recognition as part of an attack on an international labor problem: the growing dislike that today's young, comparatively well-educated workers have shown for tedious, repetitive factory jobs. In the U.S. and other countries, that attitude is reflected in heavy absenteeism and high turnover among factory work forces, poor-quality production and occasional strikes by workers desperate to get away from the line for a while. Volvo's system at

Kalmar is attracting worldwide attention as an imaginative effort to set up a factory that will keep workers interested while busy.

Instead of a clanking, high-speed conveyor line, the Kalmar plant uses 250 "carriers"—18-ft.-long computer-guided platforms that glide silently over the concrete floor. Each carrier delivers the frame for a single Volvo 264 to each of the plant's 25 work teams. The teams consist of 15 to 25 workers who are responsible for a certain aspect of assembly; one team, for example, will install the car's electrical system and another will work on the interior finish.

The teams organize themselves as they wish and work at the speed they choose. While a worker on a conventional assembly line might spend his entire shift mounting one-license-plate lamp after another, every member of a Kalmar work team may work at one time or another on all parts of the electrical system—from taillights to turn signals, head lamps, horn, fuse box and part of the electronically controlled fuel-injection system. The only requirement is that every team meet its production goal for a shift. As long as cars roll out on schedule, workers are free to take coffee breaks when they please or to refresh themselves in comfortable lounges equipped with kitchens and saunas.

The Kalmar system was worked out by Pehr Gyllenhammar, Volvo's managing director. Three years ago, when he stepped in as chief executive, he had to cope with an incredibly high labor turnover rate. At Volvo's main assembly plant near Göteborg, turnover reached an annual rate of 41% in 1971, even though the company pays some of the highest wages in Swedish industry. The company had to spend heavily to train replacements, and the rapid turnover contributed to declines in quality that have marred Volvo's reputation for durability. Gyllenhammar was convinced that the workers simply did not like their monotonous assembly-line jobs. "As

people became more educated—and Sweden spends perhaps more money per capita for education than any other country—their jobs have become less complex," he says. "That does not make sense."

Gyllenhammar assigned a task force of young executives (all under 30) to design a new plant where "machines would be the product of people and not vice versa." After two months of intensive work and study the group presented its plan. Kalmar (pop. 53,000) was chosen as a site in large part because of its high unemployment rate. Ground was broken in 1972, and 19 months later the first team-made model Volvo rolled out of the workshops.

The new plant cost $23 million, about 10% more than a conventional factory of the same capacity. It includes the most up-to-date devices to monitor production and promote quality control. At each team's work station, for example, a computer-connected television screen projects figures comparing the team's production goal with the number of assemblies it has actually completed. On top of the screen a yellow light flashes if the team is behind schedule; a green light comes on when it is ahead. So far, the plant is only turning out 56 cars a day, but by 1975 the company hopes to achieve annual production of 30,000 cars.

Many Skeptics. A steady stream of auto executives, from Henry Ford II to Fiat Managing Director Umberto Agnelli, has visited the Kalmar plant. Some have incorporated similar ideas in their own factories. In June, for example, Fiat introduced an entirely new system of engine assembly at its plant in Termoli on the Adriatic coast; work is now performed in fixed position "islands." There are many skeptics though. Most U.S. auto executives insist that the Kalmar system would not work in American assembly plants. which serve a vastly larger market and so must turn out many more cars per day than Kalmar.

Some workers and union leaders consider the Kalmar plant less than Valhalla. "The environment is better," says Göran Nillson, 38, who worked on Volvo's conventional assembly line near Göteborg, "but you should not forget that we have the same productivity objectives as any other plant. It looks like a paradise, but we work hard." Adds Kjell Anderson, an official of the militant Swedish metal workers' union, "They haven't really changed the system and they haven't changed the hierarchy. For example, we don't think it's necessary to have a foreman when you have groups."

Gyllenhammer remains convinced that Kalmar will work. "We think the extra capital involved will be offset by increased productivity," he says. Still, Gyllenhammer is a prudent manager, and Volvo is prepared to adapt if the Kalmar experiment fails. The plant was designed in such a way that it can be reconverted into a conventional assembly line at a minimal cost.

TIME, Sept. 16, 1974

Reprinted by permission from TIME, The Weekly Newsmagazine; Copyright Time Inc.

Team-building. Team-building is an effort to foster the formation of cohesive work groups which adopt a high level of performance as a "norm." The idea is that groups with a high standard of performance will pressure individual members to perform at a high level. This means that the individual is subjected to performance pressures from his peers, as well as from his superiors, and will perform at a high level in order to live up to the desires and expectations of his fellows.

The supervisor can contribute to group cohesiveness and to high performance by isolating the group from others; by assigning the group tasks which require collective effort; by putting individuals together in a group who can work well with each other; by assigning tasks of an appropriate difficulty level so that the group can experience success; by rewarding the group collectively for their high performance; and by fostering the formation of positive attitudes toward the organization. In general, supervisors seem to rate this motivational strategy as quite effective (see table 5.2). They stated in discussions that many could be pressured into high performance *only* by their peers and not by higher management.

Some problems in using the approach, however, must be taken into account. Some groups become cohesive, but adopt a low, rather than a high, standard of performance. In addition, in many work situations, it may be difficult to get the workers together in group activities, since their work is not interdependent, or because they are physically separated from each other.

Competition. Using the competition strategy, individuals or groups compete against each other for a reward. This approach is especially common in sales work, where employees participate in contests for a variety of rewards, including bonuses, vacation trips, automobiles, and so on. Competition has been used also, however, for motivating other types of employees. In an early study, it was found that a pay system which gave a bonus to only the five highest-achieving blue-collar workers was more effective than a traditional incentive wage system in which everybody received a bonus who surpassed a certain standard (Mariott, 1968).

Several case studies by Carroll (1975) indicate that competition is effective only when the reward offered is desired by all the participants and when competing individuals or groups feel they have a good possibility of winning. When the reward is not considered desirable, or when the same individuals or groups seem to win most of the time, competition strategies do not have any good effect. Competition can also lead to blocking the performance of others (Miller and Hamblin, 1963). Problems occur with this strategy when work is interdependent and competition would decrease cooperation. Sherif (1958) has shown that competition can also lead to a great deal of hostility toward one group by another.

Ego-involvement. One strategy used to obtain high performance is allowing organizational members to participate in the establishment of performance goals for themselves. It is felt that a person is likely to try to achieve a performance goal that he himself has established, since the person's self-concept or self-perception will be involved. Since most individuals think positively about themselves, they should feel positively about performance goals established by themselves. There is also evidence that individuals and groups are most likely to attain goals when they make a public commitment to do so (Hilgard et al., 1971). This may be because such commitments are promises and most people view themselves as persons who keep their word.

Korman (1966) and Vroom (1964) have described research which indicates that individuals attempt to behave in accordance with their self-concepts. They try to make their behavior consistent with such self-perceptions. Thus, individuals who promise to achieve a certain result can be expected to be strongly motivated to be successful in carrying out their promise. Vroom (1964) also reports research which indicates that individuals apply high effort to tasks which are perceived to require abilities they take pride in. Conversely, there is less effort expended on tasks which have ability requirements which do not rate high in a person's self-perceptions. Thus, we would expect people who view themselves as being high on creativity to expend a good deal of effort on tasks which they believe require creativity for success in order to validate their self-perceptions. The implications of this for motivation are obvious. An organization should be able to obtain higher performance if it can assign tasks to individuals which require the abilities the individuals take pride in. Of course, such an approach would require a personnel appraisal system that would identify each organizational member's strengths.

Ethical Considerations. Most managers evaluate the effectiveness of alternative motivational approaches in terms of the achievement of the organizational goals of higher performance. Another consideration in choosing from among alternative motivational approaches, however, might be their relative impact on individuals. In no way would the use of fear meet individual needs unless the subordinate is a masochist. Competition may break down cooperativeness, leading to a lessened satisfaction of social needs. Reciprocity, though widely used, probably contributes little to individual growth and satisfaction and can be quite Machiavellian, depending upon how it is used. The use of ego-involvement through participation in goal setting and decision making is difficult. Managers must be willing to allow subordinates to influence decisions, guarding against pseudo-participation which can have disastrous effects on morale. The team-building approach may provide social need satisfaction as well as the opportunity to experience achievement in situations where individual achievement is not possible, but the group may end up stifling the individual. The job-enrichment strategy would appear to be the approach most in line with individual needs, including growth needs, although care must be taken not to force individuals to accept more responsibility than they are capable of handling. Reinforcement methods, used appropriately, offer individuals a fair opportunity to achieve their personal monetary or advancement goals, depending upon their ability and competence.

Motivation by Lower-level Personnel

The various motivational strategies are not only used by higher organizational levels on lower levels; the lower levels attempt to motivate superiors to behave in certain ways also. For example, reciprocity is used by lower-level personnel to gain future benefits for themselves. The team-building approach can be used by a group of employees to get their supervisor, or other employees, to behave in certain ways. Subordinates often attempt to obtain commitment to a certain idea from their superior by making him believe that he originated it. Even the fear approach can be used effectively by lower-level employees. By selective slowdowns, employees can create anxiety for higher-level managers who are being held accountable for meeting a schedule.

The Development of Expectancies

Motivation in psychological terms, rather than as a management function, is an internal state of the individual that drives a person to behave in a certain way. A person may do something because he believes the effort he puts forth will yield the results he wants. These beliefs are called *expectancies*, and are basic elements in a theory of motivation called "expectancy theory." An *expectancy* is an individual's estimate, or judgment, of the likelihood that some event, or outcome will occur. These outcomes may be performance levels resulting from effort, or they may be rewards resulting from performance. Any specific act may have several outcomes. For example, working hard on a project may result in (1) high performance, (2) high satisfaction, and (3) problems at home because the person had to work late several nights.

Not all outcomes are equally desired by a person, of course. Different outcomes may have different *valences*. Valences are *anticipated satisfactions* that result from outcomes. They are the individual's estimates of the future pleasantness—or unpleasantness— of an outcome.

One way to conceive of motivation, in the psychological sense, is as a result of *expectancies* and *valences*. The force (or motivation) to behave can be stated as follows:

$$\text{Force (Motivation)} = \Sigma \text{ (Expectancy} \times \text{Valence)}$$

where all expectancies and valences a person associates with a particular act are considered.

Certain expectancies have been found to be related to performance (Porter and Lawler, 1968). The first of these, sometimes called the "effort-performance" expectancy ($E \rightarrow P$), refers to the person's expectations about the relationship of his effort expenditures to the attainment of certain performance levels. This expectancy can be related to self-esteem. In a study of managers, it was found that managers low in self-esteem expended less effort than in previous years when given goals that were perceived to be more difficult to attain than in previous years (Carroll and Tosi, 1973). On the other hand, managers high in self-esteem expended more effort than in previous years when given more difficult goals. Another study found that foremen did not try to achieve goals they viewed as impossible (Stedry and Kay, 1966).

Thus, individuals low in self-esteem will not try to achieve performance goals they feel they have little likelihood of reaching, even if they desire the rewards associated with reaching those goals, and vice versa. A student with little self-confidence in his mathematical skills, for example, will probably not try to obtain an A in a statistics or mathematics course.

Other factors may influence the effort-performance (E→P) expectancy as well. For example, even an individual high in self-esteem may not believe that efforts on his part will result in the attainment of a certain level of performance because of a lack of resources or other technological deficiencies.

Another type of expectancy is the "performance-outcome" expectancy (P→O). This refers to an individual's expectations about the relationship between achieving a particular performance level and the attaining of certain outcomes. For example, an employee may feel that if he consistently attains a particular high performance level there is a moderate probability he will become fatigued, a high probability that his co-workers will be angry with him, a high probability that he will get a pay increase, and a moderate probability that the foreman will give him a compliment.

It is obvious that some of these outcomes are positive and some are considered negative. In addition, while these outcomes are anticipated by the employee, a different set of outcomes may actually occur if the particular performance level is achieved. The degree to which a particular anticipated outcome is positive or negative depends upon the person's anticipations and expectations of the outcomes. For example, an employee may expect that there is a high probability of receiving a pay increase if he achieves a particular performance level. How positive the pay increase will be to him will depend on his perception of the consequences of his getting a pay increase. If he can use the extra pay to buy something he has long desired, then he will probably put a high positive value on the pay increase. On the other hand, he may anticipate that the pay increase will be spent by others in his family or by somebody he owes money to, and he may therefore put only a slight positive value on the pay increase.

If we subscribe to expectancy theory, we would assume that individuals tend to choose performance levels they are likely to be able to achieve and which are also anticipated to result in a set of outcomes with more positive than negative values to the individual, given his needs and his situation (Mobley, 1971). Research also indicates that the behavior of a superior can influence employee expectations. One study, for example, found that when supervisors increased the use of specific performance goals for subordinates and also reviewed their performance more frequently, employees increasingly felt high performance would result in pay increases and promotions for them (Tosi, Chesser, and Carroll, 1972). When management switches to an incentive pay plan, employees perceive a stronger relationship between high performance and the receiving of economic rewards than they did before (Cummings and Schwab, 1973).

Satisfaction—The Result of Performance

Not only does task-oriented effort produce products, but feelings of satisfaction or dissatisfaction may also develop as a result of it. The latter have been called "intrinsic reward." A person may feel good after performing a task. Work may be enjoyable, especially if the person is interested in it. His feelings of self-esteem may be enhanced when he is doing something he believes worthwhile. "Extrinsic rewards" are rewards that are controlled by others, such as pay, promotion, recognition, and so forth. Work activity may also of course lead to rewards such as these. These rewards are the incentives that are available if reinforcement motivational strategies are used.

When the individual finds work intrinsically and/or extrinsically rewarding, job satisfaction may increase. Conversely, if work is drudgery, with no rewards, dissatisfaction may increase. In general it is now believed that satisfaction follows performance when the performance results in outcomes valued by the person. Therefore, in our model in figure 5.2, we show satisfaction resulting from work, influencing the human input factor, especially the individual-need dimension. For example, if a worker high in achievement needs is successful, he is likely not only to be satisfied but also to raise his level of achievement orientation. The converse may also be true.

The Management of Performance

Our analysis shows that performance is the result of a number of factors. Motivation to perform at a high level is the result of individual ability and needs and the particular motivational strategy being used by management, along with the resources necessary to attain the desired performance level. Technological factors, and the absence or presence of certain inhibiting or facilitating forces such as those found in group norms, also play a significant role in performance.

In analyzing the causes of poor performance, management would be wise to take a systems point of view, evaluating the relative importance of human versus technological inputs on performance, and the most effective motivational strategy to obtain the performance level desired. The perspective to be taken is the management of performance rather than the usual management conception of motivation—how a person *thinks* about his job, which involves a much narrower focus.

Management should be aware of the expectancies that organizational members have and the reasons for such expectancies. House (1971) has drawn a useful link between managerial behavior (or motivational strategies, as we have called them) and motivation. He has pointed out that the supervisor can influence subordinate expectancies (E→P and P→O) by his behavior. He can clarify what he expects of the subordinates when role ambiguity exists. He can attempt to increase the payoffs to subordinates for achieving high performance levels by rewarding high performance. He may be able to build up a subordinate's self-esteem and abilities by appropriate training, support, and work assignments. He can provide facilitation of performance by insuring that supplies and other resources are available at the time and in the form needed, and he can increase the amount of productive time available to an employee through delegation or some other means of more effectively utilizing time. This linking process by the superior will be examined more extensively later, in chapter 8.

Discussion Questions

1. Think of the most highly motivated person you know. What is it about them that makes you arrive at this judgment?

2. Do you agree with the statement "Job satisfaction is *not* related to the level of performance." Why? Why not?

3. Think about a specific time you were very satisfied with your work—motivated to do more. Write down on a piece of paper what happened. What about a time when you were dissatisfied? Write that down. Go back in this chapter and read the difference between Herzberg's concepts of satisfiers and dissatisfiers. How do your answers fit with his results?

4. How does the type of technology interact with human skills to affect performance? Describe three jobs in which skill is most important. Three types in which ability is very important.

5. Which of the managerial motivation strategies do *you* believe would be most successful in dealing with subordinates? Which would you respond to most? Is

there a difference between the way you would manage and the way you want to be managed?

6. Have you ever been involved in a "team project" for which a grade was given? What problems did the grader have if each team member were to be graded on the value of (1) their work; (2) their contribution? How did you feel about the grade received by those who did not work hard? About the grade received by those who did not contribute as much?

7. Why do you believe that managers are so concerned with "motivation"?

8. What are "expectancies"? How can they affect performance levels? How does personal skill fit in? How about technology?

Part III
Organizations

Organizations, like people, are different. They differ in what they produce (cars, bread, grass seed, advertising). They differ in size (from the small independent retail outlet to firms which have more employees than some states have citizens). They differ in rigidity (some organizations have very strict work practices, while others have very loose ones). It is futile to try to understand human behavior without taking such differences into account.

To a large extent such differences are designed—or emerge—to react to the external environment within which the organization operates. Uncertainty about the environment has come to be widely accepted as a prime characteristic that affects the structure of an organization. Chapter 6 examines this environment and chapter 7 describes more fully four forms of organization which can function in different environments.

These different forms of organization attract different types of individuals to work in them. The differences in people interact with the differences in structure in such a way to require the manager to function differently depending upon the nature of the interaction if an effective level of performance is to be reached.

Chapter 6
The Environment and the Organization

We all know that differences exist between organizations. They differ in what they do, how they are structured, and the manner in which decisions are made. Managers, and students of management, must understand what these differences are, what conditions give rise to them, and how they should be dealt with.

In this chapter, two major sets of ideas which deal with these differences are presented. The first has to do with a way of categorizing the various activities of an organization. The second focuses on the external environment within which an organization operates, and some conditions of this environment which affect the shape and form of the organizational components and mechanisms which operate to adapt to the environment.

The Open and Closed Systems Perspective

All organizations are in an active relationship with their environment. Just as any organism, such as man, must learn to adapt to its environment or perish, so too must organizations. The form, or structure, of an organization must be functional: that is, keyed for survival. The functional point of view assumes that if something survives, it does so because it contributes in some way to the survival or maintenance of a larger system. Organizations must evolve or in some other way shape a form that is functional for the environmental demands placed upon them. Thompson (1967) presents this *open systems* point of view in this way:

> ... The complex organization is a set of interdependent parts which together make up the whole because each contributes something and receives something from the whole, which in turn is interdependent with the larger environment. *Survival of the systems is taken to be the goal, and the parts and their relationships presumably are determined through evolutionary processes* [our emphasis].

Dysfunctions are conceivable, but is is assumed that an offending part will produce a net positive contribution or be disengaged, or the system will degenerate.

The *closed systems*, or rational systems, approach takes a different view of organizations. It is one often taken by management scholars and practitioners. In the closed systems approach, there is an emphasis only on what is considered controllable—the internal systems of the organization. The environment of the organization, being more unpredictable, is ignored, assumed to be given, or neglected in favor of concentrating on making the internal operations of the organization as efficient as possible.

There is, of course, nothing incompatible between these two approaches, and certainly today a sophisticated management considers both the external environment and the efficiency of internal operations when making decisions. For an individual inside the organization, however, the environment must sometimes be closed off by definite decisions made by another, because unless this is done there can be no basis for formulating internal plans. There is no other way a manager can develop a strategy to achieve the objectives of his unit and the organization. On the other hand, recognition of the variations of the environment becomes extremely important from a policy-making point of view, especially for decisions of corporate strategy. Managerial strategy is used to change the general direction of an organization in response to changing external pressures or conditions. There are important accommodations that organizations must make with the environment, and these show up as different forms and functioning of the organization subsystems.

Organization Subsystems

The standard treatment of organizational components usually defines different departmental structures with the concepts of "line" and "staff." Rather than taking this view, Katz and Kahn (1966) consider a more general form of subsystems, which we use here because it provides a way to conceptualize a wide range of different organizations, from advertising agencies to manufacturing firms. To understand this more general form, we must first define a "system."

A system is a set of interrelated components surrounded by a boundary which absorbs inputs from other systems and transforms them into outputs that serve a function in other systems. Complex organizations are open systems, interacting with an outside environment and adjusting to it. A business organization must react to changes in the environments from which it takes its inputs or resources (e.g., suppliers of raw materials), and to changes in the environments in which it delivers outputs or goods and services (i.e., to clients or customers).

This, of course, is not to say that an organization does not try to influence or exert control over its environments to some extent. For example, a firm may decide to buy another which is a supplier in order to insure that it has a guaranteed source of raw materials. But no organization has complete power over its environments, and all are influenced by their environments in a number of ways.

An organization transforms inputs (or resources) into outputs (or goods and services) by means of a technological process—a complex of physical objects, procedures, and knowledges by which a certain result is obtained. Some technologies are composed primarily of physical objects, as when steel, component parts, and other materials are transformed into automobiles by an assembly line in the automobile industry, or as when gasoline is produced by the sophisticated and complex equipment used in a refinery. In other technologies, the physical objects may be quite simple but the procedures and the knowledges quite sophisticated, as when a surgeon performs a delicate operation using simple instruments. Thus technologies consist of a number of mental and physical tasks, some of which may be performed by human beings and some by machines (including computers). The mental or physical tasks may be few or many in number. They may differ widely in their complexity. Some technologies require the services of many human beings or machines and some require the services of only a few human beings. These activities are called *production* subsystems.

There are also processes (activities) which handle the transfer of inputs both into and out of an organization. The technology needs raw materials to operate. Its products must be sold, or otherwise distributed. These functions are called *boundary-spanning* activities.

It is necessary to adapt to the environment, and for this purpose some parts of the organization try to monitor the environment. For example, market research attempts to figure out what changes are likely to take place in consumer demands. These *adaptive* activities are necessary to any organization.

There are also coordination and control problems. Data must be collected, to be used for decision making. Conflict between different units must be resolved. These things are done by *maintenance* and *managerial* subsystems.

Subsystems are related groups of activities which various units perform to meet the objectives of the organization. These related activities, which absorb inputs, transform them into outputs, transfer them to users, and coordinate all of these activities are (1) production subsystems, (2) adaptive subsystems, (3) boundary-spanning subsystems, (4) maintenance subsystems, and (5) managerial subsystems.

Primary and Collateral Subsystems

All subsystems must function with some degree of effectiveness in order for the organization to survive, but some are more actively involved in the process of resource acquisition, production, and distribution than others. Those subsystems which either produce a salable or usable value for clients, or operate in the external environment to obtain information and inputs or exchange outputs, are called *primary* subsystems. They make the organization go—producing, selling, and so on. These primary subsystems are similar to the concept of "line" in an organization, as discussed by classical management theorists (Davis 1951). They are the primary functions and, according to Barnard (1938), are "fundamental requirements". Primary subsystems are the *production, boundary-spanning,* and *adaptive* subsystems.

The carrying out of support and coordinating activities is done by *collateral subsystems.* Their chief purpose is to insure smooth relationships between other subsystems. The collateral subsystems are the *maintenance* and *managerial* subsystems. The maintenance subsystem is similar to the concept of "staff," and carries out support activities. Managerial subsystems are "administrative" in nature.

These two types of subsystems are common to all organizations—business, government, health, educational, or military. In different organizations, jobs and organizational units with quite different titles from their counterparts elsewhere actually perform the same kind of work, and if we think in terms of subsystems, there is less danger of becoming confused by inconsistent terminology. The descriptions of the organizational subcomponents and individual jobs may otherwise obscure the nature of the essential functions being performed for the organizational system as a whole.

While the primary subsystems might possibly maintain the life of an organization even with ineffective performance from the collateral subsystems, in the long run this would lower the organization's effectiveness. When in economic difficulty, many organizations cut back on maintenance activities, such as training and morale improvement. They later pay for this neglect with significant losses of valuable human resources and diminished long-run performance.

The individual primary and collateral subsystems describe activities, not necessarily formally designated departments. One individual or unit may perform several functions, or be involved in more than one subsystem. A professor is part of the production subsystem of a college when he is teaching, but he participates in the maintenance subsystem when he serves as a member of a committee to establish individual faculty pay increases. He may also perform managerial subsystem activities such as resolving conflicts among research assistants assigned to him. Typically, individuals with the title of "manager" participate in several subsystems.

FIGURE 6.1 The Production Subsystem—Task-oriented Activities

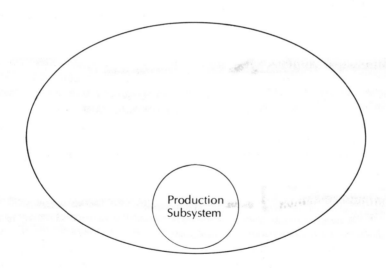

Production Subsystem

Production Subsystems

The production subsystem (see fig. 6.1) is the technical core of the organization (Thompson, 1967), producing the product, service, or ideas which are bought, or otherwise consumed, by the public. Organizations are often categorized by their production subsystems. Automotive firms, hospitals, educational institutions are designated as such specifically because of what they do, and how they do it.

Every organization has a production subsystem, whether it is a top 500 company, a hospital, a department store, or a public service agency. Too frequently the tendency is to equate production with manufacturing. This is too narrow a view. In a business firm, the production system is the task-oriented work which created the product or service—for example, an assembly line, a transaction system for tellers in a bank, or those activities in a retailing outlet which take place after goods are bought but before they are sold. In hospitals, the care facilities, operating rooms, and emergency operations are different parts of the total production subsystem. The production subsystem is important, largely because it is the "technical core" of the organization and as such it is likely to be a high-cost subsystem; that is, large sums will be required to build, create, or otherwise develop it. This large investment produces pressures for effective and efficient utilization designed to protect it from unpredictable fluctuations in the environment. (Some of these mechanisms, such as buffering and smoothing, are discussed later in this chapter.) Thompson (1967) has proposed a general classification of production technologies: long-linked, mediating, and intensive.

Long-linked Technologies. Long-linked technologies involve serial interdependence, such as task B which can be performed only after task A is completed, while task C requires both to be finished. An assembly line is a good example of long-linked technology. For instance, in a food processing plant each step must follow sequentially to obtain the correct quality of product. To process tomato juice, the tomatoes must be cleaned, mashed, strained, cooked and the juice sealed in cans, in that sequence.

Mediating Technologies. Mediating technologies carry out production activities which have as their primary function the linking of clients or customers who are or who wish to be interdependent. The phone company links callers with those called; banks link depositors with borrowers. A problem with a mediating technology is that though it may be standardized, fluctuations in demand may be very extreme and not subject to much influence from the organization. This variability in demand often requires a substantial investment in the production subsystem to handle peak loads, which means that it is underused in one period, but has high demand later. Long-distance telephone circuits, for example, are extremely busy on Christmas and Mothers' day, while it is virtually certain there will be open lines any weekday at 1:00 A.M., a time of day when there is underutilization of equipment.

Intensive Technologies. Intensive technologies are systems in which a wide range of different techniques can be used, says Thompson, to change a "specific object, but the selection, combination and order of application are determined by feedback from the object itself" (Thompson, 1967). Job-shop manufacturing (where general-purpose equipment is used to manufacture different products), construction firms, and hospitals are all examples of organizations in which the specific tools used depend on the nature of the problem or project.

Boundary-spanning Subsystems

Boundary-spanning subsystems carry on the environmental transactions in procuring the input, disposing of the output, or assisting in these functions. They are called "boundary-spanning" because while the activities themselves are performed *within* the organization, they connect it with external points of contact. They are systems which link the organization with the relevant world outside (see fig. 6.2).

The sales unit of a firm, for example, is engaged in boundary-spanning. Exchanging a refrigerator for the customer's dollars, for instance, is a boundary-spanning transaction conducted by a salesman. The purchasing department of a steel company, when buying iron ore, secures the raw materials needed to produce the final product. The function of recruiting, where the personnel department seeks human inputs, can be classified as a boundary-spanning function.

Adaptive Subsystems

Adaptive subsystems perform those activities within an organization which are designed to monitor or sense the nature of the world in which the organization operates (see fig. 6.3). Since the major objective of an organization is survival, and it does so—if it does—in some environmental context, when that context changes, the organization must change. Therefore, the environment is monitored. Research and development are one kind of adaptive subsystem activities. Efforts to keep abreast of current technology and to provide products which are being demanded by the market are organization attempts to adapt to the world.

Lobbying to influence government policy in areas which might affect the organization are also adaptive activities. Major changes in government requirements on pollution control, for example, could have a serious effect on the level of an organization's survival. Therefore, any internal activities designed to monitor the government are adaptive.

FIGURE 6.2   Boundary-spanning functions connect the inside of
the system with organizations beyond the boundary.

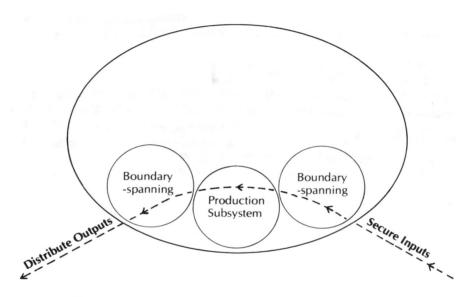

Financial and other control activities to monitor and control the
level of efficiency and performance of a firm to insure that it is profitable enough to save capital for future investment are also adaptive.

Maintenance Subsystems

Maintenance subsystem activities seek to smooth out the problems of
operating the other subsystems, and to monitor their internal operation (see fig. 6.4). One important function of the maintenance subsystem is to maintain morale. Maintenance activities include indoctri-
nation, socialization, rewarding, and punishing of organization
members, training activities, and overseeing the compensation system,
the performance appraisal system, and other systems in which all
supervisory personnel are coordinated by personnel administration
professionals.

Maintenance activities also focus on setting performance standards
for tasks, raw materials standards, and product or service quality stan-

FIGURE 6.3 The adaptive activities complete the set of primary systems.

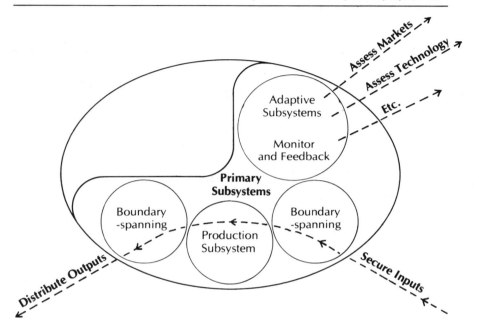

dards. Surveillance or evaluation activities are carried out to insure that such standards are met. The maintenance subsystem devises and monitors adherence to preestablished rules and norms. Specialized groups using the titles of industrial engineering or quality control may have responsibility in these activities.

The general concern of the maintenance subsystem is that of insuring predictability and the smooth operation of the rest of the organization. Its efforts to insure the effective operation of the entire system involve increasing the level of predictability. Equipment and machinery require standardized raw material inputs, and thus there must be certain minimum quality standards for such materials. Machinery must be operated in certain ways to protect it and to insure proper coordination with other machinery or the production system will break down or, at best, will operate inefficiently.

Individuals are hired to make certain kinds of contributions to the organization. Their values, motivations, attitudes, knowledges, abilities, and interpersonal orientations affect these contributions. The

---

FIGURE 6.4 The maintenance subsystem increases system predictability.

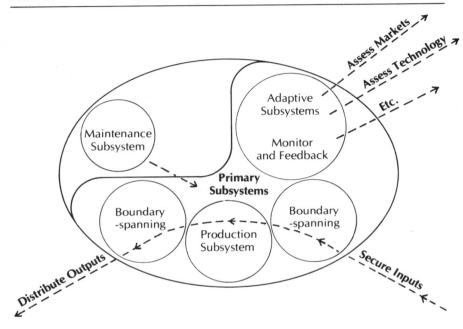

maintenance subsystem trains, lectures, motivates, punishes, evaluates, and negotiates with organizational members in order to insure that the system works as planned.

This is not to say that there is no attention paid to individual needs and personal objectives. The effective operation of the system—an integration of human resources with equipment, procedures, and other resources—often requires an organizational accommodation to such personal objectives. The organization must pay the price necessary to obtain the degree of quality and performance required from both human and material resources for the effective operation of the primary subsystems.

Managerial Subsystems

"[Managerial] subsystems," say Katz and Kahn (1966), "comprise the organized activities for controlling, coordinating, and directing the many subsystems of the structure. They represent another slice of the organizational pattern and . . . deal with coordination of subsystems and adjustment of the total system to its environment." The managerial subsystem is concerned with general policy questions. Determining general policy and strategy to interact with the environment with the intent of insuring long-term survival is a function of the managerial subsystem. The resolution of internal conflict between departments is also one of its functions, as is the use of the authority structure to disseminate directives and to resolve conflict. The total system is shown in figure 6.5.

FIGURE 6.5 The Total System

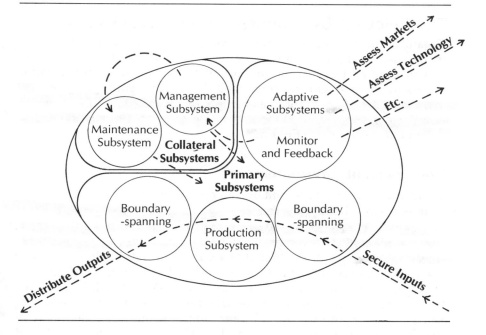

Some Concluding Ideas about Organization Subsystems

Specific forms of an organization's subsystems vary from organization to organization. The production subsystem of a hospital is different from that in a department store, for example, or in a manufacturing plant.

There is also great variation in how these subsystems are related to each other to form an organization's structure. Some organizations have extremely rigid, bureaucratic structures. Others have more flexible, colleague-oriented systems. Research and development activity, for example, may be performed very differently: people with similar backgrounds in engineering may be doing applied research in one organization, pure research in another.

What are the factors which bring about these differences? Our view is that it is the environment within which an organization tries to survive that influences the specific form its subsystems take. In the remainder of this chapter we will describe more fully the environment and its characteristics. In the next chapter, we will describe alternative forms of organization structure.

The Relevant Environment of the Organization

Organizations interact with other organizations which provide inputs, make use of outputs, exert pressures for certain kinds of decisions, and in general deal in some important fashion with the organization with which we should be concerned. This is the concept called "organization set" (Evan, 1966) and refers to the sectors of a society, institutions, or processes which have a direct bearing on what an organization does, and how it does it.

The Relevant Environment

There are many pressures outside an organization and they affect it in different ways. Its relevant environment is made up of groups, or institutions, beyond its boundaries which provide immediate inputs, exert significant pressure on decisions, or make use of the organization's output. This means that at any one point in time there are some external organizations which are closer and have a more significant effect on what goes on in a firm than do others. For instance, customers and suppliers are in immediate juncture with a business organization. They comprise the relevant environment. A sudden shift in the level of consumer demand, for example, can force internal changes, as when a slump in auto sales causes auto firms to lay off workers.

Other conditions could bring other institutions or organizations into the relevant environment. When other sectors in the organization set impose pressures, they may threaten the existence of the organization. Any outside force which is able to generate sufficient pressure to create pressures within organizations, either in the managerial structure, the production structure, or the boundary-spanning structures, must of necessity be defined as part of the relevant environment because the organization must adapt to it. When equal opportunity laws were passed, for instance, many firms had to change their hiring procedures as well as the criteria used for promotion. Laws passed to control the quality of air caused shifts in types of fuel used as well as product design of devices using fuel.

Can we be more illuminating than simply to say that the organization reacts to the relevant environment? Perhaps we can by defining certain subsectors of the environment. At the outset, let us make clear that the relevant external environment of an organization may be composed, at least, of

1. customers;	4. public pressure groups;
2. suppliers;	5. government agencies;
3. unions;	6. investors.

Here we will focus on the two sectors of the environment which are of most use in analyzing problems in the management of business organizations. These are the *market* and *technological* environmental sectors. Again, it should be noted that other sectors may be more critical in different organizations. They would, however, have similar effects, though on different subsystems from those we will outline in this and the next chapter.

The Market Environment. Organizations produce some sort of commodity, product, value, or service for a particular set of individuals, the consumers of the output. The output can obviously take many forms—automobiles, steel, television sets, bread, pencils, books—the list of products consumed by people is virtually endless. The same holds true of services. Advertising agencies sell ideas and services to clients. Welfare agencies provide services or information to clients. Hospitals provide services to patients by having available a wide variety of health care facilities in one location convenient for both patients and doctors.

For some organizations, the users of the output may be the members themselves. Interest groups form the nucleus of many clubs. Fraternal organizations such as the Elks, Masons, or Knights of Columbus essentially provide greater values to their members than to others in the usual sense of clients or customers. Even these organizations, however, frequently provide a charitable service to other parts of the community.

On a more microcosmic level, we might also consider the "market" for units (or departments) within a complex organization. The notion of organization subsystems suggests that the output of the production subsystem becomes an input for the boundary-spanning market subsystem. Departments in organizations provide some sort of product or service to other units. Indeed, demands of these users may range from specific tangible products such as subassemblies, completed units, memoranda or reports, to services, ideas, or other, more abstract values. For example, the marketing division may be viewed as the "market," or user, of the product of the manufacturing division. The shop foreman is a user of reports produced by the production control department. The marketing department may be a user of ideas generated by the advertising group; the accounting unit, when adding new employees, is a client for the services of the personnel department.

Markets may vary along several dimensions. These dimensions include time, shape, or size. The market for a particular product may exist only for a specific period of time, then dissipate until that time reoccurs. Certain food products are consumed seasonally, such as pumpkin and turkey. Toy sales soar before Christmas. Other markets vary by size. There is a vast market for automobiles, a much smaller market for cross-country skiis. The shape of the market can vary also. If we consider population age segments, we would find that some products—for example, home furnishings—are sold principally to adults in age ranges over 25. Other products—such as rock music records—may have their highest demand among younger consumers.

The Technological Environment. The technological sector of the environment has two components. The first is the availability of techniques and processes which the organization can obtain to form the production system. In this sense, technology refers to available hardware. How this is absorbed, organized, and set up internally defines the production subsystem described earlier—which means that internal production systems cannot be any farther advanced than the technology available, although it is also quite possible that production systems may not come close to using all available technology advances. (For example, customer credit accounts in a large department store might be handled by computers, while the same function in a small specialty store might be performed manually.)

Technology also refers to the ideas or knowledge underlying the processing or the distribution of the service; that is, the translation of science to useful application. Research and development, as well as applications engineering, are functions that would fall into this category. Every organization makes use of some knowledge base, some science in its subsystems.

Characteristics of the Environment

We have defined two major environmental sectors which will form the basic framework for much of the material presented later in this book: the market sector and the technological sector. We do not of course discount the possibility of other environmental sectors impinging on the organization, but if they do, the concepts in this chapter will still accommodate them.

Defining the elements of the environment only tells where an organization operates—what affects it. What causes the organization to take the form—structure—that it does is the *degree* of change in the environment. Our conceptual scheme is based on the idea that environmental variability and its potential impact on the organization must be understood before a manager can manage well.

Research has shown that degree of change is a very important aspect of the environment as it affects an organization's structure (Lawrence and Lorsch, 1967; Harvey, 1968). Degree of change may be conceived of as a continuum, at the opposite ends of which are (1) stability, and (2) volatility. These two states of the environment have substantial implications for the internal structure of the organization, the type of individual who is likely to join a particular operation, and the shaping of perceptions, attitudes, and values in the organization. Most important, however, the environment has a significant effect on the degree to which internal subsystems of the organization take on highly routine or stable characteristics. For example, when there is a large steady market for a product and a well-developed technology, a firm may invest large sums in plant and equipment to serve it. Advanced forms of mechanization can keep costs very low so that the market can be expanded, but this comes at the cost of increased mechanization, and this process in turn lowers the skill level of employees needed to run the plant, influences who will join the organization, and affects how they will adapt to it once they are members.

The Stable Environment. The stable environment is one in which changes are relatively small, occurring in small increments, with a minimal impact on the structure, processes, and output of the organization. Changes are likely to be in size (e.g., the amount of beer consumed or insurance sold) rather than in kind. For the organization, the impact of changes in the stable environment will largely be on the size of the membership of the organization. The product is unlikely to change significantly and there will be little need to alter the production subsystem of the organization with change in the environment.

With this high level of stability, it is likely that there will be extensive investment in plant, equipment, and distribution methods, and when there are increases or decreases in the market, the method of adaptation can be a short-term one, consisting of reducing or increasing the work force, rather than making changes in the product or the method of production. For example, large commercial bakeries use a fairly high-cost system of production, but the final product is still bread. Alterations in this production system come rather slowly, but steadily. If there is a shift in demand, say a drop, then the mode of accommodation is not to seek new products, but rather to lay off personnel until demand increases, or perhaps to permanently adjust to lower sales levels.

The stable environment is characterized by high levels of predictability. It is very likely that we will be able to make fairly accurate predictions of the level of the market based on some fairly common set of change measures, or indexes. For instance, the level of automobile sales may be predicted reasonably well if there are reasonably accurate data available on changes in population and income. The demand for telephone services in use may similarly be predicted rather well.

The Volatile Environment. When we say an environment is volatile, we mean that it is likely to be turbulent, with more intense changes than in the stable environment. Changes are also more rapid and random, and prediction is difficult.

When the market is volatile, it is—by definition—unstable. The customers may change. The level of demand may vary widely. The women's fashion market, for instance, may be considered in most senses as volatile. Product decisions of designers and manufacturers are based on consumer tastes and preferences, and these are highly changeable and difficult to predict. (Item 6.1 gives another example of market volatility.)

When the technology is volatile, new concepts and ideas are being rapidly generated, and these new ideas affect either the manner in which the production processes are carried out, or the nature of the processes themselves. The electronics industry, with breakthroughs in integrated circuits, transistors, and general miniaturization, presents an example of technology changes which affect the nature of the product. If these technological developments reduce the selling price of the product, marketing strategies may be affected as well. Item 6.2 tells about the problems of digital watch manufacturers. As technology changes, and prices drop, the manufacturers find themselves in a quandary, not knowing what will happen to their costs of production and uncertain about the buying strategies of the retail outlets which are their customers.

ITEM 6.1   Market Volatility

Semiconductors Take a Sudden Plunge

Enthusiastic employee-stockholders at Advanced Micro Devices, Inc. are fond of charting the integrated circuit maker's over-the-counter stock performance. Last year, as the Sunnyvale (Calif.) company basked in the glow of unprecedented growth and profitability, the price scale on the chart began at $10. But recently, the chart has been revised. "The new bottom line doesn't say 'zero,'" jokes W. J. "Jerry" Sanders, AMD president, "it says 'free.'"

AMD stock is not yet being given away, but this week's bid price of around $3.50 reflects a sudden reversal of fortunes not just for Sanders' little company but for the entire semiconductor industry. Six months ago, the producers of ICs, transistors, and other solid-state electronic components could not keep up with demand. Order backlogs had soared, and delivery times stretched out more than a year on major product lines. Big new plants were springing up in such unlikely locations as Beaverton, Ore., and Orem, Utah.

But the picture has suddenly and dramatically changed. Many of the new plants are being left half-finished or unoccupied, company after company is slashing its work force, and the first signs of red ink are showing up. During the third quarter, shipments dropped for the first time since the disastrous industry recession of 1970.

A big surprise. The rapidly deteriorating marketplace caught nearly everyone by surprise. In a few months, the industry's big order backlog was cut in half. Order cancellations and returns have reduced backlogs by $620-million since May, estimates Jon D. Gruber of Robertson, Colman, Siebel & Weisel, a San Francisco investment banker.

• • • •

Now the industry is wondering whether it faces a repeat of the 1970 debacle, in which sales of some product lines fell off more than 50% in less than a year, over-all shipments declined about 25%, and all but a few companies lost money. "This is as uncertain a business environment as I've ever seen," says Charles C. Harwood, president of Signetics Corp.

Business Week, Nov. 16, 1974

Reprinted from the Nov. 16, 1975, *Business Week* by special permission. Copyright © 1975 by McGraw-Hill, Inc.

Strategies for Adapting to the Environment

Perhaps the most important assumption underlying management process contingency theory is that an organization must operate its most costly subsystem as efficiently as possible. Generally, the production subsystem (the technical core) will be the most costly, whether it is made up of expensive equipment or highly-trained professionals.

ITEM 6.2   The Technological Environment

Prices of Electronic Digital Watches Fall As Makers Compete for a Share of Market

If you think prices of portable electronic calculators fell fast, keep an eye on electronic digital watches.

Watches that use light-emitting diodes (LED) and liquid crystal display (LCD) have been fighting each other and traditional, mechanical watches for a share of the market. Prices have begun to plummet and there is much talk of "dumping," or selling in quantity at very low prices.

"There's been a fantastic erosion in prices in the past four months," said Ardith Rivel, Benrus Corp.'s vice president for quartz watches.

• • • •

He said that electronic digital watches that had been selling for $125 to $150 are selling currently at about $30.

Trade observers note that early electronic calculators that sold for $300 or more currently can be bought for $20 and less.

Both the LED and LCD watches use as their timers the extremely high-frequency vibrations (32,768 a second) of their battery-electrified quartz crystals. The vibrations are translated into lighted digits by circuitry.

Must Push Buttons. With an LED watch, the wearer must push one or two buttons to see the time; on an LCD watch, the time is displayed constantly.

The first brand-name electronic digital watch on the market was Pulsar, by the Time Computer Inc. division of HMW Industries Inc. It sold for $2,000 in an 18-caret gold case in 1971. HMW later introduced a $250 model in a stainless-steel case.

Other major watch makers gradually began producing electronic digital watches, followed by some calculator and semiconductor producers. As more companies became involved, the technology changed and prices dropped rapidly.

At a panel discussion by retailers, sponsored by Burgess & Leith, brokers, Alice Klein, merchandise manager of Alexander's Inc., a department-store company, compared the electronic digital watch situation to what happened with calculators. Retailers are holding back orders because so many changes were made when the device caught on, she said, adding, "We have to keep our inventory low because of the changing technology." . . .

The Wall Street Journal, April 16, 1975

James Thompson describes ways in which the technical core can be protected against environmental variations—protective devices of buffering and smoothing, for example. The need for use of these devices is of course greatest when there is a substantial degree of volatility in the environment. When the environment is smooth (e.g., when demand is reasonably uniform over time), the internal systems which deal with it can be relatively simple.

Buffering attempts to protect internal operations by sealing off the production system from external variables. For example, say that a plant has a continuous-assembly operation and therefore needs a steady flow of raw materials, but the supply of raw materials is variable, uncertain, or otherwise not in synchronization with use. The solution, then, is to create an inventory of raw materials which will permit steady production even with varied inputs. The same holds true when there is smooth steady production, but variable demand. The firm simply produces to inventory.

Smoothing attempts to minimize severe fluctuations of the environment by "offering inducements to those who use . . . services during 'trough' periods, or [charging] premiums to those who contribute to 'peaking'" (Thompson, 1967). Offering discount rates to early-morning callers is a smoothing strategy used by the telephone company. Discounts offered to buyers during off-seasons is another such strategy (e.g., lower tourist rates in Florida during the summer months).

Another way to adapt to a volatile environment is to have an extremely flexible organization. The most extreme form of adaptation is to have an organization structure which has enough resiliency to cope with unpredictable demands. The "intensive technology" production system is an example. Not knowing what the demand of a customer may be, general-purpose resources are used in various ways. The emergency room of a hospital has equipment which may be used to treat heart attacks, broken legs, burns, and virtually every other possible medical emergency. For each emergency the particular configuration of equipment varies. The role of the doctor (a professional) is to know how to arrange this general-purpose equipment to be most effective in a particular situation.

Adaptation—Active and Passive. The preceding discussion could lead to the assumption that organizations are passive, subject to the buffeting of the environment, adapting to it or perishing. It is possible, however, for an organization to do many things which might influence the nature of its environment. For example, lobbying to change government regulations or laws can help insure relatively moderate to low government intervention. Or, where a stable technology exists, spending large amounts of time and money on research may produce a breakthrough, thus increasing technological volatility. In chapter 16 we will discuss in detail how an organization can influence its environment.

The Environment-Organization Linkage

In this chapter we have emphasized the idea that organization structures will differ according to the conditions of the environment. That
is, the organization's subsystems (production, adaptive, etc.) will differ, depending on whether the market and/or technology is stable or
volatile. From these ideas about subsystems, their interface with the
environment, and the character of the environment, we can begin to
form some ideas about types of organizations. One axis of figure 6.6 is
the technological dimension of environments; the other axis is the
market dimension. Both dimensions are divided into two levels of
uncertainty—stable and volatile. These two levels are used only for
analytical purposes. No environment can be characterized by only two
discrete categories, but the categories shown will be adequate for our
analysis and discussion. Figure 6.6 shows four different types of organizations. We will describe them briefly here, and in chapter 7 will
describe how the different organization subsystems look in each type.
In chapters 13 through 15 we will suggest different approaches to
managing in these four types of organizations.

FIGURE 6.6

Know

		Technology	
		Stable	**Volatile**
Market	**Stable**	Hierarchical, Bureaucratic	Technology -dominated Mixed (TD Mixed)
	Volatile	Market -dominated Mixed (MD Mixed)	Flexible, Dynamic

Hierarchical, Bureaucratic Type. The hierarchical organization develops in response to a stable market and a stable technology. It uses
standard production methods and has well-defined and fixed channels of distribution. Tasks in it change slowly. Authority/responsi-
bility relationships are specified. The hierarchical form is the appropriate adjustment to the stable environment.

Flexible, Dynamic Type.   The important characteristic of a dynamic organization—which must adapt to a volatile environment—is its ability to change. There is not an intensive investment in plant and equipment, and high skill levels are required of employees. They may be moved from one part of the organization to another as demands change. There is little centralized decision making, and authority is often not well-defined.

Market-dominated Mixed Type.   In the market-dominated mixed (MD-mixed) type of organization, the technology is relatively unchanging, but the markets are in constant flux. Under such conditions, their marketing units are their most influential subsystems. An example of a market-dominated mixed organization would be a women's apparel manufacturer. The technology for making the product has been stable for a long period of time, but the market is extremely volatile because competitors go into and out of business constantly due to price competition, because there are several distinct selling seasons, and because of unpredictable style preferences of customers.

Technology-dominated Mixed Type.   When the market is stable, but the technology is constantly changing, then the research and development (R & D) group—the scientists who deal with that technology—will be the dominant force in the organization. This is the technology-dominated mixed organization (TD-mixed). The marketing group will be much like that in a hierarchical organization, but the R & D group will be relatively flexible.

There is, of course, no such thing as a pure organizational type. But by understanding the four theoretical types we can apply their basics to any size unit (department, groups, firms) for analysis and prescription of strategy.

More than one organizational type will probably exist in the same company. Certain very large companies—such as Westinghouse, General Electric, General Motors—are actually composed of many separate organizations, some of which have relationships with each other and some of which are quite independent of each other. These organizations must carefully *differentiate* (segregate) their individual units from each other while at the same time providing some sort of *integrating* mechanism to coordinate them. Item 6.3 describes how this is done at Westinghouse.

The market and the technology are not the only environmental sectors influencing organizational structure and the managerial process.

ITEM 6.3   Changing Structure

Westinghouse Opts for a GE Pattern

Westinghouse Electric Corp. has never admitted that it is excelled by its larger rival, General Electric Corp., in anything but size and profits. But when Robert E. Kirby assumes command of Westinghouse next week as chief executive officer, he will preside over a trimmed-down corporate structure that is modeled in part on a GE management concept.

Fighting a severe profits slump, Westinghouse has recently lopped off losing businesses that account for about $700-million in annual sales. It has been preparing for the time when Donald C. Burnham, chief executive since 1963, steps down under a pre-retirement program for top officers that he himself devised. When he reaches 60 next week, Burnham will become an "officer-director" at two-thirds of his former pay. Last week, the 56-year-old Kirby, former head of Westinghouse's profitable industry and defense group, told 200 line and staff managers at a Lancaster (Pa.) meeting how the corporation will reshape itself when he takes over as chairman on Feb. 1.

Shrinkage. Instead of doing business through five operating companies, Westinghouse is shrinking back to three, each headed by a president who serves on a top, five-man management committee. The change eliminates the Consumer Products Co., already decimated by the pending sale of Westinghouse's $600-million-a-year major appliances business to White Consolidated Industries. Other consumer lines are being absorbed by two of the remaining companies—Industry Products under Douglas D. Danforth, 52, and Public Systems, headed by Thomas J. Murrin,

45. Public Systems also gets five business chunks from the old Broadcasting, Learning & Leisure Time Co., which is reduced to subsidiary status under Chairman Donald H. McGannon and contains only the money-making Group W television and radio stations. The third company, Power Systems, headed by Gordon C. Hurlbert, 50, continues as at present.

Replacing an old, seven-man policy committee, the five-man management committee will meet more often and make "more coordinated" corporate decisions. The fifth member, along with Kirby, Hurlbert, Danforth, and Murrin, is Marshall K. Evans, 57, vice-chairman and chief of staff. Faster decision-making at the top supposedly will be aided by the most interesting facet of the reorganization: the grouping of Westinghouse's 120 divisions into 37 "basic business units," each headed by a general manager. The divisions will remain profit centers, but "strategic planning" decisions on market growth and capital expansion will be coordinated at the business unit level instead of in the divisions. "We had gone too far in the decentralization to divisional profit centers and had fragmented several businesses that weren't fragmentable," says Evans.

The model for this approach is the "strategic business unit" plan adopted in 1970 by GE, which is divided into 42 SBUs. Westinghouse had been grouping its divisions by markets for some years, but now it has taken the final step to the unit concept. "We learned a helluva lot from GE," says Evans. "We struggled like mad to find something better than GE has, but theirs is as good as there is. Ours is not a copy of GE's, but we're coming out at the same place."

Other changes. In a further effort to make the new units cost-accountable, Westinghouse is reassigning corporate technical staff to the unit level. This will result in a "significant reduction" in corporate staff, Evans says.

Whether these and other changes will reverse the erosion of profits that had taken place over the last two years remains to be seen. The decline occurred in large part because the company moved too fast into service businesses unrelated to electrical equipment manufacturing and nuclear power. In recent months, in addition to the huge appliance business sale—which awaits Jus-

tice Dept. approval—Westinghouse has disposed of $100-million worth of business that had lost a total of $59-million in 1973. Included are a mail order company, water pollution control equipment operations, military and low-income housing, and a French elevator company. The divestiture program, now completed, will require write-offs of $66-million on 1974 income. But, says Evans, "we've managed to shoot all the dogs."

Business Week, Feb. 3, 1975

Reprinted from the Feb. 3,1975, *Business Week* by special permission. Copyright © 1975 by McGraw-Hill, Inc.

Considering these two sectors illustrates, however, how organizational types can vary. There are obviously many other influences as well. In this book we want to acquaint the student with the most important factors contributing to organizational structure and the process of management.

In chapter 7 we will review the organizational subsystems and their interactions with environmental forces. We will also discuss in detail each of the four basic organizational types—the bureaucratic organization, the dynamic organization, the market-dominated mixed organization, and the technologically-dominated mixed organization.

Discussion Questions

1. What is the production subsystem in a restaurant? The boundary-spanning subsystem?

2. How can the different levels of technological environmental volatility affect the reactions of two people similarly trained, but in different conditions—for example, an electrical engineer in a stable technology firm and one in a volatile technology.

3. What particular organizational environment is currently volatile for the automotive industry? Fast-food franchisers? Hospitals?

4. Is it easy for you to visualize how a unit may perform boundary-spanning functions at one time, production another, and maintenance functions another time?

Chapter 7
Organization Structural Alternatives: Adapting to the Environment

In chapter 6 we stated that an organization can be viewed as a system composed of interrelated subsystems, (production, boundary-spanning, adaptive, maintenance, and managerial). The structure of an organization (the relationship between subsystems) is influenced by the demands placed on it by its relevant environment. An organization's market and technology are especially influential environmental factors in the shaping of its structure.

Market and technological factors may take on characteristics ranging from a high degree of stability (infrequent change and thus high predictability) to high levels of volatility (frequent change and thus high unpredictability or uncertainty). Figure 7.1 summarizes the environmental/organization relationship described in chapter 6 (and shown in fig. 6.6). The subsystems which are in all four organizational types will take on different characteristics and relate to each other differently in each of the types of organization. The variations are largely determined by the external environment.

In this chapter we will describe how the five subsystems can be expected to vary within each organizational type. Of course these variances can only be expressed as theoretical, general tendencies, not as hard-and-fast rules. Nevertheless, organizations of all types do exhibit certain general structures and characteristics, depending upon their environment. Similarities and differences in structure and characteristics from organization to organization reflect adaptation to the forces and problems presented by their environments.

The hierarchical and flexible organizations represent extreme ends of a continuum of types. For both of these organizations, the different environments are relatively fixed. For the former, the market and technological sectors are stable; for the latter, they are both volatile. Many organizations interact with environments which have both stable and volatile characteristics. We call organizations which have at least one major subsystem interacting with a stable environment and another interacting with a volatile environment "mixed-form" organizations.

The mixed-form type of organization is probably more prevalent than either the hierarchical or flexible types.

There are two mixed types in our analytical framework. The first, called *technology-dominated mixed* (TD-mixed), has a relatively stable market and a volatile technology. The second, the *market-dominated mixed* (MD-mixed), has a stable technology and a volatile market.

FIGURE 7.1 Environment Characteristics And Organization Types

Characteristics of		
Market	**Technology**	**Organization Form**
Stable	Stable	Hierarchical, Bureaucratic
Stable	Volatile	Technologically-dominated (TD) Mixed
Volatile	Stable	Market-dominated (MD) Mixed
Volatile	Volatile	Flexible, Dynamic

There are two points that are important in considering these two types of mixed organizations. The first has to do with a major managerial problem: How can you develop a strategy for integrating the operations of two organizational components which take on very different structural characteristics because they interact with different environments? This particular problem is illustrated in item 7.1 which describes the managerial problems of Gulf & Western Industries.

The second has to do with power and influence over policy and strategy. As a general rule, the organizational sector which interacts with the most volatile, or uncertain, sector of the environment will exert the greatest influence in determining what the policy, strategy, and general direction of the total organization will be. It is for that reason that we have classified organizations as market-dominated or technology-dominated according to which subsystem of the organization faces a volatile environment.

The Hierarchical, Bureaucratic Organization

The hierarchical form of organization is often called a "bureaucracy," a label that immediately conjures up a vision of a vast, impersonal organization with an overriding emphasis on standardized procedures and consequent "red tape" and very little if any responsiveness to the problems of its staff and customers. Those who have studied bureaucracies agree that this is a valid criticism (Merton, 1957). On the other hand, many management researchers have found through their studies that the hierarchical form of organization is the most appropriate form of organizational adaptation when the environment is highly stable (Burns and Stalker, 1961). We can thus expect the hierarchical form to emerge whenever the market and the technology are stable and predictable. This is the case, for example, for many government agencies. The changes in technology for them are few, the markets served are fairly well-defined, and there is an absence of competition in the provision of services. The same is true for similar organizations, such as banks and insurance companies, or for, say, companies in the container industry which produce bottles and cans and which have had a very stable technology and market for a number of years. These organizations tend to be structured in the bureaucratic—that is, hierarchical —form.

ITEM 7.1   A Mixed Organization

Bluhdorn the Raider as Elder Statesman

Charles G. Bluhdorn, the 48-year-old chairman and chief executive officer of Gulf & Western Industries, Inc., is no longer the brash corporate raider of the 1960s who took over more than 100 companies in building G&W. The company's acquisitions phase is pretty much over and Bluhdorn's role today is almost that of elder statesman, watching over the management of his $2.3-billion conglomerate.

Moreover, G&W seems to be vindicating the conglomerate theory that diversification would smooth out cyclical swings in earnings. The movies *Love Story* and *The Godfather*, produced by G&W's subsidiary Paramount Pictures, pumped up earnings in 1972 and 1973. Last year, income from films and financial services trailed off, but soaring prices for sugar (South Puerto Rico Sugar Co.), zinc (New Jersey Zinc Co.) and paper (Brown Co.) saved the day. G&W

earned $100-million in its fiscal 1974, ended last July 31, a 13% increase over 1973, the third consective year of record profits.

It is not clear that the Vienna-born Bluhdorn has a winner even now. With the gloomy economic outlook for the year ahead, and with G&W's high leverage ($1.95 in debt per $1 of equity) and its massive interest costs, the company will require superior management as well as diversification to produce a fourth record year. Bluhdorn, for one, believes G&W is in good shape to accomplish this because of the emphasis the company has been giving to operating management. But few on Wall Street share Bluhdorn's optimism. . . . Most of all, they wonder if Bluhdorn the raider has really become Bluhdorn the skillful corporate manager.

Big as G&W has become, it is still very much a creature of the man who put the pieces together. Although Bluhdorn has given up trying to run the various operations himself, he remains the ultimate arbiter. "Bluhdorn is the imagination and the energy of the company," says John Duncan, former president and current chairman of the executive committee. "He is very much the player-coach. He penetrates deeply into that organization."

The coach. From his office on the 42nd floor of the G&W building in Manhattan, Bluhdorn filters his plays through three key aides. David N. Judelson, 45, president and chief operating officer, supposedly supervises the company's eight operating groups and actually does keep up with at least five of them. Don F. Gaston, 39, a certified public accountant from Nacogdoches, Tex., is executive vice-president and Bluhdorn's chief financial man. He also oversees the financial services group, which is involved in making direct installment and commercial loans and underwriting insurance. And because of his Texas background, Gaston keeps tabs on G&W's Automotive Replacement Parts Group in Houston. Martin S. Davis, 47, also executive vice-president, is a former theatrical press agent at Paramount who handles the administrative staff, some of which also reports to Gaston and Judelson.

Indeed, it is a loose management structure that could only work among long-time friends. Judelson, an engineer, has been with G&W for 16 of its 18 years. Gaston has been there for 12. It is also a harsh system, and the manager who does not produce can find himself out in a hurry. For all that, it is a more formal system, with greater stress on corporate staff work, than might have been expected.

The empire. The test in 1975 will be whether the structure can keep so many diverse elements working together in a difficult economic climate. The list of G&W subsidiaries runs nine full pages in its 10K report, in businesses as remote from one another as sugar, zinc, auto equipment, consumer finance, and motion pictures. All these units are lumped into the eight semi-autonomous operating groups: manufacturing, leisure-time, natural resources, food and agricultural products, paper and building products, and consumer products, plus financial services, and automotive replacement parts.

Top management, says Judelson, tries to strike a balance "between corporate autocracy and corporate surrender." Each unit has to compete for funds against the others, as well as against Bluhdorn's investment of G&W's cash in the stock market. The corporate staff evaluates each group's budget, Bluhdorn and his chief aides determine who gets the money for capital expenditures and acquisitions, and the operating group executives run their businesses.

G&W's corporate staff of approximately 225 not only helps the subsidiaries prepare their annual business plan, which it then monitors, but also acts as internal consultant on marketing, data processing, and cost control.

The company, in addition, has developed other controls. Each of the eight group executives must give Judelson a "flash forecast" at the middle of each month on how closely he is meeting his business goals for that month, and the company does unannounced internal audits on about half of G&W's units each year. Also, the company has a dual system of financial reporting, which means that each group controller reports to the corporate controller as well as to his own chief executive.

With this arrangement, Bluhdorn and his key executives feel confident in their ability to decide where to invest the corporate cash. The bulk of $120-million capital budget in each of the last two years has gone to New Jersey Zinc,

Brown, and South Puerto Rico Sugar, all riding the crest of the high prices in commodities, and the manufacturing group, benefitting from the boom in capital goods.

Flops and egos. Bluhdorn's style is to manage by letting others run things as long as they produce. The six groups with record earnings last year were given considerable autonomy. But there were management shakeups in both the leisure-time movie group, where pretax income dropped from $38.7-million in fiscal 1973 to $18.7-million in 1974, and financial services, where the drop was from $48-million to $20-million.

Bluhdorn's methods are plainly not to everyone's liking at G&W, and he has lost some of the management talent that came with companies he acquired. Some did not like G&W's corporate staff. "The staff used to interfere with my operating people," a former Brown Co. executive explains. "Why, I had to throw a couple of them out of my office one time so I could get to work." Another manager, who left the E. W. Bliss Co. in the manufacturing group, complains: "The staff people used to come in and try to change things they knew nothing about just so they could look like heros in New York." Both men now have top jobs at other companies.

Business Week, Jan. 20, 1975

Reprinted from the Jan. 20, 1975, *Business Week* by special permission. Copyright © 1975 by McGraw-Hill, Inc.

Production Subsystems

Tasks in the hierarchical organization's production subsystem (the subsystem whose activities are primarily directed at creating the output of the organization) are characterized by a relatively high degree of repetitiveness. That is, a standard way of performing tasks is established and routinized and all organizational members assigned those tasks must perform them the prescribed way. Tasks are repetitive in that organizational members are usually assigned only a few tasks and they perform these over and over again during the work day. The assembly-line worker is, of course, a good example of one who has such tasks, but white-collar workers in banks, insurance companies, and government agencies similarly follow a routine. This is so because most customers require basically the same kind of service and it is easy to standardize procedures for providing it.

Another aspect of bureaucracy is the extreme division of labor in many such organizations. Since the work activities can be standardized, they can be reduced to relatively small work units. This condition often leads to the case where each employee has only limited knowledge of the total situation.

The low level of worker skill required in the hierarchical form can lead to a high level of dependence of the individual on the organization. It is easy to replace workers, since low skill levels mean that probably a large number of people are available who can perform the work, and the individual who does the work has little control over how he produces or what he does. This lack of job security may give rise to a need for some protective mechanism. In bureaucratic organizations there is a need for some sort of external agent—such as a union or the civil service system—to provide a degree of job security against arbitrary actions of managers.

Boundary-spanning Subsystems

The two major boundary-spanning activities are, first, a mechanism which distributes the product and/or service and, second, the procurement mechanisms that secure the raw materials or the resources required to produce the product or service.

Marketing and Distribution. Because the market for the hierarchical organization is relatively unchanging, it is likely that the channels of distribution—those organizations through which the product or service flows to the final user—will be fairly well defined and standardized. New distribution channels will arise only if current methods of distribution become extremely inefficient. It is also likely that the organization will have a great deal of influence over the distribution mechanism. The automobile industry, for instance, strongly controls its dealers, as do steel manufacturers and petroleum firms.

In some organizations, such as banks and certain government agencies (such as employment services), the distribution system is simple because the customers come to the production system. The marketing approach of a firm of this type will base its efforts primarily on pricing strategies and attempts to increase the effectiveness of distribution. It is likely that the products manufactured or the services of organizations in an industry characterized by hierarchical organizations will be fairly similar in terms of function and use. Therefore, a consumer may use any one of a large number of products from different firms to obtain the kind of satisfaction he needs. This means that a marketing strategy might be based on pricing. That is, the firm which can give the best price can obtain a competitive advantage.

Product differentiation in such firms will be largely through advertising. Witness the automobile industry. A General Motors' product performs the same functions and has the same use as a Chrysler product. It is the "image" of the car that is important. The "better" car is better not because it is a substantially different product, but because it is perceived by the consumer as a different product.

The Procurement Function. In a stable environment there are likely to be well-developed and well-defined sources for inputs. In large industries, such as the auto industry, firms may have captive suppliers. A captive supplier is a firm which sells a large portion of its product to just one other firm. It depends primarily upon one customer for the bulk of its business. This gives the customer the capacity to influence such things as price and production techniques to such an extent that the supplier may well be considered as a subsidiary.

When there is a highly repetitive production subsystem with well-defined sources of supply, it is possible to deal with the boundary-spanning activities so as to minimize the production cost. Repetitive production subsystems operate most efficiently when they can function at a fairly level rate. Since even in a stable market and with a stable technology there are minor fluctuations, a level rate of production activities may be sustained by maintaining inventories of both raw materials and finished goods (the buffering that cushions variations in demand). Thompson (1967) points out that:

> Buffering of an unsteady environment obviously brings considerable advantages to the technical core, but it does so with costs to the organization. A classic problem in connection with the buffering is how to maintain inventories, input or output, sufficient to meet all needs without incurring obsolesence as needs change . . . .

> Thus while a fully buffered technological core would enjoy the conditions for maximum technical rationality, organizational rationality may call for compromises between conditions for maximum technical efficiency and the energy required for buffering operations.

Other Boundary-spanning Functions.   Other activities can also bring resources into the organization. Recruiting by the personnel department, for example, is a boundary-spanning activity. The personnel department must go beyond its boundaries to acquire the human inputs required to maintain a viable organization over time—it must find workers. The recruiting process may legitimately be regarded as a boundary-spanning activity, but the other responsibilities of the personnel department, such as the implementation of performance evaluation and compensation (programs designed to stabilize or obtain desired performance), belong in the maintenance subsystem.

Adaptive Subsystems

The adaptive subsystems sense the nature of the environment in which the organization operates. When operating in a stable environment, they will be relatively simple in structure, since interpreting the environment is relatively easy; that is, there will be set rules for interpreting changes in the environment because the experience of the organization will be such that it has learned what parts of the environment it should monitor. It will have a fairly good information base to be used in making decisions. An organization operating in a stable environment may be able to use standard census data, for example, or other similar market research information as a basis for deciding how to adjust internally. If this information is generally available, and if we know what it is, then collecting it can be done fairly easily. There will be no need to design elaborate research studies to examine otherwise incomprehensible market events (since there will be none), or for individuals to make subjective judgments about what is happening in the external environment (since what is happening is objectively known).

In hierarchical organizations, then, fairly simple ways of adapting to changes in the environment will emerge. For instance, management might decide on the basis of experience, as well as because of cost studies, that a sales reduction of 3 percent requires a work force reduction in Plant X of 10 percent, 3 percent in Plant Y, and the elimination of all overtime in other plants. In short, it is possible to develop a fairly systematic procedure which can be implemented in a simple way to deal with changes in the environment.

The stability of the environment, with its generally attendant high predictive accuracy, facilitates long-range planning. Long-term commitments of resources may be made with a great deal more certainty than in less stable environments, in turn facilitating the acquisition of the required capital at costs lower than where more risk is involved. The more stable the environment, the more likely that the firm will be able to make use of borrowed sources of capital rather than equity (internal) capital. There will be less need for investors to assume high levels of risk, and the organization can make long-term commitments to pay for the use of the borrowed capital.

Research and development and engineering is an important adaptive subsystem usually concerned with attempting to assess changes in technology which may alter the production subsystem of the organization. However, since by definition technological changes are relatively minimal in an organization that is in a stable environment, engineering and research and development activities in such a situation are more likely to focus on applications engineering than on advancing the science or state of the art. Thus, the job of the engineer in the stable organization will be more concerned with product improvement within the existing technology than with trying to develop a new product. The engineer will be concerned primarily with internal cost reductions to increase production efficiencies. One of the few ways to obtain increased return on investment in such an organization will be through cost reduction, because market potential is relatively limited, precluding substantial sales increases.

Maintenance Subsystems

Maintenance subsystems in a hierarchical organization will be fairly stable. For control purposes they will chiefly use historically-developed information that has achieved organizational credibility. For instance, fairly standardized auditing and budgeting procedures will collect and examine information which has come to be regarded, within the organization, as an acceptable performance measurement. Even in organizations in which no measures of profitability are available, costs which have been historically associated with sets of activities will come to be regarded as acceptable measures.

The focus of the maintenance subsystems will be on measuring performance, and employees in these activities will become extremely involved with performing their function, perhaps at the expense of not placing proper emphasis on the achievement of objectives. This is called "the inversion of means and ends." The purpose of the maintenance subsystem is to increase internal effectiveness, which means they are support systems; they should provide benefits to the organization, not cause problems. This, however, is not generally the situation when the auditor, the personnel executive, or the quality control manager argues insistently that his field of specialization must be performed at a high level of proficiency. Thus, auditors who sometimes audit for auditing's sake, or personnel executives who collect data for no other reason than that it is a "common" personnel practice, are not aiding anything other than their own status.

In a hierarchical organization, employees in maintenance activities will be extensively involved in performance evaluation, especially of managers. Since there will be a great deal of cost and other performance information available, it will be easy for someone to sit in judgment on the "numbers" which are used as performance measures. Having this kind of information gives a department—say personnel—a great deal of power, and its power can have a significant effect on decisions made in other parts of the firm. Auditing and budgeting units have the same potential power. When information is centralized and controlled, those who have it are extremely influential. Since information is localized in maintenance subsystems, these subsystems have a great deal of organization influence.

Since the production subsystem is highly repetitive and the work is divided into small activity units, it is likely that personnel testing may be a very effective means of selection. That is, as mentioned earlier, in a stable organization with jobs having lower skill requirements than in other types of organizations, a larger labor pool is available. Thus, from a large number of workers it may be a great deal more effective to screen them with some sort of performance test than attempt to make subjective evaluations of their abilities, or to test them later when they get on the job.

High morale and motivation are especially difficult to maintain when the work is routine, repetitive, or programmed. Most of the research on this topic indicates that job satisfaction and job involvement decrease as job complexity and job autonomy decrease. At the level of rank-and-file workers in the hierarchical or bureaucratic organization, boredom and alienation have been found to be higher for assembly-line workers than for workers with less structured jobs (Blauner, 1964). Boredom, of course, means the person wants a change in activity. Work alienation is a feeling that work is meaningless, or lacks significance. In addition, workers may have a feeling of isolation, of not feeling a sense of identity with the organization and what it does, and a feeling of powerlessness—helpless and controlled by various forces in the organization. Such feelings of boredom and alienation are associated with high rates of absenteeism and turnover, as well as with grievances and work stoppages. It is a fact, however, that the majority of workers on highly routined and repetitive jobs do not say they are bored or dissatisfied with their jobs (Kornhauser, 1965; Sheppard and Herrick, 1972; Wyatt and Marriot, 1956).

It is true, however, that a greater percentage of them are less satisfied and more bored than workers in other industries where the work is less routine and repetitive (Kornhauser, 1965; Wyatt and Marriott, 1956). Thus, at least most individuals in the bureaucratic organization seem to adjust to the organization's work demands. Those who cannot adjust, leave. Furthermore, some studies show that most employees in repetitive programmed jobs will not choose more complex jobs when given the opportunity to do so (Kilbridge, 1960). It is quite possible that work which demands little of the job holder attracts individuals who, because of low self-esteem or some other factor, prefer jobs of this type.

Managerial Subsystems

In a hierarchical organization, the managerial subsystem will be characterized by a high degree of centralized control at the top administrative level. The nature of the information, in organizations of this type, is such that it can be quickly collected and transmitted to the higher levels, so that decisions can be made there to change operations at lower levels without requiring a great deal of involvement of managers at those levels. Thus, decisions are made in large part by administrative management.

There will be a high degree of fairly close control and monitoring of operations, and this control will be centralized in the hands of a relatively small number of people. The amount of discretion that lower-level managers have is likely to be relatively small.

The bureaucratic organization is characterized by a fairly rigid hierarchy. Lines of authority and responsibility will be clear. Jobs will be very well-defined. Often problems will be solved by appealing to executives at higher levels, or using the formal hierarchical system as a problem-resolution mechanism.

One of the major problems with which the managerial subsystem must deal is conflict between the "management" group and employees. In industrial organizations this will take the form of union-management bargaining, and in public organizations by the relationship between the administrative staffs and civil service agencies.

People will move to top-level managerial positions in a hierarchical organization after fairly long careers. It is very likely that there will be a relatively small proportion of managers relative to the number of workers, and that the number of positions at higher levels will be relatively small. If this is true, and since the managers at the higher levels make promotion decisions, it is likely that there will be a high degree of similarity in point of view, or homogeneity of attitude, among high-level executives. Promotions will come not only for what one can do, but also because one has the "right" point of view. This can create a special problem when individuals employed by such a firm have high needs for achievement, because they will find promotion opportunities limited, leading them to go elsewhere to satisfy their advancement needs.

In the hierarchical organization, managerial control will be based on power that is a function of the particular position. Generally, there will be fairly well-defined goals. It is unlikely that the organization will be seeking to provide products or services different from its current capability. The major decision about goals in an organization of this type will be how much and when the product or service is to be provided. This will be relatively easy to forecast, since—by definition —the market is stable.

This kind of organization structure has been criticized because of its failure to adapt and cope, but in fact the hierarchical form of organization is precisely the kind which does cope effectively with a stable environment. To have a different organization form would very likely endanger survival. Those who hope for the death of bureaucracy because of its demands on its human resources must consider these points.

The Flexible, Dynamic Organization (organic)

The flexible, dynamic organization is found where the market and technological sectors are highly volatile. We call this form of organization "flexible"; it has been called "organic" by Burns and Stalker (1961). Generally, it is one in which the structure, relationships, and jobs are loosely defined, so that the process of adapting to change is relatively easy. What, then, are the characteristics of the flexible organization's subsystems?

Production Subsystems

The production sybsystem of the flexible organization is composed primarily of general-purpose equipment or technology. Essentially, it is job-shop oriented. The various production elements will be rearranged, when necessary, in order to perform the particular kinds of activities necessary to provide the required outputs as the market or the technology changes, and thus the production subsystem itself will be in a fairly constant state of change. The sequencing of operations will vary from project to project so that the development of routine, repetitive production procedures is relatively difficult, if not impossible. Thompson (1967) describes this as intensive technology, one where a variety of

> techniques is drawn upon in order to achieve a change in some specific object; but the selection, combination, and order of application are determined by feedback from the object itself. When the object is human, this intensive technology is regarded as "therapeutic," but the same technical logic is found also in the construction industry . . . and in research where the objects of concern are nonhuman. . . .
>
> The intensive technology is a custom technology. Its successful employment rests in part on the availability of all the capacities potentially needed, but equally on the appropriate custom combina-

tion of selected capacities as required by the individual case or project.

Boundary-spanning Subsystems

The method of getting the product to customers will vary from customer to customer, and channels of distribution will be relatively unstructured and will change from time to time. This means, essentially, that the organization will probably have to handle its marketing by itself. It cannot transfer this function easily to other jobbers, or develop a channel of distribution similar to that which distributes, say, automobiles or groceries. Since the distribution function cannot be routinized, highly skilled individuals in both the technical and marketing functions will be needed.

Those involved with the procurement function will also need to be highly skilled in finding different types of raw materials and resources, because both the level and type of raw material inputs will change from time to time. This means that those concerned with resource acquisition will need to keep in close touch with suppliers, and they will have to have knowledge of methods of financing purchases.

Adaptive Subsystems

Adaptive subsystem activities in the flexible organization are extremely important. They will be performed by individuals in marketing and distribution functions and procurement, as well as in engineering and research development. Individuals in the adaptive subsystems must be highly skilled at interpreting the environment. Whereas in the hierarchical form there are fairly well-defined cues which trigger internal organizational adjustments, in the flexible organization the information which might cue an internal change in the subsystem will vary from time to time and will probably occur in a random fashion. Thus, individual skill becomes essential in making some assessment as to the nature of the organization change, since it is practically impossible to specify in advance what specific aspect of the environment must be monitored. The relevant aspect may change from time to time, making the ability to read it a very individualized skill. Item 7.2 describes the nature of change in the role of purchasing agent. He is performing both an adaptive and a boundary-spanning activity. As raw material costs increase and the sources of supply become more limited, his role must take on more significance in the survival of the organization.

This same kind of clinical, analytical skill is required of those who must determine how to restructure the organization in response to external changes. In the hierarchical form of organization, a minor change in one of the external indicators may trigger a specific type of internal change. In the flexible organization, however, the process of adjustment and the resulting set of relationships will nearly always vary. This variation will be a function of different sets of circumstances and, thus, it will differ according to the circumstances. This means that the individuals in the adaptive subsystem in a flexible organization will be very influential in decision making.

Marketing activities will usually take the form of both extensive market research and a clinical subjective assessment of what the data mean. In research and development, the adaptive processes will likely be more toward the side of pure, rather than applied research.

Members performing adaptive activities must, of necessity, continually update their skills and abilities to maintain them at a high level. In order to maintain high individual skills in these critical areas, the organization may revert to a strategy of hiring individuals with the required capability, rather than engage itself in a training function. And since, by definition, these skills may be rapidly changing, there may be a fairly high level of turnover among those involved in the adaptive processes.

ITEM 7.2   Boundary-spanning and Adaptive Activities

The Purchasing Agent Gains More Clout

After years of corporate obscurity, the purchasing agent suddenly is moving into management's top ranks. First it was shortages that propelled him into the spotlight. Now it may be excessive inventories. Either way, the purchasing man today is likely to be juggling a lot of new duties under the catch-all title of "materials manager" and to be poking into practically every aspect of business operations, from new products to capital spending.

"In this suddenly .mad world," says David K. Barnes, vice-president and general manager of Du Pont's new Energy & Materials Dept., "corporate management quickly rediscovered the purchasing function and—at least in our case—came to the conclusion that planning to achieve furture supply needs and executing those plans well was going to be a major factor in determining future earnings."

Until about two years ago, purchasing

was being steadily decentralized along with other corporate operations. Then the acute shortages suddenly began showing up, and companies discovered they needed all the buying clout they could muster. "Companies are realizing they've lost leverage through decentralized purchasing," says William A. Bales, director of corporate purchasing at Quaker Oats Co. in Chicago.

Evolving strategy. Now purchasing functions are being pulled together again, but for many corporations, the change has been evolutionary. Norris Industries, Inc., in Los Angeles, for example, began by buying fuel centrally during the crunch and then started purchasing steel and other commodities the same way. At Dymo Industries, Inc., a San Francisco-based manufacturer of embossing and coding equipment, all 18 decentralized purchasing managers—even those overseas—were enlisted into a multinational mutual assistance pact. "We found some smaller divisions didn't have purchasing clout," admits Claude L. Ganz, president and chief executive officer.

Broader role. Centralized purchasing has led to broader responsibility for procurement managers. Not only are they looking for the best buy today, they increasingly are making sure there are supplies for the future. That means they participate in top-level discussions about acquisitions, development of raw materials sources, research on substitute materials, and capital expenditures.

Du Pont, for example, has had centralized purchasing since 1944, but the Energy & Materials Dept., formed this year, not only buys all raw materials, supplies, and equipment for the company worldwide, but also plans for long-term procurement of energy, conducts exploration for minerals and petroleum, plans development of alternate energy sources, and recommends investments in mineral resources, where necessary, to assure supplies.

New status. Such innovative methods are requiring more and more of purchasing or materials managers, and their status is shooting up. At Xerox, where 75% of the manufactured cost of the typical product is in materials, the job of Gaylord Powell, director of materials, did not even exist prior to last year. Now he reports directly to Robert M. Pippitt, senior vice-president. At Gillette, Jenal reports directly to William Salatich, president of Gillette North America. Purchasing jobs have been elevated to the vice-presidential level at dozens of major corporations.

Increasingly, top management recognizes that a job that affects more than half of the sales dollar should command a higher level of training and compensation. As a result, more and more companies are recruiting talent from business schools for purchasing jobs. Two years ago Rockwell began hiring two to four MBAs each year for purchasing, and Xerox is bringing MBAs directly into its buying ranks for 1975.

Business Week, Jan. 13, 1975

Since the cost of developing adaptive skills is usually too high for an organization to bear, individuals who have acquired these skills on their own will be recruited. This means that those who come to an organization and function in an adaptive capacity are likely to be more highly trained or more highly skilled than those performing other functions. This will have important implications for the levels of compensation in organizations. In the flexible organization, individuals are as likely to be paid for the level of education and training they bring to the job as for the level of importance of their job within the organization.

Capital acquisition in a firm of this sort is difficult, since there is high risk involved. With a great degree of fluctuation in an environment that is highly unpredictable, investors are less willing to take the long-term risk of lending capital for a fixed return. With the high risk that might go along with the flexible organization, the capital structure will be weighted toward equity or self-generated investments, which would provide great potential gain attendant with the high risk.

Maintenance Subsystems

In flexible organizations, the utility of historical data for control purposes is minimal, since there may be little history to go by. Therefore, cost standards used to evaluate projects will come from projected estimates. This means that control and evaluation of performance will be much more likely to be subjective than to be based on "objective" performance measures. In flexible organizations it is likely that "end results" will be less frequently used for assessment than in bureaucratic organizations, and there will be stronger focus on the manner in which individuals go about performing their work.

The control function will reside in either the person with expertise in a particular area or the person with the greatest financial interest. The expert will have great influence simply because of his capabilities. He is the one who knows the most about a particular activity. If expertise is the predominant power base, the influence pattern will shift from time to time, depending upon the nature of the project or activity and who is the house expert at a particular point in time. When influence derives from the level of financial interest, this simply means that the owner, or the major stockholder, makes the decisions. In this case, the organization will be an extension of that person's interests.

Personnel in flexible organizations are likely to have a short-range commitment to the organization. Their focus will be on their area of professional expertise or on their self-interest in promotion and advancement, since in a flexible organization there may be relatively few long-term activities to provide a basis for lengthy tenure. Individuals will be brought into the organization when they are required. When their services are no longer needed they may be relieved of responsibility, or they may move on voluntarily. This may make it undesirable and, from an individual point of view, unwise to be highly committed to the organization as a place to work.

This uncertainty may not pose a particular problem for the individual or for the organization. It is likely that people who accept employment in flexible organizations have learned that relatively rapid movement is part of the game. As in the case of the aerospace industry, engineers typically move from firm to firm as the major contracts move. Professionals who work in organizations may be willing to exercise their skills in any number of organizations so long as they are able to do what they have been trained to do and what they believe to be important.

Managerial Subsystems

The managerial subsystem in a flexible organization will be relatively less structured than in other forms of organizations. Essentially, there will be few policy guidelines to use in the decision-making process, because the variability of the environment will preclude well-defined, set policies, over time. Guidelines must be consistently changed to meet the changing requirements.

The organization structure will be flexible, one where individuals move from project to project as the need for their skills arise, with the authority structure different for each project. Individuals will move from superior to superior, depending upon what needs to be done. Teams will be composed of individuals who will work on particular projects. When the project is completed, the individuals on a team may move to different teams. If their skills are no longer required in the organization, they may be terminated either willingly or unwillingly. This mobility can cause problems unless the individual has a capacity to tolerate uncertainty, ambiguity, and role conflict.

In a flexible organization, the individual may not have the luxury of reporting to one superior. Over a period of time, he may report to several, and he will probably be placed in situations where he is faced with conflicting demands, and certainly with different leadership styles. This may be good or bad for the individual. On the one hand, it allows him to learn and grow from varied experience. On the other hand, it precludes the opportunity to build long-term relationships with a superior, which may be important for some individuals both from a personal viewpoint as well as from the standpoint of organizational advancement.

Flexible organizations, then, operate in a highly dynamic environment. It is likely that they will be relatively small compared with the size of hierarchical forms. This smallness, in and of itself, facilitates adaptability to the environment. As an organization grows, however, it begins to build-in some degree of procedural rigidity and hierarchy. This may mitigate against effective adaptation to a changing environment.

It is likely that flexible organizations will, when possible, move to a more stable sector. That is, if at all possible, they will try to increase the degree of certainty in which they operate. This is desirable in that it facilitates and eases the processes of planning and control. If it can make such a move, the organization will be able to make long-term commitments to its members, perhaps facilitating recruitment, since persons will be willing to join an organization where they can make a "career."

This last point may be an important one, especially when individuals have a high degree of anxiety about their careers. While a person might have a great deal of confidence in his own skills and abilities as a professional, the uncertainty of where he will be working can pose a problem. This uncertainty is probably related to lower levels of commitment to the organization, which in turn would make the problem of obtaining high levels of compliance from individuals extremely difficult.

Project Management.   The kind of managerial subsystem in the flexible organization, the one we have just described, is called *project management*. Project management is an important organization tool, and widely used, warranting some added discussion. When a job can be broken down into a number of fairly small segments, and when the activity will be required for a fairly long time period, then the organization can hire people to do these more narrow jobs. These jobs stay the same; they are repetitive. A manager may supervise, say, a production unit where such a situation exists. However, in the flexible organization, the nature of the work changes when the environment changes. Therefore, we can expect to see "projects" change. A project is a series of related activities required to achieve a work outcome, but one characteristic is that it may have a discrete completion time. For example, the lunar landing of U.S. astronauts was the end of a particular space project. Once the astronauts returned and the data was analyzed, space workers were shifted to another project.

Project management recognizes this need to shift both physical and human resources. Individuals are assigned to temporary, ad hoc, work teams, though they may exist for extended time periods. Still, there is a planned termination date to which planning and control are keyed in this type of organization. An important determinant of the composition of a project group is the particular configuration of skills required on the project. As skill configurations change for each project, so will the composition of the team members.

Technology-dominated Mixed Organizations

In technology-dominated mixed organizations, the major threat to survival and effectiveness stems from uncertainty in the technological environment. The market sector of the environment of these organizations is relatively stable. Scientific breakthroughs, new production technology, or other new concepts can provide their creator or early adopter with a significant competitive advantage. Therefore, it is important to monitor the technological sector of the environment carefully and make changes in the system when necessary.

The technology-dominated mixed organization, like its market-dominated counterpart, will have one major part of its structure which will take on hierarchical characteristics, with some degree of rigidity, and another part which will be less tightly structured. This combination presents the problem of achieving good relationships between these two parts of the organization. Attempting to resolve conflicts between them by using the position authority of higher management levels is likely to be ineffective, since it is improbable that individuals in the managerial hierarchy or the marketing sector will have a level of technical expertise as high as those in the technical sector or that is acceptable to the latter. The professionals, that is, are likely to react negatively to administrative decisions. (These integration problems are examined extensively in chap. 16.)

Organizational members in the stable market sector are likely to be either externally-oriented (seek satisfactions away from work and the job) or organizationally-oriented (highly committed to the organization and its values), as opposed to the professional orientation (extremely committed to the work that one does) of those in the volatile, technical sectors. This difference will result in different reactions to pressures from the maintenance system seeking to impose regularity through standardized procedures and methods. Item 7.3 describes some of problems of this type faced by Polaroid, a company that has many of the characteristics of the TD-mixed firm.

Production Subsystems

The production subsystem in a TD-mixed organization will likely use an intensive type of technology in which human beings choose from a variety of possible procedures that one which is most appropriate in a given situation. It is unlikely that we would find assembly-line technology in this type of environmental setting. Equipment would have unpredictable life, making investment in special-purpose technology or machinery highly risky. The tendency would be to use, where possible, general-purpose processes to increase the productive life expectancy.

Personnel who work in the production subsystem are likely to be highly-skilled craftsmen who have spent relatively long times developing skills on particular types of equipment. They might have done this in apprenticeship programs, or through vocational training. It is also likely that their work requires much attention to detail.

ITEM 7.3   Volatile Technology, Stable Market

The SX-70 Camera and Polaroid

"This was no Boy Scout outing, but an expedition over the Pole," sighs Edwin H. Land, founder and chief executive of Polaroid Corp. That is how he describes the $350-million industrial gamble his company has taken to manufacture and sell its much-publicized SX-70 instant camera. In essence, Polaroid has been transformed on a crash basis from a company basically oriented to research and product assembly into a largely self-sufficient manufacturer of very complex products.

One aim was to reap the higher profits of a fully integrated producer by reducing its dependence on the outside sources. Another was to protect the new technology represented by the SX-70, since Eastman Kodak, a major Polaroid supplier, threatens to become a big competitor in the instant photography market.

Polaroid's corporate transformation has been dogged by costly production problems that have sapped the company's profits and destroyed its glamour as a Wall Street favorite. The production problems have been essentially solved, Polaroid claims. But now the company faces the basic test of generating sufficient sales volume to exploit its costly new manufacturing capacity. As the vital Christmas retail sales season begins, Polaroid's test reaches a critical stage.

Inflated expectations. "What we need now is volume," says I. M. Booth, manager of the company's New Bedford (Mass.) plant that makes negatives for the SX-70. "We have all that capacity staring us in the face." Booth's plea is echoed at other Polaroid plants, some of which now run at less than 50% of capacity. Under Polaroid's "razor-and-blades" philosophy, top priority now is to sell enough cameras to generate steady, long-term demand for film.

Producing the camera and its film involves a complex blend of optics, electronics, and chemistry. The camera automatically produces a finished color photo—the user has only to press the shutter. There is no litter, as with the earlier Polaroid peel-apart film cameras. For

Polaroid the SX-70 is the key to future growth. "They're too much tied to one product and one market, like we used to be," warns the president of a Boston technology company that has recently diversified. Retorts Edwin Land: "At Polaroid, we deliberately choose to have very few products, that only we can make, and to make them very important."

Now 65 and the 15% owner of Polaroid's stock, Land continues to make the fundamental product decisions for the company as chairman and president. Pacing about his book-lined office-laboratory in Cambridge, Mass., cluttered with at least a half-dozen telephones, Land notes that he has vetoed ventures such as 35-mm photography urged on him by other executives, because they were "ordinary, not the extraordinary that we choose." Bill McCune says Land's "essential impatience" and his refusal to heed doomsayers are major reasons for breakthrough projects.

Despite his dominance of new product development, Land insists that there is less of a one-man rule flavor at Polaroid than at most companies, and that Polaroid has managers who will instinctively follow his tradition when he leaves. Says he: "I represent a framework of ideas. The men who have come with us know this framework and have chosen to live with it." As a firm believer in corporate informality, Land scornfully says that "institutionalization is an aspect of a corporate death wish ... a mausoleum drive."

No Cash Bind. But as Polaroid grows bigger, management responsibility is inevitably falling more heavily on others. Day-to-day operations are now handled by a triumvirate, consisting of McCune, 57, Wyman, 44, and Wensberg, 44. Below them, another cadre of managers, many of them in their 30s, but nearly all at least 10-year Polaroid veterans, have taken over more authority at the division level.

One reason for delegating more authority could be that Land underestimated the size and complexity of the SX-70 project. Land demanded too much perfection and too much speed in the development of the new camera.

Business Week, Nov. 30, 1974

Boundary-spanning Subsystems

In the TD-mixed organization, the channels of distribution will be fairly well fixed, or set in place. Products will perhaps change technologically, but they will be sold as they had been before any new developments. For example, item 7.3 describes Polaroid's development of the SX-70 camera. This remarkable new product is sold through camera shops, department stores, and discount stores—as were earlier Land cameras.

If a boundary-spanning unit must be in contact with an outside firm in the technological environment, however, it must be able to change with technology. New sources of supply will be needed as raw material requirements change.

In the early stages of technological change, product pricing will take advantage of the innovation and price will be high. However, if competitors enter the market with similar but lower-priced products, there will be some problems in the rigid marketing section. Customers may be reluctant to buy until there is more price stability. The example of digital watches in item 6.2 describes how retailers are unwilling to purchase and inventory the product until the technology stabilizes.

Adaptive Subsystems

Major policy and strategy influence in a technology-dominated organization comes from those in the technological sectors. In this group, a great reliance will be found on individual skill and ability of a subjective nature in assessing the environment. Research and development activities will be more extensive than applications engineering, thus placing more emphasis on advanced knowledge and skills than on pragmatic application of design.

Market research activities will be fairly simple. They will most probably focus on existing, or easily collectible, data which have become fairly widely accepted indicators to be used in decision making. In this adaptive activity, there will be a need for individuals not necessarily with experience in the firm or industry, but who know how to apply standard research techniques.

Maintenance Subsystems

Maintenance subsystems in TD-mixed organizations face a paradoxical problem. Since pressures are exerted from them for stability and predictability, the market sector will attempt to develop systematic marketing and distribution processes. If they can do so, this will result in a somewhat "bureaucratic" marketing unit. For the organization's technological activities, however, this development of a rigidly structured system may cause problems, since freedom to adjust and react to the changing environment requires that individual discretionary limits must be relatively broad. By their nature, procedures and rules that accompany the bureaucratic structure limit discretion.

For control and evaluation purposes, other problems exist for the maintenance subsystems. For example, because of the stable market, it may be easy to develop a good set of distribution cost estimates. This could result in quantified, objective "cost" estimates against which actual costs can be compared. A manager will therefore be able to measure marketing efficiency with some accuracy. When "objective" data such as these are available, they become the basis for performance evaluations.

Now consider the same performance evaluation problem in the technological sector. At the volatile boundary, the individual has little control over what outside people and organizations do. In addition, since the determination of a need for change, the internal implementation of the change, and the resulting effect on the performance level of the organization may cover a long period of time, it is difficult to develop performance criteria quite as objective as we can for, say, marketing or production costs. Therefore, there will be two obviously different types of criteria used in performance evaluation, one subjective and one objective. This is likely to lead to perceived inequities among organizational members, because no matter which criteria are used in a part of the organization, members may feel that the other type is better.

In personnel selection, emphasis will be on acquiring highly skilled and trained professionals for the technological sector. The level of *organization* commitment of this group will probably be lower than that of those in the more stable sections of the organization, since they will identify to some extent with their professional group. This identification with other professionals outside the company should be of value to the organization, however, since such contacts are a valuable source of ideas.

Managerial Subsystems

The authority structure of the TD-mixed organization will present a varied appearance. For instance, in the marketing sector we would expect to find fairly well-defined job responsibilities, accountability to specific superiors for work, and limited discretion for decisions. Those in this unit will find themselves subjected to standardized rules, policies, and procedures. On the other hand, in the technological sector, there will be more latitude of action. The production subsystem is likely to be caught in the middle, between pressures from research and engineering to adopt newer production methods and the marketing unit's desire to maintain the product relatively as is.

Market-dominated Mixed Organizations

In the market-dominated mixed form organization, the significant policy-influencing group will be from the marketing sector because of the need to stay in close touch with a constantly changing, unpredictable environmental consumer or client group.

Production Subsystems

The type of environment confronting MD-mixed organizations leads to programmed production tasks performed within a stable technology. Skill requirements for those in this system will be moderately low, and job security will probably result from union protection. The performance of the production system will be measured by relatively objective measures of cost. There will be considerable pressure from the marketing segment to change the product to meet changing consumer preferences.

Adaptive Subsystems

The relatively placid condition of the technological external environment calls for little scientific research or development in the MD-mixed organization. Where there are technical functions to perform, they will probably be of an applied nature. Engineers, for instance, though highly trained, will probably not be engaged in research on new projects but rather will spend their time trying, say, to find sources for less costly raw materials.

In the marketing sector, there will be extensive market research devoted to uncovering new markets. More than likely, those performing this function will rely on a clinical assessment, or judgment, of markets. Experience, intuition, and judgment will be more useful in determining what and where markets will be than extensive research efforts using standard market data sets such as population data, income estimates, or traditional buying patterns.

Boundary-spanning Subsystems

In general, changes in a product of an MD-mixed firm will be style or design changes, rather than changes in what the product will do. Therefore, in MD-mixed organization the acquisition of inputs will only be significant when they may directly change the character of the output, or if the market requires a product with different raw material requirements. That is, if market changes require a different type of raw material, then purchasing must seek new sources of supply. For instance, when a dress manufacturer finds that new materials are selling in the market and he must use them in his manufacturing, his purchasing staff will have to seek out various new sources of supply.

Product pricing will be controlled by the marketing subsystem, since it will need latitude and discretion in price setting to market effectively. There will be catering to customer orientations, and those in the marketing staff can be characterized as "promoters" rather than as sales managers.

Maintenance Subsystems

Primary organizational control problems will be found in the marketing segment of the MD-mixed firm and consequently it is difficult to develop internal controls satisfactory to those who perform maintenance functions. The flexible and varied nature of the marketing and distribution system will make collection of historical and relevant cost data difficult, since distribution systems may be changing, and some difficulties are likely to occur as a result of the applied nature of the required technical activities. While engineers and scientists may have been socialized through an education which has taught them to value research activities, their jobs may be concerned more with mundane applications problems. This can lead to disillusionment, dissatisfaction, and attendant problems of keeping staffed adequately. This may be an especially acute problem because of the higher status of the marketing group in the organization.

Managerial Subsystems

A hierarchical type authority structure will prevail in the technical sectors of the market-dominated firm, a more loose authority structure in the marketing and distribution sectors, which will have more individual discretion and freedom in decision making. Control systems to monitor changes in and adapt to the environment will be developed in such a way as to be triggered by decisions made in the marketing sector. It is highly likely that this type of mixed organization will be headed by someone with marketing or sales background.

As in a technologically-dominated firm, there will be problems in relating the stable and dynamic segments of the organization to each other. The well-defined structure of the technical sector may not only pose adjustment problems for the professionals who work in it, but also may present difficulties when it is interrelated to the more flexible organization structure in the marketing sector. Remedies for coping with this integration problem are given in chapter 16.

The Structure-Environment (SE) Model

We have proposed a conceptual scheme for determining what the structure of an organization will look like, given certain environmental factors. The scheme presupposes that the organization type and the way in which its subsystems function will vary with variations in the organization's market and technology situation, but there are other factors which must also be taken into consideration.

First, large organizations, especially conglomerates or multidivisioned companies, may have major divisions in different environments with different uncertainty characteristics. For example, one division of a multidivisioned firm may be in a stable industry, such as steel, while another division may be in the aerospace sector. This disparity creates problems for the parent company. Great care must be taken not to impose a managerial system inconsistent with the characteristics of the environment of the subsidiary units. For example, suppose a group of successful managers of an electronics firm acquires a clothing firm and attempts to impose a managerial structure on it that has worked in electronics. What happens? The system fails miserably in the clothing firm, because managerial strategies are imposed which work in the electronics segment but do not in the clothing segment.

A second consideration is that there is always a tendency for an organization to move toward more stable conditions, just as within most human beings there is a drive toward achieving predictability and regularity. Organizations attempt to structure themselves according to rational principles (Thompson, 1967). As this happens, the organization's growth rate inevitably begins to slow down. And when growth achieves a more deliberate rate, it may be in an organization's interest to change its environmental setting to return to a rapid growth stage. Major increases in sales, for instance, are more likely to occur in a volatile than in a stable environment because of the increased markets for, perhaps, innovation. This problem is extensively examined in chapter 16, where we deal with the changing character of the environment and the organization structure. Some of the strategies are briefly noted here, however.

A change in environmental setting can be brought about if an organization takes certain actions. By engaging in heavy research and development activities, for example, a firm in a stable environment may be able to generate a technological breakthrough which suddenly creates a technologically volatile environment. Or marketing and advertising efforts can conceivably cause enough of a shift in usage for a product so that the market changes in nature and size.

Another possibility, and perhaps a more feasible alternative, would be for a stable firm to engage in acquisitions or mergers. Thus, an automobile manufacturer might acquire an electronics firm. Or, if a particular subunit in an organization has a particular skill not suitable to the general market and technological structure, it may spin off a "division," creating an autonomous unit. Publishing firms, for instance, which produce and market textbooks may spin off a unit to create and market alternative learning devices such as tape cassettes, film strips, computer-assisted learning systems, and so on.

There are, of course, different ways that these four types of organizations should be managed. From this point on, we will consider structure as it relates to strategy—always keeping in mind that what we are discussing are theoretical constructs. While few everyday situations fit the strategies *exactly*, if a manager approaches his problems from a contingency stance, he can develop more effective solutions than if he does not.

Discussion Questions

1. If it is true that bureaucratic organizations are the most appropriate way of adapting to a stable environment, why is there so much criticism of this form?

2. Can two organizations be producing essentially the same product— say food products—and have basically different distribution methods? Why? Why not? Under what conditions would this prevail?

3. "Power is greatest at the volatile boundary of an organization." Why? Comment.

4. What are the reasons for different kinds of power in the bureaucratic and the dynamic organization?

5. Mixed type organizations have units in environments with different volatility characteristics. What type of organization is a pharmaceutical firm? A corner grocery store? A firm which manufactures electronic calculators?

Part IV
Managing
Human Resources

In this section, we consider the things that the executive does in managing people. The focus of attention is on processes which directly affect the way individuals interact, communicate, and influence others. Leadership, for example (chap. 8) is the process of influencing others. In chapter 9, problems of communicating with others are outlined. Chapter 10 explains some of the techniques used to acquire, maintain, and motivate human resources. Chapter 11 describes a broader form of organizational control—that arising from the development and implementation of plans and budgets. These plans must be implemented by others in the organization. In chapter 12, a way to achieve acceptance of plans and decisions, management by objectives, is discussed.

Chapter 8
Leadership

Leadership is the process of influencing others to do what you want them to do. Such a concept may seem simple enough on the surface, but in reality it is often complex. Suppose a foreman asks an employee to work past normal quitting time. The worker agrees. Has the foreman exercised "leadership"? Perhaps, and perhaps not. Maybe the employee needs the extra pay, or perhaps he stays because he knows he is needed, or because he is afraid he will lose his job if he doesn't.

Many things that people do at work—such as following orders, doing what is required of them, working harder than is necessary—cannot be explained in terms of leadership alone. Perhaps, then, we should start a discussion of leadership not by asking, "How does one person influence others?" but by asking, "Why do people comply?"

Why Do People Comply?

A powerful, yet relatively simple concept which can account for a great deal of compliance in organizations is the *psychological contract*. Schein (1970), states the concept of the psychological contract in this way: "The individual has a variety of expectations of the organization and the organization a variety of expectations of him. These expectations not only cover how much work is to be performed for how much pay, but also involve the whole pattern of rights, privileges, and obligation between the worker and organization."

Basically this implies that people in any situation—including that at work—will do many things *because they believe they should*. And for what they do, they expect reciprocation in the form of pay, benefits, and favors.

The terms of the psychological contract are affected by what one has learned and experienced before he arrives in an organization and by what the organization needs. The professional, the organizationalist, and the externalist all, because of their particular values, strike different "bargains" with their work organization (or more specifically,

211

its management). These different organizational types, how they view authority, and why their particular view develops was the theme of chapter 3. As noted there, individuals learn to respond to higher authority throughout their lives as a result of dealing with parents, teachers, and other authority figures. They are not only taught directly, but through films, books, TV shows, and other means which illustrate acquiescence to authority. These socialization experiences contribute to the development of personal values which usually cause the individual to feel that it is "right," under certain circumstances, for those in higher authority to tell him and others what to do. When the individual feels this direction to be right, the authority is said to have "legitimate" power.

In other words, legitimacy of power refers to whether or not the subject of influence believes it is proper for another person to influence him, and thus, legitimacy stems from the internalized values of a person. The organizationalist, for example, believes that many directives from his superior are legitimate. The professional may respond more readily to influences from colleagues. The externalist responds primarily to organization demands so long as they are made during job hours.

The legitimate power of authority figures is not unlimited. As Barnard (1938) has pointed out, organizational members believe that some directives from a leader are legitimate and some are not. Barnard uses the term "zone of indifference," similar to the concept of psychological contract, to define that collection of directives which will be followed without question, since they are clearly legitimate for a superior to make. Directives which fall outside this zone of indifference are considered nonlegitimate by those to whom they are given.

The Boundaries of the Psychological Contract. The psychological contract is not static. It often changes by mutual consent, as when a person is promoted with expectations of more effort for the increased pay, status, and privileges that come with his new position. Sometimes it is changed by pressures from one or the other of the parties, as when a union is able to obtain increased hourly wage rates from management.

So long as the requests, commands, directives, and suggestions fall within the boundaries of the psychological contract, however, there will be a response to them. Take, for example, the salesman whose psychological contract is shown in figure 8.1. In general, he will do without question anything that falls within the *public* boundaries of his contract. The public boundaries encompass those things which he leads others, especially his superior, to believe he will do as part of his job. They are generally-agreed-upon work activities. But they do not represent the effective limits of his bargain. The *real* boundaries for the salesman are broader. He will do *more* than is represented by the "public" zone. The *real* boundaries do, however, define the limits beyond which he will not go.

For tactical reasons, the salesman may wish to have his superior believe that the public boundaries of his psychological contract represent his actual limits. Then when he complies with requests that fall between his public and real boundaries, he will appear to be giving up something. He may do this in order to extract a "favor" at some future date. He has made it appear that he has gone beyond the normal call of duty and thus expects a quid pro quo—a favor—in return for exceeding the normal requirements of his job. Suppose, for example, that in the past he has created the impression that he believes it is his job to give customers the lowest possible price. When his superior asks him to charge the highest possible price and the salesman complies, he may feel that his superior now owes him a concession of some kind in return.

FIGURE 8.1 Hypothetical Psychological Contract for a Salesman

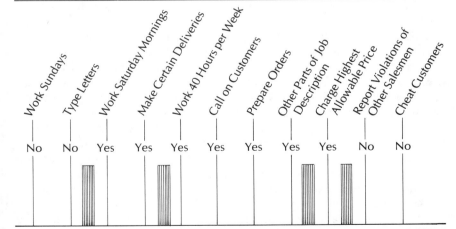

It is when an individual receives orders which fall outside the real boundaries that problems begin to occur. Any request beyond these *real* limits is excluded from the range of things the salesman will normally do. Thus, for example, if asked to work on Sundays or to cheat customers, he may resign. However, as we have said earlier, the boundaries of the psychological contract are not static. When faced with a request to act outside these real boundaries, the person may decide to comply, especially if he has no other job alternatives available. Thus, a person who is pressured by his superiors to act unethically, or in a way he doesn't want to, may do so, at great personal and psychological cost, if he cannot find a job elsewhere, or must stay in the organization for some other reason.

Leadership and Administration in Management

Accomplishing goals through others is done through administration as well as leadership, and there is a significant difference between these two concepts. By administration we mean the use of the prerogatives and rights associated with one's position in an organization, such as making decisions and giving directions. Managerial tools such as budgets, standard operating procedures, compensation systems, plans and other control mechanisms are the devices used in the administrative process. Their use to obtain compliance from subordinates, within the real boundaries of the psychological contract, is administration.

This is an important concept, for it means that a very significant part of what a manager does can be taught. The way to design these administrative tools, as well as their effective use, can be imparted to others by commonly used teaching methods. For instance, a person can learn how to prepare a budget, design a procedure, develop a compensation program, and prepare plans. Understanding the boundaries of the psychological contract and requiring subordinates to perform within the real boundaries rather than the more narrow public boundaries is part of this process. Generally, reasonable requests from a superior, although they may be outside the public boundaries of the psychological contract, are within the real boundaries, and subordinates, typically, will do more things if they are asked to do them. Generally, reasonable requests from a superior, although they may be outside the public boundaries, are within the real boundaries. Often, however, there is a need to go beyond even the real boundaries.

To obtain compliance to requests beyond the real boundaries of the psychological contract is leadership. Katz and Kahn (1965) "consider

the essence of organizational leadership to be the influential incre-
ment over and above mechanical compliance with a routine directive
of the organization." When a person is able to broaden or expand the
real boundaries of another's zone of indifference, either permanently
or temporarily, it is an act of leadership. Some of the ways in which
one might alter the boundaries of the psychological contract are: (1)
fear or threat, (2) reciprocity, (3) reinforcement, (4) job design, (5)
team building, (6) competition, and (7) ego involvement. These strategies are discussed in chapters 5, 13, and 14.

Power—The Basis of Compliance

Influence is a process, a series of actions that one initiates intended to
get another person to do something. When one is successful at influencing another—either because the influence attempt falls within the
boundaries of the psychological contract or the boundaries are moved
—it is because power has been exercised. Power is a force which one
can use to obtain compliance. Power, the force, is activated in the influence process. The use of power is leadership. People act and decisions get made. Things happen when power is exercised.

Power comes from several different bases: (1) organizational factors;
(2) skill and/or expertise; and (3) the personal qualities of the leader.
These relationships are shown in figure 8.2.

FIGURE 8.2 Bases of Power Related to Influence and Leadership

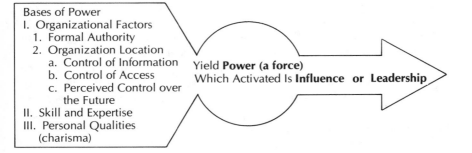

Bases of Power
I. Organizational Factors
  1. Formal Authority
  2. Organization Location
    a. Control of Information
    b. Control of Access
    c. Perceived Control over
      the Future
II. Skill and Expertise
III. Personal Qualities
  (charisma)

Yield **Power (a force)**
Which Activated Is **Influence or Leadership**

Organizational Factors

A person's position in an organization gives him power. Each position, or job, has certain activities formally specified for it which the

incumbent must perform. There are certain decisions which he is allowed to make. It is also possible that a position enables its incumbent to act as a gatekeeper for critical information, or access to important other people. These organizational factors—formal authority and organizational location—are two important determinants of power inherent in a position. Organizationally-based power resides in the position, not the person in it. He may only use it. When he leaves the position, he loses this power base.

Formal Authority. Formal authority is the right of decision and command a person has derived from the position held. These decision-making rights are delegated from higher organizational levels. In a managerial position, one has the right to allocate resources, make decisions, and distribute rewards in certain amounts and under certain conditions which are typically specified in the job description. The attendant responsibility of a person in a position is the obligation to perform well. Basically, *formal authority is the amount of designated discretion that an individual has in determining who gets what.* In most instances, the higher the position, the greater the discretion. When a decision is made in a discretionary area, it usually can be overturned only through appeals to even higher management.

Consider the case of a manufacturing vice-president. His position may give him discretionary power over how to expend funds for capital investments, who at lower levels in manufacturing should be promoted, and so forth. These will be the rights of anyone in the position of manufacturing vice-president. At lower organizational levels in manufacturing, the amount of discretion will be less than that at the vice-president's level.

There are other ways than through decision making that a manager can exercise influence. A person in a high-status position in an organization, whether deriving from its importance or its level, can exercise a great deal of control over who interacts with him, and when. For example, a subordinate generally sees his superior at the superior's convenience, not his own. And, typically, the superior will determine how long the meeting lasts. Through socialization, individuals learn that they should defer to higher-status individuals:

The very title of a position—"chairman," "chief," "planning coordinator"—may be perceived by others to represent a power base. The higher the position, the more likely it is that the incumbent will be able to determine either who gets promoted, or the criteria used to determine promotions. Thus, those in higher positions usually have significant effects on the career patterns of those in lower positions.

Organization Location. The location of a position within an organizational setting may be a base of power, sometimes without regard to the level of the position in the hierarchical structure. In some positions, for example, a great amount of important information is collected for dissemination to other organization points. Desired information, when controlled, gives power to the person who has it. The finance group may have information about future spending plans and plant site locations, for instance. If there is internal competition among managers for, say, the positions of plant manager at these new plants, having advance information that others do not have can give those who have it an advantage in making the strongest possible personal case for a plant managership. The finance group, with the information, has power.

Control over access to key people is another source of organizational power. In order to see the president, we may have to clear an appointment with his administrative assistant. When attempting to speak by phone with the director of personnel, we may find a secretary making the decision whether or not we initially see him—or an assistant. In both these instances, lower-level personnel have a great deal of influence over others in the organization at higher levels. This kind of power base is clearly illustrated in item 8.1, describing the role of the White House Staff of ex-President Nixon, which often stood between the President and those who wanted to communicate to him.

ITEM 8.1   A Power Base

Nixon's White House

Surrounding the outwardly calm White House Oval Office that is the President's citadel is a symbolic battleground pocked with shell holes and scarred with trenches. The tactical objective of the attackers is the President's attention. The besiegers include great institutions and the meekest citizen. There are the representatives of the Federal Government itself: the Cabinet en bloc and as individuals, Senators and Congressmen, military chiefs, economic advisers, satraps of the independent and quasi-independent agencies.

Those are the front-line supplicants,

but many others constantly seek to infiltrate the presidential stronghold. They include state governors and city mayors, and the senior national and state political leaders of the President's party. After them comes a helter-skelter militia of citizens, often sniping at one another, enemies of the President as well as friends: banker, lawyer, merchant, chief, cleric, doctor, scholar, journalist, student, housewife. Some advance to plead a cause, others to criticize and fix blame.

Patrolling the battlefield, defending the fortress against unwanted infiltrators, is the President's personal staff. It is his own creation. Each of the staff members is ultimately answerable to a constituency of only one man: Richard Milhous Nixon. Theirs is a hazardous occupation; often criticism aimed at the President falls short and bursts directly on them.

Throughout his first year in office, Richard Nixon's elaborately organized network of assistants, counselors, advisers and lesser factotums went largely unscathed. Any concern that it might insulate him from reality came only in sporadic muttering from Congressmen and disgruntled favor-seekers. No longer. When Nixon decided to move U.S. forces into Cambodia, evidently without realizing the outcry of protest that this would provoke, he set off angry charges that he is too isolated from many sections of American opinion. Interior Secretary Walter Hickel pleaded that Nixon pay more attention to the young, complained that he got a swift brush-off from the President's staff—and reported that he had been able to see Nixon alone exactly twice since taking office 16 months before.

Suddenly it is fashionable in Washington to fret and fulminate that a palace guard has separated Nixon from realities. In the White House, the key figures around the President are Staff Chief H. R. (Bob) Haldeman, Domestic Affairs Aide John Ehrlichman and National Security Adviser Henry Kissinger. Because of their ancestry—and their closemouthed habits—the Teutonic trio is now known as "the Berlin Wall" in the White House pressroom.

• • • •

Criticism and anger directed at the men who guard the President's doors and carry out his orders are no novelty. "This is a problem that must have started with George Washington," says one Nixon man. "If everybody went in immediately whenever he needed something, the White House wouldn't work." Harry Truman kept on his desk a sign that read THE BUCK STOPS HERE. It

was a nice, punchy slogan, but the buck got to him only after it had filtered through his personal staff. Nor is it a new idea that the men who do the winnowing can exercise extraordinary power. Clark Clifford, a perennial adviser to postwar Democratic administrations, remembers an Eisenhower aide telling him that Ike was spared night work because his staff boiled 150-page memoranda down to two pages. Clifford replied: "There is only one trouble. If I could be the fellow who prepares the two-page memo, I'd be President instead of Ike."

• • • •

Observes a White House staffer: "Everything is funneled through these two guys [Haldeman and Erlichman]. Haldeman is not at all interested in policy, and Ehrlichman is. This explains how they manage to get along. Ehrlichman views himself as a broker, a sifter of ideas, rather than an advocate." But he has taken substantive positions: in favor of Presidential Counselor Daniel Patrick Moynihan's plan for a minimum annual welfare income, in favor of the conservationists who successfully blocked a Miami jetport in the Florida Everglades. He is as critical of the liberal press as Spiro Agnew, and once told a reporter who said that a Nixon decision would not go down well in the East: "It'll play in Peoria." His staff meetings are less bang-bang-bang than Haldeman's; he moves briskly, but everyone has his say. One joke has it that Ehrlichman eats breakfast the night before.

• • • •

California Representative Paul McCloskey Jr., a liberal Republican and a college friend of Ehrlichman's, thinks that the Nixon staff has wrapped the President in a cocoon. Says McCloskey: "For the President to isolate himself from all criticism, from differing opinion is a dangerous thing. Hell, every time I see the President the band has been playing *Hail to the Chief* and everyone has been bowing and scraping. That's not the real world. I see no one who has the guts to stand up to the President down there and say 'You're wrong.' He needs that, just as a Congressman does."

That sums up the principal complaint against the entire palace guard that surrounds Nixon. It is true enough that the loudest complainers are those whom Nixon does not see, but it can well be argued that their differing views are precisely what he needs to hear in order to grasp reality firsthand. What some have called "the triumph of the advance men" has left many open wounds all over town. Says one Nixon aide: "When you come into the White House after eight years on the other side; you bring in people who are bright but not experienced in Government—especially in protocol, the proprieties of dealing with the Hill and other parts of Government, which can matter more than substance. They think they're bright—that's part of the problem—and experts in politics because they worked in a campaign. Actually, they know very little, especially about the politics of dealing with politicians."

The advance man lives for tomorrow's headlines, worries about deadlines on his flow charts, and reckons achievement by the number of specific tasks he manages to get done. These men, says a high official in one Government department, are "consumed with running the Government, but in the process they've lost sight of the fact that they ought to be running the country."

TIME, June 8, 1970

Perceived control over the future is another important source of lower-level influence. The personnel unit is a classic example of this case. Often managers, rightly or wrongly, feel that lower-level personnel staff members have a great deal of influence over who gets future assignments. So, in their efforts to insure favorable consideration, they often comply with requests from personnel staffers in order to stay on their "good side."

Skill and Expertise

Often we respond to influence attempts of others because they presumably have a greater amount of skill or knowledge in a particular area than we do. It is common practice to rely on expert opinion in our personal life, accepting the advice of accountants, lawyers, and doctors because, we believe, their training and knowledge can solve a problem. At work, the same thing happens. In designing and implementing a computer-based management information system, we rely on computer experts to define the capacity of the equipment and what it can provide. When a customer threatens legal action, the president or chief executive goes to the company's attorney for advice. When the director of engineering wants to know company policy on travel expenses, he will call the administrative assistant in personnel.

An important aspect of expert power is that it is very specific to the type of problem and to the person with the skill. We are unlikely to ask the company attorney for marketing advice, or the computer programmer for legal advice. Expert power is task-specific, but—more important for this discussion—it is generally associated with a particular person. It is not easily transferred to another person, as is the case with organizationally-based power. When a person becomes a plant manager, he generally has the same formal authority as the previous manager, but a person gets expert power only through demonstrating competence or by having it "given" to him because he has the appropriate education, experience, and appearance. When an individual with expert power leaves the organization, his replacement will probably not have the same amount of influence, even though he may have the same organizational title.

Personal Characteristics of the Leader

In some cases, individuals are susceptible to influence because they identify with another person. French and Raven (1959) call this "referent power" and say that it has its base in the "feeling of oneness" that a person has for another, or the desire for such a feeling. Referent power is based largely on the attraction exerted by an individual on another person, or on a group. The stronger the attraction, the stronger the power.

Identification with another may come about because he possesses personal characteristics and qualities highly valued by the group, such as family background, appearance, athletic ability, and so on. Or the identification may come about because of the leader's ability to articulate the values and concerns of the followers. Persons who exert this kind of influence are called "charismatic" leaders. They have the loyalty and commitment of their followers, not because they have a particular skill or are in a particular position, but because their followers respond to them as individuals. Like the skill and expertise power base, this power base is unique to the individual and the situation. Charismatic influence cannot be transferred to another person.

Leadership, Power, and Dependence

One way to view leadership is in terms of dependence. If a leader can influence others, it is because the others are dependent upon him. This can arise because of psychological identification, as discussed above, or because someone has the power to allocate rewards or impose sanctions, either objective or subjective. Objective rewards are such things as pay increases, promotions, or the bestowal of prestige and status symbols. Objective sanctions take the form of disciplinary actions, demotions, removal of rights, and so on.

Subjective rewards and sanctions are less tangible. They exist in the minds of the individual. Recognition or disapproval from a supervisor may or may not be viewed as a reward or a sanction by subordinates; it depends upon their esteem for him. One way to increase leadership effectiveness is to increase the dependency of the subordinate on either the manager or the organization. In fact, the managerial motivation strategies described in chapter 5 should be viewed in this light. In order to use reinforcement, for example, the manager must have a subordinate who desires (or wants) the reward. Reciprocity is only effective when the manager can provide "desired" favors.

Different Perspectives on Leadership

It is possible to learn and to improve administrative skills in schools and by experience, but the elusive dimension of the manager's job is the leadership process. While we can conceptualize with some ease why people comply (the psychological contract) and the bases of power (organizational, skill, and personal), it is more difficult to characterize the qualities, or behavior, of individuals who exert influence and are capable of managing in a way to achieve organizational goals. (We do not believe it is correct to consider management synonymous with leadership. We have not done so in the preceding section of this chapter, but so much of the leadership theory and research uses the terms interchangeably that we will abide by the convention in what follows.)

Leadership has long been the subject of speculation, theorizing, and research, the ultimate purpose being to select individuals likely to be able to influence others to achieve organizational goals, and to place them in a position which enhances this capacity. Early research in this century studied leadership as if it were a collection of personal traits or characteristics of those identified as leaders, and tried to identify the traits and characteristics. Subsequently, research emphasized a behavioral approach which looked upon leadership as a series of acts, or a behavioral repertoire, designed to help a group achieve its objectives. Viewed from this perspective, leadership was seen as acting out a set of behaviors which would vary, depending upon the group's need for greater task effectiveness, member satisfaction, and cohesiveness. More recently, attention has been directed toward developing "contingency" theories of leadership. This view recognizes the fact that effective leadership is a function of the situation in which leader and followers interact. These themes, then (1) the trait approach, (2) the behavioral approach, and (3) situational theories, are the main thrusts of leadership theory and research.

The Trait Approach

The underlying premise of the trait approach to leadership is that leadership is an attribute of personality, that a certain identifiable trait or collection of traits makes a person effective as a leader, and that better organizational results can be obtained by selecting as leaders those who have these identifiable qualities.

Many researchers and theorists feel that there are no readily identifiable traits related to possession of leadership status, or to effectiveness as a leader, in all situations. This may, however, be principally because the research on leaders has been done with leaders in a wide variety of situations and jobs. When studies are more situation-specific—for example, relating various personal characteristics to managerial (a special kind of leadership as we noted earlier), success —consistencies are found. Dunnette (1970), for instance, reviewing research on traits associated with executive success, states that successful executives tend to be dominant, self-confident, and assertive, and tend to have a high aspiration level as well as a general success pattern throughout life. Ghiselli (1973) found self-perceived intelligence, initiative, supervisory ability, self-assurance, and occupational level to be positively related to general management success in terms of upward mobility and rated job success. These findings are consistent with Stogdill's (1974) summary of a large number of leadership studies.

One reason for some of the difficulty in finding traits differentiating leaders from nonleaders and effective from less effective leaders is that mere possession of a characteristic is not, in itself, a sufficient condition for assuming a leadership (or management) position and then being successful in it. The individual must want the position and must want to be effective. In addition, the characteristics related to leadership do not operate singly, but in combination. Thus, individuals who seek the responsibilities of leadership and who possess the combination of traits commonly associated with success as a leader— such as initiative, self-confidence, and persistence—have an advantage over those individuals without these characteristics or those who have them but lack the interest (Stogdill, 1974; many of the references in this chapter can be found in this extensive review of research and theory on leadership by Stogdill).

Some early leadership scholars concluded that situational factors determined who would emerge as the leader (Gibb, 1954). Today it is recognized that individual characteristics and situational factors are important. As Stogdill (1974) points out: "Most recent theorists maintain that leader characteristics and situational demands interact to determine the extent to which a given leader will prove successful in a group."

Behavioral Approach

Much research on leadership has focused on leadership *behaviors*. Instead of looking at what a leader *is* (a trait), these studies aimed at finding out what he *does*. Many studies sought to relate specific behaviors of individuals in managerial, supervisory, or leadership positions to group effectiveness—that is, the productivity and satisfaction of group members. Of course, it was recognized that many leaders were only designated. Perhaps they were not individuals accepted as leaders by the group but they were in managerial positions. (This situation, however, may make it easier to study leadership, since among appointed leaders it is likely there will be a set of "bad" or ineffective leaders, necessary for comparison purposes.) Some of the earliest studies focused on very specific behavior. The different supervisors of groups with high and low performance, or with high or low satisfaction levels, were compared with respect to the amount of time they spent planning, how they disciplined employees, communication patterns, the amount of recognition given to subordinates, the amount of pressure exerted for higher production, and other supervisory behaviors.

Many studies have been conducted on how much influence the leader allowed subordinates in the decision-making process (Stogdill, 1974). From these studies, a particular classification system for describing leader and managerial behavior became popular. In these studies, flowing from the early work by Lewin, Lippitt, and White (1939), leaders were described in one or more of the following terms:

1. *Autocratic or Dictatorial.* The leader makes all decisions and allows the subordinates no influence in the decision-making process. These supervisors are often indifferent to the personal needs of subordinates.

2. *Participative or Democratic.* These supervisors consult with their subordinates on appropriate matters. They allow their subordinates

some influence in the decision-making process. In addition, this type of supervisor is not punitive and treats his subordinates with dignity and kindness.

3. *Laissez Faire*—or *Free Rein*. Supervisors in this group allow their group to have complete autonomy. They rarely supervise directly, so the group makes many of their on-the-job decisions themselves.

Thus, the amount of influence of either the superior or the subordinate can be viewed on a continuum, as in figure 8.3.

Many research studies have directly compared the autocratic and democratic styles of leadership. Such studies usually show that the democratic, or participative, leadership style is associated with higher subordinate satisfaction. High performance is also often present under democratic leadership, but there are no consistent performance differences between democratic and autocratic styles—in some studies there were no performance differences between groups even though different leaders used different approaches. However, the participative style is more often associated with greater acceptance of change and more organization identification than is the autocratic (Stogdill, 1974).

The relationship of the laissez-faire supervisory style to satisfaction and performance has not been studied as extensively as the autocratic and democratic leadership styles. What little research has been done seems to indicate that subordinate satisfaction and performance under laissez-faire is less than under the democratic approach but higher than that under the autocratic approach (Stogdill, 1974).

FIGURE 8.3 Continuum of Influence in the Leadership Process

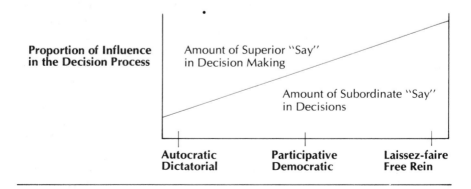

Proportion of Influence in the Decision Process

Amount of Superior "Say" in Decision Making

Amount of Subordinate "Say" in Decisions

| Autocratic | Participative | Laissez-faire |
| Dictatorial | Democratic | Free Rein |

The Ohio State Studies. Beginning in the late 1940s and continuing through the 1950s, a group of researchers at Ohio State conducted extensive studies of leadership effectiveness in industrial, military, and educational institutions. The research ranged from the development of instruments to measure leadership to the evaluation of factors which might determine group effectiveness. From these studies emerged two leader behavior characteristics often associated with group effectiveness:

1. Consideration: The extent to which the individual is likely to have job relationships characterized by mutual trust, respect for subordinates' ideas, and consideration of their feelings. High scorers tend to have good rapport and two-way communication with subordinates.

2. Initiating Structure: The extent to which an individual is likely to define and structure his role and those of his subordinates toward goal attainment. High scorers are those who play an active role in directing group activities and communicating information, scheduling, and trying out new ideas.

Effective leaders, according to the Ohio State Studies, were high on *both* these measures. That is, the leader had to show both a concern for those who worked in the group (high consideration) and an ability to plan, organize, and control (or otherwise administer) its activities (high initiating structure). The two factors are measured with a scale called the "Leader Behavior Description Questionnaire" (LBDQ), the widespread use of which facilitates comparison of results from different research efforts.

Most studies show that consideration is generally related to high employee satisfaction; it is related much less often to high performance, although occasionally it is so related (Stogdill, 1974). In a number of studies, initiating structure has been found to be related to high job satisfaction, less often to high productivity, low absenteeism, and low turnover (Stogdill, 1974). However, in other studies no relationship of any kind was found between initiating structure and subordinate behavior.

The relationship of consideration and initiating structure to performance and satisfaction varies from one study to another. Some of the inconsistencies are due to the fact that there are very different organization settings where these studies have been done. Other discrepancies may arise because researchers use slightly different versions of the LBDQ, and thus arrive at different conclusions (Schreisheim, House, and Kerr, 1975).

The Michigan Studies. The Institute for Social Research at the University of Michigan was formed after World War II. This group has made significant empirical, theoretical, and practical contributions to the study of organizational effectiveness. They conducted, for example, a number of leadership studies in offices, railroad settings, and in service industries. From the early studies, they concluded that leadership behavior could be described in terms of two dimensions similar to those used by the Ohio State group. But there was an important difference. In the early stages of the Michigan Studies, leaders were described as engaging in behavior which was *either* production-centered *or* employee-centered (Stogdill, 1974), thus differentiating the Michigan from the Ohio studies, since the Ohio Studies attempted to characterize an individual on both dimensions. The *production-centered* supervisor was defined as primarily concerned with achieving high levels of production and viewing subordinates merely as instruments for doing this. The *employee-centered* supervisor, on the other hand, was defined as concerned about subordinates' feelings and attempting to create an atmosphere of mutual trust and respect. Some early interpretations of the Michigan research concluded that the most effective leadership style was employee-centered, that employee-centered supervisors were more likely to have highly productive work groups than production-centered. Other studies, however, showed that effective supervisors engaged in *both* employee-centered and production-centered behavior at the same time (Stogdill, 1974).

A later study at Michigan by Bowers and Seashore (1966) expanded the number of leader behaviors to a repertoire of four. They found four supervisory behaviors associated with satisfaction and performance in a study of 40 agencies of an insurance company. These four basic supervisory behavior dimensions are:

1. *Support:* Behavior that enhances someone else's feelings of personal worth and importance.
2. *Interaction Facilitation:* Behavior that encourages members of the group to develop close, mutually satisfying relationships.
3. *Goal Emphasis:* Behavior that stimulates an enthusiasm for meeting the group's goals or achieving excellent performance.
4. *Work Facilitation:* Behavior that helps achieve goal attainment by such activities as scheduling, coordinating, planning, and by providing resources such as tools, materials, and technical knowledge.

The work at Michigan strengthened the case for conceiving of leadership as a complex activity. It has been instrumental in shaping much of the work of the situational theories of leadership.

The Managerial Grid.® Blake and Mouton (1964), seeking to develop a more integrated concept of leadership while the research was pointing in several directions, devised the Managerial Grid. The Grid puts the two dimensions, *people orientation* and *task orientation* together. Blake and Mouton describe five basic styles, according to these two basic supervisory dimensions. These styles are located at different Grid positions, as shown in figure 8.4. The 1,1 supervisory style shows little concern for either production or employees; it is the equivalent of the laissez-faire supervisory style described earlier. The 1,9 supervisor has high employee concern but little concern for performance, while the 9,1 supervisor has little concern for employees but places strong emphasis on performance. The 5,5 supervisor is a compromiser; he places only moderate emphasis on satisfying employee needs and on achieving satisfactory levels of performance. (Blake and Mouton feel this is the most common supervisory style.) Finally, there is the 9,9 supervisory pattern, in which there is high

FIGURE 8.4 The Managerial Grid

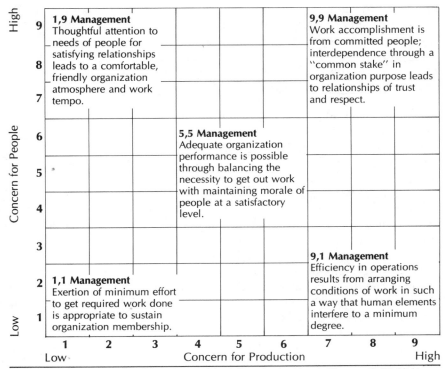

emphasis on achieving both employee needs and high levels of performance. The 9,9 supervisor is able to integrate employee needs and organizational needs with a team-building approach (explained in chap. 5 as a managerial motivational strategy). Though research on the effectiveness of these approaches is limited, one study shows improvement in both individual satisfaction and organization performance after managers participated in a change program designed to teach them the 9,9 supervisory approach (Blake, Mouton, Barnes, and Greiner, 1964).

Situational Theories

It has long been known that situational factors affect a leader's style and effectiveness in using a particular approach. The context within which a human being operates makes a difference, but until recently, these ideas were not part of the leadership research literature. Situational factors were not prominent facets of either the Ohio State Studies or the Michigan Studies, though the researchers were aware of their importance. Some of the factors which seem to be especially important to the effectiveness of a leadership style are (1) the characteristics of subordinates, (2) the organizational situation, and (3) the style of one's superior in an organization.

Subordinate characteristics are related to effectiveness. For example, the participative management style was found to be ineffective when subordinates were not used to influencing decisions of their superior. Leadership style which varies from what a subordinate expects may meet with negative reaction (Carroll and Tosi, 1973). Subordinates seem to have a better response to the participative approach when they feel it is legitimate; that is, the way a manager should behave (French, Israel, and As, 1960; Vroom and Yetton, 1974). The autocratic approach may be preferred by individuals who do not feel competent to participate in the decision-making process; that is, in a situation where, for example, the subordinate feels his superior is more expert than he, the subordinate is not likely to try to exert much influence, and he will find an attempt by a superior to use a participative style quite uncomfortable (Mulder, 1971).

The organizational situation also influences the supervisory approach. The degree of crisis and the type of work are but two possible situational factors which could be important. For example, in an emergency where a decision is quickly needed, it may be unwise to use a "participative" approach, since this would take undue time.

House (1971) and Fiedler (1967) have both theorized that the degree of task structure is an important determinant of leader effectiveness. If a person's job is well-defined, narrow, and highly routine (often the case with lower-level employees in a bureaucratic organization), then directive leadership styles might have negative effects. The employee will feel pressure from both his job and his boss. While he may perform better, dissatisfaction will be higher. When the task is less well-structured, however, directive behavior may provide the employee with needed guidance, improving effectiveness.

The style of one's superior can also affect one's own supervisory approach. Fleishman (1953) found that a manager's style was more related to the way his superior managed than whether or not he had been in a training program. Carroll and Tosi (1973) found that a subordinate models his behavior after that of his superior, especially when the subordinate finds himself in situations where he is unsure of what to do. For example, an assistant manager of a department store may be given the assignment of presenting an advertising program to the board of directors. If he has never done this before, he may pattern his approach after what he has seen his boss do. Likewise, in dealing with subordinates, a manager may handle a troublesome employee as he has seen his boss do it. The way many people learn to manage is by modeling their behavior after those who are already in management jobs.

Perhaps the two most prominent situational theories at present are (1) a contingency theory of leadership (Fiedler, 1967), and (2) path-goal theory (Evans, 1968; House, 1971). In both of these, an attempt is made to specify how a leader's or a manager's behavior is related to effectiveness in different situational circumstances. This, of course is quite consistent with managerial process contingency theory. Such work on leadership provides us with more specific prescriptions about how a manager should function in different types of organizations, and we will consider these prescriptions in chapters 12 and 14.

Fiedler's Contingency Model of Leadership. Fiedler (1967) has developed a formulation about how leadership style, the group, and the situation interact to affect group performance and satisfaction. The style of a leader is, in part, a function of his own needs and personality. Therefore like personality, Fiedler suggests leadership style is relatively well-fixed and established. The style is measured by the "Least Preferred Co-worker" scale (LPC). On the LPC, a manager is asked to describe the co-worker with whom he least likes to work. From this description, two classifications of leadership style are developed:

1. *People-centered* (Hi LPC). This style is one in which the leader is oriented toward the feelings and relationships in the work group, with a tendency to be permissive.

2. *Task-centered* (Lo LPC). This style focuses on the task, with a tendency to be directive and controlling.

Obviously, these two dimensions are much like those used in the Ohio State and Michigan studies. Fiedler, however, extends both those approaches by defining what characteristics of the situation are important in determining which style is more effective. The important situational characteristics are:

1. *Leader-member relations*, which refer to the amount of trust and how well-liked the leader is.

2. *Task-structure*, which refers to the extent to which the job is defined. High task structure refers to well-defined jobs in which each aspect is spelled out. Low task structure is present where job requirements are unclear and ambiguous.

3. *Position power*, which is a function of the formal authority structure; that is, whether or not an individual has the right to reward, sanction, evaluate, or promote those who work for him.

Figure 8.5 shows the eight possible combinations of these three factors and which supervisory style is predicted to be more effective in each. Fiedler reports that the task orientation is generally best in situations where leader-member relations are either very good or very bad. When relations are good, the group may be quite willing to accept a task orientation. Where all situational factors are bad for the supervisor, the group will fall apart unless the leader takes charge and controls their behavior. Under some of the moderately unfavorable conditions the leader must use a people-orientation approach, either to motivate group members to become involved in attempts to deal with an ambiguous task or to win their support.

Fiedler's work has some important implications. One is that if leadership style is not flexible, then when an organization is not performing well, the situation should be restructured to make it more favorable to the style of the person leading—or the leader should be replaced. In chapters 13 and 14, from a similar premise, we describe the way a leader should function to achieve best results in a bureaucratic and in a dynamic organization.

The research evidence supports some, but not all, of Fiedler's predictions as to the most effective supervisory approach for each of his eight conditions (Graen et al., 1970). Obviously, there could be other situational factors not considered by Fiedler which could also have an effect on performance.

FIGURE 8.5 Classification of Group Task Situations and the Predicted Relationship of Group Performance and Leadership Style

Task Structure	Leader-Member Relations	Position Power	Suggested Leader Orientation
High	Good	Strong	Task
	Good	Weak	Task
	Poor	Weak	People
	Poor	Strong	People
Low	Good	Strong	Task
	Good	Weak	People
	Poor	Weak	Task
	Poor	Strong	People

Source: F. Fiedler *A Theory of Leadership Effectiveness* (McGraw-Hill, 1967, p. 37).

Path-Goal Theory.   The research on path-goal theory also supports a contingency approach to leadership. As discussed in chapter 5, House (1971) asserts that the leader obtains good performance from his work unit by making sure that subordinates know what they have to do to be rewarded for good performance *and* also by reducing barriers to effective performance. In addition, the supervisor must behave in such a way as to help his subordinates satisfy their needs through high performance. Since different groups of employees have different needs and different types of work problems, the most appropriate leadership approach depends on the types of individuals involved and the characteristics of their work situation. For example, House (1971) has cited research which indicates that a leader's attempts to clarify what subordinates are supposed to do contributes to high satisfaction where the task requirements are ambiguous but may reduce satisfaction when the task requirements are quite clear. In the latter case, the supervisor's efforts to explain already clear task requirements are viewed by subordinates as unnecessary and perhaps, also, insulting. House has cited a number of other studies which indicate that a manager's emphasis on either *consideration* or on *initiating structure* can be effective, depending upon the needs of the individuals in the situation at the time.

One important aspect of House's work is that he has drawn four general propositions that link performance and leader behavior through motivation (see chap. 5). These propositions are:

1. The leader's role in motivation is to increase to the subordinate the utility (positive value) both of achieving work goals *and* of the work itself. Where there is uncertainty, he should also clarify the path (the things that have to be done) to achieve work goals.

2. With clear paths to work goals, the subordinate will be motivated because he can be more certain of how to achieve goals (or his role ambiguity will be reduced). When, for example, an employee is given a new assignment, if he does not know how to do it, then he should receive some help or coaching from his superior. Clarification of the task assignment also permits the manager to reinforce desired behavior because it may then be easier for the individual to perceive the link between performance and rewards (or sanctions), since they are now specified.

3. If the path to the work goal is already clear because of the nature of the work or the rigidity of the structure, then the leader who is directive (exercises high initiating structure) may increase performance through added pressure, but will decrease satisfaction. Close supervision of a skilled worker may upset him greatly, though he may produce more because of it.

4. If the leader acts to satisfy subordinate needs, better results will occur *only when increased satisfaction results in the individual placing greater value on the work, or goal-directed effort.* This means that if a manager provides, say, favors to a group and they are happier but still don't like their work assignment, performance will not increase.

Leader Behavior—Cause or Result of Effectiveness?

One question which arises out of much of the research cited in this chapter is whether group effectiveness is caused by how the leader behaves or whether the leader behaves as he does because of the group's performance. Put another way, "If I am a manager of an effective group, will I exert less pressure, and be more concerned about their needs and more considerate because they are a goal effective group? Or if I am head of a less effective group, will I push them, be directive, and exercise high initiating structure in an effort to improve performance?" Which comes first, chicken or egg?

The research on this subject leads to the conclusion that supervisory behavior operates in a dynamic way with performance. In some studies, it has been shown that the behavior of the supervisor caused group performance. Rosen (1969) found that when supervisors were given new assignments, group performance influenced leadership style and leader behavior also influenced group behavior. Lowin and Craig (1968) found that high-performing groups tended to cause the leader to act in a considerate way, while low-performing groups tended to cause high initiating structure behavior.

Two studies (Tosi et al., 1975; Greene 1973) indicate that some aspects of leader behavior may cause performance, while other aspects may be affected by performance. Greene (1973) concluded that the level of subordinate performance causes the leader to exhibit different degrees of initiating structure. The manager of a less effective department will be more directive than one of a more productive unit. It is the level of consideration, however, that influences the degree of subordinate satisfaction.

Can Leadership Style Be Flexible?

A number of writers have said that supervisors should be flexible with respect to the supervisory approach they use (for example, Reddin, 1970). The leader, they argue, must first evaluate the situation and then decide on the appropriate supervisory style. There is, however, a question of the extent to which supervisors can do this. Fiedler (1967), for example, considers his dimensions of supervisory style as relatively fixed, since they are aspects of individual personality. He proposes that since a particular supervisory approach is optimum for a situation, if a person with a different style is in the supervisory position, then the situation should be changed to fit the supervisory style rather than trying to get the supervisor to change his style to fit the situation. Blake and Mouton (1964), however, believe that leadership-style flexibility is a characteristic that varies among leaders; that is, they believe that some individuals can change their supervisory style and some have only a very limited ability to do this. It is our belief that it is not possible for a person, in the short run, to drastically change his behavioral style. It is possible however, to improve certain administrative skills, as we have discussed. But to the extent that behavior is reflective of personality, changes are likely to take some time to occur. It is probably more productive, then, to be concerned with effective matching of situational factors and a person's behavioral style than to try to change either.

How Leader Behavior Affects Performance

Until recently, there has been little attention paid to the specific mechanisms by which a particular behavior affects performance. We touched on this issue briefly in chapter 5, but will note here again some of the mechanisms. A manager *can* affect individual and group motivation, and in these ways:

1. *He can affect expectancies.* This can be done by spelling out relationships between efforts and performance levels and between performance levels and various outcomes such as rewards or punishments. This, of course, assumes that the supervisor has some influence over rewards or punishments (salary increases , promotions or demotions). When he does, he may be able to use this power to affect performance. When he doesn't, he still has the capacity to use social rewards, such as recognition or approval, but for these rewards to be effective, the subordinates must see this social recognition as important. Kahn (1951) found that productivity of work groups was related to beliefs by group members that high performance would lead to the receiving of the reward of supervisory approval. Such supervisory recognition must be given only for high performance. If it is also given for average performance, then subordinates assume that average performance is perfectly satisfactory.

2. *He can set goals.* Motivation may also be affected by the difficulty of work goals which the supervisor establishes for individuals or groups. In one study, it was found that when work goals set for foremen were viewed as impossible, very poor performance resulted (Stedry and Kay, 1966). On the other hand, when goals were perceived to be difficult but challenging, performance increased. In another study it was found that there was more enjoyment with goals of intermediate difficulty than there was with quite easy or quite difficult goals (Locke, 1973). It should be kept in mind, however, that personal characteristics affect the perception of the relative difficulty of goals and of the response to this perception. In one study, for example, managers low in self-esteem reported diminished effort expenditures when given goals that were perceived to be difficult, while managers high in self-esteem reported increased effort expenditures when given what they perceived to be difficult goals (Carroll and Tosi, 1973).

3. *He can clarify how to achieve work goals.* The clarification of work goals is another way that performance can be affected. As House (1973) points out in path-goal theory, a leader's high initiating structure can reduce role ambiguity, which can increase motivation by making it more probable that effort will result in goal attainment. On the other hand, confusion among subordinates as to what, when, and how something should be done wastes time and energy and contributes to personal frustrations, which in turn leads to diminished motivation.

In spite of the differences in terminology used, out of the research on leadership two basic and important dimensions of supervisory behavior emerge; one emphasizes task performance, one emphasizes satisfying individual employee needs. Figure 8.6 shows the similarity between the different approaches to leadership behavior described in this chapter. The relationship of these factors to employee needs and performance is definitely associated with the situation. Especially important situational factors are (1) the structure and nature of tasks, (2) the needs and abilities of the group members, and (3) the superior. Satisfaction with supervision would be highest where the supervisor meets the preference of group members. His ability to do this reflects his personality and motives, and the demands placed upon him by the work situation. Group performance will be highest where supervisors themselves are motivated to obtain high performance, where their supervisory style is such that their activities facilitate performance (or remove barriers to performance), and where their motivational approach allows individuals to satisfy their needs through higher performance levels stressing positive outcomes such as higher pay, increases in satisfaction, self-esteem, or recognition.

FIGURE 8.6   Similarity Between Selected Concepts of Leadership

Ohio State Studies	Michigan Studies	Blake and Mouton	Bowers and Seashore	Fiedler's Contingency Theory	House Path-Goal
Consideration	Employee -centered	Concern with People	Support	People -centered (High LPC)	Consideration
			Interaction Facilitation	**Situational Factors**	
				Position Power	Clarity of Path-Goal Relationships
				Task Structure	
Initiating Structure	Production -Centered	Concern with Production	Goal Emphasis	Leader -Member Relations	
			Work Facilitation		
				Production -centered (Low LPC)	Initiating Structure

Of course, the administrative aspect of the manager's job cannot be overlooked. Planning, budgeting, development, and training are important functions that affect performance. The manager must be both a leader and an administrator.

Discussion Questions

1. Do you agree with the concepts of leadership and administration, as presented in this chapter?

2. Think of a charismatic leader. Has this person been able to transfer his influence to another leader? Why?

3. Close your eyes and visualize a "leader"—his or her clothes, appearance, height. Is there a specific person that you have in mind? Who?

4. Close your eyes again. Visualize the chairman of the board for a large company. What does this person look like? Was it a male? Describe his clothes, height, and general appearance to your colleagues after they have done the same thing.

5. What are the problems in prescribing how one should manage using the leadership models derived from the Ohio State and Michigan studies? How are situational theories more prescriptive in helping to manage effectively?

Chapter 9
Interpersonal Organization Communication

By communicating, people put their environment under surveillance in order to cope with and adjust to it (Laswell, 1948). Communication makes human cooperation possible because through it instructions and intentions can be shared. Cultures are preserved because instructions and technical, political, and social information are transmitted from one generation to succeeding generations (Laswell, 1948).

In an organization—which is a miniature society—communication serves the same fundamental purposes as it does in the larger society. Organizations must obtain information about their environment, coordinate and motivate their members, and instruct new members in the relevant technology and management systems. The importance of communication in organizations was pointed out by Barnard (1938) who said,

> ... in an exhaustive theory of organization, communication would occupy a central place, because the structure, extensiveness, and scope of organization are almost entirely determined by communication techniques.

Barnard believed that establishing and maintaining a system of communication was the *first* function of a manager.

Communication and Management

Communication is, of course, absolutely necessary in an organization. It is the basic means by which cooperation or coordination of many different people is achieved. Cooperation and coordination require the transmission and reception of some set of signals among people so that individuals can know what others want them to do.

In carrying out their planning, decision making, staffing, and control responsibilities, managers communicate. Indeed, they often spend the majority of their time communicating. In a study of 28 managers in a single company (Carroll, 1961), managers reported random obser-

237

vations of their work behavior over a two-week period. Figure 9.1 shows that the average manager in this company spent about 43 percent of his time conversing with others, 20 percent preparing and writing reports and memos, and about 18 percent of his time reading and reviewing written communications. Thus, communication took up four-fifths of the manager's work time.

FIGURE 9.1   Average Work Time Allocations of Managers

Activities	Percentage of Total Work Time
	0 10 20 30 40 50 60
Personal activities	
Conversing with others	
Preparing and writing reports, letters, etc.	
Reading and reviewing reports, letters, etc.	
Inspecting products, procedures, etc.	
Mathematical computation	
Operating equipment of all types	
Thinking and reflection	
Minor clerical (filing, sorting, etc.)	
Walking and travel	

Contacts	Percentage of Total Work Time
	0 10 20 30 40 50 60
Superior (own department)	
Subordinate (own department)	
Manager (other department)	
Nonmanager (other department)	
Other department (person not identified)	
Person outside company	
Combination of above	
None	

Source: Dunnette, Marvin D., *Personnel Selection and Placement*. Copyright © 1966 by Wadsworth Publishing Company, Inc. Reprinted by permission of the publisher, Brooks/Cole Publishing Company, Monterey, California.   Based on observations of 28 managers over a 2-week period.

Other studies also show that communication consumes much of a manager's time (Mintzberg, 1973). This is especially the case for higher-level managers (Hinrichs, 1964). Thus, any increase in communication efficiency can result in considerable benefits to the manager and to the organization, since the time used by human resources, especially key personnel, is perhaps the most valuable of any organization's resources.

Many organizations expend considerable resources to provide employees with information about the organization and its plans. One purpose of such programs is to increase employee identification with the organization and to increase their work satisfaction and morale. There is some evidence which suggests such an approach has positive benefits. In one study, higher levels of knowledge of organizational goals was related to higher job satisfaction (Maher and Piersol, 1970). In another study, foremen who had received unclear or conflicting information on company policies had low morale (Rosen, 1970). Some other studies, however, have not shown a strong relationship between knowledge about the company and employee morale (Perry and Mahoney, 1955).

The Communication Process

Communication is the process of passing information and understanding from one person to another. The process starts with an intention to communicate—to pass information and understanding. In one study of the communication behavior of managers and nonmanagers, the purposes of communication were classified by the researchers as:

1. Information received or disseminated.
2. Instruction given or received.
3. Approval given or received.
4. Problem-solving activities.
5. Nonbusiness-related communications or scuttlebutt.

TABLE 9.1 Communications Frequency by Purpose and Position

Purpose	Position	Percentage of Total Communications
Information	Manager	53.5
	Nonmanager	54.2
Instruction	Manager	22.4
	Nonmanager	21.3
Problem Solving	Manager	11.1
	Nonmanager	12.5
Scuttlebutt	Manager	6.6
	Nonmanager	8.2
Approval	Manager	6.2
	Nonmanager	3.8

Source: Wickesberg, A. K., "Communications Networks in the Business Organization Structure," *Academy of Management Journal*, 11 (1968): 253–62.

Table 9.1 gives the percentage results of a study of the total communications for the various purposes made by managers and nonmanagers (Wickesburg, 1968). The managerial percentages were not much dif-

ferent than those for the nonmanagers. Communication for information purposes was most common; for instruction, next; for problem
solving, third.

FIGURE 9.2   The Communication Process

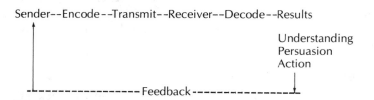

Sender--Encode--Transmit--Receiver--Decode--Results

Understanding
Persuasion
Action

-------------------- Feedback --------------------

The communication process (Davis, 1961) is illustrated in figure
9.2. The sender is the source, the person with the ideas, information,
and/or objectives to communicate. In the encoding process, ideas and
information are encoded, or translated, into a language appropriate by
the sender. The message is then sent over some channel. Any means
of transmission (bulletin board, letter, tape, film, loudspeaker) may be
used as the channel. The information is received and converted from
the language of the sender to the language of the receiver(s). Thus, the
receiver may think, "I guess what he means by that is . . . ."

After decoding, the effectiveness of the communication can be evaluated in terms of the specific objectives of the sender. A communications objective may be to make the receiver aware of a particular problem, to increase the understanding of a learner, to persuade another of
the validity of a particular course of action, or to obtain a particular
behavioral action in the future. If the recognition, understanding, persuasion, or action takes place, the communication is considered effective.

Obviously, communication objectives are not always achieved. The
receiver may not understand the communication, or be influenced to
accept a particular argument, or he may not act as the sender wishes.
There are barriers that interfere with the achievement of communication objectives. Knowing something about these barriers may make it
possible to prescribe communication approaches that increase the
possibility of achieving communication objectives. Some barriers result from the characteristics of people, some from the characteristics
of the organization. Other barriers are created by the choice of a particular communication technique in a specific situation. That is, one
communication approach will work in some situations, another in

others. And some approaches work better with some types of people than with others. Thus, which organizational communication approach works best depends on situational factors—the chief of which will be identified in this chapter. (In chaps. 13 and 14 we will suggest how communication patterns might differ in the hierarchical and dynamic organization.) Figure 9.3 shows how communication techniques, organizational factors, and personal characteristics interact to affect the success or failure of the sender's objectives.

FIGURE 9.3   The Organizational Communication Process

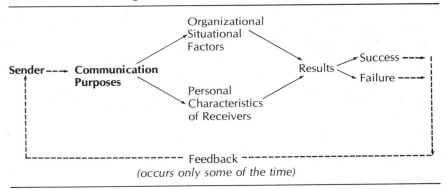

(occurs only some of the time)

Forms of Communication

Communication occurs when a message is transmitted to another person and understanding occurs. The obvious forms of communication are written and oral, but the transmission of meaning, feelings, and intentions can also take place without words. That is, nonverbal communications may convey important meanings to others. In this section, we discuss three different forms of communication—written/oral, nonverbal, and actions.

Written/Oral Communications.   Only a limited amount of research has been carried out on the relative merits of written versus oral communication. That research does indicate, however, that employees generally prefer face-to-face communication over written (Redding, 1972). And if the subject matter of discussion is controversial, some authorities believe that oral communication is better, because alternatives and ideas can be expressed more tentatively in oral rather than written form (Davis, 1968b). Moreover, if the communication is directed at attitude change, oral communication is more effective than written (Redding, 1972). However, written communications may be used to provide necessary information to support or justify a previously held viewpoint (Karlings and Abelson, 1970).

Oral communication differs from written communication in a number of ways. It provides for two-way interaction and feedback, and it provides an opportunity to develop interpersonal liking between parties. It generates social pressures to please the other party (Redding, 1972). An important difference between oral and written communication is that much more meaning can be transmitted orally than in writing. In oral communication, pauses and voice inflections give emphasis to different words, stress different parts of the message, or communicate the sender's feelings about the subject. The effect of a poem on an individual hearing it recited is different from the effect on that individual of reading the poem to himself—usually stronger in the first instance. In composing a poem the writer, in effect, reads it aloud to himself; it may, however, "read" substantially differently when transcribed on paper. The same is true, to a lesser degree, of sending a letter or memorandum as opposed to delivering the message in person, orally.

It is, of course, possible to communicate a message by both oral and written means. Dahle (1954) studied different combinations of oral and written communications. As methods of communicating information to employees, he studied oral only, written only, and oral and written together. He found that the combination of oral and written was the best approach, but not a great deal better than oral means alone.

Nonverbal Communication. People in organizations communicate by means other than words. Paralanguage, for example, refers to how something is said rather than what is said. There are several different ways that the same words may be expressed (Hayes, 1973). The volume, rate and rhythm, pitch, silent pauses, sounds such as "ah's" and "er's", laughing, and sighing may be used in a particular set of words to convey meaning. (Trager, 1958).

Kinesics is communication through body language (Hayes, 1973). Facial expressions and body gestures can all transmit information. Individual preferences and individual perceptions of the status of others may be indicated by posture (Hayes, 1973). Facial expressions such as frowns, amount of eye contact, and other factors communicate feelings (Hayes, 1973). These nonverbal actions may be useful or harmful in communication. For example, gazing is used to observe the reactions of others, to indicate the conclusion of a thought, to demand a response from another, to communicate a degree of arousal, or to attempt to suppress an anticipated response (Kendon, 1967).

"Vibes" is a popular term to express what is meant by nonverbal communication. To get vibes is to receive, nonverbally, feelings or emotions from another. When positive feelings or emotions are communicated, we receive good vibes. Bad vibes communicate the opposite. The vibrations from another person may differ from what the person is saying. He may say, "I like you," but his body language, vibes, or other cues demonstrate that this is not the case.

Some research on body language suggests that acts such as touching yourself rather than another, low levels of eye contact, and crossed arms and legs are related to feelings of conflict, a sense of distance, or dissatisfaction with another person (Beier, 1974). However, the accuracy of interpretation of body language may not be high, since some individuals communicate a different emotional state with their body than they are actually experiencing (Beier, 1974).

When nonverbal communications and oral communications carry the same meaning, they are congruent. That is, the words, facial expressions, and other nonverbal communications used, match. For example, an individual who, with a frown and in a low voice, says he is happy to do something will be perceived as communicating incongruently. And when there is an inconsistency between the verbal and nonverbal communication, it seems that reliance is placed primarily on the nonverbal aspect of the communication (Hayes, 1973). That is, the receiver uses the sender's nonverbal communication as the more meaningful indicator of the sender's emotional state and feelings. When there is a consistent discrepancy between a person's verbal and nonverbal language, the ambiguity will lead to higher tension and anxiety on the part of others than when there is high congruence between body and verbal communications.

Actions. "Actions speak louder than words." They also communicate more information. Often, a communication is intended to transmit intentions and feelings. But intentions and feelings are better reflected in what one does—behavior—than in what one says. Where there is an incongruence, for example, between what a manager says and what he does, individuals will—perforce—pay most attention to what is actually done. For instance, most organizations claim that they promote on the basis of merit, but if those promoted are not perceived to be the most competent, other organizational members will come to place little credence in what is said. Thus, for credibility, the words must be followed by appropriate actions. In a study conducted at General Electric (Miller, 1965), several approaches were used to reduce errors of production workers. In the first approach, the foreman talked to each subordinate, showing him examples of poor work, reviewing the subordinate's work methods, and stressing the need for improvement. When this approach failed, a second one was tried. Rapid feedback was given each employee about his errors. Initially, performance improved, but then it dropped back to previous levels. Finally, in the third approach, warnings and reprimands were given, in addition to the feedback. Errors were then significantly reduced. Actions, both rewards and sanctions, indicate that one is serious about what is said. Organizations often seem to say one thing verbally, but mean something else. Both words and deeds help communicate the importance, and validity, of verbal messages.

Problems in the Use of Communication Techniques

A variety of modes are available to communicate, and there are many factors which affect the various modes.

Comprehension. A prerequisite of communication effectiveness is comprehension. Readability is a comprehension problem in written communications. To evaluate comprehension levels, written material is evaluated by means of some formula which is designed to identify the average educational level required in order to understand the language used. The fog index is one such measure. It considers the average sentence length and the percentage of multisyllable words in a communication. The fog index corresponds roughly to grade levels in the school system. The higher the fog index, the higher the grade level required to understand it. The measure is very gross, but it points out the importance of using short sentences and simple words in writing, so that receivers at all grade levels can understand!

Two early studies of application blanks and company newspapers (Paterson and Jenkins, 1948) and employee handbooks (Carlucci and Crissy, 1951) concluded that most are written at too high a reading level for their audience. (In 1954, for example, one study of 100 foremen found that 40 percent read at an 8th-grade level, or below, and that of this 40 percent 8 percent read at the 5th-grade level and below [Bellows, 1954].) Application blanks, company newspapers, and employee handbooks are, at best, easily misunderstood documents—and yet it seems that often an organization goes out of its way to make their comprehension a problem.

A leading cause of comprehension problems is that the educational level of the communicators is too often greater than that of the audience, and that the communicator does not take this into account. (A survey of organization behavior textbooks, for instance, indicated that most of them were probably too difficult for their intended undergraduate audience [Villere and Stearns, 1976].)

Redundancy. Redundancy in communication has different meanings to different individuals. To some, it means repeating an idea several times, in different ways, in order to increase understanding. To others, redundancy is excessive explanation; using too many words to express an idea. The former feel redundancy is useful; the latter believe it best to avoid it.

The effects of benign redundancy (that is, repetition with variation to increase understanding) have been studied, though not extensively. Watson (1962) found that when two "popular" well-written essays were abstracted to one-fourth their original length, information recall was significantly less for the abstracted versions. Furthermore, to achieve a comparable degree of understanding, it took longer to read the abstract than the longer version. Why are there such problems with shorter versions of messages? Watson believes that one problem with the brief summary is that new information is presented at a much higher *rate* than in the longer version of the reading material. This higher rate of new information may exceed the reader's optimum information-processing capacities, causing him to take more time to comprehend the message. (Research on written reports shows that including such things as topic sentences, headings, and summaries results in significant gains in comprehension [Reading, 1972].)

Redundancy can occur in the message itself, as when explanations or words are given in several different ways, or when the same message is transmitted on several communication channels. Hsia (1968) found that both types of communication redundancy contribute to information recall by individuals. Other studies show the positive effects of communication-channel redundancy. For example, presenting information by both oral and written means combined contributes to higher levels of communication effectiveness than that achieved by using only one means (Dahle, 1954; Lawshe, Holmes, and Turmail, 1951).

Overload of Communication Channels. Individuals have a limited capacity to absorb and process information. One study showed a significant reduction in decision-making efficiency when individuals evaluated more than four alternatives (Hayes, 1962). There is probably so much communication in organizations that many important messages are not received at all. Communication overload may lead to confusion, and errors will increase (Katz and Kahn, 1966; Beach, 1967). This is especially likely to occur at higher organization levels, since, as mentioned, the amount of time spent in communication is greatest in the higher levels of the management hierarchy (Hinrichs, 1964).

Excessive information (information overload) may result in overwork of executives. This may, in turn, contribute to health problems such as hypertension, coronary difficulties, and psychological difficulties. Excessive communication may also lead to frustration for the executive trying to cope with it. This frustration may manifest itself in anger, aggression, or other dysfunctional personal behaviors.

There are a number of ways to deal with information overload. One is to have staff assistants screen both information and individuals before they are seen by an executive. This would be done with the intention of weeding out information and people not considered important or appropriate, but such a procedure, of course, can create other problems. It gives excessive power to staff. Or the executive may lose touch with what is happening. (This problem is illustrated in item 8.1, chap. 8.) Some organizations attempt to use a priority system for communications, perhaps by designating the importance by the form of a letter by using certain sizes or colors of paper.

Some organizations attempt to train their managerial personnel how to more effectively use their time communicating. For example, managers may be taught to handle all correspondence only once, or managers may be periodically asked to evaluate the relevance of all incoming communications with only relevant information communications to be continued.

Another approach to screening information is the "management by exception" principle. With this approach, only *significant* deviations from standing plans, rules, goals, standards, operating procedures, or policy are brought to the attention of higher management. That is, attention is given only to the exceptional or unusual.

The information overload problem is one reason why superiors try to limit communications from subordinates. While increased communications between subordinates and superiors improves the subordinates' satisfaction, it also typically leads to overwork, more errors, neglect of important duties, increased frustration for the superior, and so on. Thus, proposals to allow unrestricted or unlimited communication among organizational members are not realistic. Unrestricted communication creates more problems than it solves.

One-way versus Two-way Communication.   Much organization communication is one-way, from higher levels to lower. Instructions, goals, or orders are given, often without obtaining any reactions and/ or questions from the subordinates involved. One-way communication is especially likely when written communications are used. It is also likely in situations where one individual must communicate to a group. Research comparing one-way communication with two-way communication shows two-way communication to be more effective in problem-solving, as well as more satisfying to the participants (Leavitt and Mueller, 1951; Haney, 1964).

However, in such studies the problems to be solved by the subjects are usually very complex, requiring two-way communication for solution. Where understanding is difficult, two-way communication may be very necessary. Where understanding is relatively easy to achieve, two-way communication may not be so critical. There is a cost to two-way communication—the time it takes, thus wasting one of the most valuable resources an organization has. When communicators are quite skilled it is possible that two-way communication is less necessary than when they are unskilled. In highly-structured organizations, where the problems are routine and fairly simple, one-way communication may be more than adequate to achieve required task performance if care is taken.

Source Credibility.   The believability of the source is a significant factor, especially in persuasive communications (Redding, 1972). A long, long time ago, Aristotle, recognizing the importance of the speaker's "image," felt that a speaker's sagacity, high character, and good will (as perceived by the listener) were important to the listener in accepting what the speaker said. In the present day, research has sought to identify the personal factors associated with high or low communicator credibility. Whitehead (1968) identified four factors (similar to those found in other studies)—trustworthiness (honesty), competence (experience), dynamism (aggressiveness), and objectivity (open-mindedness, impartiality). Thus, if a communicator is seen as honest, impartial, and expert, he is a credible source to the receiver, especially if he articulates his points in a dynamic, energetic manner.

Personal dynamism, or vitality, as a factor in source credibility was tested in the famous "Dr. Fox" studies (Ware, 1975). In these studies an actor, Michael Fox, was hired to present lectures to students. The content of the lectures was varied, as was the style in which they were given. In some lectures, factual information was presented in a very dry manner. In others, the lecturer presented nonsense material to the students, but in a very energetic or interesting manner. When the lecturer presented his material in an energetic and entertaining manner, he was rated quite high by the students, even though the actual content of his lecture was nonsense.

In evaluating the credibility of a source, people may be limited in their perceptions by stereotypes (mental images of a certain group). The stereotype may be negative or positive, but the individual tends to perceive the group, or one of its members, according to the stereotype. The effects of stereotypes on credibility has been demonstrated in one case where a cartoon from a labor union publication was shown to union members but was identified as being from a publication of the National Association of Manufacturers. The union members were overwhelmingly critical of it, claiming it was biased and unfair (Whyte, 1952).

Stereotypes operate in organizations as well. Sykes (1964) identified a foreman stereotype among British workers. Foremen were perceived as "brutal," even though workers typically expressed satisfaction with their own individual foreman. Sykes (1964) believed this stereotype resulted from the person's feelings about the past, when managers in England were almost universally perceived to be selfish and harsh. Recent research has shown that male management personnel have stereotypes about females which influence their reactions to communications from women (Rosen and Jerdee, 1974).

Source credibility is related to a belief that the information received is unbiased. This is an important factor to contend with, because the learning of unbiased material is greater than that for biased (Zagona and Harter, 1966). Additionally, when a person argues for a position that appears to be opposite to his own best interests, he is seen as more credible than when arguing for his own interests (Walster, Aronson, and Abrahams, 1966).

In general, other things being equal, higher credibility leads to greater acceptance of a communication (Zimbardo and Ebbesen, 1969). Finally, higher credibility ratings of supervisors are associated with higher supervisory satisfaction scores (Falcione, 1973), perhaps because the characteristics of the supervisor which contribute to the high credibility ratings are characteristics of people which are generally admired.

Preferences for Different Communication Styles. Different individuals use different styles of communication, and different individuals react differently to these different styles. In one study, 18 college students and 18 noncollege students were interviewed by two interviewers, each using three different communication styles. These were:

1. "neutral"—omitting any argument or evaluation on the part of the interviewer;
2. "persuasive"—characterized by a conciliatory approach in which the interviewer tried to reason gently with the interviewee while maintaining respect for the interviewee's opinions;
3. "argumentative"—characterized by vigorous dissent expressed by the interviewer, followed by a rather blunt rejection of the interviewee's views.

The neutral style was the most preferred by the students, followed by the persuasive approach. The argumentative style ranked lowest (Redding, 1972). Maier (1958) has studied three approaches for performance review: the *tell and sell* approach, the *tell and listen* approach, and the *problem-solving* approach. The problem-solving approach is generally preferred by subordinates over the other two.

A difficulty obviously presents itself when the manager's communication style differs from subordinate preferences. For this reason, many managers have been exposed to communication training designed to help them use a communication style least likely to generate conflict or other forms of hostility from others. Most of the approaches suggested in such training involve elements of the neutral or persuasive approach sketched above, or Maier's (1958) problem-solving approach.

Openness and Candor.   An important issue in interpersonal communication is the sending of messages with full disclosure of information, both bad as well as good, or not sending them with full disclosure. Openness involves a willingness to listen, to accept "bad" news, and to be tolerant of views divergent from one's own. Argyris (1966) believes that managers are typically "closed"; that is, not candid in dealing with others. In a study of 165 executives he found that most managers discouraged open expression of ideas and feelings by others as well as by themselves. Such a closed position can result in overlooking certain organizational problem areas, inhibiting creativity, and stifling innovation (Argyris, 1966).

In one study, openness was related to performance. Indik, Georgopoulos, and Seashore (1961), studying 975 employees in a package delivery company, found openness—or a willingness to listen by supervisors—related to higher performance. The relationship was not strong, however, and was not consistent in all units of the company. This is not surprising, since many more factors than simply the receptivity of the immediate supervisor could influence performance. Willits (1967) studied openness in 20 small shoemaking companies in New England. He examined the communication pattern between the presidents and their immediate subordinates as he related such openness to company performance. He concluded that

> ... open communication of ideas, on the part of the executive group correlated with every measure of performance. In the better performing companies there is a freer, less guarded upward flow of ideas and opinions than in the poorer performing companies.

Willits also found "openness" of information associated with higher job satisfaction for the executives. In a study of telephone operators, openness was related to higher satisfaction with the company, job, and supervisor (Burke and Wilcox, 1969).

Personal Characteristics and Communications

Human beings obviously differ in many different ways—personality traits, background, and other personal characteristics. The effects of some of the differences in personal characteristics as they relate to communication are discussed here.

Status Factors.   Status differences may significantly affect the quality of communications among two or more organizational members (Halperin et al., 1976). Throughout their lives individuals are conditioned to defer to those of higher status. This deference takes the form of behavior which shows respect, submission, and acquiescence.

Higher-status individuals expect that they, rather than those with lower status, should control a conversation. The person in control of a communication event does not necessarily do most of the talking. Communication takes place by means of facial expressions, nods, body gestures, and other tactics. The higher-status person expects to dominate, regardless of the method of communication.

Level and title in an organization are determinants of status, but factors such as family background, educational level, past achievements, appearance, and dress may also affect status. Status symbols communicate an individual's status level to others. These are guides to others as to how to act with the holder of the status symbols. Offices, desks, furnishings, and organizational privileges may be status symbols. They create certain behavioral expectations about the amount of deference appropriate when interacting with another, and such symbols are often deliberately manipulated by their holders to influence others. For example, individuals may dress in expensive clothes in order to dominate those dressed less impressively. A manager, for example, may dress in such a manner, trying to give himself an edge in interpersonal interactions (Hayes, 1974).

Self-Concept. Individuals usually have a positive self-concept. They prefer to be treated in a manner which is consistent with this self-concept. If a person perceives himself to be knowledgeable about a certain subject, he wants others to acknowledge his expertise. If an individual believes he is honest, he will probably become angered if treated as a dishonest person. When a person receives a communication inconsistent with his self-concept, he is motivated to attempt to communicate to the sender of the communication what type of a person he *really* is. The original subject of the communication is forgotten; the objective becomes changing one's perception of the other.

One increasingly popular approach in analyzing the effects of one's self-concept as it relates to others is transactional analysis (Cushnie, 1975). In transactional analysis (see item 9.1), communications between individuals are classified into one of three basic types: child, parent, or adult statements (Berne, 1951). Highly emotional statements fall into the child category; judgmental statements fall into the parent category; and problem-solving interactions are considered as adult. Interactions between individuals are defined as transactions. A transaction starts when a person says something to another person, who then responds in some way. When one communicates a judgment to another, such that the other is good or bad, correct or incorrect, effective or ineffective, and so forth, this is a parent statement. It may be followed by a child statement from the other person, as when hurt or anger is expressed. Or the person may respond with another parent statement (make a judgment of the original sender).

ITEM 9.1   Business Tries out "Transactional Analysis"

Now managers are using the *I'm OK—You're OK* communications technique

Hundreds of thousands of amateur psychologists, armed with such books as Eric Berne's *Games People Play* and Thomas Harris' *I'm OK—You're OK,* have been using a behavioral technique called "transactional analysis" *since the mid-1960s* to unravel snarled communication lines with family and friends. Now the concept is taking hold in business. It has been used mainly to teach employees who deal with the public how to relate better to the customer, but managers also are beginning to experiment with TA to try to smooth out communication within a company itself.

Dozens of companies, including American Airlines, Bank of America, United Gas, Inc., Westinghouse Electric Corp., and Questor Corp., already have run executives, ranging from marketing managers to engineers, through TA courses. And some of TA's leading practitioners—Harris, Dorothy Jongeward, and Jut Meininger—are moving the TA crusade into the executive suite. In the past two months alone, the American Management Assn. has offered three-day seminars on TA in four cities.

Many executives who have been exposed to TA trainiing swear by it. Others dismiss it as just another fad. Unfortunately, results are almost impossible to evaluate objectively. And while most bosses have been more than willing to prescribe TA training for line employees, relatively few show much enthusiasm for applying the insights of TA theory to themselves.

A simpler language. Transactional analysis, developed by the Canadian-born Berne, is basically a simplified approach to psychological therapy. Impatient with the technical jargon, exclusiveness, high fees, and prolonged treatment that characterize Freudian analysis, Berne devised a new and simple behavioral vocabulary that is probably TA's fundamental strength. "TA is essentially a language," says Dr. Donald Bowen of the University of Pittsburgh's Graduate Business School. "It translates past psychological ideas into easily understood concepts which even lay people can handle."

Berne said that three primary "ego states"—parent, child, and adult—exist in all of us. In each social situation, or "transaction," one of the ego states predominates. The parent acts as he was taught to, the child as he feels at the moment, the adult after independent thought. When a person assumes the ego state, or role, that the other person expects of him, communication takes

place. Otherwise it is blocked.

The "transaction" that gives TA its name is, to Berne's way of thinking, the basic unit of social intercourse. It involves a stimulus ("Good morning") from one person and a response ("Hello there") from another. By studying transactions, Berne said, a person can determine which ego states he and those around him are operating in and respond accordingly. This may require his reacting as an adult, parent, or child—to fit the role in which the other person places him and to achieve "a parallel transaction." Otherwise there will be a "crossed transaction," and communication will end altogether.

Communication that works brings positive "strokes," a TA concept that establishes love and good feelings. This helps avoid the psychological "games" people play that make themselves and others feel bad.

Skepticism. The vocabulary and the concept leave some managers cold. "Business and industry were burned by the sensitivity training phenomena," acknowledges Dr. Hedges Capers, director of the San Diego Institute of Transactional Analysis, a center for retreats and therapy sessions. "But managers have learned that TA will make them money. TA training teaches respect for others, and that cultivates customers."

Lyman Randall, director of passenger services training at American Airlines' flight academy in Dallas, was one of the first to push for the use of TA in industry, and he admits, "It was a little difficult to sell to top management." The American program, which still is oriented to customer-contact personnel, not managers, has been the model for similar projects in banks, hospitals, hotels, and utilities. Some 15,000 employees at American have had TA training, and its program has been used to train 30,000 employees in other companies.

But the lower-level TA programs often

spark an interest in the ranks of management. At Bank of America, for example, where consultant Dorothy Jongeward has been conducting TA programs for four years, 50 executives last year attended day-and-a-half TA conferences on affirmative action programs for women. Says William Bessey, the bank's vice-president of management development: "Many of the people were tough old bankers who had some pretty firm ideas about women. But these bankers have been touched by the course. TA made affirmative action programs much easier to implement."

No one gave the program a bad review, says Bessey, and one executive, Walter W. Minger, group vice-president of the bank's national division, was so turned on by the workshops that he suggested that his entire department of some 150 persons enroll in a TA course. "I started with partial apprehension and some disbelief about TA but I found it has changed my personal life as well as my interactions with people at the bank," says Minger. "I find I take more care in my relationships with people."

From the top down. Getting management involved also helps alleviate fears of other employees that the company is trying to tamper with their personalities. "I ran into this fear at American Airlines," says Thomas Harris, whose book triggered the first use of TA in companies. "Some of the employees were afraid of being manipulated."

To avoid such feelings, United Gas is putting two corporate executives and 15 key division executives through an experimental TA seminar before offering a TA course to the 600 employees of its Houston division. "There is always the danger that management could try to play church or psychologist or Big Brother," explains Vice-President Roger D. Armstrong.

United Gas's seminars for executives are being conducted by Oklahoma City management consultant Jut Meininger,

author of *Success, Through Transactional Analysis,* a book that has sold 20,000 copies. While insisting that his corporate clients introduce TA into the company through top management, Meininger learned that there are many companies where TA "just doesn't seem to fit." That discovery led him to a study of executive and company "scripts."

Life dramas. Berne had promulgated the concept that most individuals live out scripts, or life dramas, usually based on fairy tales—Sleeping Beauty, Red Riding Hood, Cinderella, or whatever—that were heard repeatedly during childhood. "But executives don't have fairy-tale scripts," Meininger says. "They have adventure-story scripts—Batman, Robin Hood, Buck Rogers, Tarzan, the Lone Ranger and Tonto."

The type of company that tends to reject TA is the one with strongly "parented" people at the top, who believe in tough, dictatorial management, several TA consultants contend. Says Meininger: "Let the market change and they often are in deep trouble. They aren't interested in TA because they can't see that giving people autonomy is productive."

Jongeward agrees. Corporations that play the parent role "may be locked into this autocratic pattern, spending their energies maintaining the old script rather than keeping up with the times," she says.

In fact, part of the attraction of TA to businessmen lies in the fact that it can lay bare the psyche of corporations as well as of individual executives. Not surprisingly, company scripts are largely determined by the scripts of key executives, past and present, says Chicago psychologist and corporate consultant Julian S. Frank, who has worked with such companies as Sears, Roebuck, Bell & Howell, and Zenith. "If I had the life scripts of top executives of all major firms, I would know which stocks to buy and which to sell," Frank contends. "People are programmed from an early age into success or failure patterns."

Changing the script. But the script can be altered. TA's value lies in making people think about their relationships with others and giving them some kind of framework to evaluate and improve them. At Bank of New York, which has sent some vice-presidents as well as lower-level supervisory personnel through TA courses, management-training staff man Thomas C. Lincoln says: "One fellow who was strongly parental had never realized how parental his posture was. He went from recognizing it and laughing about it to doing something about it."

Most companies lump TA training with other behavioral studies. "TA is no panacea," says Lincoln. "Everyone won't be comfortable with it. For some, it will seem too psychological, and for others, it won't be deep enough. But clearly it can be valuable for all levels of management."

Today's young business recruits seem more receptive to TA than some of their predecessors. "The trend to conceptual schemes like transactional analysis is there," says Raghu Nath, director of the management training laboratory at the University of Pittsburgh's Graduate Business School, which uses TA in training executives and MBA students.

The beauty of TA. That view seems to be shared by many in business itself. All of the 68 middle managers at Bank of America who went through TA seminars believed that their adult ego states had been strengthened, 86% felt that they were better able to handle difficult interpersonal problems, and 79% found the

concept useful at home as well as on the job.

"That's the beauty of TA," says Peter J. Burton of the Mountain States Employers Council in Denver. "It's taken home by people. Spouses get together and use it on their kids. It works on a five-year-old as well as on a fellow executive."

That is why so many executives exposed to TA refer to it as "the great equalizer." With TA, the manager strives for adult-to-adult transactions whether he is dealing with a superior or a subordinate. "More than anything else," says a Sears executive, "TA has shown people here that no one is any better as a person than anyone else. We have opened up some tolerance for ideas from guys down below us."

The tolerance can work horizontally too. At Questor, a company that uses TA extensively, a severe conflict arose in a Canadian operation between the manufacturing and finance groups. "It was about to cost us money," says Malcolm Warren, Questor's director of planning and development. "TA did a lot to solve the problem and keep the division in the black."

To consultant Julian Frank, all the TA activity in business signifies the beginning of what he calls a quiet revolution. "People are adopting a transactional way of life," he says. "They want to know how to live with themselves and others. They want to learn what's going on inside their own heads."

Business Week, Jan. 12, 1974

Adult transactions are the most conducive to productive communications. Adult transactions, rather than child or parent transactions, tend to be descriptive of an actual state of affairs. Some students of behavior believe that most individuals are conditioned to make child and parent types of statements, and that consistent use of adult state-ments in communication requires training and practice.

Transactions between individuals can be classified as productive or not productive. Some unproductive transactions occur because there are two levels of transactions going on simultaneously. Thus, while two individuals are ostensibly operating at the adult level, they may in reality be communicating something else with body language. This produces confusion and a breakdown of interpersonal communica-tion.

Transactional analysis also considers various life positions and per-ceptions of the ability of one's self and others. These positions and perceptions influence approaches to solving problems and dealing with others. One of the positions, *I'm OK, you're OK*, assumes most problems are solvable and that people are capable of resolving their conflicts and accepting responsibility. *I'm OK, you're not OK* involves lack of trust in others. *I'm not OK, you're OK* is the position taken when one feels inferior, avoids risks, and attributes success to luck. *I'm not OK and you're not OK* is the position taken when a person is down on himself and everybody else, too.

Emotional State. Emotion can significantly affect the quality of communications. Feelings of anger or hostility or aggression can affect perceptions. Accurate listening and understanding is difficult when an individual's emotions are involved. Moreover, the emotional state of one individual often induces a similar emotional state in other indi-viduals in the communication process.

Another barrier to effective communication is frustration. When an individual is trying to accomplish something and is blocked from it, frustration results. Frustration can give rise to anger—and aggressive feelings—which may manifest themselves in shouting and other emo-tional behavior. In one company (a manufacturer of women's apparel) there was great environmental pressure and uncertainty because of price competition and rapidly changing consumer preferences (Wolf, 1973). Management attempted to get more information to the em-ployees of the organization to reduce this uncertainty. This resulted in too much information to be handled effectively, however, which con-tributed to further frustration, and meetings degenerated into shouting matches. After a series of such emotional experiences, some personnel refused to speak with others at all. Because of the negative emotional climate, communication completely broke down.

Selective Perception. As mentioned in chapter 3, individuals select what they perceive in their environment, and personal interests and objectives are an important factor in this selection process. Communication between individuals may contain descriptive information about the subject discussed, feelings about the topic being discussed, and feelings about the interaction. A person seeking factual information to solve a technical problem will pay attention to different aspects of the communication than will one who is primarily concerned with whether or not the other person likes him. Another person, primarily concerned about whether or not a new work procedure will be accepted, will pay attention to still other aspects of a communication.

Trust in Others.   The concept of trust is somewhat ambiguous. It can refer to one's feeling about the competence of another, or it may refer to whether or not one person believes that another intends to behave in a manner conducive to the first person's interests (Redding, 1972). Trust, as so defined, has been found related to some aspects of a manager's behavior with subordinates. When there is trust in the subordinates' competence, a superior allows them more influence in decision making (Carroll and Tosi, 1973). A superior will also monitor less the performance of a subordinate in whom he has trust (Lowin and Craig, 1968; Carroll, Cintron, and Tosi, 1971), and withhold information from subordinates that he trusts less (Mellinger, 1956; Ritchie and Miles, 1970).

The supervisor's personality is one factor which affects the level of trust. Individuals higher in "authoritarianism" have less trust in others than those lower on this personality dimension (Redding, 1972). Trust in others is probably also influenced significantly by other individuals' actual behavior—that is, their past performance, demonstrated competence, or whether or not they have acted in a way harmful to the interests of another when there was an opportunity to do so.

Interpersonal Anxiety.   Communication between individuals is affected by the interpersonal anxiety experienced by one or more of the parties. Interpersonal anxiety is uneasiness, or apprehension, which is experienced subjectively when interacting with others. It may affect some individuals and not others. It is probably related to the individual's feeling that he may not be able to meet the interpersonal demands placed by others in a communication situation. Perhaps the situation calls for humor, and one of the parties feels unable to reflect this reaction. Or the content of the discussion may be beyond a person's knowledge. In situations where a person feels that others are evaluating him, he may feel anxious because he fears that others will think him stupid, dull, or inarticulate.

Anxiety may manifest itself in an accelerated heart rate, sweating of the palms, muscle tension, higher blood pressure, or dysfunctional stomach secretions. It can lead to increased speech difficulties such as sentence incompletion, repetition, and tongue slips (Martin and Sroufe, 1970). When such speech difficulties occur, they may increase the interpersonal anxiety experienced. If anxiety increases sufficiently, it may affect the person's ability to comprehend and objectively evaluate information. Research shows significantly higher error rates under anxiety (Martin and Sroufe, 1970). In addition, the tense state of the subject may be readily observed by others communicating with him. This awareness may raise their tension levels, which, in turn, further inhibits the communication process.

Personal Concepts. A concept is a term which denotes certain characteristics applied to an object by an individual in an attempt to organize several events, behaviors, or phenomena. The concept is *meaning* for the individual, but with concepts are associated the words they are expressed in—that is, "labels." These labels are, of course, the coin of communication. Unfortunately, however, individuals using the same words often attach different meanings to them. For example, a person growing up in one home will hear the word "union" used in a positive context. Another person will be reared in a home in which the use of the word "union" is surrounded by negativism. For both persons, the concept denoted by the word "union" may be very similar, but the connotations will be quite different.

Through our experiences—our socialization—we come to link labels with the connotations we associate with their accompanying concepts. Thus, certain terms evoke positive reactions, while others generate negative or neutral reactions, and the identical term for a concept can evoke markedly different reactions from different individuals.

For example, managers and labor leaders have quite different reactions to such terms as "grievance," "arbitration," and "seniority" (Weaver, 1958). Korman (1960) found in one organization that different management levels had quite different reactions to and perceptions of such terms as "incentives," "budgets," "conferences," and "cooperation." It follows, then, that though communications may be intended to elicit particular reactions or behavior, it is quite possible that the elicited reactions will vary, simply because people impute different meanings to identical words.

Similarity of Personal Characteristics. Communication is most open and easiest when the persons involved have similar personal characteristics and attitudes. Redding (1972), in a review of research on personal similarity, says, "In general as people perceive more and more ways in which they are similar, they find it easier to communicate successfully with one another." When individuals are different from each other, they are more guarded in what they say. They may not respond as they would when they are with others whom they think are like themselves. This, incidentally, creates a problem in studying human behavior, since studies show that subjects may change their responses to certain questions if they perceive that the interviewer is of a different sex, race, or religion than themselves (Simon, 1969).

When individuals are different, there is uncertainty about the values and perspective of the other. The risk of offending another so that the second person might reject or punish the communicator increases when individuals are different. Thus, differences among individuals inhibit open communication.

Incongruent Attributions of Events. A determinant of an individual's behavior is the way he attributes events to causes. If an individual attributes success or failure in an action to luck, instead of to his skills and abilities, this will influence his future motivation and behavior under similar conditions.

A sender may attribute a problem to one cause, while the receiver of the communication will attribute it to another. This may cause the sender to recommend one course of action, but the receiver may not support the recommendation, since he attributes the cause of the problem to other factors. Such differences in attributions are frequent in organizations and are the basis of much conflict.

Organizational Characteristics and Communication

Some organizations are highly structured and bureaucratic; some are not. Some decisions and tasks in organizations are highly programmed, others are relatively unstructured, without programmed decision strategies. Some organizations have many distinct management levels, while others have few. Such differences in organizations lead to differences in effective communications behavior strategies.

Organizational Level Differences. Organizational level differences influence the quantity, quality, and effectiveness of the communication. In one study supervisors reported the most anxiety when talking to bosses, next most talking to workers, and least when talking with peers (Kelly, 1962). However, the supervisors' listening effectiveness was best when they were most anxious; that is, they listened more carefully when communicating with supervisors than with peers or subordinates. Lawler, Porter, and Tannanbaum (1968) found that managers placed a higher value on communication contacts with superiors than on those with subordinates. They point out that this is likely to lead to a manager communicating to his subordinates, either consciously or unconsciously, that the interaction with them is not valued. Because organization level reflects status, communication distortion will occur.

> In general, the larger the status differential, the more restricted the channels of communication, the greater the tendency for information to flow from low to high status persons and the more distorted the content of the message (Barnlund and Harland, 1963).

Upward communication is also subject to distortion.

> Pleasant matters are more likely to be communicated upward than unpleasant ones, achievements are more likely to be passed upward than information about errors or difficulties encountered at lower levels (Read, 1962).

Distortion of upward communication is likely when there is a great status differential between the superior and subordinate, and if the superior has the power to make or block promotions for the subordinate (Barnlund and Harland, 1963; Cohen, 1958).

Individuals will communicate what they perceive to be in their best interests (Redding, 1972). High-status individuals in organizations are trying to get better performance from lower-level personnel. Lower-level personnel are trying to obtain as many rewards as possible from higher-level personnel. These different objectives make individuals quite selective in what they bring to the attention of others.

Several research studies indicate that bosses are not aware of their subordinates' problems. In one study (Likert, 1959), 95 percent of the foremen queried said they understood the problems of their men but only 34 percent of their subordinates said that their own work problems were understood. In a study of 35 subordinate-superior pairs in four companies, Maier, Read, and Hooven (1959) found that superiors and subordinates agreed fairly well on what the subordinate's job *should be*. They did not agree very well, however, on what the subordinate's job problems and obstacles actually were.

Perhaps superiors do not fully understand their subordinates' problems because they are more interested in their own problems. Information received about topics of little interest to an individual is quickly forgotten (Redding, 1972). Perhaps when a subordinate approached his boss for the first time with a problem, the boss showed little interest. This initial lack of interest may have discouraged the subordinate from bringing problems to his boss at a later time. Or the superior may feel that problems brought to his attention are indicative of subordinate incompetence. If so, and this feeling is communicated (perhaps because the superior exhibits it through emotions to the subordinate), it would further discourage the upward communication of problems.

Organization Structure Distortions. When messages are passed from one individual to another in an organization, certain changes, 'omissions" and/or "distortions," in the content of a message may occur (Guetzkow, 1965). When a message flows through individuals, it is changed in various ways. Sometimes this change is deliberate—as when a subordinate, or a staff assistant, for example, tries to simplify information from other sources to avoid communication overload for the superior. However some "omissions" and/or "distortions" may not be intentional but may occur for other reasons. For example there may be distortion to correspond with the receiver's attitudes, distortion to please the next person in the communication chain, or distortion from excessive oversimplification (Campbell, 1958).

A common transmission problem appears to be the tendency of individuals to interpret present information in terms of the individual's previous knowledge, experience, or understandings (Campbell, 1958). For instance, Dearborn and Simon (1958) found that the way several different managers defined a problem from the same data was related to their assignments in marketing production or finance. Individuals attach meaning based on their past experiences. Individuals may "drop out" what they do not understand, or select that part of the message which supports their present beliefs or attitudes, or impute their own meanings to terms used in the message. The meaning attributed to a message by each receiver may be quite different than that intended by the sender. All of these are problems of communication, and many of them develop because of the particular organizational settings in which the communication is attempted.

However, not all communications suffer from such omissions or distortions (Redding, 1972). Some research shows that if the message is relatively *simple* and the participants have an interest in the subject, the message may accurately pass from one person to another (Redding, 1972). Nevertheless, the more individuals who are involved in transmitting a message, the more likely it is that omissions and/or distortions will occur (Redding, 1972).

Effects of "Opinion Leaders" and "Liaisons." Research has identified the effect of "opinion leaders" (influential individuals) in seeking of information or in attempts to persuade. Opinion leaders are those in a group or community who have high credibility with other members, especially in a particular subject area. Opinion leadership tends to be specific to certain topics or issues. The same person is not the opinion leader for several subjects (Lazarsfeld and Menzel, 1963).

Opinion leaders in a work group may be the formal supervisor, or some other group member. In a study of 178 civil service employees, workers were asked to identify preferred information sources for three different situations: job issues, internal organizational political situations (such as promotions or future organizational changes), and personal or nonjob-related problems (Richetto, 1969). The immediate supervisor was the most preferred source of information for job issues, but not for organizational political issues, or for personal problems. In this same study, the immediate supervisor was rated lower in credibility than other nonsupervisory members of the group. Walton (1962) found that on most topics supervisors were rarely identified as the most preferred source of information. However, in another study, conducted in a company in which counseling and coaching activities of supervisors were emphasized, and when employees felt it was easy to communicate upward, the immediate supervisor was the preferred source of help for job-related problems by more than 70 percent of the factory workers, office workers, and professional workers (Zima, 1968). For personal problems, the immediate supervisor was the most preferred source of help for the office and professional workers. The findings on this issue have been summarized by Redding (1972):

> Supervisors and managers and management spokesmen, in general do not enjoy consistently high credibility/trust ratings from their employees, especially on matters unrelated to the technical expertise or power possessed by superiors. At the same time, the evidence also demonstrates that there is nothing intrinsically prohibiting a superior from being perceived as trustworthy or credible by his subordinates. The trouble seems to be that this latter, ideal condition is more atypical than typical.

"Liaison" individuals are those in a group who *pass on* information to others (Jacobson and Seashore, 1951). Liaisons may not be the same persons as opinion leaders. They pass on information—but it is possible they are not considered as credible sources. One study found that 10 percent of the managers functioned as liaisons, passing messages on after they were received (Redding, 1972). The usual transmittal pattern was for one liaison to pass the communication to several other managers. One of these may be another liaison person who in turn would pass it on. In a study of rank-and-file employees, it was found that about 10 percent acted as liaisons, 57 percent were "dead enders" who failed to pass a message, and 33 percent were isolates who did not even receive a message (Redding, 1972).

Some "liaisons" in boundary-spanning positions in an organization secure information from outside the organization and pass it to the inside. This information is often information about the technological or market environment. In a study of research laboratories, only a few professionals acted as liaisons, transmitting scientific and technical information from the field (e.g., from scholarly journals) to other professionals in the research laboratory (Redding, 1972).

It is, of course, possible to identify those in an organization who are opinion leaders and liaisons. One way is to observe the number of times an individual contacts others in the group, then determining who is transmitting information to whom, or who has the greatest amount of influence over whom. From this information, a communication network or sociogram, can be developed which shows the communication or influence patterns in a group. An analysis such as this may well show that a particular person may be an opinion leader in spite of having only a few contacts with others. His influence may come by virtue of having influence over several other opinion leaders.

Communication Networks. Effective decision making requires information, and thus those who occupy strategic communication points in the organization are likely to have power, and to emerge as leaders (Hampton, Summer, and Webber, 1968). Some experiments which show this are those in which individuals were structured, or organized, in different ways and given problems to solve. The aim of the research was to assess the effect of different communication structures on participant performance and satisfaction. Some of the different structures—or communication networks—are shown in figure 9.4. In figure 9.4, the person in the center position in the wheel ("C") is able to communicate with all the participants in the spokes, but they can only communicate with him. The center individual emerges as the decision maker or leader, even though some individuals at the spokes may have more traits typically associated with leadership (e.g., decisiveness). These results suggest that an individual's organization position and his access to information plays a major role in determining his authority and status, and are consistent with Walton's (1962), which indicate that an organization's communication network is dominated by certain individuals ("centrals") in key positions with formal authority, power or expertise.

FIGURE 9.4 Communication Networks

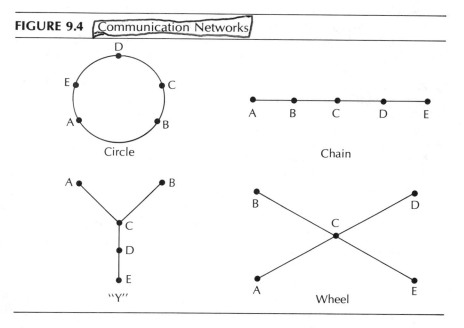

Circle   Chain   "Y"   Wheel

Some research has considered the relationship of task performance and various types of networks. Effectiveness varies with the nature of the task (Lawrence and Seiler, 1965). For example, the wheel is efficient for simple tasks, but individuals at the end of the spokes, who simply take orders, and dissatisfied with their position. Performance on simple tasks then declines from the Y to the chain and is least effective in the circle (fig. 9.4). For more complex tasks, the circle network, where each can communicate with all, seems to produce high task performance—and satisfaction. The circle network seems most effective where there are sudden and confusing changes in the task requirements.

One might conclude from network studies that communication systems where information flows through a single coordinating leader, as in the wheel network, would be best for simple and programmed tasks, as in the bureaucratic organization. Where the tasks are more complex and changing, as in the flexible form of organization, the circle network, in which individuals exchange information with each other would be more functional. However, several studies have not shown any differences in job performance when alternative communication networks are used (Redding, 1972). Obviously more research is needed to pinpoint the optimum network for a given organization.

The research on communication networks also indicates that there is a tendency for a structure to emerge which is appropriate for the task. For example, in one study (Faucheux and Mackenzie, 1966), individuals were organized into the all-channel structure, where all individuals can contact all others in the group. For simple problems, the group reorganized itself into something like the wheel structure. When more complex problems were introduced, the group shifted back to the all-channel structure because in complex problems information requirements are too great for one individual to handle.

Some research shows that, although there are often initial differences in the wheel and the circle in problem-solving ability, after a time the performance differences narrow significantly as individuals learn to cope with the problem-solving restraints imposed by the structure (Burgess, 1968). Thus, it appears that individuals can learn to solve problems and perform tasks effectively in several types of communication structures.

To achieve coordination among people, then, communication must occur. Thus, communication is one of the cornerstones of sound administration. To have managers make decisions from similar bases, they must understand concepts similarly. This will insure that policies are interpreted consistently, reducing the need for repeated and time-consuming attempts at clarification.

In this chapter we have shown that many barriers—personal and organizational—can hinder the understanding needed to achieve the desired consistency. Managers must be aware of these barriers in order to overcome them.

Discussion Questions

1. How do you sense oral communications would have a different effect than written? For social situations? In work situations?

2. Body language "communicates." Look carefully at what the next person you see is telling you. Have you ever been in a situation where someone interpreted your body language differently from what you intended? If so, what was it, and what happened as a result?

3. Why do you think redundancy can be positive? Negative? Can you relate redundancy in communication to House's path-goal theory (chap. 8)?

4. Why is Joe DiMaggio a credible source as a coffee-maker advertisement?

5. When would "openness" be undesirable in communications? Why do you think you should protect the other person? Or why shouldn't they know?

6. How do organizational settings (such as office location) affect communication patterns?

7. Think of the last time you met with a person of higher status than you. Was the purpose of the meeting pleasant for you? What kind of message was communicated? Was the purpose critical of you? Was the meeting intimidating? What caused it to be so?

Chapter 10
The Acquisition and Maintenance of Human Resources

Most managers say that dealing with people is their most difficult problem. Attempts to influence others (leadership), and to inform and persuade (communications), are interpersonal processes; that is, they deal with human interaction. In this chapter we focus on organizational systems which are intended to ease the problem of managing people. These systems are tools, if you will, that a manager has at his disposal. If they are used well, organization effectiveness will result.

Staffing

Staffing is the process of providing needed human resources to the organization. It includes the activities of recruitment, selection, and placement. Recruitment attracts applicants to the organization; the selection process chooses those to whom employment offers will be made; and placement determines the appropriate position, or role, or field, for the individuals selected. The objective of staffing is of course to increase organizational effectiveness. This objective is achieved when individuals with the necessary skills, attitudes, needs, and self-concepts are matched with organizational requirements. This matching contributes in a number of different ways to effectiveness. Outputs are achieved—products, services, and ideas—which contribute to profits or returns, and turnover and absenteeism are minimized. A review of research on turnover and absenteeism by Porter and Steers (1973) concluded that level of job satisfaction is directly related to levels of turnover and absenteeism, and one study found a significant relationship between the level of unsatisfied needs of employees and absenteeism (Hrebiniak and Rateman, 1973).

While individual needs are important considerations in staffing strategies, however, abilities may today be the easiest factor to measure, since more research has been directed at this problem than at the others. In some individuals abilities improve over time; in others, they do not. Determining which individuals have the capacity to grow, develop, and learn becomes especially important when selecting individuals for a career (e.g., managers and professionals) as opposed to selecting for just one position.

Contingency Factors in Staffing. Different individuals will perform differently in a given situation, with. the situational requirements having a significant effect on the type of individuals who will perform best in the situation. That is, individual characteristics should be assessed in terms of alternative job behaviors required in different situations in order to result in desired organization consequences such as effective role performance, organization stability, or individual growth and development. In selecting individuals for a specific organizational role, then, behavioral characteristics must be evaluated in terms of the situation, and one aspect of the organizational situation may be important in one set of circumstances, another in another. Some organizations are highly structured, of course, and some are not. In one study it was found that individuals who (1) were willing to accept authority from higher levels, (2) were willing to impose authority on lower levels, and (3) were competitive with their peers were successful in the more bureaucratic organization, but these same characteristics were not associated with success in organizations with less structure (Miner et al., 1974). Several studies show that where job complexity is high, individuals who have strong desires for satisfaction of the higher-order needs, such as those for accomplishment or opportunities to grow, will perform better and be more satisfied than those individuals concerned primarily with lower-level needs, such as security (Hackman and Lawler, 1971; Brief and Aldag, 1975). Litwin and Stringer (1968), from their research, conclude that variations in individual employee needs determines the degree to which different organizational climates produce a favorable reaction from organizational members. For certain organizational climates it is best to select individuals high in achievement needs, while in other environments individuals high in affiliation or in power needs would be more appropriate. Tests have been developed to better relate the individual to a specific work environment.

The required critical behaviors to be effective also vary with the situation. Job performance is the key factor, but in some positions, the individual's stability is most important. This could be the case when performance levels are similar for all individuals, but it is critical to minimize absenteeism because of the high cost, idle time for equipment, or because each person is an essential component in an integrated work team. On the other hand, in some roles the individual must continuously be in a learning mode, as when it is necessary to keep abreast of developments in a field to reduce the level of environmental uncertainty for the organization.

Staffing and Individual Differences. Staffing problems occur because the traits and characteristics of individuals differ, and these differences are associated with different organizational role requirements. If all individuals were alike, or virtually so, recruiting, selection and placement decisions would be relatively simple. Each person could be expected to do as well as another.

FIGURE 10.1   Frequency Distributions of Scores on O'Connor Finger Dexterity Test of Random Group (top) and Three Groups of Industrial Employees

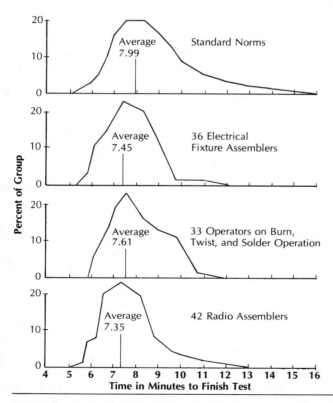

Source: Tiffin, Joseph, *Industrial Psychology* (New York: Prentice-Hall, 1947), p. 14.

Human beings differ with respect to various types of intelligence (e.g., verbal, mathematical), personality factors (e.g., authoritarian, independent, submissiveness), values, motivations, interests, sensory abilities (visual, taste, hearing, color discrimination), dexterities (finger, hand, arm), strength, quickness, perceptual speed and accuracy, and many other factors. An example of variability on such characteristics is shown in figure 10.1, a distribution of scores by various groups on a test of finger dexterity. Note that only a very small percentage of the populations are at the extremes; the largest proportion is in the middle ranges. Figure 10.1, by analogy also demonstrates that everyone has some of any required characteristic. Thus it is incorrect to say that an individual either has, or doesn't have, a particular characteristic—say mechanical aptitude. More accurately, everyone has some degree of mechanical aptitude, and this will be more or less than other individuals have.

FIGURE 10.2 Psychograph of John Doe

Test	Norm Group	John Doe Percentile Score
		10 20 30 40 50 60 70 80 90 100
Miller Analogies H	College Graduates	
Purdue Adaptability	High School Graduates	
Seashore Music	U.S. Men	
Pitch		
Loudness		
Rhythm		
Time		
Minnesota Clerical	High School Graduates	
Names		
Numbers		
Paper Form Board	Factory Men	
O'Connor Finger Dexterity	Factory Men	
How Supervise	Factory Foremen	
Kuder Preference	U.S. Men	
Mechanical		
Scientific		
Literary		
Michigan Vocabulary	College Graduates	
Commerce		
Government		
Biological Sciences		
Fine Arts		

Some personal characteristics tend to be relatively independent of one another within the same person (Tyler, 1965). Thus an individual tends to be high on some characteristics, low on others, and in the middle on others as compared to other people. Figure 10.2 shows how an individual might vary on several different tests. A person (John Doe) may score low on the Miller Analogies Test, for example, compared to a norm group of college graduates, but very high on the O'-Connor Finger Dexterity Test, compared to a norm group of factory men. It is unlikely that any particular individual will be universally low or universally high on most human characteristics. When we say that an individual is relatively low or high with respect to a characteristic we mean relative to a specific group. An applicant, for example, might be very high in intelligence, strength, or dexterity when compared to members of one occupational group, but compared with members of other occupational groups, he may be low.

Relative differences among individuals can be accounted for by both heredity and by environment. Some characteristics affected by heredity are obviously relatively unmodifiable by training and this is an important consideration in staffing.

It is important to remember that even though several individuals may differ greatly, the differences may not be relevant to the staffing decision. First, the difference among applicants may not be related to position, or job, requirements and thus are irrelevant. For example, two applicants may differ in physical appearance. If physical appearance is not related to job effectiveness, it should not be considered in the evaluation. In a listing of 7,955 job requirements, personal appearance accounted for only 3 percent (Shartle, 1952). Additionally, the difference between two individuals may not be large enough to be of significance. For example, suppose the I.Q. of one applicant is 110 and that of another is 105; this is a meaningless difference for most jobs. Sometimes a difference doesn't make a difference.

Much research has examined how groups differ on various characteristics. If large differences exist between groups, and such differences were related to job effectiveness, it would be best to select only those from the more qualified group for certain jobs.

Do such group differences exist? Yes, of course. Research has found some differences in the average scores of various personal characteristics of different groups (Tyler, 1965), but the variability between the *averages* of any two groups is almost always less than the variability *within* those groups on the particular characteristic. This has been pointed out by Tyler (1965), who in discussing the research on sex differences states:

In any discussion of average differences . . ., reference should again be made to the importance of noting variability as well as averages.

In most of the abilities we have considered, differences between the sexes are so small, and differences between individuals of the same sex are so large that it is possible to find an individual who, regardless of his or her sex, will show almost any specified degree of any special ability.

On a characteristic such as physical strength, for example, there are females who are stronger than many males, and therefore more qualified than those men for jobs requiring strength—even though there is an obvious average difference in strength of male and female groups. Even where the average differences are quite pronounced (as they are for occupational groups), the variability within the groups tends to be quite large compared to the group differences. Intelligence tests repeatedly demonstrate this. There may be, for example, large differences in tested intelligence within such groups as, say, truckdriver and miner, accountant and lawyer, but no matter how skilled or unskilled the occupation, there are always individuals in the group with extremely high intelligence test scores.

Recruitment

The more favorably an organization is viewed by those it wishes to attract, the easier it is to recruit for it. Well-known, highly reputable organizations have less difficulty in recruiting than less well-known organizations—just as certain college athletic teams have less difficulty than others in recruiting. This is probably because being associated with a high-status organization increases one's level of self-esteem.

In addition, some may feel that large, well-known organizations provide better upward mobility, or opportunities to enter other high-status organizations in later stages of life. On the other hand, many individuals feel that smaller and less well-known organizations provide them a better opportunity to meet needs such as more autonomy, more rapid advancement, or the desire not to be "swallowed up" in a large bureaucracy. Efforts to entice an individual to a particular organization will be successful when the prospective applicant believes that his needs will be better met there than in competing organizations.

Pay level is, naturally, an important factor in an organization's attractiveness. All other things being equal, of course, the higher the level of compensation, the greater will be the proportion of applicants from the available supply. Some organizations have a policy of paying significantly above the going rate to recruit the best individuals from a group of applicants. By attracting the high-performing applicants from a group in this way, overall labor costs may not necessarily be higher than those of competing firms if additional productivity offsets the additional costs of the higher compensation level. Of course this approach can only be effective when the selection system identifies the superior employee.

Usually, recruitment precedes selection—the process of choosing from among applicants—but sometimes the selection comes first. For example an organization first chooses a person it wants to become an organizational member. Then it does all it can to recruit, or entice, him to come to work for it. Supply and demand obviously influences organizational recruitment. When there is a shortage in a particular occupational group, recruitment receives great emphasis. When the demand for candidates exceeds the supply, there is no selection: You hire whomever is available. On the other hand, when the supply is plentiful, recruitment is quite easy and selection becomes a problem.

Candidates for any position may be found both inside and outside the organization. For instance, transfers and promotions fill vacancies, but often the organization must go outside itself to find viable personnel alternatives. These two sources are discussed below.

Internal Sources of Personnel. For jobs beyond the first, or entry level, the primary source of applicants is present organizational personnel, since these constitute promotions for them and most organizations have a policy of promotion from within. Since most organizational members view promotion opportunities as an important job factor, morale can be significantly influenced by promotion procedures.

The promotion process may be quite structured and well defined. For example, the organization may post a notice of job vacancies in various locations and organizational members then "bid," or apply, for the opening. In choosing from such applicants, various combinations of seniority and personal qualifications are involved. Where the organization has a union, as do many hierarchical organizations, seniority will be more heavily weighted than in nonunion (generally, dynamic) organizations. Seniority will be a more critical factor for promotions among rank-and-file employees than for managerial and professional employees.

Promotions to managerial positions above the foreman level on the basis of seniority alone are rare. Perhaps this is due to a belief that managers vary more in performance than rank-and-file workers, and that the performance of managers has more of an effect on the organization's success than that of a rank-and-file worker. Nevertheless, seniority has a powerful appeal. It is objective and not as subject to criticism or second-guessing in personnel decisions as is the use of "merit." For this reason, administrators may feel safer using seniority than merit as a basis for advancement. Culturally, there is general support for the notion that longer-service individuals should receive more recognition and respect than those with less service. In practice, this cultural value provides much support for the seniority principle. Many organizational members will feel a sense of "equity" if promotions are made on the basis of seniority.

This is not to say that the use of seniority as a basis for promotion is without its problems. Seniority boundaries—that is, limits of an individual's seniority rights—often create difficulties. Do an individual's seniority rights extend to the whole company, to a single plant, to only a department in a plant, or to just one work unit within a department? Another, more recent, problem for the seniority system has been created because of past discriminatory practices, as can be seen from item 10.1. If in the past an organization did not allow certain minority group members to hold certain jobs, but now does, such individuals will always be disadvantaged in internal personnel decisions based on seniority. In some cases, the newer employees have demanded an end to the old seniority system. In a number of organizations, this issue has created intense feelings of inequity among the newer and the older employees.

ITEM 10.1   Personnel Problems

"Last Hired, First Fired" Takes It on the Chin

When unionized companies must cut back on their work force, they almost always use job seniority as the basis for deciding which workers to lay off. But an important lower court ruling has just upset this "last hired, first fired" principle when it involves workers who owe their low seniority to past discrimination. If the Supreme Court eventually upholds this ruling, it will mean heavy costs and disruption to hundreds of companies, as well as internal trouble to unions.

In a decision almost sure to reach the Supreme Court, U.S. District Court Judge Fred J. Cassibry has ruled in New Orleans that Continental Can Co. and a Louisiana local of the United Steelworkers violated civil rights laws by using seniority as the sole criterion for laying off workers at the company's Harvey (La.) plant. The judge held that Continental's procedures were discriminatory because black workers' low seniority stemmed from the company's previous failure to hire blacks.

John Falkenberry, a Birmingham

lawyer for the Steelworkers, speaks for many attorneys when he says that "the decision will be important for a long time to come."

No easy solutions. Seniority rules have posed problems ever since Congress passed the Civil Rights Acts of 1964. Fiercely defended by union members as their historic protection against management favoritism in pay, promotions, and layoffs, seniority can work to the disadvantage of minority and women workers, whose past exclusion leaves them with few years of service. Courts and government agencies have tried to correct the resulting inequities in pay and promotion by money settlements, plantwide seniority instead of departmental seniority, affirmative action programs, and other devices. A decade of relative prosperity has postponed action in the supersensitive area of layoffs. Now the moratorium is over.

In his decision, Judge Cassibry noted that Continental Can's peak work force of 400 in 1971 included 50 blacks. With the current work force down by two-thirds, only two blacks remain: men hired during the labor shortage of World War II. The company did not hire blacks again until the 1960s, and by then those white workers still on the payroll had already accumulated seniority. Since illegal racial discrimination created this seniority pattern, said Judge Cassibry, the company and union cannot legally use it as the basis for layoffs.

But the judge also ruled that the company should not penalize longtime white employees by firing them in order to rehire laid-off blacks. Instead, he directed the company and union to submit a better solution to him. If the plan satisfies him, he will issue it as a judicial order. Judge Cassibry suggested one possibility: the payment of lump sums to tide over laid-off blacks until attrition in the work force opens up slots for them.

Whatever the judicial order, the next step almost inevitably is an appeal to U.S. Circuit Court in New Orleans where legal experts expect the decision to be upheld.

Mixed reaction. The case, brought as a class action by four laid-off blacks, "will be quite frightening to some people and quite welcome to others," says William J. Kilberg, the U.S. Labor Dept.'s top attorney. The auto industry is one with obvious reason for fright. The current slump has produced deep work force cuts, removing most of the women hired under an April, 1972, order from the Office of Federal Contract Compliance as well as many blacks hired under earlier affirmative action programs. A Supreme Court decision upholding the Continental Can ruling would have an enormous impact on the industry and its union.

Stephen Schlossberg, Washington general counsel for the United Auto Workers, says that the UAW opposes giving newly hired minorities and women false seniority because it "dilutes" the legitimate rights of senior workers who have caused no injury. Monetary damages would be an acceptable remedy, he says. Auto industry executives declined to comment on the Cassibry ruling.

Among those welcoming the decision, the National Organization for Women is considering filing its own antilayoff suits, says Marilyn Patell, past president of NOW's Legal Defense Fund. And Lynn Carcy, head of NOW's compliance task force, suggests a formula that might meet Judge Cassibry's request for a fair solution: furlough minority and women workers in the same proportion as the over-all layoff. For instance, if 10% of the work force must be fired, limit the percentage of minorities and women furloughed to 10%. "This isn't giving them an extra break," Miss Darcy says, "because they had their layoffs before they were hired."

This reasoning is already being tested in a suit in New York City.

Reverberations. Meanwhile, the decision issued in Judge Cassibry's New Orleans courtroom is causing ever-widening legal ripples. Kilberg notes that no previous ruling moves so far from helping the specific workers hurt by discrimination—that is, those blacks who could not get jobs at Continental Can's Harvey plant during the 1940s and 1950s—toward compensating totally different persons who are deemed to be in the same category. Asked how many plants might be affected, a Justice Dept. lawyer says: "That turns directly on the country's economic stability."

As for Judge Cassibry's decision, a source close to him says: "The relief he will approve is not going to penalize the man with seniority rights and it's not going to penalize the blacks, so the brunt will fall on the company."

Business Week, March 9, 1974

Reprinted from the March 9, 1974, *Business Week* by special permission. Copyright © by McGraw-Hill, Inc.

(On March 4, 1976, *The Wall Street Journal* reported that the Supreme Court allowed that federal judges could award seniority retroactively to employees who had been victims of past employment discrimination, but the Court did not deal with seniority claims of workers who contend that they did not apply for a job because they knew of the employer's discriminatory practices.)

External Sources of Personnel. There are several sources to which organizations can look for personnel, and depending on what kind of persons are needed, some are better than others.

1. *Educational Institutions.* Colleges and universities are very important sources of personnel for the managerial and professional jobs in organizations. In a typical college recruiting activity, companies visit colleges, primarily on the basis of their proximity, size, reputation, and degree offerings. Recruiters come to the campus, make their presence known through advertising, interview those students who express an interest, and then make recommendations as to which of those interviewed should be extended offers to visit the company. In rare instances, they will recommend that a firm job offer be made without a further visit.

Campus recruiters come from different subsystems of organizations. They often have experience in a department of employee relations, but may be operating personnel. If technical personnel are being sought, then professionals are likely to be recruiters. For example, in one large chemical company more than 100 professionals participated in the college recruiting program on a part-time basis (Orth, Bailey, and Wolck, 1964). They visited 125 colleges to obtain between 80 and 175 college graduates, depending on the quota for a given year.

In evaluating college graduates, employers say they rate appearance and personality as most important. Grades are next most important, and types of courses taken and work and campus experiences are rated third in importance (Endicott, 1976). In studies of the recruiting experiences of business school graduates at two universities, Carroll (1966) found that more attractive students were more successful than less attractive in obtaining visits and job offers from organizations, in spite of the fact that appearance has not been identified in research as being associated with managerial and professional effectiveness (Carroll, 1969). In another study, it was found that professional interviewers in choosing from among students preferred high scholastic standing to low scholastic standing, males over females, and more physically attractive candidates (both male and female) over less attractive candidates (Dipboye, Fromkin and Wiback, 1975).

The importance of grades in selection has been a matter of some controversy. Carroll (1969), reviewing studies which related undergraduate grades to later managerial success, concluded there was a positive relationship between good grades and effective performance. Another study found that good graduate school grades were also associated with managerial success, especially for those in staff positions (Weinsten and Srinivasan, 1974).

Since recruitment consists of selling an organization to a prospect, it is of interest to know what college graduates, especially the better ones, want in their first job. One study, by Paine (1969), compared the ratings of job factors for students from honor dormitories and those from regular dormitories. The honor students differed from regular students by giving greater emphasis to intrinsic job factors such as quality of work and self-development opportunities and less emphasis to extrinsic job factors, such as salary increases and promotions (Paine, 1969).

2. *U.S. Employment Service (U.S.E.S.)* The U.S.E.S. is the largest employment agency in the United States and places 10 million persons annually (Wernimont, 1974). This organization will conduct analyses of jobs to be filled and will also test applicants. The U.S.E.S. now operates the Job Bank, which lists jobs available in 50 U.S. cities and 22 states.

3. *Private Employment Agencies.* These organizations find personnel for organizations for a fee and jobs for jobseekers for a fee. Their activities are regulated by the various states. They do testing for clients. Many now specialize in the provision of part-time or temporary help to meet unusual work demands of employers.

4. *Walk-ins.* For well-known companies in the community it may be relatively easy to attract job-seekers without regular advertising. Walk-ins are a good source of applicants. Research shows there are many walk-ins because rank-and-file blue-collar workers tend to rely

on tips from friends and relatives about jobs rather than searching for jobs in a systematic manner themselves (Myers and Schultz, 1951).

5. *Other Sources.* Advertising job openings in newspapers and in special journals is also a much-used approach to recruitment. Many organizations, however, feel that advertising brings in too large a number of unqualified applicants. Unions are perhaps the major source of personnel in many industries such as the construction and maritime industries, and in these industries employers rely on the union to perform personnel activities for them. Organizations also recruit at high schools and vocational schools.

Selection and Placement

In the selection approach, one particular position, or role, is kept in mind when evaluating applicants, and applicants are compared against the requirements for it. With the placement approach, the individual's strengths and weaknesses are determined with a view toward finding the organization role, or situation, in which that individual's talents can best be utilized. In selection, the emphasis is on rejection. The purpose is to select from a large group of applicants the person best suited for a particular role. In placement, however, the emphasis is on how a particular individual can best be used.

In periods of labor shortage, most organizations emphasize the placement approach. Contrariwise, the selection approach is most favored when many applicants exist for a vacancy. Also, the selection approach has probably been traditionally used for lower-level personnel, the placement approach most frequently for college graduates, such as those entering the first level of management.

To use the placement approach, a number of different positions must be available, which is most likely to be the case in large organizations. The task in such a case is to maximize both role performance and role satisfaction with a given, fixed group of applicants who differ in individual characteristics and a finite group of vacancies to which they can be assigned. Perhaps the most striking example of an organization that must deal with this problem is the military, into which there flows a continuous stream of untrained recruits who must be assigned to a wide variety of specialized roles (Dunnette, 1965).

In using the placement approach, Dunnette (1965) recommends the identification of task clusters. In each cluster are jobs with some similarity in task content, although there are some differences. For example, an engineering cluster may have research jobs, applied production jobs, and technical services to customers. Prospective engineers are assigned differentially to these various jobs, based on abilities, preferences, and task demands.

Determination of Job Requirements. In staffing, characteristics of individuals are compared with job requirements. Formal procedures are used in many organizations to determine these requirements. Job analysis, a traditional approach, attempts to find answers to the questions of: *What is done? How is it done? Why is it done? What skills are needed to do it?* A variety of approaches for finding answers to such questions may be used; for example, questionnaires or interviews of job incumbents or their supervisors, or outside observers, motion picture cameras, or various other job measurement or timing devices.

Motion and time-study approaches developed by Taylor and his colleagues in scientific management are still widely used. A more recent device, the Position Analysis Questionnaire (PAQ) has been developed by McCormick and his colleagues (1972). The PAQ describes job behavior characteristics. These behavioral job characteristics specify the degree to which a particular position involves information processing, decision making, obtaining information from people, contacts with the public, structured versus unstructured work, communication to others, and other behavioral requirements. The data for each position is collected, organized, and written in narrative form. The result is a job description which contains the requirements of the job, the general authority/responsibility relationships, and other pertinent data.

The mechanistic, or bureaucratic, organization will emphasize formal approaches such as job analysis and job descriptions for developing and clarifying position prescriptions, but in the organic, or dynamic, organization, more subjective informal procedures are used, since the work assignments are constantly changing and position requirements are not stable enough for a clear definition. Of course, specificity of formal role prescriptions is greater at the lower levels of the organization than at the upper levels.

Determining the Capacities of People. Because of individual differences and differences in position requirements, individual capacities must be assessed to make the best selection or placement decision. The many different assessment or measurement devices used by organizations include interviews, application blanks, references from former employers, psychological tests, and assessment centers.

1. *The Application Blank.* The application blank can provide

staffing information of significant value. It elicits information about an individual's personal characteristics (age, marital status, etc.), as well as background and experience (previous jobs, education). Application blank information has been found to be useful in predicting the performance of professionals such as engineers and scientists, the revenue produced by salesmen, creativity in youth, turnover and absenteeism in a variety of occupations, and even proneness to theft (Stone and Ruch, 1974).

2. *The Reference Check*. The reference check is sent to former employers (if any) of an applicant to verify information provided by the applicant as well as to help predict the applicant's job success. However, most research studies on the reference check show it to be of limited value in predicting job success, basically because former employers tend to be somewhat reluctant to make negative comments about former employees (Nash and Carroll, 1970).

3. *Psychological Tests*. Tests have been widely used for selection and placement since World War I. In 1963, about 90 percent of all companies surveyed by the U.S. Bureau of National Affairs were using psychological tests. However, due to pressure from the Equal Employment Opportunity Commission in enforcing the Civil Rights Act of 1964 to use tests only if they have a demonstrated relationship to job proficiency, the proportion of companies using tests declined to 55 percent by 1971. (Stone and Ruch, 1974).

The types of tests most widely used include cognitive ability tests (e.g., ability to use words, numbers, to visualize objects in space, to perceive details quickly and accurately), psychomotor ability tests (e.g., finger dexterity, manual dexterity, finger-wrist speed), job knowledge tests (e.g., knowledge of occupational tools or language, typing speed), vocational interest tests (e.g., preferences and interests for various activities, subjects, types of people), and personality tests (e.g., measures of extroversion, dominance, self-esteem, neurotocism, cautiousness).

All tests, like other measuring instruments, should have both reliability and validity (as discussed in chap. 2). A measure is reliable if individuals receive about the same relative score when they are measured at different times or by different versions of the test. Validity is the degree to which the measure accomplishes the purpose for which it was devised. A finger dexterity test is valid if it accurately differentiates among individuals with different degrees of finger dexterity. A salesman's performance test is valid if it predicts, in advance, which individuals will be most successful as salesmen.

Tests differ in validity. Generally, abilities tests have shown a higher relationship to on-the-job behavior than personality and interests tests because cognitive and psychomotor abilities can be more accurately measured than personality and temperament. The cognitive tests have been predictive of success in training classes, but predicting an individual's learning ability is easier than predicting an individual's job performance. Job performance is a consequence of many factors, of which mental ability may be only one.

It is easier to predict failure than success on a job. To predict failure, one must identify only a lack of one factor (such as ability), while to predict success, one must identify a number of factors, all of which contribute to success.

Different tests predict better for some occupations than for others (Ghiselli, 1966). Mental ability tests have been useful at predicting success on managerial jobs. Perceptual speed tests have been predictive of success in clerical jobs. Interest tests, but not ability tests, have been useful for predicting sales personnel success. Certain psychomotor tests have been useful for predicting success at skilled jobs (Ghiselli, 1966). When tests have high predictive capacity, there can be considerable costs savings as the result of using them (Stone and Ruch, 1974).

4. *The Interview.* Research over the years has shown that the typical employment interview has little reliability or validity (Wagner, 1949; Mayfield, 1964). That is, when interviewing the same candidates, different interviewers will disagree among themselves on the candidates' qualifications. Nor do interviewers seem to be able to make accurate predictions about the later job performance of candidates.

There are a number of reasons for the ineffectiveness of the interview. First, different interviewers do not have a common standard as a reference point for judging candidates. Interviewers tend to compare the candidates they see against each other and in this way an average candidate may be judged quite good if the other candidates preceding him were quite bad (Carlson et al., 1971). Also, interviewers tend to stress appearance in making judgments (Carroll, 1964). Even when interviewers are considering the same candidates, they evaluate the same information about the candidates differently (Valenzi and Andrews, 1973). Pressure to hire a certain number of candidates has also been found to distort interviewer judgments (Carlson, et al., 1971).

5. *Assessment Centers.* Assessment centers permit controlled observation of job applicants or of organizational members being considered for different positions while they perform various tasks. They are rated on these tasks by observers. This approach, used in World War

II, has been used extensively recently to identify management potential of individuals being considered for other positions, in candidates for sales and technical positions, and potential for first-line supervisory positions (Stone and Ruch, 1974). The assessment center approach has participants carry out various exercises and group discussions while being observed and evaluated by a group of higher-level company managers. Various tests and questionnaires are also administered, and research indicates that predictions of later success made from assessment center observations can be made (Bray and Grant, 1966). An example of a variation of this technique is described in item 10.2.

ITEM 10.2   Assessment

How Rapistan Ltda. Hired a Salesman

HELP WANTED

Technical Salesman Needed. International company, expanding its market, seeks a dynamic individual with sales experience in medium and heavy machinery. He should have secondary education, good health and appearance, a proven interest in mechanical problems, and facility in communication. Salary open, plus car and other fringe benefits.

Responding to the above advertisement in a São Paulo, Brazil, newspaper, 10 job candidates find themselves in the office of Dr. A. H. Fuerstenthal, a management psychologist, at 5:30 one Thursday afternoon. They are there to participate in a unique experiment in salesman selection. Henry Hanelt, director of Rapistan Ind. e Com. Ltda. (the local licensee of Rapistan, Inc., Grand Rapids, Mich.), is present. His company needs a salesman for its materials-handling equipment and he will decide which candidate gets the job.

The candidates have been told only to appear at 5:30. When they arrive, Dr. Fuerstenthal explains that each one will have five minutes in which to stand up and sell himself; then the others, seated around the table with him, will have five minutes in which to question him and try to punch holes in his arguments. Meanwhile Fuerstenthal and Hanelt will observe the presentations, the questioning, and the emerging personalities of the candidates, and decide which ones they want to interview further.

Dr. Fuerstenthal worked out his system for selecting salesmen because "nobody has succeeded thus far in devising a reliable test for salesmen." He notes: "Sales is a communication job, while other jobs are a mixture of communication and operation, and for operation it is easy to devise tests. What I have tried to do is create a communication situation in which the pressure is similar to that of an actual sales call. I expose a man to his own competitors in the act of selling himself. When a man can define his own position, he can define a product to a customer."

Rapistan, which entered Brazil last

January, is introducing a varied line of equipment for materials handling. Management is looking for a man who can explain and describe the new products and convince prospective customers that they are not only useful but necessary to their operations. As Fuerstenthal explains, "Some salesmen hunt rabbits, others hunt tigers." Rapistan's equipment is a "tiger"—it may take a whole year of patient work to sell a full line of equipment to a factory; so the company needs a man whose sales philosophy is adapted to that kind of strategy.

Before the "testing" session starts, two candidates beg off and leave, not being sufficiently interested in the job to expose themselves to the pressure of the meeting. A third eliminates himself by refusing to speak first.

Finally, after a few words of explanation from Fuerstenthal, the session gets under way. The candidates are surprisingly poised, and talk easily and well. But as the meeting progresses, some begin to stand out—they are more convincing, convey more authority.

Candidate M leads off. He is 24 years old and has been selling throughout Brazil since he was 17. Although he talks well, he seems immature.

Candidate J is a graduate mechanical engineer with several years' experience selling various types of medium equipment. He is impressive, and the others react to the scent of competition with some probing questions in an effort to throw him off balance. Some typical questions: "What was the most expensive piece of equipment you ever sold?" "How did you convince people that your automatic welding process was more economical than manual welding in a cheap labor market?" J answers all the questions agreeably and with assurance, giving sound technical explanations. There is a general feeling in the room that here is a formidable contender.

Candidate A has years of excellent experience but is a poor communicator. He talks fluently, but he is colorless and without warmth; it is obvious that he isn't coming across.

But F makes people sit up and take notice. He is attractive, smooth, almost overconfident as he describes a bewildering series of jobs in which he has sold everything from shoes to sewing machines. He arouses a variety of reactions. Fuerstenthal, in order to provoke him, asks: "You are obviously a born salesman and could probably sell anything, but can you also play the part of a technical salesman, as opposed to a jack-of-all-trades?" Others feel that his superslick manner inspires distrust.

The questions now come thick and fast. "What arguments did you use to sell your elevators over those of your competitors?" "What real technical sales have you handled?" "Did you ever take any courses in mechanics or sales?" "How would you handle a completely new product?"

It gradually becomes apparent that most of the loaded questions are being asked by candidate L. At first that seems to indicate interest and a keen mind, but gradually it degenerates into sheer antagonism and meanness. L is asking questions framed to trip up the other candidates and to show off his own knowledge. In the end that tells against him and annuls his qualifications. Says Fuerstenthal: "A salesman should be aggressive, but not nasty."

Fuerstenthal is especially interested in knowing what outside courses the candidates have taken. He explains that that indicates not only interest and ambition but a certain dedication to one type of sales and a knowledge of the direction in which a man wants to progress.

The remaining candidates are negligible, with poor personalities and inadequate experience. The choice boils down to J, the mechanical engineer, N, or H, the two widely experienced middle-aged men.

Rapistan chooses *J*. As director Hanelt explains: "He was so eager for the job that he lowered his salary requirements considerably to meet what his competitors were asking. Frankly, I couldn't afford to turn down such a bargain." Especially, he adds, if he can sell machinery as well as he sold himself to a jury of his peers.

Sales Management, Sept. 8, 1975

Single- and Multiple-selection Methods. Selection methods can be used singly or in combination with other measures. The overall prediction may be more accurate when a number of different measures, all measuring different factors important to performance, are used. An example of combined predictors is a study conducted at Standard Oil of New Jersey. Managerial success was predicted fairly accurately by a lengthy series of tests in addition to an extensive survey of each manager's family, educational, and other personal background factors (Dunnette, 1965). The tests measured cognitive abilities, inductive reasoning, management judgment, attitudes, and personality. Differences in the test scores accounted for about 50 percent of the variability among the managers with respect to their management success (level achieved, salary earned, and rated effectiveness). Figure 10.3 shows the results of the study in the form of an expectancy chart. An expectancy expresses the degree of job success experienced by managers receiving different scores on the series of tests. As figure 10.3 shows, a manager who scores in the upper 20 percent of the test has a 90 percent chance of being above average on the overall success index used in the study. On the other hand, managers scoring in the lowest 20 percent on the test had only a 10 percent chance of being in the top half of the success index.

FIGURE 10.3   Expectancy Chart on Overall Success Index for Managers with Different Test Scores

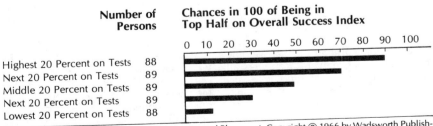

Figure 10.3 also illustrates a fact about tests used this way. Tests, and other selection approaches, when used statistically to predict job behavior, only provide results for a group, not for a particular individual. For example, figure 10.3 shows that 10 percent of the managers scoring in the bottom 20 percent of the test will nevertheless be successful (when success is judged to be a score on the success index above that of 50 percent of the other managers). This 10 percent of the managers would be rejected by the tests, even though they would perform well in the future.

Instead of a statistical approach to selection in which the scores on selection instruments are associated statistically with some measure of job success, a clinical approach can be used. With this approach, predictions are made for a single individual after that individual has been measured by several instruments. The emphasis to be placed on a particular score and on a particular measuring instrument is a matter of judgment. Often the individual making such a judgment is a clinical, or consulting, psychologist hired for that purpose. This approach is often particularly appropriate in small organizations where it is impossible to obtain a large enough sample to conduct a statistical selection study. Some comparisons of the statistical approach and the clinical approach show the statistical approach to be superior (Meehl, 1954), but other studies show the clinical approach can nonetheless be useful in many situations (Korman, 1968).

Performance Appraisal

Periodically, most organizations formally evaluate the performance of members. They do so for a variety of purposes. First, evaluation aids in allocating merit pay increases, because there is a general belief that exceptional performance should be rewarded when possible, and that some portion of the amount allocated for pay increases should be based on merit. While union contracts and salary ranges may make this hard to achieve for lower-level jobs, it is usually less difficult to do for higher managerial positions.

Formal rating systems also provide information on the training needs of organizational members and by locating skills and abilities in the organization, they are additionally useful for making transfer, promotion, and layoff decisions, as well as for contributing to human resource planning for the future.

In addition, performance review serves a feedback function. When an employee does his job well, and is told so by his superior, he receives positive reinforcement, while negative feedback about poor performance may help extinguish undesirable work habits. Of course, this reinforcement function of evaluation occurs only if the person is told his rating. In any case, discussion of ratings, and especially providing coaching in areas of deficiency, helps to identify job-related problems and is an important part of every manager's role in an organization. Performance ratings are also often needed to serve as a criterion, or the measure, of performance in selection studies, especially if there is no direct way of measuring employee output.

This process of judging the individual's contribution to an organization's success and communicating this information to him is *performance appraisal*. It has two distinct phases: (1) the evaluation stage (making a judgment), and (2) the review stage (communicating the results to the subordinate).

Performance Evaluation

The evaluation aspect of performance appraisal is the one in which a judgement is made about how well another person has performed in the job setting. It may focus on only one of several dimensions—performance and productivity, personality, or simply the degree of liking a superior has for a subordinate. There are many problems that make this evaluation process difficult. For this reason, it is a common practice for an organization to seek to standardize it. We will discuss some aspects of the evaluation problem, such as methods of rating, who should rate, and some limitations of rating efforts.

Methods of Rating. Many approaches have been used to evaluate performance: graphic ratings, critical incidents, MBO, work standards, and forced-choice methods.

1. *Graphic Rating.* The graphic rating scale is the most popular and one of the earliest approaches developed. With a graphic rating method, the person is evaluated on the basis of a number of job-related and/or personal characteristics, such as quality of work, quantity of work, reliability, cooperativeness, and so on. Typically, beside each evaluation factor is a five-point scale representing different degrees of the factor (such as "excellent," "good," "fair," "needs improvement," and "bad"). The rater simply checks the word or phrase which he believes best applies to the individual being rated.

2. *Critical Incidents Method.* With the critical incidents approach, the supervisor keeps a record of the positive and/or negative behaviors of each subordinate over a period of time, such as six months or a year. The behavioral incidents recorded over the period provide the

evidence for a high or low rating. They also provide the basis for a discussion with the employee of his performance during the period, and give specific cases to document the rating.

3. *Work Standards Approach.* With the work standards approach, performance standards are established for the tasks an employee performs. These standards may be established from a systematic analysis of the task (such as motion study), or on the basis of a past performance. The individual's performance is then evaluated against these standards. This approach was emphasized by the early scientific management writers.

4. *The Assessment Center.* The assessment center utilizes a method in which the individuals are brought together to work on different types of assignments while under continuous scrutiny by a group of observers. Many of the center's exercises and assignments involve simulations of real-life situations the employee might face if promoted to a higher-level position, and performance in the assessment center setting is evaluated and rated. Research indicates that assessment center ratings correlate positively with later job performance (Bray and Grant, 1966).

5. *Forced-choice Rating.* In the forced-choice approach, the rater must choose between two alternative behavioral statements about the individual being evaluated. The behavioral statements placed together are selected on the basis of research showing the degree of frequency with which individuals in the group exhibit the behavior, and also the degree of emotional feeling generated in the group in question by the behavioral statements. Behavioral statements are put together which are similar in "emotional tone" and in the frequency that they are used in describing the particular group. However, the statements in a pair are also chosen such that one statement has been shown by research to be more frequently applied to effective versus less effective individuals in the group, while the other statement is not associated with effectiveness. Thus, while the rater is given a pair of behavioral statements, only one of the statements is predictive of future behavior on the job—and the rater cannot tell which. An example of such a pair of statements is from a forced-choice reference check developed by Carroll and Nash (1970). The statements are: "Has many worthwhile ideas. Completes all assignments."

Research has shown that the forced-choice rating scale is most useful in predicting future success when raters are likely to be lenient (Carroll and Nash, 1972). However its acceptance by supervisors is generally not high.

6. *Behaviorally Anchored Rating Scales.* The use of behaviorally

anchored rating scales has recently become popular. As with any other rating method, their development took place in an attempt to improve the evaluation process by reducing rater leniency and other problems in performance evaluation. With behaviorally anchored scales, supervisors who are to use the ratings identify examples of good and bad performance (or behavior) from various important subordinates. These behavioral examples then provide specific reference points for raters in judging a particular characteristic of organizational members. Some research indicates that behavioral-anchored rating scales do produce better ratings (less leniency) than other rating methods, but the differences between them and some other methods have not been that large (Borman and Dunnette, 1975).

7. *Management by Objectives.* In management by objectives (MBO) the superior and subordinate together establish objectives for the subordinate (Carroll and Tosi, 1973). An objective is a desired end result with a time constraint. There is an attempt to relate individual objectives to objectives at the next higher organizational level and, ultimately, to organizational objectives. This results in vertical integration of objectives. Plans for achieving each objective are also developed jointly by the superior and subordinate. The basis for evaluating goal progress is also specified by agreement in advance. Performance is reviewed in terms of the objectives to determine the progress made toward goal attainment. Causes of performance failures can be easily identified with MBO, and thus appropriate action can be taken to prevent them.

Who Rates?   Performance evaluation may be done by one's superior, groups of managers at higher levels, subordinates, or peers. It has also been done by "rating experts" from the personnel department. For certain purposes, self-ratings are used.

There are pros and cons with each of these methods. Some research indicates that subordinates may be most qualified to rate supervisory style, peers the competence of professionals, and supervisors the job performance of rank-and-file workers (Carroll and Nash, 1970). If evaluation is intended to promote behavior change, there may be more acceptance of the need for change if self-ratings are used. In some organizations, a rating expert from the personnel department is used in order to achieve consistency in the ratings and to prevent favoritism and bias. In order to arrive at an assessment, the expert interviews the individual, his superior, and other organizational members who know the person well.

Thus, which type of rater is best depends on the situation. Generally speaking, however, the rater with the most opportunity to observe the performance or behavior in question is the better rater. In some cases this would be the immediate superior, but sometimes it would be the subordinate or peer of the ratee. In addition, several factors have been associated with the ability to judge others. These include the rater's motivation to do an accurate job, the ratee's intelligence, the similarity in background between the rater and ratee, the lack of emotional involvement with the ratee, and the ability of a rater to judge himself accurately (Carroll and Nash, 1970).

Sources of Performance Appraisal Error.   There are several factors which can lead to low reliability and validity of performance ratings. Ratings are affected by interpersonal relationships, different performance expectations, rater leniency, rater bias, limitations of the rating system itself, and the purpose for which the rating is to be used.

1. *Interpersonal Relationships.* The relationship between a superior and a subordinate has an influence in the rating of the subordinate. Kallejian, Brown and Weschler (1953) found that the interpersonal relationship was a more dominant factor in the rating a subordinate received than was the level of performance. This seems to indicate that subordinates who act in a way to satisfy the needs of the superior will be rated higher.

2. *Different Performance Expectations.* Any job includes several different activity sets. (We have already introduced this notion in our discussion of performance in chap. 5.) Different supervisors of the same kind of work emphasized different aspects of performance in rating. In a study of ratings of clerical workers, Klimoski and London (1974) found that some supervisors rated clerks highest who were more intelligent than other clerks. Other supervisors rated clerks highest who were faster at processing paper.

3. *Rater Leniency.* Some managers have a tendency to give unduly high ratings; that is, to be easy or lenient in evaluating subordinates. This can be a problem because the subordinate may overestimate his performance and potential if he receives such an unjustifiably high rating, or the organization may make a bad promotion decision because of an unjustifiably high rating and because it is impossible to determine the degree of compatability between ratings of different supervisors.

One factor which contributes to leniency is the competence of the rater. Kirchner and Reisberg (1962) found that better supervisors were more discriminating in rating subordinates. They showed more "spread" and variation in their ratings. Less effective supervisors were more lenient in ratings, and there was less of a spread given by the less effective supervisors between the top-rated subordinates and the lowest-rated subordinates.

4. *Rater Bias.* Some research has shown that raters may be biased in evaluation. It has been shown that raters tend to give higher subjective ratings to those who have personalities similar to their own. Hamner et al. (1974) show that this problem exists even when the level of task performance is similar. When different individuals performed the same task at the same pace, raters tended to give better performance evaluations to those workers who were racially similar to them. Thus, blacks give higher ratings to blacks and whites gave higher ratings to whites (Hamner et al., 1974).

5. *The Halo Effect.* One particular aspect of an individual, either performance or personality, may be extremely high or pleasant, while other aspects may be moderate or displeasing. Or one dimension may be very low, or bad, while the rest are good. The halo effect occurs when the manager gives an overall performance rating using, as a basis for judgment, only a single characteristic. The one factor provides a "halo" which casts its light over the individual, masking other characteristics. For instance, a salesperson's job may have three different aspects. Let's assume these three job requirements are (1) selling, (2) market research, and (3) customer service, and that they are of equal importance for a salesperson's success. If a salesperson has an outstanding sales record, but weak performance in research and customer service, and still gets a very high performance rating from the sales manager, sales performance is said to have generated the "halo" effect.

A number of factors contribute to the halo effect. Human beings have difficulty discriminating among various behaviors of others, and many performance evaluation systems require such discrimination. However, individuals differ in "cognitive complexity"—that is, the way they receive, store, and process information. Some can, when observing a complex situation, see many facets and patterns in it. Others, observing the same scene, can discern only a few aspects. When a person's cognitive structure is simple, they notice only a few things about their environment (Mayo and Crockett, 1964). Thus, some managers will have only a limited perceptual capacity, but must still rate subordinates. They therefore make judgments based on a more limited sample of observations.

6. *Rating System Limitations.* There may be defective characteristics built into the rating method itself. Some systems ask a rater to apply words like "excellent" or "fair" or "poor" to various kinds of

performance components. Obviously, the meaning of these terms will vary from one person to another. Also, rating systems may fail to specify reference points to be used. Is the person to be rated on an absolute standard (a student must get 90 percent to get an A)? Is the person to be rated against other individuals (the top 5 percent of the class gets A regardless of how low the highest grade is)? Or should the person be rated against his own past performance (on improvement)?

Even using objective measures, errors enter the rating. If an individual, for instance, works very well in one part of the day, but not so well in another, then the time that the rating is taken is of extreme importance. Individuals differ in how long it takes them to learn or adapt to a new task, and performance on a task in the short run may not be related to performance on the task over a longer period of time. One individual's performance may be lower than another's because one person helped co-workers and the other received help. In a factory, some machines are more efficient than others; in a retail store, some locations are more productive than others, as is also the case with respect to sales territories for salesmen. There are many other problems as well. Some performance standards assigned to workers are "tight" or difficult to achieve, and some are "loose" or easy to achieve. Generally, performance standards become "looser" over time as better materials or methods are used, and therefore comparisons among employees may not be valid if the age of the tasks are different.

7. *Purpose of the Rating.* We have seen that ratings may be used for many purposes: feedback, promotion, merit increases. The purpose for which a rating is to be used can affect the evaluation given by a manager. Taylor and Wherr (1951) examined rater leniency with both forced-choice and graphic ratings. In this study, ratings were obtained for "experimental" purposes and "for keeps." They found a large difference between those ratings collected "for keeps" and those for "experimental" purposes. The ratings given "for keeps" did not show as much variation as those given for "experimental" reasons. These ratings, collected at two different time points, were of the same group; therefore, they should have been similar. Perhaps managers tend to be more conservative in judging and recommending for promotion because recommending someone who fails will make the manager himself look bad.

Improving Performance Evaluations.   There are ways to improve performance evaluations. For example, training raters in how to use the organization's performance evaluation system can improve evaluations (Borman, 1975). The accuracy of performance evaluations is also improved when the ratings are done by individuals familiar with the performance or behavior in question (Whitla and Tirrell, 1954).

Good ratings depend somewhat on the motivation of the rater to do a good evaluation job (Taft, 1955). If raters are not motivated to do a good job, they will neither exercise sufficient care and judgment nor allocate sufficient time to the rating task. Various approaches can be used to motivate raters. One is to supervise the ratings. This is accomplished by requiring the rater to justify his judgments. Defending a judgment before a group of peers is another approach that may improve the quality of ratings.

Rating accuracy may also be improved by increasing the number of persons rated at one time. This gives the rater a basis for comparison of one person against another. Finally, pooling the judgments of several raters about an individual may also yield a more accurate assessment (Bayroff et at., 1954).

The Performance Review

In the performance review, the results of the performance evaluation are communicated to the organizational member. Performance reviews may seek to make employees aware of their performance weaknesses, strengths, or both. Carroll and Tosi (1973) also found that the performance review often serves to clarify the performance expectations of the superior.

Subordinates may react quite negatively to the performance review when it has critical content (McGregor, 1957; Halper et al., 1976). In a study of reactions to performance reviews, Meyer, Kay, and French (1965) found:

1. The average subordinate acted defensively to 54 percent of his superior's criticisms.
2. Constructive responses to criticism rarely occurred (much less than one per interview).
3. In cases with an *above average amount* of criticism, the subordinate exhibited five times as much defensive behavior as the cases with an *average* amount of criticism.
4. Those that got an above average amount of criticism showed less favorable performance 10 to 12 weeks later (and there was no evidence that they were generally poor performers).
5. Frequent criticism constituted so strong a threat to self-esteem that it disrupted performance.
6. There was more improved performance in less criticized areas than in the most criticized area.

It is not surprising that criticism in the performance review sessions generated negative reactions. Individuals have ego needs, and most people have a favorable self-concept (chap. 3). When the information content of the performance review session is incongruent with the individual's self-perceptions, this will naturally lead to a tendency to reject the information, and defensive reactions will develop to explain away any performance or personal deficiencies identified. (It is likely that negative reactions would be highest when the criticism is unsolicited rather than solicited.)

Of course this is not to say that individuals will reject all criticism. Though people being rated prefer praise to criticism (Carroll and Tosi, 1973), they do have a need to know.

Conducting the Performance Review. Maier (1958) believes the objectives of the performance review are:

1. To let subordinates know where they stand.
2. To recognize their good work.
3. To point out how and where they can improve.
4. To develop them on their present jobs.
5. To develop and train them for higher jobs.
6. To let them know how they may progress in the company.
7. To serve as a record for assessing the department or unit as a whole, showing where each person fits into the larger picture.
8. To warn some employees that they must do better.

Maier (1958) has described three basic approaches to conducting the appraisal interview and each of these has different consequences. In the "tell-and-sell" approach, the supervisor tells the subordinate how he is doing. Then he tries to gain the subordinate's acceptance of the evaluation (sell him on it). He then tries to obtain the subordinate's willingness to follow a plan of improvement. In the "tell-and-listen" approach, the results of evaluation are told to the employee. Then the supervisor listens to the subordinate to determine how he reacts to the evaluation. In the "problem-solving" approach, subordinate and supervisor discuss work-related problems of a wide variety that they feel they have. Together, they seek solutions to these. The direct communication of an evaluation is minimal. Maier has found that the problem-solving approach produces better subordinate reactions than the other two (more positive work-related results or improvements occur). The characteristics of the three approaches and typical results for each of them are summarized in figure 10.4.

The problem-solving approach seems the most appropriate to im-

prove results. It requires the greatest amount of participation of superior *and* subordinate in the discussions of performance, and most research shows that higher perceived participation in the performance
review is related to better rater reactions (French et al., 1966; Wexley
et al., 1973). One study has shown, however, that there was better reaction to the nonparticipative than to the participative performance
review when the subjects were in a training program (Hillery and
Wexley, 1974). This is consistent with Maier's (1958) belief that a
nonparticipative approach in performance review might be best if the
ratees are inexperienced in the performance which is the content of
the review.

FIGURE 10.4   Cause and Effect Relations in
Three Types of Appraisal Interview

Method	Tell-and-Sell	Tell-and-Listen	Problem-Solving
Role of Interviewer	Judge	Judge	Helper
Motivation	Use of positive or negative incentives (extrinsic in that motivation is added to the job itself).	Resistance to change is reduced	Increased freedom. Increased responsibility (intrinsic motivation in that interest is inherent in the task).
Gains	Success most probable when employee respects interviewer.	Develops favorable attitude to superior which increases probability of success.	Almost assured of improvement in some respect.
Risks	Loss of loyalty. Inhibition of independent judgment.	Need for a change may not be developed.	Employee may lack ideas. Change may be other than what superior had in mind.
Values	Perpetuates existing practices and values.	Permits interviewer to change his views in the light of employee's responses. Some upward communication.	Both learn since experience and views are pooled. Change is facilitated.

Source: N.R.F. Maier, A. R. Solem, and A. A. Maier, *Supervisory and Executive Development: A Manual for Role Playing* (New York: Wiley, 1959). Reprinted with permission.

Research generally shows that an individual likes a task more when
he perceives he has been successful at it. (Locke, 1965). This could
affect the individual's preference for tasks and, to an extent, determine what tasks are chosen in the future (Osipow, 1971). For exam-

ple, in an organization there are often many difficult tasks—that is, tasks with a higher failure rate than other tasks. Some individuals may be very reluctant to undertake such difficult tasks because of negative feedback on tasks undertaken in the past. Finally, since feedback can influence an individual's self-esteem, perhaps it may also influence his aspiration level (Carroll and Tosi, 1973).

Improving Results Obtained from the Performance Review. There are a number of things that can be done to get better results from performance reviews. Carroll and Tosi (1973) conclude that results are better when there is an agreement between superiors and subordinates about performance expectations. Increasing the number of performance review sessions has also been found related to more positive reactions by subordinates receiving feedback on their performance. With reviews several times a year rather than, say, once a year, perceived success in goal achievement is higher and subordinates react more favorably to the reviews, especially when the superior's behavior is seen as helpful and supportive (Carroll and Tosi, 1969). Self-evaluation by the subordinate also seems to improve the results of performance reviews (Bassett and Meyer, 1968).

It has also been found that if criticisms—of a personal nature or of performance deficiencies—can be converted into specific improvement goals for the subordinate, performance reviews can be improved (Meyer, Kay, and French, 1965). But even if the subordinate accepts identified deficiencies, it is often difficult to find time and energy to take corrective action, since there are so many competing time pressures. Thus, specific goals and time deadlines for correction of a deficiency should be set to mobilize and direct energy toward correcting it, thus making it more likely that behavior change will occur.

Reviewing performance will be more successful when the discussion focuses on performance problems than if its emphasis is on personal qualities of the subordinate—an emphasis which may be at variance with the subordinate's self-concept (Carroll and Tosi, 1973). Performance review sessions may also be improved by supervisors taking action to reduce the subordinate's anxiety during such sessions, allowing the subordinate to express his own reactions and grievances, active listening, rewarding self-analysis by the subordinate, and using probing questions to direct attention to critical performance problems.

Compensation

Employee compensation includes all valued resources—such as

hourly wage payments, and salaries and incentive pay—given by an organization to employees as a return for their work. Compensation includes fringe benefits such as pensions, vacations, stock options, and employee discounts, all of which require expenditures by the organization.

Compensation programs in an organization have several objectives: (1) maintaining competitive labor costs, (2) attracting qualified human talent, (3) motivating members to perform at a high level, (4) minimizing turnover by maintenance of employee satisfaction, and (5) encouraging organizational members to improve their skills, abilities, and knowledge. While the specifics of any compensation system vary from organization to organization, there are four general policy questions that any organization must resolve; these apply in both dynamic and bureaucratic organizations. According to Nash and Carroll (1975) these are (1) the wage-level decision, (2) the wage-structure decision, (3) the individual wage differential decision, and (4) the wage-method decision.

The Wage-level Decision

Wages must be high enough to attract and retain personnel, but not so high that labor costs become excessive; the organization can pay itself out of existence. Employee productivity, the proportion of total costs made up by labor costs, and the ability to pass on wage-cost increases to the consumer are among the important factors affecting the wage-level decision.

The Wage Survey.   The wage survey is a way to obtain data to make the wage-level decision. It is a study to compare an organization's wages and salaries with those of other organizations in direct competition for human resources. Sometimes the survey is carried out in a local area if that is where personnel are recruited. Sometimes the survey is broader, perhaps on a national level if certain groups of personnel are mobile over the whole nation, as is often the case with managers and professionals. The results of the wage survey can then be used to establish the wage level. The level of wages will have a significant influence on the satisfaction and performances of organizational members. The important thing to remember in establishing the organization's wage level is that it is not what an individual is paid that determines labor costs. Rather, it is how much work is done for a given wage payment. By paying more, an organization can reduce its labor costs if this higher wage increases worker productivity. (A unique approach to wage determination is described in item 10.3.)

ITEM 10.3 Participation

Arthur Friedman's Outrage: Employees Decide Their Pay

OAKLAND, Calif.—One thing for sure, Arthur Friedman will never become the chairman of the board at General Motors.

It is not just because the modish, easy-going Oakland appliance dealer does not look the part—Hush Puppies, loud shirts and denim jackets tend to clash with the sober decor of most executive suites. And it certainly is not because he is an incompetent administrator—the Friedman-Jacobs Co. has prospered during the 15 years of his stewardship.

It is mainly because Art Friedman has some pretty strange ideas about how one runs a business.

Five years ago, he had his most outrageous brainstorm. First he tried it out on his wife Merle and his brother Morris.

"Here he goes again," replied Merle with a sigh of resignation, "Another dumb stunt."

"Oh my God," was all that Morris could muster.

His idea was to allow employees to set their own wages, make their own hours and take their vacations whenever they felt like it.

The end result was that it worked.

Friedman first unleashed his proposal at one of the regular staff meetings. Decide what you are worth, he said, and tell the bookkeeper to put it in your envelope next week. No questions asked. Work any time, any day, any hours you want. Having a bad day? Go home. Hate working Saturdays? No problem. Aunt Ethel from Chicago has dropped in unexpectedly? Well, take a few days off, show her the town. Want to go to Reno for a week, need a rest? Go, go, no need to ask. If you need some money for the slot machines, take it out of petty cash. Just come back when you feel ready to work again.

His speech was received in complete silence. No one cheered, no one laughed, no one said a word.

"It was about a month before anyone asked for a raise," recalls Stan Robinson, 55, the payroll clerk. "And when they did, they asked Art first. But he refused to listen and told them to just tell me what they wanted. I kept going back to him to make sure it was all right, but he wouldn't even talk about it. I finally figured out he was serious."

"It was something that I wanted to do," explains Friedman. "I always said that if you give people what they want, you get what you want. You have to be willing to lose, to stick your neck out. I finally decided that the time had come to practice what I preached."

Soon the path to Stan Robinson's desk was heavily travelled. Friedman's wife Merle was one of the first; she figured that her contribution was worth $1 an hour more. Some asked for $50 more a week, some $60. Delivery truck driver Charles Ryan was more ambitious; he demanded a $100 raise.

In most companies, Ryan would have been laughed out of the office. His work had not been particularly distinguished. His truck usually left in the morning and returned at 5 in the afternoon religiously, just in time for him to punch out. He dragged around the shop, complained constantly and was almost always late for work. Things changed.

"He had been resentful about his prior pay," explains Friedman. "The raise made him a fabulous employee. He started showing up early in the morning and would be back by 3, asking what else had to be done."

Instead of the all-out raid on the company coffers that some businessmen might expect, the 15 employees of the Friedman-Jacobs Co. displayed astonishing restraint and maturity. The wages they demanded were just slightly higher than the scale of the Retail Clerks union to which they all belong (at Friedman's insistence). Some did not even take a raise. One service man who was receiving considerably less than his co-workers was asked why he did not insist on equal pay. "I don't want to work that hard," was the obvious answer.

When the union contract comes across Friedman's desk every other year, he signs it without even reading it. "I don't care what it says," he insists. At first, union officials would drop in to see how things were going, but they would usually end up laughing and shaking their heads, muttering something about being put out of a job. They finally stopped coming by. It was enough to convince George Meany to go out to pasture.

The fact is that Friedman's employees have no need for a union; whatever they want, they take and no one questions it. As a result, they have developed a strong sense of responsibility and an acute sensitivity to the problems that face the American worker in general that would have been impossible under the traditional system.

George Tegner, 59, an employee for 14 years, has like all his co-workers achieved new insight into the mechanics of the free enterprise system. "You have to use common sense; no one wins if you end up closing the business down. If

you want more money, you have to produce more. It can't work any other way. Anyway, wages aren't everything. Doing what you want to is more important."

Roger Ryan, 27, has been with the company for five years. "I know about the big inflation in '74, but I haven't taken a raise since '73. I figure if everybody asks for more, then inflation will just get worse. I'll hold out as long as I can."

Payroll clerk Stan Robinson: "I'm single now. I don't take as much as the others, even though I've been here longer, because I don't need as much. The government usually winds up with the extra money anyway."

Elwood Larsen, 65, has been the company's ace service man for 16 years. When he went into semi-retirement last year, he took a $1.50 cut in pay. Why? Larsen does not think a part-timer is worth as much. "I keep working here because I like it. We all know that if the Friedmans make money, we do. You just can't gouge the owner."

In the past five years, there has been no turnover of employees. Friedman estimates that last year his 15 workers took no more than a total of three sick days. It is rare that anyone is late for work and, even then, there is usually a good reason. Work is done on time and employee pilferage is nonexistent.

"We used to hear a lot of grumbling," says Robinson. "Now, everybody smiles."

As part of the new freedom, more people were given keys to the store and the cash box. If they need groceries, or even some beer money, all they have to do is walk into the office, take what they want out of the cash box and leave a voucher. Every effort is made to ensure that no one looks over their shoulder.

There has been only one discrepancy. "Once the petty cash was $10 over," recalls Friedman. "We never could figure out where it came from."

The policy has effected some changes

in the way things are done around the store. It used to be open every night and all day Sunday, but no one wanted to work those hours. A problem? Of course not. No more nights and Sundays. ("When I thought about it," confesses Friedman, "I didn't like to work those hours either.")

The store also used to handle TV's and stereos—high-profit items—but they were a hassle for all concerned. The Friedman-Jacobs Co. now deals exclusively in major appliances such as refrigerators, washers and dryers.

Skeptics by now are chuckling to themselves, convinced that if Friedman is not losing money, he is just breaking even. The fact is that net profit has not dropped a cent in the last five years; it has increased. Although volume is considerably less and overhead has increased at what some would consider an unhealthy rate, greater productivity and efficiency have more than made up for it.

None of this concerns Friedman, though. He keeps no charts, does not know how to read cost analysis graphs, and does not have the vaguest idea what cash flow means. As long as he can play golf a couple of times a week, and make money to boot, he could not be happier.

Encouraged by his success, Friedman decided to carry his revolution beyond labor relations. If it worked there, he figured, it should work with customer relations as well. So policy changes resulted in such innovations as the following 'last bill' notice, that dread purveyor of bad tidings:

"For some reasons which we really cannot understand, you have decided not to pay the bill that you owe us.

"This letter officially cancels that bill and you are no longer under any obligation to pay us. We have decided not to give this bill to a collection agency, as our gain would be small compared to your loss.

"We would appreciate it, however, if you would take a moment to tell us why you made the decision not to pay us. It would be very helpful to us for the rest of our customers."

As cute as this may appear, it could hardly be expected to work. But Friedman claims that delinquent accounts are no more frequent today.

"We don't collect any more money than we did before, but we don't collect any less either. The difference is that you learn a lot more about the problem. Anyway, it's a lot more pleasant way of doing business," Friedman says.

The Washington Post, Feb. 23, 1975

The Wage-structure Decision

The second wage-policy decision is to determine how much each job is worth relative to the other jobs in the organization. The wage structure is the system of wage relationships among jobs (not people) in the organization. Since a sense of pay equity is a determinant of the perceived fairness of compensation, the wage-structure decision is quite important.

Several methods of job evaluation can be used to compare jobs in terms of their complexity and difficulty in order to establish differences in base pay rates among them. A basic assumption in most evaluation methods is that jobs which require more education, experience, judgment, and similar factors than others should be paid more.

Job Evaluation. Job evaluation is used to facilitate the wage-structure decision. It is the determination of the relative worth of a particular job as compared to other jobs, and it offers a way to approach the wage-structure policy question. One method in use is the *point* system. The point system attempts to develop a score (based on points assigned to different characteristics) for a job. After a general analysis of jobs in a given class, a set of characteristics common to all jobs is derived. These characteristics may be such things as amount of effort required, the level of education required, the pleasantness of working conditions, the amount of responsibility attached to the job, and so forth. Each of these factors can be weighted differently, depending upon their differential importance. Because of the nature of jobs, it may be possible to develop fairly accurate descriptions of different levels for a factor. Experience levels required in jobs, for instance, may be rated in the following way:

Level Required	Points Assigned
less than 8 years	1
8-12 years	3
12-16	10

There are several other methods of job evaluation. All of them generally result in a ranking of jobs in terms of what the jobs require of the job incumbents or how the jobs differ in complexity. One of the simplest methods of job evaluation is simply to rank the jobs in units from most to least complex.

Another method, the classification method, which is popular in government agencies, arranges job *grades* in order of the level of their requirements. All the jobs in a particular grade are considered to have a similar level of difficulty and a general grade description is developed. Then the job description of each job to be evaluated is compared against the various grade descriptions to determine the appropriate grade for the job.

These procedures for job evaluation should result in a set of pay differentials among jobs that would appear to seem equitable to organizational members. However, such job evaluation procedures often do not produce differentials that individuals are satisfied with because there is disagreement as to what factors would be considered in establishing the compensation differentials. For this reason, it is often recommended that rank-and-file employees participate with managers to develop a job evaluation system that results in pay differentials acceptable to all (Nash and Carroll, 1975).

The Individual Wage-differential Decision

The third wage decision is to select a method to establish compensation differentials among individuals on the same job. For motivational purposes it is important to insure that those who contribute more effort or perform at a higher level than others on a particular job should be paid more. Also, the organization may wish to pay a premium to those individuals on a particular job who have more potential, or who have been with the organization for a longer period of time. When there is a labor union, this area is the subject of negotiation between labor and management.

Performance Evaluation. Judging the performance of workers and managers was discussed earlier in this chapter. These methods are ones that are used to make the individual wage differential decision. When it is judged that one person is a better performer than another, the difference should be reflected in wages.

The Wage-method Decision

Employees may be paid based on time worked (by the hour or week), or an organization may use incentive pay, which relates compensation to how much output is achieved. Some incentive plans are designed for a whole plant or organization. Then, too, there are supplemental forms of compensation which must be taken into account.

Compensation for Time Worked. Direct compensation is usually paid in the form of hourly wages or salaries for time worked. Hourly pay and salaries can be varied in magnitude to reflect differences in job requirements, performance, and seniority, although these differences may not be in large enough amounts to be noticeable to the organizational members. Differences in hourly rates and salaries can be an incentive for organizational members to strive for more complex jobs which pay more.

Some organizations have abolished the hourly wage, putting all employees on salaries. Some case studies show that a shift from wages to salaries is followed by higher morale and lower absenteeism (Kaponya, 1962; Gooding, 1970).

Compensation Based on Output. There are a wide variety of incentive wage plans. Some of these reward employees for individual output and some are based on the performance of a group or department in an organization. Other incentive plans are based on the performance of the whole organization. Often the bonus under an incentive plan is not made unless a certain predesignated performance standard is achieved.

1. *Individual Incentive Plans.* Individual incentive plans are applicable when the output of an individual can be measured, when the employee's effort determines his own output rate, and when the task is routine and repetitive so that the task can be performed the same way each time. Nash and Carroll (1975), reviewing research on individual incentive wage-plan installations, conclude that after they are implemented they are followed by performance increases, but at least half of the increases can be attributed to the use of specific standards where none previously existed and to the use of improved work methods.

Individual incentive plans for managers, however, may be quite subjective. Bonuses may be based on the judgment of several managers at the next higher level. Studies of organizations that pay bonuses generally indicate that their earnings are higher than organizations that do not pay managerial bonuses (Nash and Carroll, 1975). Bonuses can be expected to work best when they are very large and when they are given at unpredictable times.

Some research on individual incentive plans reveals that often work groups force their members to limit their production under individual incentive plans in order to avoid internal competition and other disruptions of group life. As indicated earlier, compliance with such norms is highest among those identifying positively with the group. Even with such restriction of output, however, performance may be higher than under hourly wage systems.

In most instances, workers prefer hourly wage systems rather than incentive wage systems, but this is partially determined by their experience with them. Individual incentive wage plans seem to work best when the individuals involved accept the plan, perhaps through participating in establishing it, when performance standards are carefully established so they are not too difficult nor too easy, when there is an acceptable procedure for changing the standards, when the employees understand how the plan works, and when the plan provides for an incentive payment of a sufficient amount to be motivating.

2. *Group Incentive Plans.* Sometimes an individual's output cannot be easily measured, and often in such cases a group incentive plan may be most appropriate. Such plans may not be as motivating as an individual incentive plan—because there is less of a relationship established between one individual's effort and the incentive received—but, as mentioned in chapter 5, group pressures may be present with

the group incentive which can facilitate higher performance.

3. *Organization-wide Incentives.* Sometimes a bonus is given to all organizational members of a particular plant based on its economic performance. Such a plan may improve cooperation among the various specialized subunits of the plant since the plant bonus represents a superordinate goal that can only be attained through the cooperation of all. And, if the bonus to be given to a particular plant for its productive efficiency is based on competition with other company plants, intraorganizational cohesiveness may be increased.

The plant-wide bonus may be based on a number of economic indicators. One is the comparision of current labor costs to labor costs in previous periods. This approach is used in companies using the Scanlon Plan. In the Scanlon Plan, production committees process employee suggestions to improve productivity. One study of ten firms using the Scanlon Plan indicated there was an average increase in productivity of 22 percent in the first year and 23 percent in the second year after the Scanlon Plan was adopted (Lesieur, 1958).

Another popular approach for determining the amount of bonus various managers in an organizational unit receive is to divide the organization into semiautonomous profit centers which are charged for the value of the resources they employ and which are given credit for the value of the services or products they produce. In practice, however, the determination of the profits made by a particular unit may be considered arbitrary and unfair by the managers involved and feelings of inequity will arise. In addition, units charging each other for products or services may create antagonism or conflict in their pursuit of maximum profits for themselves. This may result in actions detrimental to the organization as a whole.

4. *Profit-sharing Plans.* Profit-sharing plans are based on the level of company profits. Typically, a certain percentage of company profits are distributed to employees either in current payments or payments that are deferred until the employee's retirement. Companies with such programs generally claim the programs are effective and these companies usually have higher profit rates than those without (Nash and Carroll, 1975). However, it is difficult to know whether the higher profits are the result of the wage plan, or the cause of it.

Profit-sharing plans have been extensive in Japan, and the year-end distributions have been very large. In the most recent economic recession, however, when profits were low the world over, employees have realized how unstable such compensation plans can be.

Supplemental Compensation. Supplemental compensation consists of fringe benefits: pensions, hospitalization insurance, disability pay, vacations, and life insurance. Supplemental compensation presently amounts to about 30 percent of an organization's payroll costs, and this proportion is increasing yearly (Nash and Carroll, 1975). Research generally shows differences in preferences for alternative fringes by different groups of employees (Nash and Carroll, 1975). Because of this, proposals have been made to allow organizational members to choose their own fringe benefits (Lawler, 1973).

Compensation, Satisfaction, and Motivation

Compensation is, of course, one of the most important determinants of employee satisfaction. It may be *the* most important incentive that organizations can use in attracting and motivating human resources if —as we said at the beginning of this chapter—all other things are equal. Money or pay can be a *transituational* reinforcer. That is, it can be an effective incentive in a variety of situations, and incentives are more effective to the degree that they provide a means of satisfying several needs simultaneously (Opshal and Dunnette, 1966). Compensation is a transituational reinforcer because it provides a means of obtaining desired goods and services and also may reduce general anxiety, and satisfy status, esteem, and recognition needs.

Of course, compensation varies in importance to different individuals and groups. Some individuals do not view money as important as do others. Generally, higher-level occupational groups, with other sources of need satisfaction available, rate money lower in importance than do lower-level occupational groups (Nash and Carroll, 1971).

Pay satisfaction is influenced by what an individual gets as compared to what he wants and considers fair. The fairness of pay (perceived equity of pay) is determined largely by an individual's comparison of himself and his pay to other reference persons and theirs. Compensation received by the reference persons, relative to what they bring to the job in seniority, experience, skill, education, effort, and susceptibility to various role pressures, is compared to what the organizational member doing the comparing brings to a similar situation. Individuals who rate themselves higher than the reference persons on various skills, or who perceive themselves to be superior on characteristics associated with managerial success, are less satisfied with their level of compensation than individuals lower on such self-perceptions (Nash and Carroll, 1975). Interpersonal pay comparisons can produce feelings of being rewarded justly, of overreward, or underreward. A number of studies show that pay dissatisfaction is related to lower job satisfaction, and higher absenteeism and turnover (Steers and Porter, 1973). While compensation is just one job factor influencing employee satisfaction and performance, and while it is not necessarily the most important factor to many groups, such as professionals, it is still, of course, very important. Whatever its positive values, it may be the most significant contributor to employee dissatisfaction.

The techniques in this chapter are those which organizations use to acquire and maintain their human resources. Effective use of these approaches can increase returns, but—as we shall see in chapters 13 and 14—different organizations must use different variations of selection, compensation, and appraisal. In chapters 13 and 14, we shall describe what approaches can be useful in the management of different types of organizations.

Discussion Questions

1. Relate some of the concepts from chapter 3 to staffing issues for an organization.

2. Look at the expectancy chart (fig. 10.3). How would you feel if you were one of the 10 percent of the managers who could be successful, but were rejected because you scored too low on a test? Has anything like this ever happened to you? Ask your instructor if he or she knows anyone who was initially rejected by graduate school, but later went on to be a success.

3. What is your opinion on the decision on seniority and discrimination noted in item 10.1?

4. Sometimes "A difference doesn't make a difference." Can you give some examples where differences were used to make a selection but they really weren't meaningful ones?

5. People work toward the performance criteria. This means they try to do well on the dimensions which are being measured. What are we really measuring when we give students a computer-scored multiple-choice test?

6. If it is true that more effective supervisors give less lenient ratings, why would this be so?

7. Some corporate executives make in excess of half a million dollars per year. Is any man worth that much? Any woman? Why do we pay such salaries? What does an executive do that makes him worth it? By the way, who decides on salary levels of top executives? Does this have any effect on what you think about their worth? Why?

Chapter 11
Organizational Control Systems

Objectives are basic to organizations. They affect an organization's character in important ways, and they vary widely according to the type of organization they serve. The goals of government agencies, for example, often involve public service or regulation, while health-care units or social agencies have goals which involve the delivery of medical and health or social service to a community. As for business organizations, they differ from one another in stated goals. In a survey of 145 chief executives in business, the most frequently stated objective was to make profits or a living. To provide a good product or service to the public was mentioned next most frequently, followed by a concern for employee welfare, and finally, growth (Dent, 1959). Of course, these were general rather than specific goals, and their relative weight presumably reflects the bias of managers and owners. As we will see, employees or customers often have a very different set of objectives for business, and this will be an important consideration as we analyze more specifically the nature of goals and the managerial methods used to achieve them.

Though goals vary widely in kind, as well as in the purpose or clientele they serve, managers must carry out certain fundamental processes in order to direct the organization effectively toward achieving its goals and in order to influence and monitor performance to insure that events occur as intended. These fundamental processes are those of *planning* and *control*.

Planning and control are processes, but they are embedded in decisions which have been transformed into procedures and systems. These are control systems. They are the shape and form taken by the maintenance subsystems discussed in chapters 6 and 7. In this chapter we discuss control systems, their form in stable (hierarchical) and dynamic (organic) organizations, and their effects on organizational members.

Planning is the activity of determining what human and technological resources are required to reach a goal, when the resources will be needed, and at what rate they should be used. Planning is future-oriented. It may focus on the short range, from the present to one year, or it may be concerned with the long run. Long-range planning covers the proposed actions of an organization for periods beyond one year.

In planning, managers constantly make decisions about resource utilization—which to use and how to use them. These decisions are communicated to lower levels of an organization through budgets, rules, policies, and procedures, so that the probability of achieving goals is increased by increasing the likelihood of concerted action of all levels of the organization.

In today's turbulent economic and social environment, planning is becoming, if anything, increasingly complex and difficult. At one time, a planner may have been confronted with relatively discrete and manageable economic, market, and technological factors to weigh in making his plans, but the increased role of government and increasing social pressures in such areas as employment or pollution control are prime examples of the many additional variables which now have an impact on planning because of their potential effects on performance and profit. More "clients" are demanding an increasing number of goals from the organization.

For the very reason that the paths to goal achievement have become more complex, planning has become increasingly important, and managers recognize that this is so. As the world becomes more complex, and as resources become scarcer, better planning can increase the likelihood that complex goals can be met. Item 11.1 suggests ways in which a turbulent economic environment has affected corporate planning. It suggests, also, some of the ways organizations have moved to meet changing conditions through accelerated and flexible planning.

ITEM 11.1   Planning

Accurate Planning Has Never Been More Necessary Than in Today's Fast Changing Economic Environment

For corporate planners and the top executives who rely on their advice, the world has never looked as hostile or as bewildering as it does today. The very uncertainties, from the clouded economic outlook to the energy crisis, that make sophisticated forward planning more vital than ever before, also make accurate planning that much more difficult. "Annual financial plans for a number of companies are going to hell this year," says Jerome Jacobson, senior vice-president of Bendix Corp. "In a rapidly changing economic environment, some plans are out of date in three to six months."

So the very nature of corporate planning is undergoing a dramatic change, and the companies that fare best in coming years may well be the ones that adapt most quickly to the new styles in planning. Today's changes are most clearly visible in two areas:

Flexibility. Instead of relying on a single corporate plan with perhaps one or two variations, top management at more and more companies is now getting a whole battery of contingency plans and alternate scenarios. "We shoot for alternative plans that can deal with either/or eventualities," says George J. Prendergast, in charge of planning at chemical giant E. I. du Pont de Nemours & Co.

Speed. Companies are reviewing and revising plans more frequently in line with changing conditions. Instead of the old five-year plan that might have been updated annually, plans are often updated quarterly, monthly, or even weekly. Arizona Public Service Co. last year adopted a "dynamic" budget that looks ahead two years but is rolled over every month. At Ralston Purina Co., a 1% change in the price of a prime commodity kicks off a change in the company's cost models and the whole corporate plan may change accordingly.

This is heady stuff for corporate planners, because it was not so long ago that planning was a marginal blue-sky sort of operation that seldom got more than a nod from top management. But forward planning became a crucial function and the planner a central figure in the company in the complex, fast-changing business world of the 1960's and 1970's. "Planning has become intimately associated with the whole management process," says George A. Steiner, professor of management at UCLA.

And the role of planning will continue to grow because the outlook is so hazy—not just for business but for all society. What worked before may not work in the future, and a company's very survival may depend on how well it gauges the future. "Many companies feel we are moving into a new era," says Alonzo L. McDonald, managing director of McKinsey & Co. "The 1950-70 assumptions probably will not be good guidelines for the 1970's on."

Business Week, April 28, 1975

Control is concerned with insuring that events conform to plans. It is primarily a managerial function of attempting to ascertain where and how deviations from planned courses occur, so that corrective action can be taken. Control is closely related to planning. In planning, performance standards are set which become the criteria against which the execution of an activity is measured. For example, suppose we plan to achieve a 6 percent profit on sales. To do this, let us say that costs of $2.00 per unit become the cost control standard for the production department. When unit costs exceed $2.00, corrective action must be taken or the profit goal will not be reached.

For the purposes of control, mechanisms must be devised, especially in the maintenance and managerial subsystems of an organization, to monitor performance and feed back data which managers can use in identifying deviations from planned standards—such as excessive unit cost—and taking corrective action. Essentially, through planning, standards become the basis against which performance is judged. Reporting systems—whether simple or complex, and whether they deal with costs, machine accuracy, or human satisfaction, performance, or productivity—do nothing more than aid in control. These systems (managerial controls) form an important part of the work context within which individuals operate. For this reason, we consider generally how they are formed. A more specific treatment of this subject can be found in Tosi and Carroll (1976).

Organizational Goals and Individual Goals

The existence of a goal, as we have seen, is inherent in the idea of planning. Goals, or objectives, are *desired end states*. An entity, or individual, directs efforts, activities, and energies to achieve the desired end state. But as we have suggested, the desired end state differs according to who is making the claim against the organization. Customers want the product at a reasonable price. Managers want salaries and security. Employees want jobs, equal opportunity, and wages. Suppliers want prompt payment of bills. For each of these demands, corresponding contributions are made by the different groups: workers supply labor; managers, administrative skills; owners, capital; and customers provide revenues. In planning, each of these important subgroups must be taken into account.

Is it correct to say, then, that an organization has goals, since these are end states that are desired by individuals? Yes, because when we speak of organizational goals we mean what an individual, or group, desires—something that the system produces. As a customer, our goal for the local supermarket is that it has available the selection of foods we want when we want them. As an employee of the supermarket, we would expect reasonable wages and job security. *Organizational goals* are what the *system* produces and how effectively it does so.

Control Systems, Goals, and Plans

In the planning function, the manager must be concerned with determining what the goals are, what measures of goal achievement are appropriate, and how resources are to be allocated. These become the specific content of the control systems. Determining them is no easy task. Take, for example, an advertising agency. Its stated organizational goal might be to provide high-quality service to clients. What does that mean, operationally? Is this goal measured best by the number of campaigns the agency conducts, its billing, or its profits? Each of these measures of goal achievement could lead to a different plan. For instance, if the number of campaigns is the measure, the agency might attempt to increase revenues by increasing its number of clients. With a profit measure as the primary objective, the firm might focus on cost-reduction strategies, at the expense of foregoing additional clients. All this is to say that the way the goals of an organization become specific—as a control system—for its members can markedly affect what they do.

Types of Goals

In our analysis, we will consider three types of goals: environmental goals, individual goals, and internal systems goals. Since organizational survival depends on successfully dealing with a number of possible problem areas, organizations have multiple objectives. For example, an organization must concern itself with its market standing, but if it neglects innovation or physical and financial resources, it will not survive in the long run. However, often there are important tradeoffs among objectives and sometimes short-range success on one objective must be sacrificed for long-range success on another.

Even though organizations do have stated objectives, with plans to achieve them, there will often be disagreement among organizational members as to the nature and type of organizational goals. There may also be a difference between the "official" or stated objectives of an organization and its actual "operating" goals (Perrow, 1961). Very often there is significant disagreement in an organization among its constituent parts or most influential members as to what should be the short- and long-range goals (Katz, 1970). One reason for this disagreement is differing perceptions of what is the most feasible and effective direction and course of action for the organization to take. Also, the interests of a particular organizational subunit may be better served by one objective or plan than another. This subunit will therefore support plans consistent with its own interests. Yet research has indicated that an organization is most likely to be successful if its top managers agree fairly well on the organization's objectives (Child, 1974).

Environmental Goals

Environmental goal attainment is basic to the survival of an organization. Environmental goals are devised to meet the requirements, or demands, placed on the system from external sources. Groups beyond the boundaries of an organization, especially customers, expect products, services, or other relationships which provide utility, or value, to them. The customer is willing to pay for this utility. So long as utilities, or values, are provided to customers in appropriate quality, a firm can continue in existence.

Utilities may be products, such as refrigerators, pencils, buildings, clothing, and so on. They may also be services, such as health care, financial assistance, psychiatric help, and the like. So long as people wish to move from one place to another, there will be firms which build planes, automobiles, and bicycles. Fundamentally a firm must provide utilities to consumers to survive. Environmental goal attainment comes first; everything else derives from it.

Environmental goals must be based on an analysis of the environment. There are many aspects of the environment that are critical in such an evaluation. It is of course important to analyze economic trends—consumer demand, income levels, family composition, amount of leisure time, and the birth rate. These factors are important to manufacturing as well as service organizations. The need for services will change as these factors change. (For example, the demand for medical and dental care increases with income.)

It is also important to forecast technological trends. New products, services, or current research developments may significantly influence the organization's present products and services. There are, of course, hundreds of organizations which have perished because of a failure to correctly assess technological changes. An evaluation of competitors must also be made—competitor strengths and weaknesses as well as probable future competitor strategy and plans. The future actions of other organizations (such as government agencies or labor unions) may also become important. In regulated industries, or industries highly organized by unions, such forecasts may have critical effects.

Environmental goals must also be based on an analysis of the organization itself. The organization and its resources are the means by which environmental goals are achieved. The organizational analysis should focus on both strengths and weaknesses, since an organization is more likely to be successful when it capitalizes on its strengths and avoids its weaknesses, than otherwise. Its strong and weak points with respect to such factors as technical competence, capital resources, distribution system, human talent, and reputation or image are probably especially important in such an evaluation. Of course, programs can be developed to modify weaknesses in areas that need attention, and all effective organizations usually do this, at least to a certain extent.

Environmental Goals in Stable Organizations. In stable organizations, environmental goals will be fairly constant, over time, and can generally be considered as given, or having a great deal of certainty. But they take on this characteristic of certainty because we assume them to be so. We do this, for example, by examining the market environment and deciding that a particular group of customers exist and will demand our product. Suppose that the market for steel can be broken down into four general segments, automotive firms, appliance firms, defense firms, and others. A steel manufacturer may strategically, decide to focus on only one of these. Which one he chooses is important to his success or failure. To say that there is certainty in any one market is obviously incorrect, but it is possible to say that a particular market has a probability of being a certain size.

Environmental Goals in Dynamic Organizations. By definition, environmental goals for a dynamic organization will be constantly changing. The same general objective of survival is present as for the hierarchical organization, but the manner in which this goal is met varies. For example, an electronics firm may, in one time period, be producing a component for a space project, while at another time it may be building components for a computer manufacturer, and at still another time, it may be producing a device for hospitals.

Thus the product goal in the dynamic organization is not constant, since what the firm produces will vary from period to period, and consumer requirements in terms of type, quality, and quantity will keep changing. This makes it difficult to factor, or break down, these goals in similar ways over time. An appliance manufacturer, for example, may produce the exterior of refrigerators and stoves with minor changes in design in the same unit year after year. In a dynamic organization, however, there may be no set production system, except for the life of a project. When the project changes, the production system is redesigned and the staff reconstituted both in size and in the combination of skills required to satisfy the new conditions.

Internal System Goals

The environmental goal is translated, through the strategy decision, into a more refined and specific objective for the various units of the organization. These may be product goals, market share goals, productivity goals, and profitability goals.

Product goals state the character of the output. How long should the product last? How should it look? What components are to be used in its manufacture?

The answers to these questions represent how the strategy decision is translated in the system; that is, what kind of product to make to achieve the environmental goal. Design standards, quality control levels, and manufacturing methods may all be thought of as forms of the product goal.

Market share goals specify at what particular group the product is aimed and what proportion both of the total market and of the particular market segment the firm believes it can obtain. For example, for some products, some customers, of course, will continue to demand high quality and durability, even though the price may be higher. Another group will want lower price and less durability. In opting for the high volume-low price segment of the market, the firm will consider the probable size of that market segment relative to the total market for a product, as well as the total share of that market segment it is possible for the firm to obtain. Typically, they will then measure at least one aspect of market success by determining how much of the market they have relative to competitors, and their share currently relative to previous years.

Market share goals set the tone for the development of specific sales strategy and planning. What kind of advertising program is most likely to be effective in reaching the desired group of customers? Geographically, where are the majority of potential customers located? How can the sales staff sell most effectively? What channel of distribution is most efficient?

Productivity goals measure the efficiency with which resources are used. Productivity is defined as the output obtained relative to inputs. Productivity goals typically are expressed as ratios, such as sales per employee, or units produced per worker. Productivity goals may be set for manufacturing activities, marketing functions, and other areas of operation. Setting productivity goals is an attempt to give managers some idea of what they must achieve to contribute to the effectiveness of the whole system.

Productivity goals may be derived from a number of different sources—past ratios of outputs to inputs, for example. If previously 10 employees produced 1,000 units per day, then we would want to add 2 more employees if projected levels increased to 1,200. On the other hand, by adding only 1 more employee and improving the operation, perhaps we could still attain an output of 1,200 units; thereby we have improved productivity and very likely reduced costs.

Profitability goals are a form of productivity measure which refer to how well the organization has performed, overall. Typically, profitability goals are assessed by considering returns obtained on sales or investments. Profit as a percentage of sales or as a proportion of assets are common measures of profitability.

Profitability goals focus less on how well a specific component of the organization is doing and more on the whole firm, although it is possible to devise such indexes for specific units. Profitability is generally used as a measure of managerial effectiveness and may have significant effects on the acquisition of capital. For example, investors will be more willing to risk their funds in a firm that has higher profitability than another, presuming that both offer similar prospective returns in the form of dividends to the investor.

Internal System Goals in the Stable Organization. Let us say that a firm may meet its environmental goal by manufacturing a particular product, or set of related products, say steel or aluminum for a segment of the market. Its customers expect, or demand, that these products meet certain requirements of quality and quantity that are similar to the nature of demand in previous periods. Goals of this type can easily be broken down, or factored, into subgoals for each organizational unit. One segment of the firm will be allocated the task of producing iron, another of rolling steel plate, another with the marketing function, and so on. These factored subgoals represent internal subsystem objectives. The internal subsystems (various divisions) know fairly well what they are to do. For them, the important thing is to know "how much" and at "what costs."

If there is stability in the environmental goals, then following from our analysis in chapter 7, we assume that a particular method of production (the means to achievement) has been developed. It is likely that a substantial investment has been made in plant and equipment, and fixed production processes of limited purpose have been devised. In a steel company, for example, the equipment produces only steel. In an automobile company, the production system can only produce cars.

To say thus that the means of achievement is fixed implies that there is only one way for the firm to operate. It will produce its products in a particular way, and similarly have a fixed system of distribution. There is little need for extensive discussion with lower-level managerial personnel for the purpose of finding a better way to produce.

Of course, this is not to say that lower-level personnel cannot help improve efficiency, but their help will come in trying to figure out how to do, at a lower cost, things which are already being done. The purpose of having lower-level staff involved and participating in decision making is primarily to *communicate* to them desired performance levels, or levels of achievement.

For the most part then, internal system goals in hierarchical organizations will be defined in terms of *level of achievement*, as opposed to the *means of achievement*. This is so because the means is already established, and there is little need for changing it.

Internal System Goals in Dynamic Organizations. In the dynamic organization, *internal system goals* will be defined in two dimensions: both by level of achievement and means of achievement. Because each project must be designed substantially differently from previous projects, extensive coordination and cooperation will be required from lower-level personnel in order to find out what they can do, how long it will take, and when it can be done. If there are a large number of different units involved, one of the primary tasks of top management will be to perform this integrating function. Having lower-level personnel involved in these work activities necessitates that their inputs, in the form of proposals and design, be considered significantly, since they possess the technical expertise and are likely to be the most competent group to provide this information. In the stable organization, lower-level participation serves a communication function; in the dynamic organization, these groups will actually influence the way things are to be done. They will be extremely helpful in project design and in determining how a specific objective should be achieved. Item 11.1 describes the planning process in dynamic organizations. It shows the need for lower-level involvement in planning—but with a need for some centralized control.

Individual Goals

These are goals that individuals, or specifically identified subgroups, expect the organization to meet. Each person or group wants something slightly different than another in an organization. Workers want wages, managers want salaries, owners want profits. These are inducements which an organization must provide to obtain the contribution of these various groups. But to repeat: to achieve these individual goals, the environmental goal must be attained. Such a concept is based on March and Simon's (1958) inducement/contribution balance, which states:

1. An organization is a system of interrelated social behaviors of a number of persons we shall call *participants* in the organization.
2. Each participant in each group of participants receives *from* the organization *inducements* in return for which he makes to the organization *contributions*.
3. Each participant will continue his participation in an organization only so long as the inducements offered him are as great or greater (measured in terms of *his* values and in terms of the alternatives open to him) than the contributions he is asked to make.
4. Contributions provided by the various groups of participants are the source from which the organization manufactures the inducements offered to participants.
5. Hence the organization is "solvent"—and will continue in existence—only so long as the contributions are sufficient to provide inducements in large enough measure to draw forth these contributions.

Individual goals are what *people* want. They are reflected in the planning documents of an organization. Wage levels for example, will be shown and used as estimates of part of the product cost. Profit levels will be sought. The individuals and groups who expect payoffs from the system will, of course, press to increase their return. Owners will want higher profits and dividends, workers will want higher wages. The final overall plan adopted by an organization will reflect all of these subgroup goals. The final plan derives from the pressures that each brings to bear on the others. In this sense, then, plans to achieve objectives represent compromises among the subgroups.

The Planning Process and Objectives

A managerial control system begins to take its shape in the planning process, the process of trying to determine what resources are required to achieve environmental goals. One way to look at planning is as a factoring, or breaking down, of the environmental objective into system goals for both the long- and short-range. Basically, strategic decisions are made about the nature of products and markets. These are then translated into profit and cost objectives for the total firm and the specific operating units. Figure 11.1 illustrates the planning and control cycle for an organization—in it, for the coming year it is necessary to develop specific goals and strategies for marketing, production, and support functions. From these projections, budgets are developed which become the basis for evaluating how effectively the firm operates.

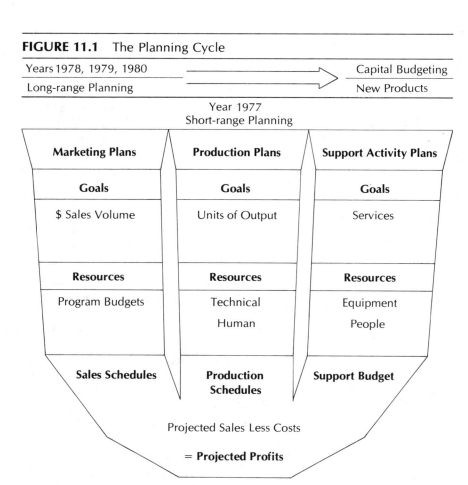

FIGURE 11.1   The Planning Cycle

There are many different types of budgets. Among those in use in industrial organizations are the production budget, the materials purchase budget, the budgeted income statement, the budgeted balance sheet, the capital expenditure budget, the cash budget, and the manpower budget. (An extensive discussion of these budgets is beyond the scope of this book. They are treated in detail in Tosi and Carroll [1976].) When the various budgets have been developed, they become the basis for other planning. For instance, the production budget can be an important source of information for a personnel manager because from it he can predict when to enter the labor market to add new staff. The cash budget will show when shortages of funds will probably occur, so that the firm may be able to anticipate and secure short-term loan commitments substantially in advance of need.

At the same time that planning is being done for the short-run, long-range considerations such as capital acquisition and development of new products must be considered and evaluated. This long-range planning requires an intimate knowledge of products and costs, as well as of strengths and weaknesses of the firm doing the planning.

Thune and House (1970) found that companies that put more emphasis than others on long-range planning have better economic performance. Longer-range planning is also related to success for individual managers as well. For example, in a study of foremen at General Electric it was reported:

> The least effective foremen spent the greatest percentage of their time finding immediate solutions to short-range production problems, while the most effective foremen spent the greatest percentage of their time on activities which involved planning and organizing the longer-range aspects of the job (Ponder, 1957).

Obtaining Compliance to Plans with Controls.   Control, then, is insuring that events conform to plans. As shown in figure 11.2, standards of performance are established, performance is periodically measured and compared with the standards, and corrective action is taken if actual performance varies from the standards by significant

FIGURE 11.2   Steps in Planning and Control

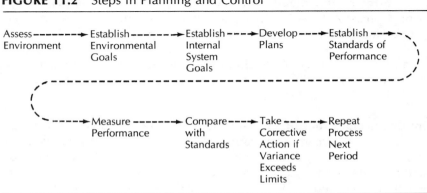

amounts. The standards are often stated in budgets, which are of course the plans in dollar and quantity amounts, and typically cover a particular time period. For example, a budget may be stated in terms of number of production units to be completed, number of manhours utilized, cost per unit produced, profit per unit produced, expenditures for raw materials, or in number of units sold in a particular month. Other standards may be expressed as number of quits per 100 employees, amount of time required to make one unit, percentage of defective pieces produced, or percentage of time machinery is idle. The data to be compared with such standards is often collected by staff units such as accountants, who may report their results directly to the highest levels in the organization. These data make it possible for higher-level management to manage by exception—that is, for them to become involved in actual operations only when significant problems emerge. In addition, the control system provides measures of success for lower-level personnel and can provide the basis for the operation of the organization's reward system.

Planning and Control in Hierarchical Organizations

A high degree of environmental certainty facilitates the use of decision strategies and resource allocation methods which are called "deterministic." In such decisions, chance elements do not exist; that is, the decision maker feels it is a realistic assumption to assume certainty, that certain situations, costs, and other conditions can be specified with accuracy. Starr (1971) gives the following example:

> Assume that an expansion in plant capacity is planned. Several strategic and tactical alternatives are considered. The possibilities are narrowed down and discarded until finally, a single plan of action is accepted. A final plan is detailed as though no worthwhile opportunities for deviating from the plan will occur.

Planning and resource allocation decisions of this type are generally preferred by managers because they offer several advantages, among which Starr (1971) notes the following:

Simple Formal Procedures Can Be Used.   There is lessened need for coordination between organizational units to develop the plans. Data such as costs and resource capacities are usually available from production units or cost accounting groups, or computer information systems may have information which is easily accessible. This facilitates the development of plans, since this information can be incorporated in existing planning models.

Efficient Logistical Support Is Possible. Once the most efficient plan is formulated, it is relatively easy to obtain help, support, and coordination from other departments. The final plan can be quickly disseminated throughout the relevant units of an organization to become the basis for planning their activities.

Control Is Emphasized Rather than Planning. With deterministic methods the planning models, (e.g., linear programming) have already been developed. These models pinpoint strategic control points and provide the manager with a specification of *what* should be monitored, and also with specific amounts, or measures, to be achieved, such as the number of units to produce or the allowable costs which can be incurred without exceeding the limits.

No Recognition of Uncertainty Is Required. It is easy to make a plan when the planner knows what is going to happen. In fact, somewhere along the line in every organization this assumption must ultimately be made in order for operations to continue, even in a volatile environment. For example, an airplane manufacturer must, in designing and building a prototype of a plane which is to be sold to the Defense Department, at some point give the go-ahead, even though the future sales depend on such unknown factors as the performance of the aircraft, approval by the military, and subsequent congressional approval.

Characteristics of Controls in Hierarchical Organizations

For control purposes, measures of performance can be constructed from historical precedent; that is, the firm will have a fairly well-accepted, and predetermined set of control points developed from past experience. For example, it may be known that marketing activities can be effectively managed by monitoring orders received. When orders drop below a particular level, added sales or promotional activity will be necessary. By knowing what to monitor, the firm can, by using historical data, remain aware of what levels are critical. Forecasts can be made of "order level activity" from previous years' experience.

Also, desired profitability levels can be set by top management. If the firm desires a 25 percent return on capital, for instance, it can work backward through its cost and revenue structure to determine how much should be produced, when, and at what cost. Since the systems of the organization are fixed, the appropriate levels of work forces and required levels of sales can be determined.

One important characteristic of these subsystem goals is that they will be objective, in the sense that they can be acceptably—though not perfectly—quantified and measured. Scrap rates, sales per employee, return on investment, number of units produced are all less subject to disagreement than more subjective criterion such as "high quality," "effective sales methods," or "the impact of advertising expenditures."

Top management usually has the most influence in the determination of the goals of stable organizations. Since the question is one of what level of achievement is appropriate, and there are years of experience from which to extrapolate, goal levels are set by top management with the aid of accountants and production engineering staffs.

Fairly rigid standards will be set, and the primary method of managing activities will follow a *management by exception* mode, which means that only when deviations occur will they be called to the attention of top management for corrective action. Because strategic control points are defined by the system, and the desired goal levels are specified, particular points in the operation can be observed, and, if these stay within the control limits, adequate performance can be expected.

When rigid standards are built into goals, there will be close, tight control, and little deviation will be tolerated, because a small deviation can magnify into a serious problem. For example, in a firm which manufactures 5 million units per year, an upward cost deviation of only 10¢ per unit can mean $500,000 in increased costs.

Planning and Control in Dynamic Organizations

Planning and control in dynamic organizations must take into account the uncertainties involved. The dynamic organization must rely on less accurate estimates of project time and costs than the stable firm. In planning and control in the dynamic organization, the control process can be facilitated by giving managers some idea about what aspects of the project are critical in order to pinpoint strategic control points. These points can then be monitored to see that events are conforming to plan.

The difficulties with which organizations operating in a volatile environment must cope arise from the fact not only that changes in the external environment must be perceived and assesed, but also that the changes themselves often alter the organization's methods of goal achievement. This means that organizations operating in a volatile environment must have a flexible structure, one in which both human and technical resources are adaptable to changing tasks. Since the opportunities to develop fixed production systems that are present in the stable organization are not present in the dynamic organization, resources in the latter must be kept mobile. What the manager in the dynamic organization must do is adopt planning strategies for short time periods, recognizing that subsequent periods may require vastly different organizational activities. Starr (1971) addresses this problem by noting that one

> approach is to speed up management's response rates and to plan for periods that are short enough to be relatively stable. Short planning periods have all the dangers of suboptimization . . ., but, if consecutive periods are relatively independent, then a good deal can be gained from faster decision making, more rapid action, and so on. Speed is accomplished largely through increased experience. . . .

The emphatic thrust, then, in dynamic organizations will be to make decisions about what environmental goals should look like, based on the changes that managers feel will occur, and to focus on the development, design, and effective managing of project-like task activities.

The manager in the dynamic organization therefore needs to know how to make decisions when there is high uncertainty in the environment. He must deal with two problems: (1) selecting a strategy likely to be successful in an unpredictable environment, and (2) implementing the strategy.

Controls in Dynamic Organizations

Thus, in the dynamic organization, the focus of control will be different for different projects because the dimensions of level and means of achievement will vary from project to project. It is necessary to define the means of achievement for projects, since in many cases, the manager will be unable to determine, during the actual conduct of the project, whether or not costs are at an acceptable level or whether or not the product performs adequately. In a steel plant, for example, performance may be monitored as the production process goes on by quality and cost measures, but in the aerospace industry about all a manager can do is determine whether an activity is completed on time and whether those who performed it have done it in a way that is generally acceptable.

Thus, because middle management and professional groups have the technical expertise, middle and lower-level management in the dynamic organization will be more extensively involved in setting both end result and activity goals than in the stable organization, and evaluation will proceed according to these goals. Of course, top management evaluates and approves the goals, but they will need to use more participative management strategies than is usually true in the hierarchical organization.

Behavioral Reactions to Planning and Control Systems

Plans expressed in terms of budgets and other control devices are designed to affect attitudes and behavior, and they do. Some of these behavioral affects may be positive and others negative from the perspective of the individual or the organization (Tosi, 1974; Argyris, 1953).

Anxiety from Budgeting. Budgets allocate resources such as man-hours, money, and supplies to units. Some research indicates that the budgeting process may work in such a way as to allocate resources to units not on the basis of the workload of the units but on the basis of their power or prestige in the organization (Pfeffer and Salancik, 1974). The fact that budgetary negotiations are usually conducted in secret and often are not based on the actual needs of the unit often creates a high level of anxiety among the managers to be affected. This may lead to political behavior, negative reactions toward control units, overstatement of needs, and the development of covert information systems.

1. Political Behavior. Managers may attempt to increase their power in an organization by political behavior. They may, for instance, withhold important information until the last minute to magnify its significance. Or they may be excessively ingratiating toward superiors or those in positions of influence. Providing favors beyond the normal courtesies and requirements of the work assignment are also political strategies.

2. Negative Reactions Toward Planning and Budget Units.
Perceived inequity of resource allocation may trigger negative reac-

tions toward those units responsible for the collection of budget data and preparation. Personnel in the controller's office (probably a group of staff specialists) are likely to have the major responsibility for putting together a budget's final figures. They may end up bearing the brunt of criticism since they are more convenient targets than line managers. After all, an individual's superior will be responsible for promotion decisions, making it unwise to alienate him by directing aggression toward him.

If this mode of adaptation becomes at all widespread, it will hinder the planning group's effectiveness because it will become increasingly difficult to interact with other units to obtain accurate and timely information.

3. Overstatement of Needs.   To protect his perceived equitable share of future resources, managers will sometimes pad estimated budgetary needs. They learn quickly that cuts are usually made in requested amounts and, in order to be equitable, all units have to experience relatively similar budget cuts. Therefore, the honest manager, estimating his needs with some degree of accuracy, is penalized. He quickly learns that an over-statement of requirements helps him secure his "fair" share.

4. Covert Information Systems.   If there is a high degree of secrecy regarding budget allocations to other units, managers will seek to make some estimate of how they fare relative to others. They will probably overestimate the amounts obtained by other units. Nevertheless, because the allocations may represent something other than need —for example, the power one has—information will be sought about the amount received by others. Secretaries, staff members from the budget offices, and those with access to data will be prodded for information. A communication network may develop which provides some information, although it may quite possibly be inaccurate.

The Use of Participation for Anxiety Reduction.   Acceptance of plans and budget requirements may be substantially increased through "participative management" strategies. March and Simon (1958) have concluded that participation may minimize problems when there is a "felt need for joint decision-making." Certainly if power is a major factor in determining budget allocations, then a participative strategy is warranted.

Participation is a decision-making process in which an individual or group can influence, or change, decisions. Of course, to move toward more participation in budget development and away from unilateral (or relatively so) determination of budget levels implies a redistribution of power to those groups involved.

Participation in the budgeting process is a promising method for anxiety reduction and increased involvement. The document that emerges will likely be more generally accepted if it is developed through a process in which line managers are involved and with overt, active support from top management.

Budget Implementation

Finally, the important question is how plans and budgets are used by the manager. He brings them to life, but the effects previously noted—anxiety in the preparation, the effects of goals, etc.—have taken place and are likely to form the perceptual base from which individual reactions will develop.

Both plans and budgets may be viewed as instruments which specify, at least partially, certain actions that a manager must take to achieve his goals. So the manager must use these instruments—make them work. Otherwise they will be useless.

The Budget and Performance Evaluation.   The seductive nature of plans and budgets is that they are "objective." Goals are quantified in a way that makes sense to the pragmatic manager—dollars and cents—and are likely to be a significant component in the evaluation of managerial performance. How budgets are used in performance evaluation is crucial, since a manager may—using them wrongly—reinforce behavior which can have negative effects on performance.

Learning theory, (chap. 3) postulates that when a behavior is reinforced (i.e., rewards or punishments are seen as its consequences), the probability that an individual will act similarly in later periods changes. Therefore, when a person is rewarded for, say, meeting a budget requirement, it can be predicted that he will later work to meet other budget requirements. It is important to ask the question, "What are we reinforcing when we use the budget as a basis for evaluation?" The answer is, of course, "It all depends."

Distorted Behavior.   Since adherence to standards in an organization is often the criteria used in the organizational reward system, there is often an attempt to look good on the standards by any means—including those which are dysfunctional to the organization. For example, a manager may stay within his budgeted costs by not performing needed equipment maintenance and this can result in serious equipment breakdowns at some future time. A manager may also engage in cost-cutting drives which so antagonize valuable employees that they leave the organization. Or to keep raw materials inventories low, managers may arrange to have deliveries made after the end of the reporting period, but the average inventory over a long period of time may be what it would have been in any case. Sales clerks or bank tellers may antagonize customers by putting first priority on avoiding financial losses, no matter how small, or on filling out data sheets for the control system, no matter what the cost in time. Quality may be sacrificed in order to achieve higher quantity, leading to revenue losses because of customer dissatisfaction. The control system may also lead to an inefficient scheduling of work so that the easy jobs or orders are done at the end of an accounting period, irrespective of their actual priorty.

There are other behavioral problems as well. Different units may blame each other for production or other problems which prevent budgeted goals from being achieved. This can create intraorganizational hostility and reduce cooperativeness in the future. In addition, it may require the frequent use of organizational arbitrators to settle such disputes among organizational units. Often, organizational members will deliberately falsify data in order to look good on control-system reports. For example, the number of defective pieces may be understated, inventory may be hidden, or production figures may be "adjusted." In addition, the control system may result in the development of a new, additional control system within the organizational units to collect the same data as that collected by staff units reporting to higher levels (McGregor, 1960). This new and unnecessary unit functions to alleviate the anxiety experienced by the unit's managers, an anxiety created by the surveillance they are already under.

When the superior's concern is with the budgeted level and it is used as described above, then those who have to live with the budget learn the ropes of manipulating outcomes with little regard for what is really intended as the purpose of the activity. This is because budgets, and most managerial controls, do not give any guidance on how to do something. Rather, they simply specify the approved level of resources to be used. Effectiveness depends both on the quantity of resources and how they are used.

To use plans and budgets effectively, then, a manager must go beyond them. He should, of course, communicate to his subordinates the intended level of achievement. But he must also monitor the way subordinates go about achieving that level. The manager may have to coach subordinates extensively about *how* to achieve goals. This means that performance evaluation must focus on both budget requirements *and* behavior so that, from a reinforcement point of view, the subordinate not only learns how much is expected, but how to do it.

Other Factors in Evaluation.   The utility of the budget as an evaluation device may be diluted by a number of other factors. First, the rewards for achievement of performance goals may not be seen as as valuable by the subordinate as by the superior. Second, the budget only contains one type of performance criterion, while overall performance may include more subjective facets. Third, the frequency of performance reviews is not great, generally once or twice a year. Such a schedule usually does not allow sufficient opportunities to link rewards strongly to performance measured against the budget. And, finally, some superiors simply may not regard the budget as a useful enough evaluative device to give it prominence in assessment.

In this chapter we have discussed control systems. Control systems result from the establishment of various types of goals and the development of plans to achieve such goals. Various types of budgets are perhaps the most common type of control system in current use in organizations. There are often contradictions between individual goals and internal system and environmental goals. For this reason, the reactions of organizational members to managerial control systems may not be satisfactory from the perspective of the organization. Obtaining acceptance of decisions involving the choice of certain goals or plans over others has traditionally been a challenging managerial task. The next chapter, when it discusses decision implementation, will focus on this issue of acceptance.

Discussion Questions

1. Using concepts of goals (environmental, system, and individual), write some goal definitions for an organization with which you are familiar.

2. What is the relationship between planning, control, and their effects on human behavior?

3. How are plans translated into restrictions?

4. Why would anxiety be reduced by meaningful participation in budgeting?

5. How can a budget "motivate" anyone? Is this motivation in a psychological sense? Or in the sense of a managerial strategy?

6. What different types of control systems can you expect to find in hierarchical organizations? Dynamic organizations?

7. Why do organizational controls seem to be more of a problem in hierarchical organizations?

Chapter 12
Decision Implementation

Decision making is the act of choosing from among alternatives—of coming to a conclusion of what should be done in a particular situation. A decision must be made when a person wants things to be different in the future. Every human being makes decisions daily about personal life. Managers not only make decisions about their personal lives but also about and for the organization in which they are employed. Decision making is an essential aspect of any manager's job and managers are evaluated on the ability to make effective decisions.

In any organization, many decisions must be carried out by persons other than the decision makers, and there may be resistance to some of these decisions, a resistance which can take many forms—verbal protest, refusal to cooperate, work slowdowns. Resistance may be directed against decisions about work methods, assignments, organizational policy or structure, or salaries or benefits—in other words, changes which impinge upon the needs or personal objectives of organizational members. Or a change may increase insecurity when its effects are unknown, or because it is a threat to an organizational member's economic well-being, his status, or his social relationships, or because to comply would be an inconvenience, or simply because the change involves a conflict with employee attitudes or values.

On the other hand, the proposal or decision may be fully accepted because it is viewed as producing benefits which exceed any negative features. Probably most decisions or changes contain both positive and negative elements (or valences) and the degree of acceptability is related to the extent to which the positive elements exceed the negative from the perspectives of the subordinates involved.

Thus decisions are made in order to achieve some goal or to solve some problem. The decision maker has some desired end result or future state of affairs in mind when making the decision. The end result or desired state does not have to be a different one than is being attained at present. A manager may wish to keep activities or performances at their present level or even to lower performance but not below a certain level.

The manager is usually evaluated on decision making to the degree that the desired end result was achieved and to the degree that the resources employed were less than those that would have been required by other alternatives. Since the decision must usually be implemented by others, the decision alternatives chosen must in most instances be acceptable to those carrying out the implementation.

Effective Decisions

Maier (1963) holds that a decision can be evaluated in terms of the degree to which acceptability (A) is important as compared to the importance of quality (Q). The *quality* of a decision refers to the degree to which technical and rational factors govern in the selection of alternatives, while *acceptability* refers to the extent to which those who are ultimately going to carry out the decision are willing to implement in it a way which minimizes problems and maximizes implementation.

An effective decision, according to Maier, takes both acceptance and quality into account as shown:

$$\text{Effective Decision} = \text{Quality} \times \text{Acceptance}$$

When either quality or acceptance is zero, (or not present if required), then a decision is a bad one. Quality is an objective characteristic which can very often be measured or assessed against some technical standard, but acceptance tends to be more of a subjective evaluation, more emotional and attitudinal.

Maier proposes three types of decisions using these dimensions. The first of these is Q/A, a decision that has *high quality but low acceptance requirements*. For these decisions, it is important that the alternative chosen is correct, since its quality has technical or economic significance for the organization. At the same time, the acceptability requirement is low, probably because the decision is not germane to the personal needs or objectives of the organizational members who are to carry it out. For example, the interest rate a bank chooses can have a significant effect on its economic situation, yet most of the bank's employees are indifferent to the choice.

A second type of decision, A/Q, is a decision in which *acceptability requirements are high but quality requirements are low*. Which of several qualified employees works on a Saturday overtime assignment is a decision of this type. Who works on Saturday is of great interest to the employees, but of little concern to management.

In an $A=Q$ decision, both the acceptability and quality requirements are high. An example of this type of decision would be the introduction of a new work procedure. It is important that the work procedure be acceptable since employees have a high degree of interest in it, and it is equally important that an efficient rather than an inefficient procedure be chosen.

How Quality/Acceptability Affects Decision Making

Obviously not all decisions made at higher levels create acceptance problems. Many fall within the "real" boundaries of the "psychological contract" (see chap. 8). Many actions taken by top management will be viewed as legitimate, and there will be little or no resistance, and often, as we have seen, the individual or group may be indifferent to a decision because it has little impact on personal needs and objectives. Many times, moreover, it is obvious to those who are to carry out a decision that very complex technical considerations beyond their competence enter the evaluation of alternatives. They will accept the advice of the "expert," or the person who "knows."

It should be noted that rational decision strategies must often be used even where a decision—perhaps because it threatens an individual's or a group's security—has a high acceptance requirement. Such decisions may well meet resistance, and strategies must be employed to overcome or adjust to such resistance. For example, some industrial firms have overcome resistance to change in work procedures by providing economic guarantees to workers affected by the change. The employees, for instance, may be guaranteed their jobs or their incomes. This may be an effective way to obtain acceptability when the resistance is caused by perceived economic threat. In other cases, acceptance of alternative work procedures, policies, or other changes has been obtained by bargaining; that is, giving the employees something they want in exchange for acceptance of the change. This will be especially applicable when the employees are represented by a union. Other approaches for obtaining acceptance include making the changes tentative instead of final, consulting with employees in advance of making the change, or allowing those who will implement the change to participate in making it.

Participative strategies, decision making in which a person has an opportunity to influence the outcome of decisions, are appropriate when *acceptance* requirements are high. The effectiveness of participative strategies was dramatically illustrated in an early study by Coch and French (1948), which set out to discover the effects of different degrees of participation in the acceptance of technological changes which were needed to increase worker productivity. In the study, some employees were told by the firm's industrial engineers what the change in work methods was to be, a second group of employees elected a representative to discuss the proposed changes with the firm's representative, and a third group, the total participation group, met with the firm's representative and suggested changes themselves. Productivity fell in all three groups immediately after the changes were implemented, but fell significantly less in the total participation group than in the other two groups, and productivity 30 days after the changes was much higher in both participation groups than it was in the nonparticipation group. These results are consistent with a series of studies conducted by Kurt Lewin and his colleagues (1953) during World War II.

Participation in Decision Making

Obtaining acceptance of a decision through participation not only has the benefit of giving the participants a feeling of influence on the alternative chosen, but provides them with an understanding of the reasons for the change and what the change will require of them, which is important, since one of the chief reasons for resistance to change is the uncertainty associated with the potential effects of change.

Participation means that a person can influence—have something to say about—a decision that is beyond his formal authority range (the degree of discretion in his job). Participation is used for more than just gaining acceptance of a decision, however. For example, it is often necessary for subordinates to participate in the making of a decision because the decision maker needs their ideas or needs information that only they possess. Under these conditions, participative approaches also increase the quality of a decision.

Some Guides to Using Participative Methods

There are various degrees of participation possible. Subordinates may be allowed complete autonomy in making the decision, or the decision maker may consult with them and then make the decision himself. (See the discussion of leadership style in chap. 8.) Which of these alternative approaches is best in decision-making depends upon the situation and the type of decision to be made. Two approaches for deciding on the degree of participation required by the decision have been developed, one by Maier (1963), the second by Vroom and Yetton (1973), who extended Maier's approach.

Maier's Decision-Making Approach. As we have discussed, Maier classified decisions into one of three categories based on the decision's acceptance and quality requirements. For Q/A decisions—those where acceptance is of little importance and thus of little concern to the decision maker—the manager may make the decision, or it may be made by an expert in the field, and it is likely that the decision will be accepted with little or no problem. For A/Q decisions—those where acceptance requirements are high and quality requirements are low— the form of participation can of course vary, depending upon the type of decision that is involved. Extensive participation and subordinate influence is appropriate and should be allowed, since it does not matter to management which alternative the group chooses. In this situation the only criterion of effectiveness is to obtain a satisfactory decision for the group involved. In the case of the $A = Q$ decision, however, it is important that the group choose an alternative which is high in both quality and acceptance. For the $A = Q$ decision, Maier recommends that the decision maker play an active role in the decision-making process. This will help insure that a high-quality decision emerges.

For any problem in which a participation approach is used, Maier recommends that the leaders follow a set of principles derived from research on group problem solving. These same concepts also apply to participation with individuals. Maier has found that the *quality* of decisions is enhanced when:

1. A discussion leader participates in the discussion.
2. The discussion leader has been trained to lead a discussion group.
3. A "developmental" as opposed to "free" discussion mode is used. That is, the members do not simply discuss anything. Rather, they attempt to move from problem definition to cause to solution.
4. Effort is directed at overcoming surmountable obstacles, such as obtaining inputs from shy members.
5. All available facts are used.
6. Group members are prevented from progressing too rapidly toward a solution.
7. The "idea-getting" process is separated from the "idea-evaluation" process.
8. An emphasis is placed on the problems to be solved rather than the alternatives available.
9. The leader refrains from suggesting solutions himself.

10. Groups are required to work on a particular problem twice rather than once.

Maier's research also shows that the *acceptance* of decisions is enhanced when:

1. The individual has an opportunity to have his opinion reflected in the group decision itself.
2. The individual feels free to express his ideas about the issue.
3. The group leader does not dominate the discussion.
4. The group leader has been trained in group decision procedures.
5. An atmosphere of tolerance for the conflict of ideas exists.
6. The group makes a high-quality decision.
7. The group leader has positive feelings about the creativity of group members.

The Vroom-Yetton Model.   There can be, as we have noted, several different levels, or degrees of subordinate involvement in decision-making. Vroom and Yetton (1973), extending Maier's work, described different methods of decision making and devised an heuristic for deciding when and how various decision strategies should be used. These range from making the decision alone to allowing a group to make it, with the manager serving as moderator of a group discussion. The alternative strategies are described below. As the decision approach moves from AI toward GII (A stands for autocratic; C for consultative; and G for group), the amount of subordinate influence over the final decision increases.

AI   The manager makes the decision alone with currently available data.

AII Necessary information is obtained from subordinates, but the manager still decides alone. The role of the subordinates is input of data only. They have nothing to do with generating or evaluating alternatives.

CI   The manager discusses the problems with relevant subordinates *individually*. Then, without bringing them together, he makes a decision that may or may not reflect their input.

CII The manager shares the problem with subordinates in a group meeting, gathering ideas and suggestions. He then, alone, makes the decision which may, or may not, take the input of the group meeting into account.

GII Problems are shared with the group. The manager functions in the "participative" style described by Maier. His role is to provide information and help, facilitating the group's determination of their own solution, rather than his.

The Vroom-Yetton (V-Y) model takes into consideration a number of factors which influence the degree of success in using a participative approach. (There is no *GI* in the V-Y model.) It is called a normative, or prescriptive, model because it describes how a decision should be made. The appropriate method is contingent upon the following properties of the situation in which the problem arises:

1. *Importance of the Quality of the Decision.* How important is it to achieve a high-quality solution? If there is no quality requirement, then any acceptable alternative will be satisfactory to management and the decision becomes a relatively easy one to make and the group can make the decision itself.

2. *Extent to which the Decision Maker Has the Information Necessary to Make Decisions.* Vroom and Yetton point out that there are two kinds of information that may be necessary to make an effective decision. One type of information pertains to the preferences of subordinates about alternatives. The second type of information is whether or not there are rational grounds on which to judge the relative quality of alternatives.

When the leader is not aware of subordinates' preferences, he must obtain this information somehow, and participative approaches are one such means. If the leader has this information, however, and the problem is such that an individual decision is more likely to produce a better solution than that of a group, then clearly the situation calls for the manager to make the decision alone.

In what kinds of situation is a group likely to make a better decision than an individual? Research indicates that an individual can do as well as a group when either (1) the problem has a highly verifiable solution, or when (2) the solution requires thinking through complicated interrelated stages, keeping in mind conclusions reached at earlier times. This same research shows that a group is superior when the problem is complex, has several parts, and the group members possess diverse but relevant talents and skills. Insight and originality can then be more likely obtained from a group than from an individual (Kelley and Thibaut, 1969).

3. *Extent to Which Problem Is Structured.* In structured problems, the alternatives or at least the means for generating them are known.

In most organizations at least some use is made of standard procedures which give individuals all or most of the information necessary
to take a previously planned action. In an ill-structured problem, on
the other hand, the information may be widely dispersed through the
organization, with a number of individuals each possessing a part.
These individuals will probably have to be brought together to solve
the problem or to make a joint decision.

4. *Extent to Which Subordinates' Acceptance Is Important.* Acceptance by subordinates is not critical where a decision will be implemented by someone outside the specific unit in which the decision is
made or where it falls in the boundaries of the psychological contract.
In the latter instance, carrying out the decision is a matter of simple
compliance rather than a matter of the exercise of initiative, judgment,
or creativity. The more commitment required from subordinates in the
carrying out of a strategy, of course, the more important subordinate
acceptance becomes.

5. *Prior Probability that an Autocratic Decision Will Be Accepted.* If
a decision is viewed as the exercise of the legitimate authority of a
manager, it will be accepted by subordinates without participation,
since it falls within the boundaries of the "psychological contract."

6. *Extent to Which Subordinates Are Motivated to Attain Organizational Goals.* Organizational members may have objectives in a particular situation inconsistent with those of management. In such cases,
participation in decision making in order to increase acceptance of a
needed change may be more risky than in those situations where the
goals of the two groups are the same. Thus, participative decision
making could be expected to work best where there is mutual interest
in the problem.

7. *Extent to Which Subordinates Are Likely to Disagree over Solutions.* Subordinates may disagree among themselves over prospective
alternatives because of different gains or losses from an alternative or
because of differences in values or other critical factors. The method
used to reach a decision must facilitate resolution of the disagreement,
and thus group involvement is necessary.

The Decision Factors and the Vroom-Yetton Model.   All of these factors are presented in the form of questions in the Vroom-Yetton model
in figure 12.1. The questions in that model are to be answered on a
yes-no basis. The decision tree format establishes the sequence of the
questions of concern to the decision maker in various situations. At
the end of every path in the decision tree is a basic problem situation.
Each of these situations gives the decision maker one or more alterna-

tive approaches for making the decision. According to Vroom and Yetton, the best method for making decisions can be determined with such an approach.

To illustrate, let us say that a manager wishes to change the work schedule so as to have at least one maintenance engineer on duty at all times between 9 A.M. and 9 P.M., six days a week, and that this represents a departure from previous work schedules. He has a number of alternative ways to make his decision. He starts with question A in figure 12.1, "Is there a quality requirement?" He decides that there is none since he will be satisfied with a wide variety of different work schedules so long as a maintenance engineer is on duty at all times between the hours of 9 A.M. and 9 P.M., six days a week. Because he answered No to question A, he must go to question D, "Is acceptance of decision by subordinates critical to effective implementation?" Suppose that in his opinion the answer to question D is Yes, since acceptance of the schedule is critical to its effective implementation. (If he had answered question D No, the decision tree shows a type 1 problem situation, and any of the decision-making methods for dealing with a group listed earlier—AI, AII, CI, CII, GII—could be used to deal with the problem.) Because he answers Yes to question D, he must next answer question E. Let us assume that he answers No to question E, "If I were to make the decision by myself, is it reasonably certain that it would be accepted by my subordinates?" A No answer to question E, according to the decision tree of figure 12.1, presents a type 2 problem situation. The recommended approach for making this type of decision is GII, which requires the decision maker to share the problem with the group and to agree to accept any alternative that the group supports. A Yes answer presents a type 1 problem situation, and any method can be used to deal with the problem.

In problem types where many alternative decision-making approaches exist, as is the case for problem types 1, 3, 4, and 8, the decision maker may want to use the alternative which requires the fewest number of man hours to make and to implement the decision—but here it should be remembered that although a manager may be able to make a decision more quickly alone, it may take more time in the long run to communicate that decision to subordinates and to achieve an understanding of what is required than would a participative decision.

Decision-making Behavior of Managers and the V-Y Model. A
number of studies have been conducted by Vroom and Yetton to determine the extent to which managers use particular decision-making

FIGURE 12.1   Decision-Process Flow Chart for Group Problems

A. Is there a quality requirement such that one solution is likely to be more rational than another?
B. Do I have sufficient information to make a high-quality decision?
C. Is the problem structured?
D. Is acceptance of decision by subordinates critical to effective implementation?
E. If I were to make the decision by myself, is it reasonably certain that it would be accepted by my subordinates?
F. Do subordinates share the organizational goals to be attained in solving this problem?
G. Is conflict among subordinates likely in preferred solutions? (This question is irrelevant to individual problems.)

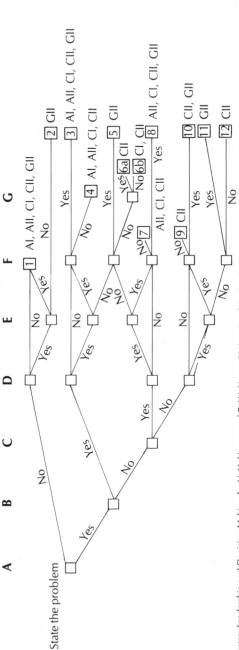

Source: *Leadership and Decision-Making*, by V. H. Vroom and P. W. Yetton (University of Pittsburgh Press, 1973). By permission of the authors and the publisher.

approaches, and the degree to which the V-Y normative model is descriptive of such strategies. In one study of 385 managers from more than 100 firms, it was found that these managers used all five of the decision-making approaches. The most frequently used styles appeared to be CI and CII, in which the manager shares problems with subordinates and then makes the decision himself. In studies of actual problems solved by more than 600 managers in many different organizations, it was found that most of the problems did not have a pressing time constraint and that most involved some degree of both quality and acceptance (Vroom and Yetton, 1973). Most managers felt that they lacked some of the information needed to make a satisfactory decision. To solve these problems, the managers used approaches CI, CII, and GII in about equal proportions. It was found that managers had a tendency to use participation more under circumstances where subordinates had necessary information, a quality decision was important, subordinates were trusted, and acceptance was considered important. There was also more participation when it was unlikely that subordinates would accept an autocratic decision. Several other studies have indicated that a continued use of participation is especially important in organizations in which individuals have become accustomed to it. In such instances, subordinates accept autocratic decisions far less readily than they do participative ones.

Vroom and Yetton (1973) also studied the decision behavior of eight different groups of managers from a variety of firms. They found that both the nature of the problem itself and the decision-making preferences of the managers influenced the degree to which participation was used. Situational factors, however, were much more important than individual preferences in determining the choice of decision-making approach. The research of Vroom and Yetton shows that middle and upper managers typically consult with their subordinates in decision making. Participation is not only used to obtain acceptance but also whenever subordinates have relevant information for the decision, when they are dealing with unstructured problems, when they need a high-quality decision, when the subordinates are not likely to accept autocratic decisions, and when the subordinates are trusted by the superior.

Dangers in the Participation Approach

Maier (1963) has suggested several reasons why managers may resist using the participative decision approach to increase acceptance of decisions. First, the manager may fear that subordinates will reject the need for any change. Second, he may fear that subordinates will make a low-quality decision. Third, a manager may feel that subordinates may expect to participate in future decisions. Fourth, the supervisor may feel that respect for him will diminish, since as a supervisor his role is to lead, not follow. Fifth, many managers feel it is their responsibility to make the decisions and that subordinates do not wish to participate in the decision-making process. Many managers probably feel they do not have the ability to lead a group discussion and are uncomfortable in such a situation.

A few research studies support Maier's contentions. For example, one study seems to show that the participation approach will not be effective when the employees do not feel their actions are "legitimate" in the particular situation (French, Israel, and As, 1960); also when employees feel they do not have the necessary information or skills to contribute significantly to a decision-making discussion, they feel inferior and resent being placed in a situation they find uncomfortable (Mulder and Wilke, 1970). In addition, those participating must be motivated to work on the problem; that is, it must be a problem they have an interest in solving.

Perhaps the most significant obstacle to the use of participation is "pseudo participation." Many managers theoretically acknowledge that decisions are more readily accepted when subordinates are "involved," so they bring together a group ostensibly to discuss a problem. After an airing of facts, there sometimes emerges a consensus among the group for an alternative unacceptable to the manager. He will then say, in effect, "Those are great ideas, but we have to do it another way." In reality, he expected the group to conclude for his alternative. Since they didn't, he overruled them. This tactic can only lead to problems for the manager. He will find it difficult to obtain much involvement later, since he will hardly be trusted.

Thus, there are certain prerequisites to making the participative approach work. These are that the problems suggested for discussion in the group should be appropriate in terms of their perceived legitimacy and with respect to the amount of interest the employees have in the problem. In addition, the manager should be trained in group discussion techniques, and he must match the amount and type of participation used to the expertise of the participants.

Lower-level employees may participate in managerial decision making through the use of elected worker representatives on decision-making boards in the organization. This can be a way of gaining acceptance of top-management decisions through the endorsement of such decisions by employee representatives, an approach used in several European countries, as described in item 12.1. This approach, however, has not been popular in the United States, where unions have generally limited themselves to the making of suggestions and the provision of advice and have typically avoided accepting any formal responsibility for the management of the organization (Sturmthal, 1968). This seems to be at least partially the result of a lack of identification of the workers with the organization and a feeling— shared with them by management—that they lack the capability of contributing in a significant way to the solution of the organization's problems (Sturmthal, 1968). With a rising level of education among the work force and a change in their values, however, U.S. unions may in the future become interested in participating in decision making to the degree that European unions do.

ITEM 12.1 Participation

Giving Employes a Say In Firms' Management Seen Gaining in Europe

DUSSELDORF, West Germany—Suppose the president of U.S. Steel couldn't name the man he wanted to head the company's top subsidiary because workers elected to the board of directors didn't like his candidate.

Or suppose management had to absorb six months of continuing losses at another subsidiary because worker-directors wouldn't agree to close it. Or suppose the company couldn't switch production from one subsidiary to another because workers didn't approve.

A preposterous nightmare for U.S. Steel, perhaps. But nothing more than the facts of industrial life for two big German companies in recent months. In one, the redoubtable House of Krupp, the worker-directors' balkiness was partly responsible for the resignation of the president, Jurgen Krackow, after only three months in office.

None of the cases, however, represented a super display of union economic power. Workers' rights to be represented in varying strength on all public

companies' "supervisory" boards are guaranteed by law in Germany. The system has been around since World War II, and it has been gradually strengthened over the years with new legislation, including big additions to workers' rights that went into effect last year.

A Common Market Model? And now the Common Market Commission has proposed that all "European-chartered companies" in the newly expanded nine-nation Market accept as a model the German system of workers' voice in management.

The Netherlands has long used a similar system, and late last year Norway adopted a law very close to the German model. Such facts lend weight to the opinion of one management consultant here that "this thing is going to spread gradually throughout Europe no matter what the Common Market ministers decide." Thus, American companies that incorporate subsidiaries in the future under a European charter or even national law could find themselves facing a whole new set of labor-relations rules.

All of which may sound scary to managers but needn't be, at least not for a while, say businessmen who have dealt with the German system. For one thing, in most cases the shareholder-elected directors have a two-to-one numerical advantage over the worker-directors, so the latter can easily be outvoted. But management men worry because unions are pushing for equal representation on the boards. Such parity already exists in the coal and steel industries and has caused some problems there, officials say.

Some Advantages Also. But while most industry officials worry about the day that parity arrives, they believe they can live with the present system and even see some advantages to it.

"My advice to Americans dealing with the German labor law for the first time is don't have it read by an American lawyer. He's likely to go into a state of shock followed by panic," says John MacDonald, a management consultant in the Dusseldorf office of McKinsey & Co. "The wording of the law sounds terribly tough. But it usually works out quite reasonably in practice."

The second bit of advice to Americans from Mr. MacDonald and others on both the labor and management sides in Germany is to familiarize themselves with the broad outlines of all German company-organization and labor law before trying to understand elements out of context.

The key to the law—and the part that the Common Market Commission wants to spread throughout the community— lies in the "two-tier board." Under the most common application of this system, the annual shareholder meeting elects two-thirds of the members of the senior, or supervisory, board. The other third are elected by the company's workers. The supervisory board, in turn, appoints the management board, which actually runs the company. Members of the supervisory cannot belong to the management board or vice versa. The supervisory board meets four or five times a year, passes on major investments or structural changes, and approves accounts. But it is restrained by law from interfering in day-to-day management.

The Works Council. Because German labor unions bargain on a regional, industry-wide basis rather than company by company, that leaves a large area of concern to workers in individual enterprises up to still another institution, the works council.

All workers in a firm with five or more employes are entitled to elect a works council, which may range from three members to 50. Members and officials of a council needn't belong to the union but usually do. They have broad rights to be kept informed by management of all developments that could affect employes' jobs. For instance, an industry-wide contract might cover only pay and hours. Within the framework of that pact, an individual works council might have equal voice with management on such matters as hiring and firing, shifting jobs, and starting and quitting times. In the U.S., these details might be covered by local plant bargaining or simply left to management; the union must use its economic power to bargain for a say. In Germany, the works council by law is guaranteed a voice.

The Common Market's proposed European company law would incorporate the two-tier board with at least one-third of the supervisory board elected by a company's works council.

Having worker-directors make up one-third of the supervisory board "is a wonderful thing; nothing could be better. You should do that in your country as soon as possible," Andreas Kleffel, a director of Germany's powerful Deutsche Bank, tells an American visitor. Mr. Kleffel sits on 14 supervisory boards and is chairman of two major German companies, Hapag-Lloyd, a travel and shipping firm, and Rheinstahl, a diversified steelmaker.

Mr. Kleffel credits this system as being the main reason for Germany's record of relative labor peace over the last 20 years, compared with the labor disputes in Britain, France and Italy. The effect, he says, is that "labor people come onto a board with the idea that they are going to teach management a thing or two and set matters straight. But when they have to look at all the company's problems, see the financial figures and participate in decisions, it changes their attitude."

In addition, Mr. Kleffel says, worker directors often provide wise and effective counsel. He cites the example of a firm in which half the stock was closely held by two members of the management board who had an argument serious enough to reach the supervisory board he headed.

One of the men became so incensed that he threatened to throw his shares on the market and enlist the public in the battle against the other. Then, Mr. Kleffel says, one of the company's oldest worker directors spoke up: "We have known you for a long time," he told his "boss," whom he was legally empowered to advise and control. "Surely you wouldn't do a damn fool thing like that and lose face with all of us."

The result was sudden and enduring silence, Mr. Kleffel says. "We heard no more about it. It was a wonderful remark but one that I could never have made," he says.

But there is a simpler reason why Mr. Kleffel and other businessmen find favor with one-third worker representation on boards. "There aren't any problems with this system," Mr. Kleffel says, "because the workers haven't any real power to force their views. When the workers' advice is good, it is listened to." Otherwise, the shareholders' directors vote them down.

For example, at Ford-Werke in Cologne, Ford Motor Co.'s German subsidiary, the two worker-directors on the six-man supervisory board almost always call for cutting the dividend and either plowing the funds back into the company or paying them out in higher wages and benefits for the workers. What happens? "Nothing," a member of Ford's management says with a shrug. "Four-to-two. That's the vote, and that's the end of it."

Ernst Lueck, the 39-year-old chairman of Ford-Werke's central plant council and a member of the supervisory board, also shrugs. On investment of profits, he says, "I don't get anywhere. I'm in the minority. We state our point of view, but we always lose the vote."

Even Horst Bergemann, Ford's director of labor relations, says the presence of worker directors on the supervisory board doesn't much influence him, even though the supervisory board must vote to appoint him. "They are in a minority," he says; "they haven't any power."

"Constant Discussion." Of more concern to Mr. Bergemann is the 12-member works council, with which he meets monthly. Its powers have been augmented by a law passed last summer. "In the past," Mr. Bergemann says, "when we wanted to hire someone, we just did it and told the works council later. All they had was a right of information. Now we tell them beforehand and get their consent. They don't withhold consent in practice, but it means constant discussion back and forth about why we're hiring someone instead of promoting from within and that sort of thing."

The works council must also give its consent to overtime and has a right to participate in decisions on who will be selected for training and who will be hired to train them. "A majority" of works-council requests involving additional costs or benefits are turned down, Mr. Bergemann says. But the council, in effect, retains a veto power over all company initiatives affecting jobs. "The most important thing is keeping the workers informed," Mr. Bergemann says. "If you explain why you want to do things, they usually go along."

Thus, despite the increased powers of the works councils, most managers are happy under the German system provided they have a "reasonable" council and a two-thirds majority in the supervisory board. "But all this may change in the near future," Mr. Bergemann says, referring to labor-union political pressure to give parity to workers on supervisory boards in all companies. "This could change our way of life completely, though we're really not sure how," he says.

Mr. Kleffel, the director of Deutsche Bank, thinks he knows. In the German coal and steel industry, where parity exists already, "It gets to be a bad thing. . . . The workers' side has real power," he says. Thus, the Confederation of German Employers Associations is bitterly opposed to extending parity throughout industry. But many believe it is coming—sooner or later. "My bet would be that we'll have a definite trend toward parity in the next two or three years," says Prof. Kurt Biedenkopf, a director of Henkel & Co., chairman of the Biedenkopf Commission on German labor law and an adviser on labor to the Common Market Commission.

Under the system as it currently operates in the coal and steel industry, supervisory boards are composed of 11 or 21 members. Of an 11-man board, five are elected by the shareholders and five by the workers; of a 21-man board, it is 10 and 10. The 11th or 21st member is called the "neutral man." But Mr. Kleffel says: "The worker-directors will only agree to a man who has their confidence. They are normally professors or politicians of leftist persuasion," though a popular one has often been Hermann J. Abs, chairman of Deutsche Bank, who enjoys a good reputation with labor. Of course, the "neutral man" presumably also enjoys the confidence of the share-

holders' directors, who wouldn't otherwise vote for him.

What management finds most distasteful about parity is the potentially high degree of worker control over investment. If workers at Ford-Werke, for example, really could cut the dividend and force the company to apply the funds elsewhere, it could do "quite some harm," Mr. Bergemann asserts. "A lot of unions couldn't care less about economic questions. We fear they would use board positions just to further their political aims," he says, echoing a theme frequently expressed by German management.

German workers naturally don't think there is any "harm" in diverting a larger share of funds from investment to wages and benefits. "You have capital on one side, the workers on the other side and the company in between," says Mr. Lueck, who is on Ford-Werke's supervisory board. As he sees it, "each side wants to take out as much for itself as possible. But both sides want the enterprise to succeed."

As for injecting national politics into the boardroom, some worker-directors do feel that they "represent the interest of labor in Germany as a whole" in the boardroom, according to Gerhard Leminski, who edits a trade-union magazine and sits on the board of Fried. Krupp Huettenwerke. "That's an abstraction, admittedly," that can lead to conflicts of interest, he says.

A Steelmaker's Problem. Mr. Kleffel, the businessman, cites the case of a big steelmaker on whose board he sits that had to face the problem of a foundry that was "losing money at a high rate." The plant "was in deplorable condition, and there was a clear decision by management to close it and fix a severance payment for the workers," Mr. Kleffel says. However, he adds, the 21st man on the supervisory board was a Social Democratic Party politician who came under pressure from party members in the foundry area.

So the board kept putting off the decision while he appeased his political following with plans to seek new orders for the foundry. "No amount of orders could have kept it going; it was just inefficient and uneconomical," Mr. Kleffel says. Finally, after three supervisory-board meetings, two special commission meetings and six months of additional heavy losses, the foundry was closed, he says.

In the case of Mr. Krackow, his rapid demise at Krupp can be laid at least partly to worker-directors' refusal to accept his nominee to head the compa-ny's biggest steelmaking subsidiary, Fried. Krupp Huettenwerke. The supervisory board still hasn't agreed on a candidate, although Mr. Krackow has long been gone. Shareholders and worker-directors have "agreed to cooperate constructively on choosing a man," says Mr. Leminski. They just haven't found the man yet, he says, adding, "It's a very complicated situation."—Neil Ulman

The Wall Street Journal, Feb. 23, 1973

Management by Objectives in Decision Implementation

One approach used rather widely in organizations of all types for purposes of implementing top-management decisions is *management by objectives* (MBO). Successful implementation is, of course, more critical for very important decisions than for those less important. For this reason, it is especially vital to obtain the successful implementation of top management decisions. Successful implementation requires acceptance at lower levels, as mentioned earlier. However, sufficient resources, effective plans, and adequate followup are also necessary in successful implementation. Management by objectives attempts to focus on all of these factors together.

MBO: A Definition. Under a management by objectives program, a superior and a subordinate attempt to reach a consensus of (1) what goals the subordinate will attempt to achieve in a given time period, (2) the plan or means by which the subordinate will attempt to accomplish the goals, and (3) the means by which goals progress will be measured and the dates for such measurements. After there is such agreement, the superior will periodically review performance. This may involve quarterly performance reviews along with a final performance review at the end of the year.

The heart of this process is *the objective and the action plan*. Success depends on how well both the objective and the plan are defined, communicated, and accepted. Objectives are goals (or ends); action plans are the maps for reaching those objectives. Thus, MBO is a process in which the individual members of an organization work with one another to identify common goals and coordinate their efforts in reaching them.

Objectives can be thought of as statements of purpose and direction. They may be long-range or short-range. They may be general, to provide direction for an entire organization, or they may be highly specific, to provide detailed direction for an individual. MBO emphasizes the *what* and the *how* of the intended accomplishments.

It is important to take note of this fact that objectives may be general, for a larger organization, or specific, for an individual, because one purpose of MBO is to make it possible to derive specific from general objectives, and to insure that objectives at all levels in the organization are meaningfully located structurally and that they are linked to each other. Sets of objectives for an organizational unit determine its activities. A set of objectives for an individual determines his job description and can be thought of as a different way to provide that job description. Once objectives are determined and assumed by organizational units and by individuals, it is possible to work out the means (performance) required for accomplishing the objectives.

Perceived Purposes of MBO. Organizations have installed MBO usually because they see this approach as an aid to solving some of their problems, especially that of achieving an integration between individual goals and organizational goals. It is a mistake to assume that all work activity in an organization is directed toward organizational goals. As mentioned earlier, research shows that individuals tend to emphasize those activities which they like to do. What an organizational member *likes* to do may not be important to the organization. Individuals also tend to do those things they feel will bring success to them. MBO may be a way of negotiating a compromise between individual preferences or goals and organizational objectives.

More time spent in planning is related to effectiveness for the organization itself and for individuals in the organization. But MBO, used well, requires more time spent in planning than might otherwise be the case. On the other hand, since individuals have a tendency to concentrate on their immediate problems rather than to look ahead to try to minimize the chance for future problems to occur, more planning insures that management is in an active mode, attempting to achieve some control over the future, rather than merely reacting to it.

Another reason some organizations introduce MBO is in a hope of improving the evaluation of individual performance, since with MBO, evaluation can focus on results, rather than on personal characteristics. In addition, with some degree of participation in the establishment of job objectives, there may be greater understanding of what a person is to be held accountable for and there should be more acceptance of the means by which performance is to be evaluated. Management of some organizations feel also that MBO facilitates problem recognition.

Under MBO the end result represents a condition or situation that is desired, a purpose to be achieved. The concept of "end" is equated with goal or objective. Objectives may be specific achievement levels, such as product costs, sales volume, and so on, or they may be completed projects. For instance, the market research department may seek to complete a sales forecast by a particular date so that the production facilities can be properly coordinated with market demands. Objectives, or end states, are attained through the performance of some activity. These activities are the means to achieve the end.

The Cascading of Objectives

In chapter 11 we discussed environmental and internal subsystem goals. Environmental goals are synonymous with the basic purpose of an organization; they seek to meet the demands placed upon the organization for its product or service, delivered in a way which will satisfy the desires of the organization's clients. Internal system goals are the objectives which organizational subsystems must meet to accomplish environmental goals.

The responsibility for developing environmental goals is typically top management's—usually the chief executive's, in conjunction with the board of directors or a group of vice-presidents. Once these goals are developed, then internal subsystem goals (marketing, production, etc.) are stated, usually in the form of general plans. When these have been developed, they are communicated to the next-lower levels. This can be done by a series of cascading meetings between superiors and their subordinates and work groups, continuing from the top management level to the lowest point of supervision.

Initially, the corporate executive officer determines his objectives and general program. Then he meets with his immediate subordinates, including staff and operating executives in charge of major divisions. At this meeting he defines his objectives and plans for the group—a statement of what he believes to be the major activities and goal areas for the following year. The purpose of this meeting, for the subordinates, is informational. They are given the opportunity to increase their understanding of how the chief executive sees the direction, goals, and plans of the company. Negotiable and nonnegotiable areas and plans are discussed, because these become operating constraints for lower-level managers. A nonnegotiable area is one in which the chief executive requires that a specific approach be taken. In these areas lower-level personnel have no discretionary power. For instance, the chief executive may insist that certain products *not* be produced, because he has been so directed by the board of directors. Negotiable areas represent activities and goals where the chief executive is willing to modify his positions.

At the first meeting, there is little emphasis on specific goals and objectives of the subordinates, but from the information received, each manager should be able to develop a plan of action, goals, and appropriate performance measures for each relevant organizational objective in his own unit or division. Then, in a private meeting with the chief executive officer he undertakes an assessment of his goals and what he will do to achieve them. When these goals and specific plans of action are agreed upon, specific goals and ways of achieving them exist for two levels of management.

Once a second-level executive knows what his objectives are, he schedules a meeting with his operating and staff personnel. At this meeting, he makes known to that group the goals and action plans that he has agreed to with his superior. This group meeting again is essentially an informational one, and subordinates are encouraged to ask questions and engage in discussion that will help them understand the kinds of commitments that have been made. The subordinate can then make a more accurate assessment of his discretionary areas, and those areas that are nonnegotiable, nondecision-making areas.

After this group meeting, each third-level executive individually prepares a set of action plans and objectives for himself and his unit and then meets individually with his superior. At this time the superior and the subordinate agree upon the goals, activities, and criteria for assessment of success.

When some consensus has been reached and the executive has his set of goals, he then schedules a meeting with his subordinates and the process continues as described. This cascading process proceeds to the lowest level of the organization at which it remains feasible. At each succeeding lower level, the range of individual discretion becomes less and less, of course. This may mean that for the lowest operating managerial level, the meetings are essentially communicational, with activities being specified and the subordinate being given a fairly well-developed set of operating measures and action plans that he must implement. The nature of the organizational beast is such that the lowest-level managers operate within tighter organizational constraints than managers at higher levels; the latter formulate the goals of the organization, and the former translate them into work.

Scope and Type of Objectives

It would be difficult to develop objectives for a manager which would cover each and every area of his responsibility, for the structure of most jobs is too complex. Yet once objectives are set for a position, they should comprise the major description of the job, and their achievement in light of what is known about total job requirements should be assessed. Once objectives are set for a person, a basis exists for insuring that there is a "balance" of activities in his job; for example, that a worker is performing the normal duties, while at the same time growing and developing. Concurrently, the relative importance of objectives or failure to achieve them should be kept in mind. For example, a man who fails on a difficult creative objective should not be evaluated in the same way as a man who fails to maintain a critical recurring operation. The former may have undertaken a high-risk project, at the suggestion of his boss, which would have had high payoffs. He may, for example, have been attempting a revolutionary product design. The latter may simply be failing at meeting normal job requirements.

Performance Objectives. A performance objective is derived directly from the job assignment, that is, from the major areas of an individual's responsibility and activity. Included in these areas would be the maintenance of recurring or routine activities, the solving of problems, or the creation of innovative ideas, products, or services. *Routine objectives* represent the normal requirements of the job, the kind of thing commonly found in a job description. Quantity requirements, the time one is supposed to come to work, or normal deadlines for reports are all routine objectives. Other objectives, however, may take on special importance for a number of reasons—emergencies, change in priorities, or management decisions. These are called *special-project objectives.*

The Action Plan

The "action plan" is the means by which an objective is attained. The action plan should summarize what is to be done. The action plan for a complex activity should be broken down into major subprograms and should represent the "best" alternative, of possibly many, which would achieve the goal level. The action plan provides an initial basis for a total action program for an individual or department. Action plans might be stated in the following manner:

1. *For a sales increase,* develop more penetration in a particular market area by increasing the number of calls to dealers there.
2. *For a reduction in manufacturing costs,* analyze the overtime activities and costs and schedule more work during regular hours.

Subordinates may base their own action plans on those developed by their manager, using his plan to guide their own roles in their unit's effort. Clear differentiation of means from ends allows lower-level use of the objectives process. Considering both means and ends permits comparing performance with some criteria and determining if events occurred which are presumed to lead to a desired outcome.

It is important to recognize the distinction between measuring an objective and determining if an event has occurred. If we are unable to measure or specify the goal level adequately, then we simply assume that the desired goal level has been achieved if a particular event or set of activities takes place. For example, while it is very difficult to measure whether or not a manager is developing the talents of subordinates, we can determine if he has provided them with development opportunities. If they have participated in seminars, attended meetings, or gone off to school, it can be assumed that the development activity is being properly conducted.

Some further benefits and opportunities which may be provided by adequate attention to an action plan are these:

1. It aids in the search for better, more efficient methods of accomplishing the objective.
2. It provides an opportunity to test the feasibility of accomplishing the objective as stated.
3. It develops a basis to estimate time or cost required and deadline for accomplishment.
4. It examines the nature and degree of reliance on other people in the organization toward coordination and support needed.
5. It uncovers anticipated snags or barriers to accomplishment.
6. It determines resources (manpower, equipment, supplies, facilities) required to accomplish the objective.
7. It facilitates control if the performance is well-specified and agreed upon; reporting need only occur when problems arise in

implementing. This is a form of planning ahead; when plans are sufficiently complete, only deviations from it need be communicated.

8. It identifies areas in which the superior can provide support and assistance.

Constraints on Action Plans. Deadlines and budget constraints can and should be strictly specified in some cases, and not in others. A great deal depends on:

1. the importance of the objective;
2. the ability to determine the time or costs required in performance;
3. whether or not written plans or objectives of other people require coordinated completion dates;
4. the amount of time and money the subordinate will spend on the particular objective under discussion;
5. the predictability of problems or barriers to accomplishment.

Discussing these constraints furthers understanding between superiors and subordinates and establishes the constraint's use in evaluation. Expectations become known; realities can be tested. Deadlines and costs should be viewed as "negotiable." Deadlines especially should not be set simply to insure that action is initiated.

Contingency Requirements. Success or failure in reaching an objective may depend upon the contribution and performance of other individuals or departments. Therefore, they must be considered. Some contingencies apply to all objectives, of course. For example, delays in the availability of resources, change in support or priorities from higher management, equipment failures, delayed information or approval, and the like, which are unplanned, should be taken into account when the assessment of objective accomplishment is made.

Other contingencies, specific to the objective, might be inadequate authority of the subordinate, lack of policy covering aspects of the objective, possible failure to gain cooperation from others, known delays in the system, and so on. Once these are uncovered, several actions are possible:

1. reexamination of the objective (e.g., alteration of a deadline) when and if the contingency occurs;
2. commitment of the superior to aid by overcoming or preventing the contingency;

3. revision of the performance required to accomplish the objective;
4. establishment of a new objective. If a contingency is serious enough, an objective aimed at overcoming the problem may be justified.

Participation and MBO.   Since MBO is intended to facilitate subordinate participation and involvement, the implicit nature of power and authority must be recognized. Unless they have the approval of their superior, lower-level managers cannot legitimately influence goal levels and action plans in areas in which they have no formal authority or discretion. Therefore, it is necessary to spell out areas in which subordinates have some latitude, so that they know what their decision limits are. Otherwise they may unrealistically believe they can participate in departmental and organizational decisions which are outside their discretion area, that their superior will allow them more extensive influence in a decision area than the superior actually will. When a person expects to participate and then cannot, negative consequences can occur.

One way to define discretion areas, or formal authority, is to determine whether or not an individual should influence the goal or action plan. In a boundary-spanning activity affected by conditions outside the organization, for example, the individual charged with performing that activity may be the person in the best possible position to determine both the goals (or ends) and the most appropriate means to achieve them, because external conditions may not be clearly known to internal managers. For instance, marketing executives in constant touch with the external environment are in a better position to determine possible sales penetration and programs than anyone else in the organization. However, not having authority over goal levels should not preclude involvement of a lower-level manager in goal setting. Here the MBO process should focus on developing the best means for goal attainment.

High levels of skill and technology required in a particular function may make the specialist better able than a nontechnical person to assess what can be done in a technical field. Thus, the specialist should be involved in determining goal levels, as well as in carrying out activities.

An important limitation on discretion, or formal authority, is organizational level. The lower the organizational level, the narrower the zone of a manager's discretion. That is, managers at the lower levels are responsible for fewer, more specific, and more measurable activities and can commit smaller quantities of resources than those at higher levels.

Another factor which causes variation in the authority range for a particular job is the changing competency levels of the incumbent. A person learning a job may need a great deal of guidance from his superior. As his skills increase, however, his superior may spend less time with him since he can capably handle more activities and make more decisions. One research study has shown that managers allow more influence in the goal-setting process to their subordinates who have the highest performance ratings (Carroll, Cintron, and Tosi, 1971).

What about those decisions that fall outside the discretion limits? In these, as we have seen, the subordinate's role may be that of contributing information and assistance, inputs to the decision-making process of his superior, which the superior may choose to accept or reject. But this type of activity must be differentiated from goal-setting participation in which the individual has something to say about the final shape and form of the goals and activities.

Discretion boundaries are not rigid. While a particular decision may fall within the discretion range under normal circumstances, emergencies might develop which would result in the decision being made by the superior. These conditions cannot be foreseen, and consequently cannot be planned for.

MBO and Managerial Control

The importance of the development and use of sound criteria (objectives) for evaluation, appraisal, and feedback cannot be over-emphasized. Sound criteria are essential if meaningful changes in behavior are to be achieved. "Hard" criteria must be used with extreme care. They are best viewed as ends or levels; they indicate nothing about attaining either. "Soft" criteria involve not a particular level of achievement, but determination that an event or condition has or has not occurred. Soft criteria are a vital and fundamental part of MBO. Without them, the approach cannot be well implemented.

To some managers, the development and communication of goals comes naturally. They are intuitively able to determine and specify appropriate measures, criteria, goals, and the most satisfactory methods for achieving them. They innately sense what must be observed and measured and can communicate this effectively to subordinates—and this is the behavior, of course, which management by objectives seeks to develop and reinforce.

Evaluating the Accomplishment of Objectives. Some goals lend themselves more easily than others to measurement—scrap rates, production costs, sales volume, and other "hard" measures. These measures pertain most to lower organizational levels and to areas such as production, marketing, or other major functional activities of the organization; they pertain least to most staff and specialist units. A distinction relevant to the measurement problem is the difference between routine and special project objectives.

Routine objectives are basic to the job, a core part of the job description. How should they be set and measured? The manager must tell the subordinate—early in the relationship—what the activities of the job are and what the desired level of performance is. Evaluation should not occur after a period of service unless there has been previous discussion of criteria.

At the same time that the criteria are being specified, acceptable tolerance limits should be developed. Assessment of routine objectives should be a major part of the objectives process, yet it should be of most concern *when performance falls outside levels;* thus minimum performance levels should be set for routine activities, and evaluation of routine goals should be by exception—that is, only when these standards are not met.

The ability to manage by exception demands good plans or clear standards from which exceptions can be specified in advance. Odiorne (1964) cites the following example:

> The paymaster, for example, may report that his routine duties cluster around getting the weekly payroll out every Friday. It is agreed that the measure of exception will be zero—in other words, the boss should expect no exceptions to the diligent performance of this routine duty. Thus, the failure any week to produce the payroll on Friday will be considered an exception that calls for explanation by the subordinate. If the cause were reasonably under his control or could have been averted by extra care or effort, the absence of the payroll will be considered a failure on the part of the subordinate.

Generally, routine job responsibilities or goals are expressed as job standards, or other "hard" performance measures. Although appraisal and evaluation essentially compare performance to the standard, this procedure may be relatively shortsighted and suboptimal. Recall that the manager should also evaluate the *manner* in which performance was carried out. For example, costs can often be reduced by foregoing certain expenditures, and a subordinate who realizes his performance is being quantitatively assessed may do this. But the expenditures foregone may be the very ones that enable a greater profit to be turned in the future—research and development expenses, for example—and thus the subordinate's "high" performance in the short run may have negative long-run effects. There can be substantial distortions of behavior when only quantitative criteria are used in measurement.

Problem-solving, special project, or creative objectives are more difficult to quantify than the essentially routine. If the ends are truly creative, determining an adequate performance level may necessarily rely on intuitive judgement. It is usually possible, however, to judge if an activity has been performed appropriately even though the ends, or the performance levels, are neither quantifiable nor measurable. Furthermore, constraints may be set on the activities. We can assess that they have occurred by some specific point in time or that a specific dollar amount has been expended. Thus, we are not only concerned with whether or not events have occurred, but also within some tolerance limit such as target dates, budget constraints, or a quality assessment by the manager. It becomes possible under these conditions to establish review points, thus giving attention to the outcomes of activities when they occur. Deliberations on these outcomes can serve to reevaluate both objectives and means. Thus changes are possible, and both flexibility and control are assured where they appear to be most needed—where predictions, plans, and standards cannot be specified or articulated in advance.

Research on MBO

The extensive research that has been carried out on MBO has attempted to identify the effect of such programs on organizational and individual performance, their effect on attitudes of organizational members, and the situational factors which seem to influence their effectiveness.

Effect of MBO on Organizational and Individual Performance.

Many of the earliest studies of MBO's effects on performance were case studies of individual companies in which the organization's performance after the MBO program was installed was compared to previous performance levels. In a number of U.S. and English firms in which MBO was introduced, substantial cost savings and improvements in productivity were reported (Wikstrom, 1968; Carroll and Tosi, 1973). For example, in one company studied by Raia (1965;

1966), before MBO was introduced, productivity was decreasing at the rate of .4 percent per month. After the program was instituted, the trend reversed and productivity increased at the rate of .3 percent per month. In one company, the authors along with the organization personnel manager improved an existing MBO program through an action research approach. There was a sudden rise in performance and in the six years after the new MBO program was introduced, productivity increased 109 percent, sales increased 252 percent, and the number of new employees increased by only 68 percent, while the dollar value of sales per salesperson quadrupled in constant (1968) dollars.

In all of the case studies, however, it is next to impossible to determine if the increase in performance is wholly attributable to MBO, since many other factors influencing performance also changed. (In other case studies of MBO, no performance improvement was noticed.)

When the unit of analysis is the individual instead of the organization, goal setting has been found to improve performance. Locke (1968) conducted some of the earliest studies in this area. In six out of eight studies, he found that students assigned specific goals performed at a higher level than students told to "do your best." Latham and his colleagues have conducted a number of similar studies in the logging industry. They found in studies of truck drivers, logging crews, and typists that employees assigned specific goals performed at a higher level than those told to do their best. In reviewing these studies and others, Latham and Yukl (1975) conclude:

> In summary, studies in organizations have examined the effects of setting specific goals. In ten of these studies, evidence in support of the effectiveness of setting specific goals were obtained, although some possible limiting conditions were discovered.

Reactions to MBO by Organizational Members. Some studies have examined reactions of organizational members to MBO, and its effects on their satisfaction. Ivancevich, Donnelly, and Lyon (1970) found improvements in need satisfaction when an MBO program was well implemented but not in a company where the program was not implemented by top management. However, even in the company where need satisfaction first increased, it later decreased, apparently because of the lack of sustained commitment to the program. A study of typists by Latham and Yukl (1975), however, indicated a drop in job satisfaction after implementation of a goal-setting program. A study by Tosi and Carroll (1975) indicated no change in satisfaction with pay or with a supervisor after the introduction of a new MBO program, but an increase in satisfaction with MBO.

Some studies indicate that these diverse results reflect the fact that individuals like some aspects of goal setting, but not others, and that likes and dislikes depend upon what is emphasized by the organization in a particular MBO program. For example, in almost all MBO programs, managers complain about the paper work and time the program requires, although this complaint seems to disappear somewhat after managers get used to the procedure (Carroll and Tosi, 1973). Managers like the MBO approach for letting them know what is expected of them and by forcing planning and boss-subordinate interactions (Tosi and Carroll, 1968). Some research shows that use of a goal-setting approach by a manager creates the expectancy among subordinates that good performance will be rewarded, and that this expectancy is followed by increased job satisfaction (Tosi, Chesser, and Carroll, 1972).

MBO and Behavior Change. An integral part of many MBO programs is the development of self-improvement or personal-development objectives. Here, objectives are established based on current or anticipated deficiencies in such areas as technical skills, managerial skills, or interpersonal skills. An early study at GE indicated that criticism of personal deficiencies did not itself improve performance (Meyer, Kay, and French, 1965). It was only when performance deficiencies were converted to specific performance-improvement objectives that positive improvements were made. Two other studies also show behavior change is greater where goal setting is used than where it is not present (Kolb and Bayatzis, 1971; Wexley and Nemeroff, 1975).

Characteristics of Goals. There has also been research on how characteristics of goals relate to the results obtained with MBO. As mentioned, research shows that performance tends to be higher when specific goals, rather than generalized, do-your-best goals are used (Latham and Yukl, 1975). Other studies have focused on goal difficulty. Hard, or more difficult, goals lead to higher performance than easy goals do, as long as they are accepted. However, goals which individuals feel they are unlikely to reach cause such individuals to give up without trying (Stedry and Kay, 1966; Carroll and Tosi, 1973).

There are other considerations in setting goals. Goals cannot be expected to improve performance significantly when there are already high levels of efficiency. In addition, when there is emphasis on errors and performance deficiencies (a punitive climate), managers will attempt to establish easy goals to minimize the risk of failure (Muzyk, 1972).

Organizational and Situational Factors Influencing the Success of MBO. One problem with many MBO programs is that it may take some time to see the results of the new program. Individuals seem to expect more of new programs than it it possible to achieve in a short time. An approach to management such as MBO will take many years to become effectively implemented (Carroll and Tosi, 1973). In the meantime, discouragement with lack of quick results often leads to abandonment of the program. Another difficulty is that organizational members often initially believe that adoption of MBO and its procedures will produce positive results. But it is of course managers, not procedures themselves, that produce such results, and a collection of procedures such as MBO is only a tool for managers to use.

Training for managers is needed, especially in how to establish goals and review performance, since very few managers are good at this (Stein, 1975). And, as implied earlier, another common difficulty of major importance is lack of top management support for the new program (Carroll and Tosi, 1973).

Still other factors can contribute to difficulty in successfully implementing the MBO approach. Stein (1975), for instance, found inadequate performance review to be an important problem in existing MBO programs. Carroll and Tosi (1969) also found more positive reactions, higher satisfaction with the superior, and more goal success with more frequent performance review. What is the ideal frequency of performance review? Stein (1975) found that most successful programs had at least quarterly reviews. Quarterly reviews were also recommended by Carroll and Tosi (1973) from their research. However, Stein (1975) concluded that semiannual reviews were probably sufficient for organizations in a highly stable environment.

In an English study of the failure of an MBO program, Wickens (1968) indicated that one important reason for the failure was that the program was not institutionalized. The MBO program must be integrated with other organizational procedures and systems to be successful (Carroll and Tosi, 1973). That is, goal setting and reviews must fit with the budgetary and other control systems.

Finally, a major complaint in many MBO systems is that of excessive ridgidity, as when each unit in an organization must use the same procedures and degree of measurability of objectives. Some research shows that MBO programs must be varied, depending upon the type of tasks and problems the various organizational units face (Tosi and Carroll, 1969).

Participation and Organizational Types

Participative group decision approaches are more likely to be used in some organizations than in others and especially at certain levels in those organizations that use them. There is evidence from research that decision making becomes more participative at the higher levels of management (Heller and Yukl, 1969). This can be expected, since higher-level managers are often perceived to be more closely identified with the organization's goals, to be more worthy of trust because of higher competence, and to have the appropriate work values. They are more organizationalist in outlook. In addition, their decisions are more important and less structured, the necessary information for a decision is possessed by more people, and the implementation of decisions requires initiative and creativity from those executing the plan.

Organizations in different types of environments will differ with respect to the frequency with which participative decision-making approaches are used. Professionals and specialists can be expected to feel that they have a right to participate in the making of decisions and will be less accepting of autocratic decisions. Also, in dynamic organizations, problems become less structured, and the information relevant to solving the problem is dispersed among different specialists. On the other hand, organizations faced with environmental certainty will have more structured problems and more narrowly defined jobs with limited discretion than those faced with environmental uncertainty; this is likely to decrease the frequency with which participative and group decision-making approaches are used.

Environmental uncertainty has an important effect on the extent to which clear-cut goals can be set and communicated to the rest of the organization. In chapter 7 it is pointed out that the environmental goals of the bureaucratic organization are likely to be relatively stable over time. This will make it easier to break them down into goals for lower units. In dynamic organizations, where the environment is likely to change, goals are less well-fixed. In the dynamic organization it will be necessary to change goals quickly in order to react to new demands placed upon the organization. One approach in this type of organization is to establish goals on a priority basis for each manager and professional. One such priority system is to classify goals as "must do," "should do," and "nice to do" (Raia, 1974). When environmental goals change, the "nice to do" internal system goals can be discarded first. In the dynamic organization, short-term goals (say, six months) can add flexibility.

Discussion Questions

1. The chapter indicates that many decisions do not have acceptability requirements because they are not of concern to organizational members. List the decisions in a university that would have acceptability requirements for students but not for faculty. List the decisions that would have acceptability requirements for both students and faculty.

2. Some advocates of the use of participation argue that employees should be required to participate in the decision-making process even if they have no interest in doing so, as a means of improving their knowledge and competence. Do you agree? Why or why not?

3. Let us assume that the administration at your university decides to change the admission standards for entering a particular college on campus (assume the college of business administration). Should students participate in this decision? Why or why not? If so, to what degree should they participate? Why?

4. List the advantages and disadvantages of using the "management by objectives" (MBO) approach at your university for directing the activities of your faculty.

5. Under the Vroom and Yetton approach discussed in the chapter, it is recommended that when several decision-making alternatives are all equally feasible the decision maker choose that which is least time consuming. This is typically the most autocratic method of making the decision. Do you agree with this strategy in these situations? Why or why not?

6. Write up a policy statement for an organization to use in guiding managers in situations involving the implementation of change.

7. Think of a recent situation in which you had a decision made which affected you? Was it a good decision? Was it an acceptance-dominated decision? Did you participate in making it?

8. The text makes it clear that in MBO there are some areas which are nonnegotiable between a superior and a subordinate. How does this fit with the concept of "participation"?

9. Why is goal-setting so important? Or is it? Under what conditions?

10. "MBO moves the point at which subjectivity enters into evaluation to a different place. It does not make evaluation objective." Comment.

Part V
Managing in Different Types of Organizations

In this part of the book, we take the position that different types of organizations (Part III), with different types of people in them (Part II), require different management approaches (Part IV). Basing our analysis on the theoretical formulations described in the preceding parts of this book, we now want to be as prescriptive as we can in proposing how managerial approaches can be adapted to the needs and character of each organizational type.

In chapter 13, we suggest how selection, compensation, appraisal—all techniques for managing people—may be applied in the hierarchical organization. Chapter 14 covers these same topic areas for the dynamic organization. In Chapter 15, the problems of managing mixed-form organizations, which focus on conflict resolution, are explained and some strategies for solving them are proposed.

Chapter 13
Managing Human Resources in the Hierarchical Organization

In the last several chapters we have discussed current research and theory in leadership, decision making, decision implementation, and communication, along with approaches to organizational staffing, performance appraisal and review, and compensation management. There are many ways that these managerial activities can be performed. Which way is best depends on the characteristics of the individual employed by the organization, the type of work they do and the type of problems they face, and the organizational structure used to cope with current environmental forces.

In this chapter we want to show how the special characteristics of the hierarchical or bureaucratic organization may affect the alternative human resource management approaches employed in an organization.

Personnel Composition

In a hierarchical organization, the largest proportion of employees will be rank-and-file workers—blue collar in manufacturing, for instance, and white collar in, say, insurance companies or government agencies. Most of this rank-and-file group can best be characterized as having an external orientation, as described in chapter 3. They tend, in general, not to be highly ego-involved or committed to their work and/or the organization. They tend to seek psychological satisfactions outside the workplace. This is partly due to their narrow job definitions; that is, the tasks are not extremely challenging, and there is relatively little opportunity for advancement to positions where rewards are greater. One reason why promotion opportunities are limited is that there are fewer positions at the higher levels. Another is that often the requisites for promotions include advanced education, which the lower-level group is less likely to have. An external orientation should not be construed to mean an unwillingness to work, however. Rank-and-file workers will probably do what is expected of them, but they do not obtain their primary satisfaction from their work (Dubin, 1956; Kornhauser, 1965).

The middle management and specialist groups in the hierarchical organization will also contain a large number of externals—in this case managers who have reached career plateaus and have little opportunity for advancement. They become increasingly committed to their life away from work rather than to the work of organization.

We can also expect, at the mid-levels, to find a group of "organization-oriented" managers and specialists, people on the way up who seek the values and rewards of the system itself, high in achievement orientation and loyal to the organization. Figure 13.1 shows this general staffing configuration for the bureaucratic organization.

FIGURE 13.1   Orientations as a Function of Level in
a Hierarchical Organization

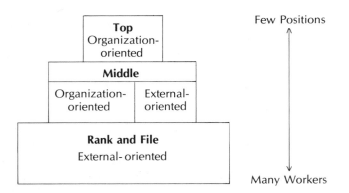

Staffing

In the natural world, if characteristics of a living thing are not compatible with a particular environment, life in that environment is not possible. In a like manner, if an individual's personal characteristics are not suited for a particular organizational environment, he will probably not be satisfied with that organization. And by the same token, the organization may not consider the individual satisfactory and the individual will eventually leave, unless, of course, no alternatives are available (Weiss, Lofquist et al., 1969). Organizations tend to attract and retain those individuals whose personal characteristics enable them to adjust to the role responsibilities and characteristics present in the situation (Porter et al., 1975). Organizations will try to predict such unsuitability in advance.

Staffing Strategies in the Stable Organization. An organization will attempt to recruit individuals who appear to have the attitudinal orientation appropriate to itself. In a study of a bank, Argyris (1954) showed that the bank recruited individuals who were nonaggressive and sought to avoid competition and conflict. He also showed that this type of personality was appropriate for all but the top-level jobs in the bank. There are other research studies which show that individuals tend to choose, and be selected by, organizations congruent with their personal goals (see, for instance, Porter et al., 1975).

Organizations carry out the staffing process in different ways. Sometimes the organization has a particular position in mind with a set of specific role requirements, and applicant characteristics are compared against certain hiring specifications to choose that particular applicant who is most congruent with the requirements. Under this "selection" approach, the emphasis is on the role or position to be filled. The emphasis in the "placement" approach, however, is on the individual person; that is, on trying to find a position or set of duties which best utilizes his strengths. In the selection approach, the perspective is that of the individual accommodating himself to the job, while the placement perspective is that of adjusting the job to fit the individual. In the hierarchical organization there is an emphasis on the "selection" approach.

In the hierarchical organization, there is also an emphasis on the statistical approach to selection, as described in chapter 10. Under this approach, scores of a group on a selection instrument (such as a test) are associated with scores on some job behavior to be predicted, such as amount of production or employee stability (absenteeism or turnover). The ideal way to conduct such a study is to administer the selection instrument (test, interview, application blank, etc.) to a large group of applicants and then to hire without reference to the scores received. Later, after the employees have been in the organization for a sufficient period of time, their scores on the selection instrument are correlated, or compared, to their job performance.

A quicker, but weaker, approach is to compare present employees' scores on the selection instrument with their job performance. The results of such a statistical analysis may indicate that employees who are older, for example, or who have lower educational levels, or who have higher degrees of finger dexterity also tend to have higher job performance scores. This statistical approach predicts only for a group, however, and not for individuals. Of those receiving any particular score, a certain percentage are likely to receive a high job performance score and a certain proportion a low score. The statistical approach requires a fairly large group of applicants for each of the specific jobs being analyzed, and there should be rather clear and unchanging job duties, along with the capacity to measure job performance. The statistical approach is, therefore, more used by large hierarchical organizations than by smaller, flexible organizations.

Different aspects of jobs may be emphasized in different organizations. In some bureaucratic organizations, for instance, predicting job stability may be more important than predicting job performance, especially for rank-and-file employees, since technological factors dominate job performance so strongly that little variation in performance can occur. This, for example, would be true for assembly-line workers. For lower-level jobs in bureaucratic organizations, it might be desirable to choose applicants concerned with satisfying lower-level needs rather than those concerned with satisfying higher-level needs, since there will be little opportunity to satisfy higher-level needs on such jobs.

Selection of Managers.   The statistical approach may be of value for the selection of individuals for first-level managerial jobs if there is a large pool of applicants and there are a large enough number of positions to be filled.

Beyond the entry level, however, managerial jobs will be filled on the basis of two factors. One is the individual's performance in his present position, and the second is the fit between the perception that decision makers have of the individual's personal attributes and those they would like.

Most promotions in the stable organization will come from present staff; that is, there will be promotion from within. This is so for a number of reasons. First, because there are proportionately fewer managerial jobs, a promotion will represent a valuable reward, or payoff. It would be demoralizing to lower-level personnel who have invested personal careers in a firm to see higher-level jobs, for which they believe they are in line, go to newcomers. Second, present managers will be known to the organization, both in terms of performance and of personality. However, though the stability of an organization and the relatively slow advancement it offers provide an opportunity to observe an individual's effectiveness over a substantial period of time, and to make a reasonably good judgment about how well he does, such observation does not necessarily suggest how well he will do in future positions. Incumbents will have an opportunity to demonstrate competence, but only in a relatively narrow range of activity. Thus, decision makers often cannot make good estimates of how well a person can perform in areas which have not been part of his job scope. In response to this problem, many organizations have in recent years developed the "assessment center," in which applicants from the organization for higher-level positions are given an opportunity to demonstrate their versatility and ability to perform effectively in a number of simulated managerial situations.

Favoring those with congruent values may not hamper organizational effectiveness if the persons selected for promotion are competent. Such selection tendencies do, however, naturally foster homogeneous attitudes among top management. In a bureaucratic organization this can become a problem if the environment changes substantially. Otherwise, it will mean a smooth-working managerial team.

Which is to say that much more than simple competence of the persons being considered comes into play in making promotion decisions, especially when several candidates with acceptable levels of competence are available for a position. In that circumstance, it is most likely that the person perceived as having values, attitudes, and behavior patterns congruent with those of top management will get the job. Generally, the bureaucratic organization's low or marginal performers will not be considered for advancement. However, they may, for reasons of their loyalty, be retained in the organization.

Seniority will play a part in promotions in the bureaucratic organization, even at the managerial level. This is especially true of government organizations. In fact, U.S. Civil Service regulations require that each person promoted to a higher grade must have spent a certain amount of time in the next lowest grade, regardless of the promotion applicant's merit.

Compensation

In chapter 10 it was pointed out that the four basic compensation decisions are the wage-level decision, the wage-structure decision, the individual wage-determination decision, and the wage-method decision. Most of the techniques described in chapter 10 were designed for the bureaucratic organization and therefore are applicable to it.

An important consideration for the wage-level decision in the bureaucratic organization is that labor costs are often quite high as a proportion of total costs, and care must be taken to insure that wage costs do not become excessive. This is especially important in stable markets, where a good deal of price competition exists.

To deal with the wage-structure decision in the bureaucratic organization, it is possible to use one of several well-developed job-evaluation approaches, because the jobs tend to be well-defined, stable, and of relatively low complexity. All job-evaluation systems require specific job descriptions; thus jobs can be compared in terms of their content. Differences in pay are based on the level of the position in the hierarchy, and this presumably reflects the level of job difficulty.

The point system is especially useful in the bureaucratic organization. With the point system certain job requirements such as level of responsibility or education level common to all jobs in a particular class of jobs such as blue collar, white collar, or managerial are identified. Each degree of such a factor in a particular job is identified and assigned points corresponding to that degree, as described in chapter 10.

In the individual wage-determination decision in the stable organization, emphasis is usually placed on seniority and consistency in pay among individuals on the same job. This is especially true at lower organization levels, since the employees are often unionized. Unions generally pressure the organization to formalize personnel procedures, especially compensation methods, and to apply them in a consistent manner to all employees. Unions, concerned with internal cohesiveness among their own members, typically try to minimize individual differences among members. Another factor contributing to an emphasis on seniority is limited variability of performance among individuals paced by machines, conveyor systems, or by specific plans.

For the wage-method decision, individual incentive pay systems may be applicable in the stable organization. Incentive pay systems can be used for tasks that are routine, done the same way each time, and repeated often. But performance standards must be available for individual incentive plans to be used. Such standards are characteristic of bureaucratic organizations. Most employees in stable organizations work for time wages rather than incentive wages, however, because individual incentive wage systems require that the employee be able to control his own work pace, that his output be identifiable, and that the union and employees accept this approach to compensation. Usually, all of these conditions cannot be met.

In addition, the stability of the external environment, the unionization of the workforce, and the prospect of longer tenure of the workforce will mean there will be greater pressures for increased fringe benefits in the stable organization than in the dynamic organization. Those in bureaucratic organizations will be spending a long part of their life in it, and they, therefore, probably feel the need to believe their future is secure. Older workers are more concerned with fringe benefits, and unions generally seek security against the risks associated with loss of income due to retirement, unemployment, or health (Nash and Carroll, 1973). Environmental stability makes it easier for the hierarchical organization to obligate itself to provide future benefits to its employees.

Motivation

Efforts to increase performance by stimulating individuals to do better and work harder are constrained in the hierarchical organization by the type of work (technological factors) and the characteristics of the people. As mentioned earlier, organizations tend to choose individuals who appear to have the motivations and personalities consistent with the job demands to be placed on them (Argyris, 1954), and individuals, in seeking jobs, look for organizations they think will fill their needs (Porter et al., 1975; Vroom, 1966; Super, 1972). Thus we would expect hierarchical organizations to attract individuals who prefer or can function well in a more highly structured work environment, with low needs for achievement and low scores on initiative measures. Some research has found that managers in the more stable and structured government organizations have higher security needs, and that this is especially true in the more structured units in the organization (Paine, Carroll, and Leete, 1965). And we would expect such individuals to perform best in that type of work environment. There is research evidence from studies of several organizations to support these assertions (Schneider, 1975). In a company studied by the authors, managers scoring highest on needs for structure were most satisfied with very well-defined goal assignments (Carroll and Tosi, 1973).

This is not to say that an organizational member must be low in achievement needs and high in need for structure in order to adapt successfully to a stable organization. However, if a person has a low tolerance, or need for, structure or unusually high achievement needs, we would predict serious lack of congruence between the organization and the individual.

Miner's role motivation theory (Miner, 1965) states that there are certain common role requirements for managerial positions: (1) positive attitudes toward authority, (2) favorable disposition toward engaging in competition with peers, (3) assertive behavior, (4) ability to exercise power over subordinates without emotional difficulty, (5) tendency to stand out from the group, in a position of high visibility, and (6) ability to keep on top of routine job demands.

Research shows that individuals who behave and feel in these ways tend to seek out managerial positions (Miner and Smith, 1969). Research also shows that managers with these characteristics, attitudinal and behavioral, are more effective in more hierarchically structured managerial positions with more formalized procedures, relationships, and communication patterns (Miner et al., 1974). They are not so effective in less rigid and less formal types of organizations.

For lower-level employees, we expect that they will be motivated by *extrinsic* factors (those rewards controlled by others) such as pay, status, and promotion opportunities, more than by intrinsic characteristics of the work itself (Kohn and Schooler, 1969).

Motivational Approaches

In chapter 5, several different managerial motivation strategies, and their advantages and disadvantages, were described, rated by different occupational groups. Now let us consider their effectiveness in stable organizations.

Fear or Threat.   The fear approach can be effective where organizational members have few alternative job opportunities. As the data in table 5.2 shows, slightly more managers from the more structured organizations (such as bank managers and manufacturing foremen) rated the fear approach higher in effectiveness than did engineering managers. In this study, however, the preponderance of the managers from structured organizations did not rate this approach as effective, and probably rightly so. The use of the fear approach can induce anxiety and disrupt performance, and it loses whatever effectiveness it has when employees are protected by a strong union or tenure rights. It can contribute to aggressive tendencies which may result in acts of sabotage or other antiorganization or antisupervisory activity. We would expect greater use of the fear approach on lower-level employees in the stable organization. Coercion or bribery would be most commonly found where job incumbents had negative orientations and were alienated from their work.

Reciprocity. The reciprocity approach involves the trading of privileges for high performance. Reciprocity will probably be most used where supervisors have little power to reward their subordinates differentially for performance and where intrinsic task motivation of the work group is low. The approach will work when the privileges that can be given are valued by the workers, but, as we have seen in chapter 5, it can cause problems. Some privileges come to be expected as normal practice. For example, one foreman allowed his men to wash up 10 minutes before quitting time so long as all the work was done. Since they finished early every day, they always left their work station early. When the foreman took away the privilege, requiring them to clean up *after* quitting time, a grievance was filed. The decision of the arbitrator was that the practice had become standard and could not be taken away from the employees.

Reinforcement Approach. Under the reinforcement approach, rewards are given to individuals for superior performance. This is indeed an effective way to improve performance. Individuals who perceive a relationship between performing at a higher level and receiving rewards try to perform at the higher level. Perhaps the most basic problem is that there is a tendency to think of this method in terms of "material" rewards, such as increased pay, but if it is not possible to separate one employee's performance from that of another, then material inducements cannot be used. As we have seen, at lower levels in particular, pay systems will probably be designed to give all individuals in the same job class the same hourly rate, regardless of contribution.

Another important way to use this approach, however, is through social reinforcements. Managers can give recognition when a job is well done and withhold it when it isn't. A freight-handling firm in which supervisors were taught to give subordinates positive social reinforcement reported striking improvements in quality of work (Organizational Dynamics, 1973). Kim (1974) reports that telephone company employees improved performance when provided with specific feedback and reinforcement about performance levels.

Ego-involvement. In the ego-involvement method, attempts are made to improve performance through obtaining personal commitments to reach higher levels. For the method to work, however, the individual must have confidence in his ability to attain a goal, and at the lower levels of the stable organization in particular, there may be many individuals who do not have such confidence in their own ability, or individuals may simply recognize that they are prevented from reaching higher goal levels because their success is too dependent on others who work on interrelated jobs, or because the capacity of the equipment is limiting.

Ego-involvement is also difficult to obtain because of the nature of certain kinds of work. It is unreasonable to expect a person to be deeply committed to a highly routine, repetitive, boring job.

Team Building. Team building seeks to foster the development of cohesive work groups committed to high performance. This would be appropriate when the task requires collective effort, and when good relationships among those doing the work can facilitate or hinder performance, but it is inappropriate if the tasks tend to be independent and coordinated by supervisors at higher levels. The team-building approach, where appropriate, can improve morale and increase the amount of helping behavior. There is, incidentally, the danger that strong groups (teams) which develop negative feelings about management could take concerted action against the organization.

Competition. Managers may attempt to motivate by inducing competition between individuals or groups. For competition to be effective, the following conditions must exist:

1. The work must be independent, not interdependent.
2. The rewards (material or social) must be attractive.
3. Participants must feel they have a chance to win.

It is not likely that all of these conditions can be met on an individual basis, but group competition, especially between departments, may work. Competition is especially effective when it arises from the members themselves, but it often is difficult for a manager to create a competitive environment, and managerial efforts to set up competition with small token rewards often do not work. In one plant, an effort was made to create a competition between departments for cost reduction. The winning groups would have a party, paid for by management. Most workers saw this as just another management effort to push them, and they did little to change their style of work.

Job Design. Job design is perhaps the most fruitful way to improve performance in hierarchical organizations, especially if the capacity of equipment sets an upper limit on the level of performance. If, for example, an assembly line can produce 60 units per hour, then improved attitudes, morale, or whatever cannot raise output. If this is the case, performance may be increased by investing in new capital resources. The technological constraint cannot be overcome by any of the approaches already outlined, and the most important question is, "Do we have the technology capable of achieving the desired output?"

The job design approach can take two forms. One is restructuring the task activities to make more efficient groupings—the classic industrial engineering or scientific management approach. The second is changing the job scope, either increasing or decreasing a person's responsibility. Job enrichment is a method which falls into this second category. In job enrichment, the employee is given a bigger job to do and is allowed to manage the job, in the sense that he plans his work, executes the plan, measures how well he is doing, and takes corrective action as necessary. Research has shown that such job enrichment programs can improve performance, especially in terms of the quality of performance (Ford, 1973).

Possibilities for improvement in motivation through job enrichment are of course most likely to be found when the tasks are programmed and repetitive, a condition which is frustrating to individuals with needs for achievement and self-control. Simple, routine, and repetitive jobs, however, are not likely to attract or retain many people concerned about achievement and the assumption of higher levels of responsibility, unless they see some opportunities for advancement, and some research indicates that a significant proportion of the operative employees in the hierarchical organization may prefer more narrowly defined jobs (Hulin and Blood, 1968). Moreover, increasing discretion at lower levels of the organization may run contrary to the climate, atmosphere, or culture of the hierarchical organization. If such a counter-climate exists, job enrichment efforts are unlikely to have any beneficial effects unless a broader program of organization development is undertaken. Organization development approaches are discussed more extensively in chapter 17.

Motivation Strategies in Practice. Our analysis here is intended to suggest the relative values of a number of approaches which can, of course, be used singly or in combination at various points in the organization. However, working toward improved performance by motivating both managers and workers requires a constant, consistent effort. Item 13.1 describes motivational efforts at General Motors. The reader should note how broadly based the approach is, but he should bear in mind that these approaches are used throughout the company. The task of the individual manager is to find the approach or combination of approaches that has the highest probability of success in his circumstances.

ITEM 13.1   Motivation

GENERAL MOTORS STRIVES TO MOTIVATE ITS WORKERS

Grey-haired Thomas A. Murphy, newly appointed chairman of General Motors Corp. (GM), takes a practical and realistic approach to improving employee motivation.

• • • •

As the world's largest industrial company, GM treats new ideas in labour relations and work restructuring with a questioning and guarded enthusiasm. "Our top management has taken a clear decision in favour of experimenting with new ways of managing people," declares Stephen H. Fuller, vice-president of personnel administration and development.

• • • •

Although the lead comes from top management, the nature and location of experiments are decided not at corporate level, nor even national level in the 29 countries where GM now manufactures, but by the individual plants. Plant managers are encouraged to initiate whatever experiments they feel most suit the circumstances of their operation. "We have no standard formula or recipe," says Fuller. "Each situation is unique."

The company's serious involvement in what the 59-year-old Murphy calls "people experiments" was highlighted by Fuller's appointment four-and-a-half years ago from an academic career.

• • • •

The company keeps a close eye on the progress of the experiments with regular meetings at executive level. For example, Morris says: "Every three to four months the executive vice-president responsible for the US car and truck body assembly divisions gets together with the general managers of his divisions, accompanied by their personnel directors and their OD specialists. At these meetings each division reports on what new people experiments they have launched as well as the progress of projects underway."

In addition, last year the company established a liaison committee with the United Automobile Workers, the largest union with which it has to deal in the US. This "quality of work life" committee, which consists of Morris and Fuller on one side and two senior union officials on the other, invites the managers of individual plants to talk about the progress of their projects. "We don't have any rigid format or pattern for these meetings, nor any rules or regulations on what the committee can do," says Morris. The quality of work life doesn't dictate to local plants how they should go about their projects. But it does encourage plants to take up new ideas.

• • • •

To stress that the committee isn't applying pressure to local management, Fuller and Morris do not keep comparative records of how active plants are initiating experiments. It might not be fair to do so, indicates Morris. "After all, the plants that have had the best industrial climate may be doing less dramatic experiments than those who have problems," he says.

Fuller is adamant that the company is concerned to do more than just make jobs easier or more interesting. He declares: "Companies have been enriching jobs in this way for years. Other things are just as important, including giving workers the opportunity to contribute to the solution of problems found in their own work relationships with superiors, and the way in which their ideas are heard and acted upon. So are structural changes which reduce the number of levels in the organization, getting people closer to top managers.''

Nevertheless, a number of experiments the company has carried out have been basically changes in the organization of work. For example, several plants have adopted pilot schemes to build some parts of vehicles in teams instead of on assembly lines.

Even so, Creason admits that some people in the group didn't like the new procedures. This is a point that all the GM executives are keen to hammer home. Group experiments may suit some people, but not all. Fuller cites several instances in US plants.

"The GM assembly division has built Chevrolet vans for many years, and this has become a fairly simplified product," he notes. "They took four men and women to a separate building and tried to educate them to build a van. They had the assistance of an engineer who worked with them to get them started. Building a van on the assembly line takes eight man hours per man. At first these people were taking 13 to 14 man hours. But eventually they got to the point where they could build the van in a little less than one and half hours per man. Finally we put that van assembly job in Detroit with another team alongside the ordinary moving assembly line.''

Some people on the team soon decided they preferred working on the assembly line and the department had to juggle its personnel until it had a group that liked team work. Adds Fuller: "We intended to put the team building approach through the whole plant. But when we surveyed the workers, they just didn't want it.''

This general apathy on the part of the employees led to the abandonment of a much publicized team experiment at GM's truck and coach division, according to Morris. In 1973 a number of workers were organized into groups of six to assemble the vehicle bodies and groups of three to assemble chassis, of mobile homes.

"We learned a lot from that," he admits. "For one thing we learned that if you are going to try the team concept of assembly, you had better try with something you know how to build, not a brand new product. We also found that the people, by and large, did not like the idea at all.

"In a typical assembly operation, the man has a fairly simple job assignment. He doesn't have a multiplicity of things to do. He can develop a style, a method and a rhythm which permit him to do the job in his own way and at his own pace.

"In a group system the individual has a lot of things to do. The whole psychology of the job has been changed for him. He has a much greater responsibility than before and he finds it quite frustrating because instead of three elements to his operation he now has 20 or 30. When he gets to number 13 or 14 he starts to think: 'Oh my God did I do number seven?' The people told us they didn't like this extra responsibility.''

While it would be unfair to say that GM regards team building experiments as a palliative towards industrial unrest, it is clear that the company sees only a limited future for them, if only on practical grounds. Explains Fuller: "In the Detroit team building experiment producing Chevrolet vans, the men performed about eight jobs an hour. On an assembly line there are 40 to 70 jobs an hour. Our Lordstown plant has run at 110 jobs an hour. You just couldn't build a plant big enough to handle that volume of production on a team basis.''

One of the biggest problems is supplying materials and parts. A car may contain upwards of 15,000 parts. "How," asks Morris, "could you possibly store that many parts where they would be accessible to five or ten men?

"You can experiment with a group if it is a very simple vehicle and if the production volume is very low.''

Adds the voluble and expansive Murphy: "I don't ever forsee the end of the assembly line. We may see different approaches to sub-assembly, to break down the job so that it can be done more effectively. But our experience in the plant is this: the greatest difficulty we have with our employees is not because the job is repetitive so much as the fact we have to change the job, which we frequently have to do because of product development or new investment."

Murphy and his colleagues show much more enthusiasm for projects which do not involve massive changes in the physical layout of the plant. Creason, for example, speaks glowingly of the US assembly division's programme of "planned leadership." The programme, which has now spread to other GM plants as far away as Sao Paulo, Brazil, is aimed at releasing the foreman from many of his routine tasks. It also involves training all the workers to take over other jobs when necessary.

• • • •

At the Oldsmobile division in Detroit the employees themselves were asked to try to determine the cause of absenteeism. Some of the managers were dubious about involving the shop floor, says Fuller. But they agreed to let the scheme go ahead. The personnel staff first interviewed foremen and their bosses, the general foremen. Then they met with a number of employees who had particularly bad absenteeism records.

These interviews, which turned up some 70 contributory causes, were followed by interviews with a random sample of 200 newly hired workers. Several foremen attended courses in group problem solving, then got together with a number of workers to form a task force to tackle the question at shop-floor level.

Direct improvements occurred as a result of the interviews and discussions. They included a programme to ease new

workers' orientation into the plants and some experiments in modifying less attractive jobs. The company claims the workers became enthusiastic at their involvement and that unofficial absenteeism fell in the plants by over 8%. In the rest of the division it rose by 25% over the same period. Turnover also fell by 38% in one plant and 25% in another, compared with a fall of only 14% in the rest of the division.

Giving employees the chance to discuss and influence decisions that affect their working conditions is becoming more and more common in GM, claims Murphy. However, he doesn't much like the idea of workers on the corporate board. "We have worker representation on the board of our German company. I think it may be right for Germany. But I'm not sure that it would be right for the US or other countries," he declares.

One of the most successful projects in worker involvement is at the Indiana plant of Delco Electronics, a division where employees participate in setting goals for their area. The goals involve, for example, absenteeism, quality levels and wastage. Each group of employees meets with its supervisor whenever a problem arises that affects its operation. The foremen have had training in group discussion techniques. So too have a number of long-serving workers who are appointed discussion leaders.

• • • •

The Adam Opel plant in West Germany took the opportunity to give a small group of workers similar control over their own workplace when it introduced job rotation to the cushion department. Many of the workers in this department were old or handicapped. The two shifts of seven people handled three operations: cutting and sewing, assembly and frame-making.

The management decided to make the cushion department workers responsible for their own production and quality control, as well as planning work schedules and ordering parts. The workers have also taken over some minor repair work to their machines.

The two foremen and their superintendent attended a short course in motivation theory, delegation and effective communications, before re-arranging the workshop. They taught the employees to handle all three operations.

Ten weeks after the experiment started, the workers all declare they pre-ferred the new work system and the foremen had overcome their initial scepticism. "Production and quality have been at least maintained," says Creason. —David Clutterbuck

International Management, 1975

Performance Evaluation

Certain evaluation methods are especially applicable in hierarchical organizations, and different approaches may be used for different purposes. Some rating systems emphasize the rating of performance only, and these may be most appropriate when using the ratings for purposes of allocating merit pay, for motivation, or when the ratings are used as criteria in research studies for organizational purposes. Other evaluation techniques attempt to identify strengths and weaknesses in terms of abilities and personality traits. These approaches are most useful when using the ratings as an inventory of talent for promotion or transfer.

Evaluating Worker Performance. The work-standards approach is widely used where jobs are repetitive, because, first, there is general acceptance of the idea that an individual can be held responsible for his own actions or performance, and second, because the programmed and repetitive tasks characteristic of the stable organization make it relatively easy to establish performance standards.

Evaluating Managers and Professionals. MBO, which also emphasizes performance, can be used as the evaluation yardstick for managers and professionals in the stable organization, since this approach works well under conditions of organization stability. However, there are problems in evaluating performance with MBO. Managers may incorrectly emphasize results, to the exclusion of the means by which goals are achieved, because there are likely to be output measures which are presented as "acceptable" standards. Excessive emphasis on objective performance standards in the stable organization can lead to dysfunctional behavior. For example, Blau (1955), in a study of a state employment agency, found that interviewers evaluated on the basis of the number of applicants processed paid little attention to successfully placing the applicants and in fact avoided those applicants who required more of their time and effort. There are many other examples of how the establishment of "objective" performance standards against which individuals or groups were to be evaluated resulted in deliberate distortion of performance records, omission of information that would reflect adversely on performance, and the generation of false statistics.

Used correctly, MBO can be an effective device, however. If the manager both sets goals with subordinates, and develops with them acceptable means of achieving those goals, it can be determined both whether or not a goal was achieved and whether or not an action plan was carried out. The supervisor can focus on problems resulting from performance, rather than on personality deficiencies, and there should be less defensiveness than with the more traditional type of rating system. A systematic comparison of the MBO performance appraisal approach with that of an existing rating system at General Electric a number of years ago found that much better results were achieved with the MBO approach (Meyer, Kay, and French, 1965).

Participation by the subordinate in setting goals in MBO has been argued pro and con. In some cases it is necessary. In others it may not be, since both task requirements and technology are known in the stable organization to both the superior and his specialized staff. However, participation in setting work goals and objectives may still be desirable for purposes of achieving higher motivation and worker commitment. As we have seen in our studies of participative decision making some studies show that when a person participates, he is more committed to the decision (Maier, 1963). If participation clarifies goals, that is good, since it is goal clarity that is related to better performance (Locke, 1968; Carroll and Tosi, 1973).

Who Conducts the Evaluation?   In the stable organization, the superior is in a position to make judgments about performance. He typically knows the task objectives and the best approach for achieving them. He is usually in frequent contact with the person being rated. The existence of objective performance data makes rating easier than in a more dynamic organization, and there is probably less of a need for the services of a staff rating expert. However, with a single rater the possibility of bias and favoritism is higher; a staff rating expert might prove useful in the stable organization to keep the superior "honest" in his ratings. On balance, however, it seems that the most preferable case is to have the supervisor himself conduct the rating and provide feedback so that an opportunity is provided to improve supervisory-subordinate relationships and to bring job-related problems to the attention of both the rater and ratee.

Timing of Evaluation.   Some research has shown that the frequency of performance review needed to achieve performance goals is higher where there is more job complexity and more job change (Carroll and Tosi, 1973). Also, Stein (1976) found that in mechanistic organizations less frequent review is needed than in organic organizations. In addition, research indicates that where organizational members were already clear as to performance expectations, frequent performance review was seen as redundant and unnecessary (House, 1971). Thus the frequency of performance review would be less in the stable than in the dynamic organization.

Leader Behavior in Hierarchical Organizations

As noted in chapter 8, leadership is an influence process—a process that affects both how one reacts to his job and how well he does it. Of course, as we have already noted, other factors—for example, a plant's technology, or group pressures—also affect performance and attitude, and thus the leader's behavior. It may be extremely difficult for a leader to have substantial positive effects on performance in a hierarchical organization since so many other factors influencing behavior are preestablished beyond his control. In addition, as Locke (1971) points out, it is easier for a supervisor to have a negative impact on performance than a positive impact in any situation. This is because a supervisor can take actions to prevent subordinates from reaching performance goals but cannot himself insure that performance standards are met since that depends on the *intentions* of the subordinates. Technology may limit the supervisor's behavior, as we have noted in chapter 8. In addition, some of the leader's behavior is affected by the group he supervises.

When performance is low, of course, a manager may exert more production pressure, and when it is high, he may be more considerate (Lowin and Craig, 1968), but task characteristics are also determinants of the most effective managerial behavior. For example, Morse and Lorsch (1970) studied two stable firms in the container industry, one successful and the other less successful, and found that different degrees of participation, or subordinate influence over decisions, were valued in the respective firms. In both firms, the tasks were programmed, and the work was mechanized and repetitive. The investi-

gators found that the effective container manufacturer was characterized by centralized management decision making and a basically
authoritarian climate. Worker morale was apparently good. The less
successful company was characterized by decentralized decision
making and a more participative climate. Morale was lower than in
the more authoritarian, more effective plant.

Results such as this suggest that in attempting to determine what a
manager should do, we must take into account the characteristics of
the situation. House's (1971) approach to leadership does this, and we
use a variant of his model for our discussion. The concepts we will
discuss in the section that follows are also applicable to the leadership problem in dynamic organizations, which we will consider in
chapter 14.

Factors Affecting Leadership Effectiveness

Our approach takes into account leader behavior, characteristics of the
situation, and the relationship between a leader and the group. There
are two leader behavior factors (structuring behavior and consideration), one task characteristic (task structure), and one situational factor
(work climate). There are also the characteristics of subordinates to be
taken into account.

Leader Behavior. Much research (cited in chapter 8) shows that
leaders differ in their behavior patterns as perceived by those whom
they lead or supervise. Two behavioral patterns which seem to be
consistently found in the study of leaders are structuring behavior and
consideration.

1. *Structuring Behavior.* Structuring behavior refers to behaviors of
a leader directed at accomplishing tasks. It includes the assigning of
tasks to individuals, letting group members know what is expected of
them, and asking the group members to follow standard procedures. It
involves planning and organizing the work.

2. *Consideration.* The establishment of socioemotional relationships between the leader and the group members is consideration.
Supervisors high in consideration create a climate of psychological
support, warmth, and helpfulness. Such supervisors show concern
and trust for others.

All managers exhibit both these behaviors to some degree, but some
tend to emphasize one more than the other. Figure 13.2 illustrates two
of the different emphases that may be possible. One manager may be

high on consideration and another high on initiating structure—or high on both.

FIGURE 13.2 Different Emphases on Initiating Structure and Consideration

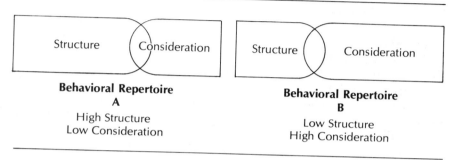

3. *Task Structure.* Task structure refers to the extent to which jobs are well-defined or ill-defined. Job requirements may be fairly well spelled out and relatively constant over time (as would be the case in hierarchical organizations) or they may not have clear requirements, as would be the case in a flexible organization. In path-goal theory (discussed in chap. 8) House refers to the ambiguity or uncertainty of tasks (House, 1971).

4. *Work Climate.* Fieder (1967) theorized that an important determinant of leader effectiveness is the relationship between the group members and the leader. House theorized that job satisfaction is an important determinant of leader effectiveness. Rosen (1967) has found that subordinates are susceptible to leader influence when the leader meets their needs through his behavior and when he has had past success in obtaining results. These various types of job satisfaction can be called the "work climate."

The work climate is the ambience that exists within the work group. It is the degree of trust that subordinates have in the leader, the level of group cohesiveness, the general satisfactoriness of leader and group relationships, and the congruence between individual and organizational needs and values.

Satisfying work climates are those in which there is high satisfaction with work and with the superior. Individual values and attitudes of members do not conflict with those of the manager or the organization. In general, there is a great deal of mutual trust and respect, and good relations exist between the leader and the members of his organization.

In dissatisfying climates, organization members have little trust in the leader's competence and fairness. There may be disagreement between the leader and subordinates about the appropriate way to solve problems. The individual values of subordinates may be different from those of the superior.

5. *Subordinate Characteristics.* There is much research on the effects of different subordinate characteristics on leader effectiveness. House and Mitchell (1975) identify two subordinate characteristics—authoritarianism and ego-involvement—as especially important. First, the individual's authoritarianism has been found to be related to how one reacts to a boss. High authoritarian people are dogmatic, rigid, and unwilling to change. Low authoritarians are the opposite. A second personal factor is ego-involvement in work. People with high ego-involvement in work see their work as particularly meaningful to them, having the professional orientation or the organizationalist orientation described in chapter 3.

Managerial Behavior. The primary factor which differentiates the managerial position in the hierarchical organization from that in a dynamic one is the level of task structure, or ambiguity about job requirements. The production subsystem is likely to be repetitive, with jobs broken down into relatively narrow tasks, and organization structures will be fairly well-fixed, with clear lines of authority, responsibility and job definition. Since goals are relatively stable, the work assignments will be fairly constant over time. The work groups themselves will tend to be stable in membership. Often there is a fairly heavy investment in fixed, specialized resources capable of producing only a limited number of products.

If this is so, then the two factors which are determinants of how a leader should act to produce effective results are (1) the level of subordinate authoritarianism, and (2) the work climate. When the work climate is satisfying and the group knows what the leader expects, the situation demands relatively low amounts of structuring behavior and greater emphasis on consideration, as shown in figure 13.3. As House (1971) points out, in some situations structuring behavior will be viewed as too much pressure and produce negative results. Structuring behavior is less necessary in the hierarchical organization since the work is already well-defined from the nature of the tasks.

In a dissatisfying climate, consideration behavior should be emphasized, as shown in figure 13.3. High levels of structuring behavior will make an already unpleasant situation more intolerable. So the leader

FIGURE 13.3 Leader Behavior Repertoire
in the Hierarchical Organization
(high task structure)

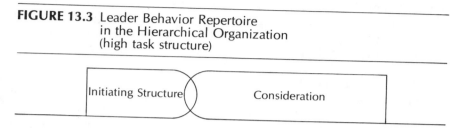

must take action to improve the attitudes of the group toward him and the situation.

Due to the routine nature of work, especially at lower levels, most of the workers will be externally oriented (as we noted earlier in this chapter) and have low job involvement, or identification with their work. The personality characteristic of authoritarianism plays an important role with regard to how a subordinate reacts. Subordinates who are low authoritarianism will react favorably when they have an opportunity to participate in job decisions. High authoritarians seem to have little need to have much influence in work decisions. House and Mitchell (1975) conclude that the high authoritarian, in fact, reacts negatively to such participative approaches. Of course the nature of participation in a hierarchical organization is restricted, since both ends and means (goals and plans of action) are already fairly well determined. Thus, participation in the stable organization will probably be seen as a form of "consideration" behavior. This may contribute to higher motivation when other positive motivational forces are absent (Carroll and Tosi, 1976b).

How a Manager Can Improve Performance

The performance of a work unit will be high when there is some congruence between leader behavior, work climate, and the level of task structure. In a hierarchical organization the task structure is fixed and well-defined by the work system; therefore, top management has at least three possible strategies to consider in the event of poor performance.

Change the Technological System. This strategy is basically one of job design or change. Suppose we find, in an assembly-line operation, that there are generally good relationships existing between the leader and his group. An analysis of the leader's behavior shows that his style is predominantly one of initiating structure. If poor performance occurs, it may be that the technological system needs to be redesigned. Improvements in efficiency may be made through methods study. Perhaps the jobs should be enriched, made more challenging. Or perhaps they should be more narrowly defined. Or it may be that old equipment should be replaced.

Clearly the suggested alternative to improve the results of the organizational unit calls for working in the technological system, not trying to change leader behavior from initiating structure to consideration. When technological limitations are the cause of poor performance, trying to change how a manager behaves may only serve to aggravate the problem.

Change Emphasis of Manager's Behavior. Performance deficiencies could also be the result of the incongruency of the manager's style with situational demands. For example, say that the technological system is producing great stress in organizational members. In this situation, if the leader's behavior pattern is dominated by structuring behavior, then he should attempt to move toward a style dominated by consideration. A manager can show greater consideration by engaging in some of the activities listed below.

1. Showing greater concern for personal problems and interests. This can be done, for example, by being willing to discuss the subordinate's personal objectives and interests.

2. Representing the interests of the employee to top management. Going to bat for members of the group or showing an interest in their advancement in the organization is a way to demonstrate concern for the individual.

3. Increasing the degree of subordinate participation in decision making. There are usually some opportunities for subordinate involvement that managers do not use. More frequent group meetings to solve problems not only may be a way to get better, more useful inputs, but could also be a demonstration of a considerate behavioral style.

4. Coaching or taking other constructive action in response to individual mistakes.

The emphasis on consideration presupposes that high task structure exists—that is, there is little ambiguity about the job. Often there is the need to provide *some* task structure through leader behavior (structuring behavior) even in a bureaucratic organization. When this judgment is made it can be done by employing a greater number of systemic factors available in an organization, such as budgets, procedures, and goals. The leader can increase structuring behavior by planning more extensively, by making more decisions, or by letting others know precisely where they stand on particular problems.

Change the Leader. Suppose that an individual manager exemplifies either a predominant structure style or considerate style and is unable to change his behavioral emphasis. The most effective strategy, may be to remove the leader and replace him with one whose style is congruent with the situation.

Communications

There is more vertical communication in the stable organization than in the dynamic organization, according to the research of Burns and Stalker (1961). There is need for more information flow between levels, managers and subordinates, to provide guidance about work requirements.

In the hierarchical organization the existence of job-descriptions and rules and procedures has been found to be related to the need for fewer meetings (Hage, Aiken, Marrett, 1971). There will be, due to the hierarchical structure, more formal communication, less unscheduled communication, and less horizontal communication (Hage, Aiken, Marrett, 1971). Managers at the same level will not have a great deal of interaction with others at the same level because of the more severe differentiation between work assignments. High mechanization through automation increases the amount of vertical communication required (Simpson 1959).

The organization structure is an important coordinating device in the hierarchical organization. By programming, in some detail, the work activities and relationships between positions and providing rewards or sanctions for compliance or noncompliance, a great deal of information is provided to an organization and members know what they should do, how they should do it, and with whom.

Status and power will be hierarchically defined. This means that power and rank will be defined in terms of organization levels. Therefore, communication between levels will be disturbed, constrained, and limited (Redding, 1972). This is one reason there will be more formal, vertical information flows.

The more highly formalized systems tend to use written communications more than oral (Hage, Aiken, and Marrett, 1971). One reason for this is the need to record what has transpired. In addition, there is less need for the rapid communication that is needed in the flexible organization.

In the hierarchical organization, the major purpose of most communicating that was not built into the procedure and work design structure will be for the purpose of informing and persuading, rather than for problem solving. Thus, decisions made at the top will be disseminated down through the hierarchy. Decisions will be largely "quality-dominated," thus most likely made by the administrator—or expert. These will be translated into requirements ("programmed decisions") for lower levels—thus the need for effective persuasion. The large imbalance toward quality-dominated problems can be a problem because managers may not learn to communicate and interact with subordinates. The manager must look for opportunities to work on "acceptance" problems with subordinates, since this provides an opportunity to communicate interpersonally.

Managing Organizational Stress

Pressures and stresses in organizations frequently derive from the demands or expectations of others at different positions in the organization. For instance, a production unit supervisor may wish to have his foremen give workers a three-day disciplinary layoff for absences, while the personnel department expects the foremen to use such extreme discipline only for drastic infractions of company policy. The foremen are being asked to take two contradictory actions, and may, as a consequence, find themselves in role conflict. Other stress occurs when a person is uncertain of exactly what his job is or how his performance is to be evaluated. This is role ambiguity. Role conflict and role ambiguity singly or combined can cause severe problems for individuals.

Stress is perhaps always present to some degree in the work situation, and perhaps it has some value in stimulation and incentive to overcome problems, but excessive stress obviously can have dysfunctional, disruptive, and even dangerous consequences to both the organization and the individual.

Role Conflict

Among the dysfunctional consequences of role conflict are these: (1) intensified internal conflicts for the individual, (2) increased job tensions, (3) reduced job satisfaction, and (4) lessened trust in superiors and the organization. (Kahn et al., 1964).

Hamner and Tosi (1974), after reviewing some of the research on role conflict, concluded that its effects are not the same for all levels in an organization. Because lower-level managers and employees in hierarchical organizations are accustomed to clear authority relationships, they find it difficult to cope with role conflict. Role conflict may not be such a problem for top managers, because individuals at this level are likely to have been selected for their ability to deal with such pressures. We would expect, in bureaucratic organizations, to find the following forms of role conflict.

Intrasender Role Conflict. Intrasender role conflicts are inconsistent expectations from a single person. A manager, for instance, may expect his subordinates to increase production but does not give them added resources. Often managers resort to this kind of demand when there are cost-cutting drives, or other programs to increase efficiency, and extraordinary demands are being made of the manager.

Intersender Role Conflict. Intersender role conflict occurs when two different individuals place incompatible demands upon a person. For example, the quality-control manager of a plant expects the foreman to reject more units of the product, while the production manager wants increased quantity and therefore fewer rejections.

Person-role Conflict. Person-role conflict is a condition where organizational demands are in conflict with one's values. This is not likely to be a serious problem in the stable organization, since it tends to be staffed by organizationally-oriented types with value systems consistent with that of the organization.

Ways to Minimize Role Conflict

In order to reduce role conflict to an acceptable level, conflicting demands must somehow be reconciled or eliminated. Here are some ways which may be used by the manager to do this:

Eliminate Authority Overlaps. An authority overlap occurs when two superiors have the formally designated right to dictate subordinate actions in the same area. In our example above, the production supervisor and the personnel department may be required to concur before an employee is disciplined for absenteeism.

Clarify Authority Relationships. Often a person experiences role conflict because he is not sure who has authority, and he responds to another who is in a higher position but outside his chain of command

simply because of the other's status. By increasing the person's awareness of those to whom he should, or must, respond, some conflict may
be reduced.

Insure that Superiors Maintain the Integrity of the Hierarchy. This
solution of course is related to clarifying authority relationships. The
"territorial" imperative here for a manager should be not to allow intrusion by other managers outside the chain of command, unless absolutely necessary. Whether or not an intrusion is appropriate is organizationally defined, as might be the case in the instance of the
production supervisor and the quality-control manager.

Role Ambiguity

Role ambiguity is defined as uncertainty about what the individual is
to do (task ambiguity), or uncertainty about how one is evaluated by
others (social-emotional ambiguity). Role ambiguity has been found to
be related to: (1) increased tension, (2) dissatisfaction with work, (3)
reduced self-confidence, and (4) poorer relations with others (Kahn et
al., 1964).

After reviewing the research on role ambiguity, Hamner and Tosi
(1974) suggest that it is most likely to be troublesome for higher organization levels than for the lower-level ranks, since top management
jobs tend for the most part to be less structured. In a bureaucratic organization of course, there is likely to be less task ambiguity even at
higher levels than is normally found in comparable jobs in dynamic
organizations. The pressing problem is likely to be ambiguity deriving
from uncertainty about performance evaluation.

Social-emotional Ambiguity. Social-emotional ambiguity may be a
problem in the stable organization because, even though there are
fairly well-defined measures for assessment of effectiveness, it is also
likely that many rewards are allocated on the basis of background
characteristics, personality, appearance, or general congruence of the
employee's values with the organization's. Carroll (1966), for instance,
has shown how appearance has affected success of an applicant in an
interview regardless of his qualifications. In the stable organization
there is often uncertainty about what one must do, or simply what one
must be, to succeed in advancing. This is especially frustrating for the
organizationalist, who seeks satisfaction from the organization. The
presence of social ambiguity means that the signals about how to be
"successful" are unclear. Organizationalists find this disconcerting.

Strategies to Reduce Role Ambiguity

To deal with role ambiguity, it is necessary to take two related steps:

1. *Define behavioral and output requirements.* Installing a management by objectives program is one approach for clarifying performance expectations, because the superior and the subordinate together determine the means of accomplishing the desired end result.

2. *Reward the achievement.* When the individual has been successful, the organizational reward system must be used to recognize it. Managers will thus communicate to subordinates what to do and what is important not only with words, but also through action. This will keep the level of role ambiguity low.

Managing Conflict

Often different parts of an organization have very different ideas about how things should be done—how the budget should be allocated, who should be appointed executive officer, what the objectives should be, how the goals should be accomplished, and so on. When there is lack of consensus, and different groups or departments attempt to have their points of view accepted over others, there is organization conflict.

Conflict causes difficulty because quite often managers don't know how to resolve it well. Also, it often creates internal tension that makes it difficult to work productively. On the other hand, conflict can be useful if it results in problem solutions that are valuable.

Sources of Conflict

Disagreement in *any* area that is important to individuals and groups can cause conflict to develop. There are some problems, however, that tend to be pervasive in bureaucratic organizations. These are:

Resource Allocation Decisions. Budgets are a frequent source of problems. The quantity of money, people, and resources available affects the ease with which a task can be accomplished. When resources are tight, managers must work harder to get the results that were more easily obtained with a larger budget. In order to make their jobs easier, increased resources are generally sought by supervisors of all organizational units.

Budgets can also be indicative of status in an organization. The larger a unit's budget, the more prestigious the unit. When a manager faces a budget cut relatively greater than others, or if his budget is reduced while another's is increased, these threats to status will be resisted.

The potential for conflict also exists when there is dependence by more than one unit on scarce resources. In bureaucratic organizations, resource allocation decisions may be made unilaterally, without lower-level participation. The budgeting unit, over time, will have developed "conversion factors" which can be used for allocation decisions. For example, it may have been determined from past experience that it takes one man-hour to produce ten units. If the budgeting unit has a projected level of production, it can arrive at an allocated labor cost. It tells the manager of a department that he has, for example, a $150,000 labor budget, and he has no say in the matter. When this kind of environment exists, it induces distrust and anxiety. Yet the nature of budget preparation in bureaucratic organizations often fosters such feelings, and they lead to conflict.

Status Differences.   The primary form of status differentiation in the bureaucratic organization is between organizational levels. There will be relatively sharp differences in privileges associated with the top management, middle management, lower management, and working levels. Workers may eat in cafeterias, lower and middle managers in large dining rooms, and top management may eat in the "executive dining room." Organizational conflict, however, is most likely to result from the distinction between management and operating levels. Since operating jobs are narrowly defined, with low skill and educational requirements, workers are easily replaced, and this, of course, is the principal basis of unionism, which provides an institutionalized system for resolving differences between management and the operating personnel.

Conflict between management levels will not be as overt as that between union-management, because, once a person has moved into a management position, he usually modifies his attitudes to be consistent with the environment—to be those of management. Lieberman (1956), for example, found that when workers were promoted to foremen their attitudes shifted toward those of management.

There will, however, be some latent conflict between managerial ranks. Lower managers will feel that the status symbols, pay, and other benefits are not equitably distributed; that top management, receives a disproportionate share of the rewards. Whether their belief is well founded or not, there is no mechanism for reducing the inequity, especially since middle-level managers do not organize into unions (although there is a growing tendency for mid-level professionals, such as engineers, to do so).

This latent conflict in the management hierarchy of bureaucratic organizations exists partly because the environment is unchanging. Top management has long tenure as well as control of important information and resources. They will insure that they have adequate resources for their purposes *before* decisions are made about resource allocation for lower levels. There *is* inequity, it will be long-lasting, and this is a source of conflict.

Different Perceptions. Dearborn and Simon (1958) have shown that different managers evaluating the same problem define the cause in a fashion consistent with their work assignments. The relatively stable organization structure of the bureaucratic organization will affect perceptions. When the firm is organized functionally (e.g., with departmental groupings based on the type of work: production division, marketing division, accounting division, and so forth), managers in each of these units will see problems and solutions in terms of their functional specialty. When departmentation is geographic (e.g., a western division, southern division, and so forth), the primary frame of reference will be geographic.

Another perceptual difference of importance flows from the union-management relationship. Managers and unions see one another as adversaries, and taking an adversarial position with another group can often be detrimental to the constructive resolution of conflict.

The Balance of Power

When groups are in conflict, it is often because one group has greater power than another; conflict seeks to bring about a change in this power relationship.

What factors affect the balance of power in a stable organization? Certainly economic factors and dependence are primary aspects of the union-management relationship. When economic conditions are favorable to a firm (high sales and profits along with high employment), the union is in the better position to assert its demands. If unemployment is high, the firm is in the stronger bargaining position.

Hierarchical status differences between management levels are maintained because of the nature of resource allocation decision processes in stable organizations. Resources are allocated from the top of the hierarchy down, and at each level how much is passed on to lower levels is usually a relatively unilateral decision. Managers are likely to hoard resources, maintaining discretionary funds where possible, which means that lower levels of management must constantly go to the higher levels to obtain additional resources. Since the organization is relatively stable, there are few external pressures to change this resource allocation process, and this leads to concentrations of power and to conflict.

Managers at higher levels also have a great degree of control over information that lower levels need. This information not only has to do with work activities, but also with important personal considerations (e.g., how one is evaluated and the likelihood of promotion). Information can be power, and like economic resources, may be hoarded at higher levels.

Power will be distributed among divisions and departments as a function of:

1. the unit's possession of important information;
2. the making of recommendations that are likely to be accepted;
3. the importance of the unit's function.

The Power of Information.   A person must understand his job before he can do it. He must know how decisions are made before he can influence them. He must know what criteria are used in making decisions before he can work to achieve them. In some organizations, budgeting units are extremely influential because they are the central point into which information from different units flows. This information is reshaped into budget proposals. It would be useful for a manager to have information about the budgetary allotments of other units in order to present his own case in the most favorable way. Because they hope to obtain such information, some managers will respond to demands from the budgeting unit that go far beyond its scope of formally defined authority.

The Power of Recommendation.   Certain individuals and departments develop, over time, the capacity to influence other's decisions. For example, the president of a major publishing firm relied heavily on advice from a trusted colleague who started the business with him but who, for personal reasons, never achieved high position. This confidante was at least four organization levels below the president, but when major decisions were under consideration, his advice was sought and usually heeded. This led many managers at all levels to seek the confidante's assistance in gaining the president's ear.

Personnel departments often have similar influence, especially in large, dispersed organizations. When the manager of the branch plant in Racine needs a production supervisor, he may turn to the personnel department for a list of potential candidates. Those who aspire to success in the firm know that the personnel department can be of great help to them. In many firms, personnel files are closely guarded to prevent individuals from learning how their performance is evaluated and what potentially they can expect in the way of promotions. This form of secrecy is not uncommon. When questioned about the reason for not telling an employee about what has been planned for him, a personnel executive said,

> It can cause more headaches than it's worth. Suppose we think someone is capable of taking over the Birmingham plant in a year and it looks like the plant manager will be moved to make room. If the economy changes, or any number of things happen to freeze the present plant manager in his position, we can't promote the person. He'll be disappointed, frustrated, and may leave because he feels we haven't kept our promise, even though we never really made one.

The Importance of the Units' Function. The balance of power between the production and boundary-spanning systems is an important relationship. Most organizations will find themselves in a situation in which one function is more critical than another, and the unit performing the critical function will generally have the most power. How can this happen in a stable environment, as we have defined it? Suppose that a firm has a captive market; suppose it is the primary producer of product A, and can sell all it can produce. So long as such demand exists, the production function will be the most powerful in the firm, especially if there are manufacturing problems which might limit output if not effectively overcome. The production function is the controlling factor, and thus the most powerful. In another firm, production problems may be minimal, while the chief problem will be to keep sales constant or growing. In such a firm, marketing will be the dominant unit.

Since the dominant unit will be more influential, it may receive proportionally larger budget allocations, and it may have access to important information. This advantaged position may cause those in other units to be more aggressive in their dealings with it, breeding discontent and coordination problems which hinder effective cooperation.

Resolution of Conflict in Stable Organizations

As we have suggested, conflict resolution should, generally, lead to improved performance. Assael (1969) notes that conflict will be beneficial if, when it is resolved, the following conditions exist:

1. critical review of past actions;
2. more frequent communications between disputants, and the establishment of outlets to express grievances;
3. more equitable distribution of system resources;
4. standardization of modes of conflict;
5. creation of balance of power within the system.

There are two kinds of mechanisms which facilitate conflict resolutions: (1) the improvement of the formal conflict resolution system, and (2) the nonstructural solution.

Formal Mechanisms

One of the main functions of organization structure is to resolve differences that arise among members. (The purpose of a labor relations department, for example, is to facilitate union-management relations.) Therefore, by definition, hierarchy can be used to resolve conflict. Managers can resolve conflicts among members by acting as an intermediary in discussion, by making the decision themselves, or by referring both parties to another location in the organization where the decision can be made.

Use of Formal Departments. Union-management conflict is often handled by a department of the firm which has been formally assigned those functions. Other staff functions can also serve to reduce conflict. Accounting department personnel, for example, can show two conflicting managers the manner in which budget allocations were decided and why. The managers then may either prepare a stronger justification for their own cases or accept the decisions because they are better informed.

Use of Committees. In some circumstances, committees may be able to resolve conflict. When a committee contains representatives of various groups, different points of view can be considered, and recommendations, proposals, or decisions made which can take the different points of view into account. Perhaps the greatest danger of this method is that the final determination may be one where everyone gets something, but no one gets all he needs. Compromises reached in committees are often alternatives which are not most effective from the point of view of the "best" way, but simply for keeping the internal peace.

Nonstructural Solutions

Quite often conflict must be treated by dealing with the people involved, rather than by using the structure of the organization. Some strategies that may be useful in the stable organization (as well as the dynamic) are increased participation in decision-making, the use of group development, and the replacement of personnel.

Increased participation in decision-making allows subordinates an opportunity to make recommendations. Discussing these recommendations with them individually and as a group will increase the information available and make them aware of potential problems. Increased participation, as we have seen in chapter 12, may take many forms, ranging from allowing the individual to make a decision to simply informing him of the grounds on which a decision has been made.

Group development and team-building training methods may also be useful in reducing conflict. With these methods individuals are brought together for the purpose of learning how to interact more effectively (see chap. 17).

Replacement of personnel is a technique to be used when the conflict can be traced to the obstinacy or personality of one or more members of a unit who are unwilling to change. It happens, though rarely, that a single individual causes many of the problems in a unit and is not willing to yield to the needs of others or the organization. Intraorganization transfer to a more compatible climate or a job where there will be less interaction with others should be considered when the individual has skills that are valued by the organization. If he does not want to transfer, managers must then terminate his employment; that is, fire him.

In this chapter, we have analyzed some of the ways in which managerial techniques are applied in organizations of a certain type. As they examine any organizational situation, management students should bear in mind that the character of the organization, its environment, and the orientations of the people it attracts are the important determinants of how it will function. Many of the techniques suggested in this chapter will work in other situations as well. They are proposed here because we believe that they are most congruent and useful in organizations of a hierarchical character. They represent the starting point from which a manager can begin to analyze his problems and deal with them.

Discussion Questions

1. What do you think of the statement "Rank and file workers will do what is expected of them, but they do not obtain primary satisfaction from their work." If true, how will this affect an organization's productivity? What will a typical manager's reaction be to such a position?

2. "Statistical selection" means making a decision to hire some one based on whether or not a score they get on a "test" is above a cutoff point. Why should such an approach be used? Why not? Under what conditions might it be of great utility to a manager?

3. Have you ever been interviewed for a job that you did not get? What do you think the interviewer found wrong with you? List the factors on a sheet of paper. Are there some which you can easily change?

4. In this chapter we suggest several alternative ways a manager might "motivate" a worker or work group. From your experience, can you recall a time when such techniques were used on you? When you tried them on others? How did they work?

5. In our discussion of leadership, we suggest that one way for a leader to improve unit performance would be to change his style; for example, move from a "structure" emphasis to a "considerate" emphasis. There is an adage "A leopard can't change his spots." Can a manager change his behavior? How?

6. Why might role conflict have more potential impact on managers at lower levels of an organization?

7. What are some added forms that status differentiation takes in bureaucratic organizations beyond those noted in this chapter?

13. List the positive and negative aspects of working in a stable organization.

14. Indicate why you would or would not want to work in the stable organization.

15. Discuss strategies for a manager to follow in getting ahead in the stable organization.

Chapter 14
Managing Human Resources in the Dynamic Organization

In this chapter and the next, we turn our attention to the dynamic organization. This chapter considers the same topic areas as did chapter 13, but it suggests strategies or approaches for dealing with the human resources of a more flexible, project-management oriented, organization. The following areas again are discussed:

1. Selection
2. Compensation
3. Motivation
4. Performance Evaluation

5. Leadership
6. Managing Stress
7. Managing Conflict

In dynamic organizations, these activities take a different shape than that of their counterparts in hierarchical organizations. The turbulent environment of the dynamic organization requires much more flexibility in relationships among members so that the system can adapt more readily.

Selection of Personnel

The selection of personnel is important in a different way in the dynamic organization than it is in the stable organization. There are not only initially higher recruitment, assessment, orientation, and training costs to be considered, but also higher potential costs should a wrong selection decision be made. If the professional hired proves to be inadequate, for example, and fails to complete a project on time, a dynamic organization may lose many hundreds of thousands of dollars through, say, the loss of a market to a competitor. Conversely, a rejected applicant who is hired by a competitor and is successful there can be very costly to the firm which rejected him.

In volatile environments, there is a high level of turnover of professional and managerial staff, since as demands for skills change, certain professionals become expendable and must be replaced by others.

The more variable the tasks over time, the higher the rate of staff change.

A reduction in the volume of work at a firm may also force the layoff of many qualified professionals who must later be replaced if the volume of work increases. An aerospace firm, for example, may have to lay off large numbers of talented professionals because of lack of work for them, only to be forced to recruit furiously a month later if it receives a large contract.

Turnover can be a problem if an organization loses someone with a particular skills configuration and must find a replacement with the same configuration, since the number of qualified applicants is usually smaller for the dynamic organization than it is for a hierarchical organization. This is so because the members of dynamic organizations must at one and the same time be highly versatile and yet possess highly specialized skills.

The Mixture of Organization Types

In the dynamic organization the mixture of organizational orientations will tend to be as shown in figure 14.1. At the lowest level of the organization there will be a professionally-oriented group of specialists, highly trained and skilled. The externalists will probably be a smaller group of operating personnel charged with carrying out routine tasks. They will be longer-term employees.

At the mid-levels, the mixture of types changes. Two groups of roughly the same size will be found, one of organizationally-oriented managers and one of professionally-oriented managers. The organizationalists will be administrators who are making a managerial career,

FIGURE 14.1   Representation of Different Orientations as a Function of Organization Level in the Dynamic Organization

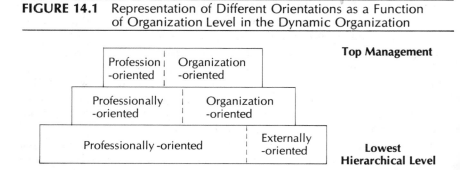

with success defined by their organization's achievement of primary work goals. The professionally-oriented group will be specialists who have been promoted to managerial positions because of their high competence, but who have retained their original value system.

The distribution of types changes again at the top level, which will have a preponderance of organizationalists. This occurs because selection decisions for higher managerial ranks are made by those already in high positions, and they are likely to place more value on the organization as such than on professional commitment. Technical skills are still important at this level, however, and some of the top management group will have a professional orientation.

Selection

The selection of personnel in dynamic organizations is more difficult than it is in stable organizations because, in the former, members do different kinds of tasks from one period to another and their tasks are often not well-defined. Therefore it is difficult to find specific predictors of effectiveness. In addition, jobs in dynamic organizations tend to have higher skill requirements than in hierarchical organizations, since a higher proportion of managers and professionals are employed. Therefore, in dynamic organizations selection will tend to be based on the clinical approach (discussed below), rather than the statistical, because the jobs are more individualized. For example, a dynamic organization may need a person to assume responsibilities for several different projects. This person may need to have the abilities to perform a number of different specialized functions, and also to have the kind of personality that fits in with other project team members. Such characteristics are difficult to measure—as well as being in short supply.

The Clinical Approach. In the dynamic organization, then, a more individualized approach to selection, called the "clinical approach," is used (Dunnette, 1966). In the statistical approach, an applicant is at least initially accepted or rejected on the basis of some score, or combination of scores, received on a test. In clinical selection, tests may be incorporated along with other important data, such as experience and education. However, clinical selection is also much more subjective. The person, or group, making a clinical decision combines the data about an applicant based on a judgment of how all the predictors of job success should be weighted and evaluated, based on the evaluator's own experience with the job.

The clinical approach to selection is suited to the dynamic organization for two reasons. First, there simply are too few jobs and too few applicants to allow an effective validation study which might insure the utility of, say, specific cut-off scores on a particular test. This means that the selector must do this intuitively. Second, there are important data which are difficult to value quantitatively but which would be useful in a selection decision; for example, the applicant's responses and behavior in an interview. This information may be important and should not be ignored, but it can only be included judgmentally.

Compensation

In the dynamic organization, the general problems of compensation policy are those described in chapter 10: the *wage-level* decision, the *wage-structure* decision, the *individual wage-differential* decision, and the *wage-method* decision. The approaches to solving these policy questions, however, must be different than those for the bureaucratic organization, because the work of specialists in the dynamic organization is highly complex, the jobs are usually ill-defined, and they do not lend themselves to the precision of the evaluation methods described in chapter 13. Because of the variability of task requirements within and between professional specialties, it is difficult to make internal comparisons to determine the relative worth of different jobs.

As mentioned, the dynamic organization has a much higher proportion of managers and professionals than the hierarchical organization, and compensation for this group will be lower in importance relative to other job factors. The lack of definition of tasks characteristic of this group makes it difficult to use individual incentive plans in which it is necessary to measure output precisely and where each individual must have control over the level of output himself. We would expect greater use of the group incentive plans and the plant-wide incentive plan in the dynamic organization. If an incentive plan is to be used with professionals, it often involves payment of a bonus to a team if a particular project is completed by a certain date and is of a satisfactory quality level.

Maturity Curves

Since the tasks in a dynamic organization are not programmed and the professional shifts from task to task on different projects, it is almost impossible to establish base rates for professional jobs through the job evaluation approaches described in chapter 13. As a substitute for job evaluation, the pay for professionals can be established using "maturity curves" developed from an analysis of salary levels attained by professionals of a certain type after certain time periods upon receiving their final college degrees. For example, the organization may subscribe to a survey which indicates the average compensation for chemical engineers for certain years after graduation. An overall judgment is then made of the quality of a particular individual chemical engineer in the company. If he is of average quality, he is paid what the average chemical engineer in that industry with a similar amount of experience is paid. If he is superior, he may be paid a certain percentage more than the base rate of the average chemical engineer.

The Classification Method

This method seeks to group different jobs into classes, or grades, based on the amount of difficulty, challenge, authority, or other important factors. This method has been used in government agencies for years. It is also used in private industry. In the federal government it is known as the GS system. Under this approach, various job grades are established. Each job grade, such as GS 1, GS 5, or GS 9, has a description in general terms of the characteristics of jobs in that group. For example, the jobs in grade GS 1 are described as involving "little or no latitude for the exercise of independent judgment," while those in grade GS 5 have "limited latitude," and those of GS 9 require "the exercise of independent judgment in a limited field." Whenever a new job is created and it is necessary to determine a wage rate for it, the description of the job is compared to the various grade descriptions to identify the one in which it belongs. The salary range for that grade is then authorized for the job. All the jobs within a certain grade are supposed to be similar with respect, for example, to the amount of latitude allowed the job incumbent. The classification method may be useful in dynamic organizations if the job characteristics represent, for example, level of training, experience, responsibility for projects, or other criteria of value in an organization of this type.

Executive Compensation

In chapter 13, we did not discuss pay methods for managers. That is because the approaches to evaluating executive and managerial positions are similar to those described above for dynamic organizations. Classification systems and maturity curve approaches are often used to determine base pay levels for executives. However, stock option plans, bonuses, and profit-sharing programs are an important part of many executive compensation plans. They may account for as much as 50 percent of a manager's pay. While we will not go into these in detail, all of them generally seek to link pay with performance. To do this, some reasonably systematic approach to evaluation is required. The reader who carefully followed the discussion of MBO (chap. 12) can see the utility of this method for dealing with these aspects of executive pay.

Performance Evaluation

Performance evaluation in the dynamic organization is also different from that in the hierarchical organization because more individuals perform a greater variety of tasks that are nonprogrammed and nonrepetitive. In addition, many organizational members, such as the professionals, are assigned to various work teams where they work with different individuals and for different supervisors.

Evaluating Worker Performance

There may be some lower-level jobs in the dynamic organization that can be routinely defined. When this is so, employees in these positions may be evaluated using the work standards approach which we saw in chapter 13. In other nonroutine and nonspecialist jobs at lower levels, the use of critical incidents (see chap. 10) may facilitate evaluation. The use of these methods, however, must be based on the existence of a clear understanding between the individual and his superior about the job requirements and how the tasks should be performed. When using the critical incidents method, the evaluator must be careful that the incidents recorded represent a true sample of the worker's behavior. That is, he must not record only the wrong things done; he must also be aware of, and record, the positive contributions of a worker so that the method does not become a "black book" of negative performance.

Evaluating Managers and Professionals

Because relatively objective output measures are difficult to obtain in the dynamic, flexible organization, management by objectives must be undertaken on a different basis than it is in the stable organization.

End results (objectives) may be specifiable only in general terms; for example, increased quality or production of a low-cost unit. But since neither quality nor cost level can be precisely defined, MBO must concentrate on the definition of means for goal achievement.

In developing a basis for evaluation with MBO in a dynamic organization, then, the general objective is stated, and an action plan is given in detail. When an individual is evaluated, the focus is on whether or not he is carrying out the action plan, and it is *assumed* that if he is, the objective will eventually be reached. In effect, this strategy attempts to get employees to go through the steps that are assumed to lead toward the goal. For example, suppose a project group has the following goal: "To develop a new product that performs better than Competitor A, and at a lower price." Such a project may take two or three years to complete. But in the interim period, the individuals assigned to it expect promotions, wage increases, and other rewards. About all that a manager can do in such a case is to make sure that the project group members are engaging in the activities which, based on experience, are most likely to achieve the desired result. The action plan for such an objective might be given in the following steps.

1. Analyze the competitor's product's characteristics.
2. Determine this company's capacity to produce a similar product.
3. Redesign the product with less expensive components.
4. Test the product for performance.
5. Prepare plans for a pilot test of the product in the market place.
6. Transfer the design to the manufacturing division for production.

If such an action plan takes three years to carry out, then a manager evaluating the performance of the project group must determine whether or not the group is carrying out the elements in the plan, and he must do this at regular intervals long before the achievement of the objective can be measured in the market place. So, periodically, the manager assesses whether or not: (1) the competitor's product was analyzed, whether or not (2) a study of capacity was conducted, and so forth, step by step through the action plan.

Participation in setting objectives of this type requires extensive involvement of those who will carry out the action plan. The supervisor may not have the technical competence needed to develop an action plan for activities which are not so routine and will vary from project to project. He often does not know what subordinates do nor how they do it, and therefore he must solicit their ideas in establishing work objectives for both individuals and project groups. Thus, because subordinates often know more about what it is possible to achieve than their superior, in the flexible organization they should have more to say about goals and action plans than would be the case in a hierarchical organization.

Who Conducts the Evaluation?

The superior in the dynamic organization will be directing individuals who are using skills and knowledge unfamiliar to him, and therefore it is difficult for him to judge their performance. In addition, if he is directing higher-level personnel who are individually working on different projects with different task teams, he will not have the knowledge—or the time—to evaluate their performances. Thus, in the dynamic organization, inputs for evaluations are more likely to come from a group of professional peers and/or the various supervisors or project team members with whom the organizational members work. While the supervisor may himself provide feedback directly to subordinates, he must rely on these other sources of information for much of that feedback.

Some Cautions about MBO. In the dynamic organization, the MBO approach may have to be used on a group basis, rather than on an individual basis, since the group's work is interdependent and the projects are often assigned to teams. Additionally, if goals are changed too often in the MBO system (because of the necessity to adapt to a rapidly changing situation), organizational members may lose confidence in it, with a resulting loss of motivation. Thus, when goals change, any documents that have the obsolete goals written in them should also be changed.

Motivation

Individuals seek organizations which provide satisfaction of needs. Because they do, we expect the dynamic organization to attract managerial and professional types with high needs for achievement, high initiative, and low needs for a structured work environment (Lorsch and Morse, 1974). And it does. Managers, professionals and technicians—those who make up the largest proportion of workers in this type of organization—generally are high in initiative, decisiveness and self-confidence and not so concerned with security needs (Ghiselli, 1971; Pelz and Andrews, 1966; Kornhauser, 1960). They also tend to be more concerned with higher-order needs, such as self-actualization. Further, a national survey of various occupational groups shows that managers and professionals rate money (an extrinsic motivator) lower relative to other job factors than do operative workers (Nash and Carroll, 1975).

However, there is a distinction, as noted earlier, between *how* managers and professionals want to achieve—be successful. Managers are more likely to be organization-oriented than professionals, and will seek recognition of their achievement through the attainment of organizational status, power, and position. The professional, who regards achievement highly, may seek recognition from fellow professional colleagues both in and out of his own organization.

Managers and professionals, then, have high intrinsic motivation to do well, as a group. In addition, tasks in the dynamic organization tend to be more complex, challenging, and interesting than in the hierarchical organization, and this, coupled with the orientation of a large group of employees who prefer such tasks, means that motivation is not a critical problem. Most individuals with such needs and who are performing tasks which are challenging will be motivated to high performance, the level of that performance being largely determined by their competence. If a highly competent staff can be selected, the chances for survival and profitability of a dynamic organization are greatly increased. This is especially so when the individual can see the relationship between effort and results and between results and rewards, whether the rewards are based on organizational payoffs or on professional recognition.

Failure to see this relationship, however, can result in goal blockage and frustration (see chap. 3). When goal blockage occurs frequently for important personal goals, a person may become sufficiently frustrated to give up and become de-motivated. He may decrease his efforts and/or seek to leave. Blocks to goal progress can arise from a number of sources in the dynamic organization. Where the work is highly interdependent, frustrations can easily arise when one individual's lack of progress leads to goal blockage of another. In addition, among scientists, professionals, and technicians, equipment failure or inadequacies in the qualities of materials may induce frustration. Thus, in the flexible organization, it is especially important that emphasis be placed on task facilitation activities, such as providing help and resources when needed. Managerial strategy should be directed toward removing goal obstacles.

Managerial Approaches to Motivation in the Dynamic Organization

As in chapter 13, some of the managerial strategies used for motivation are discussed below. Here, however, the focus is on how they may be used in the dynamic organization.

Fear or threat.   Since fear or threat can only be effective when the subject has limited job alternatives, it seems to be of little value to the manager in a dynamic organization, especially in periods of growth, when the services of specialists are in demand elsewhere. Also, the use of such pressure is inconsistent with the value orientations of professionals, and may increase their dissatisfaction with the organization to the point where they will look elsewhere for a more conducive, compatible work environment.

Threat may have some short-run effect when there is a declining market for specialist services, but as table 5.1 in chapter 5 shows, engineering managers rated the use of this approach as less effective than managers from more structured organizations.

Reinforcement.   It will be difficult to use reinforcement approaches in the flexible organization. First, professionals may find more reinforcement, both positive and negative, from their colleagues than from management. Since many of their professional peers will be outside the organization, a manager cannot influence the manner in which reinforcement is applied. For example, a university professor's work may be highly regarded by professors at other universities, and he may receive rewards and recognition from them. His superiors at his own univeristy can do little to alter these rewards. About all they can do is to make his work easier so that he increases his probabilities of success. If the work the professor does is valued by the organization, then there will be no problem, but often this is not the case, especially when professional activities impinge disproportionately on teaching, committee assignments, and other organizational work.

Since much of the work in a flexible organization is done on a group project basis, it is difficult to pinpoint a particular individual's contribution, and this makes it difficult to reward them on an individual basis. In such a setting, it is appropriate to establish a group reward system. When this strategy is used, however, there still remains the problem of obtaining a distribution of the group reward to members of the group. This problem can be solved by having group members decide how much each should get. This is the method used to distribute playoff rewards—world series shares, for instance—by professional sports teams. Typically, the decision is that all members, ranging from the team's superstars to the least-used man of the roster, share equally.

Team Building. The team-building approach is one in which cohesive work groups with high standards of performance are formed. Engineering supervisors, however, rated team building less effective than did supervisors from more structured organizations (table 5.1, chap. 5), a judgment that may reflect some of the difficulties of tying together the activities of a diverse set of specialists with different interests. In the company from which the sample was taken, project teams were *not* used frequently, and each specialist worked in a group of similarly trained personnel, rather than in an integrated task team.

Where integrated task teams of a highly interdisciplinary nature are used, team building will foster group cohesiveness and cooperation within the team. However, it may also serve to increase the potential for conflict *between* groups.

Ego-involvement. Engineering supervisors rate the ego-involvement approach higher than do other types of supervisors (table 5.2, chap. 5). This follows, since professionals and specialists are likely to be more personally involved in their work because they have spent years attaining their competency, and thus their work becomes an important aspect of their psychological make-up. If it is possible to show how their work is connected with organizational success and, at the same time, allow such groups to become more extensively involved in the planning and design of activities, performance gains will probably occur.

Job Design. Attempting to increase performance through job re-design is a useful approach in the dynamic organization. Since care must be taken to insure that a specialist's job activities draw upon his strengths, the specialist's job can be studied to identify its routine and clerical activity component, and these can be transferred to other positions. Positions such as the engineering assistant—an assistant brought in to free the professional's time so that more of the professional's time can be spent on the task itself—are already utilized in the aerospace industry, for example. In the health field, paramedics aid the physician, and the expanded-duty auxiliary performs many technical functions for the dentist.

Job enrichment of the type described in chapter 13 will have very little effect on an employee's ego-involvement, since in the dynamic organization, jobs are already filled with variety, challenge, and autonomy.

The Suggested Method—Increase Ability. Perhaps the most effective way to improve performance in the dynamic organization is to raise ability levels, especially since the personal motivation is already there. One way to increase competence is through additional training and education.

Organizations may send their specialists back to school for advanced study, seminars, and other specialized training. Many firms bring in instructors to offer advanced work on the job site.

Another way to increase the competence level of an organization is through the judicious replacement or transfer of subpar personnel. An organization may find it more effective to replace personnel with others of higher competence than to try to train present personnel up to competence. Peter Drucker, a noted management writer, comments in item 14.1 about some of the critical problems of managing the motivational setting of the workforce of a dynamic organization.

ITEM 14.1 The Motivational Setting

Managing the Knowledge Worker

Direct production workers—machinists, bricklayers, farmers—are a steadily declining portion of the work force in a developed economy. The fastest growing group consists of "knowledge workers"—accountants, engineers, social workers, nurses, computer experts of all kinds, teachers and researchers. And the fastest growing group among knowledge workers themselves are managers. People who are paid for putting knowledge to work rather than brawn or manual skill are today the largest single group in the American labor force—and the most expensive one.

The incomes of these people are not, as a rule, determined either by supply or demand or by their productivity. Their wages and fringe benefits go up in step with those of manual direct-production workers. When the machinists get a raise, the foreman's salary goes up by the same percentage more or less automatically—and so does everybody else's in the company right up to the executive office.

But whether the productivity of the knowledge worker goes up is questionable. Is there reason to believe, for instance, that today's school teachers are more productive than the teachers of 1900—or today's engineer, research scientists, accountant or even today's manager?

At the same time the knowledge worker tends to be disgruntled, or at least not fully satisfied. He is being paid extremely well. He does interesting work and work that does not break the body as so much of yesterday's work did. And yet the "alienation" of which we hear so much today (I personally prefer to use the good old word "distemper") is not primarily to be found in the working class. It is above all a phenomenon of the educated middle class of employed knowledge workers.

Two Needs We do not know how to measure either the productivity or the satisfaction of the knowledge worker. But we do know quite a bit about improving both. Indeed the two needs: the need of business and the economy for productive knowledge workers and the need of the knowledge worker for achievement, while distinctly separate, are by and large satisfied by the same approaches to managing the knowledge worker.

(1) We know first that the key to both the productivity of the knowledge worker and his achievement is to demand responsibility from him or her. All knowledge workers, from the lowliest and youngest to the company's chief executive officer, should be asked at least once a year: "What do you *contribute* that justifies your being on the payroll? What should this company, this hospital, this government agency, this university, hold you accountable for, by way of contributions and results? Do you know what your goals and objects were? And what do you plan to do to attain them?"

Direction of the knowledge worker toward contribution—rather than toward effort alone—is the first job of anyone who manages knowledge workers. It is rarely even attempted. Often the engineering department only finds out, after it has finished the design, that the product on which it has been working so hard has no future in the marketplace.

(2) But at the same time, the knowledge worker must be able to appraise his contribution. It is commonly said that research is "intangible" and incapable even of being appraised. But this is simply untrue.

Wherever a research department truly

performs (an exception, alas, rather than the rule), the members sit down with each other and with management once or twice a year and think through two questions: "What have we contributed in the last two or three years that really made a difference to this company?" and "What should we be trying to contribute the next two or three years so as to make a difference?"

The contributions may indeed not always be measurable. How to judge them may be controversial. What, for instance, is a greater "contribution": a new biochemical discovery that after five more years of very hard work may lead to the development of a new class of medicinal compounds with superior properties; or the development of a sugar-coated aspirin without great "scientific value" that will improve the effectiveness of pediatric medicine by making the aspirin more palatable for children, while also immediately increasing the company's sales and profits?

In fact, unless knowledge workers are made to review, appraise and judge, they will not direct themselves toward contribution. And they will also feel dissatisfied, non-achieving and altogether "alienated."

(3) Perhaps the most important rule—and the one to which few managements pay much attention—is to enable the knowledge workers to do what they are being paid for. Not to be able to do what one is being paid for infallibly quenches whatever motivation there is. Yet salesmen, who are being paid for selling and know it, cannot sell because of the time demands of the paperwork imposed on them by management. And in research lab after research lab, highly paid and competent scientists are not allowed to do their work, but are instead forced to attend endless meetings to which they cannot contribute and from which they get nothing.

The manager may know the rule. But

rarely does he know what he or the company does that impedes knowledge workers and gets in the way of their doing what they are being paid for. There is only one way to find out: Ask the individual knowledge worker (and the knowledge-work team he belongs to): "What do I, as your manager, and what do we in the company's management altogether, do that helps you in doing what you are being paid for?" "What do we do that hampers you?" "Specifically, do we give you the time to do what you are being paid for, the information you need to do it, the tools for the job?"

(4) Knowledge is a high-grade resource. And knowledge workers are expensive. Their placement is therefore a key to their productivity. The first rule is that opportunities have to be staffed with people capable of running with them and of turning them into results. To make knowledge workers productive requires constant attention to what management consulting firms and law firms call "assignment control." One has to know where the people are who are capable of producing results in knowledge work—precisely because results are so very hard to measure.

Effective management of the knowledge worker requires a regular, periodic inventory and ranking of the major opportunities. And then one asks: "Who are the performing people available to us, whether they are researchers or accountants, salesmen or managers, manufacturing engineers or economic analysts? And what are these people assigned to? Are they where the results are? Or are their assignments such that they could not produce real results, no matter how well they perform?"

Unless this is being done, people will be assigned by the demands of the organization—that is by the number of transactions rather than by their importance and their potential of contribution. In no time they will be mis-assigned.

They will be where they cannot be productive, no matter how well-motivated, how highly qualified, how dedicated they are.

One also has to make sure that knowledge workers are placed where their strengths can be productive. There are no universal geniuses, least of all in knowledge work, which tends to be highly specialized. What can this particular knowledge worker do? What is he doing well? And where, therefore, does he truly belong to get the greatest results from his strengths?

Most businesses and other organizations as well spend a great deal of time and money on the original employment of people who, it is hoped, will turn into knowledge workers. But at that stage one knows very little about the future employes—beyond the grades he got in school, which have little correlation with future performance capacity. The true personnel management job, in respect to knowledge workers, begins later, when one can place the worker where his strengths can be productive because one knows what he or she can do.

Skills and Ability Manual strength is additive. Two oxen will pull almost twice the load one ox can pull. Skill is capable of subdivision. Three men, each of whom has learned one aspect of a skill, e.g. glueing the legs to a table, can turn out far more work of equal skill than one man skilled in all aspects of carpentry. But in knowledge work two mediocre people do not turn out more than one man capable of performance, let alone twice as much. They tend to get in each other's way, and to turn out much less than one capable person. In knowledge work, above all, one therefore has to staff from strength. And this means constant attention to placing the knowledge worker where what he can do will produce results and make a contribution.

Knowledge is perhaps the most expensive of all resources. Knowledge workers are far more expensive than even their salaries indicate. Each of them also represents a very sizable capital investment —in schooling and in the apprentice years during which the worker learns rather than contributes (such as the five years which every chief engineer knows will be needed before the young graduate can truly be expected to earn his salary). Every young engineer, every young accountant, every young market researcher represents a "social capital investment" of something like $100,000 to $150,000 before he starts repaying society and his employer through his contributions. No other resource we have is equally "capital intensive" and "labor intensive." And only manage-

ment can turn the knowledge worker into a productive resource.

But also, no one expects to achieve, to produce, to contribute quite as much as the knowledge worker does. No one, in other words, is more likely to be "alienated" if not allowed to achieve.

Not to manage a knowledge worker for productivity therefore creates both the economic stress of inflationary pressures and the highly contagious social disease of distemper. We can indeed measure neither the productivity nor the satisfaction of the knowledge worker. But we know how to enrich both.—Peter Drucker

The Wall Street Journal, Nov. 7, 1975

Leader Behavior

In the dynamic organization, the leader contributes to performance and satisfaction to a greater extent than in the hierarchical organization because in the dynamic organization the work is not so preplanned and because more problems arise which require cooperation to solve. In addition, providing information to organizational members on the goals and activities of other employees and units facilitates task performance. Finally, as we said in chapter 5, performance is the product of motivation and ability. If ability is high, as it often is in the dynamic organization, potential performance is high. The supervisor's responsibility is to insure that the potential is achieved—that human resources are used to capacity.

How can a leader be effective in a dynamic organization? In chapter 13 we defined the factors that seem to be important in determining effective leadership style. They are briefly noted here:

1. *Structuring Behavior.* Behavior of a manager, or leader, which emphasizes task direction, planning, organizing, and controlling.

2. *Consideration.* Behavior which demonstrates concern for others.

3. *Task Structure.* The extent to which jobs are well-defined or ill-defined.

4. *Work Climate.* Two types of work environments were proposed. A satisfying climate is high on trust and group cohesiveness. Dissatisfying climates are more negative in the sense that there is lack of consensus, at least between the leader and the group.

5. *Subordinate Characteristics.* It is likely that the level of ego-involvement in work will be high in dynamic organizations. A large proportion of members will have, as noted, a professional orientation. We might also expect lower authoritarianism in the dynamic organization.

The primary factor that must be taken into account when considering leadership style for a dynamic organization is that the tasks are primarily unstructured.

Low Task Structure

In dynamic organizations, professionals and managers are often shifted from one project to another as they are needed. We have defined the nature of project management in chapter 7. Because of the volatile environment of a dynamic organization, projects will change periodically, and members of such organizations will sometimes find themselves in ambiguous situations. They will, perhaps, not know how to do a particular job or solve a new problem. This can occur when they are not sure what skills are required or, if they do know, they do not possess those skills. Another possibility is that an individual may not know how his particular competence fits with others in the organization. For example, suppose one employee is an expert on propulsion systems and another is an electronics communications specialist. Both of these persons may be extremely competent in their own fields of specialization, but if a project requires interdependent effort, then some way to integrate and coordinate their work must be devised. If they themselves are uncertain as to how to proceed, they will not function at maximum efficiency. Under the conditions of low task structure—when there is a high level of task ambiguity—and where there is a satisfying climate condition, the best leader approach is one which emphasizes initiating structure behavior, as in figure 14.2.

Structuring behavior will have desirable effects on performance and

FIGURE 14.2 Leader Behavior Repertoire
in a Dynamic Organization
(low task structure)

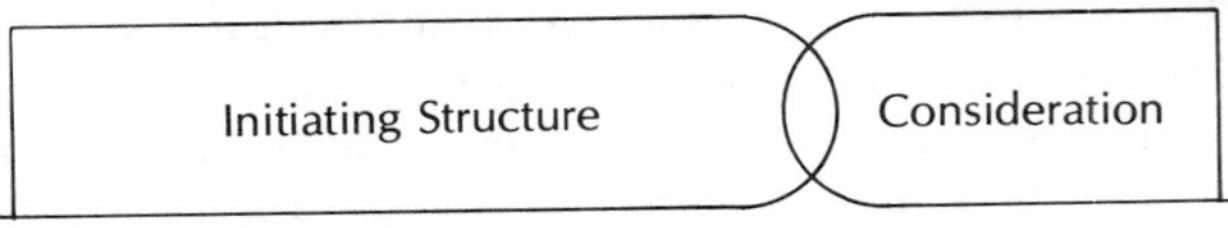

| Initiating Structure | Consideration |

satisfaction because, where "tasks are varied and interdependent and where teamwork norms have not developed within the group, initiating structure and close supervision will regulate and clarify path-goal relationships," or show the staff the way the job should be done (House, 1971). In a dynamic organization, then, a manager must exhibit a behavioral style that is more directive and work-oriented than in the stable organization. He should focus on defining subordinate tasks, fixing responsibilities, planning, budgeting, and controlling. This will impose performance pressures on the group, and, so long as these pressures are not intense enough to induce dissatisfaction, good results may be obtained. Of course when subordinates become very frustrated (see chap. 3) or come under great stress, then high consideration *in addition* to high structuring behavior may be necessary.

In the dynamic organization, structuring leader behavior will be seen as goal-oriented toward the accomplishment of organizational objectives. House and Mitchell (1975) conclude that in an ambiguous work setting, managers who are seen by their subordinates as achievement-oriented are likely to contribute positively to group satisfaction and performance. Part of the reason for this lies in the high task involvement of organization members. They desire high performance.

The research (House and Mitchell, 1975; Crandever, 1976) indicates that, in general, participation is related to both positive attitudes and performance in work settings typifying a dynamic organization. In the dynamic organization, participation is stressed not only to obtain acceptance of a decision but because the leader lacks the information necessary to make the decision himself. The low authoritarianism, high task involvement, and professional orientation characteristic of subordinates in the dynamic organization facilitates the use of participation.

How a Manager Can Improve Performance

There are a number of possibilities for dealing with poor performance in the dynamic organization, and here we will analyze some of the possibilities and suggest the circumstances under which they are most likely to be effective.

Increase Participation. One way to improve performance is to increase participation in decision making. We have already shown that MBO is especially useful in this type of work setting. (The use of MBO is discussed extensively in chap. 12).

Replace Members with Others of Greater Ability. Whereas in the bureaucratic organization, technology, plant, and equipment are important, individual skill and ability are critical in the flexible organization. When there is congruence between leader style and work requirements, but performance is still low, then it may be that employees, either managerial or professional, must be terminated (or transferred) and more competent ones hired. Of course, it may not be necessary to replace whole units. The least competent should be replaced.

Change Leader Behavior Style. The leader may be able to shift his behavioral repertoire in order to obtain the required congruence. When a considerate leader wishes to engage in more structuring behavior, he may do so by emphasizing the following:
1. Facilitate more the rough allocation of sufficient resources (time, supplies, equipment, etc.)
2. Increase emphasis on the importance of deadlines, budget constraints, and adherence to policy.
3. Schedule more meetings to develop plans for units at lower levels.
4. Take a more active part in the re-defining of tasks and the design of projects, taking more firm stands on positions, making subordinates more aware of the differentiation in organization levels that exist between superiors and subordinates.
5. Actively engaging in coaching functions, helping subordinates to understand their jobs better.

Change Leaders. The acceptability of a leader in the dynamic organization is of course as important as it is in the hierarchical. In the dynamic organization, the legitimacy of the leader may be determined by his professional credentials. If these are not sufficient to obtain "legitimacy," a change in leaders may be necessary.

Communications

There is more horizontal communication in flexible organizations (Burns and Stalker, 1961), than in stable organizations. This is due, perhaps, to the fact that in dynamic organizations, as we have noted, there is a higher proportion of highly specialized persons, professionals, than in the hierarchical organization, and the presence of such personnel is related to high horizontal communication (Hage, Aiken, and Marrett, 1971).

In the dynamic organization, there will be a substantial emphasis on committees as problem-solving devices. This condition emerges from the need to coordinate the activities of diverse professional groups. Committees will also provide feedback to members about performance. Where there is more differentiation—that is, decentralization of authorities—there will be more meetings, more upward, downward, and horizontal communication.

The loose, flexible structure of the dynamic organization, with its constantly changing work requirements, needs free-flowing information. Communications channels must be adaptive, constantly changing as different problems arise.

Status in the dynamic organization will be more related to the importance of the skill area of the person than to organizational levels. We can expect to find a good deal of interprofessional rivalry, which could give rise to a communication barrier. Resolution of this problem can be facilitated to some degree through effective use of committees.

There will be a need for quick information transmission, in order to respond to the changing environment. This leads to a greater emphasis on oral communication.

Problem solving, rather than the persuasive mode, will tend to be the dominant type of communication approach in the dynamic organization. This is because the nature of the problems is such that all organizational members will be contributing to solutions. The problem itself will be the important factor in the situation. An example of this situation was in the practices of two dentists studied by Carroll (in press). Both of these dentists had unusual practices in that they employed from 12 to 15 dental auxiliaries each, plus salaried dentists to handle very large patient loads. One dentist specialized in oral surgery, while the other specialized in trauma work—the rebuilding of a mouth after accidents. In the oral surgery practice, the work was highly programmed and all patients, auxiliaries, and dentists worked under very specific established procedures for cases, all of which tended to be quite similar. In the trauma practice, however, each patient was examined by a group consisting of two or more dentists, a technician, and several auxiliaries. A conference was held in the presence of the employing dentist in which ideas were solicited from all present, including the auxiliaries, about what to do for the patient's problem. This use of a task team in the problem-solving process was probably quite functional in this situation, where each patient's problem was unique and where a maximum number of suggestions were desirable.

In larger organizations, committees and task teams are also more common in dynamic than in stable organizations (Friedlander, 1970). In a study of 16 social welfare and rehabilitation organizations, Hage, Aiken, and Marrett (1971) found a significantly higher number of committee meetings in the less formalized organizations.

Use of Committees

Committees are contrived groups, meeting periodically. They may be established for a variety of purposes—investigation and reporting, generating new ideas, making decisions—or they may be created in order to coordinate the activities of several groups in the organization.

It is the committee meeting that is of most significance. Committee members meet together to discuss the issues before the committee. Committee effectiveness in reaching its objectives depends on several factors. One important factor is the structure and composition of the committee. Others are the communication process and the deliberation process. For example, committees should not be too large, and they should contain individuals with the necessary authority to get information and make decisions. They should be motivated to solve the problem, and they should have individuals with similar personal characteristics such as equal status, which, if different, could hinder full participation by group members. Studies have examined how differences in the way the meeting is conducted can influence the results obtained. For example, it has been found that in addition to the formal agenda, or official task, before the group, there is often a "hidden" agenda. The hidden agenda involves the personal objectives of those at the meeting (e.g., to increase one's prestige, to humiliate others, to gain control over an activity, or to sabotage a new policy or procedure). A hidden agenda may prevent attaining the group's tasks. Certain behavior by the group leader may contribute to the effectiveness of the meeting. For example, separating the *obtaining* of ideas from the *evaluation* of ideas leads to improved group meetings. Bringing opposition to proposals out in the open may also facilitate the accomplishment of a group's task objectives (Maier, 1963; 1970).

Much research has been directed at group or committee decision making. Obviously, meetings consume time that could be used for other productive purposes. As the group becomes larger, the meetings become more costly. Some research has shown that individuals working individually on a problem are more effective at reaching certain solutions than when working collectively (Bunker and Dalton, 1965). However, this depends upon the type of task on which the group is working (Bunker and Dalton, 1965). On some types of tasks there appear to be benefits in using the group meeting. Groups seem to be more effective than individuals when the problem requires a profusion of possibilities or where a pooling of information is required (Bunker and Dalton, 1965). Where the problem is such that many things have to be kept in mind simultaneously, and then developed as a whole, then the group's performance may be no better than that of its most superior member (Bunker and Dalton, 1965). Group meetings, when used for the right problems and in the right way, can result in greater acceptance and understanding of a particular decision (see chap. 11).

Committee size research shows that as groups get larger, beyond six or seven, the members lose their ability to keep track of all the other members of the group, as well as the task of the group itself (Hare, 1962). Smaller groups make quicker decisions than larger groups (Filley, 1970). As groups increase in size, their willingness to participate decreases. In larger groups, subgroups may form. Individuals identify with the subgroups rather than the larger group. In one study of 48 groups of different sizes, in larger groups there was less willingness to make contributions and the group members felt more threatened (Gibb, 1951). Bales (1954) also found a larger percentage of infrequent contributors in larger groups.

Groups may also be too small to be effective. If groups are too small, the members become overly concerned about social acceptance. Controversy is avoided in favor of superficiality. Members of small groups may be too tense to work effectively together (Filley, 1970). In odd-numbered groups there may be less disagreement and antagonism than in even-numbered groups (Filley, 1970).

Thus groups should be of size that members feel willing to express themselves openly, to work constructively on the problem, and yet to show respect for the needs and feelings of others (Slater, 1958). And of course the group must contain the skills and knowledge necessary to solve the problem confronting it. That is why, no doubt, that research has shown that in groups dealing with complex problems, groups of 12 performed better than smaller groups of 6 to 8 (Fox et al., 1953).

What are characteristics associated with effective meetings? On the basis of a review of research in this area, Filley (1970) concludes the optimum number of group members is five—assuming that there is sufficient skill in the group to solve the problem. Individuals who are similar may be able to get along with each other, but how about productivity? In one series of studies, groups composed of individuals with similar personalities were more productive, especially on tasks where there were time pressures and on which agreement was necessary (Schutz, 1955). Other studies show, however, that groups with dissimilar members are more effective. If close agreement is required to reach a solution, similarity among members contributes to reaching agreement. On the other hand, if the task is somewhat difficult, it might be best to have individuals in the group with different specialities or abilities (Filley, 1970).

The role of the committee chairman is important. There are two leadership roles in groups—a task role and a group-maintenance role. The task role includes those activities necessary to accomplish the group's objective, such as to solve a problem. The group-maintenance role includes those activities involved with maintaining group morale, harmony, or cohesiveness. (These activities are necessary in family life also.) Filley (1970) concludes that the research shows that the most effective chairman is one who is able to perform both these roles effectively at the same time. If a chairman cannot be effective in both of these roles, the task role seems most important. The chairman must perform the task role effectively to be accepted by group members.

Managing Organizational Stress

The concepts of organization stress, role conflict, and role ambiguity are discussed extensively in chapters 4 and 13. Role ambiguity is likely to be a particular problem in the dynamic organization, because the uncertainty rising out of the complex and volatile nature of the environment pervades the nature of the tasks.

Role Ambiguity

Role ambiguity has two dimensions. The first, *task ambiguity*, is uncertainty about what a person should do. The second, *social-emotional ambiguity*, occurs when a person is uncertain about how he is evaluated. Two general conditions which generate role ambiguity are characteristic of the dynamic organization:

(1) *Organization Complexity*. As the organization achieves moderate size, it may be increasingly difficult for an individual to see how his work is related to that of others.

(2) *Rate of Organizational Change*. When the environment changes, internal relationships among jobs will change. Thus, different perfor-

mance criteria may become important at different points in time (Kahn et al., 1964).

The effects of role ambiguity are increased tension, dissatisfaction with work, increased distrust, and poor relationships with others. As Hamner and Tosi (1974) note, role ambiguity may be more of a problem at higher levels than at lower. It is also more pervasive in the dynamic organization than in the bureaucratic one.

Task Ambiguity. In the bureaucratic organization, more precise task definition often flows from the narrowness of the job requirements and the stability of the organization. In the flexible organization, on the other hand, the configuration of activities (tasks) required to achieve an objective or complete a project changes over time. Since dynamic organizations are usually staffed primarily by highly trained people, including professionals, these employees will know how to do certain things well, but even though they will know how to do their own tasks, there may be a great deal of ambiguity arising from their job's relationship to other jobs. The research scientist may be extremely skillful in studying the physical properties of electrons, for example, but may not be able to understand how her work ties in with an entire project. In short, ambiguity may develop because personnel do not know the goals to which their activities should be directed.

Another type of task ambiguity may face the project manager responsible for bringing together experts from different disciplines to solve a problem. He may be uncertain of what different competencies should be brought in; his problem is one of determining which configuration of skills is required. Only after this decision is made can thought be given to the problem of integrating and coordinating their effort.

Social-emotional Ambiguity. Social-emotional ambiguity stems from lack of awareness of the criteria used in evaluation. In most flexible organizations, individuals are assessed on the basis of how well the project turns out and/or how well they carry out their tasks. When the project life does not coincide with budget and planning cycles or compensation review periods, this kind of assessment can present a problem. If a project is completed in mid-February, say, but the personnel review period is set for mid-June, months may pass before a superior makes a determination of what the success or failure of the project means in terms of promotions or changes in pay. It will therefore be difficult to link rewards and performance, since they are separated so far in time.

Strategies for Reducing Role Ambiguity

There are a number of methods by which a manager in a dynamic organization can reduce role ambiguity.

1. *Clarify the path-goal relationship.* In his path-goal theory of motivation, House (1971) emphasizes that the manager's role is one of insuring clarity of the relationship between the goal (expected results) and the path (how it should be done). Since the expert, or professional, in the dynamic type of organization knows how to perform (the path), the manager must do his best to state *expected goals* as clearly as possible. If this is done, the professional can then assess whether or not, with the competence he possesses, he has a reasonable likelihood of reaching the goal.

2. *Define expected work behavior.* Some consensus should be achieved between the manager and the subordinate about how the work will be done—unless the manager is willing to let the employee make this decision. If such an approach is taken, however, the manager must be willing to trust the judgment of the expert. He should not continually be monitoring what is being done.

If the manager has preconceived notions about the best way to accomplish an activity, whether it comes from past experiences or from his own personal bias, he should let the subordinate know his preferences.

3. *Assess performance on the consensus criteria.* If assessment is based on an agreement between the superior and subordinate on how the task is to be done, then the question becomes "Was it done as agreed?" The level of success or failure is secondary, from an evaluation point of view.

These suggested strategies for dealing with role ambiguity, the reader will note, follow closely the MBO strategy suggested in chapter 12, as well as in the early part of this chapter.

Role Conflict

The negative effects of role conflict are intensified internal conflict, increased job tension, reduced job satisfaction, and low trust. In the flexible organization the role conflict will take the following forms:

Intersender Role Conflict. This type of role conflict, caused by inconsistent demands from two or more sources, will not be as frequent a problem in the dynamic organization as in the bureaucratic organization, because under a project management type of structure it will be necessary to constantly redefine superior-subordinate relationships so that the individual will know, as a result of recent project change, to whom he is responsible in carrying out certain duties and assignments.

Person-role Conflict. Person-role conflict occurs when organization demands conflict with an employee's basic values. As we have seen, it may not occur to an important extent in hierarchical organizations, but it will present a special problem when a member of an organization has been trained and indoctrinated in a profession with high ethical standards and feels that the organization requires actions that are below this standard, or where the person has learned certain specific ways of doing his job. When this is the case, and demands conflict with these points of view, individual problems will be aggravated to the point where employees may elect to leave. Research on attitudes of professionals and scientists indicates that they often feel that managers act in unethical ways (Moore and Renck, 1955).

Interrole Conflict. When an individual is subject to incompatible pressures because he has more than one role, interrole conflict is present. A scientist who is also a supervisor may face contradictions in his feelings about his responsibilities to the organization and to his professional field. The college professor who identifies more strongly with his professional colleagues than with his school, or the lawyer who identifies more strongly with the legal profession than with his firm, both find themselves in a position where other professionals expect a particular behavior from them which is difficult to perform because of organizational demands.

Strategies for Dealing With Role Conflict

Since there are individuals who place a high value on their professional roles, provision must be made to give them—as part of their jobs—some opportunity to feel that their work has this value. Here are some strategies to reduce role conflict and to instill such a feeling.

Clearly Define Project Structures. The manager should spend time developing the authority-responsibility relationships for projects. Not only is it necessary to determine what should be done, but also who in the organization is responsible for doing it. Then this information must be communicated to those who will do the work. It will usually also be useful to specify the length of time an individual will be assigned to a project.

The specification of time limits provides the individual with important information about *who* can initiate action for him, and for what period of time. For example, an engineer assigned to a project team to develop a new communications system for a space satellite, say, may be assigned to the project team for a six-month period, and during that time the chief of the project is his superior. Unless the project assignment is then extended, at the end of the six-month period the engineer should be able to count on returning to his regularly assigned department. If the assignment is extended, the length of time of the extension should also be specified, of course.

Set Aside Time for Professional Activities.   If the person is an active professional whose external relationships represent legitimate demands, time should be allowed to maintain those external relationships. Work can often be scheduled around these, and the organization may even pay for part of the expenses connected with attending such meetings.

Select Those Who Have Values Compatible with the Organizational Requirements.   Person-role conflict can be minimized by careful screening of job candidates. If, for instance, a firm is a major defense contractor, it should, of course, screen out applicants who have strong antimilitary tendencies.

The process of screening, however, can be too carefully done. The flexible, dynamic organization needs a variety of different skills and inputs, and excessive care in a selection strategy could result in the hiring of applicants whose points of view are so narrow and rigid that they would limit the creativity required to successfully adapt to a volatile environment.

Assign People to Permanent "Groups."   One way to resolve intersender conflict is to assign each employee to a group, or department, with someone in charge. They may be loaned to other projects as needed, but they should always have a departmental contact. An engineer may be assigned to the Communications Systems Department, for instance, but could be loaned to different projects as necessary.

Managing Conflict

The management of a conflict can be especially important in a dynamic organization, partly because it is important to retain people who have special skills and partly because there are special causes of conflict in dynamic organizations.

Sources of Conflict

Resource allocation problems are found in dynamic organizations, just as in hierarchical organizations, but two other problems surface as well. The first arises from differences between professional groups. The second is conflict between specialists and managers.

Resource Allocation. In flexible organizations, budgets are likely to be drawn according to particular projects rather than departments. A project budget is one in which resources are allocated on the basis of a particular set of activities for the purpose of the achievement of a project goal. Project managers will of course compete for additional shares of a scarce resource, and since projects generally represent new or different endeavors for an organization, those who know how to develop plans and execute them will have more power, based on expertise, than the budget group, who must rely on the experts' recommendations. Project directors may tend to overestimate resource requirements to avoid being caught short—a kind of competition that bids up project cost and can be very dysfunctional for the organization.

As is the case with bureaucratic organizations, budget allocations in dynamic organizations are also thought of as indicative of the status and priority of an activity. This being so, project managers will generally seek to raise the level of this indicator to increase their own and their unit's importance. Conflict is especially likely when there appears to be an excessive level of support for one project and only minimal support for another.

Status Differences. Among professionals in dynamic organizations, status problems are more likely to exist between different professional and technical groups—that is, horizontally—than between levels, as is the case in bureaucratic organizations. Status differences may also reflect the priority of different projects in the organization.

If a dynamic organization is staffed with professionals and technical experts who have invested much personal time in the development of their competence (which is usually the case), differences in status associated with interprofessional rivalry will exist, because in their training they are likely to have been indoctrinated with values stressing the importance of their own group.

On the other hand, differences in status associated with priorities assigned to different projects is an organizationally-induced condition. In any firm, some activities are clearly defined as having higher priority than others, while at the same time, *all* projects are likely to be staffed by individuals who believe their skill and competence are important. They will be highly committed to a professional area of expertise, and yet they see that this area is not considered as important organizationally as some others. Differences between an individual's self-perceived status and the priorities associated with projects give rise to feelings of resentment.

Specialist/Administrative Conflict. The problem of authority is difficult in the flexible organization because the specialist, or professional, possesses technical expertise (a form of power) and is probably more capable of making decisions within his sphere of competence than the manager in charge of his organizational unit. Yet the line manager is still "responsible" to higher organization levels for the operation of a unit. Victor Thompson (1963) calls this "specialist/administrative conflict." It is a common problem in both flexible and mixed organizations. Advances in technology and market volatility make it difficult for those in higher-level positions who are no longer working directly in the technical field to maintain their high skill levels in those fields, and since organizations attempt to manage lower levels from higher levels, this difference in competence between lower and higher levels, and the right to make a decision and the ability to make it, causes conflict.

The feasibility of tentative goals of an organization are often technical questions. Thus they are best evaluated by specialists, although the superior in an organization has the right to approve or object to such tentative goals. The utility of a goal is a matter best left to the judgment of technical specialists, yet they do not have the power of decision. In large, complex organizations, the problem is made still more complex by the need to involve many specialists, or departments of specialists, in problem solving with managers. This problem of the "right to decide" causes both the specialist and the administrator to resort to the use of role defense mechanisms.

Specialist role defenses are oriented primarily toward the profession or the skill area in which the specialist functions or operates. He may seek peer support. The role defense of those in hierarchical positions is somewhat different. The administrator may make appeals to organizational loyalty or attempt to assert the power of his hierarchical position.

The Balance of Power

In the flexible organization, power will be based primarily on one or more of these factors: (1) technical expertise, (2) being in a role in a critical boundary position, (3) the amount of ownership interest one has in the organization, and/or (4) the priority of a project.

Expert Power. A dynamic organization succeeds or fails depending on whether or not the technical competence is present to perform the work. The organization may be more dependent on the expert than vice versa. Additionally, we have seen that it is unlikely that managers possess the technical skill required to evaluate alternatives and design projects well, because, even though they may have had technical competence early in a career, moving into an administrative job makes it difficult to maintain competence in rapidly developing and changing fields. This leads, in dynamic organizations, to the relegation of hierarchical (formal position) power to a secondary status.

Boundary Positions. Those positions in an organization which interface with the external environment are called "boundary positions." Individuals in boundary positions must possess the ability to interpret changing environmental conditions and translate them into meaningful objectives for the organization. Such individuals will have a great deal of power because of the importance of their ability to the organization. They may very well experience high levels of role conflict because of different demands from the external sector and the internal organization, but they will still have a significant effect on the determination of what the organization will ultimately do.

Financial Interest. In a smaller organization, where the ownership is not broadly dispersed to a large number of small shareholders, financial interest can be especially powerful. That is, an owner can exert a great deal of influence on the setting of organizational objectives—and he may do this completely arbitrarily, with only rudimentary competence.

The Priority of a Project. The priority assigned a project can be another base of power. Managers who are in charge of a project which is assigned a high priority will have a great deal of influence (power) in the organization. For example, a firm may have three projects under way simultaneously. One may involve several millions; the other two, only several hundreds of thousands of dollars each. Obviously, the success of the firm economically is more contingent on the first than on the last two, and the manager of the first will have much more organizational power than the manager of the last two.

Resolving Conflict

In an organization using project management, it may be difficult to create interdependencies between main projects in such a way that they will increase organizational cohesiveness. For instance, the work of a group working on project A may have no relation to the work done by the project B group. The success of either group in achieving project objectives may be independent of the other, and yet conflict arising from status differences between the two project groups may be hampering total effectiveness. Two approaches are suggested by Margulies and Wallace (1973) to resolve this problem. They are the use of team-building approaches and/or exchange of members.

Team Building. The negative stereotypes of one group concerning another may lead to ineffectiveness. In team building an effort is made to increase the accuracy of both groups' perceptions. Each group initially meets separately to compile a list of reasons why they can't interact effectively with the other—to identify the causes of the problem. The groups then meet jointly, exchange lists, and discuss them. Margulies and Wallace (1973) say:

> Reactions and questions are responded to at length, though a ground rule limiting debate helps avoid rationalizations and justifications, facilitates the process of getting data out, and establishes a norm of *listening*, a critical factor in effecting change in the relationship. At this point careful *differentiation* of the groups, their needs and their perceptions is important. It often helps to have the groups meet separately to discuss discrepancies in perceptions and the quality of the differences between groups.

Margulies and Wallace go on to say that after differentiation has occurred, the integrating process can begin. This can be started by having selected members from both groups meet to form a new group and devise strategies for solving the problems, plans for implementing the strategies, and a way to follow up to see that the solutions are implemented.

This method can be effective, according to Margulies and Wallace, when the conflict is creating critical problems, when key members of both groups are willing to face the issues, when there is acceptance between the groups of a third-party facilitator, and when there is a general agreement to utilize and follow up on the solutions proposed.

Exchange of Members. One reason why conflict often persists is that members of a specific group never leave that group and never operate in other groups. Thus, over time, they build up a loyalty to their own group and develop distorted perceptions of others. It may be possible to reduce some conflict situations by exchanging members of the two groups; for example, by transferring some staff from project A to project B, and vice versa. Such reassignment can have the effect of introducing different viewpoints into both groups, and of correcting misconceptions.

Margulies and Wallace suggest that this strategy will be effective under the following conditions:

1. There are persons [in both groups] whose technical competences overlap.
2. The difficulties are not rooted in deep-seated hostilities, prejudices and biases toward others.
3. Preliminary diagnosis indicates that the problems arise out of lack of understanding and appreciation of the other groups.

Other Approaches. Some of the techniques noted in chapter 13 may be as useful in the flexible organization as in the bureaucratic. For the most part, however, the use of formal hierarchical mechanisms and formal departments is an ineffective approach in the dynamic organization. In fact, their use often increases difficulties. The use of committees, increased participation, and replacement of personnel, however, may have beneficial effects in the dynamic organization.

As with the suggested approaches to managing hierarchical organizations in chapter 13, the techniques outlined in this chapter seem especially congruent for the dynamic organization. However, they may have some utility in other organization settings for they represent, we believe, a point of departure toward solving human problems.

Discussion Questions

1. Performance evaluation for professionals in the dynamic organization focuses on means, not ends. Discuss this point of view.

2. What are the inherent problems with peer evaluation of performance? What are the advantages?

3. Why is reinforcement, as a managerial motivation strategy, not effective in a dynamic organization?

4. Can you specify the conditions under which an effective leader (say high in initiating structure behavior) in a dynamic organization would be effective in a hierarchical one?

5. Specialist/administrative conflict exists when the professional (with the skill to make a decision) has to deal with a manager (who has the right to decide). Why can such a problem exist in an organization in which everyone works toward the same goal? Or does it?

6. One suggested approach to improving leadership is to "change the level of position power." What kind of problems do you expect to have to deal with if you reduce someone's position power?

7. List the positive and negative aspects of working in the dynamic organization.

8. Indicate why *you* would or would not want to work in a dynamic organization.

9. Some dynamic organizations eventually become more stable. Describe some of the problems that might be anticipated if this occurs.

10. What performance appraisal techniques would seem to be most useful to the organization in the dynamic organization? Which is most acceptable to the managers and professionals in this type of organization? Why?

Chapter 15
Managing in the Mixed Organization

By definition, the mixed organization contains subunits which have stable environments and subunits which have volatile environments —the level of environmental stability, of course, being relative. That is, classifying environments as *either* stable *or* volatile oversimplifies reality but is necessary for purposes of analysis and discussion.

In the market-dominated mixed (MD-mixed) organization, the market is volatile and the technological sector is stable. Lawrence and Lorsch (1969) describe a container company which had an uncertain market environment, since demand for their product (corrugated boxes for poultry, citrus fruits, beer, etc.) varied with changing geographic demand, weather conditions, and competitor actions. On the other hand, the processes for manufacturing these containers did not change significantly in any short period of time.

Conversely, the technologically-dominated mixed (TD-mixed) organization has a volatile technology but a stable market. In one firm of moderate size which manufactures picture tubes for television sets, there were some startling technological advances over a short period of time. "Quick heat," which allowed the tube to project a picture more quickly than before, was introduced, as were new methods of safeguarding tubes against the possibilities of fire or explosion. The product changed and the technology had to change to keep pace. On the other hand, the customers (manufacturers of television sets) were limited in number and readily identifiable, and demand for the new type of tube was highly predictable.

Under conditions such as this there is a need to recognize that the structure of the different parts of the organization must vary—each unit must be appropriate for the level of uncertainty of the environment with which it interfaces. We have pointed out in previous chapters the managerial processes that are the most appropriate in stable organizations and in dynamic organizations. The discussion in those chapters is relevant to the mixed organization also, since the management processes appropriate to the stable organization are also appropriate to the stable organizational units in the mixed organization, and those appropriate to the dynamic organization are appropriate to the dynamic organizational units in the mixed organization.

Many managers in mixed organizations do not understand the necessity of such a differentiation in terms of structures and management. One large company in another country, for example, is composed of a number of subsidiary companies organized into an appliances division, an electronics division, and an industrial goods division. The practice in the organization was to require all subsidiary companies to adhere closely to the organization's personnel policies even though this caused problems for certain units. For example, the technologically advanced companies had to promote from within and were not allowed to hire individuals with advanced technological training and experience, even though this was necessary to keep abreast of changing scientific and technological developments. As a result, the more technologically-sophisticated subsidiaries were falling behind competitively. In addition, the decision-making structure, supervisory style, performance-evaluation procedures, and personal characteristics of employees were not differentiated among the appliance companies (in stable environments) and the electronic and industrial goods companies (in dynamic environments). Top management felt that one particular managerial approach would be effective in *all* the subsidiaries. Similarly, Lawrence and Lorsch (1969) report that several U.S. companies they consulted were not aware of the importance of establishing the appropriate type of differentiation, given a particular state of uncertainty. Thus, a lack of awareness by managers of the research on organizational design, along with a belief in "universal" managerial principles, contributes to continued managerial problems rising simply from the existence of ineffective structures of organization.

Figure 15.1 represents the mixed organization we have been discussing. It shows two organizational units, one flexible and one bureaucratic. Manager X of the flexible unit will need to operate with a loose structure, make decisions under uncertainty, and often must manage highly trained personnel such as engineers, or marketing professionals. On the other hand, it is likely that manager Y of the bureaucratic unit will find that he is responsible for a highly routine system with well-defined decision rules and policies. These differences between the organizational units may create problems for manager X and manager Y—and also for manager Z who must manage the interface between the units.

The factor determining the severity of this interface problem is the

FIGURE 15.1 The Interface Problem in the Mixed Organization

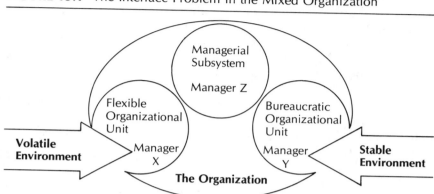

amount of interdependence between the units. In the mixed organization, it is likely that in some units the work flow requires that two units must work closely together. Obviously the greater the interdependence, the higher the need for integration. In the same organization, however, still other units may have little contact.

The achievement of integration between diverse organizational units is a worthwhile goal, since high degrees of integration are associated with high economic performance. The most integrated firms are the most successful—where integration between units is necessary because of their interdependence (Lawrence and Lorsch, 1967).

Successful integration is not necessarily a matter of avoiding conflict in all situations. Conflict between two organizational units may be reduced or eliminated, and yet the units may not work together productively in achieving organizational objectives. We know also that conflict among or between organizational units may actually be useful in terms of organizational goals if it stimulates creativity. This is an especially important factor in volatile organizational settings, particularly where the fostering of innovation is important.

In addition, since all organizations have multiple objectives, many of which do not fit together neatly, some means must be found to satisfy all of an organization's objectives to at least some degree, and this occurs often through conflict and then compromise. For example, if an organization wants to produce a product where the objectives of cost, production ease, and technological sophistication are all important, conflict between the marketing department (concerned with price), the production department (concerned with manufacturing efficiencies), and the research and development unit (concerned with emphasizing technological sophistication) may have beneficial effects, since a compromise embodying all of these considerations may result.

At the same time, conflict can be harmful if it takes certain forms. This is why in the rest of this chapter the emphasis is on the positive management of conflict, in contrast to allowing conflict to occur without taking action to channel it into behaviors that are not harmful to the organization. In any organization, efforts should be made to integrate the activities of various organizational units—most especially those with interdependent work, but before we begin to link differentiated systems together, we should be aware of the causes of problems that must be solved.

Causes of Integration Difficulties

There are some natural pressures which will drive the hierarchical unit to be separate, or differentiated, from the flexible unit of the mixed organization. As we have seen (chap. 14), the organization unit at the volatile boundary will be most influential in terms of company policy and strategy. There is some support for the notion that when one group dominates another consistently and imposes its views consistently over time, the less powerful group's negative reactions tend to produce conflict (Walton and Dutton, 1969). These differences lead to differentiation, both formal and informal, of the hierarchical and dynamic units. For example, a relationship which was strained and obviously unsatisfactory to both parties is that described between a company's engineering and marketing departments in Hampton, Summer, and Webber (1973). The situation began to develop when an engineering department was criticized for low productivity. The engineers blamed their low productivity on the time they had to spend consulting with members of the marketing department about price quotations to customers. The engineering department initiated a procedure to keep track of the amount of time they were spending with marketing personnel. The procedure, resented by marketing department representatives, required them to sign in and out of the engineering department. Although some marketing managers did sign the register, many refused to do so and the number of contacts with engineers dropped off significantly. Some marketing personnel then refused to provide information to engineers. This, of course, reduced the cooperation between the units.

In general, individuals will increase interactions which in the past have been pleasant to them and will try to avoid interactions which are emotionally distressing. Feelings of exploitation can easily arise when one individual or group feels that they are providing more benefits to another party than they are receiving in return.

Feelings of inequity which can create strong behavioral reactions in individuals can also contribute to poor relations among groups. If one group feels that another group is being unfairly favored in an organization, it may do what it can to make the other group look bad and to suggest that the favored treatment is unjustified (Seiler, 1963). A group may be favored by top management because it performs functions perceived to be very important to the organization, but in this situation other organizational units are of course likely to feel that their activities are undervalued by top management, especially if the favored groups are composed of highly specialized and educated individuals competing with the less-favored line management groups for recognition.

When groups compete against one another they tend to develop distorted and inaccurate perceptions of themselves and the other group. The differences between them are exaggerated, and the similarities are overlooked. Negative stereotypes are formed of the other group and positive stereotypes of an individual's own group, and it becomes increasingly difficult for a group to see merit in another group's ideas or position on an issue. Each group becomes more susceptible to influence from its leaders, and if such influence is directed at maintaining the conflict situation, this adds to the conflict reinforcement resulting from the perceptual distortions. The question is, what are the causes of these difficulties and how can they be treated managerially?

Organizational Differences

Figure 15.2 shows some of the differences between the internal structures of the hierarchical and dynamic units. Such differences have been shown in some research (Lorsch and Morse, 1974; Hall, 1973), and while it is true that any particular organization may not have exactly these characteristics, they seem to be very prominent generally. Specifically, there will be differences in these units in their (1) general structure, (2) objectives, (3) bases of authority, (4) bases for compensation, (5) evaluation criteria, (6) organization climate, and (7) organization status.

Objectives. Different organizational groups have different assigned objectives, and these become the objectives of the individuals in those units. The manufacturing unit is concerned about production effi-

FIGURE 15.2 Organizational Differences Between the Hierarchical and Dynamic Units

Factor	Hierarchical	Dynamic
General Structure	Emphasis on Rules More Formality Limited Autonomy in Decisions Narrow Job Definition	Less Rigid Structure Fewer Rules and Policies Greater Discretion in Decisions More Job Scope
Objectives	Short-range/ Cost	Long-range/ Development
Bases of Authority	Position Power Commitment to Organization Centralization	Skill and Expert Power Commitment to Self and Discipline Decentralization

Bases of Compensation	Level and Relative
	  Importance of the Position
	Increases Based on
	  "Merit" and Tenure
		Quality of Training
		  and Experience
		Increases Based on
		  Experience in Area of
		  Competence (Maturity Curves)

Evaluation Criteria	Objective Measures
	Focus on Results as Outcomes
	Short Time Span between
	  Performance and Results
		Subjective Criteria
		Focus on Activities
		  rather than Results
		Long Time Span between
		  Performance and Results

Organization Climate	Rules-oriented Formalism	Innovation-oriented
Status	Lower	Higher

ciency, downtime, and scrap, for example. The marketing unit is concerned about customer satisfaction through service and prompt delivery. The research group may be primarily concerned with product quality and performance. The time span for objectives also differs. The production unit tends to have short-range objectives, while the research group has long-range objectives. These different sets of objectives contribute to a great deal of disagreement among such organizational units.

Differences in objectives also contribute to differences in the way causes of problems are perceived. Dearborn and Simon (1958) showed that even though executives when faced with a problem evaluated the same set of facts, the *cause* of the problem was attributed to different difficulties. The sales executives tended to see a sales problem, the production executives saw a need to clarify the organization, and the personnel managers saw human relations problems.

Authority Differences. There is some evidence that in the better-

performing organizations, power or influence resides at higher management levels in the stable organizations or units and at lower management levels in the dynamic organizations or units (Lawrence and
Lorsch, 1969; Lorsch and Morse, 1970). These differences in power
may in themselves contribute to conflict, and they presumably relate
to differences in the origin of power and influence in the stable and
dynamic units. In the stable organization we find power and influence
based on position power or control over resources, while in the dynamic organization, knowledge of how to do the job is most critical
and influence arises out of personal skill and expertise (Friedlander,
1970).

The five types of power listed by French and Raven (1959) are: reward power, coercive power, legitimate power, referent power, and
expert power. (We have discussed variants of these in chap. 8.) Some
research shows that organizational members in dynamic units are
likely to respond best to expertise rather than to the other bases of influence (Miner, 1973). In the more stable line departments, however,
legitimate, reward, and referent power are more important (Miner,
1973).

Thus, at the interface between the hierarchical and dynamic organizational units of an organization, one group may not respond well to
the influence attempts of another group because each is using an appeal which is acceptable to its members but not to the other. Other
problems at the hierarchical/dynamic interface arise because authority
in the stable unit tends to be concentrated at the top—exercised in a
hierarchical format—while in the dynamic unit authority is dispersed
among many individuals and is weighted by the technical expertise of
the individual. This situation often creates serious frustrations for
personnel in the stable organizational units because they have difficulty in identifying the individuals in the dynamic unit who are appropriate to contact in terms of the required authority.

Authority differences also cause difficulties because as an organization has more specialists (professionals) with technical expertise, line
managers may feel a sense of frustration—of loss of control. Victor
Thompson (1963) sharply makes this point:

Modern bureaucracy attempts to fit specialization into the older
hierarchical framework. The fitting is more and more difficult.
There is a growing gap between the right to decide, which is authority, and the power to do, which is specialized ability. This gap is
growing because technological change, with resulting increase in
specialization, occurs at a faster rate than the change in cultural def-

initions of hierarchical roles. This situation produces tensions and strains the willingness to cooperate. Much bureaucratic behavior can be understood as a reaction to these tensions. In short, *the most symptomatic characteristic of modern bureaucracy is the growing imbalance between ability and authority*. . . .

Compensation Bases. For an organization with components in two different environments, we can expect two different bases for the determination of pay. In the flexible units, the quality of a person's training and experience is important. What he has done, where he has been to school, and his achievements in other organizations will be critical in determining his basic pay rate. In addition, increases in compensation may come from an assessment of how well the individual is recognized in his professional area of competence.

On the other hand, traditional methods of determining pay levels may be used in the stable sector. The background of the individual is much less an important determinant of salary level than is the level and relative importance of the position held by the individual, as determined through job evaluation procedures. Increases in compensation will be based on merit (which is more likely to be assessed in terms of hard measures of performance), as well as tenure.

When different systems of compensation are used, feelings of inequity may arise. If line managers in production groups are paid bonuses on the basis of profits of their unit, and specialists and staff personnel are paid bonuses on the basis of subjective appraisal, individuals who do badly under the pay system used for them (whichever it is) will believe the other system would be more appropriate for their situation.

Performance Evaluation Criteria. The bases for evaluating the performance of organizational members in the stable and the dynamic units of a mixed organization will probably differ. In fact, they probably should differ, since if the evaluation system is not considered appropriate for the task, the individual performing that task tends to be dissatisfied (Scott et al., 1967). In dynamic units, composed of professionals or highly-specialized managers, performance evaluation will lean toward the subjective. It is *less* easy to quantify output measures in such units, so the focus of concern must be on whether or not a particular individual has gone through the steps required to complete a particular task. Since the results of the task may not be seen for a long time (i.e., there is a longer time span between performance and results), managers in the flexible unit are faced with the problem of determining whether or not an individual's—or group's—activities are likely to yield desired results. It may also be necessary to use outsiders (in addition to insiders) as evaluators—as is done, for example, in evaluating university professors—since higher-level managers do not have the technical competence to make such judgments.

In the stable units, the superiors can typically carry out the evaluations themselves without the aid of others. In one mixed organization, a group of supervisors and peers in the research and development department evaluated the effectiveness of the technical personnel. When a management by objectives program was introduced into the company, one of the reasons for its rejection by the research and development unit was that the system did not provide for a group evaluation of the performance of the technical personnel, and their immediate superior felt he was unable to make such a judgment. In this instance, some personnel in the stable departments of the company felt that the dynamic department was simply being contrary in its opposition to the new program. They did not realize that the new performance evaluation system failed to accommodate the needs and special evaluation problems of the unit involved.

Differences in the methods of evaluation used may lead to feelings of inequity, especially when such methods influence pay. They may also lead to feelings of jealousy between groups, especially on the part of those whose performance is rated low, and this can lead to conflict.

Organization Climate. The organization climate refers to how an organization's practices and procedures are perceived by organizational members, and the relationship of such perceptions to ways of thinking about the organization and subsequent behavior (Schneider, 1974). Members of an organizational unit tend to agree on their climate perceptions, and they do, in fact, behave in ways which are congruent with their perceptions of the kinds of behaviors supported or rewarded by the organization (Litwin and Stringer, 1968).

The climate of an organizational unit will also affect certain types of orientations of organizational members (Litwin and Stringer, 1968). Higher perceived amounts of structure, or formalism, have a tendency to arouse power needs and to reduce achievement and affiliation needs for individuals. Thus, in stable organizational units we would expect higher concerns about power than in the dynamic units. On the other hand, in dynamic units where there is informality in structure, high standards of performance, encouragement of innovation, and toleration of conflicts, the need for achievement is aroused. So,

organization climate can be expected to affect the way representatives
of various groups think, behave, and attempt to solve problems when
working together in an interface situation.

Status Differences. The status of individuals is their hierarchical
ranking in a group. Individuals have high or low status depending on
their relative ranking against others in the same group. Within an organization, groups also will have different status levels. In general,
units operating in the more volatile boundary of an organization will
have the highest status because they are the units (and individuals)
upon whom the organization must depend for adaptation to change.
The dynamic unit will also tend to have highly educated specialists in
it, since such personnel are needed to cope with its environmental
uncertainties (Thompson, 1967). This means, often, that the specialist
is in a situation where his skills and ability are very important, and he
is less dependent on the organization than it is on him. Such persons
may enjoy more organizational privileges than others. Some of the factors which reflect status differences are shown in figure 15.3.

FIGURE 15.3 Factors Likely to Result in Status Differences Between
Flexible and Hierarchical Units in a Mixed Organization

Stable (low status)	Factor	Flexible (high status)
Less Years of Formal Education	Education	More Years of Formal Education
Functional Training		Technical Training
Greater Restrictions, Adherence to Rules, Policies, and Procedures	Organizational Privileges	More Freedom, Travel, Benefits, Autonomy
Individual More Dependent on Organization	Direction of Dependence	Organization More Dependent on Individual

Usually, persons with high status, or those from high-status organizational units, feel it appropriate for other units or persons to acknowledge their superior status. Thus, where the market forces involve much uncertainty, the marketing units will attempt to dominate.
When the technology is volatile, the technology or production units
will try to exert influence over the more stable units. For example, in
a small company manufacturing soaps and detergents, the production
technology was fairly stable, but competition with other firms in the
industry was very keen. Profits of the firm depended, to a consider-

able extent, on the effectiveness of the advertising and sales promotion programs. In this company, the marketing deparment dominated both the production and the research departments. On the other hand, in a company which manufactured electronic test equipment for industrial customers, successful competition was based on performance characteristics of the equipment as compared to other equipment available in the market. In this company, the research department was the highest-ranking organizational unit and it imposed its desires on all other departments (Seiler, 1963).

For a variety of reasons, there may or may not be acceptance of the dominance by the higher-status group. For example, there may be a time lag in the acceptance of a lower status on the part of a department. In one company, the production department's status had declined relative to marketing as production techniques became more standardized. But the production units refused to accept fully the higher status of sales until after the older production managers retired and were replaced by new personnel.

If a lower-status department attempts to influence a higher-status department, this violates the higher-status group's expectations of what is appropriate behavior for a lower-status group. For example, in a company making diesel engines, the product design engineering group refused to accept suggestions from the drafting section, even though the draftsmen provided a useful source of good design ideas (Lawrence et al., 1965).

In the company mentioned earlier which manufactured electronic test equipment, new product ideas were developed in the research and development department (Seiler, 1963). The research design then went to production engineering where the blueprints were drawn, specifications determined, and parts lists developed. Then the product went to production for a test run, and finally to full production. Relations between production engineering and production were not cooperative, however, and there was much delay in putting new products on the market. Certainly part of the reason for the poor relationship between these two departments was the perceived lower-status production engineering staff, who seemed to be telling production what to do, when the production staff felt no sense of inferiority to the engineers.

Differences in Individuals

Lorsch and Morse (1974) conducted a major study which shows that different kinds of organizations will attract and retain individuals

FIGURE 15.4 Some Individual Differences Between Members of Stable and Dynamic Organizational Units

Stable	Factor	Dynamic
Low	Tolerance for Ambiguity	High
Low	Integrative Complexity	High
Toward Position Power	Attitudes Toward Authority	Toward Autonomy
Low	Individualism	High
Low	Outside Reference Groups	High
Low	Professional Values	High

with different kinds of value orientations. Figure 15.4, which is based on this research, summarizes some of the differences between individuals in different groups. We would generally expect such differences to exist between hierarchical and dynamic units in mixed organizations.

Integrative Complexity. Integrative complexity is an individual's capacity to deal with a variety of information, understand it, and integrate it in order to solve problems. Lorsch and Morse found that in plants (hierarchical organizations), managers generally scored low on the measure of integrative complexity. On the other hand, managers of research laboratories (dynamic organizations) had high levels of integrative complexity.

Tolerance for Ambiguity. Tolerance for ambiguity is an individuals's capacity to function in uncertain situations. High tolerance for ambiguity means that a person is capable of operating without precise job definition and with unclear authority responsibility relationships and high degrees of uncertainty about evaluative criteria. A person with a low tolerance for ambiguity has a need for structure and definition of activities. Lorsch and Morse found that R & D managers have high tolerances for uncertainty, while plant managers have low.

Attitudes Toward Authority. If it is true that individuals in flexible organizations will have higher educational levels than those in hierarchical organizations, then we can expect their attitudes toward authority to be different than those of people in hierarchical organizations. In general, those with high educational levels are less tolerant of directive leader behavior. Thus, Lorsch and Morse found that managers in dynamic units tended to have a preference for more autonomy than those in stable units. On the other hand, managers in hierarchical organizations seemed to have a preference for strong authority relationships, or high position power. Hall (1973) found professionals to be high in preferences for autonomy, especially those professionals who work in informally structured organizations.

Attitudes Toward Individualism. Lorsch and Morse also measured the degree to which individuals prefer to work alone or with others. They found that in production plants, managers wanted more extensive involvement with others and to work in groups. The characteristics of members in the research laboratory were quite different. Their preference was to operate alone.

Orientation to Outside Reference Groups. Managers and professionals with an inside-the-organization orientation are sometimes referred to as "locals," while those who identify with outside reference groups are called "cosmopolitans." The cosmopolitans are influenced by outside groups. They attempt to adhere to what they perceive to be the values of their profession, and they therefore are less loyal to their employing organization than the locals. This contributes to value conflicts between the two groups.

Value Differences. Some research shows that differences in what is valued contribute to high conflict and low integration (Seiler, 1963). Other research has illuminated these value differences between professionals and line managers (Moore and Renck, 1955; Danielson, 1960; Pelz and Andrews, 1968; Litterer, 1970). Professionals and scientists are concerned less with money and promotions than are managers, and more with the intrinsic nature of their tasks. In addition, professionals and scientists tend to have a longer time perspective than line mangers and are more concerned with product quality and being candid in presenting information than are managers. The specialists and professionals place a higher value on research than do line managers, and value the scientific approach more than the line manager. This can create hostility, as Moore and Renk (1955) indicate in their study of the satisfactions of professionals in industry:

It seems clear from the evidence available that the professional is job-oriented. He is concerned primarily with competent performance in his chosen field. He seeks status through specialization.... General management, on the other hand, takes pride in its integrative skills and its ability to move about freely in a variety of fields. From management's standpoint, the specialist often appears to be overelaborating the obvious. . . . It is frustrating to management representatives who must try to simplify the environment and cut through a mass of detail to be confronted by specialists who seem equally bent on complicating the environment beyond reason.

From the professional's standpoint, there is often the feeling that management does not know what it is doing. The analytical mind finds the integrative mind somewhat inconceivable, perhaps even a little obnoxious. The ability to reach decisions on the basis of partial information and what might appear to be flimsy evidence is not held in high esteem by the professional. In fact, in professional circles, this borders on charlatanism.

Integration in the Mixed Organization

Perhaps the most effective way to approach the problem of integrating units with divergent tasks, values, and people is to have the appropriate form of organization structure. The primary coordinating mechanism in any organization is the managerial subsystem. A manager's responsibility is to effectively integrate the interdependent groups under his level and to resolve conflicts that occur among them. A superior can be effective in resolving conflict by persuasion if the conflict is not too serious and if the superior is esteemed by the groups involved. If the groups are not too differentiated and if both groups identify with the same objectives, the task is easier. Of course, a superior can use his authority or use sanctions to force one or both groups to take particular actions, but this can lead to enduring feelings of resentment or a perception that a superior was unfair or arbitrary. One approach to the design of structure for the mixed organization is the matrix form.

Matrix Organization

The matrix form of organization has been found useful when it is necessary to integrate the activities of many different specialists while at the same time maintaining specialized organizational units (see fig. 15.5). The two alternatives to the matrix form are usually *functional organization*, in which organizational units are formed of different specialists, and *product organization*, in which all the different specialists needed to produce a given product are in the same unit. The former approach obviously makes it difficult to achieve the integra-

FIGURE 15.5 Matrix Organization

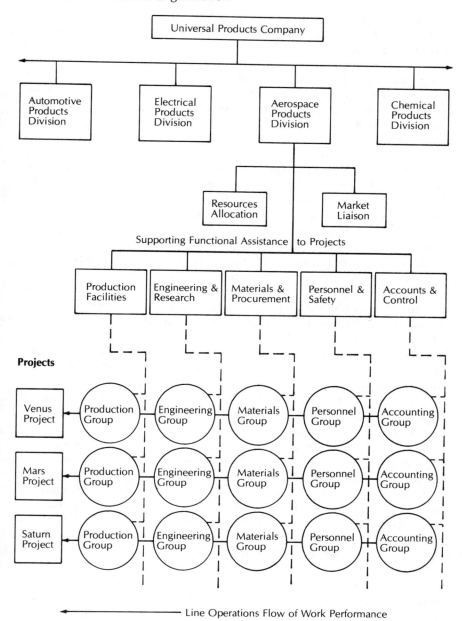

————————— Line Operations Flow of Work Performance

Copyright, 1964, by the Foundation for the School of Business at Indiana University.

tion of the different specialists, while the latter does not allow specialists sufficient access to other specialists and often results in too many specialists of a certain type working at less than their capacity on a particular product.

In the matrix organization (like the project management form discussed earlier), specialists from specialized organizational units are assigned to one or more project teams to work together with other specialists. For example, chemical, mechanical, industrial, and electronic engineers may work together in a team with physicists, accountants, human engineers, and other professionals to develop a new product. Each member of the team is subject to dual authority. He takes orders from the project manager and from the manager of his specialized department. The goals of each of these managers may be different. In the aerospace industry, for example, the project managers tend to be concerned about meeting schedules within budgetary limitations and in producing output within previously planned specifications (Galbraith, 1973). The specialized unit managers, on the other hand, are primarily concerned with full utilization of existing resources and the long-term development of such resources and high technical performance (Galbraith, 1973). The individual members of the project team should be able to integrate their efforts better within a group than when they are merely the representatives of their own specialized groups. Retention of the specialized organizational units, however, enables the individual specialist to obtain help from professional colleagues on technical problems and gives him the opportunity to identify with his professional group and to learn and grow in his profession with the help of others. The use of specialized organizational units also makes for more efficient utilization of human resources for the organization and less duplication of resources.

The matrix form of organization is also used outside industrial settings. For example, one college of business administration uses a matrix form of organization. Faculty members are assigned to their specialized departments such as marketing, finance, management, accounting, and so on. Then there are program managers for the undergraduate program, the graduate program, the management development program, and so on. Each faculty member may work for the several program managers for varying amounts of time.

While effective, the matrix form is not a panacea. Disagreements occur between managers of different projects and between project managers and managers of specialized departments. In addition, the members of the project team themselves often receive incompatible requests from their two superiors and therefore experience considerable role conflict and stress. They also often experience insecurity because they are working on temporary projects.

Even though the matrix form of organization may be the most appropriate way to structure a mixed organization, there will still be integration problems stemming from the structural and individual differences we have noted earlier in this chapter. The manager of the mixed organization may find the following approaches useful in addressing these difficulties: (1) system re-design, (2) confrontation approaches, (3) appeal systems, and (4) the use of superordinate goals.

System Redesign. If integration problems are due to the design of the work system, then the system can be restructured and the conflict reduced. For example, if the problem is that a lower-status group is initiating action for a group which perceives itself to have a higher status, the problem might be alleviated by using a liaison individual or group to coordinate both groups, by re-designing the work flow so that the lower-status group does not impose its wishes on the higher-status group, by transferring certain elements or personnel in the lower-status group into the higher-status group, or by combining the two groups into one.

Some of these possibilities are shown in figure 15.6. Let us assume that work flows from unit A to unit B and from unit B to units C and D, as shown in example 1. Let us further assume that the relationship between units B and C is quite poor. This could be true for a number of reasons. Perhaps the quality of work performed by unit C depends upon the quality of the work received by it from unit B and this dependency is resented by C. Or perhaps unit C's personnel consider themselves to be superior to the personnel of unit B, but unit B's personnel seem to be giving them orders. For whatever reason, the relationship between B and C is quite unsatisfactory, as shown in example 1, figure 15.6

In example 2, direct contact between units B and C has been avoided by placing a liaison between them. Research shows that this individual (it can be a group) is most effective if he has values approximately midway between the values of the personnel in the two units to be integrated (Lawrence and Lorsch, 1969). The title of the liaison, or integrator, commonly varies according to the kind of organization in which it is found. In an organization with many products, for instance, the liaison may be called "product manager," and be in charge of coordinating all of the various specialized units which produce particular products. The liaison individual should be a person who has high influence in the organization, which gives him power, and he

FIGURE 15.6 Examples of Possible System Relationships

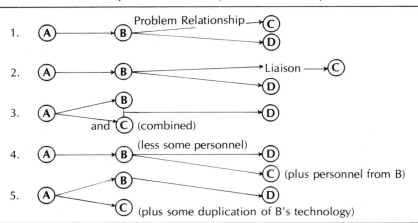

should also be expert enough in the areas he is coordinating to know when one group attempts to mislead others. The integrator is also more effective if he has the behavioral skills to be a good conference leader and if he has the reputation of operating in the interests of the organization as a whole. In some organizations, the integrator has only informal authority, but in others he has formal authority and can employ sanctions against those who are not cooperative. For example, he may be given a budget and therefore some control over resources (Galbraith, 1973).

In example 3, units B and C have been combined, a strategy that takes advantage of the fact that most individuals feel inclined to help fellow group members, as we stated in chapter 4.

In example 4, a segment of unit B has been transferred to unit C. The new personnel in unit C now no longer represent unit B but identify with their new group, unit C. Of course, there will not be an immediate identification, but it will come with time, especially if the new personnel are treated with respect by the original members of unit C. This approach was used with some success in a chemical company when chemical engineers were transferred from a research unit to an engineering unit with other types of engineers (Seiler, 1963). The chemical engineers moved from a low-status position in a high-status organizational unit to a high-status position in a lower-status organizational unit.

Example 5 shows a situation in which interactions between units B and C are no longer necessary because unit C has duplicated, within itself, those activities formerly performed by unit B. Unit C might establish its own production subunit, for example, or its own product-planning subunit, which would make it unnecessary for it to have any interaction with unit B. In many companies this kind of a situation evolves naturally when the relationships between groups become so unpleasant there is strong motivation to stop all interaction (Seiler, 1963). This approach can be taken by management consciously in a reorganization program, or informally by the parties themselves, provided they can obtain the necessary resources. Seiler reports several instances in which scientists in research departments set up and ran their own production equipment to avoid interactions with a production department.

Sometimes a procedural change, rather than a change in the structure of organizational units, can solve the problem. For example, conflict between two groups can be the result of one group frustrating another group in the latter's attempts to achieve its objectives. This frustration leads to aggressive feelings and behaviors directed at the other group. In one company, the marketing group, after receiving orders from customers, found that the credit department often did not allow certain orders to be shipped when the order exceeded the customers' credit lines with the company. The marketing personnel—not knowing a customer's credit standing—had already counted on receiving credit in the bonus system for the sales and were naturally angered by this. The situation was improved by having the orders sent to the credit department for approval *before*, rather than after, they were sent to the marketing department (Chapple and Sayles, 1961).

Confrontation Approaches. In some organizations, there seems to be a belief that if conflict is ignored—or suppressed—it goes away. There are unwritten norms against raising issues that are particularly troublesome to members. Usually problems won't go away; they need more than aspirin and rest. One way to resolve conflict is by confrontation—to face up to the conflict and allow each party to express its hopes and views. One study of six firms in the plastics industry showed that the more successful firms used confrontation more extensively than did the less successful firms in dealing with conflict (Lawrence and Lorsch, 1967).

If there are differences between the hierarchical and dynamic units of the kind shown in figure 15.2, we might then expect confrontation to be more tolerable in the dynamic unit because disagreement and conflict are considered to be part of the course of scientific investigation. In the hierarchical unit, harmony, compliance, and formality might lead to less tolerance of confrontation. If so, such differences with respect to the desirability of conflict and confrontation can create difficulties at the hierarchical/dynamic interface.

The nature of the issues in the conflict are of great importance. Research has shown that conflict over technical issues (such as differences in opinion on product design) is related to high performance, but that interpersonal conflict (based on personality factors or styles of behavior) contributes to lower performance (Miner, 1973). In confrontation it is important to keep the discussion impersonal and focused on the problem to be solved or the task to be done—not on the parties involved.

Various confrontation approaches are used in organizations in dealing with conflict. An older approach is bargaining, and there are two forms of this approach—*distributive bargaining* and *integrative bargaining*. Distributive bargaining involves a situation where one party's loss is another's gain. Conflict over the allocation of limited resources is an example of such a situation. Here the objectives of the conflicting parties are contradictory and some type of compromise is usually worked out. In integrative bargaining, on the other hand, there is the possibility of a solution that will benefit both parties. This is most likely when one group has too many resources and another not enough, or two groups can reduce costs or increase revenue by sharing.

A more recently developed confrontation approach—encounter groups—has been found to be useful in improving the relationship between two or more groups, especially where perceptual distortion and the development of negative stereotypes within each group have exaggerated group differences and provided a justification for the resulting dysfunctional interaction patterns. In the encounter group resolution approach, the conflicting groups are brought together to discuss the weaknesses in their relationship and to work out a new relationship. For example, two groups of female professionals were in conflict in a health facility. Both groups were brought to a conference site for a period of two days. The first day each group met separately to discuss the weaknesses and strengths in its own group as well as its perception of the other group. Each of the groups then selected a spokesman to communicate this perception to the other group. The groups were then brought together to provide feedback to each other on how they perceive their present relationship. Then they met separately again to discuss this feedback and to work out a plan for a better relationship.The two groups then met together once more and devised a plan to develop an improved relationship with one another. The initial reaction after such an experience was that satisfaction with the group relationship improved as a result of the encounter-group experience. After a period of six months, however, the attitudes had started to regress toward their old levels, perhaps because no changes in the structure of the organization were made, and the underlying problem (inequitable treatment of the two groups) remained. Only some of the perceptual distortions were changed by the experience. Thus, in using this approach, there must be a real change in the organizational or social system itself if relationships are to be significantly improved over the long run.

Although the research evidence supports the personal confrontation approach as a means of improving organizational effectiveness (Blake, Shepard, and Mouton, 1964; Lawrence and Lorsch, 1967), it is not easy for a manager to use this technique. Generally most people wish to avoid open conflict, avoid expressions of emotional feelings, and not openly show antagonisms toward others. Furthermore, the candid expression of feelings and individual perceptions is often seen as quite risky by the parties concerned, since they become vulnerable because of their disclosures.

Personal confrontation is most likely to be effective when certain conditions exist (Walton, 1969). First, both parties must be motivated to eliminate or reduce the conflict, and it is best if both are motivated to use this approach at the same time. Next, the organizational power of each party should be equal. In addition, the conflict dialog should contain a time period or an opportunity for both parties to describe the points of disagreement and to express their feelings about them, and then a time period when the parties can express their similarities and common goals and their wish to more effectively manage their disagreements. Results are also likely to be better when the participants know how to provide interpersonal feedback and reassurance, clearly understand what the other party is saying, and maintain a productive level of tension (neither too high nor too low) during the dialog. Managers should be taught these skills in organizations where integration problems are common and where confrontation is established as the procedure for resolving conflicts.

Appeal Systems. In many companies, formal appeal systems have been established so that organizational members can obtain another judgment on a dispute not successfully solved at a lower level (Scott, 1965). Typically, however, such appeal systems are for rank-and-file employees and not for higher-level personnel such as managers and professionals. A common approach is to send the appeal to a higher organizational level until it is either solved to the satisfaction of the parties or they accept the situation. The sequence is often this: to the supervisor, to the department head, to the personnel department, and finally to the president (Scott, 1965). In companies with unions, formal grievance procedures usually are used. The union will process a grievance for any employee at a particular level, such grievances usually involving a disagreement between the company and an employee about the employee's rights as specified in the labor contract.

Use of Superordinate Goals. Sometimes relationships between groups in conflict can be improved through the establishment of superordinate goals (Sherif, 1961), goals which are desired by two or more groups but can only be reached through cooperation of the groups. For example, the replacement of a departmental bonus system with a plant-wide bonus system may help induce the various departments in the plant to work together more effectively. Suppose that managers in a production department manufacturing a home appliance are paid a bonus based on lowering of production costs. This department is not cooperative with the marketing department, however, in its attempts to service important customers and in obtaining the cost estimates needed to provide bids to customers. The conflict between the departments could be improved if the company would shift from a "cost center" bonus system to a "profit center" bonus system in which the amount of sales and the price received for the product influence the amount of bonus that the manufacturing managers receive. The new system rewards the manufacturing managers as well as the sales managers for obtaining new customers and servicing customers more effectively.

Integration has historically been a concern of management. The degree of integration generally refers to the amount of collaboration among organizational units or the unity of effort available for the achievement of organizational goals. Integration is especially difficult to achieve in the mixed organization because the subunits have diverse characteristics. In this chapter, we have discussed integration problems and how they might be solved. The same techniques can be used in the hierarchical and dynamic organizations discussed in previous chapters, or when there is an integration problem between two stable organizational units or two dynamic organizational units.

Discussion Questions

1. Provide some examples of a market-dominated organization and a technologically-dominated mixed organization.

2. Discuss the "images" the organizational members in the stable and dynamic units in the mixed organization would have of each other. What would be some of the consequences of these images?

3. Openly confronting conflict is often recommended today. What are some of the advantages and disadvantages of this? If differences among organizational members or between groups are to be discussed openly, what rules or procedures may minimize the difficulties associated with this approach?

4. Is your university a mixed organization? Why or why not? Give examples.

5. Will increased communication between organizational subunits decrease conflict and increase cooperation? Why or why not?

Part VI
Organizational Change

People and organizations change. In chapter 16 the factors which induce the structure of the organization to change are considered. Essentially, the position in this book is that when the environment changes, the organization must also change unless it is able to find a more hospitable environmental sector.

In chapter 17, the strategies to change individuals are examined. Chapter 17 assumes that the structure is relatively appropriate for the environment and that the organization can be "fine-tuned" by seeking to better fit the individual and organization.

Chapter 18 discusses characteristics of the "effective" organization and describes some of the future forces which organizations will have to cope with successfully to remain effective.

Chapter 16
Changing Organization Structure

In chapters 6 and 7 we showed how the organization's structure is related to the nature of the technological and market environment in which it operates. Those structures, of course, should be considered only as models of particular types, not as unchangeable absolutes. The relationship between groups and departments, even in bureaucratic organizations, changes. In the bureaucratic organization the change is less rapid, more predictable, and takes place in smaller degrees than it does in the dynamic organization, but there *is* change.

In this chapter we examine ways in which the organization may change, with special concern directed at the formal structure. The basic idea is this: If an organization's structure is a function of the environment, as we have said, then when the environment changes, the structure must also change if the organization is to survive.

What causes the structure of an organization to change? First, a major change takes place when the organization grows. Everyone has seen a church group or a civic association which began as a small informal group of interested people, for some reason become popular and attract membership. Growing pains follow. Rules develop, formal procedures for the election of officers must be designed, and so forth. Business firms are no exception to this rule of change.

Secondly, major changes in the structure of an organization result from changes in its relationship to the environment. Taking the model for understanding the relationship presented in chapters 6 and 7 as representative, then if the environment of a dynamic organization becomes more stable, it must begin to take on more bureaucratic characteristics. Conversely, when the stable environment of the bureaucracy becomes more uncertain, there is no choice but to loosen up the fixed rules, policies, and guides that govern the system if the organization is to adapt successfully.

In this chapter we are concerned with the adaptation of an organization to the external environment and the changes in structure that follow from that adaptation. We will discuss four aspects of structural development and change: first, how structure, both formal and informal, develops; second, the problems associated with change in organization structure in growth periods; third, problems that an organization must face when it finds environmental circumstances changing; finally, how an organization can attempt to influence the conditions of the environment so that its existing structure is compatible with it.

The Emergence of Organization Structure

A narrow view of organization structure is to define it in terms of formal, written factors such as procedures, job descriptions, policy manuals, and organization charts. These devices prescribe behavior for workers and managers. However, they only partially explain member behavior. A more comprehensive and appropriate view is to consider organization structure as the pattern of interaction relationships among organizational members, and to analyze the degree to which behavior is predictable. When there are very stable, enduring, and clear behavioral patterns, we can say that the organization structure is rigid or "tight." The structure is easy to observe and probably simple for new members to comprehend. They can come into the organization, read the appropriate job and procedural description, and begin to contribute very rapidly.

When the pattern is not so stable and clear, or when it changes in short intervals of time, the organization structure can be described as "loose," or flexible.

Not all the patterning of behavior comes from the formal definitions prescribed in manuals, job descriptions, and procedures. As we have seen, much of it, even in bureaucratic organizations, stems from the individual characteristics of the members and pressures from groups. This is especially true in new or small organizations. Organizations represent an accommodation to members as well as to environmental demands, especially when there are changes in key members.

In newly-developing organizations, predictable patterns of behavior emerge as members interact with each other over time and find that certain behaviors are accepted by others, make their own work easier, or simplify problems of dealing with others. Consider what happens when two strangers are brought together, for whatever reason, to work on an activity. Without guidance from a third party, they will work out who should do what and when. Over time, if they continue to work together, they will begin to interact in a routine way. As new people are added to work on the activity, they will, initially, have to fit into the existing pattern. But that pattern will change over time to

pletely differentiated in the small firm. The owner-manager will keep his hand on the helm of the ship.

In a small organization, relationships between employees and the manager are likely to be highly personal. In this stage, there are few of the written, formal aspects of organization structure found in larger organizations. Assignment of responsibilities is usually done verbally, thus providing flexibility so that employees can be easily shifted from one job to another, providing the owner with a way to maintain a high level of operating efficiency. What formal structure there is will probably be imposed by governmental requirements for record keeping, such as the maintenance of wage records for social security purposes, reports that may have to be submitted to comply with health and safety laws, and financial reporting for tax purposes.

The objectives of the small firm will be a reflection of those of the owner-manager. The owner-manager expects a reasonable income and living standard (which may be quite high), and at the same time an opportunity to be independent, working for himself in a job which he likes.

FIGURE 16.2 Critical Factors in Stages of Growth

Continua of Growth	1	2	3
Objectives	Comfort-survival	Personal Achievement	Market Adaptation
Policy	Traditional	Personal	Rational
Leadership	Craftsman	Entrepreneur	Professional
Work-group bonds	Fixed Roles	Interaction-Expectation	Homogeneity
Functional development	Single	Successive Emphasis	Full Development
Structure	Power Levels	Field of Force	Rational Hierarchy
Staff	Housekeeping	Technical-Personal	Technical-Coordinative
Innovation	No Creativity	Innovation	Development
Uncertainty-risk	Nonrisk	Uncertainty	Risk
Growth-size economies	Size Benefits	Growth-Size Benefits	Size Benefits

Source: Filley, A.C., and R.J. House. *Managerial Process and Organizational Behavior*. Glenview, Ill.: Scott, Foresman and Company, 1969.

A firm may remain small (in stage 1) if the owner-manager does not want to become involved with, or feels he cannot manage, the problems associated with managing a complex organization. For example, suppose the owner-manager of a small electronics component firm who supplies highly-specialized circuitry for the space program could triple his sales and profits, but only by adding more technical and managerial staff, moving to a different part of the country, and reducing the personal control which he has over the business. Even though there is a high potential for growth, if the owner is not the kind of person who wants to take advantage of it, he may elect to stay small. Many owners of small firms have made such conscious choices, even though the conditions for growth were present.

The Transition to Growth. If an organization is to experience rapid growth, then a number of conditions must exist. Unless they are present, Filley believes, the firm cannot enter stage 2, "Dynamic Growth." The following circumstances facilitate rapid expansion.

1. *Innovation.* Something must occur which makes larger markets available. A new product may be introduced, or an old product may acquire a new potential. A firm may discover a new production method which substantially reduces costs. An invention may provide the innovation necessary.

2. *Significant Returns for Risk.* With innovation, there is usually high risk. There are many innovations that are useful to a small number of people but do not seem to have the potential of large-scale returns. Thus, the risk of undertaking the production and marketing of them may not seem worthwhile. The owner-manager of a small firm must see the potential pay-off of an innovation as far exceeding the risk involved before he will consider expansion and growth.

3. *Entrepreneurial Orientation.* The entrepreneur is an innovator willing to assume risks for expected returns. The owner-manager of the small firm must have an entrepreneurial orientation—that is, he must be willing to take risks—in order to obtain the returns associated with growth. The comfort-survival objective of the owner of a small firm must change; if the opportunities are present but the owner-manager is not entrepreneurially oriented, he will not make the decisions required to move into the second stage.

4. *Additional Resources.* In the dynamic growth stage (stage 2), substantially greater resources will be required to both produce and distribute the product. Often the firm, at this stage, does not have the capacity to generate enough resources to take advantage of the innovation and its potential. An outside source of capital must be found. If

this capital comes from borrowing (which will heavily commit the owner to financial institutions) the lending institutions themselves must see an opportunity for return.

These are the conditions which must be present if an organization is to grow. If it does, then its relatively informal atmosphere will change.

Stage 2: Dynamic Growth

The organization grows because it exploits an innovation in an increasingly larger marketplace. Sales rise, new employees are added, production increases. Growth may be very rapid, initially occurring at an increasing rate. For example, in the first stage, growth may occur at a constant rate of, say, 5 percent annually, but if the firm moves into the dynamic growth stage it may be 6 percent in the first year of stage 2, 7 percent in the second year, 8 percent in the third year, and so on. In later periods of the dynamic growth stage, the rate of growth may begin to slow down. It may move, for instance, from 10 percent in one year to 8 percent the next year, to 7 percent the following year, and so on (see fig. 16.1).

The character of leadership in the dynamic growth stage will be different from that in the first stage. It will still be highly personal, but of course more entrepreneurial and charismatic. This atmosphere will pervade the organization, especially those members close to the chief executive. It is possible that in this second stage, the leader must be someone other than the owner-manager of stage 1. While the owner-manager in stage 1 may be willing to enter the growth stage, he may find difficulties in managing a growing organization. He may want to make policy, but not get involved in the management of it. He may step aside to become the chairman of the board and hire an entrepreneurially-oriented president. He can set the tone, make policy, and handle the more ceremonial, ritualistic activities. The actual operation of the firm will be in the hands of the entrepreneur-president.

The objectives of the organization in this stage are likely to remain a reflection of those of the key executive, who of course is the entrepreneur-president. Filley (1962) describes the president's goal as "personal achievement." Growth, success, and its attendant status and prestige are reflections of the personal needs of the entrepreneur.

As the organization grows in size, and has to add new staff members, new personnel will be heavily influenced by the charismatic personality of the leader. They will be, like him, concerned with growth and willing to take risks for the possibility of substantial long-term payoffs. In the initial phase of the dynamic growth stage, while the organization is still relatively small, new members may be simply an extension of the personality of the leader. He will, through them, manage the growing organization. It is likely that they will make decisions in a fashion consistent with his beliefs, attitudes, and general policies.

During the early phase of stage 2 managers will devote their energies toward exploiting external opportunities, rather than on internal problems of efficiency and effectiveness. This lack of attention to internal managerial problems may impose a cost later, but at the time it can be ignored. For instance, both human and capital resources may lag substantially behind the level that is necessary to adequately support sales. Too, the production system may be extended beyond its capacity in order to meet market needs, thus foregoing necessary maintenance of equipment, which of course could result in earlier equipment replacement. There is a cost when a firm has to replace a capital asset before it would have had to if proper precautions had been taken.

Often at this stage decisions are made to acquire capital resources to support a projected level of activity that in the end proves unrealistic. When this happens, the organization will find itself with excess resources that become a critical managerial problem when it reaches the third growth stage. For instance, during the late 1950s and early '60s, university enrollments were expanding rapidly. During that time, many classrooms and dormitories were built on the assumption that ever-increasing enrollments would require these facilities. The buildings took three to four years from planning to completion, and during that period of rapid growth classrooms and housing facilities were crowded. The resource base lagged behind the level required. In more recent years, however, enrollments have tapered off, and now many universities have excess classroom and dormitory space.

During periods of rapid growth, the large inflow of revenues from increasing sales provides a cushion for internal inefficiencies. High sales and income can cover up many managerial mistakes. If, for example, costs increase more than they might where there was more planning and control, it may be relatively easy to pass these increases on to the consumer. This is especially true of a growing firm which has a monopoly on a particular innovation through patent control or simply because there are few other firms in the industry or market.

Changes in Structure.   As the organization continues to grow it will be necessary to add more personnel, and as more and more people are brought in, it is less likely that those selected will be reflective of the character of the leader and his initial associates. In an effort to insure consistency of decision-making, policies and procedures will have to be formalized (written) to provide guidelines for the growing number of new people, and it will not be possible completely to permeate the growing organization with the strong personality of the entrepreneur. Thus, the structure of the organization will begin to emerge more formally and clearly. The informality of earlier periods will give way to job descriptions, organization charts, and policy manuals.

The maintenance and managerial subsystems (the authority relationships) described in chapter 7 will become more pronounced and clearly separate from the production and boundary-spanning units. Greater predictability of actions from organizational members will be sought by the development of guidelines which delineate the form of the organization's structure relationships between individuals. Employees will then know what kind of decisions to make under what circumstances, to whom they must report, and the general scope of things for which they are accountable to their superior.

In the dynamic growth stage, the status system in an organization will become obvious. Those close to the leader will have access to a larger proportion of organization benefits and prerogatives, both formally and informally, than those not close to him. At the same time, as the organization develops, it may be difficult to determine exactly who is close to the leader and who is not. Some lower-level managers may misrepresent their relationship to the leader in order to enhance their own status.

Policy and procedures will become increasingly evident in order to obtain predictability and control. But their proliferation may be the beginning of such a reduction in the organization's members' freedom that the organization cannot take full advantage of the growth situation. Individuals will begin to be constrained by job descriptions, hierarchical relationships, procedural rules, and control systems. They will be reluctant to go beyond them. One reason for this is that the staff added later in the growth stage will not have an opportunity to get to know the entrepreneur personally, and if they are not as risk-oriented as he is to begin with, they will tend to stay within their position guidelines in order to avoid the risk of failure, with subsequent job loss.

The Transition to Rational Administration. As the organization moves up the growth curve, it may begin to experience competition from other firms. The market, which was once its own, is now invaded by others who see the opportunities for growth and profitability. The firm begins to lose its market advantage. As the market begins to be shared with others, profits begin to diminish. Because of competition, it is more difficult to pass on increased costs to the consumer. Growth begins to slow down because of the external factor of competition—but also because the existence of the more formal structure begins to set the organization in its ways. It becomes less able to capitalize on outside opportunities because it has built up an investment in human and physical resources with particular skills.

The transition period to stage 3 begins as market growth starts to slow. The assets begin to catch up with the output and pressures emerge for more efficient use of resources. To continue to operate at a relatively acceptable level of profit, the organization is forced to look inwardly for effectiveness. That means making better, more efficient, use of its resources.

During such a transition period, the formal structure of an organization begins to become very clear and well-defined. Policies, rules, job descriptions, and the authority structure become fairly firmly set. Managerial and maintenance subsystems to support the production and distribution functions set in place earlier in the life of the organization become more important. This is because many of these subsystem activities will have access to and control over the necessary information and technical competence required to support the increased effectiveness of internal resource utilization.

An important change in the nature of the managerial style begins to occur. In the dynamic growth period, the firm is dominated by the entrepreneur. As the organization moves to the third stage of growth, the managerial style becomes more professional, shifting toward a more impersonal form evidenced by the use of more bureaucratic structure. "Successfully achieved, the move into rational bureaucracy provides the firm with a defensive posture against decline, allowing it a solid and stable base upon which to expand further" (Filley and House, 1969).

Stage 3: Rational Administration

When the organization enters the rational administration stage, it has the characteristics of the bureaucratic form described in chapter 7. It will be structured by a well-defined set of tasks with explicit job definitions, authority-responsibility relationships, and a clear hierarchy of authority and responsibility. The managerial emphasis will be to plan, organize, and control activities in such a way as to insure long-term survival. Such a shift in strategy can be seen in item 17.1, which describes how Polaroid is moving, under its new president, toward a greater emphasis on long-range planning.

In stage 3 the rate of increase in organization size will be relatively modest compared to stage 2 rates. By now, the opportunities for rapid growth created by the existence of innovation in the early stage will be gone. Growth will slow down and markets will become more stable. Because of the stability of the external market and technological sectors, along with the internal rigidities from the development of the bureaucratic formal structure, it is unlikely that the firm will experience a rapid, dynamic growth period again. It may be too large with too much capital investment in resources that cannot be shifted easily to new and different markets where there may be extensive opportunities. If an organization in stage 3 is to experience the rapid growth of stage 2 again, it may have to do so through the process of acquisition and merger. It will likely have to join with other organizations which are in the dynamic growth stage and integrate them into the existing structure of the firm. This will often pose difficult problems of integration of the two different organizations, but it may well be the only way that rapid growth can again occur.

Relationship to Organization Models

How do the ideas of growth described above fit the organization models outlined in chapters 6 and 7? One way to look at this is to think of the small firm (stage 1) as in the quadrant with the volatile market and the volatile technology (see fig. 6.6). As the organization grows in size, it moves away from that quadrant toward the greater stability associated with either the stable market or the stable technology. Organizations in general will move toward, although they may never reach, the quadrant characterized by both a stable market and a stable technology.

Knowing something about the various stages of growth, along with the characteristics of an organization in each of the stages, permits better planning in organizations at various points in the growth cycles. Such knowledge can be critically needed by a firm in the dynamic growth stage passing to the third stage, rational bureaucracy. In this transition period, it is necessary for a stable, well-designed structural system to cope with the problems of the stable environment. The firm that can adapt effectively is likely to be among the most successful and profitable in its industry.

ITEM 16.1   Transition to Stage 3

The Team Builder

Transition—After a Genius. Shortly after William J. McCune, Jr., became president of Polaroid Corp. February 18, he had one wall of his office moved four feet to make more room for meetings. But he wouldn't let the workmen repaint the old walls to exactly match the new one.

"Bill tends to run a fairly frugal show," one Polaroid executive says. "He simply isn't one for flourishes."

Indeed he isn't. Mr. McCune has always stayed so far back in the shadows of more flamboyant Polaroid executives that he is practically unknown outside a close coterie of scientists, engineers and top executives. He joined Polaroid 36 years ago, just two years after its founding, and since 1950 he has headed all Polaroid engineering.

• • • •

Appointment Unexpected. Hardly anyone expected Mr. McCune to become Polaroid's president. He had been executive vice-president since 1969, but he had been talking about retiring since 1965. Polaroid's reclusive, 65-year-old founder, Edwin H. Land, had always been chairman, president, chief executive, chief operating officer and director of research. And even though he had repeatedly talked Mr. McCune out of retiring, most people thought one of two senior vice presidents would someday succeed Mr. Land. (Polaroid has no mandatory retirement age).

• • • •

"Traumatic" News. The news sent shock waves through Polaroid's ranks, already demoralized by a cost-cutting drive, widespread layoffs, pay freezes and rumors of further cutbacks to shore up the company's profits. "It was rather traumatic," one officer says.

Mr. McCune's promotion has only begun a probably prolonged and painful management realignment. Polaroid is a prime example of a company that has grown too big for one or two men to run but has failed to build a strong second tier of management to succeed its aging founder when he finally steps aside.

"It's one of the most difficult kinds of succession situations," a longtime Polaroid executive says. "It's the classic business school case, but it's next to impossible for an outsider to imagine how difficult the transition is going to be."

One outsider who thinks he can imagine is Eugene E. Jennings, a professor at Michigan State University's Graduate School of Business Administration. "Land is a genius, but the time has come for him to get the hell out," says Mr. Jennings. "He's going the way of Juan Trippe at Pan American, Eddie Rickenbacker at Eastern Air Lines, Al Sloan at General Motors, and other builders who stayed too long.

"The most competent people in Polaroid are those just below the top ranks," Mr. Jennings adds. "They've got some very good captains and majors there, excellent people, but their morale and team spirit have deteriorated badly. The company is at a point where it could go downhill very rapidly from here, or it could snap back and go on to much bigger things."

Profits have toppled 60% from their 1969 peak, and the company nearly lost money on U.S. operations last year. Total 1974 earnings plunged 45%, to $28.4 million, or 86 cents a share, on sales of $757.3 million. First quarter profit fell 17% from the year-ago period, to $8.2 million, or 25 cents a share, on sales of $142.6 million. Polaroid's stock hit a low of $141.25 last year, down from a 1973 high of $143.50. It closed yesterday on the New York Stock Exchange at $30.125.

Sales of Polaroid's instant SX-70 folding cameras and film, which produce dry, litter-free color prints, have fallen far short of projections, while U.S. demand for its peel-apart film products has slumped. Soaring manufacturing costs have shriveled profit margins, and technical problems still bedevil production of the film-pack batteries that power the complex SX-70.

Moreover, formidable competition looms. Eastman Kodak Co., with six times the sales and twice the assets of Polaroid, is readying its own instant cameras and instant film, perhaps for introduction next year.

In short, Polaroid is at a crucial juncture—probably its most crucial since it created instant photography with the first Land camera in 1948.

Sudden Changes Unlikely. Mr. McCune isn't likely to order sudden sweeping changes, but his new authority is being felt throughout the company. "He has known for years that certain things needed to be done around here, and now that he's got the charter he's doing them," one executive says.

"We had been trying to get certain product decisions for as long as two years before Bill became president," the executive adds. "The routine had been that one top guy thought this and another top guy thought that and the boss (Mr. Land) was waffling. So we'd go back and get more data and do it all over again. Now Bill just says, 'Okay, do it.'"

Mr. McCune is pushing decision-making to unprecedented low echelons. "You should have seen the faces of some of the nonengineering guys the first time

Bill asked them, 'Why the hell are you asking me that? Why don't you just go do it?'" an engineering man says.

• • • •

Stress on Planning. Mr. McCune confirms that the marketing people failed to lower some sales targets fast enough. "But if you talk to marketing people you'll find they had some difficulties with some projections they had from the engineering side, too," Mr. McCune says. "One of my objectives is to try to smooth that up some."

He is also emphasizing long-range planning. "A lot of people think planning is a process by which you prematurely make decisions," Mr. McCune says. "I think of it as a way to look at your options and keep those options open."

What Mr. McCune has already done "that is terribly important and terribly promising," says Mr. Wensberg, the 45-year old senior vice president of marketing, "is to lay out in a very orderly fashion the problems and the opportunities the company is facing and set people to work on them." Another officer adds, "Up to now, all the long-range planning here has been contained in Dr. Land's cranium."

"Bill's pulling people together, getting some teamwork established," says George H. Fernald Jr., 48, the assistant vice-president responsible for film manufacturing. "But we're a lot of highly motivated, bright, stubborn, opinionated people. How do you get them together?". . . .—Richard Martin

The Wall Street Journal, April 25, 1975

Adapting to Environmental Changes

Since the environment is composed of organizations and groups outside the boundaries of the firm, there may well be changes in it over which the internal management of an organization has little or no control. A dynamic organization may find its market and technological sector becoming more stable. Or a bureaucratic organization may find that its environment is becoming increasingly unpredictable. Environments may change as a result of several different sets of conditions; innovation, for example, or market saturation, or changing consumer preferences, or changes in legal requirements, or actions of other organizations, or effects of pressure groups. These causes of organizational change are reasons why an organization's structure must change. Later in this section we will show how structures can be changed to adapt to changed environments.

Innovation. We have seen how innovation is necessary for growth to occur. In some instances innovation changes the competitive character of the environment to which an established organization must adapt. For instance, the development of high-speed transportation, along with refrigeration capabilities in trucks and rail cars, made it possible to provide off-season fresh vegetables and produce nationwide. This changed the marketing patterns of both producers and processors. The development of microcircuitry made possible both cost reduction and size reduction of computers. They are now more readily available to smaller firms. The development of scanners to read data from food packages makes it possible to use data processing and computers at supermarket checkout counters. The implications of such a move in the supermarket industry are enormous. The nature of the checker's job is changed. Inventory managers must revise their systems to use the new technology; inventory levels may be determined almost instantaneously. Ordering can be more responsive to sudden shifts in demand. Such an innovation not only has implications for the supermarket and the customer, but also for the manufacturers of the scanning equipment, who must develop different sales strategies and programs to support the use of this equipment by the customer. New marketing strategies must be devised to deal with the problem of initiating and integrating a new organizational unit into the existing structure of the computer firm as well as insuring that the sales function is handled well.

Market Saturation. A firm in a dynamic market and with a dynamic technology with control of innovation may find, over time, that the market becomes more stable as demand begins to peak out. Or that the technological advantage it possessed because of patent control diminishes as other competitors develop similar processes or products.

As products become widely distributed in the hands of most potential users, then, eventually the demand may slow down to a point where the market is primarily a replacement market. Then growth will come from replacement and increases due to changes in population levels. As this happens, the managerial strategy of the firm may become more inward-looking, seeking ways of increasing profitability through internal efficiencies. This will be manifest in tighter procedures and controls.

Changing Consumer Preferences. The character of the market may change with shifts in consumer tastes. The women's fashion industry has long been cited as an example of changing consumer tastes with attendant impacts on the operating effectiveness of clothing manufacturers. This same kind of phenomenon seems to be emerging in men's fashions. Clothing styles are much more varied for men than they have been in the past. Such volatility makes it difficult for manufacturers of men's suits, for example, to predict sales levels as accurately as in the past. Production methods, procurement, and purchasing have to be more responsive to shifts in taste.

Changes in Legal Requirements. Often the environment is changed by action of the government. These changes sometimes cause a firm to shift its method of production. For example, current legislation requires automobile engines to produce lower emissions of certain chemical compounds. These requirements mean a change in the design of automobile engines which necessitates changes in production methods. Or, as another example, the Food and Drug Administration often requires pharmaceutical manufacturers to take certain drugs off the market, or imposes stricter controls on the distribution of these drugs. The subsystems of the drug company's organizational structure must respond—adapt—to these changes in their environment.

There have been instances where certain products have simply been made illegal. Perhaps the classic example is the prohibition of alcoholic sales during the late 1920s and 1930s. The ban on cigarette advertising on television forced advertisers to look for new media.

Other Firms' Action. Changes for a particular organization may be induced by what other firms in that environment do. High profitability and growing markets may bring about the entry of other firms into an area, and as competition begins to develop, prices, as we have seen, may begin to drop. The market may become saturated, bringing about a degree of market stability. Or new manufacturing processes may be developed by other firms. Or more efficient ways of production may be developed by a competitor. Or a competitor may locate its production facilities closer to the market. To all of these environmental disequilibriums organizations must adjust.

Pressure Groups. In some cases, changes in the internal structure of an organization are brought about by interest groups outside the organization. These groups may feel they should be able to affect the decision making of a particular firm. The ecology movement in the United States is an example of such an activity. Another is reflected in the study of the TVA by Philip Selznick (1953). He shows how local governments and citizens' groups applied pressure to the Tennessee Valley Authority. These pressures resulted not only in a change in the TVA's policies of operation, but also a change in its structure. Selznick describes one method for adapting to pressure groups which he calls "co-optation." Co-optation consists of absorbing the external group into the policy- and decision-making structure of the organization.

Direction of Environmental Changes

The environment can change in two directions. It can increase in uncertainty—that is, move from stable to volatile—or it can increase in certainty—move from a volatile to a stable condition.

From Volatile to Stable. There will be a "natural" tendency for all organizations to move toward a hierarchical organizational structure. This effect is similar to changes in structure that occur with growth (which we discussed in the first part of this chapter). The maintenance subsystem will attempt to increase the degree of predictability of members' behavior. Those in the adaptive sector will seek ways to reduce variance in the volatile environment. The maintenance and managerial subsystems will develop record systems to keep track of both people and resources for internal control purposes. Procedural mechanisms such as governmental reporting requirements on tax withholding and social security will require regular reports which begin to regularize behavior. As the number of systems and procedures increase and become more permanent, the organization structure becomes less flexible.

   If the environment is becoming progressively more stable, then the organization should increase the degree of specificity and rigidity of its structure. Jobs should be defined more exactly, more permanent authority-responsibility relationships should be established, and the degree of freedom of organization members to make decisions should be restricted. There will be a need for greater coordination with other units as work becomes more interdependent, and this creates a situation where it is especially important to be able to rely on another person to do his job. Thus it becomes less efficient to allow people to decide how and what to do. They must have operating definitions of their work.

The major concern in this situation, as we suggested earlier, must be the congruency between the rate of the development of structure with the changing environment. The development of a more rigid structure must keep pace with the changing, reduced, degree of volatility of the environment, but if it becomes too inflexible too soon, it may stifle creativity. A high volatility environment will not turn into a stable one overnight. The change will be gradual and thus the increasingly rigid organizational structure should also arise gradually. For example, as the rate of technological change begins to slow, the production subsystem may become more hierarchical and its methods more routine. But if the market is still volatile, the structure of the marketing department should remain flexible. It should move toward more specificity only in concert with the external environment.

The information for making such changes comes from adaptive subsystems. The market research group, for example, can tell the decision makers about the market. The engineering research group can monitor the technological sector. If the organization proceeds too swiftly in imposing structural rigidity, it may find itself disadvantaged because it cannot cope effectively in an environment that is still fairly volatile. For example, suppose a firm manufactures several lines of specialized furniture. It may decide to standardize production for a mass market. If the market isn't there, losses will occur. On the other hand, if organization structure lags substantially behind the rate of environmental change, then the organization may find itself at a competitive disadvantage. If, for example, more efficient, standardized operations can produce similar products at lower costs, then the firm that moves quickest to standardize operations will have the competitive advantage.

From Stable to Volatile. If the environment shifts rapidly from stability toward volatility, there may be great difficulty in adjusting. The stable bureaucratic organization, with a substantial investment in both people and physical resources, will find a great deal of internal resistance to change. The large organization in a stable environment will thus attempt to minimize the possibility of such a shift.

One way to minimize this possibility is through the control of technology. The large firm will control technological breakthroughs which might be transformed into useful products and will introduce them into the product line gradually. To do otherwise would require dismantling of the capital assets and an enormous reinvestment. For example, the automobile industry introduced the change from the standard transmission to the automatic transmission gradually. At General Motors, it first became available in one line, the Oldsmobile, and then in another as retooling took place. It would have required a substantial investment if the changeover had been made across the whole product line. By controlling the rate of introduction of new products, the organization is not only able to experiment, but is also able to make the change slowly enough to avoid major reshuffling of the production side of the firm.

It can be seen, then, that the rate of introduction of new products is controlled—or an attempt is made to control—because even though changing over to a new product may be technologically feasible, economically it isn't. The auto industry moved in a similarly cautious fashion in introducing small cars to meet the competition of European and Japanese imports. The market was obviously there, but the industry felt it had to make the changeover at a rate that was economically feasible.

It is more than likely that a change to a more volatile environment will be faced by industries which are composed of a large number of small organizations. For example, in the restaurant industry there were once a large number of small independents who operated in a traditional fashion. Then the rapid development of quick food service franchises, such as McDonald's and Kentucky Fried Chicken, caused a major change in the nature of the industry. The small, traditional firms were not able to take advantage of the opportunities and have found themselves losing the competitive battle with the quick food franchises. The calculating equipment industry is another example. Prior to the development of integrated circuitry, adding machines and calculators were largely mechanical, relying on electrically-driven gear mechanisms. Suddenly the development of integrated circuitry made possible extremely rapid calculation with smaller and more reliable equipment. Manufacturers of adding machines and calculators were faced with the problem of surviving in a market which was substantially changed by innovation.

There are three things that a firm can do when its environment becomes more volatile than it has been. First, it can *change its strategy* to take advantage of the new opportunities. Second, it can seek *merger* with or *acquisition* of an organization currently capable of functioning in that environment. Third, it can elect to *withdraw* from the volatile segment of the environment.

Changing strategy requires a shift in the way a firm is managed as well as in the technological processes of production and distribution. The product may be redesigned to more closely parallel that of competitors. This new design may change the way the product works, or it may simply be a change in appearance. If there has been a shift in the way the product is built (as in the case of electronic calculators), the organization may not have either the production methods or the staff to operate under the new system, and so it must acquire the services of a new group of product engineers capable of dealing with the change. If the change is a style change (as might be the case in men's fashions), new designers must be obtained. When the change in strategy requires a change in production methods, the organization will have to invest heavily in the new technology, scrapping the old production system and replacing it with a new one. The substantial investment involved, along with the attendant risk, requires a decision that should be very seriously evaluated before the change is undertaken.

Merging with a firm which is already successfully operating in the volatile environment, or one which has the technical capability but perhaps has not been profitable due to limited resources, is another way to deal with environmental change toward volatility. The joining of the two organizations is likely to produce a synergistic effect which will substantially increase the resource base and, if the fit is a good one, potentially increase the returns of both organizations involved. When this method for adapting to the environment is the one chosen, the organization which emerges will have to face the difficulties of managing the mixed organization, as discussed in chapter 15.

To withdraw from the volatile segment of the environment and continue to produce and market existing goods and services is a third possibility. The organization may elect to stay as it is, but it will face problems of managing in a retrenching position, since a segment of the market is gone. If the new environment is stable and the market is large enough, in absolute terms, however, effective managers may continue to operate a firm profitably. The remaining customer segment in the industry may be large enough for a few, but not many firms. As the less profitable and inefficient competitors who remain in the stable sector begin to drop out, the remaining firms may increase internal efficiencies to be acceptably profitable, still operating as they did in the past.

Attempting to Change the Conditions of the Environment

One should not come away with the impression that an organization in its environment is like a cork passively bobbing on the waves. Organizations need not simply react to changes in the environment; they can undertake to influence the external circumstances that directly affect them. Most organizations, either individually or collectively, as an industry or interest group, try to influence the environment, smoothing out fluctuations in demand by increasing marketing efforts during slack periods. Price policies often have the same objective. By offering discounts during periods of low demand, consumers may be induced to purchase the product or service at a time when the sales level of an organization might otherwise be low.

An obvious example of change tactics are lobbying efforts designed to yield legislation making external conditions more favorable. Agricultural groups, for example, press for government programs to insure stable prices and stable farm income in the face of foreign competition and the vagaries of nature. The meat industry seeks protective tariffs, one purpose of which is to minimize competition from imports.

Firms may use different approaches when attempting to influence the environment, but the objective is essentially the same. They seek to induce changes in the broader segment of society which will make the environment more compatible with their own method of operation.

Increasing Market Volatility. A firm may find itself selling its product or services to a set of consumers which is fairly well-defined and not increasing greatly in size. The volatility of a market may be increased by generating demand for the product in other segments of the population where the product is not used extensively. For example, Black and Decker, a manufacturer of power tools, has consistently in the recent past reduced the price of power drills. Several years ago these tools were bought primarily by professional tradesman in the construction industry and by hobbyists who used them frequently. Through the development of more efficient production systems and product redesign using less expensive components, Black and Decker was able to reduce the price of its power drills to a point where they become inexpensive enough to be bought by those who make only intermittent use of them. Thus the company made its product attractive to a larger number of consumers and substantially increased the market. Applying this same strategy to other products, such as circular saws, Black and Decker experienced very rapid growth in sales and profits from 1967 to the present. Its products have essentially the same functions as they did when they were first introduced. The market shift was caused by their strategy of cost and price reduction.

Increasing Technological Volatility. In some cases it is possible to develop a product that performs the same function as another, but uses a different technology. Electronic calculators were cited as an example earlier. Another example is the development of microwave ovens by manufacturers of kitchen equipment.

Such technical innovations can be made only if a firm is willing to expend vast amounts for research and development, at a corresponding risk. Because of the cost and risk involved, it is likely that most organizations will seek to adopt new technology after it has been developed, rather than attempt to find a significant breakthrough itself. This is especially likely to be the case where the current technological formation of a firm, or industry, represents a large investment in capital resources. Firms in the automobile or basic steel industry, for example, will not introduce technological changes which alter the basic nature of their production processes in a short time period. As we have noted, their strategy is more likely to be one of gradual introduction of the new technology.

Select a Compatible Environment. It is possible that an organization may have the capacity to function effectively within a particular environment, but for a number of reasons may choose to operate in a different one. For ease of analysis, environments were described in chapter 6 in rather sharply defined terms. Actually, of course, in the real world there is a continuum of environments. As figure 16.3 shows, there are different degrees of stability and volatility. Suppose that firm X_1 is representative of a type of firm found most commonly in an industry. It could, for example, be an automobile manufacturer. Firm X_2 in figure 16.3 may also manufacture automobiles. Their product, however, may be specialized sports cars, or racing automobiles made for a very specific clientele, with the most recent technological advances built into the product. Under these circumstances, the structure of the two firms will be quite different.

FIGURE 16.3 Continuous Nature of Environmental Variability

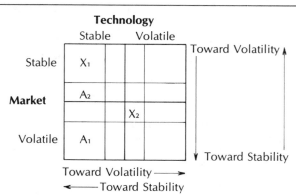

A₁ designates a firm in a volatile market with stable technology. The example cited earlier of a type of organization in this environment was a manufacturer of women's fashions, and the organizational type is characteristic in particular of the houses of certain designing manufacturers like Yves St. Laurent, or Rudy Gernriech, who attempt to remain at the forefront of the industry by introducing radical or even shocking change in each new fashion season. One reason why the market is so volatile is that this condition is fostered by designers themselves. There are, however, firms which manufacture more "traditional" clothes for women. Chanel and the Villager are noted for classic designs which do not change markedly from year to year. These houses, of course, would be in sector A₂.

Item 16.2 describes the strategy of the Rucker Company in selecting a compatible environment. In the early 1960s Rucker acquired a number of firms, increasing its asset base markedly. But the problems associated with managing so many diverse organizations (see chap. 16 for some of these problems) led to a decision to divest and return to a more familiar scope of operation.

As organization structure changes, the processes of management must also change. When the environment shifts from volatile to stable, decision making will shift from decisions under uncertainty to decisions under certainty or decisions under risk. As an organization's structure becomes more rigid, with more specific job descriptions, different personnel with different attitudes, needs and motivation should be recruited. Of course in the event the change is in the other direction (from stable to volatile), the managerial strategies should shift accordingly.

A change in the structure of an organization will create different role pressures on incumbents, and they must adapt to these if the organization is to survive and survive efficiently. Some of these structural changes can be anticipated, though not easily influenced by the firm. Other structural changes may be planned and implemented in order to increase the effectiveness of the organization within its current operating environment. Organizations interact with the environment; they do not simply react.

ITEM 16.2 Moving to a More Compatible Environment

How Rucker Cured Its Conglomerate Fever

Clarence J. Woodard, the 51-year-old chairman and chief executive officer of Oakland-based Rucker Co., knows something about the perils of conglomerate fever. In the go-go years of the 1960s, he acquired 26 companies in a half-dozen industries, a strategy that boosted sales of his tiny systems engineering company to $110-million in 1969, or a ten-fold increase in only four years. Unfortunately, Rucker's earnings disappeared in the process, as one acquisition after another failed to live up to expectations.

When Rucker lost $2-million in 1970, Woodard tried another tack, more in tune with the conventional wisdom of the 1970s. He began divesting, so Rucker could concentrate on its single, most successful operation: oil-well drilling equipment and services. With his new strategy, earnings now are beginning to keep pace with sales. As oil exploration boomed in 1974, Rucker's revenues increased 49% to $127-million and earnings more than doubled to $8.2-million.

• • • •

Control. Ironically, Rucker is emphasizing management control more now,

when it has only one basic venture, than it did when it had dozens of unrelated operations. "We are considerably more sophisticated as a company now," says Woodard. "We've gone through a maturing process. We have evolved the management philosophy that we will not invest in products where we can't achieve a significant market share, with a chance to be the leader."

That is a far cry from Woodard's scattergun approach of the 1960s, when the company was in everything from computer software to irrigation hardware. Rucker's goals, strategies, management structure, and managers have largely changed, along with the change in the nature of its operations. According to Edward M. Gibbs, a former McGraw-Edison engineer who joined Rucker as executive vice-president in 1968 and became president in 1972, there was "no instant decision one bright and sunny morning to cut the company down." The strategy just evolved, he says, as the importance of market share became clear.

• • • •

The most successful acquisitions gave Rucker a specialty in equipment for difficult drilling situations—the type of gear that could be expected to generate the biggest profits. It acquired Hycalog, a maker of diamond drill bits; Shaffer Tool Works, which produces the kind of blowout preventers used to control pressures on virtually every well drilled nowadays; and Acme Tool, a major tool rental and service company. These ventures now form the nucleus of Rucker's operations.

The slide. Yet when Woodard tried to duplicate the company's success in drilling equipment by expanding into such fields as aerospace controls and plastics molding equipment, Rucker reaped one failure upon another. It bought an aircraft controls manufacturer, for example, in 1967—just before that industry went into a tailspin. It jumped into computer software mainly to bolster a sagging systems division, than had to pick up a data processing operation to bolster the software effort.

Performance. Rucker's success in drilling equipment last year made its stock—which more than doubled—one

of the top performers on the New York Stock Exchange. It was one of the few companies that managed to sell new equity. Still, the current share price of $15 is only eight times last year's earnings, a long way from the dizzying multiples of the 1960s, and well below those of other drilling equipment companies.

Woodard has no intention of returning to the diversification tactics of the past. "As you concentrate your resources, the span of control is also concentrated so the company becomes more manageable," he says. "We are not going to divert any resources or management time outside the petroleum industry. It has all the opportunities we can handle."

Business Week, April 17, 1975

In this chapter we have described several ways in which the external environment may change, bringing about corresponding internal changes of the organization. There are many current trends which will influence organization structure in the future. Some will act to increase formalization and predictability and contribute to more of a bureaucratic design for organizations, while others will contribute to less formalization and to more of a dynamic design for organizations.

Discussion Questions

1. Why do people who continually interact with each other over time develop stable, predictable behavior patterns?

2. What is the effect of a change in the environment on structure, say as when the federal government began to impose safety legislation?

3. What kinds of decisions can an organization make which will affect the environment to make it more compatible with the organization?

4. What happens, when rapid growth occurs, to managers of small organizations?

5. It seems implicit that a person who starts a business that becomes exceptionally successful and large will have to step aside if the success is to be continued—or does it?

Chapter 17
Changing People in Organizations

In chapter 16 we noted that organizational structure must change in response to changes in the environment. At the same time, we recognized that some changes in organizational structure occur because the organization finds itself forced (for reasons of survival) to accommodate itself to the demands of its members. The reverse also holds true: members of an organization—who stay in the organization—accommodate themselves to the demands of the organization (to keep their jobs; to win promotions).

Pressures for such accommodations—for changing people—stem chiefly from management's dissatisfaction with their organization's level of effectiveness, and low levels of effectiveness are, as we have said in chapter 5, attributed by management to deficiencies in human skills, motivation, or behavior, even though inadequate resources or structure may be wholly or partly to blame.

Cultural forces operate also. Western civilization has traditionally seen as its mission the changing of the environment and of people. Nature must be transformed to serve the purposes of organizations, of society as a whole, or individuals. People must be changed as well— to conform to what some group or organization believes is suitable behavior or performance. Every organization—educational, governmental, and business—expends a large part of its efforts toward changing people for the possible enhancement of the objectives and values of the organization.

In the past few years, because of the growth of what has been called the "human potential" movement, some organizations have tried to effect change and growth on an individualized basis. That is, in some organizations programs for change try to create more diverse, rather than homogeneous individuals. The approach taken by an organization is determined by what it needs. If the organization perceives its need as the development of individuals who must fit into a specific role, change is directed toward developing homogeneous people. If the organization perceives its need as diversified individuals, however, who are creative and adaptable, its emphasis will be on individualized change. There is some research evidence that the structured or stable organization emphasizes standardization in its change efforts, while the dynamic organization emphasizes change programs that encourage diversity with growth (Friedlander, 1971).

When change efforts are organizationally planned and authorized, there is the strong implication that someone in the organization desires a change in performance. But exposing an individual to a situation that induces him to change, and then placing him in an organizational setting that supports and reinforces former behavior or attitudes leads to frustration, disappointment, and bitterness. This is most likely to happen if the systemic factors in the organization—policies, rules, procedures, job descriptions—are not structured to reinforce the change on a continuing basis.

A great deal of recent theory and research has led to the conclusion that change efforts must be more broadly based than they have been and consist of more than mere classroom exercises. Many have stressed the need for designing change efforts to be compatible with the organizational climate (Schein, 1961; Sykes, 1962; House and Tosi, 1963). This means that the management group must be willing to support change efforts with organizational reinforcements. Only when this is done can management expect change efforts to result in the kinds of behavior intended. This support can only be provided in the form of specific top management decisions and practices. It is not enough for management to "verbally" support development. They must do it with their practices and policy making.

Organization Development. Our perspective on these efforts to change individuals is our version of organization development (OD). Beckhard (1969) defines organization development as

> an effort planned, organization wide, and managed from the top to increase organizational effectiveness and health through planned interventions in the organization's processes, using behavioral science knowledge.

This view leads us to consider any particular type of training (such as specific skills in mathematics, or computer programming, or interpersonal relations), or the redesign of organization structure to be more consistent with the outside environment, as part of OD. The essential aspect is that the particular approach be planned, based on the needs of the organization, and integrated with other efforts.

This view is broader than the narrow meaning of OD given it by some training faddists. This narrower view, which grew out of sensitivity training programs, stresses humanistic values. The emphasis is on providing opportunities for human beings to realize their potential, and for allowing organizational members to influence the decision-making process, the objective being to establish open and candid human relationships.

When it was found that providing managers with a course of training and then sending them back into the existing social system where newly learned behaviors were not supported or reinforced was ineffective in obtaining change, it became evident that a systems approach was needed, that change efforts must be directed at more than just the attitudes of individuals. Relationships among individuals and among groups must also be the target of change attempts, and these relationships are affected not only by the unique personalities of people, but also by the structure of the organization.

Organization development is *not*, therefore, a particular type of training method. It includes a wide variety of methods and uses whatever is necessary to accomplish the desired change. Two factors loom large in OD. The first is whether or not the people who are the targets of change can change or are willing to change; the second is that there must be some assessment of what the change requirements are. An assessment of these factors can be made through organization planning.

Prerequisites of Change

Before individuals or groups can be changed, certain conditions must be present. First, the causes of the present unsatisfactory state of knowledge, behavior, or attitudes must be understood. If change in an individual or group is desired, it is because behavior or attitudes are not what they should be. Change attempts have the best chance of success when the causes of present behavior and attitudes can be determined. Second, the obstacles standing in the way of change must not be insurmountable. If there is to be a change in knowledge, for example, certain minimum levels of learning abilities must be present, since limits in individual learning abilities place limits on the amount and type of material that can be learned. Certain behavior patterns or attitudes are so deeply ingrained and are so important to the functioning of the individual that they can be changed only with great expenditures of time and energy, if at all. A third prerequisite of change is motivation to change. An individual—or group—must be motivated to change an existing level of knowledge, behavior patterns, or attitudes, or the influence programs will fail. Fourth, defensiveness must be minimized. Since most individuals have a favorable self-image, they are not inclined to accept information about themselves which is at variance with this favorable self-image. Organizational members who perform at an unsatisfactory level, for example, are likely to shift the blame to other people or the situation, such as a lack of resources. In general, they refuse to acknowledge that their performance is unsatisfactory or that their errors are serious. All of this hampers change.

Some research has been carried out to identify the situational factors which are related to a positive reaction to training by the participant; some of these factors have been identified in studies in two organizations of the reactions of foremen to management development training (Carroll and Nash, 1975). In these studies it was found that foremen reacted more positively to the training program if they believed that good performance would result in pay increases or promotions; when they desired a promotion; when they were relatively satisfied with their jobs and the organization; when they felt that the company was supporting the program; when they felt their superior was supporting the program; when they perceived they had the power to make changes in their jobs; and when they perceived the content of the program to be related to the solution of their current problems. In other words, participants are more favorable toward change efforts when they see them as a means of accomplishing personal objectives. Those who react most favorably to a program expect that it will help them attain outcomes they consider important (promotions, pay increases, solution of current problems). Also, those employees favorable to the company are more favorable toward training programs that the company endorses than those not favorable to the company, and those who feel they have the power to utilize the training on their jobs are also positive in attitude about the programs.

Behavioral scientists believe that if an individual participates in the making of a change, he is predisposed to accept the change. Why? First, because he has a greater understanding of it, and thus less uncertainty, which is a source of resistance to change. Second, with participation the individual (or group) becomes ego-involved with the change. If a person makes a suggestion, and if he believes it is a good suggestion, he will be motivated to try to make it work. If he does not try to make it work, and if the suggestion ultimately proves to be no good, that will be a negative reflection on him as a person, and he will have to reevaluate his opinion of himself. Third, if a person commits

himself to successful accomplishment of a change, he will be motivated to make it succeed, because people see themselves as individuals who keep their word, and they try to live up to this aspect of
their self-concept. Finally, in a group setting, the individual perceives
that the change is being accepted by his peers, whose opinion he
values.

Participation does not always overcome resistance to change, however. And participation is generally not effective when the individuals
involved do not have the competence or information needed to contribute to the development of the change, or when they lack motivation or interest in the subject of concern, or when they do not consider
their participation in the change decision appropriate.

Determination of Developmental Needs

Without the foundation of organization planning, organization development efforts cannot be related to the long-range performance requirements of the organization.

Organization planning consists of making projections of what the
organization will look like in the future—three, five, or even ten years
hence. These projections can be constructed from data available from
more extensive planning, such as long-range building or capital expansion projects. Thus, we can arrive at an "ideal" organization structure for some point in time in the future.

To bridge the gap between the ideal and the present organization
structure, the use of "phase plans" is appropriate. Phase plans are intermediate plans or steps to achieve the desired structure on a sound
and practical basis. The projected structure is broken down into
phases with respect to time and organizational units. For example, at
stated future times, certain subunits may be split off and reorganized
in an orderly manner. The various phases may be timed to coincide
with major additions, planned operational changes in plant and
equipment, introduction of new products, and the planned retirement
of executives. The final form of organization at a given point in time
will no doubt differ from the ideal structure originally conceived for
that time, but the use of phase plans allows for revision of the long-
range plan and forces planners to consider changes in economic conditions, product line, span of control, or loss of key personnel.

Forecasting organizational requirements pinpoints the primary considerations in planning the future organization structure of the firm
and should result in several benefits: (1) because the personnel selection program can be based on the future requirements of the firm, the

general skill requirements of future executives can be determined; (2) promotion decisions will be improved, since individuals can be directed into positions for which they are most qualified or for which they have the capability of being trained; (3) for those engaged in the planning of developmental efforts, organization planning provides a basis for establishing developmental objectives. Perhaps the greatest value of organization planning is the knowledge gained about the existing structure and members of the organization. Problems that need immediate attention may be uncovered. When sound organization planning is the foundation on which development programs rest, the company can avoid initiating them in response to the whims of executives or to training fads.

Requirements for Future Performance. Requirements for future performance can be inferred generally from the long-run organization plan. For example, if we assume that in the future decision making will require increased use of operations research and information technology—tools based on mathematical skills—the fundamental mathematics can be taught immediately. Then managers can be prepared for advanced training in specific applications in a relatively short time. Training in specific applications of these tools may then be included in development programs concurrently with the fundamental concepts of managing and organizing human behavior.

While there is little question of the difficulty of making determinations for specific positions, Mann's conceptual framework offers some aid for the organization planner (Mann, 1965). Basing his conclusions on a number of field studies of several levels in organizations, he concludes that managers must have technical skill, human relations skill, and administrative skill.

Technical skill is the specialized knowledge needed to perform the major functions and tasks associated with a position. Human relations skill is the capacity to work with people and motivate them in such a way that they want to perform well. Administrative skill, as we have noted in chapter 8, is the ability to make decisions and conceptualize relationships directed toward organizational goal achievement, rather than toward maximizing return to some specific subunit of the firm. These skills, of course, necessarily include the ability to plan, organize, and control the functioning of the organizational system and structure.

Mann makes two important points regarding the skills mix. There are different skill requirements for different organizational levels. At the lower supervisory levels, technical and human relations skills are primarily important. At the higher levels, administrative skill assumes major importance. Mann proposes also that the skills mix differs for different stages of organization growth and development. Therefore, as a person progresses through a career in an organization, the nature of his development experiences should change. Also, as discussed in chapter 16, as an organization progresses through various stages of growth, skill requirements can be anticipated. For example, before the firm moves into the stage of "rational bureaucracy," managers can be given training in systematic management processes.

Such an organizational planning effort will provide the overall framework for specific developmental or training experiences. In most organizations, training and development programs emerge from specific short-range situations. For example, when civil rights employment legislation made it legally necessary that more women and minority group members be moved into managerial positions, many firms attempted to reduce the resistance of the incumbent work group with training. It is important, though, that long-range organization planning be undertaken, because then it is possible to consider every training effort as it fits into an overall theme.

Development Techniques

Organizations have used many methods to change individuals and groups. These methods are the technology of the trainer. They are teaching techniques, activities which are intended to bring about a change in another. Part of the problem in doing this is overcoming resistance to change. Some of the ways industry uses these methods are discussed in item 17.1. Here we will review various off-the-job and on-the-job training methods, review what is known about their effectiveness in accomplishing various kinds of change, and then discuss how they may be applied to general programs of organizational development including the programs of Blake and Mouton and of House.

Off-the-job Methods

Off-the-job methods are learning environments other than in the work setting. Typically they present, in a classroom situation, particular training content. This content can range from typing classes to lectures and discussion of such subjects as human relations theory or quantitative decision-making techniques.

Lecture. Perhaps the most common form of training is the standard lecture, in which someone competent in a particular topic area presents a set of concepts and ideas to a group. While it is true that often questions and answers are used to determine understanding, the lecture is generally considered an "instructor-centered" method.

Films and Videotape.   Another instructor-centered method is the use of film or TV. Sometimes the instructor appears on the screen and presents material in much the same fashion as in a lecture, and sometimes he is interviewed. Usually, questions and answers are not used unless someone, such as a trainer, is present and using the film as a vehicle to stimulate discussion. Sometimes the film presents dramatization of certain incidents in order to provide examples of the concepts being taught.

ITEM 17.1   Management Development

How Companies Raise a New Crop of Managers

Eli M. Black, chairman, president, and chief executive officer of United Brands Co., who committed suicide last month, not only ran a one-man show but failed to groom a successor. The board is still searching for a replacement, while two committees run the company.

That kind of transition problem ought to be lesson enough for any company. Yet in today's recession, management development programs, which are supposed to provide in-depth backup at every level and facilitate the transfer of power at the top, are on nearly every corporate cost cutter's list. General Motors, Chrysler, Corning Glass, First National Bank of Chicago, and New York Telephone, for example, already are pruning long-established programs.

• • • •

Management development is vulnerable because it is expensive, time-consuming, and complex to administer. It means, almost by definition, having a managerial surplus. IBM, for example, has three or four potential replacements for each of several hundred top jobs. It also means moving managers in and out of jobs, sometimes just when they are beginning to make a contribution, to give them breadth of experience. That kind of talent transfer can be expensive not just because it temporarily drags down efficiency but because the physical moves that accompany many such job changes are today more costly than ever.

For all the trouble and expense of the development programs, many large corporations see no real alternative, even in today's economy. A growth company like Xerox, with sales of $3.58-billion last year, may still have to go outside to fill its management ranks, but mature companies prefer to provide for their own needs. Moreover, it is probably more than coincidence that companies dominant in their industries, such as Exxon, AT&T, IBM, and Citicorp, often have the most effective programs. Exxon Chairman John K. Jamieson, AT&T Chairman John D. deButts, IBM Chairman Frank T. Cary, and Citicorp Chairman Walter B. Wriston have all had 20 or more years of service in their companies and are products of their companies' systems.

An effective program can pay enormous dividends. It can boost morale at every level, help companies hold good men, and prevent the dislocations that come with moving an outsider in at the top. "When a chief executive is brought in from the outside," says one executive who has seen several such changes, "he brings in 50% of his staff from the outside, and they bring in 50% of theirs from the outside, and so on down the line. By the time the results are in a couple of years later it may be too late to save the company."

No two companies approach development the same way, but some common threads run through programs considered most effective:

... They are built deep into the system, involving all levels of management and affecting the way the organization works. "We don't hire management trainees," says Edward F. Krieg, IBM director of management development. "We go after competent people and provide a crucible where they can evolve into managers."

... Management development is part of every manager's job. Each executive is responsible for grooming his subordinates, and his salary and promotions are based partly on their success.

... Top management support and a long-term commitment to the program are unwavering. Otherwise, movement of executives in and out of learning jobs comes to an end.

To provide constantly challenging jobs and promotions requires that older workers must retire and mediocre ones must leave. Exxon, for one, tries to keep the top 10% of its management talent moving up by weeding out the bottom 10%. "The life-blood of our management development system is the rate at which we can move talent through the management ranks, always providing a greater challenge," says Frank Gaines,

Jr., executive development coordinator at Exxon.

Citibank uses much the same approach. For nearly 40 years, the bank has relied less on formal training than on hiring people with strong academic credentials, thrusting responsibilities on them, and closely watching their performance. "There is no alternative for doing," says Thomas C. Theobald.

Theobald likes to take people right from school, give them such rudimentary tools as cash flow accounting, and put them to work under close supervision. "We set goals for our people and they are reviewed formally every few months, but informally every few hours," he says. "The idea is to find out who can make sensible judgments and who can't, and then give those who can lots of opportunity."

He likes to "take a roll" occasionally, too, gambling on a younger person. But he monitors the person's performance through the four division heads and four staff heads reporting to him. "I spend about half my time coaching people and making judgments about them," Theobald says. "And I read every single performance report on the 300 officers in the group and see every salary action."

Companies have developed varied techniques to hasten the learning process. Some attempt to compress work experience by giving developing managers short-term special assignments on high-level task forces or making them assistants to division or corporate executives. For example, Stanley Rosenthal, now a 34-year-old partner at Peat, Marwick, Mitchell & Co. in Chicago spent two years in the company's department of professional practices in New York. The department's 12 partners and 30 managers have no direct client responsibility but work on quality control and advise the operating offices on knotty accounting problems. "You get two years of intensive problem solving and when you return to your office you are recognized as being current in SEC matters and accounting practices."

Course work. Some companies combine course study with work experience. Since 1967, The First National Bank of Chicago has tapped 167 liberal arts graduates for its First Scholar program. First Scholars attend graduate business school at nights for two and a half years and work in various line and staff jobs at the bank for from one to six months.

"It's a fast track," says Robert Bourke, 23, a First Scholar for the past 20 months. "They slot you right into the management mode and give you wide experience right away. The business school and the work mesh well so that the learning curve is straight up."

First National has retained about 82% of its scholars, and they have gone into all phases of the bank's management, where they have easily held their own with the MBAs the bank has hired fresh out of business school.

Outside course work comes in for praise as well as criticism. Peat, Marwick runs a two-week refresher course at Stanford University for partners, who may be in their 30s, 40s, and 50s, to keep them abreast of new developments in business economics and management science. And many companies send executives to the 13-week advanced course at Harvard, MIT, and other B-schools. "They are good for compressing experience and giving our people exposure to executives of other companies," Gaines of Exxon says. But Paul Anderson, vice-president of Booz, Allen & Hamilton, Inc., says that courses are "only good as supplements to work experience." Adds E. H. Clark, Jr., chairman of Baker Oil Tools, Inc.: "I send a guy to school when he's screwed up and I want to get him out of my hair."

Coordinated program. When management development fails, it is most often because top management is not directly involved. Contrast, for example, the

experience at American Airlines with that at Exxon. American's program experiments lacked strong support from top management and were wiped out during economic slumps. "We were never able to give development the proper emphasis," says Gene E. Overbeck, senior vice-president at American. The airline now has a new program in the works, and it has the strong endorsement of American's new president, Albert V. Casey. Making room for the young talent, however, may not be easy.

By contrast, at Exxon, management development is already closely monitored from the top. Chairman Jamieson, President Clifton C. Garvin, Jr., and the seven other inside directors constitute a compensation and executive development committee (curiously the acronym is COED—although there are no women members), which meets each Monday to review the development programs in each of Exxon's 12 major operating units.

These units in turn have their own COEDs reviewing fast-rising managers in the affiliates reporting to them. "Every man on the board is a product of the system, so he believes in it," Gaines says.

Exxon's program is closely coordinated with the company's business plan. Each line manager must draw up a long-range plan for the replacement needs of his organization. In it he must appraise all his key executives, forecast job openings for the next five years, and assess the most likely candidates to fill them.

Plans for more than 3,000 executives are reviewed at successively higher levels. Ultimately, the corporate COED reviews and comments on every appointment for the 250 most senior jobs and keeps track of another 500 jobs to insure adequate depth in the management ranks.

If most companies concede that management development is expensive, few can pinpoint exactly how much it costs. Many companies such as Exxon claim that it is so much a part of the management structure that the cost cannot be calculated. Peat, Marwick, however, estimates that it spends at least $10-million annually for training, including time lost during the course work. And First National Chicago calculates that it spends about $31,000 for each First Scholar.

Cutbacks. That kind of expense is an obvious target when companies start cutting back as they are doing today. First National Chicago's Scholars program, for example, is being reduced to 12 people this year, from 28 in 1974. At some companies the cutting is far more severe.

At Corning Glass Works, which since last July has laid off 9,000 employees, or nearly one-fifth of its worldwide work force, development has slowed perceptibly.

• • • •

Less drastic cutbacks in development programs are commonplace. New York Telephone Co. has reduced its work force in the last three years from 105,000 to 85,000. One result: managers are now moved laterally instead of being promoted.

Still, many companies with traditionally strong development programs are preserving what they can even in the face of deep sales slumps. GM is moving managers infrequently and has curtailed recruiting. But some of the management development survives. "Results of the program have changed," says William B. Chew, director of GM's human resources management activity, "but that doesn't change the need for the program."

Business Week, March 10, 1975

Programmed Instruction. Programmed instruction is also an instructor-centered approach. However, it is at the same time interactive, in the sense that the learner moves at his own pace, not advancing to a more advanced set of concepts until he has mastered a preliminary set. With conventional programmed instruction, concepts are presented to the learner, and then a series of diagnostic questions are asked. If all questions are answered correctly, the learner moves on to the next concept. If questions are answered incorrectly, the learner is directed to additional material on the subject. Programmed instruction is theoretically based on principles of reinforcement, the reinforcement ostensibly coming from the satisfaction of answering the diagnostic questions correctly.

Simulations—Business Games. The simulation is an attempt to involve the learner in a learning situation which approximates the real world. In most simulations the learner is faced with a series of decisions that must be made—for example, decisions about resource allocations. These decisions are then fed into computer models and their effects are shown. Simulations may be extremely complex, or very simple, and they may deal with a wide variety of problems—manufacturing, retailing, or even governmental management.

Case Studies. The case is a narrative, written presentation of a set of problem facts that the student analyzes and then solves. Cases are used to stimulate discussion of topics of all types. Like simulations, they can be simple or complex.

Conference (Discussion) Methods. The conference method may be used with or without cases and simulations. Students may be assigned material for reading and the instructor will then use a series of questions to stimulate discussion. The conference method is intended to involve the participant more extensively in the learning process than do lectures or films. It is a group-centered method of instruction, one in which the participants extensively engage, along with a conference leader, in the development of ideas that can lead to greater understanding of what is being taught.

Role Playing. Role playing is an experiential, student-centered method of instruction. In role-playing, the student (learner) is asked to act as another person. For example, in a management training program, a labor-management role play may be used. One participant assumes the role of a company negotiator while another acts as a union representative. Each has received a set of facts and is instructed to represent his side in determining the final form of a labor contract. Other problem areas—such as worker motivation, or the effect of different leadership styles and different modes of participation in decision making—may also be highlighted through role playing. Role playing is especially useful in developing interpersonal skills, in showing the consequences of behaving in different ways, and in developing an understanding of the perspectives of others.

Sensitivity Training. Sensitivity training generally focuses on exploring the nature of interpersonal relationships. Individuals are brought together in groups which have little or no structure. Group members, in an ambiguous situation, must work out, under the guidance of a leader, their own structure.

In sensitivity training there is an attempt to foster greater understanding of the participants themselves, and of other people, and an attempt to increase the interpersonal skills of the participants. It is generally felt that such objectives are achieved when the individuals become more accepting of feedback from others, more candid about expressing their own feelings, more trusting, more spontaneous, more flexible, more sincere, and more willing to face up to conflict and personal problems.

Sensitivity training sessions generally try to establish a learning atmosphere in which self-examination and criticism is rewarded, where constructive feedback is given others, and where social support is given for change efforts. Various experiential exercises, tests, and role models are also frequently used to facilitate such learning.

The Effectiveness of Off-the-job Methods

Programmed instruction, sensitivity training, computer games, television, and role playing have been widely used in training only in recent years. These newer techniques, along with more traditional methods such as the lecture, conference method, films, and case study method provide a number of training and education alternatives to use in a particular situation. While availability of resources (money, time, and personnel) play a significant part in the choice of one training method or another, another important criterion must be the relative effectiveness of the training method being considered for a particular training objective. In chapter 3 we presented a "model" of the individual, composed of the following facets:

1. skills, ability, and knowledge;
2. self-concept;
3. attitudes;
4. values;
5. needs and motives.

We can think of development as an effort to change these characteristics. However, it is unlikely that any technique noted above that is used in the work setting is powerful enough to change strongly-held values, the self-concept, or needs and motives. These characteristics are probably resistant to these change methods because they are embedded in the human personality. However, it is possible with these training techniques to change some skills, ability, knowledge, and attitudes. This conclusion is based on fairly extensive research which has been done on training methods.

Acquisition of Knowledge.   Research indicates that programmed instruction is effective for knowledge acquisition. In 20 studies which compared programmed instruction to conventional lecture and discussion in an industrial situation, it was found that immediate learning was at least 10 percent higher under programmed instruction in 7 comparisons, and there was not a practical difference between the conventional and programmed instruction in 13 comparisons (Nash,

Muczyk, and Vettori, 1971). Nash and his colleagues, however, have pointed out that most of the studies involving a comparison of programmed with conventional instruction have not used a well-planned and well-carried out conventional class as the basis for comparison.

Lectures are also effective in knowledge acquisition. Four extensive reviews of the literature where the subjects were primarily college students all concluded that on the basis of research comparisons made, lecture and discussion methods are equally effective for the acquisition of knowledge (Buxton, 1956; Dietrick, 1960; Stovall, 1958; and Verner and Dickinson, 1967).

Research results, with students as subjects, generally show no significant differences between television lecture courses and conventional lecture courses. For example, Schramm (1962b) in summarizing 393 studies of the amount learned in television courses versus conventionally-taught courses. found that in 65 percent of the comparisons there were no differences, in 21 percent of the comparisons the television approach was more effective, and in 14 percent of the comparisons the participants in the television courses did worse.

Changing Attitudes. In two fairly well-controlled studies where the lecture and discussion approaches were compared in situations involving attitude change among adults (prisoners and executives), the discussion approach was more effective (Butler, 1966; Silber, 1962). In five controlled studies involving changes in behavior of adults, the discussion approach was more effective than the lecture method in changing behavior (Bond, 1956; Levine and Butler, 1952; Lewin, 1958). Some of these comparisons were not entirely fair to the lecture method, however, since in the discussion groups the participants were usually asked to commit themselves to future actions while the subjects in the lecture groups were not asked to do this. In spite of this, it appears that the discussion approach is superior to the lecture in changing attitudes and behavior.

Several studies conducted among students show that role playing can be quite effective in changing attitudes (Festinger and Carlsmith, 1959; Harvey and Beverly, 1961). Role playing seems especially effective if the subjects participating in the role-playing situation are asked to take the point of view opposite to their own and to verbalize this opposite point of view to others (Culbertson, 1957; Janis and King, 1954; King and Janis, 1956; Janis and Mann, 1965).

Sensitivity training is fairly effective in changing attitudes. Four studies using control groups have been conducted with adults where an attempt was made to see if behavior was changed as a result of sensitivity training (Boyd and Ellis, 1968; Bunker, 1965; Miles, 1965; Underwood, 1965; and Valiquet, 1968), and these studies did find behavioral changes. With respect to attitude change, two studies using a before-and-after measure without controls and with student and adult participants found attitude changes as a result of sensitivity training (Schutz and Allen, 1966; Smith, 1964). Although there were certain methodological deficiencies in these studies, on balance the results show that sensitivity training can result in at least short-run behavioral and attitudinal change, although such change may not be related to greater job effectiveness (Campbell and Dunnette, 1968).

Problem-solving Skills.   Unfortunately, the research on the effectiveness of the case study as a training device to improve problem solving is very limited. Only a few studies were found that involved more than an attempt to obtain testimonials from course participants. Fox (1963) found that about one-third of the students exposed to case-study analysis improved significantly in their ability to handle cases, about a third made moderate improvement, and a third made no improvement. Solem (1960) found that both the case-study method and role playing were effective in learning how to derive solutions to problems but felt that role playing was better for teaching participants how to gain acceptance of solutions.

More evidence is available on the effectiveness of role playing in developing problem-solving skills. In addition to the study by Solem (1960), studies by Maier (1953), Maier and Maier (1957), Maier and Hoffman (1960a; 1960b), and Maier and Solem (1952) indicate that problem-solving skills can be improved for both students and managers with the use of role playing. Two studies (Parnes and Meadow, 1959; Cohen, Whitmyre, and Funk, 1960) found that training in brainstorming could improve problem-solving ability. Brainstorming could be taught by means of role playing.

As with the case-study method, there is little research or analysis on the effectiveness of business games as a method for teaching problem-solving skills. Dill and Doppelt (1963) conducted a student self-report study which indicated that the students did not seem to learn much about specific problem-solving solutions or strategies that could be used in other situations. Raia (1966) found that experience with a business game did not improve the ability to handle cases. McKenney (1962) found that students in sections with games plus lectures understood the interrelationship between organizational factors better than students in sections with cases plus lectures.

Interpersonal Skills. Most of the research which has concerned itself with the effectiveness of training methods in developing interpersonal skills has been on sensitivity training. Six studies of sensitivity training indicate that participants describe others in more interpersonal terms than people without such training (Campbell and Dunnette, 1968). However, research specifically measuring changes in perceptual accuracy of others as a result of sensitivity training has been inconclusive.

Some research on the development of interpersonal skills has examined role playing. A study by Bolda and Lawshe (1962) showed that role playing can be effective in increasing sensitivity to employee motivations if the participants become involved in the role play. Another study indicated that role playing can be effective in improving interviewing skills (Van Schacck, 1957). In addition, studies by Maier (1953), Maier and Hoffman (1960a), and Maier and Maier (1957), show that role playing can be used to improve group leadership skills (which are a form of interpersonal skills).

Participant Acceptance. What methods are preferred by the people who are in training? Several studies on managerial acceptance of the lecture versus the discussion approach indicate a preference among managers for the lecturer or more leader-centered approach (Anderson, 1959; Filley and Reighhard, 1965; House, 1962; Mann and Mann, 1959). Two other studies of managers and a study of adults found no difference in reactions or attitudes to the use of the lecture and discussion approaches (Hill, 1960; House, 1965).

Reviews of research on television lectures by Kumata (1956 and 1960; and Schramm, 1962a) show that television has fairly high acceptance among adults as a training method and with young children, and a much lower acceptance among high school and college students.

Raia (1966) found that business students in sections of a course which used a business game did not differ in attitudes toward the course from students who had sections without the business game. Rowland, Gardner, and Nealey (1970) found that only a few of the students participating in a business game felt that the game was a valuable learning experience and that attitudes toward the course were not improved as a result of the addition of the business game.

A series of studies in six organizations by Bolda and Lawshe (1962) indicated fair acceptance for role playing by managerial personnel. The training directors also rated the case study method as high on participant acceptance. A study by Fox (1963) found that attitudes toward the case study method in the form of student testimonials were favorable. However, Castore (1951) found interest in cases dwindled after a period of exposure to them. That programmed instruction is preferable to the lecture method is supported in a study conducted at IBM (Hughes and McNamara, 1961), and in a study by Neidt and Meredith (1966), but several studies show that participant acceptance of a training approach is a function of their experience with it (Guetzkow, Kelly and McKeachie, 1954; Harris, 1960; and Hughes, 1963).

Retention of Knowledge. There has not been much research on the retention of knowledge for the different methods. The research that has been completed has been primarily with college students and has shown no clear superiority for the lecture or discussion methods as compared with each other (Dietrick, 1960; Verner and Dickinson, 1967), for the movie film as compared with the lecture and discussion methods (Sodnovitch and Pophorn, 1961; VanderMeer, 1948; Verner and Dickinson, 1967), for the television lecture as compared to the conventional lecture or discussion approach (Kumata, 1960; Klausmeir, 1961), or for programmed instruction as compared to the conventional lecture or discussion methods (Nash, Muczyk, and Vettori, 1971). The research reviews generally conclude that the amount of material retained is proportional to the amount learned (Dietrick, 1960; Vernor and Dickinson, 1967).

On-the-job Methods

Some feel that experience is the best teacher—that putting a manager into a situation where he can sink or swim is the best approach to development. When this approach is taken in a systematic way the developmental methods are "on-the-job." Not only can an employee learn the content of his job, but he has the opportunity to observe others at higher-level managerial positions and so can pattern his behavior after them.

Members of any organization can learn from watching others and modeling their behavior. Human beings can learn from observation and/or direct experience. As Bandura (1969) concludes:

Research conducted within the framework of social-learning theory demonstrates that virtually all learning phenomena resulting from direct experiences can occur on a vicarious basis through the observation of other persons' behavior and its consequences for them.

Organizations hire certain individuals—for example, "rate busters," or someone who exceeds the production norms (in the Soviet union, such workers are called "Stakhanovites")—and place them in a group as an example to be emulated by others in an attempt to change behaviors. Research on behavior modeling shows, however, that such models will not be imitated unless the individuals to be changed are motivated to learn by, and have some respect for, the model (Bandura, 1969). The authors conducted a research study in a manufacturing organization and concluded that managers model their behavior on that of superiors when a situation has forced them to take some kind of action and they do not have previous experience to apply to it (Carroll and Tosi, 1973).

There are at least three types of experiences that can be classified as on-the-job development: (1) job rotation, (2) special assignments, and (3) delegation and coaching.

Job Rotation. With job rotation—a fairly common method—an individual is systematically moved from one position to another in an organization for the purpose of learning something about each of the positions and what the purpose and function of various organizational units are, relative to each other.

The sequence of different positions is planned in advance, with both the individual's and the organization's needs in mind, so that not always do two people get exactly the same experience. In one major aircraft company, for example, a new trainee worked for six months in production at Los Angeles, four months in the finance division in Seattle, and another six months in the marketing division in Washington, D.C. Then the employee selected the division in which she wanted to work and, after consultation with supervisors in each, the personnel department assigned her a position.

Another type of job rotation system is career progression planning. Rather than a horizontal series of jobs, a vertical sequence is planned as the individual moves up the hierarchy of the organization. For instance, the first position may be as an assistant foreman in manufacturing, then foreman. From there he may move to a higher-level position in the personnel department, after which he may be promoted to assistant plant superintendent. This type of job rotation system is usually used with employees who are considered to have high potential; that is, those destined for high managerial positions.

Special Assignments. An individual may also undergo development through special assignment. For example, a manager may be assigned the responsibility of evaluating the organization's compensation program. In completing this assignment, the manager learns a great deal about compensation. Or a marketing manager may be assigned to a production committee to obtain a better appreciation of the problems in the production area. Such assignments are often tailored to the needs of the individual.

Delegation and coaching. Delegation and coaching are also traditional developmental methods which can be quite effective. The subordinate is assigned—delegated—responsibility for a particular task, which he then carries out. He learns how to carry it out both by doing and by consulting with his superior when problems arise. Such a method works most effectively when the assignments made are challenging and when the superior spends sufficient time on coaching and provides useful feedback about the subordinate's performance. Research has shown that, as would be expected, a climate of helpfulness and supportiveness contributes to the effectiveness of coaching sessions (Carroll and Tosi, 1973), and that supervisors will do a better job of coaching when they receive credits or rewards for their efforts and when they have received training in conducting performance appraisal interviews (Douglas and Crain, 1975).

Effectiveness of On-the-job Methods

There has been no research comparing the use of the various on-the-job methods in terms of which might be better than another. Neither has there been any systematic assessment of these techniques compared to off-the-job methods. Organizations must, therefore, assess whether or not the costs of learning on the job are excessive. If so, then some sort of training away from work must be devised.

There are some problems that must be considered. Perhaps much of the value of on-the-job development comes from the "modeling" effects noted earlier. Thus, careful selection of the model and the situation in which it is hoped modeling behavior will occur can contribute to improved outcomes.

The primary problem with such a development strategy is the variability of supervisors under whom an individual will work. One may be very strong developmentally, another weak, so that the progress of the trainee is impeded. It can also happen that if supervisors are given the responsibility for such "temporary" employees they may not spend adequate developmental time with them, since they know that the employee's ultimate assignment will be elsewhere than their own units.

Some Integrated Approaches to Development

Now that we have described a fairly wide range of developmental methods and some general conditions under which they might work effectively, the question is how a manager can make use of them. He must, of necessity, understand something about how human beings change and how this can be accomplished organizationally.

Schein (1961) has analyzed a number of successful change programs in order to identify elements which such programs have in common and which can provide guides for the establishment of successful development. The change process, according to Schein (1961) and Lewin (1957), involves three basic stages: (1) unfreezing, (2) changing, and (3) refreezing.

Unfreezing.   The first step in the change process is unfreezing. At this stage attempts are made to motivate the target person to change before the actual change is introduced. Common to the unfreezing stage is the removal of social support to the individual for the old behavior or attitudes by insulating him from his habitual social system. For example, when trying to change attitudes, it may be useful, at least initially, to take the person away from his normal work setting, where he may be finding strong reinforcement of his present attitudes, to a location where he may obtain a new perspective. Next, rewards for willingness to change may be introduced, along with punishments for lack of willingness to change.

Changing.   Schein outlines two processes that seem especially effective in change programs. The first of these is *identification*, in which the target person identifies with one or more role models in his environment and thus tries to behave as they do. That is to say, the provision of appropriate role models facilitates change, since the role models exemplify the new behavior in their actions. The other effective change process is that of *internalization*, by which the target person discovers for himself that the new behavior or attitude solves his personal problems. Obviously this second change process is difficult to establish and control.

Refreezing.   In this stage, the newly acquired behavior or attitude must be supported by the social system in which the person normally functions if it is to become a part of the target person's normal behavioral patterns.

There are several "strategies," or suggested ways of going about this process described by Schein. Three of these are considered below.

What is important about each of these is that they are systematic, planned ways to induce change.

The Grid-OD Program

The Blake and Mouton (1969) approach to organizational development emphasizes changing the whole organization in a series of six sequential steps. Each step represents a particular phase of the total program.

Phase 1. This phase involves introducing managers to the managerial grid program. Phase 1 involves approximately five days of training. During this training period, managers participate in various exercises which illustrate group and intergroup problems and the advantages of certain problem-solving techniques which primarily emphasize involvement and participation. These problems focus on how other groups solve problems and what the difference is between high- and low-effectiveness groups. In addition, the group members receive feedback from the other participants as to their participant grid style. The managerial grid as an approach to describing leader behavior was discussed in chapter 8. Each person in the training is described by the other participants as having exhibited one of the five grid styles during the week of training. Each participant compares this evaluation with his self-evaluation. Then, the gap between this style and the 9,9 style (which represents excellence) is considered. An effort is made to get individuals to commit themselves to closing the gap between their present style and the 9,9 approach. During this phase, each participant also evaluates the general leader behavior patterns (a sort of leader culture) as they exist in his company.

Phase 2. In this stage, teamwork development is emphasized. An analysis of all work groups is made. Here each team member evaluates his group at work and then meets with the other members of the group to discuss their perceptions of the work culture of the group. Each member's grid style is assessed, primarily on how he relates to the group. Also, the group meets to study and attempt to resolve problems of operating together. A project, derived from some specific difficulty in the workplace, is initiated and investigated by the group. Phase 2 starts with the top group in the organization and slowly works down to the lower-level work groups.

Phase 3. In this step of the grid program, all groups review their external relationships and identify other groups with which they have problems of coordination, cooperation, or conflict. The emphasis is on developing intergroup relations. Key members of the groups with unsatisfactory intergroup relationships then meet to identify the type of relationship they actually have. They attempt to define the ideal relationship that should exist between their groups and develop a plan for overcoming the difficulties.

Phase 4. In this phase, a top management team designs an ideal strategic corporate model. This defines what the organization would be like if it were truly excellent. Consideration is given to the type of structure, the type of personnel, problems, and so on. The design team completes various instruments developed from the grid approach to help them in their task. After a long period of analysis, the model is developed and can then be evaluated by other organizational members and units.

Phase 5. Now comes the implementation of the ideal model. In this stage the organization is broken down into component parts and a planning team is created to help implement the model in each part, with the assistance of an overall phase 5 coordinator. Each team must of course implement the model with consideration for the unique character of its own organizational component.

Phase 6. This phase involves a critique of the whole OD program. Instruments are used to determine how the organization has changed since the OD program was initiated. Problems uncovered in phases 1 through 5 which hamper effectiveness are raised and form the bases for new ways of doing things.

Blake and Mouton believe that eventually such methods will become the "normal" way to do things in an organization. There will be no need to use crutches such as training sessions or analytical paper-and-pencil instruments to describe the people or the organization.

House Management Development Model

One of the most useful and well-integrated models for understanding the prerequisites for change has been developed by House (1967). He presents a systematic approach to the problem which seeks to specify the minimum conditions required for successful change efforts. This model is shown in figure 17.1. The objectives of development, which represent the kind of changes that are typically sought when develop-

FIGURE 17.1 A Model of Induced Change

Tension Experienced within the System	Intervention of a Prestigious Influencing Agent	Individuals Attempt to Implement Proposed Changes	New Behavior and Attitudes Reinforced by Achievement, Social Ties, and Internalized Values—Accompanied by Decreasing Dependence on Influencing Agent
Tension Experienced within the System ⟶	Generalized objectives established	Growing specificity of objectives establishment of subgoals	Achievement and resetting of specific objectives
Tension within existing social ties ⟶	Prior social ties interrupted or attenuated	Formation of new alliances and relationships centering around new activities	New social ties reinforce altered behavior and attitudes
Lowered sense of self-esteem ⟶	Esteem-building begun on basis of agent's attention and assurance	Esteem-building based on task accomplishment	Heightened sense of self-esteem
⟶	External motive for change (New schema provided)	Improvisation and reality-testing	Internalized motive for change

ment programs are instituted, are given, together with the input factors that are likely to affect the change and the types of conditions required to achieve a particular developmental objective.

The Input Factors. House lists five key variables which affect the outcomes of developmental efforts. Four of these represent the context in which the change effort must operate. These are the characteristics of the participants, the organizational culture, the leadership climate, and organizational structure. The fifth is the developmental method itself, which is the stimulus used to induce change in the individual.

1. Participant Characteristics. We have already noted that particular types of individuals will predominate in different types of organizations. The organizationalist, the professional, and the externalists all have significantly strong but different attitudinal orientations. These different orientations must be taken into account in developmental efforts. For example, training intended to change the attitudes toward the firm of externally-oriented members of an organization may encounter difficulty. If a program is intended to increase understanding of a particular managerial technique, however, this should not be a problem, since—for the most part—the level of intelligence of managers and professionals is above average.

2. Developmental Effort. We have detailed several of the strategies used to induce change (on- and off-the-job types) earlier in this chapter. House believes that certain techniques are more likely than others to be effective, depending on the objective of the developmental effort.

3. Leadership Climate. The climate of leadership in an organizational unit emerges from the interaction of leader (superior) and subordinates. There are two aspects of leadership of particular relevance to House's model of development. The first is the congruency of the leader's attitude with the general objectives of a particular training effort. This is especially relevant to attitude and skill change efforts, because the trainee should return to a work environment which supports the changes so that they receive reinforcement. The leader's behavior is the second important aspect. In the House model, the leader must provide guidance, counseling, coaching, and performance review based on developmental objectives.

4. Organizational Structure. The formal structure of the organization is composed of goals, policies, procedures, job descriptions, compensation systems and so on. We have already extensively discussed variations in structure in chapter 7. It would be fruitless to attempt to teach managers in a bureaucratic organization to restructure their own units as dynamic organizations when the external environment is highly stable. The structure is an important limiting factor in performance.

5. Organizational Culture. In chapter 4 we discussed the effects of groups and group norms on individuals. The culture of the organization can be defined as the values and norms that exist within a unit. It exists because of local cultural effects, the ethnic background of members, and the general social context of the location of the organization, as well as because of the structural and environmental characteristics of the organization itself.

This factor is not one easily changed by management efforts. If the culture is antithetical to organizational objectives, it can probably be changed only by mass replacement of personnel or by relocating the firm. In most instances, however, organizational culture will not be a *severe* limitation on training efforts. It is, however, a factor that must be analyzed, and the developmental content of training programs must be prepared in a way that is consistent with the culture.

Objectives of Development. The goals of development vary. Sometimes the intent is merely to increase knowledge. Often the goals are more ambitious, such as improved organizational results. House has attempted, after an extensive review of research on change efforts, to describe the minimum conditions which must be present to induce changes in (1) knowledge, (2) attitudes, (3) abilities, (4) job performance, and (5) end-operational results.

1. Knowledge Change. Knowledge change goals are considered to be independent of skill and ability change goals. They refer simply to the level of information a person has. As a developmental objective, for example, it may be desired to make employees more aware of certain technical or management techniques, such as capital budgeting or linear programming, or it may be that a developmental objective is to increase an employee's understanding of current theory about managerial practice and behavior.

According to figure 17.1, to increase knowledge the participant must be willing to learn (be motivated) and be exposed to instructor-centered methods such as lectures, tapes, textbooks, and so on. So long as the instruction is competent (contains the necessary information), it is likely that one will learn.

One problem with such development is that even when these conditions (learner motivation and competent instruction) are present and people do learn, managers (or those who are responsible for development) expect other outcomes (e.g., improved job performance). It is like expecting all those who understand and appreciate Bach to be able to play his fugues.

2. Attitude Change. In chapter 3 we defined an attitude as a predisposition to act in a certain way, an emotional feeling about something. Many firms have undertaken efforts to change attitudes of both workers and managers not only toward the company, but also toward women or minorities. They have done the latter to facilitate affirmative action programs, as well as to minimize problems in the workplace when women or minorities are hired.

For attitude change to occur, student-centered development methods are used. These are such processes as role-playing, sensitivity training, or group discussion methods in which the participants have an opportunity to consider how their current attitudes affect their work, and if and how changing them may improve the job situation. In development efforts in the organization, however, rigid attitudes—or those that are very important to the individual's psychological adjustment—will be difficult to change.

After the training, the environment to which the person returns is important. He should find a sympathetic leader, group norms that are not conflicting, and organization policies which do not make it difficult to change. For example, if the goal is to change attitudes of male managers toward women executives, then it would be necessary to have nondiscriminatory selection and promotion policies.

3. Abilities Change. If a person learns capital budgeting theory, will he be able to prepare a long-range facilities program? That is, does a knowledge change alter behavioral ability? In the House model, skills change is considered to take place in the training program itself, not necessarily on the job. A person in a training program may learn how to program a computer or run a group meeting more effectively, but whether or not these skills are used at work is determined by the job. One problem with skills training is that sometimes the new skill is not needed in the workplace, and this of course, frustrates the one who has acquired it. For example, many organizations recommend that

managers earn advanced degrees, such as the MBA. Often these degrees require courses in financial planning, but the graduate may not,
for a long time, carry out this activity.

To change abilities, the developmental effort must be experiential;
that is, the person must be able to practice the activity. For example,
he must formulate a plan, solve a problem, run a meeting. Such techniques as role playing and group discussion often provide interpersonal skill development. Business games, (simulations) and obviously
on-the-job methods such as special assignments and job rotation fall
into this category.

Behavioral modeling is an important factor here. The superior must
do the things he is seeking to develop in the subordinate. Or, if he
does not have the capacity to do so, then he should give the subordinate the opportunity to use the skill. For example, the goal of development might be to improve computer-programming skills. The superior
may not need such capacity in his own work and may have no ability
to program, but he can make available to the subordinate every opportunity to use these abilities in problem solving.

4. Change in Job Performance.   There may be a wide gulf between
having a skill and using it at work. The question with this objective is
"How can we bring skills, knowledge, abilities, or attitudes developed
away from work to the job?" For this objective of development, we
expect that the subject will possess the requisite competence, and the
responsibility of the manager and the organization is to incorporate
the ability into the work situation.

The appropriate developmental method is to provide the opportunity to use these capacities on the job. The trainee must be per-
mitted to make mistakes. The leader must offer coaching and guidance, providing help, support, and feedback about how well the
subordinate is doing. Organization structure factors must be consistent with the desired performance. For example, in promotions, we
must recognize the need to fail, and not pass over a manager simply
because he may have had some very important and useful failure experiences from which he learned, early in his career. This approach
will work effectively in conjunction with MBO.

5. Change in End-operational Results.   House does not expect improved results to be obtained unless the system (the structure) is designed so that it supports such results. For example, the compensation
system must pay, not penalize, good performance. Managers must be
able to reinforce subordinates with both objective and subjective re-

wards. All this must be consistent with, not contradictory to, the organizational culture.

Steps Involved in Development. Like Blake and Mouton, House also suggests a series of steps to move from the objective of knowledge change to organizational results. Basically, his suggestion is to progress sequentially.

After a person has increased his knowledge, he can then think about what he has learned, reconsidering his attitudes and rationally changing them, if necessary. If a change in attitudes has made him more receptive, he can be exposed to skills training. When he returns to the job with these new skills, he should then have help from his superior in the form of stated objectives and feedback about his performance to reinforce his new behavior.

If such an approach is taken at several points of an organization, and all the developmental efforts are conducted, then improved overall performance can be expected.

This is a long sequence. The costs of development are high both in terms of money and commitment. Managers must, for example, be willing to make alterations in the organization structure; for instance, changing the methods by which people are paid. Some of these changes, as we noted earlier, will meet much resistance. It is often more comfortable to go through developmental motions (offer seminars and so on), than to approach development systematically with the objective of real change.

MBO as Development

It would be more desirable not to have to resort to programs or strategies, as outlined above, but rather to build development into everyone's job. With management by objectives (MBO) this is done, because emphasis is placed on establishing goals, developing ways to achieve these goals, and providing feedback about how well someone has done. We discussed this approach in detail in chapter 12. There, however, we only examined performance objectives, which have to do with the work itself. Of course, this is developmental to the extent that a manager develops goals with his subordinates that represent learning experiences for them. In addition to setting performance goals, however, MBO should take a more pointed orientation toward development. Managers should work out, with subordinates, personal development goals.

A personal development goal is an objective which has increased human potential as an end. It should focus on improving skills and abilities, attitude change, or better interpersonal relationships. As stated, MBO builds development into everyone's job. Every manager can work out, when needed, personal development goals for those who work for him.

It is important to stress that these goals be based on problems or deficiencies, current or anticipated, in areas such as technical skills or interpersonal problems. They may also be aimed at developing a subordinate for movement within the organization. The importance of these objectives lies in their potential for combating obsolescence, given our rapid expansion of knowledge, for preparing people for increased responsibility, and for overcoming problems in organizational interactions.

Setting development goals is probably more difficult than setting performance goals, since they are personal in nature and, as such, must be handled with care and tact. This difficulty of course may be avoided by simply not setting them, and it could be argued that they should be avoided, since they are an intrusion into an individual's privacy by the superior or the organization. However, when perceived personal limitations hinder effective performance, the problem must be treated.

Thus, if at any time the superior believes an individual's limitations stand clearly in the way of the unit's goal achievement, that should be made known to the individual. He may not be aware that he is creating problems and would gladly change—if he were aware. Many technically competent people have been relieved from positions because of human problems they create. Many might have been retained had they only known that problems existed or were arising.

When there is a need for them, personal development objectives should be a basic part of the MBO program. If there is no real need, then an effort to set them probably will produce general and ambiguous objectives, tenable only if the organization wishes to invest in "education for education's sake." Personal objectives should attack deficiencies related to performance, containing specific action proposals for solving the problems. This may be done in the following manner:

Pinpoint a Problem Area. Persons involved in goal setting should continually be alert to negative incidents resulting from personal limitations. It is particularly important that the manager recognize problems. When situations occur which he believes are due to either personal or technical limitations, he should be aware of who was involved and make some determination of the cause of the problem. Other individuals in the unit may be helpful in identifying problems; those with whom an individual interacts, for example, may be in a reasonably good position to judge his technical competence or to determine when problems are due to his behavior. If colleagues continually complain about another person, additional investigation into the problem is warranted. The most important source for identifying negative incidents may prove to be the person responsible for them. He may be very aware of problems in which he is involved and by discussing them may get at the primary cause.

To be worthy of attention as a problem area, these negative incidents should be significant in effect and frequency. This does not mean, however, that an important incident which occurs only once should be overlooked if it suggests serious deficiencies.

There are several areas in which personal development objectives could be set. Self-improvement goals may be assigned to improve current performance or skills, or may be specifically designed to develop skills required at higher levels or in future jobs (where it may be impossible at the present to describe the end state of affairs to be achieved).

1. *Improve interpersonal relations.* Inability to maintain reasonably effective working relationships may be due to a person's lack of awareness or his inability to cooperate. This may arise from personality deficiencies or simple lack of awareness of his impact upon others. He may be unable to recognize that he is precipitating problems.

2. *Improve current skills.* A manager may, for instance, be unable to prepare a budget or to engage in research because he has not had adequate training in these areas or because his training is not up-to-date. His general performance may be acceptable, but his skills should be improved.

3. *Prepare for advancement.* Another possibility covers either technical or human skills required for different or higher-level positions. These are truly developmental goals which focus on preparation for advancement. There are many ways in which they may be achieved. In some cases the individual may be given advanced work assignments; in others, they may be achieved by exposure in training situations to new concepts. In any event, they represent a *potential* problem area.

Assess the Causes of the Problem.   Once it has been established that a problem exists, the cause needs to be determined. Causes should be sought jointly, a result of investigation and discussion by both the superior and subordinate after both have thought of possible causes.

The possible causes of problems may be grouped into three general categories:

1. *Procedures and structure.* The structure of the organization itself may induce disturbances. Interpersonal conflict may develop because of the interdependence of work activities. For instance, if formal requirements cause a delay in information transmission, those who need it may develop negative attitudes and feelings.

2. *Others with whom an individual must work.* Problems with subordinates or managerial peers of the goal setter may be caused by personality incompatibility or lack of certain technical skills. While this may represent an important cause of problems, it is too easy to blame negative incidents on others.

3. *The person himself.* The individual may have habits and characteristics which are not congruent with those of subordinates or colleagues. Or he may lack the technical skills requisite to carry out certain responsibilities.

Attempting to define problems and causes facilitates converting development objectives into achievable goals. Like other objectives, they can be general (attend a sensitivity training course or role-playing seminar), or more specific (attend XYZ course in financial planning, use PERT techniques on Project X).

For assessing the achievement of development objectives we can rely simply upon the determination that the action plan has been carried out and that the individual has learned something. Suppose, for instance, that a development goal for an engineer destined to be a supervisor reads as follows: "To meet with members of the financial, marketing, and production groups in order to learn how product release schedules affect their areas." Currently, he may have to know little about this since he may now have little impact on product release schedules. The question is, how do you know that the activity produced the desired learning? You don't. At some point in time, the superior, who presumably has some knowledge in the goal area, should discuss the results of the meeting with the subordinate, emphasizing particularly the important points that should have been learned. Thus, the subordinate acquires both the learning experience of the meeting and reinforcement from the discussion.

We have made the point that development must be planned. It must be pointed at fairly specific objectives, based on problems which must be solved, and the methods used should be adequate.

FIGURE 17.2 Conditions Required to Induce Change Through Development

Source: *Managerial Process and Organizational Behavior*, by Alan C. Filley and Robert J. House. Copyright © 1969 by Scott, Foresman and Company. Reprinted by permission of the publisher.

Conditions	Objectives				
	Change in Knowledge	Change in Attitude	Change in Ability	Change in Job Performance	Change in End-Operational Results
Participant Characteristics	Sufficient motivation	Flexible attitudes on part of participants; Agreement with spirit of the material to be learned	Non-conflicting habits or personality traits		
Developmental Effort	Direct method of instruction (programmed learning, lectures, films, reading, and so on); Competent instruction	Discussion of on-the-job applications and personal benefits	Practice of desired abilities; Corrective training (therapy to correct undesirable habits and behavioral patterns)	Opportunity for on-the-job practice of newly acquired abilities	
Leadership Climate		Neutral or positive attitude of superior toward development	Superior's attitude and example consistent with desired change	Coaching, counseling, and periodic performance review by superior consistent with desired performance	Performance appraisal by the superior based on practices taught in the learning phase
Organizational Structure		Goals, top management philosophy, and policies consistent with learning phase		Philosophy, practices, and precedents of the policymaking executives consistent with desired manager performance	Top management active support and interest in development; Incentive system designed to reward practices taught in the learning phase
Organizational Culture		Cultural conditions and social beliefs consistent with desired attitudes		Informal group rules and standards consistent with desired change	Positive employe and informal group attitudes toward change

Dalton (1970) found a number of factors to be associated with successful development, and these are identified in figure 17.2. First, he found that successful change is preceded by internal tensions which seem to produce a receptive environment for change efforts. A problem must exist. Second, the push for change should come from a respected or authoritative source. This also contributes to a successful change attempt since it gives credibility to the need for change. Third, it is more likely that change objectives will be achieved if they are specific rather than general. When specific development goals are known, as in the House model, then the development strategy can focus on what techniques are most likely to be effective.

The breaking off of old social relationships and the establishment of new ones also seems to facilitate change, as in the case in which people are placed in a new work environment in early stages of development. Another factor which seems important is growing self-confidence and esteem which emerges as organizational members feel they are making progress in solving their problems. A factor which is especially valuable but correspondingly difficult to achieve, is that of internalizing the change, in which individuals accept the change because they see it as valid. Finally, the change must receive reinforcement in the social system to survive. This is to say that the structure of the organization must be congruent with environmental requirements and that the people in it be capable of coping with that state of the organization. These circumstances are extensively examined in chapters 6, 7, 13, 14, and 15.

Change is proceeding at an increasingly rapid rate in our economy today and organizations must change to survive. The successful management of change is indispensable, especially in the dynamic and mixed types of organizations. All organization types, but in particular the dynamic and mixed, must give the subject of change more attention than they have in the past.

Discussion Questions

1. Using the House model of management development, what is the most likely effect of courses which you have taken in college on your performance later at work?

2. Changing organizations is an extremely expensive process. Comment. What are the costs?

3. What is the basic difference between off-the-job methods and MBO as a strategy for changing people?

4. How do personal development goals differ from work or performance goals? What responsibility does a supervisor have in setting them? Should he have any?

5. How should the environment of an organization affect the training and development strategy of an organization?

Chapter 18
The Effective Organization: Present and Future

Organizations pervade all of modern life, and where the beginning and end points are to be found is something no one can say. In various ways, organizations serve the interests of all classes of people—the owners and investors, the members of the organization, and its various publics, from consumers to those who simply have concern for the ways in which the organization and its various outputs may directly or indirectly affect the qualities of their lives.

Viewed in this way, organizations become the most significant of social institutions. Our concern in this book has been to provide the best of contemporary understanding of how organizations can be effectively managed to meet their goals.

It remains in this final chapter to address two quite fundamental questions about the character of organizations and their relationship to society. One question has to do with the goals themselves. It would indeed be difficult to define precisely the appropriate goals for any organization, but in this chapter we can perhaps clarify certain of the pressures, from within and without, which suggest the directions in which organizational goals are cast, now and for the future. We would approach this question by analyzing in more detail the question of whom the organization serves.

A second question has to do with environmental forces, inside and outside the organization, which tend further to define the types of people who are likely to be associated with organizations in the future.

Throughout this book, we have stressed that the nature of the external environment will define the structure of the organization, and that as a general rule the people who are attracted to a particular type of organization are likely to be those whose outlooks and needs are congruent with that organization. As is the case for every generation, however, we live in a time of social change. As social conditions change, so—too—do the outlooks, needs, and requirements of members of the society. If the outlooks of organizational members will change, organizations to be effective must adapt to those outlooks, or find other ways to be congruent with the needs of its members. In this chapter, we will look briefly at some of the social forces which presently are interacting in an important way with the character of organizations.

Organizational Effectiveness

First, let us consider the nature of organizational effectiveness and some common measures of this quality in an organization. The purpose of managing—of obtaining congruence among the environment, structure, people, and process—is, of course, to increase the level of an organization's effectiveness, and of course the basic measure of an organization's effectiveness is survival. In order to serve its various publics, it must survive, and, conversely, if it does not serve them well, it will fail.

Various observers have attempted to factor the basic areas of effectiveness which contribute to survival. Parsons (1956), a sociologist, states that effective organizations adapt to their environment, know their goals, and achieve behavioral integration of personal goals of organizational members with organizational goals. In a study of 100 Texas firms, Friedlander and Pickle (1968) hypothesized that the effective organization was one which provided satisfaction of owners (through profits), satisfaction of customers (through speed of service, quality and quantity of goods and services, and the helpfulness of the staff), satisfaction of employees, satisfaction of suppliers and creditors (with fair treatment and prompt payment of accounts), and satisfaction of the community (through good citizenship). Of these, only satisfaction of owners, satisfaction of customers, and the providing of certain satisfactions to employees were related to financial success for the 100 firms.

Some studies have sought to identify indicators of organizational effectiveness by surveying large numbers of managers. A study of 283 organizational units in private industry by Mahoney and Weitzel (1969) found that organizations which used and developed their human resources effectively, which had good planning, which emphasized task accomplishment, which constantly initiated improvements in their operations, and which had cooperation among organizational units were very likely to be effective according to the ratings of practicing managers. A similar study by Paine (1970) of government units indicated that effective government organizations were those which had clear goals, good planning, good cooperation between units which rewarded ability, and where superiors provided support to subordinates.

Such lists of characteristics of effective organizations are indicative, but still quite general. They beg the question of how an organization achieves effectiveness. One study by Thune and House (1970) points to the importance of planning; it shows that increased time and emphasis placed upon planning is related to effectiveness for organizations, but Mintzberg (1973) suggests further that, as we have stated throughout this book, the planning process of different organizations varies with changes in their environment and with their stages of growth. That is, planning techniques vary in utility, depending upon the environment, structure, and personnel. The approach to the utilization of human resources must vary by type of organization, since employees in different types of organizations have different values, motives, and expectations. Thus, any discussion of organizational effectiveness without reference to type of organization is too abstract and general to be of practical importance.

Measures of organizational effectiveness have always been important. If, however, it is true, as the popular press every week reports, that people are becoming disaffected with work—or with a "bureaucratic" society in general—then the rather narrow traditional views of effectiveness are less useful.

Perhaps for this reason, writers on organizational effectiveness lay increasing stress on the importance of meeting the needs of organizational members, or of using human resources in such a way as to maximize their potential. For example, Bass, as early as 1952, argued that the worth of the organization to its members should be considered as a measure of organizational value along with existing indicators of effectiveness. Caplow (1964) argues the importance of high levels of "voluntarism" (the ability of the organization to satisfy its members and their desire to participate in the organization) and "integration" (the organization's ability to control internal conflict, to increase communication about problems and procedures, and to achieve more consensus among its members about the organization's problems). Argyris (1964) has also emphasized the successful blending of individual needs and organizational goals as indicators of effectiveness, showing that achieving top-management goals at the expense of personal goal achievement leads to ineffectiveness. McGregor (1960) stresses the importance to organizational effectiveness of integrating personal and organizational goals, as have Blake and Mouton (1964) and Hill (1969). All of these writers point out that organizational members as individuals and groups must bargain with the organization in order to achieve an integration of organizational goals and personal motives.

Satisfaction of the personal psychological needs of members is increasingly viewed as an indicator of organizational effectiveness, whether such satisfaction contributes to the organization's task goals or not. The achievement of personal goals of employees is viewed as important for its own sake, and thus participation is seen not only as an effective way of obtaining acceptance of change but as an approach which is congruent with the inherent dignity of the individual.

The extent to which an organization is socially responsible is also seen more today than in the past as an indicator of effectiveness. Bass (1952) was an early advocate of the position that the worth of an organization to society must be considered in determining overall organizational value. Many critics of business have argued that responsibility to the general public—for example, in product quality or impact on the physical environment—must take precedence over concern for profits or stockholder interest. In addition, it is increasingly proposed that the private sector of the economy should carry a more significant part of the burden in helping the disadvantaged, rebuilding slums, reducing crime, improving education, and seeking other social gains (Henderson, 1968). Some surveys (Baumhart, 1961) show that managers increasingly accept responsibility in these areas and no longer see profit as their only concern, though profitability and responsibility to stockholders remain, not surprisingly, their most important concern (Lorig, 1967).

Managing in the Changing World

The world is constantly changing—politically, socially, and technologically—and these changes seem to have accelerated in recent history. Individuals, groups, and organizations adapt to this change in a dynamic way, with social and political change encouraging technological developments and these in turn contributing to further social and political change.

Some of the primary change forces with which managers must cope in the near future will be increases in foreign competition, growth of the multinational organization, continuing rapid growth of technical knowledge, growing power of government, political instability, increases in organization size, changing composition of the labor force, changes in the values of organizational members, and continued improvements in opportunities for minority group members. Such changes can well be considered as representative of the changes in environment cited throughout this book, and many of the organizational adaptations we have discussed will be in response to just such changes as these. As we discuss these environmental changes in greater detail, the reader should consider how the nature of these adaptations will be reflected in the organizational dynamics detailed in this book.

Growth in Size of Organizations

Perhaps the first factor that will be relevant to future managerial effectiveness is the sheer size of organizations. We can expect organizations in the future to be larger than they are today (Bennis, 1970). In 1947 the largest 200 corporations in the United States produced 30 percent of the value added to manufacturing output, but by 1970 the top 200 produced 43 percent of the value added (Burck, 1975). Greater size of course suggests greater formalization; whether such organizations will need greater differentiation in their own structures, however, to meet increased environmental pressures is a question for future analysis.

Increased Foreign Competition

United States firms are facing increased foreign competition. At the present time, a significantly higher proportion of the automobiles, sewing machines, binoculars, musical instruments, electrical motors, television sets and radios, clothing and shoes, bicycles, motorcycles, and other products that are sold in this country are made by foreign manufacturers than was the case a few years ago. The rapidly improving quality of some of these goods, as well as effective price competition, have made this competition difficult to cope with. Many domestic industries have been seriously affected by it in recent years, and even the U.S. automobile industry has suffered significant economic losses. Foreign competitors often have very efficient modern plants, built since the Second World War, and they have taken very quickly to modern management methods developed chiefly in the United States in the past 20 years. Their labor forces are highly motivated and often willing to work at low wages.

Increased foreign competition requires more attention by domestic producers to costs and technological improvements, and, where the technology is volatile, more specialists and more market research techniques and activities are needed. Such competition also increasingly involves the government, since economic actions, especially on the part of large firms or industries, may have an impact on national policy, imports and exports, foreign-exchange relationships, and currency reevaluations, all of which play a significant role in prices in the product or factor markets.

Growth of the Multinational Organization

In the past two decades, large firms all over the world have opened operations in other countries or have entered into joint ventures or licensing arrangements with firms in other countries. Virtually every large business enterprise in the United States has overseas operations at present; one major toolmaker, for example, has plants in England, France, Italy, Japan, Mexico, Germany, and Australia. In the past few years, Japanese firms have opened several plants in the United States as well as in other countries. A firm in Taiwan has formed relationships with dozens of firms from other countries. The growth of U.S. industry abroad has been so great that in 1968, J. J. Servan-Schreiber, a French writer and political figure, said, "Fifteen years from now it is quite possible that the world's third greatest industrial power just after the United States and Russia will not be Europe, but American industry in Europe."

There are many reasons for this expansion. Transportation cost for many products are simply too high to ship long distances and still sell products at a competitive price. New foreign markets are not perhaps as saturated with products as domestic markets, making it possible to sell the product more readily at a higher price than in the domestic market.

Foreign operations obviously create much more environmental uncertainty than do domestic operations. Market forces as well as government actions must be predicted, and this may be difficult in countries without a stable political structure or mature economy. Cultural differences and differences in needs and values of local employees suggest the need for different leadership and decision strategies. Some observers feel, for example, that the ability of middle managers or foremen in underdeveloped countries may be lower than that of the typical U.S. manager (Carroll et al., 1977). If true, this would necessitate more centralization in decision making in such operations. Intensive social change and shifts—in the value of currencies, for example—produce a very uncertain environment in many aspects of foreign operations.

Technological Change

Technology has advanced extremely rapidly in recent years, and this trend can be expected to continue. To keep abreast of such advances, firms obviously need large numbers of highly specialized professionals with knowledge of such changes and their significance for marketing and production methods.

Of significance to the business firm is the time required for ideas to be converted to products. Figure 18.1 shows the relationship of basic research to the development, distribution, and eventual death of a product. Basic research of course is not carried out to produce specific new products, but typically produces new concepts, ideas, or modifications of existing models or theories. In the applied research stage, the new idea is tested in terms of its specific product application, and technological advantages are considered for the first time, while in the product development stage, the product is developed, evaluated, and subjected to cost analysis.

Research and development expenditures in the United States have steadily increased on an absolute basis every year and are significantly higher than in any other country in the world. However, research and development expenditures are not rising as fast as gross national product. In Europe and Japan, on the other hand, the percentage of national income devoted to research and development is rising, a development which has worried a number of analysts (Dean, 1974; Boretsky, 1974), though it should be noted that Japan and the European nations started at a very low base rate. However, U.S. firms often have access to technological developments from other countries through joint ventures, licensing agreements, or imitation, and the reverse is also true. Clearly, the fact that other nations are investing more heavily in research and development accelerates product change, making the technological environment of firms ever more volatile. Some of the nations which formerly imported technology, such as Japan, are now exporting it, particularly to the less-developed nations (Ozawa, 1973).

There is some disagreement among authorities over how long it takes a new concept or idea to be developed into a marketable product. Some say the period averages 14 to 19 years (McLoughlin, 1970) but others believe that the time has shortened in recent years. Ayres (1969) believes both that the lead time has shortened and that new technological processes saturate an industry much more rapidly than was the case a few years ago. Thus, today it is more important than ever for an industrial organization to be able to discern new tech-

FIGURE 18.1   Product Life Cycle

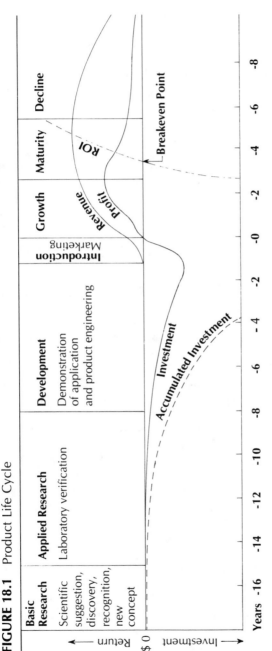

The product life cycle represents the history of a commodity or service from the time of its initial conception to its ultimate withdrawal from the market because of inadequate profit margin. There are four distinct phases of the life cycle after the initial introduction to the market: introduction, growth, maturity, and decline. Profit during these phases may be defined as the margin realized after both fixed and variable costs have been covered. The return on investment (ROI) does not begin until breakeven on the total accumulated investment is realized. The position of the breakeven point is determined by the effectiveness of management in controlling the investment prior to market introduction and in providing a correct pricing policy thereafter.

Source: McLoughlin, W. G. *Fundamentals of Research Management*. New York: American Management Association, 1970, p. 17.

nological and scientific developments quickly and to convert them to products or new technology. The boundary-spanning and adaptive subsystems are of course especially critical to this process.

Changing Composition of the Labor Force

The relative proportions of different occupational groups in the U.S. labor force has changed over the years, and this is perhaps not surprising in the light of both technological and social change. Presently, the number of professional and technical workers is increasing the fastest, with an estimated increase of 50 percent between 1968 and 1980 (Bureau of Labor Statistics, 1971). The number of service, clerical, and sales workers is also increasing more rapidly than such occupational groups as craftsmen, foremen, and factory workers. The average educational level of a United States employee is above 12 years of school, and white-collar workers now constitute just about 50 percent of the labor force. This change in composition in the labor force of course has implications for management in terms of effectiveness. It is also important to note that the advantages of job opportunities are not uniformly available to all Americans.

Employment of the Disadvantaged Worker

As a concluding note in this book, let us consider some of the challenges and responsibilities confronting managers in the matter of equal opportunities and, finally, how certain changes in societal values may further affect the design of organizations and approaches to managing them.

Pressures have increased upon every organization to employ more disadvantaged workers. In considering this question, it is fundamental to examine the socialization that has affected the attitudes and position of persons who are disadvantaged in the U.S. labor force. For our purposes, the disadvantaged are defined basically as ethnic or other groups who historically have not enjoyed the same educational and social opportunities as other Americans. Because of this long history of reduced participation in U.S. society, the disadvantaged often have low levels of self-esteem (Ausubel and Ausubel, 1969; Coleman, 1966). Such persons tend to have a short-run perspective and do not expect future benefits to result from current behaviors (Rosen, 1959). As personal frustrations increase, they become less optimistic and less motivated to find a job or to exert effort on a job (Means, 1966). Lack of success at work contributes further to reduced self-esteem and a feeling of irrelevance (Liebow, 1967). Money may not be an effective motivator for such groups because their pay checks often are spoken for in advance by creditors, relatives, or friends; they are expected to share whatever they have with those close to them and thus cannot fully utilize the fruits of their own labor (Davis, 1964).

The employment of disadvantaged workers unquestionably constitutes a contribution to the community and an appropriate exercise of corporate responsibility. It calls for a number of adjustments in management technique. The outlook of such individuals, for example, clearly calls for new motivational approaches, such as one proposed by Porter (1973), which calls for daily pay and attendance rewards. Perhaps special confidence-building programs and greater job security might work better, since they would address themselves to some of the primary problems involved. Special training programs have been launched in a number of companies (Doeringer, 1969), and some positive results have been obtained when the proper "supportive" climate has been established (Friedlander and Greenberg, 1969). Special training is needed not only for the disadvantaged employees themselves, but for the personnel who will carry out programs for the disadvantaged, since those people seem most resistant to changing company procedures or policies in order to meet the special needs of the disadvantaged (Goeke and Weymar, 1969).

Increased Employment of Minority Group Members in Higher-level Management Positions

There is considerable evidence of discrimination against blacks and other minorities and women in compensation and promotion (Commerce Clearing House, 1972; Matich, 1970; Upjohn Institute, 1973; Cates, 1973; Equal Employment Opportunity Commission, 1972). Government and private groups in the past have placed substantial pressures on organizations to eliminate such discriminatory practices. Initially, conciliation procedures were used, but these have not been effective, and more stringent procedures are now in effect (Adams, 1972). The number of blacks and women in management and professional positions has slowly increased, but there is still resistance to their employment in such positions. Part of the bias lies in sexual and racial stereotypes which result in negative evaluations by incumbent managers (Rosen and Jerdee, 1974a). It does not appear that such stereotypes are disappearing quickly. Some research shows that even female managers are likely to favor males over females in promotion, selection, and placement decisions (Schein, 1975).

There seems to be no empirical justification for such general discrimination at work. Research has indicated a great deal of overlap among the white male group and female, black, and other minorities on various abilities relevant to job performance (Tyler, 1965). Research also shows no differences in personality factors, values, and job satisfactions between white males and minority group members that cannot be accounted for by variations in social situations (Tyler, 1965). Research also shows, finally, that minority group members have lower job satisfaction than the dominant white male group (O'-Reilly and Roberts, 1973), which could be accounted for largely by differences in social situations facing the respective groups. In sum, this line of research suggests strongly that competent employees can be found for any job among members of various minority groups.

There are some average differences in values and motives of males and females, but these differences may simply reflect tendencies for men and women to fulfill various sex roles imposed by the culture (Tyler, 1965). It is possible that organizations are forcing women managers to adopt for themselves the male role stereotype (Schein, 1975). Perhaps, as we discussed in chapter 3, individuals are often forced to adapt to the organization's value system.

Changing Societal Values

There is, finally, growing evidence that the younger age groups in our society are changing their values, particularly those values that interface the world of work. As compared to previous generations, today's high school students put less emphasis on security and promotions and more on autonomy and interesting work. They are also less accepting of authority today than in the past (Sheppard and Herrick, 1972). Miner (1973) has found the same to be true of college students. He has found that there are fewer individuals with positive attitudes toward those holding positions of authority, who are competitive with peers, and who are willing to exercise power over others—all factors, obviously, which would be associated with attraction to management as a career, especially in structured organizations.

Business executives themselves predict a shift in national ideology in the United States by 1985 (Martin and Lodge, 1975). Among 1,800 executives surveyed, there was a preference for the traditional U.S. emphasis on individual rights and responsibility. The vast majority, however, predicted a new dominant ideology by 1985 which would stress rights stemming from the group and the use of property according to the goals of the community. If these studies reflect a coming permanent shift in values, contemporary management strategies must change. Newer motivational and leadership approaches will be needed.

Effect on Management

In this chapter, we have outlined briefly some of the major conditions that will impact organizational structure and management style in the future. Other factors—the effects of pollution, for example—are perhaps too evident from the information we receive daily to warrant discussion here, but the discerning reader will see their relevance to our theme.

The various environmental changes taking place today will have consequences that can hardly be predicted with accuracy, but which can be analyzed to some degree in the light of contingency framework set forth in this book. Clearly, certain of the changes will contribute to increased stability of certain types of organizations; for example, increases in sheer size may in many cases result in increasingly stable organizations, and whether this will be an advantage or a disadvantage, in view of changing social values, is something that remains to be seen. Certainly, managers will find it necessary continually to reassess the relationship of their organization structures and its goals to the values of the various publics, internal and external, with which it interfaces. One assumption might be that increasing environmental pressures of the kind outlined in this chapter will result overall in substantially greater differentiation among organizational subunits with respect to structure, personnel, and the way the managerial process is carried out.

The applied behavioral sciences will become increasingly important in management, since human resource problems in organizations will be more complex. The tremendous increase in the literature of applied behavioral science and a similar increase in management training and consulting programs are also indicative of this trend. The trends will continue, and knowledge in the behavioral area, as well as other areas of management, can be expected to increase as greater resources are committed to its development.

Discussion Questions

1. If the changes in values and personnel take place as predicted in this chapter, and management becomes more participative and humanistic, what will be the consequences of this for the increased international competition that is also predicted? Give reasons for your answers.

2. It is predicted that relationships among organizations will become increasingly important in the future. How can such relationships be improved?

3. Make a list of the technological developments which will have occurred by 2025. How will these influence the management of organizations?

4. Evaluate the various criteria of organizational effectiveness cited in this chapter. Were any important characteristics left out? Which ones? Why are they important?

5. As noted in this chapter, many U.S. companies are establishing branches or subsidiaries in other countries and other countries are now operating in the United States. Make a list of the responsibilities that such companies have to the people and government of the foreign country in which they are located?

6. Some critics of current writings on the social responsibilities of a business say that the only responsibility of a business is to perform an economic function to society. Providing quality goods and services at the lowest possible cost should be the only concern of management. Do you agree or disagree? Why?

7. Write up a policy statement on social responsibility for a business organization. Do the same for a government organization. Discuss these.

References

Adams, A. V. "Toward fair employment and the EEPC: A study of compliance procedures under Title VII of the Civil Rights Act of 1964. EEOC Contract 70-15." Equal Employment Opportunity Commission. Washington, D.C., 1972.

Aldag, R. J., and A. P. Brief. "Some correlates of work values," *Journal of Applied Psychology,* 60 (1975): 757–60.

Alderfer, C. P. *Existence, relatedness, and growth: Human needs in organizational settings.* Free Press, 1972.

Allison, D. "The motivation of the underprivileged worker," in W. F. Whyte (ed.), *Industry and society.* McGraw-Hill, 1964.

Anderson, R. C. "Learning in discussions: A resume of the authoritarian-democratic study," *Harvard Educational Review,* 29 (1959): 201–15.

Andrew, G. "A study of the effectiveness of a workshop method for mental health education," *Mental Hygiene,* 38 (1954): 267–78.

Argyris, C. "Human problems with budgets," *Harvard Business Review,* 31 (1953): 97–110.

———. "Interpersonal barriers to decision making," *Harvard Business Review,* 44 (1966): 84–97.

———. *Organization of a bank.* Labor and Management Center, Yale University, 1954.

———. *Personality and organization.* Harper & Bros., 1957.

———. *Integrating the individual and the organization.* Wiley, 1964.

Asch, Solomon E. *Social psychology.* Prentice-Hall, 1952.

Assael, H. "Constructive role of interorganizational conflict," *Administrative Science Quarterly,* 14 (1969): 573–83.

Atkinson, J. W. *Introduction to motivation.* Van Nostrand, 1964.

———. "Motivational determinants of risk taking behavior," *Psychological Review,* 64 (1957): 359–72.

Ausubel, D. P., and P. Ausubel. "Ego development among segregated Negro children," in A. Ferman, J. L. Kornbluh and J. A. Miller (eds.), *Negroes and jobs.* Univ. of Michigan Press, 1969.

Ayres, R. U. *Technological forecasting and long range planning.* McGraw-Hill, 1969.

Bales, R. F. "In conference," *Harvard Business Review,* 32 (1954): 44–50.

Bales, R. F., and P. E. Slater. "Role differentiation in small groups," in Parsons, T. R. et al. (eds.), *Family, socialization, and interaction process.* Free Press, 1955.

Barnard, C. *The functions of the executive.* Harvard Univ. Press, 1938.

Barnlund, D. C., and C. Harland. "Propinquity and prestige as determinants of communication network," *Sociometry,* 26 (1963): 467–79.

Bass, B. M. "Ultimate criteria of organizational worth," *Personnel Psychology,* 2 (1952): 157–73.

Bassett, G. A., and H. H. Meyer. "Performance appraisal based on self-review," *Personnel Psychology,* 21 (1968): 421–30.

Baughman, J. P. *The history of American management.* Prentice-Hall, 1969.

Bayroff, A. G., H. R. Hafferty, and E. A. Rundquist. "Validity of ratings as related to rating techniques and conditions," *Personnel Psychology,* 7 (1954): 93–113.

Beach, L. R. "Multiple regression as a model for human information utilization," *Organizational Behavior and Human Performance,* 2 (1967): 276–89.

Beckhard, R. *Organization development: Strategies and models.* Addison-Wesley, 1969.

Beier, E. G. "Non verbal communication: How we send emotional messages," *Psychology Today,* 8 (1974): 53–56.

Bellows, R. *Psychology of Personnel in Business and Industry.* Prentice-Hall, 1954.

Bendix, R., and L. N. Fisher. "The perspectives of Elton Mayo," *Review of Economics and Statistics,* 31, 49, 312–21.

Bennis, W. G. "Toward a truly scientific management: The concept of organizational health," in Ghorpade, J. (ed.), *Assessment of organizational effectiveness: Issues, analysis, readings.* Goodyear Publishing, 1971. 116–43.

Berne, E. *Games people play.* Grolier, 1963.

Berscheid, E., and Elaine H. Walster. *Interpersonal Attraction.* Addison-Wesley, 1969.

Bigonness, W. J. "Effect of applicant's sex, race, and performance on employer's performance ratings: Some additional findings," *Journal of Applied Psychology,* 61 (1976): 80–84.

Blake, R. R., and J. S. Mouton. *The managerial grid.* Gulf, 1964.

————. *Building a dynamic corporation through GRID organizational development.* Addison-Wesley, 1969.

Blake, R. R., H. A. Shepard, and J. S. Mouton. *Managing intergroup conflict in industry.* Gulf, 1964.

Blake, R. R., J. S. Mouton, J. S. Barnes, and L. E. Greiner. "Breakthrough in organization development," *Har-*

vard *Business Review,* 42 (1964): 133–55.

Blau, P. *The dynamics of bureaucracy.* Univ. of Chicago Press, 1955.

Blauner, R. *Alienation and freedom.* Univ. of Chicago Press, 1964.

Bolda, R. A., and C. H. Lawshe. "Evaluation of role playing," *Personnel Administration,* 25 (1962): 40–42.

Bond, B. W. "The group discussion-decision approach: An appraisal of its use in health education," *Dissertation Abstracts,* 16 (1956): 903.

Boyle, B. "Equal opportunity for women is smart business," *Harvard Business Review,* 53 (1975): 85–95.

Boretsky, M. "U.S. technology-trend and policy issues," in *Twenty-Seventh National Conference on the Administration of Research.* Denver Research Institute: Univ. of Denver, September, 1973.

Borman, W. C. "Effects of instructions to avoid halo error on reliability and validity of performance evaluation ratings," *Journal of Applied Psychology,* 60 (1975): 556–60.

————., and M. D. Dunnette. "Behavior based versus trait oriented performance ratings: An empirical study," *Journal of Applied Psychology,* 60 (1975): 561–65.

Bowers, D. G., and S. E. Seashore. "Protecting organizational effectiveness with a four-factor theory of leadership," *Administrative Science Quarterly,* 11 (1966): 238–63.

Boyd, J. B., and J. D. Ellis. *Findings of Research into Senior Management Seminars.* Toronto: The Hydro-Electric Power Commission of Toronto, 1962. Cited by J. P. Campbell and M. D. Dunnette, "Effectiveness of T-group experiences in managerial training and development," *Psychological Bulletin,* 70 (1968): 73–104.

Bray, D. W., and D. L. Grant. "The assessment center in the measurement of potential for business management," *Psychological Monographs no. 625*, 80 (1966): 1–27.

Browne, P. J., and R. Golembiewski. "The line-staff concept revisited: An empirical study of organizational images," *Academy of Management Journal,* 17 (1974), 406–17.

Bunker, D. R. "Individual applications of laboratory training," *Journal of Applied Behavioral Science,* 1 (1965): 131–48.

———, and G. W. Dalton. "The comparative effectiveness of groups and individuals in solving problems," in Lawrence, P. R., and J. A. Seiler (eds.), *Organizational behavior and administration.* Dorsey Press, 1965.

Burek, C. G. "The intricate 'politics' of the corporation," *Fortune,* April, 1975.

Burgess, R. L. "An experimental and mathematical analysis of group behavior within restricted networks," *Journal of Experimental Social Psychology,* 4 (1968): 338–49.

Burke, R. J., and Douglas S. Wilcox. "Characteristics of effective employee performance review and development interviews," *Personnel Psychology,* 22 (1969): 291–305.

———. "Effects of different patterns and degrees of openness in superior-subordinate communication on subordinates job satisfaction," *Academy of Management Journal,* 12 (1969): 325.

Burns, T., and G. Stalker. *The management of innovation.* Tavistock, 1961.

Butler, E. D. "An experimental study of the case method in teaching the social foundations of education," *Dissertation Abstracts,* 27 (1967): 2912.

Butler, J. L. "A study of the effectiveness of lecture versus conference teaching techniques in adult education," *Dissertation Abstracts,* 26 (1966): 3712.

Buxton, C. E. *College teaching: A psychologist's view.* Harcourt-Brace, 1956.

Cameron, J. "Black America: Still waiting for full membership," *Fortune,* April, 1975.

Campbell, D. T. "Systematic error on the part of human links in communication systems," *Information and Control,* 1 (1958): 334–69.

Campbell, J. P., and M. D. Dunnette. "Effectiveness of T-group experiences in managerial training and development," *Psychological Bulletin,* 70 (1968): 73–104.

Caplow, T. *Principles of organization.* Harcourt, Brace and World, 1964.

Carey, A. "The Hawthorne studies: A radical criticism," *American Sociological Review,* 32 (1967): 408–16.

Carlson, R. E., P. W. Thayer, E. C. Mayfield, and D. A. Peterson. "Improvements in the selection interview," *Personnel Journal,* 50 (April, 1971): 268-75, 317.

Carlucci, C., and W. J. Crissy. "How readable are employee handbooks?" *Personnel Psychology,* 4 (1951): 383–95.

Carman, H. J. and H. C. Syrett. *A history of the American people.* Knopf, 1955.

Carpenter, C. R., and L. Greenhill. "An investigation of closed circuit television for teaching university courses," *Instructional Television Project Report #2,* University Park, Pennsylvania: Penn State Univ., 1958.

Carroll, S. J., Jr. "A central signalling technique for measuring the time and allocations of managers." Unpublished research study, 1961.

———. "The relationship of various college graduate characteristics to recruiting decisions," *Journal of Applied Psychology,* 50 (1966): 421-23.

———. "Beauty, bias, and business," *Personnel Administration,* 32 (1969): 21–25.

———. "Some personal and situational correlates of reactions to management development programs," *Journal of the Academy of Management,* 13 (1970): 187–96.

———. "Effectiveness ratings of motivational methods by different groups of supervisors." Unpublished study, Univ. of Maryland, 1973.

———. "Two cases of failure in using competition for motivation." Unpublished study, Univ. of Maryland, 1973.

———. "Factors related to job involvement of dental assistants." Unpublished study, Univ. of Maryland, 1974.

———. "Danyau Picture Tubes Co. Ltd." in Carroll, S. J., F. P. Paine, and John B. Miner (eds.), *The managerial process: Cases and readings,* 2d ed., Macmillan, 1977.

———, D. Cintron, and H. L. Tosi. "Factors related to how superiors set goals and review performance for their subordinates," *Proceedings of the American Psychological Assn.,* 1971: 497–98.

Carroll, S. J., Jr., and A. N. Nash. "Effectiveness of a forced choice reference check," *Personnel Administration,* 35 (1975): 42–46.

———. *The Evaluation of Performance.* University of Maryland, 1970.

———. *The management of compensation.* Brooks/Cole, 1975.

Carroll, S. J., Jr., F. T. Paine, and J. B. Miner (eds.). *The managerial process: Cases and readings,* 2d ed., Macmillan, 1977.

Carroll, S. J., Jr., and H. L. Tosi. "The relationship of characteristics of the review process as moderated by personality and situational factors to the success of the MBO approach." *Proceedings of the Academy of Management Annual Convention,* 1969: 134–43.

———. "Goal characteristics and personality factors in a management by objectives program," *Administrative Science Quarterly,* 15 (1970): 295–305.

———. *Management by objectives: Applications and research.* Macmillan, 1973.

———. "Relationship of various motivational forces to the effects of participation in goal setting in a management by objectives program." Paper presented at 1976 Industrial Relations Association 29th annual meeting.

Carzo, R. "Organizational realities," *Business Horizons,* Spring, 1961, 95–104.

Castore, G. F. "Attitudes of students toward the case method of instruction in a human relations course," *Journal of Educational Research,* (1951): 201–13.

Cates, J. N. "Sex and salary," *American Psychologist,* 28 (1973): 929.

Chapple, E. D., and L. R. Sayles. *The measure of management.* Macmillan, 1961.

Child, J. "What determines organizational performance? The universals vs. the it-all-depends," *Organizational Dynamics,* 3 (1974): 2–18.

Cleland, D. "Understanding project authority," *Business Horizons,* 10, (Spring, 1967): 63-70.

Coch, L. and J. R. P. French, "Overcoming resistance to change," *Human Relations,* 1 (1948): 512–32.

Cohen, A. R. "Upward communication in experimentally created hierarchies," *Human Relations,* 11 (1958): 41–53.

Cohen, D., J. W. Whitmyre, and W. H. Funk. "Effect of group cohesiveness and training upon creative thinking," *Journal of Applied Psychology,* 44 (1960): 319–22.

Colby, A. N., and J. Tiffin. "The reading ability of industrial supervisors," *Personnel,* 27 (1950): 156–59.

Coleman, J. S. *Equality of educational*

opportunity. U.S. Department of Health, Education and Welfare; Office of Education; and U.S. Government Printing Office, Washington, D.C., 1966.

Commerce Clearing House. *Employment practices guide*. Washington, D.C., 1972.

Costello, T. W., and S. S. Zalkind. *Psychology in administration*. Prentice-Hall, 1963.

Crockett, H. J., Jr. "The achievement motive and differential occupational mobility in the United States," *American Sociological Review*, 27 (1962): 191–204.

Culbertson, F. "Modification of an emotionally held attitude through role playing," *Journal of Abnormal and Social Psychology*, 54 (1957): 230–33.

Cummings, L. L., and D. P. Schwab. *Performance in organizations: Determinants and appraisal*. Scott, Foresman, 1973.

Dahle, T. L. "An objective and comparative study of five methods of transmitting information to business and industrial employees," *Speech Monographs*, 21 (1954): 21–28.

Dalton, G. W., "Influence and organizational change," in Dalton, G. W., Laurence, P. R., and Greenier, L. G. (eds.), *Organizational Change and Development*. Dorsey Press, 1970.

Danielson, L. *Characteristics of engineers and scientists*. Ann Arbor, Mich.: Bureau of Industrial Relations, Univ. of Michigan, 1960.

Davis, A. "The motivation of the underprivileged worker," in W. F. Whyte (ed.), *Industry and society*. McGraw-Hill, 1964.

Davis, K. *Human Relations at Work*. McGraw-Hill, 1962.

———. "Readability changes in employee handbooks of identical companies during a fifteen-year period," *Personnel Psychology*, 21 (1968): 413–20.

———. "Success of chain-of-command oral communication in a manufacturing management group," *Academy of Management Journal*, 11 (1968): 379–87.

Davis, R. C. *The fundamentals of top management*. Harper, 1951.

Davitz, J. R. *The communication of emotional meaning*. McGraw-Hill, 1964.

Dean, R. C., Jr. "Why is U.S. technological prominence withering?" in *Twenty-Seventh National Conference on the Administration of Research*. Denver Research Institute: Univ. of Denver, September, 1973.

Dearborn, D. C., and H. A. Simon. "Selective perception: A note on the departmental identification of executives," *Sociometry*, 21 (1958), 140–44.

De Charms, R., and W. Bridgeman. *Leadership compliance and group behavior*. Tech. report no. 9. St. Louis: Washington Univ., 1961.

Dietrick, D. C. "Review of research," in R. J. Hill (ed.), *A comparative study of lecture and discussion methods*. Pasadena, Calif.: The Fund for Adult Education, 1960.

Dill, W. R., and N. Doppelt. "The acquisition of experience in a complex management game," *Management Science*, 10 (1963): 30–46.

Dill, W. R., T. L. Hilton, and W. R. Reitman. *The new managers: Patterns of behavior and development*. Prentice-Hall, 1962.

Doeringer, P. B. *Programs to employ the disadvantaged*. Prentice-Hall, 1969.

Douglas, J., and C. Crain. "Activity reaction forms: Measurement of dyadic perceptions of managers using a management by objectives program." Working paper presented at Midwest Academy of Management. Univ. of Michigan, Ann Arbor, Mich., April, 1975.

Drucker, P. *The practice of management*. Harper and Bros., 1954.

Dubin, R. "Industrial workers' worlds: A study of the central life interests of industrial workers," *Social Problems,* 3 (1956): 131–42.

Dunnette, M. D. *Personnel selection and placement.* Wadsworth, 1965.

———. "Predictions of executive success," in F. Wickert and D. McFarland (eds.), *Measuring executive effectiveness.* Appleton-Century-Crofts, 1967.

———., J. P. Campbell, and K. Jaastad. "The effect of group participation on brainstorming effectiveness for two industrial samples," *Journal of Applied Psychology,* 47 (1963): 30–37.

Dunnette, M. D., R. D. Arvey, and P. A. Banas. "Why do they leave?" *Personnel* (1973): 25–39.

Endicott, F. S. *Trends in employment of college and university graduates in business and industry.* Northwestern University Press, 1976.

England, G. W., and D. G. Paterson. "Selection and placement—the past ten years," in H. G. Henneman, Jr., et al. (eds.), *Employment relations research: A summary and appraisal.* Harper, 1960.

"At Emery Air Freight: Positive reinforcement boosts performance," *Organizational Dynamics,* Winter, 1973.

Equal Employment Opportunity Commission. *Promise vs. performance.* An Equal Employment Opportunity Commission report, Washington, D.C., 1972.

Erikson, E. "Identity and the life cycle," *Psychological Issues,* 1 (1959): 140–41.

Evan, W. M. "Conflict and performance in R and D organizations," *Industrial Management Review,* 7 (1965): 37–45.

Evans, M. G. *The effects of supervisory behavior on worker perceptions of their path goal relationships.* Doctoral Dissertation, Yale Univ., 1968.

Falcione, R. L. "The relationship of supervisor credibility to subordinate satisfaction," *Personnel Journal,* 52 (1973): 800–3.

Faucheux, C., and K. D. MacKenzie. "Task dependency of organizational centrality: Its behavioral consequences," *Journal of Experimental Sociology and Psychology,* 2 (1966): 361–75.

Fayol, H. *General and industrial management,* C. Storrs (trans.). Sir Isaac Pitman and Sons, 1949.

Fernandez, J. P. *Black managers in white corporations.* Wiley, 1975.

Festinger, L. *A Theory of cognitive dissonance.* Row, Peterson, 1957.

———, and J. Carlsmith. "Cognitive consequence of forced compliance," *Journal of Abnormal and Social Psychology,* 58 (1959): 203–10.

Fiedler, F. *A Theory of leadership effectiveness.* McGraw-Hill, 1967.

Filipeti, G. *Industrial management in transition.* Irwin, 1946.

Filley, A. C. *A theory of small business and divisional growth.* Ph.D. Dissertation, The Ohio State Univ., 1962.

———. "Committee management: Guidelines from social science research," *California Management Review,* 13 (1970): 13–21.

———, and R. J. House. *Managerial process and organizational behavior.* Scott, Foresman, 1969.

Filley, A. C., and F. H. Reighard. "A preliminary survey of training attitudes and needs among actual and potential attendees at management institute programs," Madison: Univ. of Wisconsin, 1962, cited in R. J. House, "Managerial reactions to two methods of management training," *Personnel Psychology,* 18 (1965): 311–19.

Fleishman, E. A. "Leadership climate, human relations training and supervisory behavior," *Personnel Psychology,* 6 (1953): 205–22.

Ford, R. "Job enrichment lessons from AT&T," *Harvard Business Review,* 1973 (Jan.-Feb.): 96–106.

Fox, W. M. "A measure of the effectiveness of the case method in teaching human relations," *Personnel Administration,* 26 (1962): 53–57.

Franklin, B. "How to make a decision," 1772, as quoted in MacCrimmon, K. R., "Managerial decision making," in Joseph W. McGuire (ed.), *Contemporary management: Issues and viewpoints.* Prentice-Hall, 1974.

Freedman, J. L. "The crowd: Maybe not so maddening after all," *Psychology Today,* 4 (1971): 58–61, 86.

French, J. R. P., E. Kay, and H. H. Meyer. "Participation and the appraisal system," *Human Relations,* 19 (1966): 3–20.

French, J. R. P., and B. Raven. "The bases of social power," in D. Cartwright (ed.), *Studies in social power.* Research Center for Group Dynamics, Univ. of Michigan, 1959.

French, J. R. P., Jr., J. Israel, and D. As. "An experiment on participation in a Norwegian factory," *Human Relations,* 13 (1960): 3–19.

Fretz, C. F., and J. Hayman. "Progress for women—men are still more equal," *Harvard Business Review,* 51 (1973): 133–42.

Friedlander, F. "The relationship of task and human conditions to effective organizational structure," in Bass, B. M., R. Cooper and J. A. Haas (eds), *Managing for accomplishment.* D. C. Heath, 1970.

Friedlander, F. and H. Pickle. "Components of effectiveness in small organizations," *Administrative Science Quarterly,* 13 (1968): 289–304.

Friedlander, G. and S. Greenberg. "Work climate as related to the performance and retention of hardcore unemployed workers," *Proceedings of the 77th Annual Convention,* American Psychological Association, 1969.

Galbraith, J. *Designing complex organizations.* Addison, Wesley, 1973.

Gannon, M. J. "Sources of referral and employee turnover," *Journal of Applied Psychology,* 55 (1971): 226 –28.

George, C. S. *The history of management thought.* Prentice-Hall, 1968.

Georgopoulos, B. S., and A. S. Tannenbaum. "A study of organizational effectiveness," *American Sociological Review,* 22 (1957): 534–40.

Ghiselli, E. E. *Explorations in managerial talent.* Goodyear, 1971.

———. *The validity of occupational aptitude tests.* John Wiley and Sons, 1966.

Gibb, C. "Leadership," in *Handbook of Social Psychology,* vol. 4, 2d. ed. Addison-Wesley, 1968, pp. 205– 82.

Gibb, J. R. "The effects of group size and of threat reduction upon creativity in a problem-solving situation," *American Psychologist,* 6 (1951), 324.

———. "Defensive communication," *Journal of Communication,* 11 (1961): 141–48.

———. "Fear and facade—defensive management." In R. E. Farson (ed.), *Science and human affairs.* Science and Behavior Books, 1965, pp. 197 –214.

Goeke, J. R., C. S. Weymar. "Barriers to hiring the blacks," *Harvard Business Review,* 47 (1969): 144–52.

Gollin, E. S., and M. Moody. "Developmental psychology," *Annual Review of Psychology,* 24 (1973): 1– 52.

Goode, W. J., and I. Fowler. "Incentive factors in a low morale plant," *American Sociological Review,* 14 (1949): 619–24.

Gooding, J. "It pays to wake up the blue collar worker," *Fortune,* 82 (1970): 133–35, 158–68.

Gordon, W. J. J. *Synectics*. Harper and Row, 1961.

Gouldner, A. "The role of the norm of reciprocity in social stabilization," *American Sociological Review*, 15 (1960): 161–78.

Graen, G., K. Alvares, J. B. Orris, and J. A. Martella. "Contingency model of leadership effectiveness: Antecedent and evidential results," *Psychological Bulletin*, 74 (1970): 285 –96.

Greene, C. N. "Causal connections among managers' merit pay, job satisfaction and performance," *Journal of Applied Psychology*, 58 (1973): 95–100.

Greene, Charles "The path-goal theory of leadership: A replication and analysis of causality," *Proceedings, Academy of Management*, 1974.

Greiner, L. E. "Patterns of organizational change." In G. W. Dalton et al. (eds.), *Organizational change and development*. Dorsey Press, 1970.

Grove, B. A., and W. A. Kerr. "Specific evidence on origin of halo effect in measurement of employee morale," *Journal of Social Psychology*, 1951, 165–70.

Guetzkow, H. "Communications in organizations." In J. G. March (ed.), *Handbook of organizations*. Rand McNally, 1965, pp. 534–613.

Guetzkow, H., E. L. Kelly, and W. J. McKeachie. "An experimental comparison of recitation, discussion, and tutorial methods in college teaching," *Journal of Educational Psychology*, 45 (1954): 193–207.

Hackman, R., and E. E. Lawler, III. "Employee reactions to job characteristics," *Journal of Applied Psychology* monograph 55 (1971): 259–86.

Hage, J., M. Aiken, and C. B. Marrett. "Organization structure and communications," *American Sociological Review*, 36 (1971): 860–71.

Haire, M., E. Ghiselli, and L. Porter.

Managerial thinking: An international study. Wiley, 1966.

Hall, D. T., and K. E. Nougaim. "An examination of Maslow's need hierarchy in an organizational setting," *Organizational Behavior and Human Performance*, 3 (1968): 12–35.

Hall, E. T. *The hidden dimension*. Doubleday, 1966.

Hall, R. H. *Organizations: Structure and process*. Prentice Hall, 1972.

———. "The concept of bureaucracy: An empirical assessment," *American Journal of Sociology*, 69 (1973): 32–40.

Halperin, K., C. R. Snyer, R. J. Shenkkel, and B. K. Houston. "Effects of source status and message favorability on acceptance of personality feedback," *Journal of Applied Psychology*, 61 (1976): 85–88.

Hammond, L. K., and M. Goldman. "Competition and noncompetition and its relationship to individual and group productivity," *Sociometry*, 24 (1961): 46–60.

Hamner, W., J. Kim, L. Baird, and W. Bigonness. "Race and sex as determinants of ratings by potential employers in a simulated work setting," *Journal of Applied Psychology*, 59 (1974): 705–11.

Hamner, W. C., and H. Tosi. "The influence of role conflict and ambiguity on the relationship of various role involvement measures," *Journal of Applied Psychology*, 59 (1974): 497 –99.

Hampton, D. R., C. E. Summer and R. A. Webber. *Organizational behavior and the practice of management*. Scott, Foresman, 1973.

Haney, W. V. "A comparative study of unilateral and bilateral communication," *Academy of Management Journal*, 7 (1964): 128–36.

Hare, A. P. *Handbook of small group research*. Free Press of Glencoe, 1962.

Harrell, T. W., and M. Harrell. "Army general classification test scores for civilian occupations," *Educational and Psychological Measurement,* 5 (1945): 231–32.

Harris, C. W. (ed.). *Encyclopedia of educational research.* Macmillan, 1960.

Harvey, E. "Technology and the structure of organizations," *American Sociological Review,* 33 (1968): 247–59.

Harvey, O., and G. Beverly. "Some personality correlates of concept change through role playing," *Journal of Abnormal and Social Psychology,* 63 (1961): 125–30.

Hayes, J. R. *Human data processing limits in decision making.* Air Force Systems Command, Electronic Systems Division. ESD-TDR-62-48. AD283384. July, 1962.

Hayes, M. A. "Nonverbal communication: Expression without words." In R. C. Huseman, C. M. Logue, and D. L. Freshley (eds.), *Readings in interpersonal and organizational communication.* Holbrook Press Inc., 1974.

Heckhausen, H. *The anatomy of achievement motivation.* Academic Press, 1967.

Hegarty, W. H. "Using subordinate ratings to elicit behavioral changes in supervisors," *Journal of Applied Psychology,* 59 (1974): 764–66.

Heider, F. "Attitudes and cognitive organization," *Journal of Psychology,* 21 (1946): 107–12.

Heller, F. A., and G. Yukl. "Participation, managerial decision making and structural variables," *Organizational Behavior and Human Performance,* 4 (1969): 227–41.

Helmreich, R., R. Bakeman, and L. Scherwitz. "The study of small groups," *Annual Review of Psychology,* 24 (1973): 337–54.

Henderson, H. "Should business tackle society's problems?" *Harvard Business Review,* 46 (1968): 77–85.

Heneman, H. G. III. "Comparisons of self and superior ratings of managerial performance," *Journal of Applied Psychology,* 59 (1974): 638–52.

Herzberg, F., B. Mausner, R. O. Peterson, and D. F. Capwell. *Job attitudes: Review of research and opinion.* Psychological Services of Pittsburgh, 1957.

Herzberg, F., B. Mausner, and B. Snyderman. *The motivation to work.* Wiley, 1959.

Hilgard, E. R., R. C. Atkinson, and R. L. Atkinson. *Introduction to psychology.* Harcourt, Brace, 1971.

Hill, R. A. *A comparative study of lecture and discussion methods.* The Fund for Adult Education, 1960.

Hill, W. "The goal formation process in complex organizations," *Journal of Management Studies,* 6 (1969): 198–208.

Hinrichs, J. R. "Communications activity of industrial research personnel," *Personnel Psychology,* 17 (1964): 193–204.

Hoagland, J. "Historical antecedents of organization research," in W. W. Cooper et al. (eds.), *New perspectives in organization research.* Wiley, 1964.

Homans, G. C. *The human group.* Harcourt, Brace and World, 1950.

House, R. J. "An experiment in the use of management training standards," *Journal of The Academy of Management,* 5 (1962): 76–81.

————. "Managerial reactions to two methods of management training," *Personnel Psychology,* 18 (1965): 311–19.

————. *Management development: Design evaluation implementation.* Bureau of Industrial Relations, Univ. of Michigan, 1967.

————. "A path goal theory of leader effectiveness," *Administrative Science Quarterly,* 16, 1971.

————, and H. L. Tosi. "An experimental evaluation of a management training program," *Academy of Management Journal*, 6 (1963): 303–15.

Hrebiniak, L. G., and M. R. Roteman. "A study of the relationship between need satisfaction and absenteeism among managerial personnel," *Journal of Applied Psychology*, 58 (1973): 381–83.

Hsia, H. J. "Output, error, equivocation, and recalled information in auditory, visual, and audiovisual information processing with constraint and noise," *Journal of Communication*, 18 (1968): 325–45.

Hughes, J. L. "Effects of changes in programmed text format and reduction in classroom time on achievement and attitudes of industrial trainees," *Journal of Programmed Instruction*, 1 (1963): 143–55.

Hughes, J. L., and W. J. McNamara. "A comparative study of programmed and conventional instruction in industry," *Journal of Applied Psychology*, 45 (1961): 225–31.

Hulin, C., and M. Blood. "Job enlargement, individual differences and worker responses," *Psychological Bulletin*, 69 (1968): 41–55.

Indik, B. P., B. S. Georgopoulos, and S. E. Seashore. "Superior-subordinate relationships and performance," *Personnel Psychology*, 14 (1961): 357–74.

Industrial Research. $33 Billion for research," *Industrial Research*, 16 (1974): 38–41.

Industrial Research. "Europe not catching U.S. in R & D yet," *Industrial Research*, 16 (1974): 24.

Inkeles, A., and P. H. Rossi. "National comparisons of occupational prestige," *American Journal of Sociology*, 61 (1956): 329-39.

Ivancevich, J. M. "A longitudinal assessment of Management by Objectives," *Administrative Science Quarterly*, March, 1972, 126–35.

———, J. H. Donnelly, and H. L. Lyon.

"A study of the impact of management by objectives on perceived need satisfaction," *Personnel Psychology*, 23 (1970): 139–51.

Jacobsen, E., and S. E. Seashore. "Communication practices in complex organizations," *Journal of Social Issues*, 7 (1951): 28–40.

Janger, A. R., and R. G. Schaeffer. "Managing programs to employ the disadvantaged," *Personnel policy study 219*. New York: National Industrial Conference Board, 1970.

Janis, I., and B. King. "The influence of role playing on opinion change," *Journal of Abnormal and Social Psychology*, 49 (1954): 211–18.

Janis, I., and L. Mann. "Effectiveness of emotional role-playing in modifying smoking habits and attitudes," *Journal of Experimental Research in Personality*, 1 (1965): 84–90.

Jarrett, H. (ed.). *Science and resources: Prospects and implications of technological advance*. The Johns Hopkins Press, 1959.

Jasinski, Frank J. "Technological delimitation of reciprocal relationships: A study of interaction patterns in industry," *Human Organization*, 15, (1956): 24–28.

Jeswald, T. A. "The cost of absenteeism and turnover in a large organization," in W. C. Hamner and F. L. Schmidt (eds.), *Contemporary problems in personnel*. St. Clair Press, 1974.

Jones, E. W., Jr. "What it's like to be a black manager," *Harvard Business Review*, 51 (1973): 108–16.

Kahn, R., D. Wolfe, R. Quinn, and J. Snoek. *Organizational stress: Studies in role conflict and ambiguity*. Wiley, 1964.

Kallejian, V., P. Brown, and I. R. Weschler. "The impact of interpersonal relations on ratings of performance," *Public Personnel Review*, (1953) 166–70.

Kaponya, P. G. "Salaries for all workers," *Harvard Business Review*, 40 (1962): 49–57.

Karlins, M., and H. I. Abelson. *Persuasion: How opinions and attitudes are changed.* 2d ed. Springer, 1970.

Katz, D., and R. Kahn. *The social psychology of organizations.* Wiley, 1966.

Katz, R. L. *Management of the total enterprise.* Prentice-Hall, 1970.

Kaufman, H. G. "Relations of ability and interest to currency of professional knowledge among engineers," *Journal of Applied Psychology*, 56 (1972): 495–99.

———. "Individual differences, early work challenge, and participation in continuing education," *Journal of Applied Psychology*, 60 (1975): 405–8.

Kelley, H. H. *Attribution in social interaction.* General Learning Press, 1971.

Kelley, H. and J. Thibaut. "Group problem solving." In Lindzey, G. and E. Aronson (eds.), *Handbook of social psychology*, vol. 4. Addison-Wesley, 1969.

Kelly, C. M. "Actual listening behavior of industrial supervisors as related to listening ability, general mental ability, selected personality factors, and supervisory effectiveness." Ph.D. dissertation, Purdue University, 1962.

Kepner, C. H., and B. B. Tregoe. *The rational manager: A systematic approach to problem solving and decision making.* McGraw-Hill, 1965.

Kerlinger, F. N. *Foundations of behavioral research.* Holt, Rinehart, & Winston, 1964.

Kerr, Clark. "What became of the independent spirit?" *Fortune*, 48 (1953): 110–11.

Kilbridge, M. D. "Reduced costs through job enlargement," *Journal of Business*, 33 (1960): 357–62.

———. "Do workers prefer larger jobs?" *Personnel Journal*, 1960, 45–48.

Kilmann, R. H., and B. McKelvey. "The MAPS route to better organization design," *California Management Review*, 17 (1975): 23–31.

Kim, J. "Effect of feedback on performance and job satisfaction in an organizational setting," unpublished doctoral dissertation, Michigan State Univ., 1974.

King, B., and I. Janis. "Comparison of the effectiveness of improvised vs. nonimprovised role playing in producing opinion changes," *Human Relations*, 9 (1956): 177–86.

Kirchner, W. K., and D. J. Reisberg. "Differences between better and less-effective supervisors in appraisal of subordinates," *Personnel Psychology*, 15 (1962): 295–303.

Klausmeir, H. J., *Learning and human abilities.* Harper, 1961.

Klimoski, R. J., and M. London. "Role of the rater in performance appraisal," *Journal of Applied Psychology*, 59 (1974): 445–51.

Kohn, M. L., and O. Scheeler. "Class, occupation and orientation," *American Sociological Review*, 34 (1969): 659–78.

Kolb, D. A., and R. E. Boyatzis. "Goal setting and self-directed behavior change." In D. A. Kolb, I. M. Rubin, and J. M. McIntyre (eds.), *Organizational psychology: A book of readings.* Prentice-Hall, 1971.

Korman, A. K. "A cause of communications failure," *Personnel Administration*, 23 (1960): 17–21.

———. "Self esteem as a variable in vocational choice," *Journal of Applied Psychology*, 50 (1966): 479–86.

———. "The prediction of managerial performance: A review," *Personnel Psychology*, 21 (1968): 259–322.

———. *Industrial and organizational psychology.* Prentice-Hall, 1971.

———. "Hypothesis of work behavior revisited and an extension," *Academy of Management Review*, 1 (1976): 50–61.

Kornhauser, A. *Mental health of the industrial worker.* Wiley, 1965.

Kornhauser, W. *Scientists in industry: Conflict and accommodation.* Univ. of California Press, 1960.

Krasner, L. "Behavior therapy," *Annual Review of Psychology,* 22 (1971): 483–519.

Kumata, H. *An inventory of instructional television research.* Ann Arbor, Michigan: Educational Television and Radio Center, 1956.

———. "A decade of teaching by television." In W. Schramm (ed.), *The impact of educational television.* Univ. of Illinois Press, 1960.

Landsberger, H. A. *Hawthorne revisited.* Cornell Univ., 1958.

Laswell, H. D. *Power and personality.* W. W. Norton, 1948.

Latham, G. P., and S. B. Kinne, III. "Improving job performance through training in goal setting," *Journal of Applied Psychology,* 59 (1974): 187–91.

Latham, G. P., and G. A. Yukl. "A review of research on the application of goal setting in organizations," *Academy of Management Journal,* 18 (1975): 824–25.

Lawler, E. E. *Pay and organizational effectiveness: A psychological view.* McGraw-Hill, 1971.

———, L. W. Porter, and A. Tennenbaum. "Managers' attitudes toward interaction episodes," *Journal of Applied Psychology,* 52 (1968): 432–39.

Lawler, E. E., and J. L. Suttle. "A causal correlational test of the need hierarchy concept," *Organizational Behavior and Human Performance,* 7 (1972): 265–87.

———. "Expectancy theory and job behavior," *Organizational Behavior and Human Performance,* 9 (1973): 482–501.

Lawrence, P. R., and J. W. Lorsch. *Organization and environment: Managing differentiation and integration.* Graduate School of Business Administration, Harvard University, 1967.

———. *Developing organizations: Diagnosis and action.* Addison-Wesley, 1969.

Lawrence, P. R., and J. A. Seiler. "Experiments in structural design." In *Organizational behavior and administration.* Richard D. Irwin and Dorsey Press, 1965.

Lawshe, C. H., W. Holmes, Jr., and G. M. Turmail. "An analysis of employee handbooks," *Personnel,* 27 (1951): 487–95.

Lazarsfeld, P. F., and H. Menzel. "Mass media and personal influence." In W. Schramm (ed.), *The science of human communication.* Basic Books, 1963.

Leavitt, H. J., and R. Mueller. "Some effects of feedback on communication," *Human Relations,* 4 (1951): 401–10.

Leiberman, S. "The effects of changes in roles on the attitudes of role occupants," *Human Relations,* 9 (1956): 385–402.

Lesieur, F. G. (ed.). *The Scanlon plan: A frontier in labor management cooperation.* Wiley, 1958.

Levine, J., and J. Butler, "Lecture vs. group decision in changing behavior," *Journal of Applied Psychology,* 36 (1952): 29–33.

Lewin, A. Y., and R. L. Weber. "Management game teams in education and organization research: An experiment on risk taking," *Academy of Management Journal,* 12 (1969): 49–58.

Lewin, K. "Studies in Group Decision," in D. Cartwright and A. Zander (eds.), *Group dynamics.* Row, Peterson, 1953.

———. "Group decision and social change," in E. E. Maccoby, T. H. Newcombe, E. L. Hartley (eds.), *Readings in social psychology.* Holt, 1958.

Lewin, K., R. Lippitt, and R. K. White. "Patterns of aggressive behavior in experimentally created social climates," *Journal of Social Psychology*, 10 (1939), 271–99.

Liebow, E. *Talley's corner: A study of streetcorner men.* Little, Brown, 1967.

Likert, R. "Measuring organizational performance," *Harvard Business Review*, 37 (1958): 349–66.

Ling, C. C. *The Management of Personnel Relations: History and Origins.* Richard D. Irwin, 1965.

Lippit, R., and R. K. Whyte. "An experimental study of leadership and group life." In E. E. Maccoby, T. H. Newcomb, E. L. Hartley (eds.), *Readings in social psychology.* Holt, 1958.

Litterer, J. A. "Research departments within large organizations," *California Management Review*, 12 (1970): 77–84.

Litwin, G. H., and R. A. Stringer, Jr. *Motivation and organizational climate.* Graduate School of Business Administration, Harvard Univ., 1968.

Locke, E. A. "The relationship of task success to task liking and satisfaction," *Journal of Applied Psychology*, 49 (1965): 379–85.

———. "Personnel attitudes and motivation," *Annual Review of Psychology*, 26 (1975): 457–80.

———. "Toward a theory of task motivation and incentives," *Organizational Behavior and Human Performance*, 3 (1968): 162.

Lorig, A. W. "Where do corporate responsibilities really lie?" *Business Horizons*, 10 (1967): 51–54.

Lorsch, J., and J. Morse. *Organizations and their members: A contingency approach.* Harper & Row, 1974.

Lowin, A., and J. Craig. "The influence of level of performance on managerial style: An experimental object lesson in the ambiguity of correlational data," *Organizational Behavior and Human Performance*, 3 (1968): 440–58.

McClelland, D. C., J. Atkinson, J. Clark, and E. Lowell. *The achievement motive.* Appleton-Century-Crofts, 1953.

McCormick, E. J., P. R. Jeanneret, and R. C. Meachem. "A study of job characteristics and job dimensions as based on the position analysis questionnaire (PAQ)," *Journal of Applied Psychology*, 56 (1972): 347 –68.

MacCrimmon, K. R. "Managerial decision making." In McGuire, Joseph W. (ed.), *Contemporary management: Issues and viewpoints.* Prentice-Hall, 1974.

McGregor, D. "An uneasy look at performance appraisal," *Harvard Business Review*, 35 (1957): 89–94.

———. *The human side of enterprise.* McGraw-Hill, 1960.

McGuire, J. W., and J. B. Parrish. "Status report on a profound revolution," *California Management Review*, 13 (1971): 79–86.

McGuire, W. J. "The nature of attitudes and attitude change." In G. Lindzey, and E. Aronson (eds.), *Handbook of social psychology*, vol. 3, 2d ed. Addison-Wesley, 1968.

McKenney, J. L. "An evaluation of a business game in an MBA curriculum," *The Journal of Business*, 35 (1962): 278–86.

McLoughlin, W. G. *Fundamentals of research management.* American Management Association, 1970.

Maher, J. R., and D. T. Piersol. "Perceived clarity of individual job objectives and of group mission as correlates of organizational morale," *Journal of Communication*, 20 (1970): 125–33.

Mahoney, T. A., and W. Weitzel. "Managerial models of organizational effectiveness," *Administrative Science Quarterly*, 14 (1969): 357–65.

Mahoney, T. A., T. H. Jerdee, and S. J.

Carroll. *Development of managerial performance: A research approach.* South-Western, 1963.

———. "The job(s) of management," *Industrial Relations,* 4 (February, 1965): 97–110.

Maier, N. R. F. "An experimental test of the effect of training on discussion leadership," *Human Relations,* 6 (1953): 161–73.

———. *The appraisal interview: Objectives, methods, and skills.* Wiley, 1958.

———. *Problem-solving discussions and conferences: Leadership methods and skills.* McGraw-Hill, 1963.

———. *Problem solving and creativity in individuals and groups.* Brooks-Cole, 1970.

———, and L. R. Hoffman. "Quality of first and second solutions in group problem solving," *Journal of Applied Psychology,* 44 (1960a): 278–83.

———. "Using trained 'developmental' discussion leaders to improve further the quality of group decisions," *Journal of Applied Psychology,* 44 (1960b): 247–51.

———., and R. A. Maier. "An experimental test of the effects of 'developmental' vs. 'free' discussions on the quality of group decisions," *Journal of Applied Psychology,* 41 (1957): 320–22.

Maier, N.R.F., W. Read, and J. Hooven. "Breakdown in boss-subordinate communication." In *Communication in Organizations.* Ann Arbor, Mich.: Foundation for Research on Human Behavior (1959): 19–23.

Maier, N. R. F., and A. R. Solem. "The contribution of the discussion leader to the quality of group thinking," *Human Relations,* 3 (1952): 155–74.

Maier, N. R. F., L. R. Hoffman, J. J. Hooven, and W. H. Read. "Superior-subordinate communica-

tion in management," *American Management Association* (1961): 9.

———. "Superior-subordinate communication: A statistical research project," *American Management Assn. Research Report,* 52 (1961): 9–30.

Mann, F. "Toward an understanding of the leadership role in formal organization." In R. Dubin et al. (eds.), *Leadership and productivity.* Chandler Publishing, 1965.

Mann, J. H., and C. H. Mann. "The importance of group tasks in producing group-member personality and behavior change," *Human Relations, 221 (1959): 75–80.*

March, J. and H. Simon. *Organizations.* Wiley, 1958.

Margulies, N., and J. Wallace. *Organization change: Techniques and applications.* Scott, Foresman, 1973.

Margulies, S., and L. D. Eigen. *Applied programmed instruction.* Wiley, 1962.

Marriott, R. *Incentive wage systems.* Staples Press, 1968.

Martin, B., and L. A. Sroufe. "Anxiety." In C. G. Costello (ed.), *Symptoms of psychopathology.* Wiley, 1970.

Martin, W. F., and G. C. Lodge. "Our society in 1985—Business may not like it," *Harvard Business Review,* 53 (1975): 143–50.

Maslow, A. H. "A theory of human motivation," *Psychological Review,* 50 (1943): 370–96.

Mayfield, E. C. "The selection interview: A reevaluation of published research," *Personnel Psychology,* 17 (1964): 239–60.

Means, J. E. "Fair employment practices legislation and enforcement in the United States," *International Labor Review,* 93 (1966): 211–47.

Meehl, P. *Clinical versus statistical prediction.* University of Minnesota Press, 1954.

Mellinger, G. D. "Interpersonal trust as a factor in communication," *Journal of Abnormal and Social Psychology,* 52 (1956): 304–9.

Merton, R. K. *Social theory and social structure.* Free Press, 1957.

Meyer, H., E. Kay, and J. R. P. French. "Split roles of performance appraisal," *Harvard Business Review,* 43 (1965): 123–29.

Miles, M. B. "Changes during and following laboratory training: A clinical-experimental study," *Journal of Applied Behavioral Science,* 1 (1965): 215–42.

Miller, D. *The Structure of Human Decisions.* Prentice-Hall, 1967.

———, and M. Starr. *Executive decisions and operations research.* Prentice-Hall, 1960.

Miller, G. A. "Human memory and the storage of information," *IRE transactions on information theory,* 1956 (IT-2): 129–37.

Miller, L. *The use of knowledge of results in improving the performance of hourly operators.* General Electric Co. Behavioral Research Service, 1965.

Miller, L. K., and R. L. Hamblin. "Interdependence, differential rewarding, and productivity," *American Sociological Review,* 28 (1963): 768–77.

Miner, J. B. *Studies in management education.* Springer Publishing, 1965.

———. *Personnel psychology.* Macmillan, 1969.

———. *Personnel and industrial relations.* Macmillan, 1969.

———. "The real crunch in managerial manpower," *Harvard Business Review,* September-October, 1973, 146–58.

———. *The management process: Theory, research and practice.* Macmillan, 1973.

———, and H. P. Dachler. "Personnel attitudes and motivation," *Annual Review of Psychology,* 24 (1973): 379–402.

Miner, J. B., and N. R. Smith. "Managerial talent among undergraduate and graduate business students," *Personnel and Guidance Journal,* 47 (1969): 995–1000.

Miner, J. B., J. R. Rizzo, D. N. Harlow, and J. W. Hill. "Role motivation theory of managerial effectiveness in simulated organizations of varying degrees of structure," *Journal of Applied Psychology,* 59 (1974): 31–37.

Mintzberg, H. *The nature of managerial work.* Harper and Row, 1973.

Mobley, W. H. "An interorganizational test of a task-goal expectancy model of work motivation and performance," Ph.D. thesis, Univ. of Maryland, 1971.

Moore, D. G. and R. Renck. "The professional employee in industry," *Journal of Business,* 28 (1955): 58–66.

Morse, J. J., and J. W. Lorsch. "Beyond theory Y," *Harvard Business Review* (May-June, 1970): 61–68.

Mott, P. E. *The characteristics of effective organizations.* Harper and Row, 1972.

Mulder, M. "Power equalization through participation?" *Administrative Science Quarterly,* 16 (1971): 31–38.

———, and H. Wilke. "Participation and power equalization," *Organizational Behavior and Human Performance,* 5 (1970): 430–48.

Myers, C. A., and G. P. Schultz. *The dynamics of a labor market.* Prentice-Hall, 1951.

Nash, A. N., and S. J. Carroll. "A hard look at the reference check," *Business Horizons,* 1970: 43–49.

———. *The management of compensation.* Wadsworth, 1975.

Nash, A. N., J. P. Muczyk, and F. L. Vettori. "The relative practical effectiveness of programmed instruction," *Personnel Psychology,* 1971, 397–418.

Neidt, C. O., and T. Meredith. "Changes in attitudes of learners when programmed instruction is interpolated between two conventional instruction experiences," *Journal of Ap-*

plied Psychology, 50 (1966): 130–37.

Newcomb, T. M., R. H. Turner, and P. E. Converse. *Social psychology: The study of human interaction*. Holt, Rinehart, & Winston, 1951.

Nord, W. R. "Beyond the teaching machine: The neglected area of operant conditioning in the theory and practice of management," *Organizational Behavior and Human Performance*, 4 (1969): 375–401.

Odiorne, G. *Management by objectives*. Pitnam, 1964.

Opshal, R. L., and M. D. Dunnette. "The role of financial compensation in industrial motivation," *Psychological Bulletin*, 66 (1966): 94–118.

O'Reilly, C. A., and K. H. Roberts. "Job satisfaction among white and non-whites: A cross-cultural approach," *Journal of Applied Psychology*, 60 (1975): 340–44.

Orth, C. D., J. C. Bailey, and F. W. Wolek. "The Houston Corporation." In *Administering research and development*. Richard D. Irwin and Dorsey Press, 1964.

Osborn, A. F. *Applied imagination: Principles and procedures of creative thinking*. Scribner's, 1957.

Osipow, S. H. "Success and preference: A replication and extension," *Journal of Applied Psychology*, 56 (1972): 179–80.

Ozawa, T. *Transfer of technology from Japan to developing countries*. Unitar Research Report No. 7. United Nations Institute for Training and Research, 1973.

Paine, F. T. "What do better college students want from their jobs?" *Personnel Administration*, 32 (1969): 26–29.

————. "Organizational assessment dimensions as related to the overall effectiveness of assessment terms." In W. Frey, (ed.), *Management Research and Practice*, in *Proceedings of the Seventh Annual Conference*.

Eastern Academy of Management, Univ. of Massachusetts, Amherst, 1970, 114–123.

————, S. J. Carroll, and B. Leete. "A study of need satisfactions in managerial level personnel in a government agency," *Journal of Applied Psychology*, 50 (1966): 247–49.

Parnes, S. J., and A. Meadow. "Effects of brainstorming instructions on creative problem solving by trained and untrained subjects," *Journal of Educational Psychology*, 50 (1959): 171–76.

Paterson, D. G., and J. J. Jenkins. "Communication between management and workers," *Journal of Applied Psychology*, 32 (1948): 71–80.

Pearlin, L. I., and M. L. Kohn. "Social class, occupation, and parental values: A cross-national study," *American Sociological Review*, 31 (1966): 466–79.

Pelz, D. C., and F. M. Andrews. *Scientists in organizations: Productive climate for research and development*. Wiley, 1966.

Perrow, C. "The analysis of goals in complex organizations," *American Sociological Review*, 26 (1961): 855.

————. *Complex organizations*. Scott, Foresman, 1970.

————. *Organizational analysis: A sociological view*. Wadsworth, 1970.

Perry, D., and T. A. Mahoney. "In-plant communications and employee morale," *Personnel Psychology*, 8 (1955): 339–46.

Pfeffer, J., and G. Salancik. "Organizational decision making as a political process: The case of the university budget," *Administrative Science Quarterly*, 19 (1974): 135–51.

Ponder, Q. "The effective manufacturing foreman," Proceedings of the Industrial Relations Research Assn., 1957.

Porter, L. W., and E. E. Lawler, III. *Managerial attitudes and performance*. Irwin-Dorsey, 1968.

Porter, L. W., and R. M. Steers. "Organizational work and personal factors in employee turnover and absenteeism, "Psychological Bulletin, 80 (1973): 151–76.

Porter, L. W., E. E. Lawler, III, and J. R. Hackman. Behavior in organizations. McGraw-Hill, 1975.

Raia, A. P. "Goal setting and self control," Journal of Management Studies, 2 (1965): 34–53.

———. "A second look at goals and controls," California Management Review, 8 (1966): 49–58.

———. "A study of the educational value of management games," The Journal of Business, 39 (1966): 339–52.

Read, W. H. "Upward communication in industrial hierarchies," Human Relations, 15 (1962): 3–15.

Reddin, W. C. Communication within the organization. New York: Industrial Communication Council, 1972.

Rice, A. K. "Productivity and social organization in an Indian weaving shed," Human Relations, 6 (1953): 297–329.

Richetto, G. M. "Source credibility and personal influence in three contexts: A study of dyadic communication in a complex aerospace organization." Ph.D. dissertation, Purdue University, 1969.

Ritchie, J. B., and R. E. Miles. "An analysis of quantity and quality of participation as mediating variables in the participative decision making process," Personnel Psychology, 23 (1970): 347–59.

Ritti, R. R. "Job enrichment and skill utilization in engineering organizations." In Maher, J. R. (ed.), New perspectives in job enrichment. Van Nostrand Reinhold, 1971.

Rizzo, J., House, R. J., and Lirtzman, S. "Role conflict and ambiguity in complex organizations," Administrative Science Quarterly, 15 (1970): 150–63.

Roethlisberger, F. J., and W. J. Dickson. Management and the worker. Harvard Univ. Press, 1939.

Ronan, W. W., G. P. Latham, and S. B. Kinne. "Effects of goals setting and supervision on worker behavior in an industrial situation," Journal of Applied Psychology, 58 (1973): 302–7.

Rosen, B. and T. H. Jerdee. "Sex stereotyping in the executive suite," Harvard Business Review, 52 (1974): 133–42.

———. "Influence of sex role stereotypes of personnel decisions," Journal of Applied Psychology, 59 (1974): 9–14.

Rosen, N. Leadership change and group dynamics: An experiment. Cornell Univ. Press, 1969.

———. "Supervisory behavior as perceived by subordinates: Cause or consequence of performance and group cohesion?" In Bass, B. M., R. Cooper, and J. A. Haas (eds.). Managing for accomplishment. D. C. Heath, 1970.

———. Supervision: A behavioral view. Grid, 1973.

Rosen, R.A.H. "Foreman role conflict: An expression of contradictions in organizational goals," Industrial and Labor Relations Review, 23 (1970): 541–52.

Rowland, K. M., D. M. Gardner, and S. M. Nealey. "Business gaming in education and research," in Proceedings of the 13th Annual Midwest Management Conference Academy of Management, Midwest Division, East Lansing, Mich., April, 1970.

Sartre, J. P. Existentialism and human emotions. New York: Philosophical Library, 1957.

Schachter, S. The psychology of affiliation. Stanford Univ. Press, 1959.

Schein, E. "Management development as a process of influence," Industrial Management Review (May, 1961): 59–76.

———. "How to break in the college graduate," *Harvard Business Review*, 42 (1964): 68–76.

———. "Organizational socialization and the profession of management," *Industrial Management Review*, 9 (1968), 1–16.

———. *Organizational Psychology*. Prentice-Hall, 1970.

Schein, V. E. "Relationships between sex role stereotypes and requisite management characteristics among female managers," *Journal of Applied Psychology*, 60 (1975): 340–44.

Schramm, W. *The research on programmed instruction: An annotated bibliography*. Stanford, Calif.: Institute for Communication Research, 1962a.

———. "What we know about learning from instructional television," in *Educational Television–The Next Ten Years*. Stanford University Press, 1962b.

Schreisheim, C., R. J. House, and S. Kerr. "The effects of different operationalizations of leader initiating structure: A reconciliation of discrepant results," *Academy of Management Proceedings*, 1975.

Schuler, R. S. "A new test of the path-goal theory of leadership: The effect of leader behavior on subordinates' responses via subordinate motivation." Unpublished paper, Cleveland State University, 1973.

Schutz, W. C. "What makes groups productive?" *Human Relations*, 8 (1955): 429–65.

———, and V. L. Allen. "The effects of a T-group laboratory on interpersonal behavior," *Journal of Applied Behavioral Science*, 2 (1966): 265–86.

Scott, W. G. *The management of conflict: Appeal systems in organizations*. Irwin, 1965.

Scott, W. R., S. M. Dornbusch, B. C. Busching, J. D. Laing. "Organizational evaluation and authority: Incompatibility and instability," *Administrative Science Quarterly*, 12 (1967): 105–16.

Searfoss, D., and R. Monczka. "Perceived participation in the budget process and motivation to achieve the budget," *Academy of Management Journal* (Dec. 1973): 541–54.

Seashore, S. E. *Group cohesiveness in the industrial work group*. Survey Research Center, Univ. of Michigan, 1954.

Seiler, J. A. "Diagnosing interdepartmental conflict," *Harvard Business Review*, 41 (1963): 121–32.

Selznick, P. *TVA and the grass roots*. Univ. of California Press, 1949.

Sereno, K. K. "Ego-involvement, high source credibility and response to a belief-discrepant communication," *Speech Monographs*, 35 (1968): 476–81.

Shartle, C. L. *Occupational information*. 2d ed. Prentice-Hall, 1952.

Shepherd, C. R. *Small groups: Some sociological perspectives*. Chandler, 1964.

Sheppard, H. L., and N. Q. Herrick. *Where have all the robots gone? Worker dissatisfaction in the 70's*. Free Press, 1972.

Sherif, M. "Superordinate goals in the reduction of intergroup conflict," *American Journal of Sociology*, 63 (1958): 349–56.

Silber, M. B. "A comparative study of three methods of effecting attitude change," *Dissertation Abstracts*, 22 (1962): 2488.

Simon, H. A. *Models of man*. Wiley, 1957a.

———. *Administrative behavior*. Macmillan, 1957b.

———. *The new science of management decision*. New York Univ. Press, 1960.

Simon, J. *Basic research methods in social science*. Random House, 1969.

Simpson, Richard L. "Vertical and horizontal communication in formal organizations," *Administrative Science Quarterly,* 4 (1959): 188–96.

Smith, A. *An inquiry into the nature and causes of the wealth of nations.* A. Strahan and T. Cadell, 1793. The Modern Library, 1937.

Smith, P. N. "Attitude changes associated with training in human relations," *British Journal of Social and Clinical Psychology,* 3 (1964): 104–13.

Sodnovitch, J. M., and W. J. Pophorn. *Retention value of filmed science courses.* Kansas State College of Pittsburg, 1961.

Soelberg, P. "Unprogrammed decision making," *Papers and Proceedings, Academy of Management,* 26th Annual Meeting, 1966.

Solem, A. R. "Human relations training: Comparisons of case study and role playing," *Personnel Administration,* 23 (1960): 29–37.

Starr, M. *Management: A modern approach.* Harcourt Brace Jovanovoch, 1971.

Stedry, A. A., and E. Kay. *The effects of goal difficulty on performance.* General Electric Company: Behavioral Research Service, 1964.

Stedry, A. C., and E. Kay. "The effect of goal difficulty on performance: A field experiment," *Behavioral Science,* 11 (1966): 459–70.

Steers, R. M. "Task goal attributes, in achievement and supervisory performance," *Organizational Behavior and Human Performance,* 13 (1975): 392–403.

Stogdill, R. M. *Individual behavior and group achievement* New York: Oxford University Press, 1959.

————. *Handbook of leadership: A survey of theory and research.* The Free Press, 1974.

Stone, C. H., and F. L. Ruch. "Selection, interviewing and testing." In D. Yoder, and H. D. Heneman, Jr. (eds.), *Staffing policies and strategies.* Bureau of National Affairs, 1974.

Stovall, T. F., "Lecture vs. discussion," *Phi Delta Kappan,* 39 (1958): 225–58.

Sturmthal, A. "Worker's participation in management: A review of United States experience." International Institute for Labour Studies, Geneva (bull. no. 6), 1968.

Super, D. E. *The psychology of careers.* Harper & Bros., 1957.

————. *Occupational psychology.* Wadsworth, 1972.

Sykes, A. J. N. "The effects of a supervisory training course in changing supervisors' perceptions and expectations of the role of management," *Human Relations,* 15 (1962): 227–43.

————. "A study in changing the attitudes and stereotypes of industrial workers," *Human Relations,* 17 (1964): 143–54.

————. "Economic interest and the Hawthorne researches," *Human Relations,* 18 (1965), 253–63.

Taft, R. "The ability to judge people," *Psychological Bulletin,* 52 (1955): 1–23.

Taylor, C. W. *Creativity: Progress and potential.* McGraw-Hill, 1964.

Taylor, E. K., and R. J. Wherry. "A study of lenience in two rating systems," *Personnel Psychology,* 4 (1951): 39–47.

Taylor, F. W. *Scientific management.* Harper, 1947.

Thompson, J. *Organizations in action.* McGraw-Hill, 1967.

Thompson, V. *Modern organization.* Knopf, 1967.

Thorndike, E. L. *Individuality.* Houghton Mifflin, 1911.

Torrance, E. P. "The Minnesota studies of creative behavior: National and international extensions," *Journal of Creative Behavior,* 1 (1967): 137–54.

Tosi, H. L. "A reexamination of personality as a determinant of the effects of participation," *Personnel Psychology* 23 (1970): 91–99.

———. "Organization stress as a moderator of the relationship between influence and role response," *Academy of Management Journal,* 14 (1971): 7–22.

———. "Improving management by objectives with a diagnostic change program," *California Management Review,* 16 (1973): 57–66.

———. "The human effects of budgeting systems on management," *Business Topics,* 22 (1974): 53–63.

———, and Stephen J. Carroll. "Some structural factors related to goal influence in the Management by Objectives process," *MSU Business Topics* (Spring 1969): 45–51.

———. *Management: Contingencies, structure, and process.* St. Clair Press, 1976.

Tosi, H. L., L. Baird, and L. Foster. "Relationships between different levels of superior and subordinate performance and subordinate attitudes and perceptions of leader behavior in the work setting," *Proceedings, Academy of Management,* 1975, 164–66.

Tosi, H. L., and S. J. Carroll. "Managerial reactions to management by objectives," *Academy of Management Journal,* 11 (1968): 415–26.

Tosi, H. L., R. J. Chesser, and S. J. Carroll. "A dynamic model of certain aspects of the superior/subordinate relationship," *Proceedings Eastern Academy of Management,* Annual Meetings, Boston, 1972.

Tosi, H. L., J. Hunter, R. J. Chesser, J. Tarter, and S. J. Carroll. "How real are changes induced by management by objectives," *Administrative Science Quarterly,* 21 (1976): 276–304.

Trager, G. L. "Paralanguage: A first approximation," *Studies in Linguistics,* 13 (1958): 1–12.

Trist, E. L., and K. W. Banforth. "Some social and psychological consequences of the long wall method of coal getting," *Human Relations,* 4 (1951): 3–38.

Turcotte, W. "Control systems, performance and satisfaction in two state agencies," *Administrative Science Quarterly* (March, 1974): 60–73.

Tyler, L. *The psychology of individual differences.* Rev. ed. Appleton-Century-Crofts, 1965.

Underwood, W. J. "Evaluation of laboratory method training," *Training Directors Journal,* 19 (1965): 34–40.

W. E. Upjohn Institute. *Work in America.* MIT Press, 1973.

Ulrich, L., and D. Trumbo. "The selection interview since 1949," *Psychological Bulletin,* 63 (1965): 100–16.

U.S. War Department. *What the soldier thinks: A monthly digest of War Department studies on the attitudes of American troops.* Army Services Forces, Morales Services Division, I (1943): 13.

Valiquet, I. M. "Contribution to the evaluation of a management development program," Unpublished master's thesis. Massachusetts Institute of Technology, 1964. Cited by J. P. Campbell and M. D. Dunnette, "Effectiveness of T-group experiences in managerial training and development," *Psychological Bulletin,* 70 (1968): 73–104.

Van de Ven, A. "A panel study on determinants of authority structures within organizational units. *Proceedings of 36th Annual Meeting, Academy of Management,* 1976, pp. 256–61.

VanderMeer, A. W. *Relative effectiveness of exclusive film instruction, films plus study guides, and typical instructional methods. Progress report no. 10.* Instructional Film Program. Pennsylvania State College, 1948.

Van Schacck, H., Jr. "Naturalistic role playing: A method of interview training for student personnel administrators," *Dissertation Abstracts,* 17 (1957): 801.

Verner, C., and G. Dickinson. "The lecture, an analysis and review of research," *Adult Education,* 17 (1967): 85–100.

Villere, Maurice F., and G. K. Stearns. "The readability of organizational behavior textbooks," *Academy of Management Journal,* 19 (1976): 132–37.

Vroom, V. H. *Work and motivation.* Wiley 1964.

———. "A study of pre- and post-decision processes," *Organizational Behavior and Human Performance,* 1 (1966): 212–25.

———. and P. W. Yetton. *Leadership and decision-making.* Univ. of Pittsburgh Press, 1973.

Wagner, H. *Principles of operations research.* Prentice-Hall, 1969

Wagner, R. "The employment interview: A critical summary," *Personnel Psychology,* 2 (1949): 17–46.

Wainer, H. W., and I. M. Rubin. "Motivation of research and development entrepreneurs," *Journal of Applied Psychology,* 53 (1969): 178–84.

Walker, C. R., and R. H. Guest. *The man on the assembly line.* Harvard Univ. Press, 1952.

Walster, E., E. Aronson, and D. Abraham. "On increasing the persuasiveness of a low prestige communicator," *Journal of Experimental Psychology,* 2 (1966): 325–42.

Walton, E. *A magnetic theory of organizational communication.* U.S. Naval Ordnance Test Station Publication III, 1962.

———. "Motivation to communicate," *Personnel Administration,* 25 (1962): 17–19, 39.

———. "Project: Office communications," *Administrative Management,* 23 (1962): 22–24.

Walton, R. E. *Interpersonal peacemaking: Confrontations and third party consultation.* Addison Wesley, 1969.

———, and J. M. Dutton. "The management of interdepartmental conflict: A model and review," *Administrative Science Quarterly,* 14 (1969): 522–42.

Walton, R. E., and R. B. McKersie. *A behavioral theory of labor negotiations.* McGraw-Hill, 1965.

Wanous, J. P. "Organizational entry: From naive expectations to realistic beliefs," *Journal of Applied Psychology,* 61 (1976): 22–29.

Ware, J. "Seduction in the classroom: The Doctor Fox effect," *Proceedings of Midwest Division of Academy of Management Conference,* 1975, pp. 349–50.

Wason, P. C. "The retention of material presented through precis," *Journal of Communication,* 12 (1962): 36–43.

Weaver, C. H. "The quantification of the frame of reference in labor-management communication," *Journal of Applied Psychology,* 42 (1958): 1–9.

Weber, Max. *The theory of social and economic organization* (T. Parsons, trans.). The Free Press, 1947.

Webster, E. (ed). *Decision making in the employment interview.* Montreal: Eagel, 1964.

Weinstein, A. G., and V. Srinivasan. "Predicting managerial success of master of business administration (MBA) graduates," *Journal of Applied Psychology,* 59 (1974): 207–12.

Weiss, D. J., R. V. David, G. H. England, and L. H. Lofquist. *The measurement of vocational needs.* Bulletin 39, Industrial Relations Center, Univ. of Minnesota, 1964.

Wernmont, P. F. "Recruitment policies and practices." In D. Yoder and H. G. Heneman, Jr. (eds.), *Staffing policies and strategies.* Bureau of National Affairs, 1974.

Weston, J., and F. Brigham. *Managerial finance.* Holt, Rinehart, 1972.

Wexley, K. N., and W. F. Nemeroff. "Effects of positive reinforcement and goal setting as methods of management development," *Journal of Applied Psychology*, 60 (1975): 446–50.

Wexley, K. N., J. P. Singh, and G. A. Yukl. "Subordinate personality as a moderator of the effects of participation in three types of appraisal interviews," *Journal of Applied Psychology*, 58 (1973): 54–59.

Whitehead, J. L., Jr. "Factors of source credibility," *Quarterly Journal of Speech*, 54 (1968): 59–63.

Whitehill, A. M., Jr., and S. Takezawa. *The other worker*. East-West Center Press, 1968.

Whitla, D. K., and John E. Tirrell. "The validity of ratings of several levels of supervisors," *Personnel Psychology*, 1954: 461–66.

Wickens, J. D. "Management by objectives: An appraisal," Journal of *Management Studies*, 5 (1968): 365–79.

Wickesburg, A. K. "Communications networks in the business organization structure," *Academy of Management Journal*, 11 (1968): 253–62.

Wikstrom, W. S. "Managing by—and with—objectives," *Studies in Personnel Policy*, 212 (1968): 1–21. National Industrial Conference Board.

Wild, R., and Kempner, T. "Influence of community and plant characteristics on job attitudes of manual workers," *Journal of Applied Psychology*, 56 (1972): 106–13.

Williams, F. "Analysis of verbal behavior." In E. Brooks and W. D. Brooks (eds.), *Methods of research in communication*. Houghton Mifflin, 1970.

Willits, Robin D. "Company performance and interpersonal relations," *Industrial Management Review*, 7 (1967): 91–107.

Witkin, H. A., R. B. Dyk, H. F. Faterson, D. R. Goodenough, S. A. Karp. *Psychological differtiation*. Wiley, 1962.

Wolff, P. J. "Casual Togs, Inc." In S. J. Carroll, F. T. Palne, and J. B. Miner (eds.), *The management process*. Macmillan, 1965.

Woodward, J. *Industrial organization*. London: Oxford University Press, 1965.

Wren, D. A. *The evolution of management thought*. Ronald, 1972.

Wyatt, S., and R. Marriott. *A study of attitudes to factory work*. London: Medical Research Council, 1956.

Yuchtman, E. and S. E. Seashore. "A system resource approach to organizational effectiveness." In Ghorpade, J. (ed.), *Assessment of organizational effectiveness: Issues, analysis, readings*. Goodyear, 1971.

Zagona, S. V., and M. R. Harter. "Credibility of source and recipient's attitude: Factors in the perception and retention of information on smoking behavior," *Perceptual and Motor Skills*, 23 (1966): 155–68.

Zaleznik, A., C. R. Christensen, and F. J. Roethlisberger. *The motivation, productivity, and satisfaction of workers: A prediction study*. Division of Research, Harvard Business School, 1958.

Zalkind, S. S., and T. W. Costello. "Perception: Some recent research and implications for administration," *Administrative Science Quarterly*, (Sept., 1962): 227–29.

Zima, J. P. "The counseling-communication of supervisors in a large manufacturing company." Ph.D. dissertation, Purdue University, 1968.

Zimbardo, P., and E. B. Ebbesen. *Influencing attitudes and changing behavior*. Addison-Wesley, 1970.

Name Index

Subject Index

individual differences in, 442–44
individualism, attitudes toward,
in, 443
integration and competition, 435
integration and conflict in, 433–34
integration and confrontation
approaches in, 449–451
integration in, effects of inequity
on, 435
integration and objectives in, 433–34
integration and system redesign
in, 446–47
integration between units in, 432–33,
444
integration between units and matrix
organization in, 444–46
integrative complexity and, 442
organization climate in, 439–40
organizational differences, 435
organizational differences and
authority in, 437
organizational differences and
compensation in, 438
organizational differences and
objectives in, 435–36
performance evaluation in, 438–39
reference groups within, 443
status differences in, 440
structure of parts vary in, 431–32
values and conflict in, 443–44
Motivation, 408–11, 119–53, 372–75,
406–11
and compensation, 303–5
competition, 374
defined as management, 121
defined psychologically, 121
in dynamic organizations, 406–7
job design, 374–75, 409
ego involvement, 373–74, 410–11
fear as, 372, 409
in the hierarchical
organization, 371–75
and job satisfaction, 121–27
managerial function, 121, 136–37
and manipulation, 136–37
and need for structured
environment, 371, 4067
and performance, 121–23, 128–30
reciprocity, 373
reinforcement approach, 373, 408

strategies, 136–50
strategies, in practice, 375
team building as, 374, 409
threat as, 372
and work ethic, 120
Motivational strategies, 137–51
competition, 146–47
ego involvement, 147–48
fear, 137–38
job enrichment, 143–44
reinforcement, 140, 43
team building, 146–48
threat, 137–39
Multinational corporations, 522

Needs
Alderfer's need structure, 78
definition of, 75–77
determinants of, 78–79
ego, 77
existence, 78
growth, 78
importance of, 78
Maslow's hierarchy, 76–77
motivating effects of, 77
physiological, 76
primary vs. higher order, 76–78
relatedness, 78
satisfiers, determinants of, 78
security, 76
social, 76
self-actualization, 77
Nonverbal communication, 242–43
Norms, 93–94, 106–7
definition of, 93
effect of educational level, 107
effect of personality factors, 107
effect of position in the group, 107
enforcement of, in groups, 106–7
group, 106
learning of, 106
pivotal vs. peripheral, 94

Objectives
Objectives, 17. See also Goals
conflicting, 116
evaluating, 356–57
organizational differences
and, 435–36
of organization growth, 459–67

77 78 79   L   6 5 4 3 2 1